The Browns of Providence Plantations

The Colonial Years

The Browns
of Providence
Plantations

The Colonial Years

James B. Hedges

Brown University Press
Providence   1968

PREFACE

This is the first volume of a projected three-volume history of the Brown family of Providence. It includes only their activities which were of Colonial or Revolutionary origin. These are followed through to their liquidation in the score of years after 1783. But meanwhile, in the early post-Revolutionary period, the family had entered into new forms of business enterprise which will constitute the subject matter of the next volume.

This volume is based primarily upon the Brown Papers in the John Carter Brown Library of Brown University, and to a lesser degree upon the papers of Moses Brown in the Library of the Rhode Island Historical Society in Providence. The first-named collection includes the major portion of the manuscript records accumulated by the various members of the Brown family in the course of their multifarious business activities during the period from 1723 to 1913. It numbers about 350,000 separate items.

The Brown Papers are notable in several respects. They illustrate many facets of the economic and business development of the country. They are extraordinarily complete. Successive generations of the family preserved their business records with great fidelity; and along the way no one in a house-cleaning mood ever conceived the idea of feeding them to the flames. Because of the completeness of this manuscript collection, newspapers and government records can add little to the story of the Browns, especially for the period covered by this volume. The Papers span a period of almost two hundred years. Although there are numerous collections of papers covering one or two generations of a given business, it is doubtful that there is another large body of documents representing six generations of one family whose dominant business interests shifted from one generation to another. The Browns were a flourishing business concern at the time of the Seven Years War; their activities were on a much greater scale and more complex when the American Civil War broke out a hundred years later. A more detailed description of these manuscripts is to be found in my article on "The Brown Papers," in the *Proceedings of the American Antiquarian Society,* vol. LI, Part I, pp. 21-36.

Decade by decade through the nineteenth century these records accumulated in the counting house of Brown and Ives at 50 South Main Street in Providence. Near the turn of the century George Parker Winship, first Librarian of the John Carter Brown Library, moved some of the papers for the earlier period to the Library, with a view to the preparation of a volume dealing with activities of the Brown family. Unfortunately, the pressure of other duties prevented the consummation of this plan. In 1923 the remainder—and by far the greater portion—of the collection was deposited in the John Carter Brown Library.

In the 1930's I spent considerable time over a period of two or three years in an examination of these manuscripts. Carefully folded and tied neatly in small bundles according to subject matter, they had remained undisturbed in their boxes for decades. On a spike file were documents apparently untouched since 1771. This investigation revealed not only the richness of the collection but also the magnitude of the task of making it available to the student of history. In 1941 the timely interposition of William G. Roelker and others enlisted the interest of Arthur H. Cole, Chairman of the Committee on Research in Economic History. As a result, that Committee, with the coöperation of Brown University, the Rhode Island Historical Society, and John Nicholas Brown, provided the funds necessary for calendaring and indexing the Papers, and making them readily accessible to the investigator.

I am happy to acknowledge my indebtedness to the many persons who have generously given of their time and wisdom. Arthur H. Cole, of Harvard University, Anne Bezanson, of the University of Pennsylvania, Lawrence C. Wroth, of the John Carter Brown Library, and William G. Roelker and Clarkson Collins III, of the Rhode Island Historical Society, all read the volume in manuscript and made many valuable suggestions, some of them fundamental.

Hillman M. Bishop, of the College of the City of New York, kindly made available to me material on the security holdings of the Brown brothers. Henry M. Wriston, President of Brown University, made possible my release from teaching for an extended period. The friendly interest of Bruce M. Bigelow, Vice-President of Brown University, has been an encouragement at all times. James P. Adams, formerly Vice-President of Brown University, gave enthusiastic support to this project in its early stages.

Miss Mary Rugh, Mrs. Florence Clapp, Mrs. Stella Duff Neiman, and Mrs. Constance Farwell Thurlow all rendered valuable assistance to me while they were engaged in the work of calendaring the Papers.

At the Rhode Island Historical Society, William G. Roelker, Clarkson

Collins III, and Clifford P. Monahon gave the most prompt and cheerful compliance with my every tedious request.

My obligation to the John Carter Brown Library is especially heavy. Lawrence C. Wroth placed at my disposal, as my particular workshop, the most pleasant room in the Library. He and his staff—Miss Marion W. Adams, Miss Jeannette D. Black, Mrs. Raymond M. Watts, and Mr. Woodley L. Wright—by their ready coöperation, their uniformly courteous manner, and their unfailing good nature made my long sojourn in their midst a most delightful one.

My greatest debt is to my wife, Nina Leonard Hedges, to whose completely honest criticism this volume owes much of whatever merit it may possess.

Brown University   James B. Hedges

CONTENTS

[*A partial genealogy of the Brown family and a list of family companies or partnerships mentioned in the text precede Chapter 1.*]

ILLUSTRATIONS

INTRODUCTION

The business activities of the Brown family span a period of six generations. The first entry made in 1723 in the ledger of a small shop in a New England village records the beginnings of a business which has been continuously adjusted and adapted to fit the pattern of the expanding economy of the nation. By skillful management and shrewd foresight, the Browns from one decade to another were able not only to make the most of successive opportunities in new enterprises but in many instances to assume positions of leadership.

Other American business families have achieved greater prominence within a single generation; but it is doubtful that the chronicle of any other family would show so much substantial achievement in so many areas through so many years of changing conditions and circumstances. The story of these varied commercial and industrial undertakings of the Browns becomes then in a sense the history in microcosm of many of the evolving forms and facets of the growth of business in the United States.

As colonial merchants the Browns were first concerned with sea-borne trade and, in a small way, with that important adjunct to the maritime commerce of the period, the distilling of rum. Gradually, in line with the pre-Revolutionary trend, they began to transfer their capital from sea to land. They became important manufacturers of spermaceti candles and of pig iron; by 1775 their mercantile and maritime interests had become ancillary to those of manufacture.

When conditions after the Revolution rendered early forms of manufacture obsolete, they returned for a period to the sea. Their ships were dispatched to China, to the East Indies, to the Baltic and Mediterranean countries, and to South America. While this profitable and globe-girdling maritime trade was still at its peak, the Browns began another series of investments which involved another transfer of capital from sea to land.

The last decade of the eighteenth century was propitious for pioneering in new forms of business. There was a spirit of confidence in the business community, inspired by the adoption of the new constitution and the inauguration of Hamiltonian fiscal policies. The Browns, with ample funds at their command, were active participants in a variety of new enterprises. They went into banking and insurance; they promoted the building of turnpikes and, later, of canals; and, most important, they introduced the cotton manufacture into this country. This last venture was financed originally by the transfer of funds acquired in maritime pursuits. After the embargo of 1808, which placed heavy burdens upon foreign trade, these transfers continued at frequent intervals for two or three decades. As a result of their investment of money and managerial skills, the Browns attained a dominant position in this significant industry.

By the 1840's the cotton manufacture, once a capital-consuming industry, had become capital-producing. No longer was it possible to reinvest in the business all the profits which it returned to the owners. New forms of investment must therefore be found. Men with resources and imagination turned their attention to the West. The result was another migration of capital—this time from the factories of the Atlantic seaboard to western lands, to mining, and to railroads. In this stage of economic development the Brown family again played a conspicuous part. When the process had run its full course, the rounding out of the continent was complete, and the passing of the frontier was at hand.

Throughout the decades, the business of the Browns in all its ramifications has been conducted from Providence, now the capital of the smallest state in the Union. In the story of the colonial and Revolutionary phases covered in the present volume this location has special significance.

The settlements on the shores of Narragansett Bay which came to be known as the State of Rhode Island and Providence Plantations had their beginnings in a religious and political secession from the Colony of Massachusetts Bay. The separatist trend thus begun persisted at least through the eighteenth century; and there are those who believe that separatism exercised a significant influence upon the course of events in Rhode Island even in the nineteenth century.

However great may have been the differences between Rhode Island and her neighbors in religion and politics (and they undoubtedly were very real), they were less marked in economic affairs. In its broader outlines the economy of the colony closely resembled that of the section of which it formed a part. The physical features of Rhode Island encouraged maritime activity. The colony consisted of a mainland section bordering three sides of Narragansett Bay, together with a series of islands within the bay. With dimensions of forty-eight by thirty-seven miles, no part of it was far distant from salt water; and with a coast line (including both bay and sea) of about four hundred miles, it was not lacking in good harbor sites. Rhode Island merchants, like their neighbors, early turned their attention to the sea. Their ships carried the fish, lumber, and provisions of New

England to the West Indies, bringing back molasses, rum, sugar, specie, and bills of exchange. Later they carried the shingles, flour, beef, and pork of the Middle Colonies to these same islands, and at a still later time they freighted fish, flour, and lumber to the countries of Southern Europe.

But important as maritime trade was to New England, it was relatively more vital to Rhode Island because of her more limited area and resources. The Narragansett Bay area abounded in excellent harbors; but the towns located on the bay had a severely limited hinterland from which to draw raw materials and in which to sell manufactured goods. Rhode Island lacked Boston's easy access to the Newfoundland fishery and to the forest resources of northern New England. It was also largely denied the grains and meat products of Connecticut, New York, and Pennsylvania. Reference in the Rhode Island Remonstrance of 1764 (to be discussed later) to the "deficiency" of the colony's "natural produce" was no figment of the imagination. That deficiency explains the fact that Rhode Island merchants first largely imported the products which they reëxported in raw or processed form to other colonies and to the West Indies. Lack of "natural produce" also helps to account for another lack within the colony—lack of specie which was so chronic as to force the merchants to depend upon other colonies for supplies of it. Under these conditions merchants in colonial Rhode Island labored under a considerable comparative disadvantage.

The commercial beginnings of Rhode Island go back to the year 1639, when William Coddington and his associates separated from the Portsmouth settlement and established the town of Newport, located at the southern end of the Island of Aquidneck in Narragansett Bay, and possessing an excellent harbor. "Not liberal politics so much as maritime adventure guaranteed its future." Newport was a prime beneficiary of the Anglo-French wars of the early eighteenth century. Privateering activities of John and William Wanton, Benjamin Ellery, and others, together with the clandestine trade with the Dutch and the Caribbean buccaneers, contributed greatly to the expanding commerce of the town. In years of peace, merchants concentrated their trade chiefly with the West Indies and Surinam, exporting horses, lumber, beef, pork, candles, cheese, and wool; and receiving in exchange sugar, rum, molasses, and specie from the Spanish Main. The hard money paid for English manufactured goods which Newporters procured at Boston. Newport began to make inroads upon Boston's domination of the coasting trade with Connecticut, Philadelphia, and New York. After 1720 the African slave trade increasingly attracted the attention of merchants in the town.

In 1740 the Governor of Rhode Island reported ownership of 120 vessels within the colony, "some on the coast of Africa." By 1763 this number had grown to 184 engaged in foreign trade, not to mention 352 employed in the coasting business. This fleet gave employment to 2200 seamen, while the manufacture of the rum for this growing trade sustained more than twenty "distill houses" in Newport alone. That town had become the great mart of the slave trade in America, the commercial metropolis of Southern New England, and the home of an imposing group of merchant grandees.

Earliest of the great business princes of Newport had been John and William Wanton, with whom "shipbuilding, privateering and mercantile adventuring were interchangeable occupations." In the middle of the eighteenth century there appeared on the roster of Newport merchants such names as Abraham Redwood, William Ellery, Henry Collins, Daniel Ayrault, Godfrey and John Malbone, John Channing, Samuel Vernon, and Joseph Wanton. These men of Newport's "Golden Age" were persons of "magnanimous minds." So marked was this quality in Henry Collins that he was termed by Dr. Waterhouse "the Lorenzo de Medici of Rhode Island." This group of merchants depended "more and more for emolument upon the slave trade."

A third group of men conspicuous in the commercial life of Newport in the generation before Independence comprised a number of outstanding Jewish merchants who pushed their trade into the Mediterranean and the Levant. Jews were to be found at Newport as early as 1658. In 1694 a number of Jewish families arrived from Curaçao. It was eminently fitting that Jews should come to a colony designed by its founder for the benefit of persecuted races, including the Children of Abraham. Outstanding among the members of the Jewish colony at Newport were the Rivera, Polock, and Lopez families. These Jewish merchants were drawn into the spermaceti candle manufacture in such numbers as to make Newport the center of that business in Colonial America.

Perhaps the most conspicuously successful of Newport merchants on the eve of the Revolution was Aaron Lopez. Arriving in the town in 1752, he began to trade in a small way strictly within the limits of Rhode Island. Soon he was in the candle manufacture, marketing the product through the coastwise trade. In the middle 1760's he overindulged in trade with Bristol in England from which he emerged heavily in debt, but with a realization of the importance of diversifying his risks. He then entered the West Indian trade, where his success was such as to enable him greatly to expand his maritime activities. Soon his vessels could be seen "riding the bounding main to Jamaica, Hispaniola, Surinam, Honduras, Newfoundland, England, Holland, Spain, Portugal, Africa, the Azores and Canaries."* So extensive were the ramifications of his business that he owned, in whole or in part, a fleet of over thirty vessels. Small wonder that Ezra Stiles referred to Lopez as "a Merchant of the first eminence; for Honor & extent of commerce probably surpassed by no Mercht in America . . ."

But Newport's "Golden Age" was not restricted to the accumulation of wealth and leisure. Its cultural growth kept pace with the expansion of its commerce. When Dean Berkeley, the English philosopher, and John Smibert, the painter, arrived there in 1729 they found an urbane and aristocratic society of cultivated tastes. If the Dean's presence in the community marked the "advent of a renaissance," that would have been impossible without a congenial environment. Although there were no less than seven churches in the town representing five different sects, Berkeley was able to write that "notwithstanding so many differences, here are fewer quarrels about religion than elsewhere, the people living peaceably with their neighbors of whatsoever persuasion." Men of intellectual interests were sufficiently numerous to make possible, with or without the Dean's influence, the formation in 1730 of a society for the discussion of literary and philosophical subjects.

When Berkeley's brief stay came to an end in 1731 other men were not lacking to provide leadership in the cultural life of Newport. Abraham Redwood and Henry Collins were conspicuous for their patronage of the arts. Peter Harrison and Richard Munday gained distinction in architecture, while John Smibert, Gilbert Stuart, Robert Feke, and Samuel King were no less outstanding as painters. Prominent in theology were John Callender, Isaac Touro, Ezra Stiles, and Samuel Hopkins. Dr. Thomas Moffatt and Dr. William Hunter were active in a scientific way, as were the Franklins and Solomon Southwick in the field of printing and publishing.

But during these years of the development of the Island metropolis, the dreary hamlet on the mainland remained little more than a trading post for the scanty agricultural products grown on the poor soil of the northern part of the colony. Providence as late as 1740 "was still, as in the seventeenth century, but a long straggling street by the water front, where on summer evenings the inhabitants sat in the doorways, smoked their clay pipes, and fought the swarms of mosquitoes that rose from the marsh opposite." By 1740, the Browns had been in business for twenty years. Many times they and other ambitious men in the community must

*See the sketch of Lopez by Bruce M. Bigelow in *Dictionary of American Biography*, XI (1933), 402-403.

have felt that "the good Providence of God from whom the Plantations have taken their name" had largely deserted them.

But slow and painful as was the process, business once established inched slowly ahead. After 1720, the growth and development of Providence may be traced through the activities of the Brown and Hopkins families. Together they finally were able to challenge Newport's supremacy in the political and intellectual life of the colony. As the leader of the political faction which bore his name, Stephen Hopkins with valiant support from the Browns brought to an end the almost unbroken control which Newport had maintained over the government of Rhode Island. The Brown brothers with Hopkins' help won for their home town another notable victory when they succeeded in bringing the College of Rhode Island (now Brown University) to Providence.

These political and cultural accomplishments were made possible by the striking success in business which the Browns and other mercantile families had finally achieved. By 1775 they had become the peers of the Newport businessmen and on occasion had proved themselves to be more than a match for the merchant grandees of the Island. But the fortunes of war resolved all questions of divided leadership in the small state. For three years during the Revolution, Newport was occupied by British troops. Some of the prominent residents became Loyalists, many others moved away. Several hundred buildings were destroyed. Years later, a competent observer could write of the once proud city of Newport that "Commerce & all the Jews are fled. The wharves are deserted & the lamp in the synagogue is extinct." But he added that "the town of Providence has risen to riches & elegance from the ruins of this once beautiful spot" which had been the home of the "best bred society in N. England."

The rise of Providence was of more than local significance. The basic business structure of the Browns was intact at the close of the war. More fully perhaps than any other business family in the country, the Brown family enjoyed equal success and prominence in both the colonial and national periods of our history. Like the Hancocks of Boston, they had been in business for fifty years when news came of Lexington and Concord. But unlike the Hancocks and scores of other families, their business history did not come to an end with the war for Independence. The continuing postwar expansion of the business of the Browns was a powerful force in the development of Providence as the commercial metropolis of southern New England and the emergence of Rhode Island as one of the most important industrial states of the Union. Financially successful at home, the Browns were able to take full advantage of new opportunities offered by the rapidly growing economy of the young nation.

The Colonial Years

PARTIAL GENEALOGY OF THE BROWN FAMILY

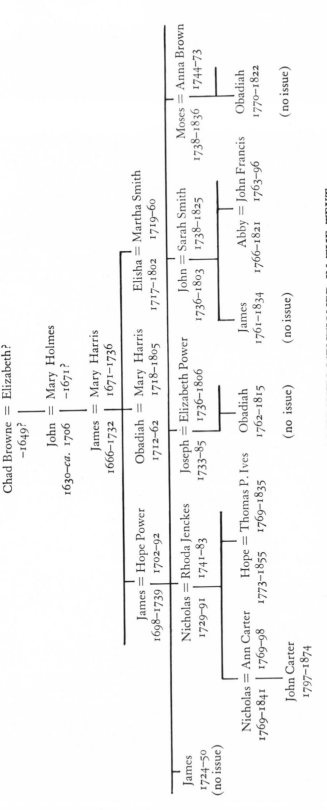

FAMILY COMPANIES OR PARTNERSHIPS MENTIONED IN THE TEXT

James Brown, 1721–1739
Obadiah Brown, 1739–?
Obadiah Brown & Company, —1762
Nicholas Brown & Company, 1762–1774
Brown & Benson, 1783–circa 1794

Brown & Francis, 1786–1796
Brown, Rogers, & Brown, 1784–1791
Brown & Power, circa 1776–1784
Brown, Benson, & Ives, 1792–1796
Brown & Ives, 1796—

CHAPTER 1

The Browns of Providence Plantations

IN July 1638 the ship *Martin* brought to Boston one Chad Browne, his wife Elizabeth, and their son John, a small boy of eight. Of their English years before that July day nothing is known, nor of the motives that prompted their journey. But tradition has it that young Chad brought his family from Salem to Providence "for conscience' sake," and it may be reasonable to assume that conscience was responsible also for the long Atlantic voyage to the new country that was America.

Available records give only glimpses of the life of Chad Browne and his immediate family. Soon after their arrival in the Bay Colony they came from Boston by way of Salem to join the young colony which Roger Williams had founded two years before on Narragansett Bay and which came to be known as Providence Plantations. The head of the family did not long remain a mere "first comer." As a surveyor he was a member of the committee which compiled lists of lots for the first settlers on the "Towne Street" and marked out for himself a lot of ample proportions which extended from the "Towne Street" at the foot of the hill (now South Main Street and Market Square), up the hill and well beyond to the "Highway," known to present-day residents as Hope Street. He was interested in the religious life of the community as well as the practical, for in 1642 he was ordained as the "first settler Pastor" of the first Baptist Church in America.[1]

Chad Browne passed this dual interest in civic and spiritual affairs on to young John. Grown to manhood, he, too, became a surveyor and a Baptist elder. In 1672 for some reason he sold the fine parcel of land originally marked out for his own by his pioneering father, and it was not until 1770, when two of John's great-grandsons repurchased the land as the site of the new College of Rhode Island, now Brown University, that the land came back to Brown ownership.[2]

John Brown had seven children. Of these, his son James seems to present the first evidence of the family bent for business. James was born in 1666, three years after King Charles II granted a charter to Rhode Island and Providence Plantations, a charter which recognized that the Rhode Island colonists had seized and possessed "such lands, islands, rivers, harbors and roads as are very convenient both for plantations, and also for building ships, supply of pipe-staves and other merchandise; and which lie very commodious, in many respects, for commerce, and to accommodate our southern plantations . . ."; and granted permission for the Rhode Islanders "to hold forth a lively experiment . . . with a full liberty in religious concernments" and with "true piety rightly grounded upon gospel principles."

During his life James Brown must have developed some interest in "commodious" commerce, while maintaining the family interest in "religious concernments." He followed in his forebear's footsteps in civic and religious activities, as member of the town council, town treasurer, and pastor of the church, but he found time to become a man of substantial property as well, and left behind him generous provision for his sons and grandsons. That his life was not all austerity and stern Baptist piety was attested to by the inventory of his personal estate which included "2 Hogsheads of sider," "4 Hogsheads of apple beere," and 133 pounds of tobacco.[3]

This bequeathed property must have been accumulated from some form of trade. There is no evidence, however, that James himself ever sailed to England's southern plantations in search of lively barter or profitable exchange. This phase of family activity was initiated and developed by two of his sons, James and Obadiah.[4] During their careers as successful merchandisers at home and traders abroad they laid the foundations for the long succession of business firms bearing the Brown name. The records left by James and Obadiah are only fragmentary, but those that are available serve to show something of the versatility and ingenuity of the businessman of pre-Revolutionary days.

James, fourteen years older than Obadiah, became interested as a young man in the art of navigation and the building and sailing of ships. One of his books on geometrical and nautical problems bears the notation "Begun October the 24th-1719."[5] He was then twenty-one years old. Two years later he was one of five partners, all of Providence, who contracted with John Barnes for the building of a sloop of about 73 tons. Colonel Nicholas Power, one of the leading shipowners of the town, was one of the five, and before the sloop *Four Bachelors* sailed from Providence, James had married his daughter Hope. So it was as Captain James Brown that he set out in the new vessel bound "to Some of the Leeward Islands in the West Indies." Colonel Power signed the Captain's instructions "for myself & Company" with the invocation "and so God send you a prosperous Voyage." [6]

Apparently the trip was successful, for after his return to Providence Captain James Brown opened a shop on Towne Street, near the corner of present-day College Street and Market Square. But James was not yet ready to settle down as a storekeeper in the small town beside the Providence River. On February 24, 1727 he again sailed from Providence. This time he was master of the Sloop *Truth and Delight,* with "a Brave Gail and fair Weather . . . Bound to Martinneco." [7] The cargo comprised 11 horses, 15 hogsheads of Indian corn, 16 hundredweight of tobacco, 700 pounds of cheese, 6 barrels of tar, 12,600 feet of boards, and 12,000 shingles, a cargo typical of the goods available for shipment from colonial Rhode Island; and from Martinique *Truth and Delight* brought the equally typical cargo of molasses and rum. With his return to Providence from this second voyage Captain James Brown's career as a mariner came to an end. Others were to sail the ships which he later owned.

It may have been regretfully that Captain James laid aside the role of shipmaster, but his expanding commitments must have made it inevitable. During his comparatively short life he became a money lender, proprietor of distilleries, owner of a slaughterhouse, shopkeeper, and shipowner. The age of the specialist had not arrived, and James Brown, like many another colonial businessman, turned his hand to many things. Free enterprise there was indeed, but it took ingenuity and foresight to succeed at it. It is obvious that knowledge of the sea and of sailing ships was an essential ingredient of that success.

The young shopkeeper's first ledger refers under date of October 9, 1723 to the "Sloope *Four Bachilors.*" [8] This ledger and a second book bearing the title "James Brown His Book of Accounts both Debt and Credit," begun in 1731 after his sailing days were over, show a good deal about his methods of doing business. [9] The commodities he sold to his customers were for the most part the homely, day to day essentials for frugal living: salt, fish, beef, turnips, sugar, butter, lamb, and mutton to feed the large colonial families; iron pots to cook in, and wood to supply the capacious fireplaces; cotton wool, cotton, linen, Osnaburgs, leather, and hats for wearing apparel; occasionally a looking glass for vanity; staves and hoops for the barrels so essential in shipping various and sundry articles; rum for the honest workingman, wine and brandy to grace the gentleman's table, and tobacco for a little solace in a grim world.

Little money crossed Captain James's counters. His customers paid him in goods and services, for money was notoriously scarce in early Rhode Island. To be successful, a merchant was forced to develop great skill. The exchange of his calico for the countryman's cheese was a delicate operation involving an inherent knowledge of human nature. Both traders must conclude the transaction convinced not only that they had made a good bargain but that they had a little the better of it.

Captain Brown's letters reveal that in the exercise of his shrewdness he drew within his business orbit all parts of Rhode Island, various points in Southern Massachusetts, and portions of Eastern Connecticut.[10] He trafficked regularly with such commercial centers as Newport, Boston, and Nantucket. Farmers from Worcester and intermediate points drove their cattle to Providence to barter for the Captain's merchandise. From local Rhode Island farmers he procured tobacco, pork, and cheese, as well as boards, hoops, and staves, although his order that "if there should come in a Piscataqua Man we shall want all his load" indicates an increasing dependence on areas to the north for products of the forest. Occasionally, there came a consignment of flour from New York or of rice from distant Charleston, in South Carolina.

Successful trader though he was, Captain Brown's letters lack the chattiness so characteristic of most eighteenth-century business letters. In general they have the cryptic quality which we associate with present-day business documents. They are direct and to the point. To "Mr. Turtolow" [Tourtellot] he wrote simply "I want my money very much." He asked Mr. Davis of Pomfret, Connecticut "please to gett tan horsis for me that is sutabil to go to Surray nam [Surinam] and bring tham downe naxte Mundy Cum fortnit and bring me all the Butter and ottes that falls in your way." From "Mr. Cutler" he wanted "teen or a dusin Surnam horses." Writing to "Mr. Bulfinch" (sailmaker at Boston and grandfather of Charles Bulfinch, the great architect) about sails for a sloop, he said that he had a "Vessell at Nantucket a Whaling, and if she gets any quantity of oil or bone I shall order it to be sent to you, in order that you may sell it to the best advantage for my use."[11]

Even when the social amenities crept into a business letter, they were quickly and brusquely dismissed in favor of the matter at hand. In a letter to a lately bereaved widow, he commiserated with her upon the death of her husband. "So Shure as we come into the World we must go out," he wrote consolingly. But in the next sentence, "he had of me 100 bushels of salt—for which he was to pay last fall £23-15/. I will take any of your moveables at what it were apprised at, if money be scarce with you, provided you will send it soon—I understand you have a pair of oxen that was prised at £22—I will take them, or I will take corne, or oats, shingles, staves, bedding, hay, sheep or hoggs, or any of your moveables at what they are worth."

While keeping store in Providence with one hand, Captain Brown was expanding his Caribbean trade with the other. His ships made many voyages to the British Islands, to those not in the British domain, and to Surinam, or Dutch Guiana. The "tan horsis sutabil for Surray nam" which he hoped to purchase in Connecticut were to be exchanged for molasses and sugar from that Dutch colony. Prior to the enactment of the Molasses Act in 1733 the importation of foreign molasses or sugar into Rhode Island was subject to no legal impediment. Subsequent to that Act, of course, the payment of the sixpence duty per gallon was required. But the statute interfered only slightly with the traffic to the foreign possessions in the Caribbean area, for like many another colonial merchant, Captain Brown soon learned how to circumvent it. To one of his ship captains he wrote in 1736: "Sr. Received yours . . . wherein you say you carried all your horses in well but came to a porr market. I hope you observed my orders in selling them as soon as you could lett them be low or high, for fear there should come more in and make them lower, but I hope there well sold before this time." He then gave the captain orders as to his procedure on the return from Surinam: "I would have you enter in the West Indias [meaning the west inlet between the mainland and Conanicut Island avoiding Newport] if you can, and if you cannot come to down the River and go to unloading, send me word as possible when you arrive."[12]

In the same year he wrote to Captain Field: ". . . it is ticklish times here my neighbors threaten to inform against us, so I hope you will not be too bold when you come home, enter in the West Indias if you can, and if you cannot bring too down the River and send your cargo some to Rhode Island and some up here in boats, so as not to bring but a few hhds. up to my Wharff. . ."[13] The Rhode Island coast was admirably suited to the thwarting of His Majesty's customs regulations. It was a comparatively simple matter to avoid the payment of the duty on the illicit molasses which constituted the bulk of the good captain's cargoes.

Captain Brown built up his shipping interests to include, in addition to *Four Bachelors* and *Truth and Delight,* whole or part ownership of numerous craft. He was jointly concerned in a voyage of the Sloop *Humbrid* to New York. The Sloops *Dolphin, Rainbow, Hopewell,* and *Mary* also appear frequently in the record. His Schooner *Ann* seems to have been the first Providence vessel larger than a sloop. The Sloop *Mary* enjoyed the dubious distinction of being the first slave-trading vessel to sail from Providence.

Captain James Brown died in 1739, sixteen years after he sailed his first ship out of Providence. But during these years he had been training his younger brother Obadiah in the technique of sailing ships and trading goods. One of Obadiah's books was *A Guide to Book Keepers according to the Italian Manner,* published in London in 1729.[14] The several pages of printed matter at the beginning and end of the book describe double-entry bookkeeping and contain "Instructions for Super-Cargoes." It was probably at James's insistence that the younger brother taught himself accounting methods and disciplined himself in the ways of the super-cargo. In any event, he used the originally blank pages, which principally composed the book, to keep a journal of his early voyages as master of his brother's vessels.

The first item in this journal reads: "On ye 11th of September 1733 ye Sloop *Dolphin* with her cargo from New England (Jeames Brown Esq owner) arrived at Antigua concined to me Obadiah Browne." Obadiah gives a day-by-day account of the sale of the cargo and the purchase of goods for the return voyage, including the names of those with whom he transacted business. By October 25 he was ready to weigh anchor for the return to Providence.

But almost immediately Obadiah again sailed from his home port. On November 29, 1733, on board the Sloop *Mary,* he embarked on a huck-stering voyage with cargo to be sold wherever he could find a market. On January 7, 1734 he was at Antigua; on the 8th at "Stasha" [St. Eustatius], where he sold 8 hogsheads of tobacco, 2 shoats, 1 hogshead of corn, 18 hogs, and a half barrel of oats. At St. Christopher he succeeded in disposing of a large part of his remaining cargo. He called again at St. Eustatius, visited St. Martins and Anguilla, and finally spent the summer of 1734 at Surinam.

Late in 1735 Obadiah was again in Surinam with *Mary,* as is indicated by "A Journal of our intended voig by God permicion in ye Sloop *Mary* from Suranam to Rhoad island." While on this voyage Obadiah received instructions from James: ". . . I would not have you sell your vessel without a pretty good price for her, and if you bring her home we will send her direct to Guinnia, for rum is like to be very plenty . . ." These words give the first hint of the idea which lay behind the initial slave-trading voyage from Providence—that of Obadiah in the Sloop *Mary* in 1736-37, to be discussed in another connection.

In February 1738, Obadiah, as master of the Sloop *Rainbow,* a relatively new vessel of eighty tons, sailed under instructions from Captain James Brown. He was to "make the best of your way to Barbadoes—Speak with no vessel on your passage if you can help it; when you are Arrived, do with your Cargoe as you think will be most to my advantage, if you think best Sell there, but if not goe Else where"; and a bit of brotherly advice, "be Sure to keep your Selfe in your right mind if possable, if any Misfortune attend you lay it not to heart, but consider there is a higher power that governs all things, and if you are likely to meet with good fortune consider the same"; as to business arrangements, "you Must not charge me but five pr Cent Sales & two & halfe Returns." The orders conclude with the confident assurance that "in doing as near as possable you can to my directions I make no doubt but the heavens will bless you in your proceedings."[15]

Within a few weeks Obadiah wrote from St. Eustatius that he had sold "nothing but my Candels and them at a very low rate." Discouraged by the prospect there, he had "a Desire to try for Martinnecko," where the burning of "the town of St. peairs" [St. Pierre] had occasioned an unusual demand for lumber. To this end he had acquired the available supply at "Stasha"—about thirty thousand feet. At St. Eustatius and at the "Inglise Islands," he could "not do that you sent me for: that is to gett Money." But he added that "it is thought . . . the french trade will soon be opened. I shall take as much Cair of your Bisines as Posibel I can and if I Dont light of no misfortin I shall make you a good voige; for I have a good prospect at present, but you have all ways had Misfortin in this Vessel which Maeks me afraid, but . . . If I Should never Venter nothing I should never have nothing." Taking no chances on the law's delay in opening the "french trade," he announced in a postscript that he was "agoing to Marteneck to load," hoping to open the trade by private negotiation with the local authorities.[16]

The "misfortin" which had always dogged the course of *Rainbow* seems to have persisted throughout the voyage. She probably failed to arrive at "Marteneck." On May 5, 1738 Obadiah wrote from Montserrat that he "was tacken at St. Luse [St. Lucia] by his Majesty Ship *Rawbuck* Charles Craford Commander: when ye ship Come first in I went on bord with my Rigestor and Clearanc in order to Lett him know from & wheir I came." Captain Crawford sent for Obadiah's "trunck and all my papers and two hands and cep me thare five days."[17] He then took Obadiah and *Rainbow* to Montserrat, where he "Libeld ye Sloope for landing of tobacker in St. Eustasha and in St. Luse." Tobacco was one of the enumerated articles of colonial production which by the Act of Parliament of 1660 must be sent only to England for sale. Obadiah's story of his capture in unlucky *Rainbow* is the only record of British interference with a Brown shipment of Rhode Island tobacco to the Caribbean.

The young shipmaster somehow made his way back to Providence. But the following year he was again in the West Indies. On July 16, 1739 he wrote from "Hispanyoler" a confused letter indicating that he was once more involved in the toils of the law. More serious than his difficulties with French officialdom, however, was his concern over the death of his older brother. The letter, addressed to his "Onerd Sister," the wife of Captain James Brown, informed her that he had "heard ye heavy nuse of ye Death of my brother which is no small Con sarn to me for he was ye only frind to me."[18]

As soon as Obadiah finished his business in Hispaniola, he returned to Providence, and his days at sea came to an end when his vessel arrived at his deceased brother's wharf. The cycle had again been completed—the apprenticeship at sea in preparation for the career of the merchant on shore—and Obadiah, like James before him, turned his training to good account. There was a greater urgency in his case, however, for he was to stand *in loco parentis* to his brother's five sons ranging in age from fifteen years to six months.

Obadiah prospered both as a shopkeeper and a shipowner. Ledgers beginning in 1739 show an expanding business. A decade after the first entry, clerks in the Brown counting house as they worked at the ledgers could see the evidence of his maritime trade tied up at the docks below: a "Privateer sloope" calling for supplies and the "Sconer *Ranger*" being fitted out as flag of truce; the Sloop *Sarah,* the Brigantine *Warren* and the Sloop *Bachelor* awaiting their cargoes for the Caribbean.[19]

But the next decade found Obadiah seeking wider areas of business, abroad as well as at home. In 1750, the ship *Smithfield* left his wharf bound for London. She was embarked upon an epoch-making undertaking. The captain carried an order for English goods which filled three closely written folio pages.[20] With the sailing of this ship with this order, Obadiah Brown was in a sense proclaiming the mercantile independence of Providence. He was by-passing the great men of Newport and Boston, from whom Providence shopkeepers had largely purchased their English goods, and he was sending out a ship under his own direction to bring back his own supplies from London and Bristol. In the fifties, too, other new ports of call were visited by ships dispatched by Obadiah. Cuba, Newfoundland, and the Bay of Honduras appear in sailing orders of Brown ship captains, along with the familiar ports of the British, Dutch, and French Islands. After the outbreak of the Seven Years' War these same Brown ships docked with increasing frequency at that notable center of trade with the enemy, the "Mount," or Monte Cristi, on the Island of Hispaniola.

The business within Providence was also growing in various directions. Obadiah began to venture into the field of manufacture. His first undertaking was a natural outgrowth of his shopkeeping activities. One of the products that came into the colonies in the holds of sailing ships was the cocoa bean. By one crude method or another the beans were ground and widely used by the colonial housewife. Obadiah decided that there were extra shillings to be made if he processed the cocoa bean himself. As water power was easily available, he proposed to use it to grind "chocklit" wholesale. He built the mill, probably the first of its kind in Rhode Island, and began to solicit orders. To "Mr. Spencer" of Newport he wrote on March 19, 1752: "I have been at considerable charge to git a chocklit mill going by water which have now completed. I am advised by Mr. Nichols that you have occasion for a considerable quantity of chocklat in you er way. I shall be glad to supply you with all you have occasion for at ye cheapest rate you can have it at Newport or any whair else."[21]

Letters making the same offer were written to "Mr. Momford," "Mr. Pitman," and "Mr. Codenton."[22] Obadiah was not only prepared to do custom grinding of chocolate for merchants throughout Rhode Island, but to Peleg Thurston, the well-known distiller of Newport, he wrote: "I shall be glad to supply sum of your shops with chocklat; or grind their nuts for them which will do for 19d clear of all charges."[23] The "chocklit" mill achieved an early sucess. Entries in Obadiah's day book for 1753 charged "Jabesh" Carpenter of Newport £7:13:6 for "griden 78 lbs. of chocklat"; and John Tweedy of Newport £24:4:3 for "grinden 349½ lbs. of chocklat."[24]

But while Obadiah was profitably grinding chocolate for the merchants at Newport, he was making a significant start in another field. He began to manufacture and sell spermaceti candles, laying the groundwork for a business which was in later years to become one of the most successful and far-reaching of all the Brown enterprises.

The precise time when Obadiah began to manufacture candles is not certain. Moses Brown in his old age thought it was in 1754. But there is some indication that the construction of a spermaceti works was under consideration in 1751.[25] The earliest documentary evidence upon the subject is in the entry in Obadiah's daybook for March 31, 1753: "Spermaceit House Dr to 500 nails delivered Blake"; and for April 11, 1753: "Amasa Killam Cr By 8 days work on ye Spermasita Hous 35/— £14-0-0."[26] A receipt dated April 14 of the same year refers to "framing a candle house."[27] So the spermaceti manufactory must have been in process of building in the early spring of 1753. By June, Obadiah was buying essential supplies. On June 9 he paid one John Beard £ 52 4/ Old Tenor for the freight on 87 barrels of head matter.[28] This is the first recorded Brown transaction in this vital raw material from which spermaceti candles were made. Not long after, fifty boxes of candles were shipped to James Apthorp of Boston.[29] From 1753 on, the Browns were manufacturers as well as merchants and shipowners. The conduct of their business came more and more to be shaped and influenced by the fact that they were seeking markets not only for goods purchased at home and abroad, but also for the products of their own making in their Rhode Island plants.

With so many of his interests dependent upon the voyages of his ships, Obadiah was drawn into the marine insurance business. In March 1747 he entered into a curious reciprocal agreement with Elisha Brown, by which the latter insured for £100 "ye Brigt. *Desire*," owned by Obadiah, who in turn insured for a like amount the Brigt. *Wainscot*, presumably owned by Elisha.[30] From February 1753 to 1762 Obadiah kept an "Insurance Book" bearing the notation "Providence February 29, 1753 Memorandum of what vessels I have insured that is now abroad and not heard of."[31] For the nine years he has listed more than 130 voyages by many different vessels. Some of these are known to have been owned by him; in others he had a financial interest and controlled their management. Still others, however, can be identified as the property of other merchants in Providence. His accounts, unfortunately, do not make clear the specific policies in individual cases. But it seems likely that his memorandum of vessels "I have insured" refers not merely to policies he had taken out on his own ships but also to insurance he underwrote on other vessels.

In the 1750's Obadiah Brown with his various enterprises was one of the outstanding business figures of the small town of Providence, and was well on his way to equal standing with the great merchants of Newport, the commercial metropolis of the Narragansett country. In retrospect, however, important as Obadiah's achievements were in their own right, his training of a new generation of businessmen in the Brown family was more significant. Since his own sons died early, Obadiah trained the five sons of his brother, Captain James Brown, to carry on the family business. Four of these nephews—Nicholas, Joseph, John, and Moses—were actively associated in the late 1750's with Obadiah Brown and Company. But James, their older brother, died in his twenties while on a voyage to the Chesapeake.

Like the other young men in the Brown family, James had acquired early education in nautical techniques. His book of *Geometrical Problems,* bearing the inscription "James Brown His Book February the 10th 1742/3," contains sections on "Rectangular Trigonometry," "Oblique Trigonometry," "Plain Sailing," "Mercators Sailing," "Traverse Sailing," etc.[32] The many problems and exercises requiring the application of fundamental principles of nautical science are carefully solved in the handwriting of the youthful James. A well-thumbed copy of *The English Pilot,*

The Fourth Book Describing the West India Navigation from Hudson's Bay to the River Amazones, published in London in 1745, with the notation "1748 August Then this was Bought in Boston by James Brown pris £10-10" inscribed on the flyleaf, was a companion volume.[33]

James was in Barbados in April of 1743, but in what capacity and on what vessel is not known. "A Journal of a voige from Rhoad island to Sincristophers [St. Christopher] to be kept by James Brown on board the Brig *Hope* Rufus Hopkins Master 1747/8 February ye 9th came to sail from . . . Newport" describes visits to "Antego" and St. Christopher.[34] In July 1748 he sailed aboard the Sloop *Desire* on a "voige to New York and Philadelphia." Shortly after his return to the home port he must have embarked on the coastwise trip to Carolina about which he wrote from Newbern, North Carolina in February 1749.[35] Addressing his brother as "Mr. Nicholas Brown Distiller in Providence Rhoad island," he told of the hardships and difficulties experienced on the voyage, "to Whrite the Whole" of which "Would take a quire of Paper." In a passage of thirty-one days he had been compelled to "Lay two Part of twenty-four days With Such Gales of Wind that It Is Impossibel to Expres Beat and toar my Sails and Riging more than I should have Dun in Six months moderate Wether. The Vessel Sprung A Leak the second Night after I came out and Continewed The Whole Passage So that Wee had a smart Spel at a pump Every half hour . . ." Continuing his account, he told of vessels which "have had 30-35 and 40 and 45 Days Passage and Vessels are Lucked for that have Been out Boston and York six and seven Weeks; . . . markets Are Very Bad So that our Goods Will Not fetch the firs Cost and Theirs dearer and scarcer than Ever they Was Known . . . Remember my harty and obedient Respect to my dear mother Brothers and Sisters Likewise to Unkel Elisha."

James must have been back in Providence by summer, as he embarked in the "Sloope" *Dolphin* for Barbados on July 23, 1749.[36] This voyage finally took him to "Sant Eustata," where he seems to have transferred to another vessel as indicated by the notation "1749 November ye 25th at 6 PM Wee came to Sail in Stasha Road on board the Schooner *Smithfield,* Darius Sessions master."

The last known bit of information from James Brown's own pen is that on "Satterday September ye 15th AD 1750 at 4 o'clock I came to sail in Rhodeisland harbur on board the Sloop frelove and am bound to Maryland." *Freelove* carried a cargo of sugar, molasses, rum, beef, port, etc., on "account and risk of Obadiah Brown and Company." From this voyage James never returned. His devoted brother, Nicholas, wrote this obituary on the last page of James's copy of *The English Pilot:* "York in Virginy February 15 ye 1750/1 Capt. James Brown Died half a Oure Past 6½ at Nite."

The remaining brothers—Nicholas, Joseph, John, and Moses—during their lifetimes brought the Brown family to a vital and significant position in the business life of Providence, of Rhode Island, and of all New England. On the solid foundations laid by older generations, the sons of Captain James Brown built a chain of enterprises which touched almost every phase of economic life in their period. The written records which they have left of their numerous activities tell much about the problems of the colonial businessman and of his methods of solving them. But those records also show a great deal about the characters, talents, and temperaments of the men conducting the business. The four Brown brothers, although similarly trained to carry on the commercial tradition of the family, developed into diverse and dissimilar personalities. Each had abilities and aptitudes which the others lacked. For almost twenty years they turned their talents to good account in joint effort as partners. Eventually the partnership was dissolved. But as the brothers went their separate ways, whether in the China trade, in cotton manufacture, or in banking, they maintained a family solidarity through the years. It was this combination of unity and diversity of the four men which made the impact of the Browns on New England so significant; and which makes it possible to secure from their records an over-all picture of eighteenth-century business and economic life in New England.

As a businessman Nicholas was methodical, patient, plodding, persevering, and thorough, trusting little to inspiration or improvisation. In contrast to the somewhat reckless daring of his brother John, he was cautious in the extreme. His mind had little if any of the reflective quality so marked in Joseph and Moses Brown. He was not the first in Rhode Island to turn to manufacture, produce pig iron, send a ship to China, or spin cotton yarn with power-driven machinery, but his achievements in several fields of business were notable. The countless pages of computation which he has left us in his own handwriting exhibit him as the conservator of funds and fortune rather than as the creator of original ideas. Content with something less than the "most" or the "best," he was never tempted to recklessness or extravagance. In all his dealings he appears firm but reasonable. If he expected to be paid to the last farthing, so he expected to pay in the same degree. Without doubt it was these very qualities of caution, calculation, and moderation which enabled him to serve so successfully in a business family where fraternal bonds were sometimes unduly stretched by the individualistic bent of its different members; and perhaps these were the qualities which were indispensable to the founder of a successful business dynasty.

The most unobtrusive of the brothers in a business way was Joseph, next in age to Nicholas. None of his business letters has survived, if indeed he ever wrote any. He served no apprenticeship at sea. There is no evidence that he made trips to New York, Philadelphia, Boston, or Nantucket in the interest of family business affairs. His personal connection with most of the family pursuits often is so attenuated that he seems in many cases to have been merely a silent partner. Yet he long served as manager of the spermaceti candle manufactory, and as such he held a key position in the firm. But even in this capacity there are only occasional fleeting glimpses of him. Joseph's interests and aptitudes clearly were not in commerce, not in financial speculation, not in mere buying and selling. He had a reflective, inquiring mind and was interested in philosophy, in architecture, in electricity, in the steam engine, and in other things mechanical. But he was largely unfitted for mercantile pursuits which would take him into the rough and tumble of the market place.

A rather confused letter which Joseph wrote to Nicholas in 1774 shows the qualities of vacillation and indecision which must also have helped to disqualify him for overactive participation in trade and commerce:

I have all along been pretty much undetermined about sending for goods to come next fall upon my own account, so that when I considered on one particular it would incline me one way, and on considering another I should be inclined the other way. Many different circumstances operated in this manner upon my mind, until at length I thought I had gone through every consideration. Yesterday when I wrote the billet you was speaking of today, and determined accordingly notwithstanding all which, while we were talking this afternoon, another quite new matter came into my mind. I have taken a turn out and considered it (I hope) properly. The Thing is this, as I observed before, I have been so undetermined on the matter that small or light consideration has wrought considerably upon me, and now as it will certainly make a very material odds to your interest between my sending for goods and not, I say considering this and that I set little or no store on bringing any, I think it is my duty to postpone it, for why should I do a thing which I think there is an almost an equal chance to hurt me as to benefit me, when it is obvious that it must injure you. I can truly say I never considered the thing in this light before. If I had, should have declined as readily as now.[37]

When the Brown brothers built the Hope Furnace and went into the iron business, Joseph took an eager and active part. Here he seemed to find a suitable outlet for his mechanical aptitude, skills, and interests. A more positive side of his personality came to light, a side which had seemed vague and nebulous in previous business affairs. This more forceful facet of his character was especially evident during the Revolution when the furnace was converted to the uses of war. Joseph then displayed, in addition to an easy mastery of mechanical problems, a surprising degree of business acumen, and an over-all grasp of policy which he had hitherto successfully concealed.

There must have been times when Joseph's doubts and uncertainties in commercial concerns provided a much-needed foil to the complete self-assurance of his brother John. The latter's apprenticeship in business was thorough in the extreme. At twenty-one he was a seasoned factor or super-cargo on ships of Obadiah Brown and Company bound for New York, Philadelphia, Newport, Boston, and Nantucket. He was responsible for disposing of the cargoes at those ports and for the purchase of goods for the return voyages. He was not a mariner, and his nautical experience was confined to the coastwise trade; but he obviously was well acquainted with the varied business interests of his uncle Obadiah. At twenty-two his reputation as a businessman was such that the Judge of the Admiralty Court at Newport commissioned him, together with brother Nicholas, to dispose of the cargo of a prize snow.

Seldom have fraternal differences been more marked than those between John and Joseph Brown. There was nothing of the dreamer about John. His was not the contemplative, reflective, inquiring mind, but rather the cold, calculating, practical one. He was as ubiquitous as Joseph was retiring and self-effacing. Throughout life he displayed the same cocksureness which had prompted him as a boy to write at the foot of the page in his "Cipher Book" the words "John Brown the cleverest boy in Providence Town."[38] Although of only medium height, he was otherwise a man of huge physical proportions; and much of his career was cast in a similar mold. It has been said that "he was the Elizabethan merchant-adventurer type in a new setting."[39] It is easy to imagine him in the rôle of one of the promoters of a Muscovy, a Levant, or a London company, and it was altogether in character that in 1772 he was the instigator of the *Gaspee* affair as well as a participant in it. His life abounded in superlatives. It was no mere accident that he sent the first Rhode Island ship to China or that he built the finest house in Providence.

Moses, the youngest of the brothers Brown, was a mere infant at the time of his father's death in 1739. As a small boy he showed the discernment which characterized his later life. Catching the drippings from molasses casks as they were unloaded from vessels at his uncle's wharf, he early acquired a reputation as a shrewd judge of molasses. When an importer was asked "What casks are your best?", he admitted his ignorance, but added "Ask that little molasses-faced Moses; he will tell you." But Moses' training for business was not confined to molasses. Like John, he frequently served as a supercargo on coastwise voyages of Obadiah's vessels. His frequent trips to Newport and Nantucket in other capacities rendered him familiar with the diverse aspects of the family's business.

Less aggressive than Nicholas and John, Moses possessed a breadth of interest far beyond either of them, an interest which in the long run was left unsatisfied by the daily routine of invoices, bills of lading, receipts, and sailing directions. He combined a broad humanitarianism, reflected in his Quakerism and his devotion to the anti-slavery movement, with a deep interest in basic economic problems. His observations of the disastrous results of currency depreciation aroused in him a concern for a sound circulating medium. This, in turn, enlisted his interest in banking, in pursuance of which he supplied the ideas for the Providence Bank. His inquiring mind enabled him to grasp the importance of manufacture in a young country. Not content with mere theorizing upon the subject, he put his ideas into practice and thereby became one of the pioneers of the industrial revolution in this country.

Collectively the four brothers were a redoubtable combination. Nicholas, the cautious, methodical partner, John the born adventurer, Joseph the technician, and Moses the balance wheel represented an aggregate of qualities and aptitudes which promised well for the results of their joint endeavors. Perhaps this complementary character of their capacities was the secret of the success which enabled Moses to write to his brothers: ". . . let us remember and be thankful few in our Days have been Crowned with Such Blessings in Business as we have."

Upon Obadiah's death in 1762 the four brothers continued the business under the name of Nicholas Brown and Company. The change in name brought no immediate change in the scope or character of their activities. Only gradually did the scale of operations expand as the company turned its attention to the promotion of the Hope Furnace in 1765, and to competition with Boston and Newport merchants in the supplying of small-town shopkeepers with English goods in the late 1760's.

There was no break in the solidarity of the four brothers until 1771, when John withdrew from Nicholas Brown and Company while retaining his interest in the furnace and the spermaceti candle manufactory. His departure probably was prompted by his brothers' disapproval of his eagerness to expand the business, and his inclination toward undue risk-taking. These tendencies on John's part are subjected to mild criticism by Moses in a letter outlining to the others his ideas as to the general policy the company should pursue.[40] He referred disapprovingly to the sum of 7950 dollars.

we must pay interest for not having so much Stock as our present Business requires. [Continuing, he wrote that] if Nicholas Power can be agreed with to carry on & oversee the rope Walk on terms that would be Equal . . . and this would Satisfye the Views of Brother John to extend Business as far as he inclines to So as to give him intire Sattisfaction I will agree to come into it; but with this Express Stipulation that for the futer no One Enter into any Kind of Business of a Publick or private Nature whereby the Time or Moneys of the Company will be Imployed to any ones particular advantage or Immolument without first Consulting the Rest of the Company and Either having Their approbation or giving Sufficient opportunity for the Company to adjust their affairs and make a friendly and Honorable Separation in Case the Inclinations of such part of ye Company as Incline to do a further Business is not come into by the rest.

Becoming more pointed in his criticism of John, Moses wrote:

In regard to the Principle proposed by Brother John of Augmenting our Business Annually as our proffits may be (or the Contrary Lessening as we Loose which aut [ought] to be Considered) I conceive if duly Examined will not Hold Either prudent or advantageous . . . who Ever plays any Game the Rubbers, or plays the last for the Value of the Whole gain of the Preceding many, will Sooner or Later Loose the Whole at one Throw. The same is applicable in Trade the Business of which is Truly to get Something to Lay by in Safety and finally to Leave it with Independence from the Various [illegible] of fortune Incident to Trade.

Moses thus rejected John's proposal to expand the business through reinvestment of the profits as likely to result in the loss of everything "at one Throw." And he remarked that "it appears to me most Rational that the Laws of Society or of the Injoyment of our Selves by no means will Extend any mans business beyond what he can attend with due Care and Leave time to Injoy his family and Connections."

Lest his observations thus far should have left anyone in doubt as to his attitude, Moses concluded cryptically: "Therefore from these Considerations I would be Understood by no Means to Expect to Enlarge [the business] hereafter should We be So fortunate as still to Thrive . . . fortune is a Round Stone that Easily Turns Every way and when once moved from the Long Rested Successful Past may not again revolve in the same place."

Nicholas, cautious, conservative by nature, must have shared Moses' disapproval of John's expansionist plans. Nor is there reason to suppose that Joseph, with his indifference to business, would sympathize with John's grandiose ideas. Outvoted, but undoubtedly unconvinced, John decided to go his separate way so far as maritime trade and shipowning were concerned. His relations with his brothers, however, remained entirely cordial; and he shared with them the management of the spermaceti works and the furnace.

On February 7, 1771 Nicholas, Joseph, and Moses met at the spermaceti works and agreed to continue their business in company, notwithstanding John's withdrawal.[41] It was agreed that Moses' "Store Room Down Town & his Three Looer Rooms in his Uptown Store [were] to be Improved by the Company as is Nicholas and Joseph Stores Wholey, and all the Wharf at all times without any charge against each other." In addition to their existing stores, they planned "To build a Shop and Store on the Lott belonging to Mother . . . Two Rooms on a floor the Height of Thos. Green's House." The first floor was to serve as the store. On the second floor was a counting room "16 feet by 19½ feet to be plastered, the back room on the same floor of counting room to be cealed with Grubbed cealing." The upper chamber was to be plastered "before the Shelves are put in." There was to be "A Scuttle through each floor in the back rooms for hoisting up Goods about 4 feet Square with a Trap door to Each & a conveniency to fasten a tackle to in the Garret."[42] The three brothers pledged that for the period of three years from January 1, 1771 "Neither of us be at Liberty to Improve any part of ye Stock in any other Branch or to Ingage with any other Stock in any new branch of Manufacture or Merchandize without the Approbation of both the Others."

During the three years which followed this agreement, Nicholas Brown and Company undoubtedly attained the high point of its success and influence. But in 1773 Moses withdrew from the partnership. This resulted neither from personal incompatibility among the three brothers nor from disagreement regarding business policies of the Company. The death of Moses' wife in 1773 had affected him profoundly. He turned from worldly pursuits into more contemplative channels of the mind and spirit. He became troubled about the traffic in slaves, freed the six slaves whom he owned outright, and gave up his one-quarter interest in four others employed at the spermaceti works. Later he joined the Quakers and participated in the organization of the Rhode Island Abolition Society.

Writing to Nicholas and Joseph under date of August 27, 1773, Moses gave expression to the spiritual travail through which he was then passing:

It has for Some Months layn before me to Leave off Business finding my Ingagements of Mind such as Suffered me not to do what the Curcumstances of Our affairs has Seemed to Require, but having Waited Sometime not Knowing but this Restraint might pass away having before Experienced a degree of the same that has been Measureably Worn off tho not Intirely. But after the most Deliberate Consideration and Waiting what I hope & Trust is the best Council, I verily believe my Business and Ingagements in the World has been a principal Means of preventing my Injoying any Increase of that better part that has Foundation and Will Indure when all thing here below will Vannish and be no more.[43]

Moses therefore asked Nicholas and Joseph to "Take the Whole Business" into their hands. He then remarked that he had no

Other Motive for this proposal than a Desire to pursue such a Cours of Remaining Life as will Afford the Most True peace of Mind here & prepare for its Futer Injoyment in a better Country for I Seek one to Come. The Nature of Our Business is such as dont well admit of a Division and if it would that is not what I Seek for I am Sensible it Wold not Lesson my Cares & Ingagements but it is freedom from it which appears to me best if not absolutely Necessary for Me. I am going a Little Journey Southward with a publick Friend how far is Uncertain by My Return you will be at Leisure after Commencement [at the College] when it would be Agreeable to Confer with you upon the Subject.

In order to be completely certain in his own mind about "a Matter of so great Consequence," Moses withheld this letter from his brothers during his "Little Journey Southward." But far from changing his mind, further consideration merely strengthened his conviction that he could never be "Easy and truly Sattisfyed in a Continuation in Business."[44] Accordingly, he renewed the request made in his previous letter that the brothers take the business into their hands. The brothers accepted Moses' decision. In a letter to the Company's London correspondent announcing the retirement of Moses from the firm, Nicholas wrote that "our Moses Brown has been for some time meditating withdrawing from business & has removed to his seat out of town where he (having a sufficient capital) may enjoy himself and his friends consistent with a serious contemplative mind."[45]

But the withdrawal of Moses from Nicholas Brown and Company involved more than his own preference and convenience; it involved, too, the future of the Company itself. With John already gone, the departure of Moses inevitably raised the question whether Nicholas and Joseph should continue their association in the firm. Given Joseph's indecision, if not downright indifference, in matters of trade, it was not likely that he would care to assume the added duties and responsibilities incident to

Moses' separation from the business. Nicholas, however, expressed Joseph's boredom with business more euphemistically by saying he was "much engaged at present other ways."[46] Announcement of the final dissolution of the Company came in May 1774. Although never again were the four brothers to be united in one over-all concern, Nicholas, Joseph, and John retained their respective interests in the spermaceti works and the furnace, and thus continued to be associated in those two branches of business. During the War for Independence Nicholas and John were jointly concerned in numerous trading ventures.

Despite Joseph Brown's increasing preoccupation with science or natural philosophy, he never entirely dissociated himself from business. Besides his connection with the spermaceti works and the furnace, in the latter of which his interest was both scientific and financial, he was a member of the mercantile firm of Brown and Power during the Revolution, and later he was associated with Joseph Rogers and his own son, Obadiah Brown, in the partnership of Brown, Rogers, and Brown. That his heart was ever in this latter enterprise seems doubtful in view of his acceptance of the chair of natural philosophy at the College of Rhode Island while identified with it. If Joseph regarded this partnership as a means of establishing his son securely in trade and thereby perpetuating his branch of the family in business, he was destined to disappointment. This firm never achieved notable success, and little is heard of it after Joseph's death in December 1785. The son died without issue in 1815.

With his zest for the market place, John Brown must have wished to see his children successful in trade. But of his two sons, only James lived to maturity, and he, unfortunately, had no taste for business. John, therefore, counted heavily upon his son-in-law, John Francis of Philadelphia, who became the junior partner in Brown and Francis after the war. With a mercantile tradition inherited from Tench Francis, pre-Revolutionary Philadelphia merchant, and with John Brown for a mentor and partner, young Francis began his business career with the fairest of prospects. But his death in 1796, followed by that of John Brown himself in 1803, terminated prematurely the business history of that branch of the Brown family.

Moses Brown, who had retired from business in 1774, gradually re-emerged in a mercantile way in the late 1780's. During the next decade he not only became one of the founders of the Providence Bank, but with his son-in-law, William Almy, and with the aid of the mechanical skill of Samuel Slater, he successfully launched the cotton manufacture which his son Obadiah pursued successfully and profitably until his death in 1822. But like John, Moses at his death in 1836 at the age of ninety-eight left no one to carry on the business tradition of the Browns.

Whether or not the descendants of Captain James Brown would achieve distinction in business beyond the lifetime of his own sons thus depended on Nicholas. Fifty-four years old at the close of the war in 1783, and somewhat infirm in body, though not in mind, he gave careful attention to the selection of a partner who, in the event of his own early death, could provide a business training for his two young sons, Nicholas, Jr. and Moses Brown. His choice fell on George Benson, thirty years his junior, who in the previous decade had served as a clerk in the firm of Nicholas Brown and Company, and who had subsequently acquired business experience in other capacities. To insure an adequate apprenticeship for the two young sons, the articles of agreement stipulated that the partnership should continue for seven years, even though Nicholas might depart from this "transitory life" the day after the signing of the bond.

Brown and Benson began under auspicious circumstances, in the midst of the wave of optimism which swept the country with the return of peace in 1783. But events were soon to prove the confidence unwarranted, as the young nation plummeted into the postwar depression of the middle eighties. Although Brown and Benson weathered the crisis, Nicholas Brown's death in 1791 cut short his enjoyment of the era of prosperity which the country was then entering.

As Nicholas' son Moses predeceased him, there remained only Nicholas, Jr. to carry on the name of Brown within the firm. After several years of experience, he became a member of the new partnership of Brown, Benson, and Brown a few months before his father's death. But meanwhile Brown and Benson had been training another young man in the ways of the countinghouse, Thomas P. Ives, a native of Beverly, Massachusetts. Ives, left an orphan at an early age, was placed in the care of relatives. In 1782, when only thirteen years old, he became a clerk for Nicholas Brown. Accepting employment with Brown and Benson in 1783, he continued with the firm for several years. For a short time he was in business with George Sears in Baltimore, a venture in which he appears to have had the blessing, if not the actual financial support, of Brown and Benson who doubtless desired that he should have the added experience of responsible membership in a business firm. In 1792, following his marriage to Nicholas Brown's daughter, Hope, he became a partner in Brown, Benson, and Ives.

Lack of harmony quickly became evident in the new company. With the passing of Nicholas Brown, Sr., George Benson had lost his original mentor. Soon charges and countercharges were flying between the two brothers-in-law on the one hand and George Benson on the other. Perhaps the family solidarity of his two partners made Benson an outsider. The unpleasantness was finally terminated in 1796 by the retirement of George Benson. The partnership of Brown and Ives then entered upon its long history. Thomas P. Ives continued in the firm until his death in 1835, while young Nicholas carried on until his death in 1841. By that time younger men bearing the names of the two families were trained to take over the business. Today, two hundred and thirty-one years after Captain James Brown made his first entry in his book of nautical problems, the sixth generation of his family perpetuates the business tradition which he then established.

CHAPTER 2

"Molasses an Engine in the Hands of the Merchant"

IN a larger sense the primary purpose of the commercial economy of colonial New England was to obtain the means with which to purchase English manufactures, an objective which the Virginia planter accomplished by the simple expedient of exporting tobacco. New England traders, without a staple in ready demand in England, resorted to a variety of indirect trades to secure the wherewithal to pay for goods from the mother country. Most notorious of these was the triangular slave trade from New England to Africa, to the West Indies or the southern continental colonies, and back to the home port. Seldom, however, was the slave trade the chief commercial interest of the New England merchants, and many of them were not concerned in it at all; far more important were other types of trade involving the Caribbean area. Some of these voyages were complicated in the extreme and traced strange and many-sided geometrical figures on the surface of the sea. But probably the majority of them represented a direct reciprocal trade between one of the New England commercial towns and a Caribbean port.[1]

The importance of this trade to the merchants, individually and collectively, cannot be overemphasized. The Rhode Island Remonstrance of 1764 did not exaggerate the energizing influences of molasses upon the economy of the colony when it said that "it is this quantity of molasses which serves as an engine in the hands of the Merchant to effect the great purpose of paying for British manufactures."[2]

Once established in it, the merchant found the Caribbean trade largely self-perpetuating and self-financing. He procured the cargo for each new voyage to the Caribbean with the products he had brought back with him on the voyage before—molasses and the rum distilled therefrom. At the risk of oversimplification one might say that he found the first voyage the hardest. If he could somehow scrape together the initial cargo, future ventures would finance themselves, provided, of course, he employed due enterprise and prudence, and was reasonably favored by wind and weather.

The mercantile history of the Brown family began in this simple fashion. Captain James Brown sailed his ships out of Providence laden with the limited assortment of Rhode Island products which could command a market in the West Indies. Sometimes his vessels proceeded directly to a particular port in the islands, where the goods were sold and a return cargo obtained. At other times his ships went on huckstering voyages in which they shopped about from island to island. In either event, his vessels returned to Providence loaded mainly with molasses, but with perhaps some rum and sugars. The pattern thus established by James Brown was continued by Obadiah.

About 1755 Obadiah Brown and Company began to save the records of many of their Caribbean voyages, a practice which Nicholas Brown and Company continued after 1762. From the invoices, bills of lading, orders to ship captains, receipts for labor and supplies, accounts of sales of cargoes, masters' letters to the owners, and various other documents it is possible to reconstruct many of these voyages.

By this time trade from New England to the Caribbean was so well standardized that a merchant need not puzzle his brain as to the proper ingredients of a suitable cargo. Allowing for variations in volume, an invoice selected at random is likely to be typical. The Brig *George* on one occasion carried 72½ bushels of salt, 2600 feet of pine boards, 9867 feet of oak boards, 8 barrels of pork, 12 barrels of "beef new & 3½ old," 94 barrels of alewives, 400 bricks, 80 barrels of flour, 46 shaken hogsheads, "31 dozen & 7 axes," 13 hogsheads of codfish, 27 hogsheads and 4 barrels of tobacco, 1 hogshead of loaf sugar, 2911 feet of heading, 5600 staves, 1 horse, 8 sheep, and 200 boxes of spermaceti candles.[3] Barring some temporary fluctuation in the Caribbean market which might depress the price of a particular commodity, the articles named above were accepted as staples of the trade.

But such a cargo did not assemble itself. Careful thought and planning went into the accumulation of the assortment of goods required for any given voyage. Some of the articles were produced in Rhode Island or in adjacent areas of neighboring colonies. For example, bricks came from nearby Taunton in Massachusetts. By an agreement of May 1, 1761 one James Hart of that town was to make for Nicholas Brown 110,000 bricks.[4] For the "faithful performance" of his bargain Hart was to be paid at the rate of fifteen shillings lawful money per thousand. He was to receive fifty dollars in cash and the balance in "West India goods or other as he shall want" at the market price. Thus about four-fifths of the cost of the bricks was paid in goods, almost certainly in molasses and rum.

Boards and other forms of lumber were originally procured locally by simple barter agreements. Moses Cooper promised to deliver to the Browns 6000 feet of pine boards to be cut at his mill in Glocester, Rhode Island. He was to be paid at the rate of 65 pounds Old Tenor "or lawful money equivalent" per thousand and to receive his compensation in "goods," meaning molasses or rum.[5] By the 1760's, however, reliance could no longer be placed solely on the forest resources of Rhode Island and adjoining areas. More and more the lumber, hoops, staves, etc., which the Browns' vessels carried to the Caribbean were obtained to the "Eastward"—meaning Maine.

Axes were contracted for locally, as were beef and pork, although the Browns came increasingly to rely upon Connecticut sources for meat products. Payment was made, of course, in the customary currency of rum and molasses. Various kinds of fish, flour, bread, and oysters, all of which were conspicuous in Caribbean cargoes, were obtained from other colonies through the coastwise or intercolonial trade. They, too, in the face of the scarcity of money in Rhode Island, were largely paid for in molasses, rum, candles, and spermaceti oil. Purchases of these commodities, however, were usually negotiated through correspondents or agents in other colonial towns and therefore called for more complicated processes of exchange than the simple barter transactions which characterized trading within the borders of Rhode Island itself.

After 1754, spermaceti candles manufactured in the Browns' own spermaceti works appeared in almost every invoice. The Browns did not need to make intricate financial arrangements to get this product of their own factory into the holds of their ships. But the raw material which went into the candles had been brought into Rhode Island at great cost in money and planning. The story of the trade in head matter with all its ramifications is told in another chapter.

The lack of adequate amounts of gold and silver in all of the colonies made the reckoning of the accounts of the Caribbean trade and of any colonial business an intricate operation. Moreover each transaction had to be scrutinized carefully with an eye to the amount of "hard" money which it might bring in. The situation in Rhode Island was particularly acute. A brief glance at the colony's financial history indicates the chaotic framework of exchange in which the eighteenth-century merchant operated.

The scarcity of hard money inevitably provided a strong temptation to resort to bills of credit. In 1710, Rhode Island followed the example set by Massachusetts twenty years before. The Assembly issued bills of credit to the amount of £5000 to be redeemed in specie within five years. To provide for their retirement a tax of £1000 per year for the five-year period was voted.

A second and somewhat different issue of bills of credit came in 1715. This new issue of £40,000 was secured not by tax but by mortgages on land. Anyone might mortgage his land to the government and receive bills of credit to the amount of the mortgage. Upon these he paid 5 per cent interest up to ten years, when the principal was to be retired. This plan seemed ideally suited to the needs of a community which was land poor. By it the landowner could, with the aid of the government, convert his real property into money, even though the land was so little in demand that it was impossible to borrow upon it in the open market on reasonable terms.

During the next thirty years the Assembly authorized several additional "banks" (the name applied to paper emissions on land security). In 1731 despite the fact that the bills in circulation exceeded £120,000 and depreciation was increasing, the Assembly voted another "bank" of £60,000. By 1740 Governor Richard Ward admitted that the bills outstanding amounted to £340,000, but attributed the prosperity of the colony to "paper money and a right application" thereof.

In 1750, when bills of credit had increased to the amount of £525,335, the lower house of the Assembly authorized another "bank." In consternation, seventy-two members of the mercantile elite of Newport signed a petition to the Crown praying that the colony be prevented "from emitting any more bills of credit upon loan" except with royal consent. Whether because of this petition or not, Parliament in 1751 forbade all "banks" of paper money. Henceforth bills of credit might be issued only for current expenses of the colony or to meet the costs of war. Adequate provision for redemption of the paper must be made at time of issue.

Meanwhile, the paper issued in such excessive amounts had greatly depreciated. In recognition of this fact, the Assembly when authorizing the "bank" of 1740 stated the precise amount of silver and gold the new bills of credit would purchase. Silver was valued at 6 shillings, 9 pence per ounce and gold at £5 per ounce. The term "New Tenor" was applied to this latest emission of paper to distinguish it from the earlier issues which were henceforth referred to as "Old Tenor." Old Tenor bills were supposedly worth exactly one-fourth as much as the New Tenor. But, of course, it required more than mere legislative fiat printed on the new bills to maintain their stipulated value.

When in 1756 there arrived from England six chests of silver and one of gold in partial recompense for Rhode Island's outlay in support of the Crown Point expedition of the previous year, the money was applied toward redemption of the paper. The Assembly authorized the issuance of £8000 in lawful money which was declared the equal of the lawful money of Massachusetts. In 1763 there was drawn up a table of depreciation of the Old Tenor bills in terms of the Spanish dollar. As of 1751, £2, 16 shillings Old Tenor was equivalent to one Spanish dollar; for 1760, £6 Old Tenor was equal to one dollar, and for 1763 the rate was £7 for a dollar. In 1764 the courts fixed the ratio of Old Tenor to lawful money at 23½ to 1; in 1769 it was established at 26⅔ to 1. In the same year the Spanish milled dollar was worth 4 shillings, 6 pence Sterling, and 6 shillings in lawful money. To the undoubted satisfaction of the mercantile interests within the colony, these ratios continued to 1776, thereby providing the colony with a stable currency for the first time in more than half a century. Even so, the merchant still found it necessary on many occasions to reckon accounts in any one of several different currencies: Sterling, lawful money, Old Tenor, New Tenor, livres, stivers, and Spanish milled dollars.

The cost of the goods which the Browns over the years sent to the Caribbean must be figured against this background of exchange. The value of the cargoes varied, of course, according to their size and the state of the market in which they were purchased. Goods shipped on board the Ship *Nancy* in 1764 the Browns charged in the vessel's invoice at £24339 Old Tenor or £782 Sterling.[6] In the same year the cargo of the Brig *George* was charged at £26749 Old Tenor, or about £860 Sterling.[7] Thus within a period of three months Nicholas Brown and Company had shipped goods to the value of more than £1600 Sterling. This outlay, moderate even for that time, is fairly representative of the scale on which the Browns conducted their trade to the Caribbean area. Usually the value of a single cargo was not excessive. These conservative and careful Rhode Island merchants seldom made the mistake of risking too much of their hard-won capital in a single venture. They knew too well from actual experience the hazards of the sea. They knew that once a vessel had weighed anchor in the Providence River, its fortunes were out of their hands. The captain with the orders from the owners in his strongbox was master of the vessel and its cargo. Much depended upon his integrity and judgment. But, in the last analysis the success or failure of the voyage was beyond human control. The operation of the law of supply and demand, the market conditions at the port of call, and always the whims and vagaries of the weather were factors that must be hopefully and helplessly accepted.

In the face of all these contingencies, the captain of the ship carried heavy responsibilities. In the majority of cases the cargo was consigned directly to him. It was his job to get it to its destination, sell it, and buy satisfactory merchandise on satisfactory terms, in exchange. Only occasionally were factors employed to assume part of the burden of buying and selling. The orders to the captains varied in detail. They might give reasonably specific instructions or they might grant substantial measures of discretion.

Fairly typical were the orders given to Captain Christopher Sheldon of the Brig *George* in 1768. Captain Sheldon was to proceed with all convenient dispatch to Surinam, there to dispose of his cargo "to the best advantage for a load of good molasses and the remainder you'll send us in good bills of exchange as soon as possible, as we shall want the money in November at the furdest."[8] The owners urged Captain Sheldon to take care not to raise the price of molasses but "to use all prudent methods to endeavor to lower it." If he should find Captain Burrough (of the Sloop *Four Brothers*) at Surinam he was to assist him "in the best manner . . . that he may sail as soon as possible with as many Bills of Exchange as the whole of his cargo net clear of charge."[9] These orders were simple and to the point—sell the cargo at the highest price, buy molasses at the lowest, and send back good bills of exchange at the earliest possible moment.

Oddly enough, instructions of a more detailed character might allow greater discretion to the captain. In 1764 Captain Abraham Whipple of the Brig *George* received orders to dispose of his cargo at Surinam "to our best advantage for molasses if to be got at not exceeding 6½ stivers per gallon along side," and to lay out the "overplus" in good Russia duck.[10] Should molasses exceed that figure, and duck be available at 22 Holland guilders per bolt, he was to ballast his vessel with molasses but invest the bulk of his funds in duck "which you are to pack in dry molasses hhds. or other proper package and secrete in the most effectual manner possible and proceed home." Should he be unable to procure either molasses or duck at the prices stipulated he was to go to such of the Islands "as you may think best and load with salt and proceed home."[11] Under these instructions, Captain Whipple was free to buy molasses and Russia duck in varying proportions at Surinam or to buy salt at any of the islands for his return cargo. Generally, instructions to a shipmaster left entirely to him the decision as to whether he should sell his cargo wholesale to merchants at his port of destination, or dispose of it at retail to the local residents. On this particular voyage, however, Captain Whipple was told of vessels from Taunton and Swansea, "in the Massachusett Bay Colony," which were bound for Surinam. Should he arrive before them, he would be well advised to "sell to the Merchants," but should he arrive later he was to retail his goods.[12]

The letters and reports which the ship captains sent back to the owners give many details of the actual processes of trade at the Caribbean ports.

Many of these are pessimistic in the extreme—markets were bad, prices unsatisfactory, and prospects gloomy. But year after year the ships plied back and forth. The molasses and other goods which they brought into the colony must have been so indispensable that the disappointing results of individual voyages could be viewed with some equanimity in the light of the net results. Reports such as this from Captain George Hopkins from Surinam were frequent: "It is now very dull Times. Nor ant anything in demand." But despite the lack of "demand" he had sold a large part of his cargo at prices not too ruinous. But he added that he had "lost three horses on the passage . . . The smallpox is very plenty here . . . We are all well on board as yet but a miserable gang at best."[13]

The letters of the shipmasters also show the leisurely pace of commerce in the eighteenth century, the guesswork and uncertainty involved in transacting business at such a distance, and the lack of adequate standards of quality. Sale of a cargo at Surinam and purchase of molasses for the return voyage frequently required as much as four and one-half months. The delay might result from any one of several causes beyond the control of the captain: the slow sale of his wares, the difficulty of collecting for goods sold, the scarcity and high price of molasses, or the faulty local facilities for assembling the cargo he was to take home. Sale of the cargo at retail was not only time consuming, but it also accentuated the problem of debt collection, which occasioned further delay. On November 20, 1768 Captain Sheldon of the *George* hoped to have all his molasses on board by the following January first, but he was "very uncertain when I shall sail as I have my affairs in upward of 80 different hands, and none bad as I know of yet."[14] With money "very scarce and hard to collect" the problem of securing payment from so many different purchasers required time.

The procuring of the return cargo of molasses at Surinam was difficult because of the lack of any central agency with which the shipmasters could deal. There was no middleman between the planter and the captain to expedite the process. There were no hogsheads of molasses piled high on the wharves awaiting the incoming vessel. The ship captain sought out his own cargo. He carried with him the staves, hoops, and heading which his cooper fashioned into hogsheads. He took his turn in engaging his molasses from the planter. He distributed his empty hogsheads and then waited for the return of the punts or small boats which brought them back filled with molasses from the plantations.[15] All of this might consume weeks or months. Yet the delays were taken for granted and seldom if ever was a ship captain reprimanded for the loss of valuable time. Although stoically accepted, these delays occasioned great inconvenience, disrupted many plans, and caused much actual financial loss.

If the loss of precious time blighted many fair prospects, that was equally true of the lack of information regarding market conditions. With nothing to guide him in the planning of a voyage to a distant port except the latest price current therefrom (already weeks out of date), even the shrewdest merchant had to proceed blindly with his preparations for the dispatch of a particular vessel. Relying upon his latest information, he might decide that flour would answer well at Surinam. But before he could assemble and start his cargo on its way, half a dozen vessels might have arrived with flour from Philadelphia, with a resulting demoralization of the market. Of course the evil effects of such a situation were somewhat alleviated by the assorted nature of the cargo. But in the absence of really current market reports even the most careful selection of goods afforded little protection against disastrous over-all loss on an entire shipment.

The lack of fair standards of quality of products involved in trade added to the uncertainty of profit and loss. Complaints were constant that the weevil was in the flour, the tobacco "touched by frost," oysters tainted, beef or pork spoiled, fish decayed, and oil "very foul." Even spermaceti candles were sometimes of doubtful purity. And, of course, a cargo in perfect condition at the beginning of a voyage could easily suffer heavy damage en route to its destination.

Such annoyances as these, added to the basic difficulties of money and exchange, demanded that the successful eighteenth-century businessman use continuously every ounce of wit, imagination, patience, and perseverance which he possessed. Business of necessity called for continual improvisation and adjustment. It could not be conducted with streamlined efficiency. It could not be hurried. But even so the merchant made the most of his opportunities and met his problems with surprising skill and ingenuity.

During the decades when the Browns traded in the Caribbean, Surinam, the Dutch Colony in South America, was a favorite port of call. In the years 1763 to 1774 the vessels of Nicholas Brown and Company docked there more frequently than at any other port in the area. The preference of the Browns for the Dutch Colony is easily understood. It was a satisfactory source of supply for that necessary "engine" of trade, molasses. It was also a good market for horses and tobacco, two of the most important of the few articles for export produced in Rhode Island. The Dutch Government had opened Surinam to British traders in 1704 on condition that they bring horses with them to supply draft animals for the sugar planters. Captain James Brown made the most of this opportunity. He often purchased "Surinam horses" in lots of ten or a dozen; and his successors enlarged the trade. On occasion they shipped as many as thirty horses on a single voyage. Between March and October 1765 Nicholas Brown and Company contracted with Isaac Tripp for

ninety horses suitable for the Surinam market. By one agreement Tripp
was to purchase forty of them, "the whole not amounting to more than
£180 Lawful money." He was to pay for them with rum, sugar, molasses,
and "one negrow garl," and was to receive compensation at the "rate of
6/ lawful money per day for my time and trouble in selling these articles
and purchasing the horses." Another contract with Tripp required that
he procure and deliver twenty "of the small snug kind of Dutch horses,"
for which the Browns allowed him twelve dollars per head. By still another
agreement Tripp promised to purchase and deliver thirty horses "in good
care and free from lameness and to have two good eyes and otherwise to
be young enough to have good teeth." Again he was to receive twelve
dollars per head.[16]

In the same year one Chad Brown agreed to procure "6 choice good
Surinam horses" for which Nicholas Brown and Company allowed him
"70 gallons molasses for the best and in proportion for the others." By
another agreement he was to deliver four Surinam horses "by Saturday
one hour before sunset" at £120 Old Tenor per head. The following year
he contracted to deliver twenty horses, "each having two eyes," at the
maximum price of "48 gallons New England rum for each."[17]

Sometimes the agreements were more elaborate. Amos Babcock purchased thirty horses for the Browns at the rate of four pounds ten shillings
lawful money per head. He received his pay in 400 pounds of coffee, 10
hundredweight of brown sugar, 200 pounds of loaf sugar, two hogsheads
of West India rum, six hogsheads of salt, and the balance in New England
rum, the price of each article being carefully stipulated. In the event of
failure to deliver the animals at the stated time, Babcock must "make
good all damages that the same may ocation to the s^d Browns."[18] Transactions of this type for voyages to Surinam were carried on for many
years, but they never assumed the importance of the business in tobacco.

Rhode Island tobacco was of inferior quality and could not compete
with the Virginia and Maryland varieties in the English markets. But it
appealed to the less discriminating taste of the Surinam residents, who
allegedly purchased it in preference to the finer grades. Strangely enough,
during the many years in which they engaged in the export of Rhode
Island tobacco to the Caribbean region the Browns appear only once, as
mentioned before, to have run afoul the British mercantile regulations
requiring the shipment of colonial tobacco to England, a laxity on the
part of the British which undoubtedly reflects their lack of esteem for the
weed grown in the Narragansett country.

The speculative features of the tobacco trade with Surinam had a
strong attraction for Nicholas Brown and Company, and they watched
with care the various factors governing the price of tobacco both in Rhode

Island and in the Caribbean. On September 16, 1764 Captain Abraham Whipple sailed from Providence with a consignment of tobacco for the Surinam market.[19] On that very day there "was the most remarkable frosty knight ever known in America for the season."[20] As a result the bulk of the Colony's tobacco crop was totally destroyed. And the little that was "not quite spoilt" was "so much touched with the frost" as to be but "very ordinary." The Browns recognized, of course, that the resulting "scarcity and dearness of this article," while nullifying the plans of all the merchants for large purchases and shipments of tobacco to Surinam, would increase the price of that article in the Dutch colony.

At this time Connecticut also produced tobacco which was shipped to the Surinam market. Careful investigation indicated that "nary a vessel is like to go" from the "Nutmeg" colony that season.[21] The reason was not the ravages of the elements upon the crop but rather "the great danger they apprehend in trading to foreign parts." All of which suggests that Connecticut merchants and mariners were either more law-abiding or more timorous than those in Providence Plantations. At the moment, of course, Britain was tightening her commercial regulations with respect to the colonies. The Sugar Act had recently been enacted; and its provision for the collection of the threepence duty on foreign molasses imported into New England evidently made Surinam voyages seem less attractive than they had been. Either respect for the law or fear of the consequences of breaking it was about to restrain the Connecticut exporters. This would still further increase the scarcity and dearness of tobacco at Surinam. Hoping to make the most of this opportunity, the Browns wrote to Captain Abraham Whipple that "if you should have any of this article left when this reaches you by no means part with it until you can get a good price for it."[22] Unfortunately, because of the slowness of eighteenth-century means of communication, this intelligence came too late to the good Captain at Surinam; he had sold his tobacco in complete ignorance of circumstances which were about to cause an appreciation in its price.

If nature had been unkind to the Rhode Island tobacco growers in 1764, she smiled on them the following year and blessed them with a bountiful crop. And the merchants of the colony, undeterred by British regulations, shipped it to Surinam and imported Dutch molasses in return, with or without the payment of the threepence duty, as circumstances might dictate. The shipments of tobacco to Surinam from the crop of 1765 were so great, however, and the price so much depressed that the merchants decided that something must be done to prevent a recurrence of the situation in 1766. They could, of course, do nothing to control the total production of tobacco within the colony, that being in the hands of God and the tobacco planters; but they believed they could greatly influence, if not absolutely control, the shipments to Surinam, and the price at which the tobacco sold there.

Accordingly, Nicholas Brown and Company, Daniel Jenckes and Son, and Nathan Angell, all of Providence, devised a scheme for that purpose. On September 5, 1766 they jointly addressed a letter to Captain Esek Hopkins, later Commander-in-Chief of the Continental Navy in the Revolution but then in the service of Nicholas Brown and Company at Surinam, in which they carefully outlined their plan.[23] "In consequence of the low price tobacco was reduced to last year, occasioned by the great quantity and its being consigned to the different masters,"[24] they had agreed to ship to Esek's care 155,000 pounds in three or more vessels in the following proportions: Nicholas Brown and Company, 75,000; Daniel Jenckes and Son, 45,000; and Nathan Angell, 35,000.[25] The tobacco was to go at the risk of the several shippers until its arrival at Surinam, there to be consigned to Esek Hopkins and sold at the "best price it will fetch and the net proceeds to be equally divided according to each shipper's proportion." Should any part of "either company's tobacco . . . be lost or damaged on the passage they who shipt it to abide by the loss and if any bad debts should be made each shipper to lose in the same proportion as what he shipped is to the whole quantity."

The three contracting parties then signed an agreement in which they pledged themselves "not to give for tobacco directly or indirectly any more or better terms than five shillings old Tenor per pound by presents, promises or otherwise, to be paid in six months from delivery."[26] They further agreed to continue to purchase "all the tobacco that may be bought on the above terms until the whole quantity that is raised [in the colony] be bought."[27] In short, the three subscribers to this covenant planned nothing less than a corner on the tobacco grown in Rhode Island in the year 1766.

That the Providence mercantile houses successfully achieved this part of their audacious scheme is shown by an urgent letter which Nicholas Brown and Company received from their old friends, the firm of Joseph and William Wanton of Newport.[28] "We want," they wrote, "about 3000[wt] good tobacco for our Guinea men. Dont know where to apply for it as you have monopolized all in the colony, but the true reason of applying to you is the want of cash without which dont expect to get it if I knew where it was." While recognizing the monopoly which the Browns and their associates had achieved, the Wantons promised that "if you will befriend us so much as to send that quantity by the first boat will pay you in Duck at as low a price as any man in the colony will sell for. Mention this article because cash is generally given for it, but you may exact of us any other article you please at cash price." Should this proposal be unsatisfactory, the Wantons desired the Providence house to purchase it "for us on your credit payable in four months provided it can be done this week." If this should not be feasible, they hoped the Browns would "send us that quantity and supply yourselves again for which shall pay as you shall agree with the seller. We shall be greatly obliged to you to purchase it on same terms and send it forthwith."

This humble plea to the Browns from one of the oldest and proudest of the Newport houses is significant. That three mercantile firms in the commercially immature town of Providence should have the imagination, the enterprise, the boldness to conceive and execute such a stroke at the expense of, and to the embarrassment of, their Newport contemporaries was indicative of the business awakening of Providence under the leadership of families such as the Browns. To get the jump on the Newporters was no ordinary achievement; for they had shown themselves to possess resourcefulness and daring in business equal to any on the continent. By this move the Providence merchants served notice that they were no longer to be treated as country cousins accepting without question the commercial leadership of Newport.

Having laid their plans for a monopoly of the tobacco crop in Rhode Island, the Browns and their confederates carefully mapped the strategy to be employed at Surinam. On October 24, 1766 they jointly wrote to Esek Hopkins giving the details of their plan.[29] The 155,000 pounds of tobacco were to be shipped in three different vessels. One was to sail from the Browns' wharf at the end of October; a second from "the Jenckes house" in ten or twelve days thereafter; and the third from "Angells house" by the middle of November.[30] The entire quantity was to be consigned to Esek Hopkins, who received instructions to sell none of it at less than five stivers per pound. Explaining the purpose of the plan, they wrote:

We have two things in view in consigning this tobacco to you. The first is that we think it will be of advantage to our interest; the second is we think it will be of service to yourself. We doubt not of your being able to get five stivers for the whole as we shall buy near all the tobacco that is raised this year in the colony and have engaged under writing that neither of us will ship any tobacco over and above the 155 thousand aforesaid, not till after the first of February next.

Confident that only a very limited quantity of tobacco would be shipped to Surinam from other sources, they instructed Hopkins to buy all "that is equally good with ours from the time you receive this till the whole of our 155 thousand wt is sold," provided it could be had at not exceeding four stivers. In other words, Hopkins would purchase all tobacco that was offered at four stivers, as a means of maintaining the price and with a view to enabling him to dispose of his consignment at the agreed figure of five stivers per pound.[31] But this clearly fell short of the mark, as tobacco could be freely sold at any figure between four and five stivers in competition with that which Hopkins was instructed to hold for five. Before the letter was dispatched someone discovered this loophole and inserted a paragraph directing Hopkins to do everything in his power to maintain the price at five stivers, even to purchasing on the owners' account whatever quantity of good tobacco might be offered under that price.

As a special inducement to Esek Hopkins to remain in Surinam "to complete our business," he was to receive rewards over and above the customary 5 per cent commission on all tobacco sold by him, with 2½ per cent on all molasses purchased for the return voyages of the vessels. His principals allowed him, free of all freight charges, 8000 pounds of tobacco on his own account, together with "a privilege home in each of our vessels that carries . . . the tobacco as much molasses in each vessel as is equal to 4 per cent on the whole molasses you ship in said vessels and to have your casks free if you choose it; and to live on board either vessel that may suit you best on the same terms as though you went from here her master."[32]

These instructions were carried to Esek Hopkins by Captain Abraham Whipple, the Brig *George,* belonging to Nicholas Brown and Company. Hopkins was told that

Capt. Whipple is permitted to open this letter after he gets southward of Bermuda and is the only person besides ourselves that knows anything of our plan and we particularly recommend to you your keeping the same between you as much as you possibly can. Our dependence on Capt. Whipple not divulging any part to any person whatever arises from our favorable opinion of him which is expressed in furnishing him with about 7000 [pounds] tobacco.[33]

On October 29, 1766 the Sloop *Mary Ann,* Captain Jeremiah Hawkins, pushed off from the Browns' wharf with the first shipment of tobacco covered by the agreement. Besides 100 hogsheads of that article, the vessel carried 122 boxes of spermaceti candles, eight horses, and small consignments of bricks, staves, heading, beef, pork, onions, and flour.[34] But this was primarily a tobacco voyage and the letter to Esek Hopkins which Captain Hawkins carried from the three contracting firms was concerned with tobacco to the exclusion of every other article in the cargo. To enable Hopkins the more effectually to obtain the stipulated price of five stivers per pound, the shippers enclosed a letter of credit authorizing him to draw on them to the extent of 10,000 guilders, if necessary, to purchase all the good tobacco offered under that price.[35] He was to continue his purchases until convinced that "there is as much arrived as will supply the place the year or until you can get five stivers for yours." They observed that "tis possible some vessel may go from Connecticut with tobacco but at present we have no certain advice of any."

There then follows a bit of rationalizing designed to salve their consciences. They had been brought into "this union" not primarily with a view to "engrossing" so much as "in our own defense."[36] This latter conclusion was arrived at, and the whole procedure justified, by a strange species of reasoning. They wrote that "we separately engaged all the tobacco we could before in order to get away first before we united, and having given the planters here their usual & asking prices and not stipulated you to sell for more than it has been often sold for we think we are clear from any Reflection on that acct." To this point the three houses were content with the thought that their procedure would injure neither the tobacco grower in Rhode Island nor the consumer in Surinam.[37] But then it occurred to them that their conduct might be justified on positive grounds. Accordingly, they said "tis probable if we did not do this the price abroad would be so reduced by the Quantitys Raised being forced to Market in such Hast that it would Greatly Discourage and Injure the Planters in their Next years crops."

Here we have a good eighteenth-century example of business practice with which the American public was to become thoroughly familiar a hundred years later. Attempting to avert the danger to themselves inherent in continuation of their competitive buying and selling of tobacco, the three Providence houses had entered into a monopolistic agreement. Somewhat less callous and less indifferent to the consequences of their conduct than some of their later counterparts, they comforted themselves with the thought that they were injuring neither the Rhode Island tobacco grower nor the Surinam buyer, and that their actions were probably a positive boon to the planters.

The results of this elaborate plan of the Providence merchants must have been disappointing to them in the extreme. In the spring of 1767 Esek Hopkins wrote that "I have Not Sold but Twenty Six hhd tobacco in the whole Sent me by the Several Vessels and Sum of that at 4½ and I See No prospect of Seling it at aney Price. When the Sloop Come in I Could have Sold hers for 4st but Indavering to gitt 5 I Do not Now Expect to gitt 4. The Times Luckes Dull for me at present."[38] This seems to be the final unhappy word on the great tobacco speculation of 1766. The papers of *Mary Ann* are strangely silent on the subject. There is no further word from Esek Hopkins telling of sales when times "lucked" less dull. But there is every evidence that the plan failed completely. The reasons for the failure are a matter of conjecture.

In part, the failure of the scheme was doubtless the result of conditions then prevailing in Surinam, where the large carry-over from tobacco shipments of the previous year had a depressing effect upon the price of the product. More important, perhaps, was the disorganized state of the world tobacco market. A break in the price at Amsterdam in 1764 began a decline which by September 1768 amounted to 50 per cent. So the Browns and their Providence friends were attempting, by means of local arrangements, to correct an international price situation. Viewed in this light, the agreement to monopolize the tobacco crop of Rhode Island could not indeed have been injurious to the planters, as without it they would have had no active market for their product.

In 1767 Nicholas Brown and Company, in pursuance of some sort of agreement with Daniel Jenckes and Son, dispatched at least two vessels to Surinam with tobacco.[39] But again, because of the carry-over, they were unable to maintain the price and in the end sold the cargoes at $2\frac{1}{2}$ and $2\frac{1}{4}$ stivers.[40] To make matters worse, the tobacco was in such a bad condition that it was necessary "To over haul every cask by taking out both heads." The resulting shrinkage in weight caused heavy financial loss.[41] In 1768 Nicholas Brown and Company once more sold their tobacco at $2\frac{1}{4}$ stivers.[42]

The persistence of the low price year after year finally led several Providence mercantile firms to make another attempt to correct the situation by concerted action. On October 10, 1770 five houses, Nicholas Brown and Company, Daniel Jenckes and Son, Nathan Angell and Job Smith, Thomas and Nathanael Greene and John Wiley, and Thurber and Cahoone and Edward Thurber signed articles of agreement "which is to be by each and every party fully observed upon principles of honor pledged each other without mental reservation whatsoever."[43] The five houses were jointly to ship to Surinam not more than 200,000 pounds of tobacco prior to February 1, 1771. The quantity assigned to each firm ranged from 60,000 pounds allotted to the Browns down to 28,000 pounds for each of the two companies last named in the agreement.[44] The covenant fixed the price of "good merchantable tobacco delivered in Providence" at not more than five shillings Old Tenor per pound, with six months' credit, and not more than four shillings, ninepence "cash down within three months from date."[45] In lieu of consignment to a factor, as in the venture of 1766, the tobacco was to be shipped to the care of the various ship captains. The signatory firms agreed to "give all our masters express orders not to sell his tobacco within thirty days after their arrival under three and one-half stivers per pound unless the last price should be less, in which case or in any case of a necessity of falling under that there should be a free consultation of our respective masters present for our general advantage." As a safeguard against a device frequently employed to violate the spirit of price maintenance agreements, no ship captain was to "lessen the sale of his tobacco by adding any greater price on any other article of his cargo but shall give a true account of what his tobacco sells at without connection with any other articles." On the return of all the vessels the merchants were to have a meeting at which they were "to put the sales into one sum and settle the whole accordingly; and those who shall sell for more than an average price shall pay to those that shall fall short in sales, in money as Bills then pass or Dutch bills."[46] In short, by the agreement of 1770 the Browns and their associates sought to guarantee themselves a minimum price of three and one-half stivers per pound. The difference between this figure and the five stivers mentioned in the covenant of 1766 reflects not only the growing demoralization in the tobacco trade at Surinam but also the world-wide decline in tobacco prices during the intervening years.

For a time it seemed that it might not be necessary to implement this agreement. On September 4, 1770 Captain Smith sailed from Providence aboard the Brig *Sally,* owned by Nicholas Brown and Company. He was bound for Surinam with a cargo of tobacco. On November 10, 1770 he wrote that he had sold all his tobacco at "from six to seven stivers."[47] But this was too good to last. Soon the heavy autumn shipments of tobacco to Surinam began to depress the price. On November 15, 1770 Nicholas Brown and Company ordered Captain Christopher Sheldon to proceed to Surinam in the Brig *George* with eighty-four hogsheads and three tierces of tobacco. They directed the Captain "not to sell your tobacco under the greatest price you can get for that article alone and not undersell in order to get a higher price for any other article."[48] They provided him with a copy of their agreement with the other houses which they asked him "to see so far as you can that the other contractors' masters follows." But evidently the price yielded to the pressure of heavy receipts in the late autumn and winter. On March 22, 1771 Captain Sheldon wrote that the last tobacco at Surinam had sold at two and one-half stivers.[49] Whether this was the result of consultation among the various masters or of the action of an individual ship captain it is impossible to say; but it is apparent that in the long run the agreement of 1770 had achieved little if any more success than that of 1766.

Although a large carry-over might on occasion prevent it, the price at Surinam usually advanced in the summer and early autumn prior to the arrival of tobacco in large volume. Thus, notwithstanding the depressed state of the market in the spring of 1771, when Captain Simon Smith arrived with *Sally* in the autumn of that year he was able to sell his tobacco at three to four stivers, chiefly at three and one-half, the price which the Browns and their friends had sought the previous year.[50]

Aside from its importance to the Browns as a source of molasses and the rum distilled therefrom, the Surinam trade provided them with the Dutch bills of exchange which they so much needed in other branches of their business. Only on rare occasions did they instruct their ship captains to invest the entire proceeds of their outbound cargoes in molasses, for only a short cargo could be balanced entirely in molasses. But it was only on equally rare occasions, when their need for cash was urgent, that they directed their captains to remit the proceeds of their goods wholly in bills of exchange. In the majority of instances the proceeds were returned in molasses and bills, the amount of the latter representing the difference in the value of the two cargoes.

This discrepancy in the value of the cargoes naturally varied with each voyage.[51] Sales of goods from the Brig *Sally* in 1769 amounted to 22,436 guilders, while the cost of 290 hogsheads of molasses, plus disbursements and port charges, came to 15,792 guilders, leaving a balance of 6643 guilders to be remitted in Dutch bills.[52] In the same year when sales of merchandise from the Brig *George* amounted to 15,174 guilders, her return cargo of 21,686 gallons of molasses cost 8132 guilders, while disbursements and port charges were 2779 guilders. The captain, therefore, remitted 5562 guilders in bills of exchange.[53] As there was nothing unusual about the business situation at that time, these figures may be regarded as reasonably typical. Sometimes, of course, a vessel made a bad voyage; occasionally one met with unusual success.

Arrival of ships at Surinam was timed to take advantage of the new crop of sugar and molasses; and, fortunately, this fitted admirably into the Browns' larger scheme of business. Their heaviest outlays of cash came in the late autumn and winter when they purchased at Nantucket their annual stock of head matter for the spermaceti candle manufactory. A steady flow of bills of exchange during those months was, therefore, very welcome. Sometimes the need for those bills was too urgent to await the sale of the cargo at Surinam. In such cases the captain received instructions to borrow in anticipation of the disposal of his goods and to remit in bills. In 1767 Captain Nicholas Power was asked to obtain 9000 or 10,000 guilders in this manner.[54] Thus the Caribbean trade of the Browns, once their major concern, was now secondary to the candle business. To them, commerce was becoming the servant of manufacture.

Trade at Surinam must have been conducted in an atmosphere of distrust and suspicion. Surinam merchants appear in the letters of Brown ship captains as a hard-bitten lot, against whose trickery one must be constantly on the alert. Esek Hopkins, seldom given to exaggeration, believed there was "more honour and honesty in so many highwaymen in England than in the merchants" of Surinam.[55] Captain John Burrough of the Sloop *Four Brothers* wrote that "as for a price current it is almost impossible to make one out here is so much biting and lying that no man knows anothers price but do each other all the damage they can."[56]

Unfortunately, there is little direct evidence as to what the Surinam folk thought of their visitors from the British continental colonies. But it is not difficult to imagine their reaction to some of the sharp practices of which the shipmasters sometimes convict themselves by their own letters. When Captain Simon Smith wrote that, in accordance with instructions from the ship owners, "we are now about to fall the price of molasses" through agreement among the captains, he was referring to a practice which the sugar planters thought reprehensible.[57] And their opinion of the visitors from Rhode Island would not have been enhanced could they have known that the captains sometimes lacked the honor to abide by their own solemn covenants. Captain Christopher Sheldon gave an instance of this when he advised the Browns that he was "sorry now to Acquaint you of the Unhappy Affair of our Scheme of Falling molasses being put to an End by Nick° Bogart Arriving from N York has nockt it all in head. it is now at 8S^t at plantation and Every one that Can take is a takeing it at that price."[58] When the same ship captains, acting on instructions from their principals, sought to maintain an artificial price for tobacco they probably branded themselves in the eyes of Surinam merchants as men who would bear careful watching. It was clearly a struggle for financial advantage and no holds were barred for any of the participants.

There is, however, still in existence one bit of direct evidence of a phase of the hurly-burly of life as it was lived at Surinam during the days when it was the port of call for ships from the New England colonies. John Greenwood, a colonial artist, lived at the Dutch port for six years when the Caribbean traffic was in its heyday. In his painting, "Sea Captains at Surinam," he has portrayed with "breezy candor" a drinking orgy in one of the local taverns. The dimly lit room presents a scene of chaotic disorder. Chairs are overturned, and tables are cluttered. Men in varying stages of conviviality quaff their drinks from enormous bowls handed out by a Negro at the bar, sleep in slovenly disarray, or with wigs awry, three-cornered hats askew, stumble towards the door carrying bed-time candles tilted at precarious angles. Providence tradition has it that the two reasonably sober and upright gentlemen in the room are Esek Hopkins himself and Nicholas Cooke, later Revolutionary Governor of Rhode Island. But quite apart from the depiction of individual faces, Greenwood has brought to his canvas in realistic fashion something of the rugged, roistering quality of the Yankee traders as they relaxed after their long sea voyages or fortified themselves for matching wits with the Surinam "highwaymen" on the morning after.

Frequently ship captains found it difficult to collect from Surinam merchants to whom they had sold goods. Captain Abraham Whipple of the Sloop *Four Brothers,* complaining of two of his debtors, wrote that "the reason they say that did not pay it before [is that] I cheated them in the tobacco and they say that it all rotted on their hands."[59] Captain Nicholas Power, referring to his debtors, wrote: "I dont see that ever I shall get paid for the tobacco by Mr. Wolff, for some times when I go for the money he is in a great passion & at other times he tells me a foolish story that we delivered him more by 60 hhd. then Capt. Esek Hopkins told him there was."[60] Emphasizing his further difficulties, Captain Power wrote that "he [Mr. Wolff] told me yesterday he would pay me as soon as he could get the money, on which I told him where I had hired the money to send home." As the "hiring" of the money had been made necessary by Wolff's failure to pay his debt, Captain Power tried to persuade him to pay the interest on the loan. This Wolff declined to do on the ground that he would lose enough "without paying interest for the money."[61] The Captain was sure that in the end he would be forced to sue Wolff for the debt, "as also Mr. Kobeart . . . and Grifanger and De le Mare . . . and John Welch." It was his plan "to get all I possibly can this month and then sue them all that wont settle." A month later Captain Power wrote that "four days ago I paid your lawyer . . . to carry on that affair of Bampers & Co. The lawyer tells me it will be settled next month. Mr. Bampers ran away in a Sloop bound for Barbados last week, but that is no detriment to your case . . . for the longer he staid the more he got in debt."[62]

Along with runaway debtors and increasing litigation there was another difficulty. Surinam bills of exchange met dishonor in Amsterdam in ever-increasing volume. At one time the amount of this paper under protest was no less than eight million guilders.[63] Nicholas Brown and Company received their share of the protested bills. When the outbreak of the Revolution in 1775 interrupted the normal course of their trade, they not only held many of these Surinam bills but they also had there a long list of debts which they were unable to collect.[64]

After 1771 the trade of the Browns to Surinam became relatively, if not absolutely, less important. The decline of the Dutch colony in popularity may well have been due to the various difficulties just mentioned. And the depressed and fluctuating state of the tobacco market there also tended to make it less attractive than formerly. Although the Browns continued to send vessels to Surinam, they now tried the islands more frequently than in the sixties. Hispaniola, St. Eustatius, St. Christopher, Antigua, and St. Lucia gained favor. Numerous voyages to these ports can be identified. Letters from captains of unidentified craft make it clear that St. Eustatius enjoyed a popularity with the Browns which it had not had in the previous decade.[65]

Although it continued to be the policy of the French government to permit ships from the British continental colonies to bring to the French Islands the provisions which the French themselves could not supply, local officials on Hispaniola sometimes sought to exclude vessels flying the British flag. But Nicholas Brown and Company knew how to deal with such situations. In 1772 they decided to dispatch the Brig *George,* Captain Peter Ritto, to Hispaniola. At that moment they had conveniently at hand a Frenchman whom they addressed as "Stephen Gregory," but who signed himself as "Gregoire."[66] They directed Captain Ritto and Gregoire to proceed to any French port on Hispaniola and have the "Vessel made a French Bottom." To this end they provided the two men with a bill of sale by which Captain Ritto conveyed the Brigantine to Gregoire for 4600 Spanish pieces of eight.[67] As they explained to Gregoire, this was for "the purpose only of qualifying you to make said Brig a French Bottom or otherwise to get a permit for to Trade at any port in said Island."[68] At the same time they required Gregoire to sign a "Writing of Defeasance" which invalidated Captain Ritto's bill of sale and thus protected Nicholas Brown and Company's ownership of the vessel.[69] In return for bearing the cost of making the ship a French bottom, Gregoire was to be the sole owner of all papers connected therewith, subject to one reservation: that the Browns should have "the Preference of said papers . . . for another voyage before any other persons whatever." *George* sailed from Providence early in July 1772. On August 28 Gregoire wrote from Port au Prince, on Hispaniola, that he had his French papers.[70] In December the vessel arrived at Providence with 176 hogsheads, 11 tierces and 7 barrels of molasses and with 3155 pounds of coffee.[71]

Along with coffee, Brown invoices from the Caribbean area sometimes included salt, gin, various kinds of wine, and sundry other articles. Nevertheless, molasses remained the staple import from that reign, regardless of the particular port visited by their ships. And, unlike many other New England merchants, they never dispatched their vessels from the West Indies to England or other ports of Europe. To the end of the colonial period, their Caribbean trade was a direct and reciprocal one.

Doubtless this primary concern of the Browns with the molasses trade has strengthened the very natural assumption that in a colony noted for the number and excellence of its distilleries a mercantile firm of the prominence of Nicholas Brown and Company must have been important distillers of rum. Indeed the company was supposed to have processed not only the molasses imported in its own ships but also to have engaged extensively in custom distilling for others. The author of *Providence in Colonial Times* says "it seems evident that their busy distilleries supplied the 'Guineamen' of their old friends the Wantons, and other Newport merchants . . ."[72]

Undeniably there was a well-established history of rum distilling in the Brown family. Captain James Brown was a distiller. His brother Obadiah and his son James were known in the same capacity. Nicholas Brown as a very young man had mastered the art. In the division of the estates of the elder and younger James Brown in 1760, Nicholas received, along with other property, the "40 ft. Lot whereon the Distill House standeth, together with the Wharff Distill House and all the utensils with the Ware Houses on said Lot."[73] When one particular member of a company owns two "distill houses" it is a reasonable inference that the company distills. Yet there seems to be no direct or positive evidence of the operation of the distilleries by Nicholas Brown and Company during the years 1762 to 1774. On the other hand, it is clear that other merchants did distilling for them.

Further doubt is cast upon their operation of the distilleries at this time by a proposal for a division of property submitted by John Brown to Nicholas in 1770. John's suggestion was that "you [Nicholas] to have your house, household furniture, clothing, etc., lot, wharf, store, land adjoining Isaac Field, the old Still & still head and neck now on the wharf, with the worm and still head in your store . . ."[74] This proposition obviously refers to two distilleries—the two which had been allotted to Nicholas in the division of his father's and brothers' estates in 1760. With the formation of Nicholas Brown and Company in 1762 the distilleries became part of the company's stock in trade. It is hardly open to doubt, however, that John's reference is to distilleries which are either wholly dismantled or in a state of disuse.

If this evidence, positive and negative, warrants the conclusion that the company did not include distilling in its business repertoire, the question as to why men who owned two distilleries did not make use of them remains. It seems plausible to surmise that their expanding maritime interests, a spermaceti candle business which made increasing demands upon their time and attention, a ropewalk, a sugar house, and an iron furnace to be established, made it necessary for them to draw the line somewhere. As they remarked when asked to sell goods on commission, "we have and still do business in more branches than one ought but have not sought any in the commission way."[75] But this, of course, does not explain why, when confronted with the necessity of choice among their various interests, they chose not to distill the molasses which they so freely imported.

Not all of the molasses imported by the Browns came in legally. Captain James Brown had discovered ways and means of circumventing the Molasses Act of 1733. With the passing of time, however, British enforcement of the Act became so lax that subterfuge was no longer necessary; the law could be openly and brazenly violated with complete impunity. But all this was changed at the close of the Seven Years' War, when the British government, as part of the plan of imperial reorganization, enacted the Sugar Act of 1764. This piece of legislation cut in half the duty of sixpence per gallon imposed by the Act of 1733 on foreign molasses imported into the continental colonies; and at the same time the government in London laid plans for the effective enforcement of the measure. The Sugar Act was a blow to all the commercial colonies of Britain and produced strong reactions. But from none was the protest more notable than that from Rhode Island, set forth in the famous Remonstrance of 1764.

The essential point of the Remonstrance was the statement that of 14,000 hogsheads of molasses imported into the colony annually, only 2500 came from the British Islands in the West Indies; and that the actual collection of the threepence duty per gallon on the 11,500 hogsheads brought from foreign possessions would be wholly destructive of the molasses trade. This would, in turn, seriously cripple the entire economy of Rhode Island and thereby render the people of the colony incapable of paying for their annual importation of British goods. Thus in the end Britain would be the loser by the Sugar Act.

The Rhode Island Remonstrance, of course, set forth the strongest possible case against the Sugar Act. Yet, after due allowance is made for exaggeration of the effects of the law, the fact remains that the threepence duty was a consideration to which colonial merchants could not be indifferent. On a cargo comprising 20,000 gallons of molasses the duty amounted to £250 Sterling. Even after the reduction of the duty to one penny in 1767 the duty was still no small sum. Regardless of whether the threepence figure was actually prohibitive, as the merchants alleged, it was sufficient to encourage widespread attempts to evade its payment.

In January 1764, when the enactment of the Sugar Act was assured, Nicholas Brown and Company sent the Ship *Nancy,* Captain George Hopkins, on a voyage to the Caribbean. The captain's fictitious orders directed him to proceed to Bridgetown in Barbados, where he was to sell his cargo, invest a portion of the proceeds in rum, and then continue to Saltatudos and load with salt.[76] His genuine orders dispatched him to

Surinam, where he would find Captain Whipple in the Brig *George.*[77] As the latter had been ordered to sell his cargo wholly for molasses, he would require funds to cover his various disbursements. Captain Hopkins was to supply him with the money for this purpose, as well as to defray the cost of procuring English papers to cover Captain Whipple's homeward voyage in the Brig *George.* Upon the completion of his business at Surinam, "observing to take nothing on board by which your vessel will be made liable to confiscation," Captain Hopkins was to sail to Prince Rupert Bay in the Island of Dominica "and there endeavor in the best and safest manner you can to get a complete set of English papers for your vessel and cargo, expressing the molasses to be of English produce." If unable to procure English papers there, his orders directed him to continue along the "Leward Islands to St. Eustatius and from thence to St. Kitts in your boat and touch at any or as many ports with your vessel as you may think any way likely until you effect your desired clearance or gone through the whole and proceed home for this place."

Captain Hopkins obtained his complete set of British papers, not at one of the British Islands, but at St. Eustatius. Before he had an opportunity to use them in Rhode Island, however, developments had convinced his owners that any such attempt would be inexpedient. Unfortunately, many merchants had thought to employ false English papers as a means of evading payment of the duty on foreign molasses. The Browns were watching the course of events and they had sources of information about occurrences in other colonies. One William Barnet of Boston wrote Nicholas Brown in September 1764: ". . . I have nothing new to acqt. you of only the Devil to Pay with the Custom officers. 30 Masters and Oners are to Answer this Day at the Cort of Admiralty for falls Clearens from St. Stasha. The Governor of Anguila hath sent word he hath never cleared such vessels out and the consequences is much dredded here."[78]

A month later Nicholas Brown and Company had learned that fourteen vessels with Anguilla clearances had been prosecuted at Boston; and that they had been obliged to pay £2900 Sterling, "being the amount of the Dutys at 3^d per gallon."[79] The Rhode Island collector had a copy of the proceedings of the Boston court and the Browns daily expected "a prosecution of all ours this way being 6 vessels."[80] Doubtless it was this intelligence which prompted the decision that Captain Hopkins should not use the false English papers he had obtained at St. Eustatius. Yet, the burden of the duty on molasses seemed so great that they urged Captain Whipple, still at Surinam in the Brig *George,* to endeavor to get his vessel and cargo "entered without paying any charges, or the expense of getting her there will be so great shall make a bad hand on it." But they gave him no instructions as to how he could enter "without paying any charges." [81]

In view of the demonstrated futility of fictitious British papers as a means of averting payment of the duty on molasses, the Browns employed another procedure in the case of Captain Hopkins and the Ship *Nancy*. This is described in a letter from the Company to Captain Whipple: "We landed the ship's [*Nancy's*] cargo . . . clear of the duty and paid £66.13.4 Sterling for a fine, not making any use of the papers Capt. Hopkins obtained at St. Estatia. His voyage was very bad, although we saved the dutys or otherwise it would have been Shoking in Deed." [82] This savors strongly of connivance by British officials; for surely the Ministry in London, seeking funds with which to finance imperial reorganization, must have found the fine a poor substitute for the payment of the full duty.

There still remained the problem of getting Captain Abraham Whipple and the Brig *George* safely home from Surinam; and the instructions given him throw a good deal of light upon the techniques of smuggling. Nicholas Brown and Company wrote that "as times are now we think if can get the Brigg buy Conimicutt without their knowing in Newport of her arrival unload and land her cargo pritty safely without much danger of being seized, but how the severity of the officials may be by the time of your arrival we cannot say." Weighing the alternatives open to them, they added: "But as there will be a very great difference to us between paying the whole dutys (which we must if we pay any) and paying the fine, we desire you'l either come in to the westward of the lite House (which is now in very good order) in the nite in the Secunnit way." If successful thus far, he was to "proceed up [toward Providence] as fast as you can with the vessel in case the Wind is so can come along as fast as a man can buy land." Should the wind be unfavorable, Captain Whipple would "sett your mate Mr. Hopkins on shore to proceed to us as fast as possible, not stopping for nite nor foul weather nor telling no person from winth he come and we will meet the Brigg with schows and as many hands as is needful to unload." [83]

For several years after the reduction of the molasses duty to one penny per gallon in 1767, there is little evidence of smuggling by the Browns. But in 1772 it reappears. In that year they wrote to the captain of one of their vessels at Hispaniola: "If you are loaded full enter about 75 hhd 86 tierces and the remainder in barrels to make up all the casks you have on board." [84] Actually he had 176 hogsheads, 11 tierces and seven barrels of molasses. Continuing, they directed him to "tell at the Custom house that you dont know exactly the number of each cask only that you have so many in all on board. If any difficulty advise with Coll. Wanton Mr. Benjamin Mason & Mr. John Lawton."[85] In a postscript they informed the captain that if he entered coffee, of which he had 3155 pounds, it must be for exportation.

By depositing the coffee at the customhouse for exportation, the captain avoided payment of the duty. As the vessel cleared out for her next voyage the captain received instructions to load the coffee, ostensibly for exportation. He was then "to get Some of the Packets to take it out if you can, or take it in your bote & Land it at Coll. Wantons store till we can get it brot up."[86]

Notwithstanding the frequency of smuggling, the bulk of colonial peacetime trade was carried on within the framework of the law. Molasses was one of the comparatively few articles extensively smuggled. The duty on molasses stood as the symbol of a distant and oppressive government, entirely callous to the interests of the colonies. It was easy for the eighteenth-century businessman to justify his smuggling operations on this basis. Even so, over the long pull from 1733 to 1775, most of the molasses brought into the colonies was imported in conformity with the regulations or with the connivance of British officials.

To the Browns, trade with the Caribbean region was of major importance. So closely were other features of their business integrated with this commerce that stoppage of it for any length of time would have thrown their whole way of life out of gear. Not content merely to traffic with British possessions, they constantly sent their ships to the foreign colonies in the area. Where other merchants showed a strong preference for the French Islands, the Browns were more disposed to deal with the Dutch at Surinam. But to the extent that they traded with either the French or the Dutch their conduct contributed nothing to the prosperous commerce with England's "Southern Colonies" envisaged in the Rhode Island Charter of 1663.

One should not accept too literally the gloomy reports which ship captains sent back from the Caribbean area. Doubtless many voyages to the region returned a very slight profit. But the long persistence of the Browns in the Surinam trade hardly accords with the idea that the traffic was not profitable in the long run. However, the direct financial gain derived from this commerce is not necessarily the measure of its importance to the Browns. Quite apart from the immediate returns from the trade, it provided the Browns with molasses, rum, sugar, and bills of exchange which were vital to them in other branches of their business.

CHAPTER 3

"Prohibited Trade with the Vassalls of the French King"

FROM time to time in the eighteenth century, England became involved in war with other European countries owning islands in the Caribbean whose trade was so important to the economy of Britain's continental colonies. Three times between 1702 and 1763 Britain was arrayed at arms against France, and in each of these wars, of course, British control of the seas made it difficult for France to maintain commercial ties with her islands in the West Indies. Unable to supply them adequately with provisions in time of peace, France was almost powerless to do so in time of war, when British men-of-war swarmed about the Caribbean. Her islands were dependent on Britain's northern colonies for foodstuffs; and the colonies were quick to take advantage of the opportunity offered them. In the War of the Spanish Succession British colonials did a thriving business with the French and Spanish colonies. Again in the War of the Austrian Succession the commercial contacts of the British colonies with the French West Indies were so constant that Admiral Knowles believed them responsible for the failure of the Royal Navy in the Caribbean.[1]

Mindful of the aid her own colonies had given to the enemy in the two previous wars, the British Government moved quickly to prevent a recurrence when the Seven Years' War broke out in 1756. On October 9th of that year the Board of Trade sent a circular letter to colonial governors instructing them to lay an embargo on all ships carrying provisions from any place in the colonies unless bound for some British colony.[2] In the latter event bonds must be given requiring the vessel to go to the port designated in the papers. While this doubtless occasioned some inconvenience to colonials trading with the enemy, it in no sense put an end to the trading. Through loose interpretation of the regulation by certain colonial governors or by their connivance in its outright violation, merchants in some of the colonies were able to trade with the enemy without material interference.[3]

Traffic with the enemy was carried on in two ways—one direct, the other indirect. Direct trade was in part made possible by the indulgence of French colonial officials who were well aware that it provided them with supplies otherwise unobtainable. Vessels from the British colonies participating in it were not seized by French men-of-war because they usually had "lycences from the French governors who refused them to none who applied for them."[4] Direct trade with the enemy was also carried on extensively under passes from English colonial governors authorizing colonial vessels to proceed to French colonies for the ostensible purpose of effecting an exchange of prisoners. Vessels armed with these passes were commonly known as "flags of truce."[5] Occasionally the passes were used to effect a legitimate exchange of prisoners; but they were subjected to flagrant abuse. All too often they merely cloaked a trading venture with the enemy. Many times, perhaps usually, the flag of truce carried only one or two prisoners; sometimes it carried none at all.

Indirect trade with the enemy was conducted through neutral colonies in the Caribbean. In the early years of the Seven Years' War the Dutch port of St. Eustatius was the principal emporium for this trade. British colonial vessels carried cargoes there, whence Dutch ships took them to the French Islands. Within a period of four months in 1758 three fleets of Dutch vessels sailed from St. Eustatius to Martinique.[6] Without this aid the French could not have fitted out their privateers. This trade the British broke up through seizure of the Dutch vessels under the "Rule of 1756"—the principle that a trade forbidden in time of peace could not be opened to a neutral in time of war.[7] Since France disallowed Dutch trade with the French Islands in peace, she could not allow it in wartime.

But the British colonials were not thwarted so easily. They found a more convenient neutral port through which to trade with the French. This was Monte Cristi, known to colonial merchants and ship captains as the "Mount."[8] It was a Spanish settlement situated on the north coast of the Island of Hispaniola, on which both France and Spain had colonies. Contiguous to the French boundary, Monte Cristi was an ideal spot through which to conduct an illicit trade. In its prewar insignificance it had been closed to foreigners. It produced nothing which the British colonies wanted, nor did the handful of residents in its fifty houses offer a market for provisions. Its imports went immediately to the French; its exports were entirely of French production. Indeed, the trade with the enemy at the Mount was indirect in name only, as the exchange of goods was sometimes effected directly between British and French vessels in the

Spanish harbor. In 1759 and 1760 as many as one hundred North American vessels were at the "Mount" at one time.[9] For the latter year the total was estimated at four hundred.[10]

A less extensive, but by no means unimportant, phase of the traffic with the enemy was that with the French by way of Louisiana and Florida.[11] Trade with New Orleans was direct by means of flags of truce. That with Florida, of course, was indirect until Spain became a belligerent in the later stages of the war.

The colonies which were especially notorious for their traffic with the enemy were Pennsylvania, New York, Massachusetts, and Rhode Island, with the highest honors going to the first and last of these. The flag of truce trade from Pennsylvania became a public scandal.[12] In Rhode Island, Newport merchants had acquired a wealth of experience in enemy trade in the first two French wars of the century, particularly in the War of the Austrian Succession. Providence merchants, still in the stage of commercial adolescence at the time of that war, had not been prepared to take much of a hand in such a game of chance. Yet, an entry in one of Obadiah Brown's account books does show a try at it even in that period: "Stephen Hopkins Dr to ye Balance of ye Sconer *Ranger* fiting out for a flag of truce, March 19, 1746."[13]

But between the second and third French Wars some of the Providence mercantile firms began to grow up. As a result, in the Seven Years' War they were ready to take a conspicuous part in the trade with the enemy. According to Governor Stephen Hopkins, in the first four years of the war no less than thirty-two flags of truce sailed from Rhode Island to the French colonies.[14] He asserted that in these cases officials had not connived at the violation of a colonial law forbidding the export of provisions and military stores. He admitted, however, that the Rhode Island flags of truce had carried lumber and British manufactures to the French, bringing back molasses and sugar. He further acknowledged that it was "highly probable, that some Vessels from this Colony as well as from others, have taken in cargoes under pretence of being bound to Jamaica" only to sell them to the French in Hispaniola.[15] Direct trade of Rhode Island with the enemy was so generally well known and understood that Francis Bernard, in reference to it, wrote the Board of Trade: "These practices will never be put an End to, till Rhode Island is reduced to the subjection of the British Empire; of which at present it is no more a part than the Bahama Islands were when they were inhabited by the Buccaneers."[16]

Obadiah Brown, with his four nephews, participated actively in this illegal French trade. In Obadiah's Insurance Book under the date of 1756 is the entry "Snow *Dolphin* from St. Eustatius."[17] As *Dolphin* belonged to Obadiah, it is evident that in the first year of the war he was trying the indirect trade with the French by way of the Dutch port.

Within a short time Obadiah and the four nephews were engaged in the flag of truce traffic. In 1758 they sent the Brigantine *Prudent Hannah,* Captain Paul Tew, under a flag to Hispaniola. In latitude 36°50' and longitude 71 the vessel was seized by the British "man-of-war" *Chesterfield,* and taken into York River in Virginia. Captain Tew in a long letter to the Browns told of his unhappy experiences not only with the British navy but with the residents of the southern colony, who evidently looked askance at some of the doings of their northern neighbors. When all the eloquence at his command had failed to secure his release, Captain Tew wrote that he endeavored by "remonstrance, etc." to induce Captain Legge of *Chesterfield* to send him into some port to the northward. This plea was denied him, but he was assured that he would be given liberty to go ashore and solicit for his defense. But, added the Master of *Prudent Hannah,* "he [Captain Legge] was so far from keeping his word that after our arrival here he confined me 36 hours on board the King's Ship until he had went up to Williamsburg and . . . engaged all the attorneys of note (save one) against me." To add insult to injury, Captain Legge represented him so "ungenerously" to the "merchants and gentlemen here (if there be any such)" that when he was finally allowed to go ashore they looked on him as an enemy and traitor to his country because his captor had published the fact that he "was loaded with provisions" destined for the enemy.

In this state of affairs "none of them would engage" for Captain Tew on any terms. He was not permitted to go on shore until after his vessel had been seized by the Marshal of the Admiralty and he had been served with a citation to appear at Williamsburg to answer in six days. "In this deplorable condition" he prevailed "with George Wythe, Esq., an eminent attorney (more by entreaty than money) to put in an answer and defend the vessel and cargo." This man, later famous as professor of law at William and Mary College and as Chancellor of Virginia, made a clever defense by arguing the sacredness of flags of truce among all nations; and by his contention that the provisions on board in excess of the ship's manifest were legal by virtue of the collector's clearance; but all in vain, because "had Cicero himself been present and argued the case would have availed nothing." *Prudent Hannah* and her cargo were condemned August 26, 1758, ostensibly, Captain Tew asserted, in accordance with an act of Parliament in 1756 to prevent the exportation of provisions from the plantations, but actually "according to popular clamor" in Williamsburg, Virginia.[18]

Captain Tew believed that the "popular clamor" against him had been augmented and his condemnation hurried by the revelation of the contents of letters found on a French flag of truce also captured by Captain Legge and taken into Williamsburg along with Captain Tew. This French vessel was proceeding from Port-au-Prince, in Hispaniola, to New York, laden with molasses, rum, and sugar. The letters she carried were destined for "Old France" and set forth "the miserable condition of the inhabitants" of Hispaniola for want of provisions. They said that the suffering of the French colonies would steadily increase unless relieved by flags of truce. To the residents of Williamsburg, Virginia, Captain Paul Tew and *Prudent Hannah* seemed to be a disloyal Englishman's answer to the French prayers for provisions as set forth in the captured letters.

The Judge of the Admiralty Court ordered that *Prudent Hannah* and her cargo be appraised and sold by September 19, 1758. Captain Tew prayed an appeal which was granted on condition that he produce bondsmen for £100 sterling within fourteen days after completion of the sale. "How I shall conduct myself in this affair God only knows," wrote Captain Tew. He saw no likelihood of procuring bondsmen. "In this wretched place no person will advance a single farthing for me, there being no manner of trade from hence to any port of New England, New York or Philadelphia." He planned, therefore, to set out from "this accursed place designed by God & Nature for convicts" in an effort to secure bondsmen in Norfolk, "where there is some gentlemen that trade to the Northward." Captain Tew asked for instructions from Obadiah Brown and Company, and also for a letter of credit, both of which he hoped would arrive "before the time be expired for giving in bond to prosecute the appeal." To show that his troubles were not all of the spirit, the Captain concluded his long, melancholy letter with the remark that "on the whole and to crown my misfortune the D——nd gout has seized my right foot. Every reflection has a dreadful aspect and my thoughts are too confused."

The Browns received Captain Tew's letter by the post in twenty days.[19] But the deadline for posting the bond was but seventeen days away. They expressed their great surprise at his condemnation, "the first instance of that nature that has ever happened," and resolved to prosecute the affair. Upon reflection, however, they added, "but as we all know the expense that attends appeals, and the weight of a fifty gun ship, we should be glad if the affair could be any way accommodated, so that we should not be too great sufferers."[20] Forwarding to him their letter of credit, they submitted the matter to Captain Tew's "prudence," but with a reaffirmation of their determination to prosecute the appeal should he find it impossible to reach an accommodation.[21]

Bond for the prosecution of the appeal was finally obtained. All necessary papers in connection with the case were to be forwarded from Virginia to Tench Francis, Philadelphia correspondent of Obadiah Brown. As late as January 10, 1759, however, Francis had not received them.[22] Thereafter there is no mention of Captain Tew in the letters and papers of the Browns. But there are no records to show whether her carriage of provisions in obvious excess of the needs of her crew and "prisoners," and in violation of the law, operated to prevent recovery on the insurance by her owners. The complete silence surrounding the whole affair seems to indicate that the voyage of *Prudent Hannah* ended in utter disaster.

The story of the Brigantine *Brittania,* another flag of truce vessel in which the Browns were interested, also had an unhappy ending. In order to spread the risk as thinly as possible, vessels bound on voyages to the enemy frequently, if not usually, went as the joint venture of several "owners & hyrers." In 1758 Obadiah Brown, George Corlis, William Rhodes, George Hopkins, Nicholas Cooke, Christopher Lippitt, Samuel Chase, and Ephraim Bowen sent the Brigantine *Brittania,* Nehemiah Rhodes Master, under a flag of truce to Hispaniola.[23] The thin veneer of legality which covered this type of traffic is well illustrated by the records of *Brittania*'s cargo. At the time Daniel Jenckes (later to be the father-in-law of Nicholas Brown) and Elisha Brown (uncle of the four brothers) constituted a Committee of two, responsible for the inspection of all flags of truce granted in the County of Providence. It was the Committee's particular duty to decide upon the quantity of provisions such vessels might take on board "for the victualing the prisoners and mariners." The foodstuffs for this "victualing" were the only provisions which flag of truce vessels could carry according to law. So a friendly, coöperative committee at the home port was a great asset. When the owners of *Brittania* appeared before the Committee, they were authorized to take for "victualing" purpose 25 barrels of beef, 5 barrels of pork, 20 barrels of flour, 2600 pounds of "sea bread," 4 firkins of butter, and 3 barrels of peas.[24] In addition to the provender for the crew and prisoners, the cargo supposedly included 120 barrels of pickled fish, 1000 pounds of spermaceti candles, 4 pipes of wine, 30 boxes of soap, and 18 desks and tables. But the Committee apparently took no interest in what was actually shipped, once the official papers were out of its hands. According to the receipt which Captain Rhodes signed for *Brittania*'s cargo, the vessel's final assortment of goods was considerably different from that approved by the Committee.[25] The quantity of beef had increased to 30 barrels, a more varied shipment of lumber was on board, the 4 pipes of wine had become 8 tierces of claret, and the amount and kinds of fish had changed. It would seem that 30 barrels of beef and 5 barrels of pork were a generous allowance for the prisoners and mariners, the more so since there is no evidence that any prisoners were aboard the vessel.

Besides his consignment of goods, Captain Rhodes carried about 825 dollars in gold which he was to "dispose of for the best advantage" of the owners. He was accompanied by one Captain James Bardin, a sort of supercargo. Captain Rhodes was to proceed to Port-au-Prince, in Hispaniola.[26] Upon arrival there he was, with Captain Bardin, to go to the General "for directions concerning your prisoners," of whom he had none, and to deliver up Captain Bardin "all our goods together with our gold and silver." Captain Bardin's instructions were to dispose of the cargo and lay out the net proceeds, together with the gold, in the best sort of muscovado sugar.[27] As he had a number of water casks on board, he was "to have them filled with good molasses if to be got." The owners enjoined him to "enter and clear all . . . goods properly so as not to give umbrage to the officers on shore."

Brittania reached her destination safely. But on her homeward passage she was taken by the Privateer *Spry,* Captain Spring, of Philadelphia.[28] Her supercargo, Captain Bardin, was taken from her and detained on board *Spry*. From this point the history of *Brittania* is uncertain and obscure. More than nine weeks after her capture, Tench Francis wrote from Philadelphia that "your flag of Truce Capt[n] Rhodes is not yet arrived and I am afraid never will."[29] Referring to a libeled vessel whose case was similar to that of *Brittania,* he remarked that "should [it] be acquitted, perhaps you will recover from the Owners of the *Spry* though Capt[n] Rhodes never be more heard of." But after the lapse of seven months Tench Francis was more doubtful. He then wrote "from what I can now gather you will have but a very poor chance of recovering anything . . ."[30] Yet the owners of *Brittania* persisted and Francis did his utmost to arrange a settlement of the affair. Because of the continued procrastination of the lawyers the case was still unsettled as late as October 1760. Thereafter all reference to the Brigantine disappears not only from the letters of Tench Francis but also from the papers of the Browns generally. Whatever happened to Captain Rhodes and Captain Bardin, *Brittania* and her cargo were probably a total loss.

Another Hispaniola venture of 1758 was more rewarding. In the autumn Obadiah, George Corlis, and Joseph Rhodes, of Boston, by a charter party "granted and unto freight letten" to Esek Hopkins, Arthur Fenner, Solomon Drowne, Daniel Tillinghast, John Cole, Nathan Angell, and Thomas and Nathaniel Greene, "9/16 parts" of the Sloop *Speedwell,* a vessel of 53 tons.[31] Esek Hopkins and his associates were to pay Obadiah and his fellow owners at the rate of £300 per month "for the whole vessel for the whole time, hire to begin November 6, 1758." Should the Sloop be "lost, taken or seized" during the voyage Hopkins was to pay for the "9/16 parts" at the rate of £4400 Old Tenor bills of Rhode Island [about 733 dollars] for the entire vessel, "but no hire money." *Speedwell* and her papers were submitted to the careful scrutiny of the Committee appointed to "examine every Flag of Truce fitted out" at Providence and received a certificate saying she had "no goods on board contrary to law."[32] Her provisions consisted of 10 barrels of beef, 5 barrels of pork, 15 barrels of flour, 1000 weight of bread, 5 firkins of butter, 4 bushels of beans, and 20 bushels of potatoes. These, in the opinion of the Committee, were "no more than a sufficiency for the subsistence" of the crew and "such French prisoners" as she might carry.[33]

This generous supply of foodstuffs must have been more than enough for the "subsistence" of the two French prisoners of war on board *Speedwell*. But besides the Frenchmen, Captain Updike carried a type of human freight not usually found on craft trading with the enemy, namely, ten Negroes valued at £800 Old Tenor per head. Along with the provisions and slaves, the cargo included a parcel of spermaceti candles and 15 casks of wine.[34] Lending a sort of sporting touch to the whole venture is a notation on the memorandum of the cargo which reads: "A bever hat waged between EH [Esek Hopkins] and NB [Nicholas Brown] on acct wine and candles answg. best. Ditto EH with GC [George Corlis] wine and negros."[35]

Captain Updike's destination was "New Orleans or some other port or place in the River Mississippi." But his false sailing orders, intended for the eyes of inquisitive naval or customs officers, directed him to proceed to the Bay of Honduras, where he was to dispose of his cargo to the best advantage.[36] After loading his Sloop with logwood he was to deliver the remainder of the proceeds over to Captain Nehemiah Allen, "Master of our Snow *Dolphin,* who will sail in ten days after you." If, through some misfortune, Captain Allen should fail to arrive at the Bay, Captain Updike was to leave the balance with Captain William Cahoone, with orders to ship it in logwood on board any vessel bound from the Bay to Providence. In conclusion the orders read: "We look upon it that there will be the least danger of the French privateers through the Gulph and recommend that you go that way."[37] Actually the attraction of the "Gulph" route was not its relative freedom from French men-of-war but its proximity to the French port of New Orleans. In view of the frequency with which English colonial vessels visited the Bay of Honduras, the false orders were perhaps plausible enough, although the Browns in their legitimate trade seldom sent a ship to the Bay.

Speedwell appears to have arrived at New Orleans without untoward incident; and once there Captain Updike was at particular pains to smooth the way for the success of his mission. His account current with the owners of his Sloop shows the notations: "To a negro boy to Governor as present" and "To one negro boy to the Intendent as present."[38] He sold two Negro slaves at £1500 Old Tenor each; and five Negro slaves at £1450 Old Tenor per head; which leaves one Negro unaccounted for. Of his provisions, supposed to be entirely for his "prisoners" and crew, he sold 9 barrels of flour and 3 firkins of butter. He brought back with him 12 casks of indigo, 88 packs of peltry ("Indian dressed deer skins"), 36 packs of parchment and 19½ tons of logwood.[39] The sale of his cargo at New Orleans amounted to £37,248 Old Tenor; the goods for the homeward voyage cost £36,298 Old Tenor. The notation "Cash obliged to leave behind £5000" suggests that *Speedwell* may have made her departure under circumstances of undue haste. After Captain Updike arrived safely at his home port, the parchment skins were sent to Francis and Relfe, Philadelphia agents of Obadiah Brown and Company, for sale on commission.[40] The fact that *Speedwell* had made the voyage to New Orleans and back, when two ventures to Hispaniola had failed, encouraged her owners to the point where they were to undertake a second venture to the "River Mississippi."

For the voyage of 1759, Obadiah, Nicholas, and John Brown, George Corlis, and Joseph Rhodes by a charter party "granted and letten" to Nathan Angell, John Cole, Daniel Tillinghast, Esek Hopkins, and Thomas and Nathaniel Greene "7/16 parts & one half" of *Speedwell*.[41] Although Captain Updike carried two French prisoners, the Rhode Island authorities did not go through the usual ritual of listing provisions for them. Except for 100 barrels of flour mentioned in the bill of lading and 75 barrels referred to in the invoice there is no mention of foodstuffs. Dry goods accounted for two-thirds of the total value of the consignment.[42]

Again Captain Updike carried false sailing orders, directing him to proceed to the Bay of Honduras.[43] After disposing of his cargo he was to "take in a load of logwood & go to the Island of Jamaica & there lodge it in the hands of Mr. Henry Livingston, merchant, to whom we have given orders how to proceed." As his cargo would purchase several loads of logwood, he was to employ the Sloop between the Bay and Jamaica until he had carried his "whole effects" to the latter place. He was then to take in a load of molasses and proceed directly home, leaving the remainder of his effects in Livingston's hands. Once more his owners urged him to go through the "Gulph" as the most probable way to avoid French privateers. Captain Updike's genuine orders directed him to proceed to

New Orleans in "The River Mississippi," dispose of his wares, and purchase "such a cargo as you shall judge most for our interest and benefit."[44]

Captain Updike was stopped at the mouth of the Mississippi and forbidden to continue to New Orleans.[45] He must have successfully eluded capture by British men-of-war, however, for he was back in Providence before the end of the year.

On January 7, 1760 Captain Updike sailed *Speedwell* out of Providence River on her third voyage to the Mississippi. After a stormy passage he arrived at the mouth of the river, whence he sent a report of his presence to the Governor at New Orleans. That official wrote that there "was about 400 Indians in town," that he was obliged to keep guards on flags of truce, that numerous persons had made a great disturbance "about Englishmen coming there," and that the townsmen were in no want of goods or provisions.[46] The recent arrival of a "storeship" from France may help to explain the rather cavalier treatment accorded the master of *Speedwell*. In Updike's words, the Governor had written him that "I must Begone from his Government." When the Captain demanded liberty of the Commandant to go to New Orleans to collect the money he had left on his first voyage, he received "Absolute Orders for . . . Departer."[47] He was allowed. however, to appoint an agent to collect the money.

Rebuffed at New Orleans, Captain Updike went to "Penzacola," where he obtained permission to rest his "Vessel which she much wanted." Much of his goods had suffered damage from water, while the "Ratts have Eat Great part of the Bales in a Bad Manner."[48] There he sold goods to the value of about 4000 livres "to not much advance." He could have disposed of his entire cargo but refused because there was little money in the place. He then decided to try the "Mount," the great haven of the indirect trade with the enemy. There he found "Times Very Dull." There, too, he received the melancholy news of the capture of another flag of truce belonging to the Browns, intelligence which he wrote them was "But too true." Altogether, the Captain appears to have been somewhat disillusioned by his experiences with the enemy, as he observed that "a Frenchman's Friendship goes no Farther than his necessity." From the "Mount" *Speedwell* went to Cap François on Hispaniola, a place so glutted with all kinds of merchandise that Captain Updike found his dry goods a slow sale.[49] Sugar, with which he hoped to load, was very high. At the "Cape" was Captain Abraham Whipple, also in the service of Obadiah Brown and Company. But eventually, at one of the ports Captain Updike sold the bulk of his cargo and purchased 44 hogsheads of white sugar, 13 hogsheads of brown sugar, and 10 hogsheads of molasses, with which he arrived safely in Providence on July 30, 1760. His troubles with the "ratts," "dull times," and the uncertainty of the "Frenchman's Friendship" must have persuaded him that this sort of business was not to his liking. His service with the Browns was terminated with his return from this voyage.

But not so his sturdy Sloop *Speedwell,* clearly a boat well suited to surviving the risks and dangers of trade with the enemy. With two different captains she made three more successful flag of truce voyages.[50] On one of these made in 1761, although her captain carried a certificate signed by Governor Hopkins permitting her to sail under a flag of truce, her papers did not even mention French prisoners of war. Evidently the trade had become so much of a commonplace in Rhode Island that the authorities did not feel the necessity of making any effort whatsoever to give it a semblance of legality. On one occasion with Captain Kinnicutt in charge, she had a brush with two frigates off Port St. Louis. But it came to nothing. After purchasing flour and onions out of her cargo, the officers of the frigates allowed her to proceed with the warning "not to be catcht so near a French Harbor again." In the course of the war *Speedwell* made no less than seven voyages to the enemy. No other vessel in the service of Obadiah Brown equaled her record.

Meanwhile another Sloop *Speedwell,* "new and well found," in which the Browns were interested was less successful. Her second voyage, surrounded by most unusual circumstances, put a humiliating end to her career. The Master of *Speedwell,* Captain Silas Cook, accomplished the first voyage to St. Mark on Hispaniola in the new vessel quickly and successfully.[51] On January 5, 1760 he sailed again, ostensibly bound "for Jamaica."[52] Governor Hopkins certified that the vessel carried one French prisoner. This prisoner was positively identified as one who had been captured near Curaçao some six months before. But before the Rhode Island Assembly had approved Governor Hopkins' certification it had listened to an unusual story from Captain Cook—a story involving three redskins and nine Negroes.

The tale as the Captain told it began with his earlier capture by the French while in command of a privateer in which the Browns were concerned. At that time, he said, he and his company had been taken to St. Mark on Hispaniola, where all except Captain Cook had been imprisoned. Later, he and the majority of his men had been sent in a flag of truce to Jamaica, where they were exchanged. Among those left behind in prison at St. Mark were three Indians, "all freeborn & liege subjects of our Lord the King" of England. Besides the three redskins there were nine Negroes, "very valuable slaves belonging to gentlemen" in Rhode Island. Knowing the slaves to be highly esteemed by their masters, Captain Cook had agreed with a "certain French gentleman" at St. Mark to purchase them, so that their former masters might be able to redeem them. Captain Cook asked the Governor and the Assembly for a flag of truce in order that he might go to St. Mark in *Speedwell,* and there procure the liberty of the three Indians and the redemption of the nine slaves. So the Rhode Island authorities, knowing that the real destination of *Speedwell* was the enemy port of St. Mark and not the British colony of Jamaica, ratified the Governor's flag of truce certification.[53]

Captain Cook, according to his own story subsequently related to the Admiralty Court, did not accomplish his mission. When he arrived at St. Mark in *Speedwell,* he found that the three Indians had been set free by the French and were not to be found. For the nine Negroes he had offered 2200 pieces of eight, but "could not obtain them for that price or any other consideration." While at St. Mark Captain Cook wrote, March 22, 1760, to John Randall, master of another of the Browns' ships, then at Port-au-Prince, Hispaniola: "If Brother Burgess arrives from Jamica present my compliments to him who I hope to see safe with yourself in Providence soon if it be our good fourtains to escape our enemys."[54] In this instance, of course, "enemys" meant British men-of-war, an interesting commentary on the state of mind which trade with the enemy developed in English colonials.

Captain Cook cleared from St. Mark for Providence on March 25, 1760. Five days later he was taken by the British privateer *Little John* and carried into the port of New Providence in the Bahama Islands. In the trial there before the Court of Vice Admiralty Captain Cook again told the story of the three Indians and nine Negroes, in whose interest, he alleged, the flag of truce voyage of *Speedwell* had been largely conceived.[55] The Court evidently was less impressed with the story than had been the Rhode Island Assembly. In the decree it is passed over in silence. And grave doubt and suspicion must have been cast upon the reality of the French prisoner of war supposedly carried to St. Mark, as the Court asserted flatly that, after clearing out for Jamaica, *Speedwell* "did fraudulently and clandestinely proceed to St. Mark . . . without carrying thither any French prisoners"; and that her captain, "submitting himself to the laws . . . of the said French colony was permitted to . . . sell the . . . cargo consisting partly of sundry eatable provisions," by all of which "it is manifest the said Sloop in her present voyage hath been employed in a fraudulent, illegal and prohibited trade with the subjects and vassalls of the . . . French King." On May 11, 1760 the vessel and cargo were condemned and ordered sold.[56]

A similar fate awaited a more ambitious project of the Browns for trading with the enemy. On September 20, 1759, Obadiah, Nicholas, and John Brown entered into an agreement with one Elijah Cobb of Taunton, Massachusetts, by which Cobb promised to deliver to the Browns by November 10, 1759 a certain Brigantine of about 120 tons "Burthen," then on the stocks in Taunton.[57] The contracting parties reckoned the cost of the vessel at £60 Old Tenor money of Rhode Island for each ton—a total of about 1200 dollars. The contract called for the payment of 100 dollars in cash on the execution of the bond, a similar amount on the delivery of the Brigantine, and 200 dollars in cash by January 10, 1760. The balance of 800 dollars the Browns agreed to pay in West India goods at the current market price upon delivery of the vessel. The Browns also promised to provide Cobb with two pounds of good refined bar iron for every pound of worked iron in the ship. Should Cobb fail to deliver the Brigantine at the stipulated time he must allow £1000 Old Tenor "to be taken out the monies, merchandize & things by them covenanted to be paid."[58]

The Brigantine *Providence* represented something of a new departure in her owners' trade with the enemy. Hitherto they had tried to spread the risks inevitably involved in such traffic by sharing with others the ownership and management of their ventures. But *Providence,* in her forthcoming voyage, was to be entirely a family affair. Prudential considerations should have dictated a different course.

Providence, a flag of truce, carrying no French prisoners of war, sailed on January 8, 1760, with Captain John Randall in command. That both the Brigantine and her large assorted cargo were highly prized by the Browns is indicated by their request that Tench Francis of Philadelphia "make insurance" for £1000 Pennsylvania currency on the vessel and an equal sum on the goods she carried.[59] The Captain's orders directed him to go to Port-au-Prince in the "Bite of Leogan" [Bight of Leogana], Hispaniola, to dispose of his cargo, and to load the vessel with molasses and barrels of the best brown sugar "to be Stow'd where Hogsheads or Tierces Can't be Stow'd."[60] At his discretion he might invest the "overplus" in cotton and indigo according to the "Prices There, Compared with the Value here." He carried with him, "Going passenger" one Captain John Burgess whose business it was, should a suitable opportunity offer, to purchase "some proper vessel . . . to Load her home for this place with Molasses etc upon the Acct and Risque of himself" and the owners of *Providence.*[61] Should Burgess purchase a vessel, Captain Randall would deliver the "overplus" of his sales to him to be employed as the best judgment of Burgess might dictate. If unable to gain entrance to Port-au-Prince because of men-of-war or privateers, Captain Randall was directed to "Use your best Endeavors to beat up the South side for Port Lowe" or any other port thereabout and to "Follow the same orders with Capt. Burgess." Obadiah and his nephews were risking not only *Providence* in this precarious trade but were planning to extend the risk to an additional vessel.

Captain Randall arrived at Port-au-Prince without incident. On February 14th he wrote that he had come to a "glutted" market. He added that he had landed all his prisoners "and some of them in a veray bad State of helth I have yett Some affairs to Do With them befoure I Can Give you a particklar Account"—a strange bit of news from one who carried no French prisoners of war.[62] But it might serve a useful purpose if British naval officers became too interested.

Meanwhile Captain Burgess was endeavoring to mature the somewhat nebulous plan for the joint venture which he and the owners of *Providence* had considered. With James Chambers, a resident of Port-au-Prince, he bought the Snow *Warring*, with the understanding that a one-half interest was to be taken by Obadiah Brown and Company. Then, for the good of the Consarn," he felt it necessary to visit Kingston, Jamaica. There he learned to his sorrow that "the best Consarted Scames may Be by Divine Providence Disconsarted";[63] although in the interest of strict accuracy he should have substituted the words "British Navy" for "Divine Providence." In a letter to Captain Randall written from Kingston, Captain Burgess clarified one of his "scames." He regretfully stated that he had "not been able to Do anything With the admerl." And he added that "for him to give me a protection would Be Directly Opposet to what he has set out on That is to take all shuger & molasses Laden Vessels That Comes out of any french port if posable." For this purpose, Captain Burgess said, the Admiral had "Two men of war Crossing In the Bit of Leugan And on the south side of Highspanola so That Thare is not the Lest Prospect of Ascaping."[64] Evidently Burgess had gone to Jamaica in the hope that, somehow, he could persuade the Admiral to close his eyes while *Providence* and the Snow *Warring* sailed out of Port-au-Prince with handsome cargoes of sugar and molasses.

When his best efforts failed with the Admiral, he was ready to give up the project. The increasing effectiveness of the British blockade of Hispaniola, long the favorite haunt of colonial traders with the enemy, seemed too much for him without help from high places. He wrote that he was assigning to a merchant in Kingston all his "Pretentions" to *Warring;* that James Chambers, copurchaser of the Snow, would reimburse Captain Randall for all the funds he had advanced on account of the half-interest in *Warring* which Burgess had been holding for Obadiah Brown and Company; and that the part "of your [Captain Randall's] Cargo that was To be Deliverd to me if I sucseded in my Scames" Captain Randall might remit in accordance with his original orders. Burgess then proceeded to give the Master of *Providence* some sage advice, based upon his observations of the British blockade. Randall should not attempt to clear indigo out of Port-au-Prince for Rhode Island. Instead, he should send it "in Sum Jaimaica flag of truce" to Kingston; and he warned that "if you should Go out before there is a better prospect you have Teen to

one aganst your getting clear, and all the Indigo that is taken in any Vessel Laden with suger or molasses is as Lyable as any other part of the
cargo as I have been informed." He concluded with words of warning to
Captain Randall which were wiser than he knew: "I am heartily sorry
that things is so Surconstanced, on your Accout, for you will have but a
pore Chance of getting out Clear of the men of war."[65]

Meanwhile Captain Randall and *Providence* were having difficulties.
Early in March 1760 the Captain wrote to the Browns that he had re-
ceived "Accounts of 20 Sail Flaggs of Truce being Carried" to Jamaica
and "a Moungst the Rest Godfree Malborn [of Newport] and none yet
Treyed but all Libled. Cool Angle [Colonel Angell] stopt at the Mount
and from thence was going to the Cape and was Taken by an Antegua
Privetear." Captain Randall had found that "all marketts here is Verey
Low & Their produce on the Rice . . . I cant advise you in being concerned
in aney to come here at present by Reason of the place being overdone."
Port-au-Prince was glutted with goods from "York, Philadelphia and
Jamaica. Everey Store Full." He hoped to make first cost, even though
"numbers are obliged to Sink 20 & 30 & 50 per cent who has purch[d] affects
befoure the sale of their Goods." Despite the dismal outlook, Captain
Randall optimistically trusted that his "Voige will Turn to Account if
ascape the Rovers of the Seas."[66]

On March 19, 1760, Captain Randall wrote that he had 70 hogsheads
of molasses on board and expected to be loaded within three weeks. But
he complained that the French themselves were contriving to make
the trade difficult. He added that "The Super Entendent of this place is
Ded and a New one appointed which Dubled the Duty on Suger and
Laid a Duty on Molass which Never was done befoure." As the Captain
explained it, the French "by the multitude of trade . . . have determined to
fleece all they can." Not only was he troubled by French profiteering but
he was uncertain about his voyage home "for most all that attemted the
passage has been taken but I shall take the Safest Methods I can."[67]

The sale of *Providence*'s cargo moved slowly in the dull market at
Port-au-Prince. Some of the dry goods could not be sold at all. Equally
slow was the job of obtaining his return cargo at that place. The sugar
and molasses shipped from the port came in by land carriage, the motive
power supplied by oxen. As Hispaniola had been visited by a severe
drought "Their Cattle are So poor and Die So . . . They are put to Grate
difficulty in Gitting their Goods Down by that Means."[68] In the end, however, Captain Randall not only procured a full cargo for *Providence* but
also a surplus of 15 hogsheads and 12 barrels of molasses which he shipped
on the account of Obadiah Brown and Company aboard the Snow *Winsor*,
owned by Gideon Cornell of Rhode Island.[69] The cargo of *Providence*

from Port-au-Prince consisted of 166 English hogsheads of molasses, 24 tierces and 7 barrels of molasses, 25 hogsheads of brown sugars containing 30699 wt., and 500 pounds of the best indigo—a very valuable freight indeed.[70]

Captain Randall sailed from Port-au-Prince at night on May 12, 1760. He went to "Lougan and gott the best Intiligence" he could respecting the "Cruzers in the boight." Hearing that there were two men-of-war cruising off the south side of the bay he decided "it would not do to attempt that passage." He heard of "no Vessels the North Side . . . there foure took a Dark Squally Night: Weighed Anker about candle liting: With a Vew of Running over to St. Mark and there weight a Good time to Run into the trade and go through the Gulf." Unfortunately, the day the Captain sailed from "Lougan" there had arrived off St. Mark a small Schooner called *Polley's Revenge*. The latter part of the night "the Wind Died away and left us all Calmd. at the Brake of Day we aspeyed the Schooner Rowing for us to Whome we fell a Sacrey fice the 17th day of May."[71]

Providence was taken by *Polley's Revenge* into New Providence in the Bahama Islands, where Captain Randall made his protest against the privateer. Writing to his owners, he expected "but a poor Chance for they Condem Vessels and Cargo of all flaggs without exception being Combind a neast of pirats alltogether."[72] Several weeks later he wrote that "after a long & Teadeious Law Sute with these Pirattical People am Condemd hul & Cargo."[73] The only solace he could find was the fact that three other Rhode Island flags of truce were condemned at the same time. In the course of the hearings before the Court of Vice-Admiralty it was established that *Providence* had carried no French prisoners of war to Port-au-Prince, but that she had two English prisoners on board at the time of her capture.[74] Not only was she charged with being employed in a "wicked, Illegal, unwarrantable, Clandestine and prohibited trade," but also that she had "not on board all the Legall, Necessary and Customary Papers, which all Fair Traders ought to have and Carry, or that if she had such they have been concealed or destroyed."[75]

Having lost a valuable ship and cargo, of which they were the sole owners, Obadiah, Nicholas, and John Brown hoped to salvage something from the disaster by means of insurance. They had insured the Brigantine for £1000 Pennsylvania currency, and the goods for a like amount. But should they recover the full amount of the insurance they would still be losers, as they estimated that the lost cargo had cost them £1611 Pennsylvania currency, and that the total cost of the vessel, with sails, rigging, iron work, etc., was £1218 in the same currency.[76] Some of the Philadelphians whom Tench Francis had persuaded to underwrite the policies on *Providence* paid promptly; but others, frightened by the large claims for insurance on colonial flags of truce lost in the enemy trade, sought by every conceivable legal loophole to escape liability. This was notably true of two of the underwriting firms.

Suit against one of these companies was brought in the Pennsylvania courts prior to the death of Obadiah Brown in 1762. It was carried to the Supreme Court of the Province which in April 1763 ordered the defendants to pay to the Browns the sum of £127:10/3^d lawful money of Pennsylvania.[77] The underwriters thereupon appealed to the Privy Council in England which on July 26, 1765 confirmed the decision of the Pennsylvania Court.[78] The other firm seized upon a technicality in an effort to escape liability. The policy had stated that *Providence* carried no provisions other than for her own use. The Browns pointed out that the Committee appointed by the Rhode Island Assembly for the examination of all flags of truce had certified that the vessel's cargo contained provisions sufficient only for her own needs—a warrant which meant little in view of the notorious laxity of colonial officials in this matter of trade with the enemy. The underwriters, however, contended that the inclusion of beef, pork, flour, and bread in the invoice and bill of lading, together with Captain Randall's certificate on the back of the bill of lading that he had the owners' order to sell the cargo, rendered the policy null and void. Thereupon the Browns procured affidavits from several of their ship captains showing that Obadiah Brown and Company had customarily included a ship's provisions in the invoice and bill of lading.[79] Sworn testimony from other prominent merchants in Providence showed that this was the prevailing practice of the mercantile fraternity generally.[80] By way of controverting the contention of the underwriters that the large quantity of fish carried by *Providence* was in violation of the law, the Browns obtained an affidavit from the Collector of the Customs in Boston asserting that fish were not deemed to be "provisions" within the meaning of the law, and, therefore, could be cleared without giving bond to land them at a British port.[81] The court, however, was not impressed. In 1767 it held that the presence of the provisions in the cargo rendered the insurance policy void.[82] The most it would do was to order the underwriters to reimburse the Browns to the amount of the premium on the policy, with interest thereon.[83] Nicholas Brown and Company continued to press the case, but such were the law's delays that in 1774—fourteen years after the loss of *Providence*—the affair was still unsettled. In the confusion of the Revolutionary years it quietly sank into oblivion.

The loss of the Brigantine *Providence* in 1760 was at least partially balanced by a successful voyage to the enemy in the same year. In February, Obadiah Brown and Company dispatched the Sloop *George,* Captain

William Earle, as a flag of truce to Hispaniola.[84] Although Jaquemel was supposedly the Captain's destination, he was free to visit other ports on the Island. Except for the fact that it contained a quantity of dry goods, little is known of the cargo *George* carried to the West Indies. In July 1760 she arrived safely at Providence with a cargo of sugar and molasses.

In 1762 the Sloop *George,* commanded by Captain Abraham Whipple, visited Barbados, where she sold her cargo. She then continued to Martinique. While en route from St. Pierre to another port on the Island she was captured by a Spanish privateer, which plundered *George* to the value of 500 pieces of eight.[85] Captain Whipple then ransomed the vessel for 400 pieces of eight. His captors gave him a "ransom bill," good for two months, which the Captain hoped would protect him against other privateers. Either the ransom bill or lady luck provided the necessary protection, as *George* returned to Providence with 114 hogsheads of molasses.

Besides the many flag of truce voyages in which the ships can be positively identified, the Browns were concerned in numerous others in which the names of the vessels are not known. The remark that "we ... have been concerned in many voyages to your Island, several of which to your particular address," contained in a letter of 1761 to the Hispaniola firm of Detruce & Lecount, suggests flag of truce voyages to the French colony on the Island by Brown ships which cannot be individually accounted for.[86]

While pursuing the direct trade with the enemy under cover of flags of truce, Obadiah and his nephews had also participated in the indirect trade carried on through neutral territory. During the first year of the war they sent *Dolphin* to St. Eustatius. When the British broke up the traffic through the Dutch port, the Browns, in company with other colonial merchants, shipped to the "Mount." In the spring of 1758 they dispatched five vessels to this Spanish island port. One of these was the Sloop *Speedwell*, Captain Uriah Davis, almost certainly the vessel which later in the year sailed on the first of her three voyages to the "River Mississippi."[87] The others were the Sloops *Ann, Deborah, Esther,* and *Hazard.*[88] Obadiah consigned the cargoes of boards, candles, oysters, codfish, beef, pork, etc., carried by these vessels to Captain John Wheaton, his factor at Monte Cristi. From his vantage point at the "Mount" Captain Wheaton was in a position to trade advantageously with such French ports on Hispaniola as Fort Dauphin and Cap François. After the safe arrival of *Esther* at the "Mount," he reported that she had gone to the Cape. In the late summer of 1758 the five ships returned from the "Mount" with various quantities of sugar and molasses. The Sloop *Hazard* brought more than 70,000 pounds of sugar, while *Ann* seems to have carried an even larger cargo. Obadiah advised Captain Wheaton that he was fitting *Ann* as fast as possible for another voyage to the "Mount." Obadiah and his nephews must have viewed with satisfaction the five successful voyages to the enemy in that year.

Lack of evidence of voyages to the "Mount" in 1759 and 1760 might be construed to mean that Obadiah shunned that port in those years. Yet this hardly seems probable in view of the success achieved there the first year. But be that as it may, he dispatched the Sloop *George* to the "Mount" in 1761. False orders directed the captain to proceed to Kingston, Jamaica.[89] If captured he was to ransom his vessel on the best possible terms, "endeavoring as much as possible to have the Ransom money to be paid in some English port as the Difficulty of Sending a flag of truce to any French port (by reason of ye Repeated Interruption by his Majesty's cruisers) is too great." Captain Earle's genuine orders directed him to Monte Cristi, but should he be "drove by your Port by a Man of War or Priveteer so that you Cant get to the Port bound to, you are to use your endeavour to get into any French port on Hyspaniola." From the "Mount" the Captain wrote of the dull market for flour (of which he had 200 barrels), candles, hoops, and provisions, the last of which was "very plenty." A month later he had a cargo of molasses on board but he feared to sail because of men-of-war. After the lapse of another six weeks he still had not sailed because "several vessels has gone out and been taken." *George* returned safely, however, as she sailed from Providence again in January 1762 on another voyage to the "Mount."

From the evidence at hand it is apparent that the Browns were persistent traders with the enemy. In the course of the war they had been concerned in more than twenty trading ventures with the French in which the vessel can be identified by name. But it is obvious that these by no means exhaust the list of their excursions into this trade. They began it in 1756, the first year of the war, and they continued to be actively engaged in it to the end of hostilities. They clearly elected the enemy trade in preference to their customary traffic with Surinam, which remained open to them, and in which they occasionally engaged during the war years.

Like other colonial merchants, the Browns had entered the trade with high hopes of large profits. In the absence of a balance sheet of the trade, no categorical statement with regard to profits is possible. On the one hand, they almost certainly lost four vessels, with their cargoes, in consequence of the trade. Of these, at least one was entirely owned by Obadiah, Nicholas, and John. Severe as these losses must have been, they represent the only complete failures among the many voyages in which the Browns were involved. And over against these are several voyages which returned very valuable cargoes of sugar and molasses to Providence. The persistence of the Browns in the trade over a period of seven years, in spite of occasional losses, and largely to the neglect of their opportunities at Surinam, must create a strong presumption that over the long pull they found the profits of this commerce sufficient to justify the risks involved in it.

If in the wars of the eighteenth century British colonial merchants eagerly pursued trade with the French, thereby providing the enemy with the sinews of war to prolong the conflicts, they also indulged in another form of maritime activity which, in part at least, neutralized the effects of their traffic with the foe. From one point of view it seems rather irrational that merchants who indirectly aided and abetted the enemy in the conduct of the war should at the same time "patriotically" fit out private men-of-war to prey upon the commerce of that same enemy. They appear to be giving with one hand and taking away with the other. But perhaps the contradiction between traffic with the enemy and privateering was only on the surface, for the two activities did have a common denominator—the prospect of lucrative profits to the merchants.

Although less active in the privateering game in King George's War of the 1740's than were their Newport friends and neighbors, Providence merchants were keenly aware of its possibilities. In 1745 and 1746 the privateer Sloop *Reprisal,* owned by Stephen Hopkins and others, enjoyed a brief season of success. One of Obadiah Brown's ledgers for 1747 contains an entry which refers to a "Priveter Sloope," whose home port was probably Providence. When war broke out anew in 1756 the mercantile interests in the town readily seized the opportunity to fit out private men-of-war. The privateer Brigantine *Providence* (not to be confused with the later Brigantine of the same name, owned by the Browns and lost in the trade with the enemy) was owned by Nicholas and John Brown, Benjamin Bowen, Allen Brown, Ambrose Page, and Esek Hopkins. In the years 1756-1758 *Providence* made four privateering voyages.[90] On the first three Esek Hopkins was the master. On the fourth, on which she was captured, Captain Silas Cook was in command.

A state of war was proclaimed in Providence on August 26, 1756. *Providence* went to sea soon thereafter. On January 8, 1757 she captured her first prize, the Snow *Desire.* Amid the cheers of the excited townspeople, the captured vessel arrived at Providence on January 30, 1757. Her cargo was a varied one. But along with the usual everyday essentials there were 57 barrels of red wine, 15 baskets of white wine in bottles, 103 chests of "best wine," and a "cask or chest unknown for the governor of Hispaniola."[91]

The captors of *Desire* were greatly intrigued by the "cask or chest" for the governor of Hispaniola. Referring to it in a letter to Nicholas and John Brown, Silas Cook said they had "reason to believe it is of great value, the Capt. of the prize being very fond of ransoming the vessel."[92]

All were well on board *Providence* and in high spirits, he wrote. "Having had so good success the first of the cruizes we do not despair of making our fortunes before we have done."[93] He hoped the next news from him would be "by as good a prize as this." Whether his optimism about the treasure in the governor's chest was justified is not made clear. The cargo of *Desire* was finally valued at £78,000 Old Tenor, one-half of which went to the owners of the privateer. Each member of the crew received £354:10:10. *Desire* was sold at auction to Daniel Tillinghast and Company.

Before sending *Desire* off to Providence in command of her prize crew, of which Rhodes Arnold was the acting captain, the company on board *Providence* drew up articles of agreement appointing Nicholas and John Brown to be "our whole and sole agents . . . to take and dispose this prize . . . and also to dispose all goods, merchandize & other effects whatever and to act and do in our behalf anything that they shall think will be an advantage to the company. . ." The document was signed by 56 men, including Esek Hopkins and Silas Cook.[94] That John Brown should have been appointed one of the agents is eloquent testimony to his business precocity. He was then but twenty years of age.

By a charter party the new owners evidently shared with the Browns the management of *Desire* on a voyage to the Caribbean. In June 1757, Joseph Hillborn of Philadelphia wrote to John Brown that he had insured the goods aboard her for £178 Pennsylvania currency. The master of *Desire* for this voyage was Rufus Hopkins, nephew of Esek. As she "saild out of the River Surinam" en route to Providence with "One hundred and Eighty nine Hogsheads and eight Tearses of Molasses Containing 19040 Gallons Net," she was taken by the French, who dispatched her to Martinique. But before her arrival there she was recaptured by a Philadelphia privateer and sent to the latter port. When Tench Francis, the Browns' Philadelphia correspondent, heard of this he immediately applied to the owners of the privateer and informed them that he intended to claim *Desire*.[95] Discovering, to his disappointment, that she had been in possession of the enemy a sufficient time to entitle her latest captors to one-third for salvage, Francis, without instructions from the Browns, conceived a plan designed to benefit both them and the owners of the Philadelphia privateer. He proposed to realize a handsome profit from *Desire*'s cargo by avoiding "the extortionate Duty of 6^d Stl. p Gallon, to get the Molasses privately on Shore and sell it." The Judge of the Admiralty Court "being luckily out of town" gave him a "fair opportunity to execute our Scheme." He landed the cargo successfully and disposed of the molasses at 2 shillings, 4 pence per gallon. Of the resulting £2200, the owners of the cargo received two-thirds, the Philadelphia privateer, one-third. Tench Francis, of course, charged a commission for transacting the business.

Writing to Obadiah Brown and Company, Francis said:[96] "We have acted in this affair as we would have done for ourselves. Indeed our friendship for some of the owners obliged us to run so considerable a risk in serving them. Had we miscarried and the molasses been seized, we depended solely on your honours, for no doubt in strictness of law, we were accountable, not having your orders for what we did." But the affair was "now happily over" and Francis awaited the owners' pleasure regarding the net proceeds of their two-thirds of the cargo.

While *Desire* was being thus buffeted about by the tides of fortune, the privateer *Providence,* which had originally made her a prize, had not been idle. Indeed, excitement in the town of Providence attending the capture of *Desire* had hardly subsided when *Providence* captured the Snow *Seven Brothers,* placed aboard her a prize crew commanded by Silas Cook, and dispatched her to Rhode Island. Again the company on board the privateer chose Nicholas and John Brown to be their agents. On February 26, 1757 the Judge of the Court of Vice-Admiralty at Newport directed the agents to take the cargo of *Seven Brothers* into their custody and to deliver an account of it to the Court under oath. The goods carried by *Seven Brothers* were less diversified, but more valuable, than those on *Desire.*[97] They were valued at £93,000 Old Tenor net.[98] One-half went to the owners; and £422:14:6 to each member of the crew of *Providence.*

It would be easy to exaggerate the profits of privateering. Fortunes supposedly were made in this way in every one of the eighteenth-century wars, but doubtless many of these existed only in the imagination of contemporaries. As for the Browns' privateering exploits in the Seven Years' War, they certainly yielded nothing approaching a fortune. True their privateer took two prizes, but in the end this ship was lost. And the value of the prizes has been greatly overestimated. The author of *Providence in Colonial Times* gives the value of the cargoes of *Desire* and *Seven Brothers* as £78,000 and £93,000 respectively; and she remarks that "with facts such as these fresh in their minds we can well understand that the naval service of Great Britain would offer few attractions to the stalwart seamen of Narragansett Bay."[99] She evidently believed the value of the cargoes was computed in pounds Sterling, and such is the inference which the reader would draw from her statements. A prize cargo of £93,000 Sterling, approximately $450,000 (our money), in the mid-eighteenth century would indeed have been a handsome one. But unfortunately the value was not reckoned in Sterling but in the Old Tenor currency of Rhode Island, which was then worth about £6 to the dollar. So the value of *Desire*'s cargo was about 13,000 dollars and that of *Seven Brothers* somewhat more than 15,000 dollars. These may have been satisfactory figures but they were hardly spectacular. Many prizes of that sort would be required to found a fortune, especially when balanced by the loss of the privateer which took them.

CHAPTER 4

"That Unrighteous Traffic"

EW aspects of colonial commerce have excited so widespread an interest as the African slave trade; and in the popular mind none of the British continental colonies has been more closely associated with the trade than has Rhode Island. The first recorded instance of the visit of a slave-trading vessel to the shores of the colony is that of the Brigantine *Seaflower,* owned in Boston, which arrived at Newport in 1696 with a cargo of forty-seven Negroes, fourteen of whom were sold there.[1] In 1700 two sloops and a ship, all fitted out in Rhode Island, sailed from Newport for the African coast, where they obtained slaves who were disposed of in Barbados.[2]

Little evidence exists as to the extent of the African trade carried on from Rhode Island during the next twenty years. Whether it underwent a steady expansion it is impossible to say. But the authors of the Rhode Island Remonstrance of 1764 stated that the trade had attained a considerable importance by 1723.[3] In that year some enterprising merchants of Rhode Island introduced rum upon the African Coast, where "from small beginnings" its consumption soon increased to several thousand hogsheads yearly; "by which the French are deprived of the sale of an equal quantity of brandy." According to the Remonstrance, for thirty years prior to 1764 Rhode Island sent "about eighteen sail of vessels" annually to the Coast, carrying about eighteen hundred hogsheads of rum. There they exchanged "some of the rum with the traders from Britain, for a quantity of dry goods, with which each of them sort their cargoes to their mutual advantage." The Rhode Island ship captains then bartered their assorted cargoes for slaves, elephants' teeth, gold dust, and camwood. They sold the slaves in the English Islands, in Carolina, and in Virginia for bills of exchange; and the remaining articles they sent to Europe. This trade, it was estimated, provided Rhode Islanders with the means by which to make remittance of £40,000 Sterling annually to Britain.

The early Rhode Island slave traders were, of course, from Newport.

Not until 1736 did a Providence merchant presume to enter this hazardous traffic. On January 28, 1735/6, Captain James Brown, father of the four brothers, wrote to Obadiah, then in the West Indies with the Sloop *Mary:* "I would not have you sell your vessel without a pritty good price for her, and if you bring her home we will send her direct to Guinnia, for rum is like to be verry plenty."[4] Obadiah brought *Mary* safely home to Providence, where, true to James's design, she was fitted out as the first "Guinea man" to sail from the Providence Plantations. Although commanded by Captain Godfrey, her supercargo was Obadiah, who was "one-eighth concerned" in the vessel and cargo. Although no record remains of her invoice of goods, it undoubtedly included a quantity of rum and, perhaps, some tobacco. *Mary* arrived on the African Coast at an inauspicious moment. The place was surfeited with rum but short on slaves. In the "Rhoad" there were nineteen craft at one time. Instead of prime slaves, once so plentiful, the traders were forced to take "any that comes."

But the depressed conditions which young Obadiah reported from the slave coast did not discourage the elder brother. In a letter which combined distressing family news with business, James wrote: "But you are well, which is good news, for health in this world is better than welth, you wrote Something Concerning your Mother, these may informe you that She died about two Months after you Sail'd, and I hope She is now more happy than either of us are we being burthened with this world and She at rest as I hope." Turning to the business at hand, with characteristic directness James Brown urged "dispatch in your business if you cannot Sell all your Slaves to your mind bring some home I believe they will Sell well, gett Molases if you can, and if you Cannot come without it." His closing injunction was to "leave no debts behind upon no Account, gett some Sugar & Cotten if you Can handily, but be Sure make dispatch for that is the life of trade."[5]

Conditions on the Coast proved to be less distressing than first reports had indicated. Obadiah procured Negroes who, when sold in the West Indies, purchased a substantial cargo of coffee, Osnaburgs, duck, cordage, and salt. Three slaves brought to Providence were valued at £120. Offering the cargo for sale, Captain James Brown wrote to one of his customers: "Sr if I Remambor Rite you deziared me to Right you a few Lines at the Arivol of my Ginemon. Theas may in forme you that she is Arived and you may have A slave if you Cum or sand Befoar they air Gon." He added that he had "solte plantey if you want and savoral other Sortes of Goods if you desaine [design to come] down you Cannot be two soon."[6]

From the somewhat fragmentary evidence which has survived, it is apparent that the first "Guinea" voyage of the Brown family was not a fail-

ure; on the other hand, it was not a conspicuous success. During the brief
span of life remaining to him James Brown seems not to have succumbed
again to the lure of the slave trade. Or, perhaps the temptation was not
so great as we have supposed! In any event the extant records of the Brown
family reveal no indication of another slave voyage until 1759[7] On January
31 of that year Tench Francis of Philadelphia advised Obadiah Brown
and Company (successors to Captain James) that the underwriters would
insure the Schooner *Wheel of Fortune,* William Earl, Master, to the Windward Coast of Africa, while on the Coast and back to Providence at 25
per cent, and would engage to return 10 per cent if she "dont arrive at the
Coast."[8] Before the policy was actually written, however, there occurred
a further advance in insurance rates; and Tench informed Obadiah that
he had insured for £400 the "Goods in ye schooner *Wheel of Fortune*
from Providence to the Windward and Leeward Coasts of Africa and at
and from thence to Providence @ 28 pct to return 13p^{Ct} if she doth not
arrive at the Coast or 3 p^{Ct} if she arrives at the Windward Coast and doth
proceed to the Leeward."[9] There are but two subsequent references to the
Wheel of Fortune. A letter from the Browns to Tench Francis reported
her safe arrival on the Windward Coast of Africa.[10] The other mention of
her is found in Obadiah's Insurance Book, where her name appears in
Obadiah's own hand, followed by the somber notation "Taken." As it
was the menace of French privateers off the African Coast that had
driven insurance rates to the 28 per cent level, it seems evident that the
vessel fell a prey to an enemy raider.

This appears to have been the last slave-trading venture of Obadiah's
career. Perhaps the discouragement which inevitably attended the loss of
Wheel of Fortune dampened whatever ardor he may have had for the
slave traffic. Perhaps, too, preoccupation with trade with the enemy during the remainder of the war years left no time for the planning of slave
voyages. Before peace finally came in 1763 Obadiah was dead, leaving to
his four nephews, Nicholas, Joseph, John, and Moses, the responsibility
of deciding whether the Browns should return to the Guinea trade.

Nicholas Brown and Company, probably at John's insistence, soon
decided to risk another ship in the slave trade.[11] The plan for the
voyage was first mentioned in one of the Company's letters to Carter
Braxton of Virginia. Braxton, later one of the Virginia signers of the
Declaration of Independence, writing "on Pamunkey River" in the Old
Dominion, had advised the Browns that he had accidentally met up with
Nicholas Power, supercargo aboard *Four Brothers,* a sloop which the
Browns had dispatched on a voyage to Virginia and Maryland on January
1, 1763. Braxton wrote that he had traded "with him for Better than Half
his Cargo of Goods."[12] Sensing that Power was "desirous of fixing a Cor-

respondent" in Virginia for his owners, Braxton was moved to offer his services to the Browns in that capacity. He would gladly transact their business for a 5 per cent commission on sales, with an equal amount on purchases, notwithstanding the fact that their correspondents in Philadelphia, New York, and Boston received but 2½ per cent on purchases. He could provide them with flour and corn as "cheap as any man," as he was a large manufacturer of the one and lived in a part of the country where the "other generally sells cheaper than anywhere else." Of New England products, he thought rum would best answer in Virginia, but he suggested that they "clear it out as West India and enter it here as such," as by that means they would save half the duty, as the impost on rum made in the islands was only fourpence per gallon, compared with eightpence on the New England variety.

Braxton understood there was a "great Traid carried on from Rhode Island to Guinea for negroes," and he would be pleased to enter into partnership with "some Gentlemen" for a voyage or two, the slaves to be sent to Virginia where they would sell as well as anywhere. The "common price" of them was £30 to £35 Sterling—two-thirds of the money paid down, the balance in three months. He added that should the Browns "incline to enter such a Scheme" he would be glad to hear from them "particularly" about it; and he asked them to urge their friends to consign their slave cargoes to him "on the best terms you can."

All in all, the picture of Braxton painted in this self-revealing letter is not that which we commonly associate with prominent Virginians of that day. He may have been a courtly, aristocratic planter, lord of broad acres, utilizing slave labor in the cultivation of his fields, while he devoted his leisure time to politics or the social graces. But if he was all this, he was also a businessman, eager, aggressive, and self-assertive, willing to drive a hard bargain, with an eye to the main chance, prepared to evade the customs duties, and to play the rôle of commission merchant in the African slave trade.

Because preoccupation with other business prevented them from dispatching a vessel to Virginia in the spring of 1763, Nicholas Brown and Company delayed their reply to Braxton until September 5.[13] They then advised him that they planned to send a ship to Virginia in the autumn; and that they would be glad to "enter into a Correspondency" with him on condition that his commission should be identical with that charged elsewhere in the colonies. As for Braxton's slave-trading proposition, they wrote:

You mention of being Concerned in the Guine Trade & that the Vessels Return with negroes to your place, as we shall be Largely Concerned in the

Navigation this Fall which will bring Mell° [molasses] in the Spring & we living in a place wair we Can procure a Large quantity of Rum Distilled Amediately, its Very Likely if its Agreeable to you to be Concerned that we may Fitt a proper Vessill for Guiney in the Spring, & as a Considerable quantity of Tobacco will answer their, You'll advise us in your next wither you Could Send a Quantity of Tobacco Clear of Duty by our Vessill, if Comes to your Address this Winter, & at What price, so as not to Indage the Vessill nor Cargo from Confiscation.

Carter Braxton's reply of October 16, 1763 seemed to remove the one obstacle to the proposed joint venture in the "Guine trade."[14] He acknowledged that the commission fee he had sought to charge was excessive, and offered his services as correspondent at the commission the Browns customarily paid. He would gladly be

concerned in the African Trade and will be a fourth of the Voyage if you Choose it. Tobacco I can send any quantity at 20/ phund^d and I believe free of duty if your Skiper will take it. I should choose to be Insured and what ever Expense come to my Share more than the Tobacco sent I would remit by the Return of the Vessell that brought the Slaves. The whole of the Voyage I should leave to you to conduct and you may begin to prepare if you please. But you will let me know the Terms and every Thing relating to the Voyage before the Vessill Sails. It ought to be forwarded so as to have the Vessill here in May, because the Negroes will sell better then than later. The Gold Coast Slaves are Esteemed the most Valuable & Sell best. The prices of Negroes keep up Amasingly. They have sold from £30 to £35 Sterling ahead Clear of duty all this Summer & I should not doubt of rendering Such a Sale if the Negroes were well and come early. I find two or three Vessills have been here this summer from the Northward & I suppose the trade will be carried on with more vigour for the future.

Thus far in the letter Braxton, the potential adventurer in a slave voyage, had spoken; now Braxton in the capacity of the commission merchant dealing in slaves wrote that

if you will undertake to befriend me in Soliciting the Consignment of some of them I will give you for your Trouble ⅓ of my Commissions which will be a Pritty thing if the Vessill is consigned wholly to me. But if she is only half to me, I will give you ½ of my Commissions for all that you get and will make my remittance in any manner they desire.

In December 1763 only a few weeks after the Braxton letter was written, the Sloop *Four Brothers* was again in Virginia. Captain Pardon Sheldon was instructed to inform himself of markets at Norfolk and "at other towns within the Bay."[15] The cargo included "the negro man Corodan," whom the Captain was to "sell for the most he will fetch." The return cargo included none of the tobacco which Braxton had planned to smuggle out. And what is more, there is no evidence that Captain Sheldon made contact with Braxton. In fact the Virginian disappears completely from sight in the records of the Providence business house. The Browns continued to trade with Virginia but Braxton was not one of their correspondents; nor was their traffic to the Chesapeake region in any way connected with the "guine trade." Unfortunately there is no explanation for the abrupt termination of this potential partnership with Braxton. It is possible that Nicholas Brown and Company decided that business with the gentleman from the South might prove too costly. But, whatever the reason, there can be no doubt that an interesting chapter in our economic and social history was lost through this failure of the sons of New England and the Old Dominion to get together in the trade to the Gold Coast.

The miscarriage of the plan for a joint venture with Braxton did not mean that the Brown brothers had given up the slave trade. It merely delayed for a few months the slave voyage which they had already planned for the spring of 1764. In the summer they devoted much of their time and attention to the fitting out at Newport of the Brig *Sally,* command of which they placed in the hands of Esek Hopkins, who was so closely associated with them during the twenty years before Independence. On the eve of *Sally*'s departure Nicholas, writing from Providence, gave some last-minute instructions to Joseph, John, and Moses who were at Newport helping Hopkins with the final preparation for the voyage. He advised them that

Jno. Jenckes asks 6/ for his Tobacco perhaps it might be got of the Judge at less, tho making him an Offer while at Newport may put him in Mind of selling it in Newport where its much wanted for the Guneamen . . . Inquire of Malbone whither there Brigg Caried Any qy. Onions—if they did not it may be worth while to get 100 bshl. more at Bristol . . . I believe that if a Stroke were put in the Newport paper Truly giveing a State of the Rum Trade upon the Coast of Guinea it may prevent Menny Vessels from Pushing that way this fall, this is a subject worth our Attention. a Small matter as 2 dols. will get from the Newport into the Boston & York Papers, or Phila.[16]

Here was a more or less subtle proposal to use a news story to their own advantage. But if the "Stroke" suggested by Nicholas was ever put in the paper, its influence must have been negligible, as the Guinea coast fairly thronged with slave traders during the autumn and winter of 1764-1765.

The cargo of *Sally* consisted of 159 hogsheads and 6 tierces of rum, amounting to 17,274 gallons, 25 casks of rice, 30 boxes of spermaceti candles, 10 hogsheads of tobacco, 6 barrels of tar, 40 barrels of flour, a quantity of loaf sugar, 2 tierces of brown sugar, 96 pounds of coffee, and 1800 bunches of onions.[17] The ship's stores emphasized the desperate nature of the voyage upon which *Sally* was embarked. She was carrying a small arsenal—7 swivel guns, 1 cask of powder, "40 hand Cufs" and "40 Shakels," 3 "Chanes," 2 pair of pistols, "8 Small arms," 13 "Cutleshes," 1 dozen "pad Locks," 1 pair of "Blunder Bursses."[18] The combined value of the merchandise and stores on board the Brig was £97,723 Old Tenor, or about 14,000 dollars.

Because of his owners' "Thoraugher acquaintance and Satisfaction" with Esek Hopkins' ability and integrity, their sailing directions, dated September 10, 1764, allowed him a large measure of discretion on the voyage.[19] He was free to dispose of his cargo for slaves or "any other thing" which would net as good a "proffet." It was suggested that he proceed to Barbados with his slaves, although he was at liberty to visit any other port in the West Indies which he thought best for his owners' interest. Failing a satisfactory market in the West Indies, he might sell in Carolina, Virginia, or Maryland. He was to accept only "Hard Cash or good Bills of Exchange" in payment for his slaves. Should he deem it advisable, he was authorized to sell the Brig along with the cargo. The Browns requested that he bring "four likely Young Slaves Home for Owners about 15 Years old." Captain Hopkins' privilege was to be ten slaves, with a commission of four slaves for every 104 obtained, plus 5 per cent of the net proceeds of the sales of the Negroes.

On December 30, 1764 Nicholas Brown and Company wrote Hopkins that they had nothing new by way of orders "only that you dew as you Shall Think Best for Our Interest its an old proverb and we doubt not you will veryfye it, Despach is the Life of Business."[20] They asked him to make all possible inquiry into the "trade of ye Brazil for hope Something may be done there to advantage from this Quarter of ye World."

Captain Hopkins arrived aboard *Sally* on the Guinea coast in early November 1764. Few, if any, records of African slave voyages as complete as those of *Sally* now exist. Captain Hopkins faithfully wrote down his day-to-day transactions. His account reveals the method of doing business. It shows the hardships, the bribery, the greed, and above all the horror that went with this traffic in human flesh.[21] The first Notation in "Brige *Saley,* Trade Book" bears the date of November 10, 1764. On that day the Captain traded one gallon of rum for some wood, another gallon for "1 Small Tooth" and "3 botles powder for Corn & fowels." Two days later he sold "2 bunches onyons" at one shilling, sixpence per bunch and 10 pounds of loaf sugar at one shilling per pound. The following day Captain Hopkins made his first overture to the tribal hierarchy when he gave three "galons Rum to alkade and his people." He obtained his first slave on the 15th when he sold Captain "Heweet 156 galons Rum" and "1 barel flower" for £17, balancing his account "by 1 garle slave" at £10 and 1 boy at £7.

That times were dull and slaves scarce is indicated by the complete absence of entries between November 16 and December 1. On the latter date Captain Hopkins made his first important deal. He sold "Mr. Hudson" rum, loaf sugar, and onions to the value of £70:11:0; and he purchased "1 man & 1 man boy slave," 1 "woman" and "2 garles & 1 boy," all for £70:11:0. The next day "195 galons Rum," valued at £19:10:0, fetched 1 "garle" and 1 boy slave. Nine days elapsed before more slaves were to be had, when goods worth £164:11:0 brought 13 Negroes, including "5 prime slaves" and "2 grone slaves."

In a sense the trade which Esek Hopkins had thus far carried on was of a preliminary nature, as he had not yet paid his proper respects to tribal officialdom. But that diplomatic mission was soon accomplished. He tells us in his "Trade Book" under date of December 21st that he "wated on the Kinge with 2 barels Rum and 1 Cagg of Snuff for him and his officors." The following day he gave "1 cask to alkade" and "a bout So much more give a way to the Retenna on board." The next several days were similarly occupied with matters of protocol. On the 23d the Captain "Went a Shore to meet the King under the palavor Tree Cared 5 Caggs 14 flask Rum and paid the King 75 galons for his Customs and Recd a Cow a present." But the 24th was a really notable day. The entry for that date reads: "Wate on the King with a Cagg of Rum & he opened my Trade by Sending of a Slave for which I give 112 galons Rum." But the purchase of a slave did not mean that official ceremonies were at an end. The African king knew how to bargain. Captain Hopkins records that later in the day he "Paid King fodolgo Talko his Customs—36 galons Rum"; and with various quantities of rum, "Tobacor" and bar iron he paid the "Customs" of the "Kings Son," and the "King arger or high Cunstable," the "geograff," the "Alkade," and the "owner of the founten." While "paying the Customs" of these dignitaries he "Expended to all their Retinue . . . at Lest 50 galons Rum besides Sugar and vitles."

Even after all formalities had been completed, Captain Hopkins was careful to see that the King's thirst was kept well slaked. Thus his pages are dotted with notations such as "1 Cagg Rum to the King . . . 4 flask Rum give fodolgo Talko . . . 1 cask Rum give Talko." Other functionaries were also kept in the proper attitude of mind by the judicious use of rum. An entry for January 19, 1765 reads "1 flask Rum to the owner of the founten."

As the weeks lengthened into months the trade became more complex. In the early stages slaves were frequently obtained by means of simple, bilateral transactions, such as that described by the entry "48 galons Rum give for garle Slave" or "52 galons Rum for a boye Slave." But soon the day-to-day trading involved the exchange of many articles, of which slaves were not one. In this process dry goods brought to the coast in British ships occupy a prominent place. "Country Cloths" appear constantly, while silk stockings, "manchester" cloth, "cargoson" cloth, and various other kinds are frequently found. One of these transactions reads "10 flask Rum for 5 C——y Cloths."

Further light is thrown upon the process of slave trading by the notation that "Mr. York returned with the boat from Jabe brought 1 man 1 boy 1 garle slaves and 3 Country Cloths . . . 165 lbs beas wex, for which he give and expended 328 galons Rum, 28 bushels onyons many more wasted, 1 pr silk stockins 20 galons Rum drunk and Stole Mr. York being Sick." On January 16th Captain Hopkins gave 3 flasks of rum to the "alkade for birning [bringing] a Run a way Slave on Bord." On the 21st he gave a like amount to "2 men that brought Slaves."

Although his primary purpose was the procurement of slaves for sale in America, the Master of *Sally* disposed of some of his Negroes while still on the Coast. On February 18th he "Sold . . . 4 Slaves 2 men 2 women" for 270 iron bars. On March 25th he bought "a Small garle Slave" whom he sold the same day to Captain Rotto, making a profit of 4 bars. In the next month he disposed of "4 Slaves 2 old woman & 2 old man" to Captain Portages Snow for 240 bars. Thus Esek Hopkins parted with nine of his slaves by sale prior to his departure from the Guinea Coast. On August 1st he recorded the exchange of "a man Slave with his foot bitt of by a Shark and goot a boy in his Roume."

But sale was not the only means by which the total number of *Sally*'s slaves was reduced. Long before she was ready to leave the Coast death began to take its toll. The first occurred on April 1, 1765 when Captain Hopkins noted that "a boye Slave died." On June 8th a "woman Slave hanged her Self between Decks." By August 20th, when he purchased his last slave, he had already lost twenty. Captain Hopkins had then been on the Coast for more than nine months. By dint of constant trading he had procured 196 slaves. As he had sold nine and lost twenty by death, his net cargo comprised 167 Negroes.

With so much at stake in *Sally*, Nicholas Brown and Company sought to keep in close touch with Captain Hopkins. In the course of the months he was on the Coast they addressed several letters to him at Barbados and gave him news of potential markets for the cargo he was purchasing. In one letter written on June 3, 1765 they advised him that by several accounts from the Windward Islands slaves were a slow sale.[22] On the other hand, all reports indicated a good market in South Carolina, partly because of the eagerness of the planters to supply themselves before an increase in the provincial duty on slave importations became effective. The Browns suggested, therefore, that he go to Charleston; if the market were unfavorable, he might try Virginia. In either case he was to "get what Hard Cash" he could.

In mid-July Nicholas Brown and Company received an indirect report that the Captain had lost all his "Hands in the River Basa."[23] But almost immediately thereafter came a letter from the Captain himself, written on May 25th, which Moses Brown said "Quite aleviates our Misfortune" by its favorable account of his circumstances.[24] Replying to this letter Moses, in behalf of the Company, advised Captain Hopkins, as the South Carolina market was now glutted, that he sell his slaves at Barbados if he could get £28 Sterling for them. Otherwise, he was to proceed to Jamaica.[25]

Unfortunately, the letters which Esek Hopkins wrote from the Guinea Coast, which undoubtedly explained the reasons for his long stay there, have not survived. But from his "Trade Book," from the Browns' letters in reply to his, and from collateral sources it is clear that the Coast was so crowded with British and New England traders that slaves were procured with difficulty. Undoubtedly the high "customs" which the Captain was forced to pay as the price of "opening the trade" reflected the spirited competition for slaves. In those circumstances a nine months' sojourn was necessary to acquire a cargo of Negroes.

The internal evidence contained in the "Trade Book" indicates that Captain Hopkins took his departure from African shores shortly after he recorded the purchase of his last slave on August 20th. Scarcely had he set Sally upon her course through the Middle Passage when misfortune, which was to make a financial disaster of the voyage, began to plague him.[26] Under date of August 21st he recorded the somber fact that "1 garle Slave Dyed," being number twenty-one taken by death since April 1st. On the 25th "one boye Slave Dyed," while "1 woman & 1 boye slave Dyed" on the 27th. More ominous were the events of August 28th when the "Slaves Rose on us was obliged to fire on them and Destroyed 8 and Several more wounded badly 1 Thye & ones Ribs broke." This brought the number of dead to thirty-two. Through September, as Sally sailed toward the Caribbean, deaths were almost daily occurrences. On the 8th "2 women and 2 boys dyed." Another day Hopkins recorded the deaths of "3 boys & 1 garle." On the 19th "1 man slave Dyed of his wounds on the Ribs when Slaves Rose." Early in October Sally arrived in the West Indies, calling at Barbados in accordance with the original instructions to Captain Hopkins. Failing, apparently, to find there any of the letters the Browns had addressed to him, Captain Hopkins continued on his own initiative to Antigua. In a letter from that port, he told the story of the last tragic days of *Sally*'s voyage.[27] The uprising of the Negroes on board ship and its suppression brought heart-breaking results. The surviving Negroes were "so disperited" that "some drowned themselves, some starved and others sickened and died." Eighty-eight of the slaves were dead and the remaining were in a "very sickly and disordered manner." *Sally* had traded her cargo of rum for tragedy, disease, and death.

On November 25, 1765, Alexander Willock, merchant at Antigua, wrote Nicholas Brown and Company, enclosing bills of exchange for £417:4:3 Sterling, being the net proceeds of the sale of twenty-four slaves placed in his hands by Captain Hopkins for sale.[28] Willock remarked that these "Slaves was verry Indifferent." Had the "Negroes been Young and Healthy" he would have been able to sell them "pritty well." As there is no record of the further sale of Negroes from this voyage, some of the slaves procured by Hopkins cannot be accounted for. The records show that on December 20, 1765 there occurred the 109th death. Allowing for these deaths and for the sixteen slaves constituting the privilege of the Captain and crew, there should have been left for sale on account of the Brown brothers a total of 62 Negroes. Of these only 24 are known to have been sold. What became of the remaining 38? Were they so "indifferent," in such "bad order," so "sickly," so old and infirm as not to be disposable at any price? And, if they were not sold, what disposition was made of them? These questions cannot be answered.

But, from a business standpoint, whether twenty-four or sixty-two slaves were sold does not greatly matter. In either event, the voyage was a financial disaster for Nicholas Brown and Company. If only the 24 Negroes were sold, the loss on the voyage was approximately 12,000 dollars. If the 38 unaccounted for were sold at the same average price as the 24, the loss was still close to 9000 dollars. In the face of this staggering blow the owners of *Sally* were stoical in the extreme. Writing to Esek Hopkins the day after the receipt of his disappointing letter of October 9, 1765, they said: "We need not mention how Disagreeable the Nuse of your Luseing 88 Slaves is to us & all your Friends, but your Self Continuing in Helth is so Grate Satisfaction to us, that we Remain Cheirful under the Heavy Loss of our Ints."[29] Although they had some suggestions with respect to his conduct of their affairs, they remarked that "we Knowing your Capatity Submitt the Whole Management of the Voyage to Your best Judgment and you may assure your Self that what ever you think best we shall be fully Satisfied with." Notwithstanding his "Misfortin" they assured him that "we will on your Arival at Home Imploy you in Aney Businesses you may Chuse and we are able to Execute. Your Famaly, ours & all Friends is well, We are, your Friends & owners."[30]

Although Captain Hopkins' voyage was unsuccessful, the record of his transactions while on the African Coast was sought by the Browns' friends, the Wantons, to guide them in planning a slave venture of their own. In June 1766 they wrote to John Brown that they would be "obliged if you would ask the Favour of Capt. Esek Hopkins for a Sight of his Trade Book at the coast of Guinea, if not Inconsistant with his and your Interest, with a few Directions with regard to the Customs and the Government of the Captain with such observations as his Inspectious Eye has made."[31] Replying to this request, Nicholas Brown offered the Wantons the use of the book at their pleasure and convenience.[32]

According to all available evidence, to 1765 the African slave trade engrossed but a small proportion of the time and energy which the Brown family devoted to commercial affairs. They had sent three vessels to the Guinea coast, one of which was lost, another of which was a financial failure, while the third was not a notable success. Nor does the trade appear to have become more important to them after 1765. It is virtually certain that Nicholas, Joseph, and Moses never again participated in a slave voyage after the ill-starred venture of *Sally* in 1765.[33] But not so with John, who continued to be intrigued by the African trade almost to his dying day. In 1769, while still a member of Nicholas Brown and Company, he was concerned in the voyage of *Sultan* to Africa. Writing to his friend Benjamin Mason, of Newport, he explained his need for "about 2000 Gallons of Rum more than Can be Got here" by the time scheduled for *Sultan's* departure.[34] He wished to know the lowest price at which Mason could obtain that quantity, to be paid "Either Gallon for Gallon in Good Surinam Mello. [molasses] & the Distilling in Sp. Cands at 1/9^d or wholly in Cands at this price." In a postscript he added that "if it Sutes You to Recommend the Gentlemen in the West Indies who sold your Last Cargo of Slaves, plese to Give us their Names, as its possible, if Mr. Smith who goes in the Ship should git Safe Round to the West Indies may Value on your Friends."[35] John arranged with Hayley and Hopkins in London for insurance on the voyage.

There was a hiatus in the African trade of Rhode Island during the War for Independence. British occupation of Newport was of course an obstacle to the continuation of the traffic. But probably John and his fellow-traders found privateering and other wartime opportunities more attractive for the moment. It has been said that, at the close of the war, "Newport cast back a longing glance . . . upon the slave trade." Its merchants, together with those of nearby Bristol and Warren, showed a zeal for it which, by comparison, made those of Providence appear apathetic. But John Brown did not share the indifference of Providence. During the score of years remaining to him, John became the foremost defender of the Guinea traffic in Rhode Island. And by a curious trick of fate it was his brother Moses who shared with the Reverend Samuel Hopkins of New-port the honor of being the most distinguished leader of the opposition to what he termed "that Unrighteous Traffic."[36]

As early as June 1774 the General Assembly of Rhode Island had passed an act providing that "no negro or mulatto slave shall be brought into this colony."[37] In 1784 the Assembly enacted a law authorizing the gradual abolition of slavery in the state and repealing the provisions in the act of 1774 allowing the importation into the colony of slaves which could not be disposed of in the West Indies.[38] Although this was a substantial gain for the opponents of slavery, both Moses Brown and Samuel Hopkins were disappointed. Alluding to the failure to obtain a more drastic measure directed at the African trade, Moses wrote that the influence of the mercantile interest "in the House was greatly Exerted, and the Justice of the Subject thereby Overbourn."[39] Sorrowfully Moses had to say that his "Brother John was deep in the Opposition,"[40] although, as a member of the General Assembly at the time, he was instructed by the Providence town meeting to support the measure. John thought emancipation a "shallow policy."[41]

John's principles, however, were sufficiently flexible to permit him to shift his attitude on the African trade as circumstances might require. In 1787 he was making his plans for the dispatching of his Ship *General Washington* on the voyage which inaugurated the East India trade of Providence. In an effort to purchase the financial coöperation of brother Moses, he promised that, should the venture materialize, he would "not be aney more Concerned in the Guiney Trade."[42] He also urged Moses to become a member of the Rhode Island Assembly, pointing out that "if you are in the House You can do what you think Right Respecting the proposed proabbition to the Guiney Trade or Reither the Slave Trade."[43]

In that same year Moses Brown and his fellow abolitionists won a notable victory when the Rhode Island Assembly, much to their surprise, enacted the first law in America prohibiting the African slave trade.[44] The act forbade citizens or residents of the state to be in any way concerned in the transport of Negroes from Africa for the purpose of selling them into slavery. Violation of the law incurred a penalty of £100 lawful money for each Negro thus transported, plus £1000 for every vessel employed in such traffic.[45] Realizing that Rhode Island slave traders were preparing to circumvent the law by fitting out their vessels at Norwich and Middletown in Connecticut, Moses and Hopkins quickly turned their propaganda to that state. In particular they sent their literature to the younger Jonathan Edwards, minister at New Haven and member of a committee of the clergy chosen to petition the legislature of Connecticut for a law abolishing the African trade.[45] In October 1788 they had the satisfaction of seeing such an act placed upon the statute books of Connecticut.

Continuing his opposition to slavery in all its aspects, Moses Brown in 1789, with the assistance of several friends of like mind, organized the Providence Society for Promoting the Abolition of Slavery.[46] One of the functions assumed by this Society was that of guarding against violation of the Rhode Island Act of 1787 forbidding citizens of the state to participate in the African trade. And when Congress, in 1794, enacted a law designed to close that traffic to all American citizens, the Society became the self-appointed agency for the enforcement of that measure within the limits of Rhode Island. Moses probably did not anticipate that his brother John would one day be one of those to be prosecuted at the instigation of the Society. In 1797, however, John succumbed once more to the lure of the "Guiney" trade and thereby found himself the defendant in litigation brought against him by the Abolition Society. Although the vessel was condemned, Moses tells us that John "found means notwithstanding, by the Peculiar Turn of the Jurors, even before the federal Court at Newport to get acquitted on Tryall for the Penalty on part of the Slaves."[47]

This court battle occasioned an exchange of letters between John and Moses in which the former appears in no very favorable light. In them John's customary arrogant bravado gives way to a whining, plaintive note. He implies that he deserves special consideration for "never having been Concerned in but one Voyage Since the Law passed."[48] And he sought to plead as an added extenuation that he had undertaken the slave voyage "from Nessesity Seeing no other way to pay the Reveneu of the United States to whome I then owed near 100,000 Dol[s]." Continuing, he wrote that "Not Constering the Law as it has since beene, I did not suppose I was doing Rong but to the Conterary that I was doing the best I could to Inable me to help pay this Grait Sum to the Government for Import Dutys."[49] To John's plea that these alleged alleviating circumstances justified an "accommodation," Moses was quite unsympathetic. He observed that the "terms offered at Newport were Moderate & Such as he [John] would have accepted had it not been for the flatterings of his friend."[50] And he added that "there were those at Newport & elsewhere who would have prosecuted him more severely had it not been for the Influence of those he calls his enemies."[51]

Once the litigation was safely behind him, John quickly recovered his accustomed self-assurance. As a candidate for the national House of Representatives in 1798 he solicited the votes of Moses Brown and his son Obadiah, of George Benson and other leaders in the abolition movement in Providence.[52] As a member of Congress he still continued to be a source of mortification to Moses. In January 1800 the latter wrote that John "has now a Ship he has been refiting which if he does not Sell I fear he would, again, be tempted to send on a Slave Voyage."[53]

It is doubtful that this "Guiney" venture ever materialized. But, in any event, John Brown had experienced no charge of heart. In May 1800, Congress passed an act intended to strengthen the law of 1794 prohibiting the carrying on of the "slave-trade from the United States to any foreign place or country."[54] As a member of the House of Representatives, John not only cast one of the five votes against the bill, but he also spoke in opposition to it.[55] He thought it improper to deny to American citizens the benefits of a trade permitted by all the European nations. He was sharply critical of the influence of "certain persons who would not take no for an answer" in the enactment of the Act of 1794. Those persons were members of the "Abolition Society, otherwise the Society of Friends," of which his brother Moses was one. Those people, John asserted, "did not do much to support the Government, but they did as much as they could to stop the measures of the Government and particularly our defensive system," on which national security depended. Believing that an American law against the slave trade would not prevent the exportation of a single slave from Africa, he thought his fellow countrymen should enjoy the trade rather than leave it wholly to others. Prohibition of the trade was morally wrong, as by the "operation of the trade" the slaves themselves "much bettered their condition." Financially the trade was desirable since it "would bring in a good revenue to our Treasury." John was reliably informed that on the African coast New England rum was much preferred to Jamaica spirits and would command a higher price. "Why then," he asked, "should it not be sent there," thus providing employment for the New England distilleries which were lying idle for want of an extended commerce. "Why should a heavy fine and imprisonment be made the penalty for carrying on a trade so advantageous?"

That John Brown was one of the foremost champions of the African slave trade in his day there can be no doubt. But his defense of it was dictated only in part by his own self-interest. As the arch individualist, he was inalterably opposed in principle to any interference by government with so-called free enterprise in business. In and out of Congress he could see no reason why the humane spirit of the time should be permitted to limit the freedom of the merchant to augment his capital in any way he might choose.

It would be easy enough to argue that Nicholas, Joseph, and Moses Brown abandoned the slave trade after 1765 because they were convinced that it was unprofitable. But in the light of the strong differences of opinion which later developed between Moses and John, the moral factor in the decision cannot be ignored. Nicholas and Joseph did not follow Moses into active participation in the movement for the prohibition of the slave trade, but neither did they continue in the buying and selling of slaves in which John persisted after the financial failure of the earlier years. There was as much need for them to try to recoup their losses by new slave voyages as there was for him. Instead, they chose to concentrate their attention on other phases of their businesses. Years later, Moses Brown wrote that three of the brothers had lived to regret their participation in the disastrous voyage of *Sally*. But John had no such regrets. Moreover, after many of the citizens of the community in which he lived had branded the buying and selling of human beings as immoral, he continued to condone it by devious and superficial argument.

CHAPTER 5

"Spermaceti Candles Warranted Pure"

WHILE exploiting the commercial opportunities of the Caribbean, while trading with the enemy in the Seven Years' War, and while indulging in an occasional voyage to the Guinea Coast, the Browns were engaged in another type of economic activity, far more important to them and far more permanent than either the wartime traffic with the French or the African slave trade. This was the manufacture of spermaceti candles, which largely conditioned their peacetime trade to the Caribbean, and prompted them to pursue the whale fishery on a modest scale.

Few groups of men have received a more handsome or a more merited tribute than that which Edmund Burke paid to the whalemen of New England on the eve of the War for Independence: "Look at the manner in which the people of New England have of late carried on the whale fishery . . . Falkland Island, which seemed too remote and romantic an object for the grasp of national ambition, is but a stage and resting place in the progress of their victorious industry . . . No sea but what is vexed by their fisheries. No climate that is not witness to their toils."[1] The great orator's compliment would have been no less apt had he paid it to the men of Nantucket alone; for in this one phase of maritime activity the merchants and sailors of the New England mainland had to be content with second place. The great names in the whale fishery of the eighteenth century—the Rotches, Macys, Starbucks, Husseys, Folgers, and Coffins—and the countless mariners who manned their ships, were the pride and boast of the little island off the New England coast.

Although Nantucket dominated whaling, almost every coastal settlement from the Kennebec to Long Island engaged in it at one time or another. In Rhode Island, Newport and Bristol men were the first to send out whaling ships. Providence merchants, as usual, were not the pioneers.

But in due course the Browns and many others were actively engaged in the whale fishery.

The records of the whaling voyages of the Browns are more fragmentary than those for almost any other branch of their business. They are brief and purely factual in character. They show that several ships went on many whaling voyages; sometimes they include the results in terms of physical volume or monetary value of the cargoes, but the color and excitement so often associated with these bold undertakings is almost completely lacking. There is no evidence that whaling occupied a prominent place in Obadiah Brown's business roster. In 1754, he and three associates purchased a sloop of about fifty tons which went on a whaling voyage in that same year.[2] There are no records of other voyages undertaken by his Company.

But Obadiah's nephews, associated as Nicholas Brown and Company, were much more active. Probably they turned seriously to whaling after the slave voyage of *Sally* had chilled their enthusiasm for the Guinea trade. Between 1769 and 1777 they sent out a small whaling fleet with reasonable regularity.

On December 24, 1767 John Brown wrote to Joseph Nicholas at Nantucket: ". . . I want 3 wale boats for a Brigg that's going wailing to the Western Islands—2 of them to be 6 ored and 1 of 5 ores, and all to be reddy by the last of March, and desire you'l procure them made according. Pray let them be good."[3] Two years later, in December 1769, the Sloop *Abigail* was sent to "Cape Blankco" on the coast of Africa to keep "a good look for whales" on a voyage "which we suppose will be 9 or 10 months long."[4] Captain Coffin's share of the proceeds of the voyage was to be one-seventeenth and "his peoples" shares from one-twentieth to one-fortieth. In September 1770, Captain Coffin returned to Providence in the Sloop *A*, with 77 barrels of oil and 11 barrels of head matter.[5] As the crew of the Sloop *A* was partially the same as that of *Abigail*, it is probable that the two references are to one and the same vessel. At any rate the Sloop *Abigail* disappears, while the Sloop *A* made six voyages to the West Indies and Africa during the next four years with instructions which followed the same general pattern: ". . . crews till you get a full load of oil & Head Matter or as much as all your Casks will hold & by no means return home without a full Load as aforesaid."[6] The first voyage of the Sloop *A* brought back 1170 gallons of oil, the last, 2904.[7]

The Sloop *Betsey*, the Brig *Rhoda*, and the Sloop *Katy* made whaling voyages in 1770 with varying results. The second voyage of the Sloop *Betsey* was one of the Browns' most successful. Her cargo of oil and head matter was valued at 417 pounds.[8]

Vessel number five in the whaling fleet was the Sloop *Defiance*. From her cruise of 1770, she returned with oil and head matter worth £400 lawful money. Christopher Folger, member of the prominent Nantucket whaling family, was the Captain on the second voyage of *Defiance* in 1772-73. Captain Folger's orders directed him to go "to the Whaling ground on the Coast of Africa & if you do not find Whale sufficiently plenty to get your vessel Loaded with Oile & Head Matter you are to proceed from there to the Coast of Brazele & there Whale it till you get a full Load."[9] It is doubtful if Captain Folger "whaled it" until he secured a load profitable for the owners. In October 1773 in a letter to one of their customers in Connecticut, Nicholas Brown and Company wrote, "But there is nothing like money . . . If you would do what you can to bring a sum it will never be more wanted than at this time . . . as our whaling voyages and other trade has not turned to advantage this season."[10]

Although there are many other references in the Brown papers to whaling in the years 1767-1774, these five vessels seem to have constituted the bulk of the Browns' whaling fleet. It seems clear that with a few exceptions their whaling ventures were only an indifferent success. The scope of their operations could in no way compare with that of the Nantucket men. Perhaps outstanding achievements in the whale fishery called for a degree of specialization of which unspecialized merchants were incapable. But be that as it may, Nicholas Brown and Company achieved far greater success in the manufacture and sale of spermaceti candles, a by-product of the whale fishery, than they did in the fishing itself.

The principal products of the fishery were whale fins and bone, several different kinds of oil, and spermaceti, or head matter. The best grade of oil was obtained in the autumn when the vessels went to the eastward, carrying try works, in which they tried out the oil as the whales were caught. This very white and clear oil was known as Bank or white oil. It enjoyed a wide preference in both colonial and British markets. Next in order of quality was the yellow oil obtained in the early spring. In the absence of try kettles on late spring and summer voyages, the vessels carried the blubber back to the home port. When thus subjected to the heat of the warm season, the oil changed in color and often became exceedingly rank. This was known as brown oil. The spermaceti or head matter was a white, waxy substance found in the cranial cavities of the sperm whale, and was widely used in the manufacture of spermaceti candles. The bone, fins, and oil from the colonial whale fishery provided New England merchants with one of their chief forms of remittance to the mother country. Theoretically the spermaceti or head matter was processed in the colonies themselves, but actually much of it was surreptitiously shipped to England in the guise of ordinary whale oil.

The spermaceti candle manufacture was established in the colonies about the middle of the eighteenth century. There are several versions of its beginnings.[11] According to one account, Abraham Rodrigues Rivera, a Portuguese Jew, brought the secrets of the process from his native land to Newport. Another story is that Dr. John Vanderlight (husband of Mary Brown, sister of the four brothers) introduced into Rhode Island the technique used in Holland. Neither of these claims is well documented. It is a matter of record, however, that in 1749 one Benjamin Crabb (or Crab), an Englishman living in Rehoboth, Massachusetts, petitioned the General Court of that Province for the "Sole priviledge" of making "Candles of Coarse Sperma Caeti Oyle." Although his request was granted, Crabb did not choose to exercise his "Sole priviledge" in the Bay Colony. Instead, he moved to Rhode Island, where he built a candle manufactory which was soon destroyed by fire. When Obadiah Brown built his spermaceti plant, he engaged Crabb to conduct the business for him. But he "was disappointed of the information which he expected to receive from Crab and was obliged to learn the secret of refining by his own experiments." These "experiments" by Obadiah are, perhaps, an early indication of the Brown family's bent for manufacture.

Once the necessary information regarding the business was in the country, it was disseminated so quickly that by 1763 there were probably as many as a dozen spermaceti candle manufactories in the British colonies. But in none of the colonies were the merchants so much attracted to the business as in Rhode Island, where the growing community of Jewish merchants at Newport took readily to it. Indeed, Rhode Island became as conspicuously associated with the candle manufacture as with the slave trade and the traffic with the enemy.

Obadiah Brown's candle factory was under construction in the winter and spring of 1753. The following year he was marketing candles in Boston. His "Spermaceti Works" at Tockwotton in Providence were a flourishing concern in the late 1750's. By 1763 Nicholas Brown and Company were recognized, even by their competitors, as the leading manufacturers of spermaceti candles in the colonies. Prior to 1767, when the Company seems first to have turned the attention seriously to whaling, the head matter, the raw material from which the candles were made, came almost wholly from outside sources. And even after that date the Browns' own whaling vessels provided only a minor part of the head matter consumed annually at the spermaceti works. In 1769 their ships brought in 33 tons of head matter out of a total of 125 tons received by the Company.[12] The Starbucks, Rotches, Husseys, Folgers, and other whaling families of Nantucket provided the bulk of the head matter needed, but commission merchants, such as Henry Lloyd of Boston, made extensive purchases on account of the four Brown brothers.

The candles found their way to market through a variety of channels. Spermaceti candles were a part of the cargo of virtually every ship the Browns sent to the Caribbean area during the score of years preceding the outbreak of the War for Independence. Their established correspondents or agents in New York and Philadelphia received consignments of candles regularly which they sold on commission to merchants in their respective cities. In Boston, Henry Lloyd not only purchased head matter for the spermaceti works, but he also disposed of very large quantities of candles for the Browns on commission. In Newport, itself a leading center of the candle manufacture, Benjamin Mason, long a close friend of the Browns, sold their candles on commission and purchased extensively from them on his own account. Their friends, the Wantons of Newport, regularly bartered rum, molasses, sugar, coffee, etc., for large consignments of candles. Francis Malbone, Samuel Goldthwaite, John Mawdsley, and Charles Wickham were other Newport merchants who consistently received shipments of candles from the Providence works. In Providence itself, the firm of Joseph and William Russell; Nicholas Cooke; and Jabez Bowen were leading customers. In Bristol, Rhode Island, Simeon Potter, the well-known Guinea trader, and Mark Antony De Wolf were frequent purchasers of substantial quantities. The Newport and Bristol merchants, in turn, shipped Brown candles to New York and Philadelphia, and sent them aboard their own ships to the West Indies.

Candles made in the works at Providence were wrapped in blue paper, which in the early 1760's was obtained in large quantities from Philadelphia. The candles averaged about three to the pound and were usually shipped in boxes whose gross weight was from twenty-eight to thirty-five pounds. On occasion, however, the Browns packed their candles in much larger boxes; and upon special request they could turn out a candle of superior craftsmanship. In 1759 they shipped to Tench Francis in Philadelphia a box of candles "made in the best manner for a gentleman in London." They wrote that "we recommend [them] to be equal to any made in Europe or America, the difference between these and the common sort is in their being harder & consequently freer from oil, whiter, clearer and neater cast."

Product differentiation made its appearance in the candle manufacture fairly early. Obadiah Brown and Company had a label which they affixed to every box of candles which they placed on the market. After Obadiah's death in 1762 the four brothers in the new association of Nicholas Brown and Company neglected to have a new label made and so marketed their candles without any distinguishing mark upon the boxes. Within a few years, however, their friend Henry Lloyd in Boston ventured the opinion that their candles would command a higher price were they to employ a label as had their uncle.[13] They thereupon resurrected the old copperplate, sent it to Henry Lloyd, and requested him to have the word "Obadiah" changed to "Nicholas." Although this required the insertion of an additional letter, Nathaniel Hurd, the Boston engraver who had executed the original copperplate, made the change with such skill that, even with the aid of a reading glass, no traces of the change can be detected.[14] Sold under this label, the Browns' candles were known by name in every market in the continental colonies, as well as in the West Indies, British and foreign. Brown ship captains, writing from Surinam or the Islands in the Caribbean, frequently mentioned the arrival of Brown candles by way of Philadelphia, New York, Boston, or Newport.

In general the label was a guarantee of high quality, although there were occasional criticisms. Gurdon Saltonstall, of New London, who had shipped 146 boxes to Anderson and Company at Gibraltar, complained of short weight. Anderson had protested to Saltonstall that the weight of the candles did not correspond with the invoice because the "tare of the boxes run short."[15] Saltonstall in turn held Nicholas Brown and Company responsible for the faulty "tare." In 1765 John Relfe wrote from Philadelphia that he had some "complaints that your last candles are not so good as formerly."[16] In 1774 Henry Lloyd wrote that he was "sorry to say the quality of your candles is not liked so well as heretofore. It is very material to keep up their reputation, especially now there are so many manufacturers, as the purchasers will certainly give the preference to those in the highest credit."[17] Later Lloyd wrote in explanation that "the occasion of my mentioning the quality of your candles (though I have some time past observed them inferior to what you used to send) was my selling a quantity to a person for present pay that engaged me at first to let him have them all of your manufacture." But, Lloyd added, when this person "came to view them and found them inferior to what they used to be . . . I lost the sale of 96 boxes of yours."[18] From what he could learn, Lloyd expressed the belief that candles made by Nicholas Brown and Company were "as good as most that are made now, though what I have had of Mr. Rome this spring is as good as any that was formerly made.[19] From this letter by Henry Lloyd the conclusion might well be drawn that on the eve of Independence the quality of spermaceti candles generally had deteriorated. And it may well have been that the increasing number of spermaceti works (a development which the manufacturers viewed with alarm) so disturbed the equilibrium within the industry that the various houses attempted to reduce costs at the sacrifice of quality.

The Brown candle works at Tockwotton appear to have been managed by Joseph Brown, even during the lifetime of his Uncle Obadiah. This was a wise recognition of the fact that to Joseph's mechanical turn of mind the spermaceti works had a far greater appeal than did ordinary mercantile pursuits. A memorandum under date of November 18, 1762, a few months after Obadiah's death, reads: "This day it is agreed between Nicholas, Joseph, John & Moses Brown owners of the spermaceti works that Joseph live at the spermaceti works and manage them as usual, board the workmen and find the labour, etc. necessary for that purpose," for which he was to receive "£9.6.8 per week for board of men, washing, lodging, mending, etc. as also £1400 Old Tenor yearly and find him his wood, house rent, garden spot, the house stuf, etc. now there belonging to the Company."[20] The agreement was effective from the 18th of the previous October, "the money to be reckoned dollars at £7."

One by-product of the candle manufacture, namely, the oil from which the spermaceti was strained, was of financial importance both to the manufacturers themselves and to their section of the country. Explaining the processes involved in the handling of the oil, the Browns wrote to Tench Francis in Philadelphia that the "Manner we keep our Oil is this, When it Comes to us we Carefully Trim it, for which purpose we Keep a Cooper whose Constant Business is when aney Leaks to over hall it and Trim it a new."[21] They stored the oil in "Valts" which were "no More than common Cellers only Something Deeper, where in we Keep it Stored [in casks] One Two Three or four Heights as our Stock happens to be." In conclusion, they said that "in the Oil Works in England, we are Informed the Bottoms of their Valts are Lead or Copper. We think it Two Expensive here."

The strained spermaceti oil obtained in this manner was always a valuable stock in trade. Although the bulk of this oil was undoubtedly shipped to London, much of it was consumed in the colonies. Some of it served to light the street lamps of colonial towns. In 1759 Tench Francis at Philadelphia wrote to Obadiah Brown and Company: "Since Mr. Brown's departure we have agreed with wardens of our city to supply them with sixty barrels of oil at 70/. so that you will please to send them by the first convenient opportunity."[22] But oil shipped by the Browns to Tench Francis did more than light the streets of the "City of Brotherly Love." It also lighted the lamps of the thrifty German housewives living on the farms of eastern Pennsylvania.[23] Prior to 1763 the Brown family sent most of their oil to Tench Francis, who shipped to London the large amounts he was unable to sell locally. From 1763 to about 1768 Henry Lloyd and other Boston dealers, including John Hancock, purchased oil extensively from Nicholas Brown and Company, as did also the Rotches of Nantucket, who once spoiled Hancock's scheme for a corner on oil shipments to the mother country. Although the Browns occasionally shipped oil to London on their own account in the earlier years, it was not until the half dozen years before the Revolution that such consignments became a regular feature of their business. In that period oil constituted their most important single form of remittance to England in payment for manufactured goods received from their British correspondents.

In its early stages, the spermaceti candle manufacture in the colonies must have shown unusual promise of large profits. The business spread rapidly, especially in Rhode Island and in the Boston area. As the number of spermaceti works increased, the demand upon the limited supply of head matter produced by the whale fishery increased accordingly. While the amount of this raw material available for the candle manufacture varied from year to year with the fortunes of the Nantucket men, the total potential fund of it was apparently incapable of marked permanent expansion. The catch of a given year might be greater or less than that of the previous year, but over a period of years the increase in the amount of head matter failed to keep pace with the increasing capacity of the spermaceti works established in the colonies. By 1760 it was accepted as a truism that three or four plants could transform into candles all the spermaceti obtained by colonial whalemen. As the number of manufactories increased, their competitive buying of head matter tended, of necessity, to force up the price. The result was that the whalers and the commission men who bought from them occupied a very strategic position. Theirs was a seller's market, which inevitably placed the makers of candles on the defensive. Should the competitive buying of head matter continue without interruption, the day seemed not far distant when the price would become so prohibitive that the manufacturers would be forced to close their plants.

Theoretically, the candle manufacturers could have dealt with this problem in either of two ways: by increasing the price of candles in conformity with that of head matter; or by agreeing among themselves to establish a ceiling price on head matter. The first of these alternatives was not feasible because spermaceti candles were in competition with tallow candles and also with the wax variety. Furthermore, the oil, which was a by-product of the candle manufacture, was itself used as an illuminant in competition with candles of various kinds; and when whale oil was scarce and high in price it had to compete with seal oil. Any progressive advance in the price of spermaceti candles must inevitably result in the loss of business to the competing illuminants. The other alternative—a ceiling price on head matter—was practicable only within limits. The manufacturers dared not control the price too rigidly, lest they thereby give offense to the Nantucket whalers and drive them into the candle manufacture. They lived in constant fear of such an eventuality, and on the eve of the Revolution their fears were realized when one of the leading whaling families turned to the manufacture.

Over the years, therefore, the aim of the candle manufacturers was not to prevent all appreciation in the price of head matter, but to avert an unduly rapid advance. They tried to realize this objective in two ways: by means of periodic agreements fixing a ceiling price; and by allocation of the limited fund of head matter among the manufacturers in stated proportions. The first effort in this direction came in the autumn of 1760 when the manufacturers were laying their plans for the purchase of their fall supply of head matter. On September 23d John Brown, then at Newport, wrote Nicholas that "it was with a good deal of difficulty" he had "procured a letter from Mr. Collins to limit the price of Head to Mr. Rotch, but at last have got his letter signed by him Mr. Lopez and us."[24] John added that "Mr. Hart agreed it to be a good method the first time I mentioned it to him, but never could git him to write till this evening." The Browns, in conjunction with three of the Newport manufacturers, were in effect serving notice on Joseph Rotch of Nantucket, a leading whaler and also an important commission dealer in head matter and whale oil, that they would not purchase head matter priced above a figure named by them. Unfortunately, the letter does not mention the price at which they "limited" Rotch or the manner in which they had determined it.

Assuming that the establishment of a ceiling price for head matter was the proper solution of the problem confronting the manufacturers, the agreement of the four concerns mentioned above was only a first step toward the consummation of such a plan. The success of a plan of price limitation required a more general acceptance of the idea than had yet been achieved. Concerted action by the four manufacturers could avail little so long as others were free to bid up the price and thereby largely monopolize the supply. In the course of the following year this fact seems to have become generally understood among the candle-making fraternity. On October 8, 1761 Obadiah Brown and Company wrote to John Brown, again at Newport, that they had just conferred with William Belcher and Joseph Palmer, representing Richard Cranch and Company of Boston, "on uniting our endeavors to reduce the price of head matter and the plan presented by these gentlemen we think contains all the necessary articles to obtain it."[25] Evidently Belcher and Palmer, upon the conclusion of their visit to the Browns in Providence, called on the candle manufacturers of Newport, as Obadiah recommended John Brown's "assistance to the gentlemen in inducing Messrs Collins, Hart & the rest of the gentlemen manufacturers to join in a plan so much for our mutual interest."

At Newport the efforts of the gentlemen from Boston, in combination with those of John Brown, brought quick results. On November 5, 1761 Richard Cranch and Company and Edward Langdon and Son, both of Boston, Collins and Rivera, Isaac Stille and Company, Naphtali Hart and Company, and Aaron Lopez, all of Newport, and Obadiah Brown and Company combined to form the "United Company of Spermaceti Chandlers." This was the beginning of the association of candle manufacturers which has often been referred to as the "Spermaceti Trust."[26] Within little more than a year, therefore, after the four had named the maximum price to Joseph Rotch, this larger group had entered into a more comprehensive agreement governing the price of head matter from whatever source derived. Credit for the precise terms of this improvement upon the covenant which John Brown had negotiated with the Newport chandlers belongs to Richard Cranch and Company, which was soon to become the firm of Joseph Palmer and Company.

This agreement among the candle manufacturers is a prime example of colonial interdependence in the economic sphere. But it is merely one of many such instances in the annals of the Browns. From generation to generation, no feature of their business was more conspicuous or more constant than their reliance upon merchants in the other continental colonies for markets, raw materials, technical data, information as to the state of trade, the settling of balances, and for the procuring of much-needed supplies of specie.

The articles of agreement drawn up at the meeting of November 5th stipulated that the union was to continue for a period of seventeen months from that date. The parties to it promised to instruct their buyers of head matter not to pay more than £6 Sterling per ton above the price of "common merchantable spermaceti body brown oil." The price of this oil was to be that currently given by the merchants of Boston for the London market. It was one thing to agree to place a ceiling on the price of head matter, but to provide a rational formula by which to determine the price was something else. The aim of this formula was to keep the price of spermaceti in line with another product of the whale fishery; to prevent too great a price divergence between head matter and common whale oil. And it was hoped that indirectly the formula would maintain something of a price balance between head matter and strained spermaceti oil.

The signers of the covenant promised not to pay any buyer of head matter a commission in excess of 2½ per cent. Within the limits of New England the signatories were not to sell candles for less than one shilling, ten and one-half pence per pound, with one shilling for each box containing about twenty-five pounds of candles. No one would manufacture candles for anyone not a member of the United Company. The parties to the agreement pledged themselves to employ all "fair and honorable means" to prevent the "setting up" of new spermaceti works. They further agreed that, should the price of head matter exceed their limits in spite of their union, they would "fit out at least 12 vessels upon our joint concern" to be employed in the whale fishery, each manufacturer to "furnish and receive an equal proportion in and from said vessels." The danger to the "catchers" and sellers of head matter implied in this threat was probably more apparent than real. It is doubtful that twelve additional vessels in the whale fishery could have exercised much control over the price of head matter.

The articles of agreement stipulated that there were to be two meetings each year "at the best tavern in Taunton," Massachusetts, with at least one representative from each house. But should the occasion demand it, Obadiah Brown and Company, together with any two of the houses, were empowered to call a special meeting at Taunton. This last provision may have been a recognition of the central location which the Browns enjoyed with respect to the Boston and Newport members of the association. Or, it may have been the result of the dominant position which they had acquired as the leading producers of candles within the colonies. But whatever the reason, it placed the Providence firm in a position of initiative and responsibility in the Union which they retained to the end. The Browns served as a clearinghouse for all correspondence and official transactions of the United Company; and this undoubtedly explains the completeness of the documentary record of the Association preserved in their papers.

In the articles of union no attempt was made to assign quotas of head matter to the members of the association. This made it theoretically possible for one or more members to obtain an undue portion of the total supply without exceeding the limited price, since there was no provision in the agreement to prevent the exercise of improper influence by members upon the buyers of head matter in Nantucket and elsewhere. True the amount of the commission was stipulated but other considerations might prompt a buyer to favor a particular manufacturer with more than his fair share of the supply. This weakness was subsequently corrected. Finally, it will be observed that the articles were less far reaching with respect to the price of the finished product of the candle manufacture than that of the raw material used in the process. Only in New England was the price of candles fixed. A wide field remained open to price cutting.

The houses which entered into the United Company of Spermaceti Chandlers did so with the hope that the solution of their difficulties had been found. Each firm was no doubt profoundly conscious of the rectitude of its own intentions, regardless of reservations it might have with respect to the good faith of fellow members. Unfortunately, the parties to the covenant soon discovered that it was easier to effect an agreement among themselves than it was to secure strict observance of its various provisions. Long before the expiration of the term for which the Association was to continue, the different companies were charging one another with a breach of the articles. In late July 1762, Collins and Rivera, Naphtali Hart and Company, and Aaron Lopez, leading Newport manufacturers, addressed a letter to Richard Cranch and Company setting forth alleged violations which, if true, were tantamount to a destruction of the union.[27] They had "certain information" that most of the buyers at Nantucket had purchased head matter at a price substantially above that stipulated in the articles of association. Although they were not sure for whom it had been purchased, they assumed it was for members of the union. They further charged that Robinson and Company and Stille and Company, two Newport houses, had received head matter whose price had not been ascertained.

After suggesting various other alleged violations of the articles, the writers continued: "Besides the above hints you'l please to excuse our once more observing that Messrs Brown, being allowed the liberty to give to the sellers 2½ more than the restricted price, has given them the opportunity of exceeding every manufacture, who acts upon principle, from the benefit of purchasing a single cask." In their opinion, this was "diametrically repugnant both to the letter & spirit of the articles which were intended for mutual benefit; and not to give one manufacturer the advantage of the rest." Although they felt that "these circumstances" had vacated "our articles" to all intents and purposes, they nevertheless promised that "if such judicious measures can be concerted, as will put this affair upon such a basis as to admit of no violation, they shall have our ready concurrence."

At this distance the allusion to the Browns is not easily understood or explained. Certainly the articles of agreement had not given them the "liberty" to exceed the stated price of head matter. The mystery is deepened by the fact that in the correspondence which passed between Richard Cranch and the Browns regarding the Newport letter this accusation against the Browns is not mentioned, although other charges made in the letter are.[28] While Cranch and Company expressed the belief that the other "indiscretions" were serious violations of the agreement, they were prepared to join the Browns in a move "either to confirm the old articles with such additions and alterations as shall be agreed upon . . . or making new ones." Should Nicholas Brown and Company arrange a meeting for this purpose Cranch would send a representative. Although all the manufacturers must have shared with the Browns and Cranch the belief that "the destruction of the articles will be the destruction of the manufacture," the suspicion and ill will prevailing thwarted all efforts to convene them in a meeting. In writing the obituary of the United Company, Cranch and Company remarked "that they will, when too late, see the evil of their precipitancy in departing from the articles."

A few months sufficed to demonstrate the truth of Cranch's prediction. On February 21, 1763 Nicholas Brown and Company wrote to Joseph Palmer and Company (successor to Cranch), proposing a general meeting of the manufacturers at the earliest possible time, and asking them to choose the time and place.[29] The Providence firm assured the Palmers that their choice would be readily approved by the Newport manufacturers as well as themselves. In reply Palmer and Company asked to be excused "as the roads are at this season very bad, our business urgent and as we think can do better (everything considered) without us."[30] However, lest they should be thought averse to a union, they forwarded a "rough draught for a general plan." Although Palmer and Company's "draught" contained several new features as compared with the articles drawn up in 1761, the Boston house can scarcely claim originality in this respect. As sad experience with the earlier agreement had revealed its weakness to all the members, there was general accord in regard to the new provisions necessary to make the association more workable. When the meeting was finally held in Providence on April 13, 1763, Joseph Palmer was present in person even "tho clouds and darkness" seemed to "invelop the whole plan."

The agreement of 1763 was to continue for one year, during which the subscribers promised not to pay for head matter more than £10 Sterling per ton above the current price of "common merchantable Spermaceti Body Brown Oil."[31] Unlike the covenant of 1761, this one named the persons from whom the manufacturers were to procure head matter. They were Joseph and William Rotch, Silvanus Hussey and Company, Folger and Gardner, Robert and Josias Barker, Obed Hussey, Richard Mitchell and Jonathan Burnell, all of Nantucket; Henry Lloyd of Boston, George Jackson of Providence, and Benjamin Mason of Newport. Most, if not all, of the Nantucket men were engaged in the whale fishery. Henry Lloyd was a commission merchant, while Jackson and Mason were in the unspecialized mercantile business. The parties to the agreement promised not to "give or allow" these men more than 2½ per cent "considered as commissions or otherwise, for their trouble."

The most important innovation in the agreement was the allocation of definite quotas of head matter to the various members of the union, which included six Newport manufacturers, two from Boston, one from Providence, and "the Philadelphians." All head matter caught in North America was to be considered as one "common Stock or Dividend," to be divided into one hundred parts and allotted to the members in stated proportions. In recognition of the fact that theirs was the largest plant, Nicholas Brown and Company received twenty barrels out of every one hundred. Next came Joseph Palmer and Company with fourteen barrels. Thomas Robinson and Company received thirteen barrels, while Aaron Lopez and Collins and Rivera each obtained eleven barrels. "The Philadelphians" were assigned seven barrels, and Isaac Stille and Naphtali Hart were allotted nine parts each. Bringing up the rear were Edward Langdon and Son of Boston with four parts and Moses Lopez of Newport with two.

The factors at Nantucket were to be directed to retain in their own hands about four hundred barrels of the "Fall Headmatter" undivided "until they know from each of our Houses, how much each House has had, in order to make a final division agreeable to the above proportions." The factors were to be further directed to transmit to the various houses frequent accounts of head matter sent to each member, to report any breach "of these articles," and to "give the most early notice" of any attempts to establish new spermaceti works.

With the exception of Edward Langdon and Son and "the Philadelphians," all those to whom proportions were allotted signed the articles of 1763. But as the quotas assigned to these firms were ample, they could have no incentive to exceed the stated price of head matter. However, violation of the covenant came quickly from other sources. When the compact was scarcely two months old, Joseph Palmer and Company reported that "by certain advice from Nantucket" one of the factors there had purchased head matter at a figure in excess of the stipulated price.[32] They observed that the factor had acted either upon specific instructions from some of the members of the association or upon the knowledge that he could sell the head matter to one of them. The Boston firm suggested, therefore, that appropriate action be taken with respect to the offending factor. Their proposal was that the other factors be authorized to contravene the letter of the law in order to maintain the spirit of the agreement; that they be instructed to bid up the price for a time and "give Such purchaser a Surfeit," after which they could lower it "so as to Serve our general Interest." Palmer's proposition seems not to have commended itself to the association generally. The guilty factor was not punished, and the manufacturer for whom he had purchased was not identified. But the incident is significant as an example of the atmosphere of suspicion and petty bickering which surrounded this and every other covenant signed by the candle makers.

But for the next dozen years, in good times and bad, the manufacturers never faltered in their conviction that, in view of the limited quantity of head matter available, they must fix its price. They felt that to do this a union was imperative; and that union, to be effective, must include all the spermaceti works within the colonies.

Unlike the articles of 1761, those of 1763 contained no provision with respect to the price of candles. But on July 6, 1763 Nicholas Brown and Company and the six Newport houses signed a supplementary agreement by which they promised upon "our word and honors" that they would not directly or indirectly sell candles in "Rhode Island, Providence and Boston" for less than two shillings and threepence lawful silver money per pound.[33] In New York the minimum price was to be three shillings currency, while in Philadelphia it was two shillings and tenpence Pennsylvania currency. Allowing for the differences in value of the currencies in terms of the Spanish milled dollar, the prices in the three areas were as nearly identical as it was possible to make them without reckoning in fractions of a penny. The manufacturers were prepared to absorb the cost of transporting the candles to New York and Philadelphia. The merchants in those cities could scarcely fail to see the essential fairness of such an arrangement.

In reply to an invitation to join in the agreement fixing the price of candles, Joseph Palmer and Company wrote: "We are very sorry to find that you think it necessary to lower the price of candles; for you can't but know that candles cannot be offered under 2/6 at the present price of Head Matter."[34] They added that if they could as readily reduce the price of head matter "by an agreement among ourselves as we can the price of candles, we would very readily join you, but we must beg to be excused joining in your present proposal, at least until you have very seriously reconsidered this affair, which we do most earnestly recommend you." Palmer and Company had no doubt of selling all their candles "at 2/6 unless you spoil our market by underselling us." They would very readily join in fixing the price at that figure. It was their conviction that "if we should reduce 'em to 2/3 the exporters will again try as hard to reduce 'em to 2/; and we really think that tis as easy now to keep 'em at 2/6 as it will be to keep 'em at 2/3."

Nicholas Brown and Company's reply to Palmer's comments pointed out that the opening of the French Islands to candles during the Seven Years' War had led to a marked increase in demand for them; but, they observed, the market must necessarily shrink when France excluded them from her colonies in time of peace.[35] Unless new markets could be found, therefore, it would be impossible to sell all the candles even at the new price of two shillings and threepence. Evidently this view of the Browns was shared by the Newport manufacturers who had joined with them in fixing a new minimum price.

This agreement which attempted to set the price of candles was even more productive of suspicion than were the Articles of Union. The charges and countercharges centered largely about the sale of candles in Philadelphia, where each of the houses had a correspondent who sold on commission. The agreement had not been long in operation when rumors of price cutting began to fly. Typical of these is a passage from a letter of Thomas Robinson and Company to the Browns: "I this day saw a letter of yours to my neighbor Rivera in which you complain of Thomas Richardson's selling candles at Philadelphia under the stated price. You may depend on the intelligence to be wrong."[36] Robinson had written Richardson immediately "after we concluded on the price of candles what we had done & ordered his strict compliance therewith, which he has advised me from time to time he has done." In conclusion Robinson said "he had a letter from him by last post when he had not sold a box under since we stated the price, which I showed to Rivera who is satisfied." The Browns had complained to Rivera that Thomas Richardson, Robinson's Philadelphia correspondent, was selling candles below the stated price. Rivera had reported the charge to Robinson who, of course, had absolved his correspondent of all guilt.

A few days later Rivera received a letter from Anthony Stocker, his Philadelphia correspondent, stating that the agent of one of the Newport houses, whose "brand mark" contained the initials "I.S.," was selling candles below the stipulated price. This, Stocker said, made it impossible for him to sell Rivera's candles at the figure named in the agreement. Evidently on this occasion it was Isaac Stille and Company who were violating the compact. Two months later Stocker advised Rivera that "nobody [in Philadelphia] asks above 2/8," whereas the agreed price was 2/10.[37]

Others were soon to have the accusing finger pointed at them. On November 15, 1763 Tench Francis, the Browns' correspondent at Philadelphia, wrote that candles were "quite a drug, so many people having them to sell." He then proceeded to explain in detail the manner in which "we are undersold." Candles were brought to Philadelphia, where they were bartered for "our commodities and to save appearances they fix them at 2/10, the price agreed upon by your manufacturers, but then they take goods at an advance price and when people have got the candles they sell them for the most they can, being under no restrictions." Tench Francis knew this to be a fact "and particularly was the case with that very gentleman you mention, Mr. Rivera, who bartered a large parcel with Messrs Willing and Morris."[38]

The Browns passed this on to Thomas Robinson and Company who promptly showed it to Jacob R. Rivera. An indignant denial was forthcoming.[39] He asserted that he had never "had any trade or connection with Messrs Willing & Morris," nor had he bartered candles in Philadelphia for any other commodity; in proof of which he pointed to the fact that Stocker, his agent in Philadelphia, complained of being undersold by others. Rivera said he would not "take these pains . . . to remove the falacy of your complaint was I not so tender of my integrity, which I have the vanity to say . . . have always maintained, though many times to my prejudice." Thus far Rivera had been on the defensive; but he quickly resorted to countercharge. "What difference," he asked, "is there between bartering candles at Phila. for commodities at an advance price, or doing it here; pray don't we all do it." Or "what privilege has one manufacturer above another" that those persons who, at the "first groundless representations, exclaim against me, should be at liberty to offer candles at 50/ here to discharge a draught from Phila., or something of the kind, without having any regard to our agreement . . . and there should no notice be taken of it." This charge, Rivera alleged, could be more easily proved than "Mr. Francis's representation" against him. At this point in the letter Rivera assumed the role of martyr by asking "why should Mr. Slocum be allowed the advantage of Breaking through all our agreements, both here, there and everywhere, and no notice taken but of me, which looks as if I was the person that must only keep up the articles when the rest are left to do as they please." Rivera ended his letter with the remark that "if this be the case I should not care how soon our agreement of the price of candles was put to an end, for I am confident no person concerned suffers more than we do, for adhering closer to the tenor of the agrement than any of the rest."

In effect, Rivera had in general terms accused all the subscribers to the agreement of underselling; and he had specifically charged two houses with violation of the compact. His reference to "Mr. Slocum" was an indictment of Isaac Stille and Company with which Slocum was connected. The allusion to the offering of "candles at 50/ . . . to discharge a draught from Phila." was aimed at Nicholas Brown and Company. This charge had been passed on to Rivera by Thomas Robinson and Company of Newport, who in turn had been told by Godfrey Malbone (not one of the manufacturers) that to his "certain knowledge" the Browns had resorted to this form of price-cutting. Here is another illustration of the extent to which rumor and gossip were bandied about by the candle makers. When Nicholas Brown and Company advised Tench Francis of Rivera's denial of the alleged barter arrangement with Willing and Morris in Philadelphia, Francis insisted that "Mr. Rivera may show & tell you what he pleases, but I aver he did barter with Messrs Willing & Morris a large parcel of candles for Bohea Tea; some of these very candles they now have on hand."[40]

It appears, therefore, that the Philadelphia correspondent of each manufacturer was convinced that the agents of all the other candle makers were underselling him. Much of this feeling was justified. The temptation to cut prices often proved too strong to resist. On the other hand, it was very easy to persuade an agent to blame his slow sales on the dishonesty of his competitors rather than on the glut in the market. The manufacturers were quick to listen to the charges. But the persistent stories of price-cutting, real and fictional, created such a heavy load of suspicion and distrust that the agreement collapsed under its own weight. The candle makers did not try again to fix the price of their product.

The unpleasant business relations were only the surface indications of the underlying cause of the abandonment of the agreement. It had been drawn up at a most inauspicious time. During the depression following the Seven Years' War every businessman was searching frantically for markets. Solemn covenants could easily be forgotten in the scramble for new customers. Human nature being what it is, inflexible price agreements in periods of price readjustment have usually failed to accomplish their purpose. The attempt to fix the prices of spermaceti candles was no exception.

Over the years, however, the price of candles was not the major worry of the manufacturers. The scarcity and resulting high price of head matter was always a more pressing problem. There were too many houses engaged in the business of buying this vital ingredient. Common sense required, therefore, that the established manufacturers should seek to discourage new comers. Realistically, the Articles of 1761 pledged the members of the Association to the use of all fair and honorable means to prevent the setting up of new works; and the covenant of 1763 required that the factors should give their principals the "most early notice of any attempt to set up other spermaceti works."

One way by which the manufacturers tried to prevent the establishment of new plants was through the careful guarding of the mechanical equipment required in spermaceti works. The two prime pieces of machinery were a press and a screw. Although these appear not to have been particularly intricate, it was not everyone who could reproduce them. Indeed there were only a few men in the colonies who possessed the mechanical skill necessary to construct an approved spermaceti works. The course of the manufacturers, therefore, was clearly indicated. Just as Britain forbade the exportation of textile machinery, and those who had a knowledge thereof, so the candle makers sought jealously to hoard the machinery and mechanical know-how required in their business.

This policy on the part of the manufacturers first became evident in 1761 when Moses Brown wrote from Newport to his uncle and brothers:[41] "Mr. Hart tells me Mr. Robinson applied to him in an earnest but friendly manner for the favor of the method of refining which was refused. Mr. Robinson has since been seen trying ye experiment at his own house. He complains of our Mr. O. Brown injoining Mr. Wilkinson to secrecy and forbearance." After expressing his surprise that Mr. Robinson should have this last bit of information, Moses mentioned "one Wm Finch of this town who has made Mr. Robinson's press and I am told is going to undertake making ye screw. This man, Mr. Collins tells me is well acquainted in all parts of ye work. Mr. Levay is to try if he can to prevent his undertaking." Moses then penned a postscript saying that he advised "a little caution in Bro Jos that he is not too free with strangers lest this Mr. Finch should go to Providence for information." Evidently Moses feared Joseph, as manager of the spermaceti works, might allow his mechanical interest to triumph over his business acumen, and thus unwittingly betray the secret of the process. But Moses might well have spared himself his pains; for, whether from "Mr. Finch" or elsewhere, Thomas Robinson and Company obtained the mechanical secret. In November 1761 that firm appeared as one of the subscribers to the Articles of Agreement of the candle makers.

Although they had failed in this effort to prevent the building of one competing plant, the Browns were more successful in their next attempt. Among the select company who had mastered the mechanical aspects of the spermaceti business was Israel Wilkinson, who, as Thomas Robinson, alleged, had been "injoined" to "secrecy and forebearance" by Obadiah Brown. Members of Israel's family were well known for their mechanical bent. He himself had had a hand in the setting up of a number of plants in New England, and his reputation had spread at least as far as Philadelphia. In 1763 two Philadelphia Quakers, Benjamin and John Mifflin, decided to enter the candle manufacture, probably at the urging of an enterprising promoter. On September 14, 1763 they wrote Israel Wilkinson that they had "entered" into contract with Samuel Delucena to carry on the spermaceti business and "being desirous to have our works done in the most complete manner, we are recommended to thee by Lucena as a person well qualified for that purpose."[42] To induce Wilkinson to come, the Mifflins were prepared to pay "thy reasonable expenses from thy house to Philadelphia, one dollar per day from the time thou leaves and for and during the time thou act in our employ here together with thy accommodation for that time. As the season is so far advanced there is no time for delay. We therefore beg thy speedy answer that we may know what to depend on." In a postscript they requested that "if thou dont conclude to come we beg this favour of thee which we hope thou will not refuse us to send what light and instructions thou can in the affair which will oblige thy friend."

The first reaction at finding a copy of this letter of the Mifflins to Wilkinson, in the handwriting of Moses Brown, in the papers of Nicholas Brown and Company is one of surprise. Its presence there, however, is not the result of mere chance. Israel Wilkinson was well known to the Browns and his talents were much respected by them. Furthermore, they had prepared themselves against the possibility of losing him to a competitor. Their forehandedness is aptly described in their letter to J. R. Rivera and Company of October 9, 1763.[43] On that day, they related, they had been shown a letter from the Mifflins of Philadelphia "to a certain ingenious mechanic this way" regarding the building of a spermaceti works for them. "This person," they said, "sould doubtless comply with the offer from Phila . . . were he not under a tye for the sum (500£) t'was thought best he should have which we accordingly gave him, for which he barred himself from erecting or repairing, etc. any spermaceti works without our consent." Wilkinson had repeatedly offered to return the money with interest "that he may be free but we think it our duty to inform you of this affair as also to prevent any new works being set up if it can be done at not too great an expense to our particular house, as well as the loss of freedom to our friend." The Browns were willing to bear one-fifth "of the sum gave" and they thought "the remainder ought to be borne by the other manufacturers." Speculating upon the probable results of Wilkinson's compliance with the Mifflins' request, they said that "we . . . most naturally think the business wont be worth carrying on in this colony as we are pretty sure that when this person gets to Phila he will not come away without erecting more than one complete set of works, and also stop at New York where we are assured they want nothing but just such a person to direct them." The Browns requested a reply from Rivera "as soon as may be, as this person proposes to answer the Philadelphians by the return of the post but we must get him to omit it for one week longer."[44]

Clearly the method employed by the Brown family to restrict the exercise of the "ingenious mechanic's" skill had been ingenious in itself. Although they had apparently tied his hands completely, the letter seems to suggest some hesitancy on their part about the method of using the hold which they had on him. Evidently his loss of freedom was annoying to Wilkinson and somewhat disturbing to the consciences of his principals. But whatever qualms the Browns may have had regarding their bargain with Wilkinson must have been somewhat eased by certain revelations concerning him contained in Rivera's reply to their letter.[45]

To the suggestion of the Providence house that the other manufacturers share with them the burden of the £500 retainer fee given to Wilkinson, Rivera wrote: "As to what relates to the offer made to your ingenious mechanic & the type he lays under for the consideration he received, we say that Mr. Robinson is of opinion that as this was done prior to his having any connection with this business, that they think themselves not bound to any proposition."[46] Rivera assured them that "as for our parts and I dare say the same for Mr. Aaron Lopez, we are ready to bear at all times our proportion of anything that may be thought necessary for the preservation of this manufactury . . ." Although the Browns had not mentioned the name of Wilkinson in their letter, his fame as a mechanic was such that Rivera and Company knew him to be the one in question. In reference to him they remarked that "we cant help saying that by tying the old gentleman and living [leaving] his son (who works with his Father's ingenuity) at Liberty is really doing of nothing."[47] Rivera and Company then related that when Robinson and Company in Newport were "about setting up their works they applied to the old gentleman who readily told them he could not on any account assist them, but hinted that he was under no obligation not to teach his son anything he knew and the consequence was that his son undertook and the Father directed." Rivera thought the "Philadelphia gentlemen" might thus indirectly avail themselves of Israel's mechanical skill, in which case "our securing the old and living the young to do the mischief can be of little service." Rivera's statement that the "Son undertook and the Father directed" the building of Robinson's works makes one wonder whether the "Mr. Finch" whom Moses Brown had previously mentioned in connection with the building of the Robinson manufactory was really Wilkinson's son. In any event, the facts brought out in Rivera's letter make the restriction imposed upon Israel's freedom by his acceptance of the fee from the Browns appear somewhat less unpleasant. He himself had, on occasion, found a devious way of circumventing that restraint.

Rivera's letter was written on October 12, 1763. Meanwhile, Nicholas Brown and Company had written Joseph Palmer and Company on the 10th, advising them of the proposition made by the Mifflins to the "ingenious mechanic" and expressing their expectation of "prevailing on ye person to do nuthin."[48] Israel Wilkinson's reply to the Mifflins was dated October 18, 1763.[49] It would be interesting to know just what had occurred between Israel and the Browns during the week preceding the writing of that letter. But the fact that a copy of the letter exists in the papers of Nicholas Brown and Company, in the handwriting of Moses Brown, indicates pretty conclusively that the Company dictated it. Perhaps Moses even penned the original for Wilkinson. The letter makes it clear that the Browns had prevailed upon him "to do nuthin," but it fails to indicate the precise means which they had employed. Moral suasion may have sufficed to discourage him, or it may have been necessary to invoke the veto provided by the £500 "tye" on Wilkinson.

Regardless of the manner by which he was dissuaded from going to Philadelphia, Wilkinson's letter contained a very plausible explanation of his inability to accept the Mifflins' offer. He wrote that he would be glad to embrace the opportunity could he "attend the business" to their mutual advantage; but, unfortunately, he was engaged in a "furnace that is now going and in which my concern and engagement are such that I cannot attend on any account."[50] Having given his reasons for not appearing in person, he then addressed his attention to their plea that he "send them what light and instructions" he could. The Browns were careful to see to it that this part of his letter painted such a black picture of the candle manufacture generally that the Mifflins would give up their plans. Israel wrote that "as you desire the favor of me that I would give you what instruction in the business I could, to do which in the most friendly manner possible, I must recommend you to have nothing to do with it on any account." But if they were determined to carry on the business contrary to his advice, he suggested that they purchase "a complete set this way which may be got at less than one quarter of what a new one would cost." He said that Josiah Quincy of Boston had the most approved spermaceti manufactory in America, "allowed by all who has seen them which has been frequently advertised in the Boston prints and other ways offered at private sale and I have been lately informed they would dispose of any part and I doubt not but almost every set in this colony can be bot for much less than they can be built for."[51] Similarly, Thomas Robinson and Company, after building a very complete works only two years before, had offered theirs at a bargain price. Wilkinson had been intimately acquainted with the building of three different plants. "The biggest part of the materials of one went through" his hands and on "summing up the bills they each amounted to near double the sum they calculated for although informed by me and those in the business . . . could not be convinced but by experiment." He remarked that when "Messrs Brown first entered the business they bought head matter at three pounds Boston money per ton more than oil and it is now got to be at least 100£ above oil and headmatter generally adulterated with oil to that degree as not to make more than 3/4 the quantity of candles it formerly would."

Then follows a passage which shows the unmistakable influence of the Browns:

I am assured by the quantity of candles by the manufacturers I work for have by them that they are now by far the greatest drug they have ever been.

They have most of their last years stock by them made up and unsold. If we examine the estate of those in the business we should find little encouragement. Mr. Henry Collins who has been long in the business and done near as much as any body has failed the most in debt of any body this way. Mr. Quincy himself who is acquainted with the business and had a workman from England has lay still for several years and can do nothing to advantage, tho his works are advantageously situated. Mr. Gorham who in his lifetime was concerned with Messrs Cranch & Company has been declared insolvent and Mr. Belcher of the same Company has failed and gone to the West Indies, not to mention Mr. A. M. Crabb, Mr. Moses Lopez and sundry others . . .[52]

Although the letter was written with the clear intention of discouraging a potential rival, the description of the state of the industry at that time was fairly accurate. With the end of the war and the depression which followed it, and with the ban upon their further importation into the French Islands, candles had become a drug on the market. In the spring of 1764 much of the stock of the previous year remained unsold even at reduced prices. And the further stagnation attending the enactment of the Sugar Act did not improve the situation. It was true that the spermaceti works owned by the Quincys were then idle and could not be sold at any price. Nathan Gorham had separated himself from Cranch and Company, although it is not certain that he had been declared insolvent. William Belcher had also retired from the same company, perhaps in financial distress. And it was all too true that the price of head matter had appreciated out of all proportion to that of oil.

Word soon came from Philadelphia that the Mifflins would not build a spermaceti works, even though they must forfeit 70 or 80 pounds as the price of breaking their agreement with Delucena. Several considerations must have contributed to the final decision. Their inability to enlist the aid of Wilkinson or his son may well have been one. Wilkinson's bleak picture of the state of the business had probably done its work well. But there were other influences which had not been without their effect. Thomas Robinson and Company of Newport had quietly played their part through Thomas Richardson, their correspondent in Philadelphia. By innuendo Richardson and others had worked to undermine the Mifflins' confidence in Delucena's character.[53] Richardson wrote that he had "left no stone unturned to discourage 'em [the Mifflins] and from Lucenas behavior to me believe have had my share of success, as I saw him the other day at the coffee house and he would not speak to me."[54] The Robinsons, obviously upon the authority of Richardson, informed the Browns that the Mifflins, "upon inquiring into Lucena's character found it bad."[55]

While making their plans to build the works, the Mifflins had purchased a considerable stock of head matter. Once the plans were abandoned the head matter must be sold. Thomas Richardson, as a gesture of good will, suggested to the Robinsons that the manufacturers should take it off the Mifflins' hands. More than good will prompted the proposal. It was an added safeguard against any revival of the plans for another candle factory. The Robinsons and the other Newport houses naturally thought well of the idea, sent their respective proportions of the required sum of money, and asked Nicholas Brown and Company to forward £144 as their share.[56] The transaction ended the threat of trouble in that quarter.

But danger again threatened before many years had passed. This time the danger point was Providence itself. In January 1767 Nicholas Brown and Company advised J. R. Rivera that Judge Jenckes and his son, Dr. Jabez Bowen, and Captain George Jackson were "about erecting a sett of new spermaceti works."[57] Although the Browns promised their "best endeavors" to prevent the execution of this plan, they entertained little hope of stopping it. Appealing to the Newport houses for assistance, they said that "if anything in your or any other you brethrens power can be done toward preventing them it doubtless will prove greatly to the advantage of all, as they are gentlemen able to pay for as much stock as they can want." The Browns then came forth with a specific suggestion as to a possible means of dissuading the new promoters. "Query," they said, "whether if one of the manufacturers in Newport was to give the judge a letter & offer to sell their works it might not discourage them."[58] They then added that "we shall in a most solemn manner offer to sell them ours."

An interesting feature of this incident is that Judge Jenckes was the father-in-law of Nicholas Brown; which seems to indicate that business allowed little place for sentimental considerations. It is significant, too, that on this occasion there was no suggestion by the Browns that the proposed new project could be stopped by the hoarding of mechanical skill. By this time there doubtless were numerous men possessed of the technical knowledge necessary to build new plants. The Browns were preparing, therefore, the use of more subtle and more indirect means of achieving their ends.

But all of their efforts, and those of their Newport "brethren," were unavailing. The new group evidently were not deceived by offers to sell existing spermaceti works. By 1769 the capacity of Daniel Jenckes and Company's plant was excelled only by that of the Browns' manufactory. The size of their operations attested to the truth of the remark that they were "able to pay for as much stock as they can want." By 1772 they had in contemplation the building of a new plant, in which event they planned to sell their old works to Joseph and William Russell of Providence.[59] Alarmed at this threat of still another works in Providence, John Brown wrote to "Messrs Jenckes" on June 24, 1772: "You must be sensible that the business is not worth following when the price of head matter is as high as at present, viz £325 to £330 Boston Old Tenor per ton." Continuing, John remarked that "as we understood you or your partners are under negotiation with Messrs Russell to be concerned in the old works, we think it our duty to our own interest as well as yours to give you our opinion on the consequences which will naturally arise on their being concerned." He suggested that it would be much more to the interest of all concerned "to unite with your old works & continue them on the best terms you can," rather than to sell to the Russells. In that event John thought "there may possibly be an agreement this year on the price & proportions, but if you should continue to build and there should be some new owners to the old works we have no hopes or expectations of any articles."[60]

Coming to his specific proposition John said that "if you object to stopping your new works on account of your having layn out a considerable expense thereon, we doubt not but this may be obviated by the present manufacturers taking their proportion of the materials & paying the cost at least of all such as you choose to dispose of." John assured "Messrs Jenckes" that his company were "quite willing to do anything in this way you may desire." From his discussion "with the other owners of your old works," he was sure that they were "ready to continue the works with you in any reasonable method you yourselves may point out." John then added a postcript saying that he thought it "needless to take up your time in mentioning any consequences that may arise in your building new works at this time—by way of encouraging others."[61]

This latest effort of the Browns to discourage the construction of new works proved unsuccessful. Two years later Daniel Jenckes and Company were still in business, while the new firm of Russell and Howland had made its appearance. It is a reasonable inference, therefore, that this concern had taken over the old works of Jenckes and Company, who had, in turn, carried their new plant to completion.

If the self-interest of the manufacturers required that they should endeavor to defeat plans for the erection of new spermaceti works, it should also have demanded that they prevent a plant once abandoned from resuming operations. It will be remembered that the Quincy family had closed their works (perhaps the most approved in America) at Green's Point, Weymouth, Massachusetts. In 1762 they had offered the plant for sale but there had been no bidders.[62] Edmund Quincy had then written to the Browns that he had decided to sell the utensils separately at private sale, "and to turn the place into a fishery." He offered them "what part . . . you want at what they cost after deducting what any indifferent man shall say they are worse for use." He enclosed an inventory of the utensils which may well constitute the most complete record now extant of the equipment of a first-class spermaceti works.[63]

Evidently Nicholas Brown and Company were not interested, as they appear to have done nothing about Quincy's offer. Almost a year later the works were still unsold. In August 1763, Edmund Quincy offered to sell the plant to Joseph Palmer and Company. As Quincy was "going to London in about a Months time" and was in need of the money, he was prepared to "sell em cheap."[64] Palmer and Company then wrote the Browns that "as he is going abroad, 'tis probable this is the best time that has yet offered for to purchase; and we think he is *now* in earnest." Palmer and Company offered to purchase the plant for Nicholas Brown and Company provided they received a commission for their time and effort. Or, if the Browns would take the iron screws, "the Plates & Barrs," the "Copper & Moulds" at a moderate price, Palmer and Company would then "try to purchase the whole so as to make it worth *our* trouble to take all the rest of the Rubbish."[65] They suggested that "notwithstanding the present ruinous situation of the manufacture, it may be worth while to lose a little in order to finish the destruction of these Works."[66]

In reply to this offer, the Browns wrote "That at present we have no notion of purchasing as there is nothing in the inventory that we have any occasion for and the destruction of the works seems already accomplished by the business being so poor as barely worth pursuing by those already engaged."[67] It is not easy to reconcile their indifference on this occasion with their eagerness to prevent the Mifflins from building new works, especially when the two incidents were separated by only a few weeks. If they could trust the distressed state of the manufacture to discourage new owners from buying the Quincys' old plant, why did they fear that the Mifflins would erect a new one? Perhaps they felt that awareness of the doldrums of the candle manufacture was greater in New England than in Philadelphia, and could be relied on as a deterrent in the one case but not in the other.

No categorical statement can be made as to the success of the manufacturers in their attempts to prevent new houses from entering the business. It may be said, however, that through 1769 the number of spermaceti works remained relatively constant. The articles of agreement of 1761 were signed by seven different companies; those of 1769 were entered into by ten houses. There had, of course, been some changes in the composition of the association within the period. Some familiar names had disappeared; some new ones had made their appearance. Nevertheless, five of the seven subscribers of 1761 were represented among the ten signers of 1769. This relatively stable condition of the manufacture over the nine-year period was surely in part the result of the various devices employed by the candle makers to discourage newcomers. But other factors were involved. The postwar depression, the scarcity of money, the apparent surfeit of candles, and the abandonment of existing works all conspired to dissuade men from building new plants.

After 1770 the number of houses engaged in the business increased sharply and conditions within the industry became more unstable. The articles of December 7, 1774 allotted shares of head matter to twenty-four different manufacturers. In Providence, where the Browns once held undisputed sway, there were now four plants in operation. Boston was represented by three houses. The "Philadelphians," who had participated in the United Company for many years, had disappeared, their places taken by the "Yorkers," comprising Isaac Stotenberg and Company and Solaman Simson and Company. Newport, with a representation of thirteen houses, retained its place as the leading center of the candle manufacture in the British colonies.

Among the important newcomers to the association was a representative from Nantucket. Although the bulk of the head matter which went into the candle manufacture was caught by the whaling fleet of the Island, and passed through the hands of dealers there en route to the spermaceti works on the mainland, it was only when the golden age of Nantucket was approaching an end that one of its whaling families entered the candle business. While the Rotch family had long been prominent in the whale fishery, as well as in the purchase of head matter and oil, it remained for William Rotch to establish a spermaceti works at Nantucket. Late in 1772 it was rumored that he and one David Harris were planning to establish a plant there. By 1774 it was a going concern, and by the Articles of Agreement of that year William Rotch received a quota of 13 parts out of every 181 parts of head matter. It was probably well that the outbreak of hostilities soon made a union of the manufacturers impossible; for it was evident that in William Rotch the association was confronted with a new problem.

Although many of the manufacturers had engaged in whaling as a side line, Rotch was preëminently a whaler. Like other members of his family, he was no shrinking violet. On January 24, 1775 he addressed a long letter to the Newport and Providence houses.[68] He called attention to the fact that at the meeting of the previous year he had proposed that his works should receive head matter "equal in proportion to any one on the continent." His fellow candle makers disregarded his suggestion, however, "the division being made more according to the numbers concerned than their interest in procuring head matter." He then pointed out that his own vessels in a less than average season had caught more head matter than was allotted to his house, not to mention the very large interest of his brother Francis in the fishery, "with whom you may reasonably suppose I have some influence." He concluded with this note of warning: "Now if upon consideration you still insist keeping me to the proportion you allotted me, I believe I shall comply with it, but I certainly know it will not be for your interest to drive me to such an unreasonable complyance."

The other manufacturers disapproved of these suggestions. They naturally felt that the existing division of head matter was a just one. But the Union would eventually have to decide what to do if Rotch's whaling fleet should catch more head matter than was assigned to him. The members would also have to determine whether William Rotch, candle manufacturer, should continue to purchase head matter for other manufacturers. But before these issues could be fairly faced in a full meeting of the Association, Lexington and Concord had intervened.

The Browns in 1774 still held their rank as the most important single firm in the business, although their proportion of the total fund of head matter had declined, as shown in the quotas assigned to the various concerns. In 1763 they had received 20 parts out of every 100; in 1764, 20 out of every 104. Their relative position had improved in 1765 when their share was 20 parts out of 89. The next year the articles assigned them 20 parts out of 92, a proportion which remained unchanged in 1767. By 1769 they were receiving 20 barrels out of every 112; in 1771, 20 out of every 114. But by 1774 their quota was only 23½ barrels out of 181.[69] Over the long pull from 1763 to 1774 their percentage of the total fund of head matter distributed among the members of the association had declined from 20 per cent to 12.9 per cent. Yet their proportion had declined less than that of their competitors. In 1763 their closest rival had received 14 parts out of every 100; in 1774 the house ranking second had a quota of 13 barrels out of 181. This represents a decline from 14 per cent to 7.2 per cent of the total. During the decade before the Revolution the Browns had not only held first place but they had retained their position in relation to the runner-up.

All this suggests certain questions. Was the total fund of head matter greater in 1774 than in 1763? In view of the decline in their percentage of the total amount, did the Browns receive a greater weight of head matter in 1774 than in 1763? Or, to put the second question in different form, were the Browns able to manufacture more candles in 1774 than in 1763? The answers to these questions seem to be in the affirmative. While incompleteness of the Browns' records for 1763 makes a comparison between that year and 1774 impossible, comparison can be made between 1769 and 1774. In the former year when they received 17.8 per cent of the total amount of head matter, their quota had a weight of 125 tons.[70] For 1774 when their share was 12.9 per cent of the total they received 133 tons.[71] It may be reasonably inferred from this, therefore, that the Browns were manufacturing more candles in 1774 than in 1769; and it appears that the total output of candles must have increased substantially in the same period.

The increased production of head matter, the larger output of candles, and the growth in the number of spermaceti works between 1769 and 1775 undoubtedly reflects the gradual recovery from the postwar depression of the sixties, from the stagnation which the Sugar Act had accentuated, and from the monetary stringency of the earlier years. The early seventies were years of relative political tranquillity and economic prosperity. In such an atmosphere men evidently turned to the spermaceti manufacture with renewed confidence and with greater hope of success. By this time, too, the mechanical skill, so closely guarded a decade before, was more generally available; and with bankruptcy less prevalent in the business, existing manufacturers found it more difficult to deter enterprising newcomers. The candle manufacture seemed to be enjoying an illusion of prosperity before the gathering storm clouds of war.

The best efforts of the United Association of Spermaceti Chandlers did not keep the price of head matter from rising steadily during the period the Union was in existence. In 1761 the Articles had fixed the differential between oil and head matter at £6 Sterling per ton. The Agreement of 1763 increased this differential to £10 Sterling. The Covenant of 1764 set a ceiling price of £27:6:8 lawful money on head matter. By 1774 this ceiling had increased to £40 Sterling per ton.

The price of candles failed to advance in harmony with that of head matter. In the Agreement of 1761 the subscribers had agreed not to sell candles in New England for less than one shilling, ten and one-half pence Sterling per pound. In 1763 the Browns and six Newport houses gave their "word and honors" that in "Rhode Island, Providence and Boston" they would not charge less than two shillings and threepence lawful silver money per pound. By 1772 candles were selling in Boston at "1/9³/⁵ cash" and "1/10 on 9 months credit."[72] A year later Henry Lloyd advised the Browns that, having no candles "by me at present & but few in the hands of the Manufacturers believe I could obtain a ready market for a considerable quantity at 2/3 to 2/4."[73] In 1774 Lloyd acknowledged the receipt of sixty boxes of candles from the Browns, which he would sell "either at 2/7 cash or 2/8 on three months credit to those I think safe."[74]

Thus while the price of head matter doubled in the decade 1764 to 1774, the price of candles in Boston (a chief outlet for them) advanced from two shillings and threepence to two shillings and eight, an increase of less than 20 per cent. Evidently the prosperity of the candle manufacture in the early seventies was more apparent than real.

One reason for the persistent advance in price of head matter was the purchase of it for shipment to the London market, a business in which Henry Lloyd of Boston and the Rotches were largely engaged. On these purchases London houses paid a commission of 5 per cent, without limitation of price, at a time when candle manufacturers allowed only $2\frac{1}{2}$ per cent. With this differential, it was little wonder that some men preferred to purchase on London account. And as head matter moved across the Atlantic in quantity, the dearer it became to the candle industry. All this was bad enough. But even worse was the fact that much of the head matter bought for the London market was actually shipped as oil in order to avoid the duty on head matter in England.

This charge was first made in 1764 when someone informed the British Customs officials in America that Joseph Rotch was loading a ship with head matter for London under guise of whale oil. In a long letter to some of the Newport manufacturers Rotch indignantly denied the allegation, which he said originated with some one of the candle makers.[75] According to Rotch, the collector at Boston had "told us we might easily obtain an act of Parliament either to prohibit the manufacturing of any head matter in this country or to have the duties taken off & either of them would be equally fatal to you." Rotch then remarked that he should be sorry "if ever this branch of business is wholly stopped in this country for we always was willing to do all of you as much good as we possibly could (without doing too much injustice to ourselves)." He assured his Newport friends that he "might have sent more head matter out of the country than we have, although we never have had more thanks or notice taken of us by some of the fraternity than to those that never looked to anything but their own interest intirely." The hard-bitten philosophy of Rotch was well expressed when he added, "now gentlemen . . . you know that all the Friendship that can be expected in trade is to let your Friend have a thing at the same Price that others would give for it." He received "5 per cent Commission for all we Ship out of the Country & Draw bills when we Please for the Money If it's even before we ship it, so that there is a grait difference between that & $2\frac{1}{2}$ per cent." In conclusion, Rotch promised his correspondents that "if it is Possible for you to keep the Headmatter in this Country we will do all in our Power to help keep it forward, if it is not against our interest."

It is significant that Rotch came under attack at the very moment he was engaged in his great oil-purchasing duel with John Hancock, in which he spoiled the latter's plan for a corner on whale oil for shipment to London. It may be significant, too, that Hancock was not charged with shipping head matter as oil. Perhaps Rotch was technically correct in his assertion that the head matter was cleared out as such. Yet, the fact remains that this and all other shipments of head matter were entered at London as oil.[76] Rotch and his fellow purchasers of oil could hardly have been unaware of the fact that they were the beneficiaries of this device.

This sort of thing went on without interruption through the decade of the sixties. In 1769 two notable instances of it came to light in the course of a few days. A Boston factor, buying for Jacob Polock of Newport, had exceeded the ceiling price of head matter. When reprimanded by Polock, he said he had followed the example of Henry Lloyd. After he was told that Lloyd had purchased for London, he remarked that he was "an entire stranger to Mr. Lloyd's order being from England, as I could not think he would have accepted of such an order to the detriment of persons by whom he had been employed for some years."[77]

The other offender was again Joseph Rotch and Son of Nantucket. In a circular letter to the Rotches, the Rhode Island manufacturers expressed their hope that the Nantucket house "should not put such an unfavorable construction on our conduct in this affair as to suppose it a combination, for we consider that the interest of the mfg. & catchers are reciprocally connected & we who are best acquainted with the profits on mfg. have regulated our conduct accordingly." If the Rotches would consider the "low price of oil, loss per bills, low price of candles & slowness of sale," they must be "persuaded the good of the whole is the principle that governs our breast." The Newport manufacturers added that they must "conclude that if any of you gentlemen after this candid open declaration should ship it to any foreign market, will not act favorable to his country & may in the end have cause to repent when *too* late, as we are convinced it cannot be to his interest to ship it home at more than our limits."[78]

This is one of the numerous occasions when the manufacturers sought to represent themselves as the friends and promoters of American industry, as opposed to the shippers of head matter, who, by playing false to the interests of their country, were aiding British commerce and industry. Of course no purchaser for the London market ever thought of himself as acting in a manner adverse to colonial interests; and doubtless all could say with Joseph Rotch that they were willing to do as much as they could for the candle manufacture "without doing too much injustice to ourselves."

Protests notwithstanding, buying of head matter for shipment to London as oil continued unabated. Reluctantly the manufacturers decided to substitute warning for protest. On October 22, 1771, Nicholas Brown and Company wrote "to the Manufacturers in Newport," advising them to make a "proper draught" directed to all the purchasers of head matter for the London market "purporting in the firmest (though decent manner) that information will be made by us as a body (or some persons for us) to the Commissioners [of the customs] in such a manner as to prevent any H. M. being shipped without being cleared out in such a manner as will oblige them to pay the duty."[79]

The Newport manufacturers lost no time in acting upon the suggestion made by the Browns. Within three days they had drafted a letter to "Henry Lloyd, Nathaniel Wheatley & all other purchasers of head matter for Great Britain."[80] In it they said it gave them "great concern to observe the embarrassing state of the spermaceti manufacture for several years past, owing chiefly to Head Matter being shipped to Europe as oil, to the great injury of the fair trade." They had endeavored to establish the "most salutary regulations" they could devise in an effort to render the candle business "beneficial to the colonys, promote the fishery and support ourselves & families." In "the most dispassionate manner" they appealed to the "breast [of the purchasers] whether we are to set contented and see it carried from us contrary to the Acts of Parliament."

Posing as the friends of home industry, the Newport men went on to say that "if the British Legislature loaded it [head matter] with the heavy duty in order to encourage the Fishery, navigation and growth of the colonys, every person or persons who violated the acts stops the operation of the good intentions of the Mother Country, to the great injury of America & us in particular who have at so much expense established the trade." They requested the purchasers not only to refrain from buying for London "unless shipped as head matter," but also "to acquaint your correspondents that it is in our power to come at the knowledge of every barrel caught; will have an attentive eye to the disposal of it & that we cannot in justice to ourselves permit it any longer to be carried in a clandestine manner and in open violation of the law." Not content to warn against further purchases for the London market, they also frowned on the shipment of stock already on hand. Should their warning be disregarded, they would be "drove to the disagreeable necessity of making or causing to be made, such information at home and in America, as we think we ought in duty to ourselves to make." Nor did they think they were injuring the purchasers "as private individuals" by such procedure, "as the same advantages will arise to you by purchasing for us as for the European market." This last statement was not entirely accurate. Even at the same rate of commission, purchases for London were likely to be more profitable because they were usually made at a figure well above the stated price of the candle manufacturers.

On the same day Nicholas Brown and Company, together with the other Providence manufacturers, penned their warning to Henry Lloyd and his fellow purchasers for London.[81] They expressed their concern over the declining state of the spermaceti business "owing to head matter being bought up and shipped to Europe." They had been at great expense to erect works which would be wholly useless unless head matter could be purchased "at a rate that we can work it." In fixing the price of head matter they had in mind the good of the fishery as well as their own private interests. But they had had the mortification of seeing that price "greatly exceeded," which if persisted in must result in the destruction of the candle manufacture in America. They thought it very hard to "be thus treated by our own country-men, especially as you can have as good a commission for purchasing that article for us, which we are ready & willing to give you." The manufacturers could not look "tamely on" and see themselves injured "in so sensible a manner" when they had "law, reason and self-preservation as our justification." Unless the purchasers desisted from their baleful practice, such information would be lodged both in "England and America" as would prevent "head matter's being shipped to Great Britain under the character of oil."

It remained to communicate with the Boston candle makers. On October 29, 1771, Nicholas Brown and Company addressed to "Mr. Oliver Wendal" [Wendell] a letter "to be communicated to the Manufacturers at Boston." In it they expressed the opinion that there was no "other remedy to be applied than to make immediate information to the commissioners of every vessel that has any head on board for London." They also suggested that the Boston men write to "the Lords Commissioners of the Customs or other proper officers" in England, setting forth in the strongest terms the "great disadvantage this clandestine trade is to the revenue." The Browns promised that a similar letter to the Customs officials would go forth from Providence. In conclusion they expressed their conviction that "we must make an earnest of this matter or resign the business to our good friends the other side of the water."

On November 13, 1771 the Browns wrote to the Nantucket factors, enclosing a copy of a letter, signed by the Providence and Boston manufacturers, and addressed to the purchasers of head matter for London.[82] They thought it "but friendly to give notice hereof to you . . . though we have no reason to think any of our friends in Nantucket have shipped any head matter this year to London."

There is reason to doubt that the manufacturers gave the threatened information to the Customs officials at that time. It obviously had been their hope that a warning to the offenders would suffice to put an end to the practice. Henry Lloyd, perhaps the chief sinner, promptly gave his promise that he "should not for the future buy any head matter for the London market." Such a pledge from Lloyd undoubtedly gave hope of similar ones from other sources.

But the surest indication that the officers were not informed is the fact that buying of head matter for shipment to London continued; and soon Henry Lloyd had maneuvered the manufacturers into a position where he was able to break his promise with impunity. On April 7, 1772 he informed Nicholas Brown and Company that "agreeable to my promise to you I wrote my friend in London who employed me to purchase head-matter for him that I could continue it no longer."[83] But Lloyd added that he had "by the late vessels from London a further application made to me . . . to purchase a few tons of head matter now & to purchase a few more at a time during the season as opportunity shall offer." If he should decline, "another is to do the business in my stead, which will deprive me of the advantage of purchasing oil and pot ash also for him in the future, which will be greatly detrimental to me and of no advantage that I can perceive to my friends the manufacturers of spermaceti candles." Henry Lloyd was conveying this intelligence to the Browns for their consideration and "permission to purchase." In somewhat ominous fashion he informed them that "this correspondent of mine is a man of some importance in his way of business and resents the opposition that is made to him and is meditating some return of opposition to your manufacture if he is still opposed in his purchases and he may effect some things to the prejudice of the manufacture, which I should be glad to be instrumental in preventing."

Having employed this thinly veiled threat, Lloyd told the Browns that he had consulted the Boston manufacturers, who desired that he "should be the purchaser [for London] . . . in preference to any other person." Then, in a more conciliatory vein, he added that if he were the purchaser he would be prepared to agree "to such terms as may be judged most for the interest of the manufacturers which it is probable the person to be put in my room cant be brought to consent to."

The upshot of this whole affair was that the Browns, as well as the Boston manufacturers, acquiesced in Henry Lloyd's continued purchase of head matter for London.[84] The one concession he had made was an implied promise not to bid the price up above their limits. On their part, the manufacturers had retreated from their earlier demand for a complete cessation of shipments to London. In the absence of "an information" to the customs officials, perhaps no other course was possible; and their hesitancy to inform is understandable. As almost every colonial merchant violated British regulations on occasion, only the greatest provocation would prompt one segment of the fraternity to "inform" on another.

So the purchasing of head matter for shipment to London went on unabated during the next two years. The purchasers may have refrained from bidding up the price, although the figure of £40 Sterling fixed by the Articles of 1774 hardly suggests as much. In any event, the long-threatened "information" to the Customs officials was finally made by an unidentified person on this side of the Atlantic in the winter of 1774-75. Hayley and Hopkins, London correspondent of the Browns, writing with reference to the shipment of head matter, remarked that in this "there has been a fatal mistake made by some gentlemen on your side of the water." They explained that in the importation of head matter into England "the greatest care" had always been taken to see that the "inspectors should never get sight of it." The customs officers had never "seen a single cask of head matter from its first . . . importation . . . till this winter." It had always been kept out of their sight "to prevent their calling upon the importer for a very heavy duty which it is liable to." Refuting the Browns' charge that the inspectors had connived at its shipment as oil, they remarked that the officials had "never had any opportunity of returning it as oil for they never saw it till this winter." But, they were sorry to say, "this winter a very heavy expence has been brought on every oil cargo by some mistaken man in your province who watches the shipping of head matter & gives regular information to the Commissioners of the Customs here of every parcel which is shipped." This had subjected every cask of head matter to the payment of the heavy duty in England.

But this was "not all of the mischief." Fearing that some shipments of head matter might escape the vigilance of their good friend and informer in America, the Customs officers had ordered that "every cask of oil shall be landed and opened immediately before it is put into any store." This entailed considerable expense "and will continue upon every cargo of oil from henceforth." Furthermore, the inspectors had become so very exact that they examined the "quantity of settlement at the bottom of every cask of oil and charge duty on such quantity of spermaceti as they suppose may be in the bottoms" of all oil cargoes. "These are the consequences," said Hayley and Hopkins, "of the zeal of the gentleman informer whosoever he is that has taken upon himself the office of informer. He has brought a heavy burden upon the whole oil trade which it will never get rid of."[85]

A Rhode Islander turned informer had thus been instrumental in suppressing the shipment of head matter under the guise of oil, but at the cost of a "heavy burden" imposed on every cask of oil. As manufacturers of candles, the Browns and their associates could only look with approval upon this new order of things. But they were also large shippers of oil, and whether their gains in the one capacity would more than offset their losses in the other is not certain. Coming as it did upon the eve of hostilities between the colonies and the mother country, the new dispensation had no adequate opportunity to prove itself one way or another. But a practice against which the manufacturers had long inveighed had finally been terminated.

Were we to believe the manufacturers, the buying of head matter for clandestine shipment to London was *the* cause of its steady appreciation in price during the period 1761-1775. It was a factor and a very important one; but it was not the only one. The sharpest advance in the price of head matter came in the prosperous years of the early seventies, when the number of spermaceti works increased markedly. The resulting increased demand for head matter created a strong additional pressure for price increases. In the face of this pressure the manufacturers dared not sit too firmly on the price lid. They lived in constant fear lest by setting the price of head matter too low they would antagonize the "catchers" and purchasers of head matter at Nantucket and drive them into the candle manufacture. As it was, William Rotch had built spermaceti works and others on Nantucket might easily emulate his example. It behooved the manufacturers, therefore, not to stand too adamant against the strong trend toward higher prices.

On March 29, 1775 an adjourned meeting of the Association of Spermaceti Candle Manufacturers was held at Newport. As "the small number of members present" made it impossible to draw up Articles of Agreement for the year, those in attendance "appointed Wednesday the 26th April next for meeting to settle & fix upon another union." They urgently requested all "members to attend to a matter of so much consequence." Before the appointed day of meeting had arrived the country was at war, and there is no indication that the meeting was ever held. That of March 29th, therefore, may well have been the last. The ensuing war was to deal the business of candle manufacture a blow from which it was never to recover. Many of the manufacturers were no longer in business at its conclusion. Although the Brown family weathered the storm, they were unable to restore the spermaceti manufacture to its earlier position of importance in the family's scheme of business.

Aside from its importance as a form of business enterprise, offering opportunity for the investment of capital, yielding profit to the owners, and providing employment to workers, the spermaceti candle manufacture had another and perhaps greater significance. It gave to eighteenth-century America its outstanding example of attempted monopoly and price-fixing under private auspices. In any specific sense the United Association of Spermaceti Chandlers largely failed to achieve the ends which its architects had in mind. Its efforts to fix the price of candles were a complete failure. It was unable to prevent the establishment of new spermaceti works. And it was unable to maintain a ceiling on the price of head matter for any length of time. Yet from 1763 to 1775 it was the considered opinion of the manufacturers that the annual agreements were the salvation of the business. Granted the strong propensity of human beings to humbug themselves (when no one else will do it for them), it seems unlikely that all the candle makers could have fooled themselves all the time during the dozen years before the Revolution. Undoubtedly the Union provided a degree of stability within the business which would otherwise have been absent. Without it there would have been such reckless competition in the purchase of head matter that the business must have perished.

The Association functioned in an atmosphere strongly surcharged with mutual suspicion on the part of its members. Its records abound in instances of bad faith. Yet it cannot be said that the Articles of Agreement were "honored more in the breach than in the observance." If for no other reason, the various provisions of the covenant were observed by most of the subscribers most of the time because of the zealous watch which each member maintained over his fellows.

Perhaps the marked increase in the number of spermaceti plants on the eve of the Revolution, in spite of the growing disparity between the price of head matter and of candles, is evidence in support of Louis Hacker's contention that colonial merchants possessed capital which they were eager to invest in manufacture if only British regulations would allow them so to do.[86] The candle business was one form of manufacture with which the mother country in no way interfered. Indeed, the duty on head matter imported into England, in so far as it was collected, served as a protection and an incentive to the manufacture of spermaceti candles within the colonies. Finding other channels of investment closed to them, merchants may have been attracted to an industry which seemed to enjoy the complete benediction of the British government.

CHAPTER 6

"A Furnace for Making Pigg Iron"

IN 1765 the Browns went into the iron business. Their spermaceti manufacture was well established and they were easily the leading candle makers in the colonies. Many other Rhode Island merchants, such as Aaron Lopez of Newport, were enlarging their maritime commerce, but the Browns had become manufacturers first and merchants second. When capital was available for business expansion, it went not into a larger merchant fleet but into another branch of manufacturing.

Prior to 1765 the Browns had each year planned their navigation to the Caribbean with an eye to the acquisition of funds to purchase head matter. But the major objective of their maritime ventures in 1765 was to secure working capital for the newly projected iron works. Three of their vessels were to rendezvous at Surinam. One of them was later to go to Barbados to meet Captain Esek Hopkins, fresh from his slave-trading voyage to the Guinea coast in *Sally*. Another carried an especially valuable cargo, including "the best parcel [of horses] shipped out of this place," several of which were too superior to be used in the sugar mills and were, therefore, to be sold as riding horses. From the sale of this and the other two cargoes at Surinam, plus the anticipated profits from the sale of Esek Hopkins' slaves in the British Islands, Nicholas Brown and Company hoped to realize handsomely. The profits were to pay part of the initial costs of their new experiment in iron. In a letter to Captain George Hopkins of the Ship *Nancy* they wrote: "send us all the bills you can collect before you come away . . . as the building of the Furnace calls for all the stock that all the owners are able to supply and more if we had it." And they added that "as your vessel & cargo will be very valuable by no means bring anything that will make her liable to confiscation." The disastrous outcome of Esek Hopkins' voyage in *Sally* materially reduced the "stock" realized from the sale of the three cargoes. But the Browns and their Providence associates made up the deficit somehow and continued construction of the new furnace.

It was an auspicious moment to enter a new field of manufacture, particularly the manufacture of iron. The time seemed too favorable for the project to be abandoned, even though the results of the Surinam voyages were disappointing. No one had forgotten that iron manufacture in the colonies had been very profitable during the boom which accompanied the Seven Years' War. Moreover, the colonials were disturbed by the Stamp Act. As a result they were urging the nonimportation of British goods and talking vigorously about the importance of home industry. There was also the very practical consideration that it was a period of depression, and costs of materials and of labor were very low.

The iron industry in America is almost as old as English settlement. The earliest colonists at Saugus or Lynn, in the Bay Colony, discovered the bog iron ore deposited in the peat bogs and ponds of eastern Massachusetts. Specimens of this ore were taken to London in 1643, where there was organized the "Company of Undertakers for the Iron-Works" for the purpose of exploiting this natural resource. Among those who came to New England under the auspices of this company was Joseph Jenks, a native of Hammersmith, near London, a man "held in high estimation for his extraordinary ingenuity as an artificer." At the forge which he built at Lynn he earned the distinction of being "the first founder who worked in brass and iron on the Western Continent."[1]

A new arrival from the Massachusetts Bay Colony introduced iron manufacture into the Narragansett country. He was Joseph Jenks, Jr., son of the builder of the pioneer forge at Lynn, who not only erected the first house in Pawtucket but in 1655 built a forge to utilize the iron ore recently discovered at that place.[2]

The iron ore of Rhode Island was not of the best quality. In the town of Cumberland there was a magnetic ore which yielded "a red short iron not good."[3] Even so, before the Revolution there were three furnaces making use of this mineral.[4] In the southern part of the Colony the bog ore produced a "cold, short iron" which in most instances was not "sufficiently tough for nails, spikes or tools of good quality."[5] The chief deposits of bog ore seem to have been in the towns of Scituate and Cranston. Daniel Waldo is reported to have purchased an ore bed there in 1735 and to have erected a furnace and foundry on the Pawtuxet River, near the present village of Hope.[6] The assumption of various writers that this was the beginning of Hope Furnace is in error; for in 1765 the Brown brothers referred to the bog ore, which they were about to exploit, as recently discovered; and the Hope Furnace in which they were concerned for almost fifty years was built *de novo* by them in 1765-66.[7]

The colonial iron industry, however, was not confined to New England. Prior to the Revolution, ironworks were to be found in every colony except Georgia. By 1775 there were more blast furnaces and forges in the colonies than in England and Wales; and colonial production of pig and bar iron exceeded that of the mother country. In that year the colonies produced not quite one-seventh of the world output of iron.[8]

Although the iron industry was widely dispersed in the colonies, it attained its highest development and concentration in southeastern Pennsylvania.[9] There the characteristic unit was the "iron plantation," usually comprising several thousand acres of land, where wood for charcoal was present in abundance and where food for the workers could be grown. Important, also, in determining the location of the plantation was availability of iron ore and the presence of water power. Proximity to markets seems not to have been a governing consideration, as the plantations were usually at considerable distance from the larger urban centers.

The mansion house, the homes of the workers, the furnace and forge or forges, the iron mines, the charcoal house, the dense woods which furnished the material for making charcoal, the office, the general store where supplies of all kinds could be obtained, the gristmill, the sawmill, the blacksmith shop, the common bake oven, the barns, the grain fields and orchards, were part of a very interesting and almost self-sufficing community.[10]

The furnace was built into the side of a small hill so that the ore, charcoal, and limestone could be fed into it from the top. It was kept filled continuously with alternate layers of these materials.

The gaseous products escaped at the top of the stack. At the fuyère of the furnace the ore melted and dropped down to the hearth below . . . About twice a day, sometimes oftener, the molten iron was run into the casting bed of sand, which was prepared for its reception by molds occasionally made from mahogany wood patterns but usually from other wood patterns. Some imaginative early ironmaster compared the casting bed to a sow and her litter of sucking pigs. Thus the main stream or feeder for the furnace was called the sow, while the side gutters were called pigs, a term which is in use today. Before the iron became cold, the pigs were separated from the sow, and the latter broken up into smaller pieces.[11]

Nearby the furnace usually stood the forge, in which the pig iron was refined and hammered into bars of wrought iron. "The dull, unvaried turning of the water wheel, the irregular splash of falling water, the rhythmic thump of the hammer, and the droning sound of the anvil, were a part of life on the plantation."[12] Blacksmiths fashioned the bar iron of the forges into various sorts of tools, implements, and ironware.

Besides blast furnaces and forges, there were more highly developed forms of the iron manufacture within the colonies. In various towns there were rolling and slitting mills where bar iron was heated and slit into strips called slit iron, or nail rods used in making nails. There were also small furnaces, where "blister" steel was produced by hit or miss methods. In plating mills powerful hammers driven by water power hammered bar iron into thin sheets. Coated with tin, these were known as tin plate. Toward the end of the colonial era there appeared the air furnace, resembling the blast furnace but smaller, and used for making castings from pig iron. During the War for Independence air furnaces were extensively employed in the casting of cannon.

Unfortunately, no record has been preserved of the deliberations which must have taken place among the four Brown brothers and their fellow proprietors of Hope Furnace before they arrived at their decision to venture their time, their talents and, above all, their capital in the iron industry. But if the incubation stage of the furnace idea is undocumented, that is not true of the implementing of the idea in the furnace structure itself. For few, if any, eighteenth-century business undertakings is there a more complete record than for the building of Hope Furnace and the development of a market for its product.

The men who were to control the destinies of the furnace were inexperienced in the iron business, and possessed little if any technical knowledge of it. But they had the sound sense to secure an associate who had the necessary skill. This man was Israel Wilkinson, the "ingenious mechanic," whose knowledge of the mechanical side of the spermaceti business the Browns had so jealously guarded. At least two members of his family operated iron forges and manufactured a variety of iron products. Israel himself seems to have combined with his facility in the candle manufacture "the business of making iron."

On May 14, 1765, Israel Wilkinson entered into an agreement with one Jeremiah Burlingame, of Cranston, Rhode Island, on whose land "a quantity of iron" had lately been discovered, the "goodness of which . . . was quite unknown." As Wilkinson was "about to make an experiment of said ore at his own proper cost and expense," Burlingame, to encourage him to "make proof" of the ore, "bargained and sold" to Wilkinson "all the Iron ore that was then or might at any time thereafter be found or discovered in a certain tract or parcel of land . . . in Cranston." The consideration was three pounds lawful money. Wilkinson was to have "full power & free liberty" at all times "forever thereafter peaceably and quietly [to] dig after, raise, carry away & convert to his own . . . proper use all such iron ore as was then or at any time thereafter might be found within or upon the tract of land . . . without any manner of interruption or molestation." He agreed for himself and his "heirs, executors or assigns" to pay for every ton of ore "dug and carried from" the land the sum of sixpence lawful money. Should Wilkinson, his heirs or assigns neglect to "dig at said ore" within the term of three years from the date of the agreement, Burlingame or his heirs were to have "free liberty" to dispose of the ore as might seem proper, and the agreement was to be null and void.[13]

Six days after the signing of the covenant between Israel Wilkinson and Jeremiah Burlingame, Moses Brown purchased of John and William Page, both of the town of Glocester, for the term of 999 years "all the iron ore in a certain tract of land lying in said Gloucester" for the consideration of twenty shillings lawful money. Moses further agreed to pay sixpence lawful money per ton for all the iron ore to "be dug and carried away from the said land."

Although ostensibly the Brown family had no hand in the compact between Wilkinson and Burlingame, later events showed that they and Stephen Hopkins had almost certainly conceived the plan. The full design became apparent when on July 9, 1765 Stephen Hopkins, Israel Wilkinson, Nicholas, Joseph, John, and Moses Brown, Job Hawkins, and Caleb Arnold, "in consideration of the trust and confidence which every one of them reposeth in the other," joined themselves "to be co-partners in the business of making pig metal commonly called pig iron or any other form of cast iron and settling such measures of vending and selling the same as the parties shall and may from time to time agree."

By the same articles of agreement, Israel Wilkinson, to promote the experiment in making pig iron, to further the general purpose of the copartnership, and in consideration of the sum of fifty-two shillings and sixpence paid him by his fellow partners, granted, bargained, sold, assigned and made over to his copartners, "seven-eights parts" of all the iron ore "discovered and to be discovered" in the tract of land described in his covenant with Jeremiah Burlingame of May 14th. To Stephen Hopkins he conveyed one-quarter, to each of the four Brown brothers one-eighth, to Job Hawkins one-sixteenth, and to Caleb Arnold one-sixteenth. He retained one-eighth part for himself. Thus the Browns collectively obtained one-half interest in the ore.

Again in the same covenant, Moses Brown "for promoting" the iron manufactory, "for furthering the general purpose of the copartnership," and in consideration of seventeen shillings and sixpence lawful money paid him by his copartners, conveyed to them "for the term of 999 years" seven-eighths of "all the iron ore discovered or to be discovered" in the tract of land covered by his contract with John and William Page.[14] As the proportion assigned to each of the copartners was the same as in the Burlingame land, the four Brown brothers again received one-half of the total.

The copartners mutually agreed that before August 31, 1765 they would "make experiment of the quality of the . . . Cranston ore or of any other which they shall think fit at the Furnace Unity in Cumberland," each of them agreeing to pay his proportion, according to ownership of the ore, of all costs incidental to the making of the trial. The owners further agreed that if the ores should, in the opinion of the "major part" of them, "turn out on trial to be good," they would immediately proceed with the building of a furnace "for making pig metal or pig iron or any other form of casting as they shall think fit." This, together with a "damn," coal house, and "such other houses, offices and accommodations" as might be deemed necessary, should be complete within one year.

The subscribers to the agreement were to provide coal and "all other necessaries" for making a blast as soon as the furnace was "so far completed as to be in readiness therefor." The copartners were, of course, to furnish their several proportions of "stock" or capital for carrying on the business "as fast as the same shall be wanted." Should any one or more fail to do so, the other partners might proceed with the business without accounting to the absentees for "any profits or for the use or wear of the works or for any accidents to the works by fire or water." Anyone thus refusing to carry on his proportion of a "blast or blasts" might, "upon repentance," participate in the "next succeeding blast" on condition of reimbursing the other partners for all costs and charges "they may have been at in repairs and implements."

To prevent any part of the ownership from falling into unfriendly hands, the articles stipulated that

none of the . . . co-partners shall sell or lease his part of the . . . works . . . without first giving in writing to his fellow partners . . . an offer to buy or sell together with the price he will give or take, giving to his partners 40 days time to accept or reject his proposals under penalty of £100 lawful money for his one sixteenth of the said works and in that proportion for any other part or parts.

If the partners should not accept such an offer, the one making it would then be at liberty to sell according to his pleasure. Finally, it was mutually agreed that should doubt, question, or controversy arise among the copartners regarding any clause of the articles, it should be "referred unto indifferent persons" before bringing any legal action. Each of the partners in dispute was to choose one "indifferent person." The award of "such indifferent persons" was to be binding if "made in writing under their hands and seals."

It was characteristic of the cautious and methodical Nicholas Brown that he should seek all possible light upon the iron industry, once he had committed himself to the furnace project. He turned logically to Pennsylvania, where the industry had been most highly developed. Just one week after the Wilkinson-Burlingame agreement, and many weeks prior to the formation of the copartnership, he addressed a letter to John Relfe in Philadelphia.[15] In it he explained that he and his brothers were "about making trial of some iron ore lately found here and purpose in case it proves to make good pig iron to be concerned in erecting a furnace for that purpose." He added that he had noted some "querays" which he hoped Relfe would answer by the return of the Browns' sloop. Nicholas anticipated some reluctance on the part of the ironmasters to reveal trade secrets. He himself was always wary about disclosing the details of the candle business. To forestall any such reserve of the Pennsylvanians, he remarked that they "need not decline answering them fearing it might encourage our undertaking, as we are determined in case the ore . . . will answer . . . to proceed immediately in erecting the works." The "querays," therefore, were more a matter of "speculation and curiosity than importance." The Browns were already committed to the project, and were not to be stopped by any conspiracy of silence from Pennsylvania.

As the queries called for a bit of research and investigation by John Relfe, he was unable to send the answers by the return of the sloop. Nevertheless, he did forward the information in such good season that it was in the hands of Nicholas Brown very near the time the partnership agreement was executed. The data which Relfe sent in reply to the questions put to him covered various phases of the iron business. First of all came the "Names of all the Furnaces in Pennsylvania," fifteen in number. Their distance from Philadelphia varied from thirty-nine to seventy-five miles. In all but two cases the carriage to the busy Quaker metropolis was entirely by land. Opposite the name of one furnace was the notation "abt. 40 Miles to Maryland a Town called Baltimore." Land carriage of pig iron to Philadelphia cost one shilling per ton mile. The iron ore must be carted from one half mile to twenty miles. "Raising" the ore cost five shillings per ton. One and one-half to three tons of ore made a ton of pig iron according to quality. A load of "cole" consisted of 144 bushels. The charcoal was carted from one to seven miles. The furnaces employed an average of twelve men, who received fifty shillings per month, but the founder or foreman was paid five shillings per ton extra. They were in blast roughly from April to November of each year, during which time they turned out from sixteen to twenty tons of pig iron per week, or from 700 to 800 tons per year. Only two of the questions put to him by the Browns did John Relfe leave unanswered. One asked the cost of coal per load delivered at the furnace; the other, the value of the ore in the "Bank before raised (or in its Natural State)."[16]

Allowing for certain differences between New England and the Middle Colonies, the substance of the material from Philadelphia was relevant to the Browns' project. Forewarned by the tested experience of the Pennsylvania producers they could go into the iron business with their eyes wide open and with positive criteria and standards for judging their own progress. Here was another example of the extent to which local barriers were breaking down in colonial America a decade before the Revolution. Men in one colony were well informed about developments in another. Ideas and information, as well as goods, flowed freely across colonial borders. Of course the Browns were fortunate to have a correspondent like Relfe to expedite the process.

The data from John Relfe arrived close to the time the trial of the Cranston ore was in process at the Furnace Unity in Cumberland. On July 28, 1765 Stephen Hopkins wrote Nicholas Brown and Company: "Yesterday I was at the Furnace . . . Last night they began to feed, and tomorrow will begin to Blow. There is Wanted 20 or 30 yards of the Most Worn poor old Sail Cloath . . . for the use of the People to cover them from the Violence of the Fire. and Joseph Lapham wants a Barrel of good Molasses to make Beer for the People."[17] Six days later Nicholas Brown and Company wrote John Relfe "they were then upon trial of our iron ore which we find will be good, though not quite so rich as the ore your way."[18]

Once the quality of the ore had been demonstrated to their satisfaction, the partners quickly laid their plans for the building of the furnace. The first question requiring a decision was that of the location of the "works." The governing consideration, of course, was proximity to iron ore, stone, wood, and water power. The site finally chosen as the most desirable was not included in the area covered by the agreements with Burlingame and the Pages. On August 9, 1765, Joseph Remington, of the town of Scituate, in return for "one Mil'd Dollar In Hand" gave to the partners a "Good Dead or Lease of about three Archors of Land for there use for Iron works with free Priviledge of the River."[19] At about the same time Thomas Collins, also of Scituate, relinquished title to a small tract for the same purpose. Hope Furnace was to be built on this land at a point a "Little Southward of . . . Collins' Bridge upon the . . . Pawtuxet River, a little below a place called the Salmon Hole in Scituate in the County of Providence."[20] An important element in favor of the particular site was the reasonable price asked by Remington and Collins. In contrast to the "one mil'd dollar" paid to them, one James Matheson had tried to obtain 100 dollars plus a yearly quit rent of four dollars for a nearby two-acre tract. The spot selected was four miles from the ore beds, and separated from them by a rather formidable ridge over which the ore must be carted. But

John Relfe had reported that ore in Pennsylvania was carted as far as twenty miles. A distance of a steep four miles could not be considered a handicap in Rhode Island.

A careful reconnaissance of adjacent timber resources had been made before the furnace was finally located. The copartners had interviewed no less than thirty-two landowners within a narrow radius of the spot contemplated for the structure. They had asked these men what it was worth to them to have the furnace located near their farms. They may have painted a glowing picture of a thriving industrial center springing up around the new furnace, with land values rising rapidly. But they did not ask the farmers to buy shares of stock or make any cash payments. A monetary contribution of any sort would have been out of the question for most landowners of colonial Rhode Island. The furnace owners did stress the fact that a furnace could not be built without timbers, and that it could not be operated without charcoal and stone. The direct question, then, was how many cords of wood would each farmer in the vicinity contribute if the furnace were near his land. The thirty-two men, it was hoped, would answer this question to the entire satisfaction of the managers.

On August 10, 1765 the copartners incorporated these ideas in a document which they circulated among the landowners for their signatures.[21] The subscribers "being Desireous of Incouraging so Useful an Undertaking and more particularly to Induce said Hopkins & Associates to erect the Said Works at the place aforesaid" agreed to "Furnish and Supply the Several Quantities of Wood to Each of our Names Set, Gratis." In other words, the landowners agreed to donate the wood on condition that the furnace be located on the "Salmon Hole" of the Pawtuxet River. The only "Priviledge" the signers asked of the copartners was that of "Cuting Carting or Coling the Said Wood on the Same Terms as other People will do it for." Should they not "cut, cole and cart at Such Times and So Offten" as the furnace proprietors might require, the latter would be free to "Imploy who they please." They further promised that the wood subscribed "Shall Lay within the Distance of Two miles" from the furnace. Should it be at a greater distance, they agreed to "Cart it at the Same Price as is given for Two Miles Distance." Their final promise was "to furnish and Supply the Said Owners with as Many Stones as shall be Wanting for the Building, Waterworks, etc. as they Lay on Each of our land Gratis."[22]

A safeguard which took the form of a threat was added later. There was a real possibility that the total subscription might fall short of expectations. Four days after the original document was drafted the property owners were told that if they subscribed five thousand cords of wood within a radius of two miles, together with a sufficient quantity of timber and stones, "with the proper rodes laid out Direct to the Place," the furnace would be located at the Salmon Hole.[23] But should the men default on their subscriptions in any respect, it would be built elsewhere. This threat, so prophetic of the methods employed by railway promoters of a later day to make or break towns, appears to have brought the desired results. Subscriptions of wood were satisfactory as individual landowners made donations which varied from twenty to thirteen hundred cords within the proscribed two-mile radius. The owners had cleared another hurdle on the road to the launching of Hope Furnace.

There was a sharp contrast between the iron plantations of Pennsylvania and the very slender landed estate on which the Browns and their associates projected Hope Furnace. In the former the acquisition of larger tracts of land with the necessary iron ore, timber, and water power seems to have presented no great difficulty. The Browns, however, were seeking to develop the iron manufacture in close proximity to the town of Providence, in an area long settled, with much of the land already under cultivation, and with much of the timber already destroyed. The problem of procuring an adequate supply of wood for charcoal, therefore, was one which greatly exercised the ingenuity of the promoters of the furnace. Their arrangements with the farmers for cutting, carting, and burning the wood were absolutely essential. Had the farmers understood that fact, they could have exacted a high price for these services. Later the company bought farms in order to obtain wood, but on these the timber must have been partially depleted. At no time in its history did the furnace possess a large or an assured backlog of timber. During one of its busiest periods it had but "75 Acres of Wood Land." In no respect did the furnace proprietors display their entrepreneurial ability to greater advantage than in their maneuvering to obtain an adequate fuel supply for an industry located in the midst of a settled agricultural community.

While negotiating for the necessary fuel, the copartners were making plans to build a "New House" at the furnace site. One Job Manchester was to occupy the house as soon as the chimney was completed and to continue there for one year. He was to provide lodging, board, and washing for all the men the owners "hath amind to put in said House not Exceeding Twenty . . . at any one time." For these services Manchester was to be paid by the proprietors at the rate of seven shillings lawful money per week for each man, payment to be made in molasses, rum, sugar, salt or any other goods "that the said Manchester wants" and that the owners "can get . . . at the common Merchantable Truck Price in Providence." He was also to have the use of the new "Dwelling House . . . Excepting Two Rooms only," and to enjoy the "whole and sole Advantage of Retailing all the goods that can or may be Retail'd" at the furnace.[24] Under this arrangement, Manchester would retail the goods supplied him by the owners in return for the keep of the men employed at the works.

To men occupied with numerous other pursuits, as were the Brown brothers, it must have seemed that the building of the furnace called for no end of decisions about comparatively minor details. At a meeting of the copartners on October 1, 1765 they listed some of the "Determinations [which] Wair agreed to be executed as Fast as may be." Among them was a "Suffitient Stone Wall 5 Feet thick at bottom & Top [to] be Built from Each End of the Dam Down the River to Support the Ground on the Back Side of S^d Wall." They must decide on the location of the coal house and of the "well to be Dug." The strip of common land had to be laid out and the "Smith Shop" to be located. Should they buy the "Adams" farm and at what price per "Acor?" Should they employ all the men at the "Ditch" or should they "set some to Cut Wood?" The price of "Carting per Day" was to be set, the depth of the furnace foundation to be agreed upon, a complete plan for all parts of the furnace to be drawn, and the account for the experiment at "Furnis Unity" to be settled. Finally, they must arrange for "ye Bellows stuff which must not be neglected," and they must come to some agreement about the purchase of Edward Potter's farm.[25]

These joint "Determinations" were translated into action within the next few months. The owners gave one Edmond Johnson "Free Liberty to Erect a Blacksmith Shop upon our Land near S^d Furniss there to Have and to Hold as his own Proper Estate." His contract stated that should either party "take any Dislike after S^d Shop is Erected," the owners might take over the shop by reimbursing Johnson.[26] Subsequently Johnson did relinquish title to it upon the receipt of £230 Old Tenor from the owners. An agreement with Francis Brayton provided that he should do all the iron work that "may be wanting in building and carrying on" the furnace, including deck nails, hooks, staples, and the "heaviest" iron work, except "the bellows noses."[27] Jeremiah Lippitt was engaged to convert into charcoal all the wood he subscribed to the furnace project. For the "coaling" he was to receive nine shillings lawful money for every eighty bushels.[28]

As the work progressed the owners continued to draw upon skill and experience from sources beyond the confines of Rhode Island. Joseph Brown and Israel Wilkinson paid a visit to Salisbury, Connecticut, where there was a well-known furnace bearing the name of the town. There they arranged with Elisha Painter for the construction of "one Good Pair of wooden Furnes Bellowses . . . not exceeding Twenty Five feet for the Length of the Wood Work and five feet wide."[29] The copartners promised to have the necessary plank ready by February 1766, and to provide the bellows pipes and other iron work when needed. For his labor Painter was to receive £25 lawful money of Connecticut, and to "find himself" en route to and from Rhode Island, the owners "to find him" while he was engaged at the furnace. Painter expressed to the partners the hope that "your Plank will be well Seasoned for your Bellowses: Otherwise the Damage will Be great unto the oners thereof."

From the same Salisbury Furnace in Connecticut the owners obtained James Sturdefant to serve as founder.[30] Sturdefant agreed to bring with him a faithful workman who would make a suitable fireman. Founder and fireman were to be paid five shillings lawful money per ton for all pig iron made in the furnace; twelve shillings per ton for all iron prepared for potash kettles, and forty shillings per ton "for Moulding of all Open Casting." The iron might be "Run into any form the said Owners shall Direct, provided . . . the . . . Founder and Fireman are paid to as much Profit as though it was made into the Form of Common Pigg Iron." Sturdefant was to arrive at the furnace by March 20, 1766, and was to assist in laying the hearth, lining the same and "to do any other thing towards forwarding the Blast." The copartners considered themselves fortunate to have enlisted the services of Sturdefant as founder, as he not only understood "all parts of the Business of a founder," but also "had the longest experience of any man in America."

Having drawn upon the furnace lore of Pennsylvania and the furnace personnel of Connecticut, the promoters of Hope Furnace next called upon the mechanical skill of Boston. Although bellows pipes were then commonly made of iron, the partners believed they might be made more cheaply of copper. Accordingly, they submitted elaborate specifications to Martin Gay, a Boston coppersmith, with the request that he give them an estimate of the cost.[31] Their idea as to the comparative cost proved to be correct. Orders were placed with the Boston man to proceed with the construction of the copper pipes. The furnace was fast becoming an intercolonial project.

On December 23, 1765 the partners were again in conference with a full agenda under consideration. They authorized the cutting of 2500 cords of the wood donated by the owners of adjacent land.[32] This proved to be insufficient; so within a fortnight they ordered an additional 5000 cords, for the carting of which they would pay forty shillings Old Tenor per cord. They further planned to give public notice that they would pay "1½ Dolar" for every eighty bushels of "Good Merchantable Cole" delivered at the furnace, one-half to be "paid down In Cash" and the remainder in goods or cash in six months. At the same meeting the owners decided to contract for the carting of 200 tons of iron ore during the winter "on the best terms we can." They also arranged for "Proper Boards to cover the bellows house, tap house, casting house and cole house," and voted to build two "Compleat Carts" for ore and two for "cole," with two pairs of "cartwheels" to serve both for "cole & ore."[33]

By February 1766, plans for the building of the "works" were almost complete, as were arrangements for the delivery of the wood for charcoal and the iron ore for the first blast, which was to begin the following summer. But final plans must be made for the casting of hollow ware, which the partners planned to make a principal feature of the business. Here again sources beyond the boundaries of Rhode Island were tapped. At Bridgewater, Massachusetts, Josiah King was no longer operating his furnace. His hollow-ware patterns and flasks would be useful to the new enterprise. A man was sent to Bridgewater with instructions to obtain all the patterns in King's possession, and also to procure three or four hollow-ware moulders, a "Tapman," and a "good man for a gutterman." Within a fortnight the proprietors asked King for "patterns of other things usually cast in Furnaces." In fact, they could use "every kind of Pattern & Flask" belonging to King's furnace "that's not so much out of Repair as not to Answer the Purpose." They would omit none, "be it ever so Simple a thing if a good One of the Kind, as we Should not Chuse to have any Clumsy Ware."

From Joseph Washburn, Jr., of Bridgewater, and from Abner Lapham came information about the price paid for molding hollow ware. A furnace in Cumberland, Rhode Island, perhaps the Unity, provided a list of the prices at which hollow ware was sold at that furnace.[34]

On June 20, 1766 the owners wrote that the fire had been going for about ten days and that they would begin to "blow in about a Week." Attention must be given, therefore, to the completion of their labor force. Once again the call went forth to persons residing outside the jurisdiction of Providence Plantations. The furnace proprietors secured Paris Simmons of Middleboro, Massachusetts "to make moulds, Flasks, etc. before the Blast begins."[35] Naming seven molders of Middleboro and Taunton, who had been recommended to them, Nicholas Brown and Company asked Simmons to bring "these persons or Some others which you know to be good men to make a Sortment of Ware to the Number of Eight, besides Pot Ash Kettle Moulders, which we Desire you'l make application to & get them to come to the Furnace in a Fortnight from this time at Farthest." Referring by name to three men who had been recommended to them "for Tap & Bankmen,"[36] they added "we shall want 3 or 4 of these sort of Faithfull Men the best you can get," more of the "best & Faithfullest Colliers," and about six men to work as "under colliers." The partners would pay the wages of these men in any sort of West India or British goods, in any of the "Ware made in the Furnace" or in good pig iron at the cost price, and "Rather than fail will agree to give some Cash for Colliers."

First reports of the furnace at work were mildly favorable. On July 18 Moses Brown wrote to John, then in Boston, "they have made one Potash Kettle and are going on making Hollow Ware. The furnace is in good order but dont Increase making Iron." Two days later the third potash kettle had been cast "and it provs Sound"; the furnace was still going well and "makin Iron as fast as can be Expected." But this was not to last. Before the end of the month, Job Hawkins, one of the copartners, wrote that "the Furnace has been in a Very Likely Way of Stopping Ever since yesterday Break of Day." The founder had then "Discovered a very sudden alteration in the fire . . . all that Could be Done was Done But to no purpise. She Remains Still in Likelyer way to Stop than not." Hawkins added that "the Governor [Stephen Hopkins] is Very much Indisposed and all the Rest of us almost Tired out Not Resting any Since the Misfourtin Happened." A week later Nicholas Brown and his brothers received an appeal from Stephen Hopkins himself: "The Furnice hath not gone well since our last misfortune, and yesterday morning the Iron began to grow Slack the Furnace to work Stiff & both continue growing worse. Sturdefant alters with em, and the other workmen discouraged so that I am much Afraid of the consequences." Stephen desired, therefore, "Some of you to come up directly that all mảy be done that can be done. To say more is in Vain."

In spite of the difficulties, something more than a ton of hollow ware had been cast and carted to Providence. But it came "Down in Very Bad order." Nearly a quarter of the "Vessils" had "Hooles" in them, while many of the "Tea Kittles . . . has not Holles to put in the Bales." Whether this was the result of some defect in the ore, of faulty handling of the blast, or of lack of skill on the part of the molders was not immediately determined. And before the cause could be ascertained, labor troubles developed in one department after another. First to become disgruntled were the colliers brought in from the Taunton-Middleboro area of Massachusetts. Nicholas Brown was "very fearful of the consequences of their going away" but was powerless to prevent them. He felt that the utmost care must be taken with respect to colliers "or we Shall finally fail in the Grand Plan."[37] When the teakettle molders became disaffected, Stephen Hopkins advised a settlement with them to their satisfaction, "so that the bad impressions may be removed that Zechariah Whitman hath used every means to infuse into all the People here, and doubtless will exert the same Scandalous faculties to the full when he gets Home."[38] The shortage of both wood choppers and colliers became acute. Nicholas Brown, writing from the furnace, appealed to his brothers to "spair no pains to collect wood choppers & Colliers by Constantly applying to every Countryman that Comes in to Town."[39] There were fourteen men and boys chopping, "which by Calculation is not half enough." The need for choppers is something of a mystery, as the promoters had anticipated that the landowners who donated the timber would do the cutting and carting of the wood.

Although not all of these problems were solved immediately, the furnace appeared to be going somewhat better as the months wore on. In November it turned out two and one-half tons of pig iron within a period of twenty-four hours, and Nicholas remarked that it "would easily make 3 Tons if Could be prevailed on to Blow as hard as they might."[40]

After this inauspicious beginning, the owners of the furnace met again in the autumn of 1766. Far from discouraged, they readily agreed to raise 2500 dollars in coin. Two thousand cords of wood were to be cut "off our Adams Farm," recently acquired. To relieve the shortage of colliers, six good master colliers were to be employed at the "cheepest Rate they Can be Got for." The colliers were to do all but cut the wood and cart the coal. Israel Wilkinson and Caleb Arnold agreed to oversee the digging of at least one thousand tons of ore within two months; "Governor" Hopkins undertook to procure a "Rode Layd out streight from the Furnis" to the land on which the wood was to be cut. The price of pig iron at the "works" was fixed at 25 dollars per ton, with a dollar extra in Providence. Hollow ware was to be 50 dollars per ton at the plant, with the cost of carting added if sold in Providence. The owners voted to make 150 potash kettles and 2000 teakettles. Finally, they made provision for the construction of a second coal house, 45 by 90 feet, "in order with the Other Cole House to Contain all the Cole . . . Necessary to Continue the Blast Threw the Winter."[41]

At the termination of his contract, Job Manchester was not reappointed as manager of the furnace. His successor was Rufus Hopkins, eldest son of Stephen, who thus began a long career in that capacity.[42] As Rufus had been a sea captain, he naturally brought to the furnace no technical experience and no particular mechanical skill. His duties at the "works," therefore, were really those of business manager rather than supervisor of production of pig iron and hollow ware. He was to "cause a sufficient Quantity of Cole to be procured and brought to the Furnace," to obtain the proper "Quantity of Ore to be dug . . . as also Sand, Clay and every other necessary Material," to weigh and "pile up in Tons all the pig iron once every week," to take an account from each molder once a week "and to examine and receive his wares," and to keep "regular Books of Account wherein fair entries shall be made of every thing that shall be transacted in the whole Business of the Furnace." Although the owners were to pay

Hopkins for boarding and housing the workers, his chief remuneration would come from the "sole and exclusive Right and Privilege of Retailing whatever [goods] shall be sold at the Furnace."

Judging from the length of his tenure, Hopkins must have been a satisfactory manager. His chief weakness appears to have been a certain lack of decision with respect to furnace affairs, especially in the employment of workers. Nicholas Brown and Company were sorry to see in him "a Diffidence, and Too Much dependence on the Approbation of the owners before you Close Agreements with the Imployed or Contracts for What is Wanted as hereby Time is Delayed & the Business Consequently postponed."[43]

In 1767 the owners took other steps with a view to the more efficient conduct of the furnace.[44] To the "Eastward," meaning Massachusetts, they planned to engage "8 Tonage ware Moulders," together with a "Moulder of Bakepans." They agreed to pay colliers six shillings per hundred bushels, one-fourth in money, the remainder in goods. Molders were to receive money in the same proportion. Laborers and carters were to receive no more than one-fourth part money and "all possible Pains [were to be] used in getting the business done without any money." Six master colliers "with their gangs" were to be employed in coaling "and more if can be with Convenience."

In June of that same year, in the general interest of the firm, John Brown went on a mission to the "westward." As one of his commissions, he was to "Endeavor to procure an Experienced Founder to Come hither, and also an Experienced Refiner, and to Discover the Value of Piggs to Ship hom." The "westward," of course, meant the iron producing colonies of New Jersey and Pennsylvania. John was to find a founder to replace James Sturdefant, who had not been too satisfactory, even though he was reputed to be the founder with "the longest experience of any man in America." At East Greenwich, Rhode Island, John tried unsuccessfully to interest young Nathanael Greene in the purchase of Caleb Arnold's one-sixteenth part of Hope Furnace. From Lime, Connecticut, he wrote to his brothers saying that it would be well "to advertise nearly the time we begin to blow." He particularly urged them to mention "Iron Keels for Boats," experiments for which "has bin made & answers the intent Exceeding well." He said he mentioned it "coming over the Ferry in New London and it was immediately observed to be a Fine Invention and Doubted not but would become Very Common."[45] It was characteristic of John to be looking ahead to new worlds to conquer before he and his associates in the infant furnace had mastered even the simple technique of making pig iron.

By June 11 John was at Philadelphia where the search for the founder began in earnest. He addressed a letter to "Mr. William Hick" at "prince Town," who seems to have been recommended to the Browns by the Reverend James Manning, President of the newly established College of Rhode Island, as "a Compleate Master of the Iron Business."[46] John explained that he came from Providence in New England to engage "such a Gentleman" to oversee a furnace and the "Building and working of a Forge." He said that the company in which he was concerned "has now Got a Compleate Furnace (perhaps the largest in America)." John hoped to hear from Mr. Hicks, either in writing or in person during the several days he expected to be in Philadelphia. "But," he added, "if I do not here from you within the time above mentioned I shall go to most of Furnaces in this province to procure a proper person." Mr. Hicks did visit John in the Quaker City, but after the interview John wrote his brothers that "its doubtfull whether he will do as we must have a founder besides him he not pretending to do any Labour & to have him & Capt. Hopkins both to be over Seears maint Answer."[47] On June 20 John wrote that he had not yet heard of a founder, but that within a few days he would set out for the "Furnaces to the westward and Northwestward of this City and from them Strike over in the Jerseys & go to them in that Province."[48]

One of the places visited by John Brown on this pilgrimage into Pennsylvania was the Elizabeth Furnace in Lancaster County, owned by Henry William Stiegel, commonly known as "Baron von Stiegel," the ironmaster, glassmaker, townbuilder," whose eccentricities and baronial style of living have given rise to so many stories, real and fancied. Stiegel, a native of Cologne, Germany, had arrived in Philadelphia in 1750. In 1758, in company with Charles and Alexander Stedman of Philadelphia, he purchased the furnace of his father-in-law in Lancaster County and named it Elizabeth.[49] From a visit to England in 1763-64 he returned with skilled glassmakers whom he employed in a glass manufactory which he erected at Manheim, the town he had built near the Elizabeth Furnace. To later generations he is better known as the maker of the beautiful Stiegel glassware than as ironmaster. Nevertheless, it was Baron Stiegel, proprietor of Elizabeth Furnace, not Stiegel the glassmaker, upon whom John Brown called on that day late in June 1767.

At Stiegel's Elizabeth Furnace John found the man he wanted. He engaged one Jacob Shower "to set out tomorrow morning" for "Furnace Hope," where he was to work "in making pigg Iron, potts, kittles, Hammers or any other Castings." For his work Shower was to receive compensation at the rate of five shillings Philadelphia currency for every ton of pig iron; ten shillings per ton for all iron run into pots, kettles, or other closed castings; fifteen shillings for all forge castings such as hammers or anvils; and forty shillings per ton for "all open Castings which are Ladled." John advanced to Shower twenty pounds Philadelphia currency, for which he took a "Receipt from Mr. Henry Wm. Stiegel to Repay it in Case the s^d Shower should not go to Said Furnace." The agreement, to which Shower subscribed with his mark, was witnessed by Baron Stiegel. The fact that Stiegel gave the receipt for the money advanced to Shower suggests the probability that the latter may have been one of Stiegel's indentured servants.[50] John's visit to Pennsylvania and his successful negotiations there continued the pattern of business interchange between that faraway colony and Rhode Island. Hope Furnace had been launched against the background of Pennsylvania experience. Jacob Shower, the new founder, would now add the skills which he had acquired with one of the great ironworkers of the Quaker Colony.

But not even the magic of a new founder could make Furnace Hope a complete success in the summer of 1767. Many were the difficulties encountered that year which were more than a match for the collective experience and ingenuity of the owners and their employees. The furnace was still in the experimental stage. Proper techniques and procedures were being perfected slowly and painfully through trial and error. Founders and other workmen borrowed from other furnaces were making the disappointing discovery that the bog iron of Rhode Island, when subjected to the charge and blast of a furnace, did not react in precisely the same manner as did ore in Massachusetts, Connecticut, or Pennsylvania. Indeed they seem to have found that ore mined within a narrow radius of Furnace Hope varied sufficiently to justify the use of the terms "Cranston ore" and "Scituate ore." They had to discover the proper proportions of each type of ore; whether scrap iron should be used; whether the charge and the blast should be increased or decreased in unison or separately; and whether "lump ore" should be "pounded without burning." Only a repetition of experiment could give the correct answer, and experiments took time.

Several weeks after Shower had taken over as founder, Rufus Hopkins wrote to the Browns: "We had a Casting at 4 P M this Day and find the Iron as bad as has been at any time for this week past. What few Vessels that Com hole flew all to peaces in Cooling. I don't find any Liklyhood of the Iron being any Better without Some body moor Capable of giving Direction than aney body her." He quoted Paris Simmons as saying that for "Hollow Ware the Charge is to Light and the Blast too Strong." He found that Jacob Shower, the new founder, "dont Care to follow aney advice, but his own Judgment . . . The General Oppion of all the molders and fireman that Pretend to know anything about a furnace is that the Charge is Vastly to Light for the Blast." The new founder was off to a bad start

Silhouette of Moses Brown.

Silhouette of Nicholas Brown.

Mansion designed by Joseph Brown for his brother John. Built in 1787.

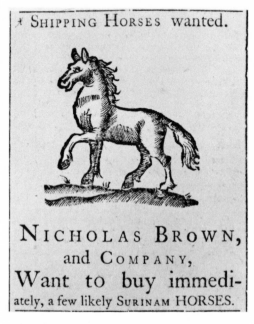

Advertisement of Nicholas Brown & Co. which
appeared in the Providence Gazette, *1764.*

*Label, engraved by Nathaniel Hurd of Boston, used on boxes of spermaceti
candles manufactured by Nicholas Brown & Co.*

The College Edifice and President's House, College of Rhode Island (now Brown University), circa 1795.

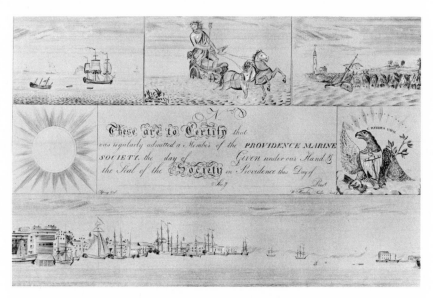

View of the Providence water front, circa *1795*.

"*A Surinam Planter*," *from J. G. Stedman*, Narrative, of a five years'
expedition, against the Revolted Negroes of Surinam *(London, 1796)*,
engraved by the celebrated William Blake.

if both the manager and the workmen lacked confidence in his ability and judgment.[51]

Four days later Hopkins continued his protest: "Iron Continues as bad as has been at any time for Hollow ware." He suggested that Simmons be allowed to take charge during the hollow ware blast.[52] After weeks had passed without any appreciable improvement, the owners wrote that they had fully considered "the present order of the furnace and are unanimously of the opinion that the present slow method of making iron without more moulders will not answer." But they did not accept Hopkins' suggestion about Shower. Instead they directed him "to give Showers the full and absolute command of the furnace as a founder in all its parts and that you assist him in his orders, to see that they are fully obeyed as to charge, blast, etc. in order to make as many piggs as possible."[53]

For the next several months the results were alternately better and worse. In one period of seventy-six hours the furnace turned out seven and one-half tons of iron. Steady production at this rate would mean an output of approximately sixteen tons per week. Such a rate would compare favorably with the sixteen to twenty-four tons produced in Pennsylvania furnaces.[54] During another eight-day period the furnace actually produced eighteen tons.[55] And later in the autumn within seven days there was an output of fourteen and one-half tons of pigs particularly good in appearance.[56] But a week later Hopkins sent the doleful report that "We have Daily Decreast in the Quantity of Iron maid the Week past."[57] More bad news soon followed. Just before Christmas, Paris Simmons, in charge of the hollow-ware department, came to blows with Shower, the founder, who "happened to be a good Deal in Liquor." This incident strengthened Hopkins' conviction that the Pennsylvanian was not the man for the job. "If aney of the owners Could spare the Time to Come up for a Day or two it might be of service," he wrote. "I thing [sic] the affairs hir are managed but very indifrantly at Present and see but Little Prospect of there Mending."[58] Early in February 1768 the furnace was "in greater Distress than has been the Blast." Those on the scene were unable to determine whether the difficulty was owing "To the Sand that is amongst the bad Coals or in the Flux as the Sinder is greatly altered Since we put Lime Stone for the Worse . . . have sent for a few shells . . . by which hope to find whether it is owing to Lime Stone or not."

Persistent labor troubles went hand in hand with technical problems. It still was difficult to keep enough woodcutters on the payroll. On occasion the "choppers are in number between 30 & 40 every good day, Sunday not excepted," but more often the number was quite inadequate. The Labor force in other departments was also erratic: "the Molders are all apacking up to go off together as they seem to be fully convinced that it

is out of the Power of Mr. Showers to make the Iron fitt for their Youse."
The division of labor between whites and blacks created tension. The
owner of a Negro slave, serving as "overseer of the Blacks" at the ore beds,
complained that, after the Negroes had "uncovered" the ore, white men
were allowed to dig it, which he thought was "Ill usage." But the slave
owner added incidentally that he had permitted his Negro, "Sharper," to
work in the mine "on the first day of the week" because he believed it
might be the means of keeping him "out of mischief as there is but few
negros troubled with Religion and no first days to furnaces."[59]

The second blast of Furnace Hope approached its end in the late winter
of 1768. Although the results were not entirely pleasing, there had been
a decided improvement over the blast of the previous year. In some weeks
the output of pig iron had been excellent, judged even by a rigorous standard. Furthermore, the owners had learned from the very failures of the
furnace. They had finally accepted that fact that Jacob Shower, the founder,
was not the ideal man for his position, and they allowed him quietly to
fade out of the picture, perhaps because James Sturdefant, the original
founder, had reappeared before the end of the blast. He came back with
great confidence that he could overcome every difficulty and make the
furnace a complete success. Rufus Hopkins reported that "Sturdefant told
me last Evening that he is Sure by the Experience he had here last year
and by the Tryal now maid that he can make 21 tons per week with a
good Harth if he cant he would Ingage to having nothing for his Labor,
and he thinks a Hundred Ton per month might be maid."[60] Twenty-one
tons per week or "nothing for his Labor" was an alluring prospect. On
April 5, 1768 Sturdefant was reëmployed as founder for the new blast to
begin in June. He was to find "two good and able Firemen," while the
owners were to be free to "Imploy whom they Please as Moulders in the
Furnace for the Future." Sturdefant was to be paid at the rate of five
shillings lawful money per ton for pig iron, twelve shillings for closed
castings, and forty shillings for every ton of iron run into open castings
and "Moulded," one-quarter to be paid in cash, the remainder in any
kind of goods "that he may want." The owners agreed to find Sturdefant
house room, firewood, and one-quarter of an acre of land for a garden,
and to supply him with "Provisions and other Necessarys." These terms
were more favorable to Sturdefant than those of his first agreement. He
must have convinced his employers that he could produce the results
which he promised.

Along with a change in the technical management of the furnace there
were minor changes in ownership. Israel Wilkinson, Job Hawkins, and
Caleb Arnold disappear from the records of the business in which they
had collectively held a quarter interest. Caleb Arnold had from the first

been a nebulous figure in the enterprise, and Job Hawkins had been only slightly more active. Israel Wilkinson, however, had been prominent from the very beginning. He had been the only partner with technical knowledge and experience. Furnace Hope could hardly be the same without the "ingenious mechanic." The newcomer in the ranks of the copartners was Jabez Bowen, Jr.

The year 1768 marked a turning point in the history of the furnace. Until that year it had been the plan of the owners to build a forge as soon as the furnace was a going concern. John Brown had stated as much in his letter written at Philadelphia to "Mr. Hick of prince Town" in 1767. The same idea had been expressed in a letter by Nicholas Brown and Company to the firm of Welch, Wilkinson & Startin, in Birmingham, England. They told the English company that they were interested in a "Bead of Iron ore," lately discovered near Providence and had built a furnace in which they had made about "300 Ton" of pig iron, and were "about erecting a forge to manufacture the piggs into Barr Iron." As good workmen for "refining Iron" were scarce in New England, but were plentiful in the region tributary to Birmingham, the Browns asked their correspondent to find three or four "good workmen for refining of pigg Iron to come over to this colony as soon as may be and we will engage to employ them immediately upon their arrival." Should twice that number come it would be worth their while, "as there is a grate number of forges already built and many more now building, and but few workmen."[61] To a ship captain sailing for England at this time they had mentioned "refiners of iron being very difficult to be got," and asked him to endeavor to secure three or four such men for them. And they had written to Sherwood, the Rhode Island agent in London, in much the same vein.[62]

But no workmen came to Rhode Island as a result of these appeals, perhaps because Britain discouraged the emigration of such skilled artisans. The forge where they were to work at "refining ore" was never built. After 1768 the plans were abandoned. There was not necessarily any causal relationship between these two facts. Lack of skilled labor probably played some part in the decision not to build the forge. But the "grate number" of forges already built and the "many more building" must have been a more important consideration. Moreover, the furnace was not yet an assured success and the added responsibility of a forge might further retard its progress. Caution seemed to argue against expansion under these circumstances.

Until 1768, too, the owners had planned to make the casting of hollow ware a principal feature of the furnace business. They had assiduously collected hollow-ware patterns from the Taunton-Middleboro sector, and had gathered all available data regarding costs, prices, etc., of that branch of the business. They had asked their Nantucket friends to advise them about the potential market for such goods on the Island. They had instructed one of their ship captains to find out what could be done with hollow ware at the "Mount," and "which kind of iron vessels will sell best"; to find out the value of iron grates "and what quantity will sell"; to inform himself as to the "worth of sugar boilers by the hundred weight"; and to send them the dimensions and size of each, "that is the diameter, depth, etc."[63]

In the blasts of 1766 and 1767 the operation of the furnace had been largely geared to making hollow ware. During those two years substantial amounts of such goods were turned out. Consignments were sent to Nantucket, to Newport, to New York, to Boston, and to the West Indies. But in the main the goods were a slow sale. In some cases the reports came back that the markets were glutted with such ware, which seemed to suggest that the owners of Furnace Hope may have come a little late into the hollow-ware game. Henry Lloyd wrote from Boston that the

discouragements . . . the potash kettles labour under and the vast quantity of kettles on hand render them at present almost unsaleable at any price. The first kettles I have some hopes of selling but can't contract with Mr. Webb or any other person to take any sort of your ware. Webb tells me he has all the hollow ware from 6 or 7 works & has the supplying of them with what they want & gives no money.[64]

Perhaps a more important reason for the slowness of the sale had been lack of quality. In this connection Christopher Hussey, one of their Nantucket friends, had given the Browns a word of warning in the very beginning when he wrote that he would "not advise you to make run very largely upon either pots or kettles until they are proved, as many of our N. E. kettles will not stand the fire. Perhaps that may be the case with your ware."[65] The Browns themselves had observed to Rufus Hopkins that the breakage of hollow ware was greater at Hope Furnace than at any other which they knew. Faulty craftsmanship may have been partially responsible for the poor results. But unsuitable material was the major cause. By 1768, it was unmistakably clear that production at Hope Furnace should not be so largely devoted to hollow ware.

As the idea of the forge passed into the discard and hollow ware received less attention, the proprietors concentrated their efforts very largely upon the production and marketing of pig iron. In the blast of the summer of 1768 the difficulties which had plagued the furnace during the two previous years were largely overcome. The trial and error method had gradually given way to a more assured procedure. From that year to the outbreak of the Revolution, therefore, the problem confronting the proprietors was not how to make pig iron successfully, but how to market it to advantage. In the solution of the problem they showed zeal, energy, and imagination, and their efforts were rewarded with no small measure of success.

Since it was the policy of Great Britain to encourage the production of pig iron in the colonies and its export to England, it was logical for the furnace proprietors to look for markets in the mother country; it was practical, too, because of the chronic need of the northern colonies for a satisfactory form of remittance to Britain. As early as October 1766 one of the New York correspondents of Nicholas Brown and Company had suggested the idea of shipping pig iron to England.[66] He wrote that he was "surprised as you abound in Bog ore, that none of the furnaces to the Eastward have made a tryal to send piggs made of that ore to England as they are the sort that will answer best for air furnaces." He added that if his information was correct "they fetch almost the same price as mountain ore piggs."

Nicholas Brown and Company sent eight tons of Hope pigs to England in the spring of 1767. They instructed the captain of the vessel aboard which they were shipped to endeavor to dispose of the pigs to some person "concerned in having the same made up into Barr Iron." They asked him to enjoin "on the purchaser to give . . . a particular account how they work and how they are esteemed, what the value per ton for a quantity." It was their hope that the consignment might be sold partly to a refiner "and partly to be worked on air furnaces," that their suitability for both purposes might be known.[67] The captain placed the pigs in the hands of Vardon and Franklin, in London, extensive dealers in iron and steel products. These men, in turn, engaged one Benjamin Parker to make a trial of them. Parker reported that he had made an "Essay on the pig iron marked Hope both in our air and blast furnaces. Find it not fit for a founder as its extremely hard, but am of opinion it will do for a forge provided the piggs are made all alike as to texture." He found that "some of these piggs tried are harder than others, which apprehend must arise from want of care in charging the furnace . . . therefore would advise you recommend to the gentlemen to be careful in fluxing the iron ore."[68]

Common sense dictated that more than one experiment should be made; and it seemed to be equally the part of wisdom to have these experiments carried out in various parts of the country. Accordingly, on September 19, 1768 Nicholas Brown and Company wrote Henry Cruger, Jr., of Bristol, England, that they were sending him forty tons of pig iron, which they requested him to have assayed by different ironmasters with a view to discovering the purposes for which it was best suited. Henry Cruger could easily comply with this request, as he frequently had "large parcels of various sorts of pigg iron to dispose of and frequent assays made." He wrote that "if your piggs are of a tough good quality they will sell readily; if brittle 'twill be difficult to dispose of them even at the lowest rate."[69]

Henry Cruger sold the iron to five different "manufacturers" in England, one of whom took twenty-two tons, another twelve tons.[70] After a trial of the pigs, three of the men expressed the belief that they would probably be well suited to the needs of a foundry, an opinion exactly contrary to that of Benjamin Parker who had made a trial for Vardon and Franklin in the previous year. One wrote to Cruger that "could your friend send them of a dark & light gray & some mottled, would be more in esteem for making bar iron." Another said he found them "of a very bad quality and not worth £5 per ton." The summary of these reports which Henry Cruger sent to Nicholas Brown and Company was moderately encouraging. Cruger came to the conclusion that the quality of Hope pigs would "not do for Barr Iron by themselves, nor without being mixed with a much larger proportion of some very tough pigg." It was his belief that he could sell "what Piggs . . . you may in future send me" at five pounds, fifteen shillings per ton, as compared with the figure of six pounds the Browns had hoped to get. This opinion, combined with that received from Vardon and Franklin, prompted the Browns to write to Henry Cruger that they were "sensible our piggs suit the foundry very well and that different workmen make different estimates of their values for Barr Iron."[71]

Meanwhile, Nicholas Brown and Company had been exploring other possibilities of the English market. In 1767 they had made the firm of Hayley and Hopkins their London correspondent, and the following spring they sent a shipment of fourteen tons of Hope pigs to them. Hayley and Hopkins disposed of the consignment to Vardon and Franklin, who had tested the pig iron the previous year. As John Brown had been told on his journey to Pennsylvania in 1767 that "pretty good" pigs would sell for £6 per ton in London, the furnace owners had hoped Hayley and Hopkins would be able to obtain that price for the fourteen tons. In this they were disappointed, as the iron sold for only £5-17-6 per ton. But the Browns insisted that Hayley and Hopkins should not sell again under £6 per ton. During the next eighteen months the latter had little difficulty in obtaining the stipulated figure.

Not until August 1770 did sales at six pounds become difficult. At that time the arrival in London of fifteen tons of Hope pigs along with sixty tons from other sources depressed the market. Hayley and Hopkins wrote that "the buyers aim at taking the advantage of a large quantity being on sale at one time, but we shall not part with them under that price [£6] if we can help it." A month later they reported that they had "sold the several parcels of pigg iron at £6 per ton."[72] During the seven years preceding the Revolution the pig iron from Furnace Hope took its place alongside oil and potash as an important form of remittance to England. Proceeds from the sale of these products financed the purchase of the large quantities of British wares which Hayley and Hopkins sent to the Browns in return.

On this side of the Atlantic, Nicholas Brown and Company found various ways of placing their pig iron on the market. Once they had abandoned the idea of building their own forge, they began to negotiate with neighboring refiners of iron for the sale of Hope pigs. Among the prominent ironmasters not far distant from Providence was Peter Oliver, at Middleboro, in the Bay Colony. Oliver, a man of many interests, was a gentleman farmer of note, as well as a successful ironmaster. He is best known to history as the Tory Chief Justice of Massachusetts on the eve of the Revolution, and as the brother of Andrew Oliver, Lieutenant Governor of the same province.[73] In August 1768, the Browns wrote to Peter Oliver explaining that they had been concerned "in erecting a furnace at a great expense for the making of pig iron, and we now make such as we think very good for refining." Knowing that Oliver was largely interested in the "refining business," and assuming that he was "filled with that patriotic disposition of encouraging every useful manufacture of our country" (perhaps an unwarranted assumption with respect to one with Oliver's undoubted Tory tendencies), they hoped he would take some of their pigs on trial. Should the iron answer his purpose, they would agree to supply him regularly "on easier terms than . . . can be had anywhere else." Moses Brown and Jabez Bowen, "junior owners . . . in the Furnace," were to visit him and would furnish "any particulars" about Hope pigs. "Besides, Mr. Brown being a curious farmer will want to see your drill plough, and being informed of all your curious and useful improvement in husbandry."[74]

Peter Oliver's encouraging reply prompted the Browns to send him three tons of Hope pigs for trial. They remarked that "workmen this way have tried them who say they work as well as Mr. Livingston's but the yield we haven't had information about."[75] After the lapse of several months, Oliver wrote that he had at last made a "thorough experiment" of the pigs.[76] He thought that Hope Furnace was "drove too fast" to make a good yield. "But We apprehend the greatest difficulty is in the quality of your ore which I fear cannot be avoided. There is something in it that burns off the fewel irons very often so that we were obliged to put in new ones frequently, sometimes two in a day." Although the metal went very much to cinder, it made "as good bar iron as can be," and it plated well. Then Oliver conveyed the welcome news that he had also "slit the iron into rods [for nails] and it makes the very best of rods." This last bit of information was especially welcome to Nicholas Brown and Company because it came at a time when nonimportation was placing a premium upon domestic nails as opposed to those of British manufacture. Impressed by the evident inclination of the Browns to "promote the Iron manufacture," Oliver proposed that "if you have a mind to send 30 tons" of pigs "of not a worse quality than what you sent us we will give you 21 dollars per ton . . . and let you have nail rods in pay at five dollars per hundred, although we sell none under six dollars."

The Browns, in reply, pointed out that the adverse comments with respect to Hope pigs were applicable only to the white ones, "the gray ones yielding little cinder." They were unable to accept Peter's offer to buy the thirty tons of the white variety because they had none of that sort on hand. But they would be glad to send him three tons of the gray pigs if he were disposed to make a trial of them.[77] Oliver was willing to try them if that would serve the interests of the Browns, but he observed that there "are Forges around us from whence we have heard of their working."[78] He made a significant comment about the Browns' intention of carrying on the nail manufacture: "we could each of us promote our mutual Interests. For our own Parts we should gladly do any Thing to encourage the Iron Manufacture as we imagine it would be of universal Benefit." He could not see why the making of nails "may not be carried on here to equal Advantage as in Pennsylvania, where they make great Quantities."

But Oliver realized that there was a larger labor force available in Pennsylvania, and that wages were lower. To offset this disadvantage, he observed that although "their Labour is cheaper through the Number of their Foreigners, but how many idle Boys are there in the Colonies, whose Idleness might be exchanged for Industry?" In a sense Peter Oliver was anticipating Hamilton's idea of manufacture as a means of making the labor of children useful. Oliver believed that if the boys of New England could be put to work it would increase the labor supply in New England so that "we are upon equal Footing with others."

For the Browns' information, the "case of the Nail Manufacture" was developed in great detail. Oliver estimated that labor at one shilling Sterling per day could turn out nails at six shillings lawful money per thousand. "One hundred of Rods" would make seven thousand nails. An experienced hand could make one thousand nails per day. "We have," he said, "put everything at as high a Rate as we need to have done. In short it only wants Spirit to make it a profitable Manufacture."

Peter Oliver's arguments were effective. Nicholas Brown and Company decided to "make an experiment of it." In December 1769 advertisemnts for nail workers appeared in the *Providence Gazette and County Journal:*

Wanted, a number of experienced Nail-makers to work on Hire, or on the Day. Coal to be found gratis, and the Rods to be supplied and paid for in Nails. There being a great quantity of small coal suitable for a Nail Manufactory, at the Furnace Hope . . . a number of workmen might be usefully and advantageously employed . . .

In a few months they reported that "we have just now begun to make nails.[79] Have 2 men at it that make near 2 M 10^d nails a day & propose to learn a number of boys and keep the business going if it answers."

The Browns also persuaded Oliver to make an experiment of Hope pigs in the manufacture of iron hoops, and they found that the hoops "proved very good." They used the "greatest part of them" for "Guinne" hogsheads.[80] It was their plan to encourage the use of them in the whaling business "which this town has begun and is likely to do considerable at." They expressed surprise that iron hoops had never been introduced at Nantucket, "as we find by experience that the wooden hoops on the Blubber hhd will not stand a long voyage & very often cause as much leakage as would pay the extraordinary charge of iron hoops." Although three of the four Brown brothers had by this time foresworn the slave trade, they nevertheless asked Peter Oliver to convert some of their pigs into bar iron "fit for the Guinne market," the bars to be "neatly drawn" so as to make eight bars to a hundredweight of iron. Thus Hope pigs moved to Peter Oliver's iron works at Middleboro and returned to Nicholas Brown and Company as nail rods, iron hoops, and "Guinne" bars.

Peter Oliver was not alone in his esteem for nail rods made from Hope pigs. Nicholas Brown and Company shipped considerable quantities of their iron to Henry Lloyd, their Boston friend and correspondent. At a slitting mill in Milton, Massachusetts, Lloyd had the pigs made into nail rods, not for return to the nailery of the Browns, but for sale to nail makers in the Boston area. In August 1770, he wrote that "the iron made of your piggs proves the best of any for nail rods, slits the best and works the best into nails," and since the "non-importation scheme" was likely to continue to the next spring a large quantity of rods might be vended.[81]

Special arrangements were made with forgemen in many localities for the use of Hope pigs. Among these forgemen was Nathanael Greene of Coventry, Rhode Island, for whom Griffin Greene served as agent. On one occasion the Browns promised to deliver to Greene ten tons of pig iron on condition that he return to them bar iron at the rate of one ton for three.[82] By another contract, he made twenty-five tons of bar iron at the same ratio. This was but the beginning of an important traffic with Greene.

Silas Wood, of Middleboro, Massachusetts, sent the Browns forty-one bars of good refined bar iron which he thought they would find the "best iron that ever you had made out of your pig iron, and drawn in the most workman-like manner." He needed fifteen tons of their pig iron per year, which he asked them to provide.[83] Other forgemen habitually worked Hope iron with Livingston pigs and reported the mixture made better bar iron, more economically, "then either worked alone."[84] Winslow and Tilson, in the Bay Colony, agreed to take six tons of Hope pigs, mix them with other pig iron, and return to Nicholas Brown and Company two tons of good, refined bar iron.[85] The Browns themselves frequently exchanged their own pigs for those from other furnaces. They sent Hope pigs to James Obiel in New York in return for an equal quantity of Hibernia pigs.[86] And they agreed with Moses Ogden, "one of the partners with Messrs Edward and Wm Laight in Vesuvius Furnace in New Jersey" for a shipment of fifty tons of Hope pigs. In return, Ogden sent ten tons of Hibernia pigs, and paid for the remaining forty tons at the rate of £9-10 New York currency per ton, or £7-10 Rhode Island currency.[87]

Besides these outlets in New England and the Middle Colonies, Nicholas Brown and Company tried to develop a market in the Old Dominion. A report had reached them that Colonel Archibald Cary, later the author of the famous Cary resolutions adopted by the Virginia Assembly in 1776, had tried some of their pigs in his forge with successful results. On the basis of this report the Browns shipped to the colonel forty tons at the price of £5-10 per ton.[88] The next year they shipped another fifty-seven tons at the same price, payable in Virginia produce at the cost price, or in Colonel Cary's bar iron at the rate of one ton for two and one-half tons of pig iron. If he did not wish to take the iron on these terms, and if the captain of the vessel carrying it should be unable to dispose of it, the Browns asked Colonel Cary to ship it on their account to Bristol, London, or Hull in England.[89] But this trade with Archibald Cary was neither satisfactory nor long sustained, although the negotiations for payment continued for a long time. After a bill of exchange drawn by Colonel Cary had been protested, the Browns wrote that the "renewal of this protested bill with a good one and a punctual payment of the balance of £467-12-11 Sterling in the fall can alone restore that intire good opinion of your punctuality and ability which we before with the highest reason entertained of you." Evidently Colonel Cary did not care to restore himself to the "intire good opinion" of the Providence firm. For years he ignored all the urgent appeals for the liquidation of his debt.

But Nicholas Brown and Company were not content merely to have Hope pigs made into bar iron. They were strongly intrigued with the idea that their iron was well suited to the making of steel. Perhaps this notion was put into their heads by the arrival in Providence of a parcel of English steel which they were told had been made from pigs which they had shipped to Britain.[90] Although they could not vouch for the accuracy of the report, it was "well known that the steel came from the person who bought our pigs in London." If the quality of their pig iron justified shipment to England and its subsequent reshipment to Providence in the form of steel, how much more would it justify fabrication into steel in New England. As Dr. Benjamin Gale, in association with Aaron Eliot, was experimenting with steel manufacture at Killingworth, Connecticut, a shipment of three tons of their Hope pigs was sent to him for trial. After considerable delay, Dr. Gale wrote that he had made about sixteen hundredweight of steel from the iron; and he concluded his rather enigmatical letter with the hope that "some better method can be found out for Manufacturing it, as we Suppose it will make excellent Steel."[91]

Aaron Eliot continued the experiments with Hope pigs. He made steel from them and from other pig iron, but its quality was not such as to enable the Browns to sell it in competition with British steel. Nevertheless, they continued to believe that English steel sold in New England had been made from pigs which they had shipped to England. By an agreement of 1774 Nicholas Brown supplied Eliot with equal quantities of Hope and Hibernia pigs from a New Jersey furnace, from which mixture Eliot was to make steel.[92] Execution of the agreement was delayed, first by Eliot's illness and later because his workmen "armed themselves and went off" upon hearing the tidings of "the Battle of Boston." He finally sent some of this steel to Providence in June 1775. The success of this experiment was not put to the test. The increasingly critical political situation in New England at the time of the arrival of the steel diverted Nicholas Brown's attention to other things.

The colonial purchasers of Hope pig iron thus far mentioned were men engaged in the iron business in one form or another—as forgemen, proprietors of slitting mills, makers of steel, etc.[93] There was, however, one extensive buyer who was not himself an ironmaster, namely, Aaron Lopez, the Newport merchant who achieved such prominence in the dozen years before the Revolution. The pig iron traffic with Lopez began in 1768 when the Browns sent eight tons "to go aboard your ship" for London. This was the first of many such shipments. Within a period of seven days in the spring of 1769 there were three separate consignments of fifteen, thirty, and ten tons respectively.[94] Between October 18 and November 8 in that same year Lopez placed three orders for ten, four, and fifteen tons.[95] The following year within a period of seven weeks there was one shipment of twenty tons and two of fifteen tons each.[96] On two different occasions there were consignments of forty tons,[97] while shipments of eight to twelve tons were common. Sometimes Lopez's instructions called merely for delivery at his wharf in Newport; at other times he desired the iron before the sailing of his ship for London. Thus the Hope pigs which Nicholas and his brothers shipped directly to England were supplemented by other shipments passing through the hands of Aaron Lopez. Besides shipping the product of Hope Furnace to England on his own account, he sometimes freighted pigs to London on the account and risk of the Browns. On at least one occasion he purchased pigs for shipment to Kingston, Jamaica, whence he had a call for forty tons.[98] In addition to pig iron, Lopez sometimes ordered other products of Furnace Hope. On one occasion he desired two cast iron plates for the "use of iron screws" in his spermaceti works. At another time he wrote that Meyer Polock was to deliver to him an anchor weighing eleven hundred pounds, "which he tells me is to come from your works." In payment for furnace goods Lopez might proffer Jamaica spirits, flour, or European wares.

Undoubtedly the greatest single outlet for Hope pigs on either side of the Atlantic was in New York. There Peter T. Curtenius combined a general mercantile business with an extensive iron works. His air furnace, in which he fashioned a variety of metal products, required a regular supply of pig iron. Informed of the fledgling Furnace Hope by a ship captain in 1766, Curtenius wrote to the Browns asking them to send by the return of the skipper's vessel two or three tons of pig metal so that he might make a trial of it.[99] He gave a careful description of the "kind of metal" that would serve his purpose. "It must be of a dark dead grey without any white shining specks in it & the softer it is the better." Pigs available to him in New York sufficed for pots, kettles, cart boxes, bars, etc., but he wanted the sort "that will stand for chimney backs, stoves, forge hammers, & in short for all kinds of uses, because when we have it soft we can always make it hard enough with our jetts, scrapps & old stuff." Curtenius explained that he had once purchased a basin made at Hope Furnace, had broken it, and "found it grey, though it was Thin, from which I judge your metal will answer our purpose." As he would have need for at least one hundred tons a year, should the pigs prove suitable, his letter opened up an altogether pleasing prospect to Nicholas Brown and Company.

The sample which the Browns readily sent must have proved to be quite satisfactory. On July 3, 1767 they signed an agreement with Curtenius, Richard Sharpe, Thomas Randall, and Gilbert Forbes, by which they promised to deliver to the New Yorkers "Sixty Tuns of pyg iron of the Darkest Dead Gray kind within one year" at 25 dollars per ton, the iron to be shipped in consignments of about twenty tons at intervals of four months.[100] This shipment began a trade which continued unbroken to the Revolution, despite an occasional complaint from Curtenius that the Browns had included a few pigs "that were quite white," and infrequent protests from the other party that Curtenius was a little slow in paying for the iron.

Transactions for the year 1771 may be regarded as typical. On May 9 Curtenius wrote: "We have contracted with the Corporation of this City to make an iron fence round the Bowling Green, for which we shall want about fifteen ton of your best dead grey piggs, such as you sent last, which please to send us by the first opportunity."[101] Three weeks later he repeated this request and asked the Browns to send "us 15 or 20 tons more by Capt. Garver." Within a month he acknowledged the receipt of both of these shipments and pronounced them "the best we have ever had of you."[102] He therefore urged them to send by the first opportunity another fifteen tons "of the very same sort"; and he asked that they "lay by at your furnace all of that sort, for I reckon we shall want 70 or 80 ton more" within the next six months.[103] In view, therefore, of the eminently satisfactory character of these several consignments of Hope pigs, it seems pretty certain that the iron fence around the Bowling Green in Battery Park on Manhattan was made from the product of the Furnace Hope.

Early in 1772 Nicholas Brown and Company sent to Curtenius four consignments of pig iron, containing twenty, twenty, fifteen, and twenty-one tons respectively.[104] On another occasion Curtenius acknowledged the receipt of eighteen tons of Hope pigs, and remarked that he would take all the Browns had on hand.[105] The importance of this trade to the Browns is evident. They reminded Curtenius in March 1773 that the balance in their favor was £793 New York currency. At another time he owed them £560.[106] Sometimes Curtenius remitted in flour, sometimes in Russia duck, sometimes in bills of exchange, and sometimes in specie. On March 24, 1774, he shipped £187 in gold and silver.[107] In the main, however, in 1774 and 1775 he remitted in Hibernia pigs produced at the Vesuvius Furnace in New Jersey. This he did by the simple device of exchanging a quantity of these for an equal weight of Hope pigs. Thus on March 21, 1774 he offered to exchange one hundred tons of Hibernia pigs for an equal weight of Hope pigs, an offer which the Browns accepted.[108] On August 3, 1774 Curtenius acknowledged receipt of fifteen tons of Hope pigs; and he sent twenty tons of Hibernia pigs by the return of the vessel.[109] On August 28 he received twenty-seven tons from the Browns and sent twenty-one tons in return.[110] Thus Hope pigs passed through the hands of Curtenius to various refiners in the Middle Colonies, by whom they were probably worked with other pig metal, just as Hibernia and Livingston pigs were blended with Hope pigs by forgemen in New England. The Browns sold the Hibernia pigs received from Curtenius to refiners within their section of the country. [111] When, on one occasion they had taken fifteen tons more of Hibernia pigs than they had contracted for, Curtenius agreed not "to send any more . . . to any body in your place until yours are sold."[112]

The outbreak of war in 1775 brought to an end an era in the history of Furnace Hope. During the war it was devoted chiefly to the casting of cannon, a use of which the proprietors had hardly dreamed when they launched the enterprise in 1765. This new phase in the life of the furnace forms a part of the record of the Brown family in the War for Independence.

From the point of view of the number of men employed, Hope Furnace was for its time a sizable concern. If we add to the thirty or forty wood choppers, the carters and coalers of wood, the diggers and carters of ore, the molders, the tap and bankmen, the founder, the firemen, and the carters of pig iron, it must have had a labor force of some seventy-five men.

As ironmasters the Browns had shown a nice regard for the realities of their situation. Realizing that forges were numerous in their section of the country, they abandoned their original plan to do their own refining of their pig iron. They began the furnace with ambitious plans for the hollow-ware business; but they early sensed the fact that success for them lay not in that phase of the iron manufacture. Accordingly, they were content to concentrate upon the production of pig iron, which they were able to sell freely in the markets of both Britain and the colonies. Had they elected to pursue the hollow-ware branch they would have been entirely dependent upon the colonial market which they were late in entering.

From small beginnings, on a limited area of land, the furnace owners achieved a degree of success which must have compared favorably with that of other ironmasters of the period; and it was attained without jeopardizing in any way the position of preëminence which the Browns enjoyed in the spermaceti candle manufacture.[113] Their prominence in the two industries, at one and the same time, goes far toward stamping them as among the most conspicuous families of their time in the field of manufacture. Indeed, it may be said that they had come to think primarily in terms of manufacture; their commerce was increasingly conditioned by the needs of the candle and iron business. A major purpose of their Caribbean and intercolonial trades came to be the procuring of good bills of exchange and specie with which to pay for the raw materials of their candles and the wages of the workers at the furnace. And the pig iron produced at the latter provided them with one of their chief forms of remittance to England, once they had entered extensively into the importation of goods from that country.

CHAPTER 7

"Settled Correspondents in the Neighboring Governments"

WRITERS have disagreed sharply as to the extent of commercial relations between and among the continental colonies of England in the eighteenth century. Some tend strongly to minimize this intercolonial traffic; others believe the amount of such intercourse was substantial.[1] In the most recent work touching upon this question the author takes a position intermediate between these extremes. Although he recognizes that there was considerable trade across colonial boundaries, he nevertheless concludes that the subject of his investigation—the Hancocks of Boston—maintained far closer relations with Britain and the West Indies than with Newport, New York, Philadelphia, Baltimore, or Charleston.[2] Their intercolonial contacts were primarily with village and country storekeepers in New England rather than with leading merchants in the larger commercial towns of the colonies. Whether the Hancocks in this respect were typical of the mercantile fraternity generally, or even of the merchants of Boston, is a question which can be answered only when the papers of many business houses have been carefully examined.

Close and constant as were the ties of the Browns with the Caribbean area, their contacts with the leading seaports of the continental colonies were no less intimate and vital. The ease with which they were able to borrow ideas and personnel from other colonies for the purposes of Hope Furnace suggests that they possessed a wide acquaintance with persons and conditions beyond the boundaries of Providence Plantations. This acquaintance was no mere accident. It was the result of the stern realties of their situation. They lived in a colony where hard money was a rarity. This condition, from which Rhode Island undoubtedly suffered more acutely than did its neighbors, was chiefly caused by that "deficiency of its natural produce," so much emphasized by the Rhode Island Remonstrance of 1764. Huddled closely about the shores of Narragansett Bay, with a severely limited hinterland, and blessed with no important staple product, the people of Rhode Island were hard put to find articles for export. Denied the forest products and fish of Massachusetts Bay, and the flour and provisions of New York and Pennsylvania, Rhode Island merchants must first largely import the articles which they subsequently reëxported in raw or processed form. The flour, beef, pork, fish, and lumber for a West India voyage came chiefly from outside the colony, and in the process of assembling such a cargo there was little opportunity to retain hard money.

For the Browns, this dearth of gold and silver in Rhode Island was the more serious because of their extensive concern with the manufacture of spermaceti candles, a business which called for the outlay of considerable amounts of specie. With head matter in short supply, the Nantucket whalers enjoyed a privileged position in which they could demand gold, silver, or "good" bills of exchange in payments to them. To the Browns the laying in of the annual supply of head matter was of prime importance; and the problem of paying for it constantly exercised their "skill and invention." They planned their navigation to the West Indies with this in mind, and they instructed their ship captains to return the "overplus" of their cargoes in bills which would be acceptable at Nantucket. But the funds thus obtained were rarely if ever sufficient to square their accounts.

Writing to a New York firm Nicholas Brown and Company explained that they carried on the "Spermaceti Manufactory" and were largely concerned in "Navigation." Living in a "colony where we have but little gold and silver passing," they were "obliged to have settled correspondents in the neighboring governments."[3] To these, they said, "we ship spermaceti candles, oil, rum, molasses, etc. in order to raise hard money without which the spermaceti business cannot be carried on." Expressing the same idea in terser form to their friend Tench Francis, they lamented that "the inconvenience of our being obliged to raise hard money from our neighboring colonies to carry on our business is very great."[4]

That the Browns were not exaggerating the stringency of hard money in Rhode Island is shown by their inability to procure it in Newport. If Providence was a fledgling commercial town, that was not true of Newport, then one of the thriving maritime centers of colonial America. It commanded the entrance to Narragansett Bay. It was visited by most of the ships bound to or from Providence. It abounded in merchants as successful and prominent as those the Browns sought elsewhere as agents. The Brown family maintained commercial relations with most of the important mercantile houses there. Why could these houses not supply the Providence firm with the necessary amounts of hard money or good bills? The answer is that, unfortunately, their business was cut to the same pattern as that of the Browns. Their economy duplicated that of the Browns.

They, too, lived in a colony with "but little silver and gold passing." They also suffered from that "deficiency of its natural produce" which the Rhode Island Remonstrance suggests was such a handicap to the colony and its people.

Trade with Newport did little to relieve the shortage of specie and good bills under which the Browns labored. Aaron Lopez, Joseph and William Wanton, and Benjamin Mason were fairly typical of their mercantile connections in that town. The sale of pig iron to Lopez brought some little remittance in hard money or bills; but most of their trade with him was on a barter basis. Lopez was glad to receive cables made in the Browns' ropewalk and anchors cast in Hope Furnace in exchange for English goods.[5] The two houses might exchange broadcloth for Irish linen.[6] The Browns might send 11 hogsheads of sugar "to be paid for in goods."[7] For a time they supplied Lopez with oil in exchange for merchandise. Although himself a candle maker, Lopez tried to procure Brown candles in exchange for goods, a request which was refused.[8]

Trade with the Wantons was much the same. They needed 30 or 40 barrels of oil for Jamaica, for which they would pay in molasses.[9] They proffered the same sort of payment for 10,000 feet of boards. They desired Guinea hogsheads to be paid for in English or West India goods.[10] For 500 pounds of cheese they wished butter in return. Although the Browns regarded candles as "a cash article," they were willing to accept West India rum or Jamaica spirits from the Wantons in half payment for a consignment of 10,000 pounds of candles.[11] Just what reply the Browns gave to a request for 50 boxes of candles, for the payment of which the Wantons had neither goods nor money, we cannot say.[12]

Traffic with Benjamin Mason was very similar to that with the Wantons. On October 31, 1763 the Browns asked Mason for 20 hogsheads of molasses, for which they would pay in candles.[13] In 1768 they offered candles in exchange for 100 to 150 barrels of sweet flour. Mason dealt constantly in Brown candles, taking some on his own account, selling some on commission for them. In neither case does the process seem to have been productive of much cash. Mason might purchase flour for the Browns, paying for it in rum or molasses, and receiving rum for the flour at Providence.[14] It was only an extreme financial emergency which prompted Nicholas Brown and Company in 1763 to ask Mason to sell his draft on David Van Horne of New York in order to raise for them the sum of £500 New York currency.[15]

Trade of the Browns with Newport seldom produced such amounts in cash. In the main they and the Newport merchants dealt in the same articles which they bartered chiefly with a view to obtaining a better assortment of goods for their stores and for use elsewhere. Before they be-

gan to import English merchandise on their own account the Browns procured much of it through this traffic. Obviously, their commerce with
Newport was incapable of providing them with the means of meeting
their obligations at Nantucket.

Constantly in need of hard money, and unable to procure it in Rhode
Island, the Browns had no choice but to develop close commercial ties with
Boston, New York, and Philadelphia. Other merchants of Providence
and Newport did likewise. As a result, in the decade before Independence
both Boston and New York maintained more constant and more intimate
trade relations with Rhode Island than with each other.

Had proximity been decisive, Boston would have been the seat of the
first of the "settled correspondents" of the Brown family. But from their
point of view, Boston had disadvantages which more than counterbalanced
its nearness. The products on whose sale, actual or potential, the Browns
expected correspondents to advance hard money to them were candles,
whale and spermaceti oil, molasses, and rum. As Boston was in the 1750's
an important center for the manufacture of spermaceti candles, it was not
a likely market for candles made in Providence. Like the Rhode Islanders,
Boston merchants were largely engaged in the West India trade and in
the distilling business. They were not, therefore, ideal customers for
molasses and rum. Boston was the leading mart of the oil trade. But the
sale of oil alone would not provide the Browns with the means of making
their payments at Nantucket. They must, therefore, have a correspondent
in a town where all of these articles were in demand. In the middle 1750's
Philadelphia seemed best to meet their specifications.

It was in 1756, shortly after their entrance into the candle manufacture, that Obadiah Brown and Company made arrangements by which
Tench Francis and Son became their correspondent in Philadelphia. For
the sale of New England wares consigned to them Francis and Son received a commission of 5 per cent. The Browns were then free to "draw
for the amount either in specie or produce." Whenever they had occasion
for a larger sum than "the amount of the goods shipped" they gave
"timely advice" to Tench Francis and Son from whom they always "had
the most exact compliance." On all sums advanced to them in anticipation
of sales of goods by their correspondent they paid interest at 6 per cent.
For all goods purchased for them in Philadelphia they allowed the correspondent the usual 5 per cent commission.[16]

In accordance with this arrangement, the Sloop *Charming Molly,* which
the Browns maintained chiefly for the coastwise trade, shuttled back and
forth between Providence and Philadelphia for the next several years.
Besides candles, oil, molasses, rum, and sugar, the staples of the trade, the
Browns sent from time to time sundry articles which they happened to

have on hand. These included packs of parchment skins or "Indian dressed deerskins" brought back by the Sloop *Speedwell* from her first voyage to New Orleans in the Seven Years' War, and surgical instruments, "iron three pound cannon," swivels and cutlasses captured from the French by the Privateer Brigantine *Providence* in the same war. The letter accompanying the invoice of goods shipped to Philadelphia ordinarily enumerated the articles which Tench Francis was expected to forward by the return of the sloop. A typical consignment to "the westward" might comprise 86 boxes of candles, 39 hogsheads of rum, and 5 hogsheads of molasses; or 19 hogsheads of rum, 1 hogshead of sugar, 63 barrels of sugar, and 39 boxes of candles.[17] A typical return shipment was 188 barrels of flour, 32 barrels of ship bread, 4 barrels of pork, 5 tons of pig iron, with small amounts of bar iron and cordage.[18] Before the opening of Hope Furnace, pig and bar iron were familiar items in the invoices from Tench Francis. And he supplied a substantial part of the flour and ship bread, as well as pork and butter, which the ships of the Brown family carried into the Caribbean. In the year 1759 Obadiah Brown and Company sent to Francis nine different consignments of goods which he sold for £5315 Pennsylvania currency.[19] From July to December 1764 he sold for them candles, oil, rum, cider, and potatoes to the amount of more than £3700.[20]

Of course this traffic with Tench Francis was important to the Browns as a source of numerous articles which they used in other branches of their trade. But its most vital function was to provide the hard money and bills of exchange so necessary in their business. They sent him goods of substantially greater value than those which came in return; and they received the balances due in specie or approved paper. Frequently shipments of specie accompanied the goods sent by Tench Francis. In December 1757, he forwarded an invoice for a quantity of merchandise, together with "one bag containing 267 milled pieces of 8/8." A year later a consignment of goods arrived in Providence with "one bag containing 667 Spanish Milled pieces of 8/8." An invoice of 1759 lists "2 bags containing 1600 pieces of 8/8 (amount £660)," and goods to the value of more than £400. In the same year the Browns wrote to Tench Francis, enclosing a bill of lading of an assorted cargo of goods consigned to him. They asked that he ship by the return of the sloop 160 barrels of flour, small amounts of ship bread, pig and bar iron, pork, rigging, two cables, and £800 Pennsylvania currency in cash, "gold if to be had."[21] The goods requested came to £718. Francis sent "£800 this money in silver," as gold was not to be had because flag of truce adventurers paid an "advance price" for it.[22] A short time later Obadiah Brown and Company shipped candles, rum, and molasses, in return for which Tench Francis was to send them 200 barrels of flour, together with pig and bar iron, beef, cocoa, white oak hogshead staves, and "£600 your currency in gold or silver." In June 1761 Tench wrote that he had sent by the Sloop *Victory* "two thousand Spanish milld pieces of 8/8." A year later he forwarded 1000 pieces of eight.

The transactions just cited involved the actual shipment in specie of balances due to the Browns. But frequently the Providence firm asked their Philadelphia correspondent to advance substantial sums for which he was not in debt to them. Thus in September 1762 they wrote that "we have some expectation that we shall want to draw on you this fall for about £800 or £1000 your currency & desire you'll acquaint us in your next whether its agreeable to you to advance it in case it is not due to us & charge no interest 'till paid you by remittance in goods, which we shall endeavor to do as soon as possible."[23] Francis replied in the affirmative. The Browns then advised him that they had drawn on him in favor of Silvanus Hussey and Company of Nantucket for £800.[24] On another occasion Francis reported to them that he had "supplied Mr. Gardner" of Nantucket with "£350 this money which we debit you with." In September 1765 Nicholas Brown and Company wrote that "the scarcity of money this way and the situation of our stock not bringing us money so soon this fall as we expected" prompted them to ask for the advance of £1000 or £1200. They assured Francis that he could depend on full remittance within six months after the advance of the money. Naturally they would prefer specie or "bills of exchange on England" but other bills payable at a short sight would be agreeable.[25]

Goods shipped by the Browns to Tench Francis were in most instances sold by him on commission to persons in Philadelphia and its environs. This was true even of whale and spermaceti oil. For a brief season in 1761, however, the two houses coöperated in the purchase and shipment of oil to Europe. They had dreams of diverting the bulk of the oil trade away from Boston. In view of the relative remoteness of Philadelphia from Nantucket, it was a bold undertaking for the men of that city to risk competition with Boston merchants in the purchase of whale oil for the trans-Atlantic trade. The first suggestion of this idea is found in a letter by Tench Francis saying that "we expect a vessel in every day which we should be glad to send to London, but can find nothing here to load her with. Therefore if you can send us 400 or 500 barrels of good white spermaceti oil and are willing to sell it for £3 we will take it."[26] The plan seems to have been to capitalize upon the Browns' proximity to Nantucket and Tench Francis' ability to command the necessary shipping. Within a fortnight Francis wrote that "we shall be very desirous to bring the oil trade to this place, but the risk would be great on account of leakage."[27] A few weeks later the Browns received instructions to buy 2000 barrels. As Francis was "extreme desirous to push the oil trade so that it may be brought through this channel," he engaged to procure them an exceptionally favorable price.[28] As the months passed his enthusiasm continued unabated. In September he was prepared "to give you the same price that it sells for at Boston, which must be a very advantageous circumstance to you." Meanwhile, Moses Brown was at Nantucket purchasing superfine Bank oil for which Tench Francis engaged to procure £16 Sterling per ton.[29]

This bold attempt on the part of the two firms to challenge Boston's supremacy in the oil trade was undoubtedly foredoomed to failure. It hardly made sense to purchase oil at that city's front door for shipment to London by way of Philadelphia. Such a procedure would have been particularly unwise from the standpoint of Nicholas Brown and Company. But at this time they had developed closer relations with Philadelphia than with Boston. They were quite willing to join in this attempt of Tench Francis to turn business in his direction at the expense of their neighbor in Massachusetts.

Details as to the outcome of the oil gamble are meager. But in September of the following year Nicholas Brown and Company commented upon the silence of Tench Francis "about purchasing oil which we suppose is by reason of your suffering with all others who shipped oil for England last year." They hastened to assure him though that the "business will be much better this year as there is not half the quantity got . . . as was last." Should he be inclined to "ship a quantity" they would do their "best endeavors to serve you in purchasing it."[30] Francis, however, showed no desire to burn his fingers a second time.[31]

Tench Francis and his partners rendered various other services to the Browns. He offered advice and counsel concerning business affairs generally. He kept them carefully informed on matters affecting their interests. He arranged for the writing of most of the insurance on their shipping. He handled their litigation in the courts of Pennsylvania and of England. And it was his partner, John Relfe, who gathered for the Brown brothers the information about the iron furnaces in Pennsylvania. Over and above his strictly business functions, for which he exacted commission and interest fees, the faithful correspondent, in his capacity as friend and adviser, performed many acts of kindness for his principal, for which he expected no compensation. In his old age Tench Francis could still recall with satisfaction the pleasant relations which had always prevailed between the two houses. Ultimately, his son married the daughter of John Brown.

Upon the withdrawal of Tench Francis and John Relfe from active business, it became necessary for Nicholas Brown and Company to find a new correspondent in Philadelphia. They chose Clement Biddle and

Company. But from the beginning of the correspondence between the two houses in 1768, the relationship wore a formal and restricted aspect never found in their dealings with Tench Francis. The Providence firm shipped only candles to Clement Biddle, who disposed of them at a 5 per cent commission, plus "a small storage fee," as the candles "take up room and rents are very high here." One month after the receipt of a quantity of candles Clement Biddle would "answer" the Browns' bill at ten days' sight, "or remit in such manner as you shall direct . . . whether they are then sold or not."[32] The one commodity purchased for the Browns by Clement Biddle was flour. By this time they depended largely upon their own Hope Furnace for iron. Beef and pork they now obtained elsewhere, as they did staves and rigging; cables they made in their own ropewalk.

Balances due to Nicholas Brown and Company were not settled by the shipment of specie to Providence as was so often the case when Tench Francis was the correspondent. Instead, the Brown brothers drew upon Clement Biddle to meet their obligations elsewhere. Although Biddle was never able to take the place of Tench Francis in the Browns' scheme of business, he continued as their agent in the Quaker City until 1771. By that time their connections in New York and Boston were such as to render a Philadelphia correspondent no longer necessary. Only after the Revolution had largely interrupted their relations with those two cities did the Brown brothers again have a "settled correspondent" in the Pennsylvania town.

The Browns had no such representative in New York prior to 1760, when Walter and Samuel Franklin became their agents in Manhattan. Their first consignment of goods to the Franklins consisted of 20 hogsheads of rum, 70 barrels of oil, and 60 boxes of candles.[33] The rum was a "dull" sale, but the oil and candles sold readily, which evoked from the Franklins the opinion that "a considerable quantity" of the two articles could be disposed of "if no other persons should not import them."[34] Within three months the Franklins made remittance by means of bills to the extent of about £500. As time passed the Browns consigned to their new agent only candles, oil, and molasses. In return the Franklins occasionally sent nails, pig iron, wine, cotton, coffee, bread, and bran, but the mainstay was flour which they shipped in large quantities. Again, balances due to the Browns were settled not by the shipment of specie but by bills of exchange or by orders on the Franklins to make payment to creditors of the Browns. In 1763-64 the two houses became involved in a controversy over commissions charged by the Franklins on goods purchased for the firm in Providence. Whether because of this, or because they found a more satisfactory correspondent, Nicholas Brown and Company had only the most occasional contacts with Walter and Samuel Franklin thereafter.

The new correspondent in Manhattan was David Van Horne, recommended to the Brown brothers by their friend Benjamin Mason of Newport. Explaining to Van Horne their need for a "settled" agent who could supply them with the hard money demanded by their spermaceti business, the Browns outlined the terms on which Tench Francis had conducted their business for the past seven years in Philadelphia. After expressing the hope that Van Horne would serve them on the same terms, they informed him that they were shipping "as an introduction 100 boxes of spermaceti candles and shall want by the return of the vessel two hundred pounds your currency in cash." [35] They added that they would have occasion for "one thousand pounds your currency" within three or four months, for which, if Van Horne were not "in cash of ours for goods sold," they expected to allow interest until replaced by consignment. It was their plan to keep candles constantly in Van Horne's hands, as well as "other goods according as we have them on hand and as they answer at your market."

David Van Horne was entirely willing to "undertake" the Browns' business for the commission which they customarily paid, but as the legal rate of interest in New York was 7 per cent, "at which any sums can be put out on the best security," he could not agree to accept a lower interest on money which he might advance on their goods. [36] The sale of candles seems to have been a new venture for Van Horne. He complained that the venders of them in New York were "constantly falling the price," a practice which he believed could be prevented by an agreement of the candle manufacturers to fix the price of candles. Such a procedure, he thought, would be completely logical in view of the fact that they had already placed a ceiling price upon head matter. Although the Browns were able within a month to advise him that the candle-makers had agreed upon a minimum price for candles, this action had not been inspired by Van Horne's suggestion. [37]

The correspondence of the Brown brothers with Van Horne could hardly have begun at a more inauspicious moment. The Seven Years' War was just coming to an end, leaving in its wake the depressed economic conditions which have usually accompanied postwar periods. The candles sent to Van Horne in the summer of 1763 sold with painful slowness. Although this fact in no way diminished the Browns' usual autumnal obligations at Nantucket, it did affect adversely Van Horne's ability to remit. Nevertheless, they drew upon him in favor of Nathan Fordham of Long Island, from whom they occasionally purchased head matter. [38] They also sent to Van Horne two bills of exchange drawn by Henry Lloyd on two gentlemen in New York, asked him to collect the £324 which these amounted to, and, in addition, to advance them £200 on the candles which were still largely unsold.[39] Thus they were requesting him to send them more than £500 in gold and silver within the course of a few weeks. These requests brought from Van Horne the observation that "silver and gold is become so scarce that it is a rare thing to meet with any and it will be attended with considerable difficulty to collect such a parcel."[40] The imperious necessity under which the spermaceti business placed the Browns is shown by their reply to Van Horne. They were sorry to hear that gold and silver were so hard to come by. They would gladly draw on him from New York currency (which he had suggested), if they had an opportunity. But, as they had none and were "much in want for the money," they urged him to send the amount in silver or gold.[41] They added that "if the hard money cannot be had without too much difficulty we expect you'll charge us with the common discount." But firmness was of no avail, as Van Horne found it impossible to obtain gold or silver in New York even at a premium. Having correspondents in different cities, the Browns were able to appeal elsewhere when they suffered a disappointment such as this. To their friend Henry Lloyd, of Boston, they wrote that they had never before found it out of their power to make the most punctual payment to their creditors at Nantucket. They therefore asked Lloyd to procure £450 for them by selling their draft on New York, by taking the amount upon loan for them, "or otherwise on the best terms you can."[42]

To Nicholas Brown and Company it seemed that the depressed conditions of 1763 were intensified by the Sugar Act of the following year. As they expressed it, "all business seems to wear a gloom not before seen in America," a view which Van Horne reciprocated when he wrote that he had never known "a time when money was so scarce and difficult to get."[43] It gave him concern that their two houses had begun a correspondence at a time when trade was "so dull and extremely declined." Nevertheless, business relations between them made headway in the dark year 1764. The Brown brothers sent molasses to Van Horne, receiving in return 250 barrels of flour, 25 barrels of beef, a ton of ship bread, and the definite promise of £500 to be forthcoming in the autumn.[44] Before the end of the year they had sent two large consignments of candles, from the proceeds of which Van Horne was to send them 100 barrels of flour and to pay £400 to one of their creditors.[45] They further requested him to send them a Sterling bill for £200, for which they were prepared to pay 7 per cent interest until he was in cash for their goods.[46] They were sure he could obtain such a bill with New York currency more easily than he could procure the hard money. The Browns closed the year by introducing Van Horne to the oil trade. Sending him large consignments of spermaceti oil and right whale oil, they explained that the former was "of the best kind for lamps."[47] And recalling that the street lamps of Philadelphia had been lighted with oil they had shipped to Tench Francis, they suggested to Van Horne that he approach the "lighters of the city & light house lamps." The right whale oil, they informed him, was principally used by the curriers of leather, by soap makers, and "in the West Indies for stills." In this fashion, the two houses managed to turn the corner in 1764.

From 1765 to 1773 inclusive, David Van Horne was one of the most valued of the correspondents of the Brown brothers. In their plan of business he played much the same role that Tench Francis had in the period 1756 to 1763. Thanks to his efforts, the New York market for candles expanded as that in Philadelphia declined; and he found that the candles made by the Browns grew steadily in favor within the city. As a further result of Van Horne's energetic conduct of affairs, New York completely supplanted Philadelphia as a market for the oil which the Providence house shipped to the "westward." Thus candles and oil became the staple articles on bills of lading sent to Van Horne. In return he supplied large quantities of flour, together with substantial amounts of beef.

As a result of these transactions, large balances remained in favor of the Browns. These Van Horne remitted in various ways. The record of 1768 is typical. It reveals the scope and importance of the business which Nicholas Brown and Company carried on with Van Horne. In February, the balance in their favor was £700.[48] They asked Van Horne to supply them with a Sterling bill for £400 for a firm in Birmingham, England. At the same time they enclosed William Richardson's bill on the Franklins of New York, which Van Horne was to present for acceptance.[49] Van Horne sent the Sterling bill for £400, the equivalent of £730 New York currency, and promised to send "the £500 you desire in gold and silver" as soon as he could collect it.[50] Less than three weeks later, he sent this amount in gold. In October he wrote that he had collected an additional £1000 in gold for them, and on the following day he forwarded to them a bill of exchange for £500 payable at Philadelphia.[51] In November the Brown brothers asked him to pay John Brush of Huntington, Long Island, an order on account of Christopher Hussey and Company of Nantucket.[52] A few days later they advised Van Horne that they would soon draw on him in favor of "Nantucket friends" for £400. In December they asked him to pay Nathaniel Marston of New York £330 New York currency for Rowland Chambers, Huntington, Long Island, on account of Christopher Starbuck and Company, Nantucket.

Throughout the period of the association of the two firms, the Browns' demands on Van Horne were numerous and varied. They might request him to pay Silvanus Hussey and Company, at Nantucket, £240 and charge it to their account. They might ask him to remit £300 New York currency to Samuel Smith and Son in Philadelphia.[53] In a typical letter they "desired" the advance of the value of 200 boxes of candles "on interest" until replaced. Advising Van Horne of a large consignment of goods sent to him, they asked him to send £300 in silver or "Joannes" by the return of the vessel; and they wanted a good bill of exchange for the net proceeds of the goods.[54] Through their trade at Surinam, Nicholas Brown and Company came into possession of Dutch bills of exchange in considerable amounts. This prompted them to ask Van Horne "the price of bills drawn in Surinam on Amsterdam," and "whether the hard money for 5 or 6000 guilders may be got."[55] On another occasion they enclosed two bills for 1000 and 700 guilders respectively, which he was to dispose of for their account. In the same letter they announced that they would draw on him within a few days for £130; and they desired £400 in silver "by Capt. Warner's return." Otherwise they would be obliged to draw bills on London at a considerable loss, they "being now 1½ per cent under par."[56] By one form of remittance or another, Van Horne supplied large amounts of the ready funds so essential to Nicholas Brown and Company.

The growing importance of New York to the Browns in the decade before Independence is attested not only by their ties with David Van Horne, but by the mutually advantageous business relations which they maintained with Peter T. Curtenius in the same city. As Curtenius purchased pig iron from the Browns on his own account, rather than selling it for them on commission, he was not, strictly speaking, one of their "settled correspondents." Nevertheless, he often made remittance in goods, bills, and specie; and as such he was almost as essential to them as David Van Horne. Probably in no other commercial center were there two men so vital to the Browns as were Van Horne and Curtenius.

Meanwhile, the Browns had long since acquired a "settled correspondent" in Boston, which they had once passed by in favor of Philadelphia and New York. Although they had dealt with numerous Boston merchants, it was not until 1761 that they selected there an agent to buy and sell for them "in a commission way." This was, of course, five years after Tench Francis had begun to conduct business as their representative in Philadelphia. Their first correspondent in the metropolis of the Bay Colony was William Hunt, to whom they consigned spermaceti candles in substantial amounts. Oil was conspicuously absent from their invoices to Hunt, as this was the time when the Browns were seeking, in coöperation with Tench Francis, to divert the oil trade from Boston to Philadelphia. Although Hunt purchased sundry articles for the Browns on occasion, he ordinarily remitted either in cash or draft. The account current of January 1, 1763, shows that Hunt had paid to John Brown £914 lawful money in cash and had honored a draft in favor of Silvanus Hussey and Company of Nantucket for £350.[57]

In 1762, while Hunt was still serving as their agent, Nicholas Brown and Company secured the services of Henry Lloyd in the same capacity. This marked the beginning of a business association which was to continue unbroken until severed by the War for Independence, in which Lloyd became a Loyalist. So successful was he in the management of their affairs at Boston that within a year or two he had taken over the complete management of the commission business of Nicholas Brown and Company there. Although annoyed by Lloyd's persistence in buying head matter for shipment to London, the Brown family always maintained the most amicable relations with him.

The most important article which Lloyd purchased for his principals was head matter, the raw material of the candle manufacture. In November 1764 he wrote that he had engaged head matter of Joseph Rotch and Company, Nantucket, to the "amount of your bills and other money in my hands."[58] The quantity was 27 tons. A week later he sent the invoice for 191 casks of head matter.[59] Within a fortnight he announced that he had bought 20 tons more from Rotch.[60] Before many days had passed he forwarded the invoice for another 142 casks of head matter.[61]

The Browns paid for this head matter in part by consignments of oil which Lloyd sold on their account. From 1762, when they and Tench Francis abandoned the attempt to divert the oil trade to Philadelphia, to 1767, when they began to ship oil direct to London, Nicholas Brown and Company disposed of much of their oil through Lloyd's commission agency. Sometimes Lloyd sold the "spermaceti drained oil" to Joseph Rotch and Company, of Nantucket, from whom he also purchased head matter on the account of the Brown family. In December 1764 his sale of oil to Rotch netted the Browns £319 lawful money.[62] In April of the following year the net proceeds of the oil thus vended came to £246.[63] Lloyd also disposed of large quantities of oil to Samuel Hughes, "Mr. Rowe," Richard Derby, James Mortimer, John Melville, and Benjamin Parker. The importance of this oil trade to the Providence house is apparent. On June 13, 1763 Henry Lloyd submitted his account of the sale of 639 casks of oil, the net proceeds of which were £1432 lawful money.[64]

But, as the head matter purchased by Lloyd exceeded in value the oil sold by him on the account of Nicholas Brown and Company, there remained a balance which had to be paid in other ways. This was done chiefly by the consignment of spermaceti candles to Lloyd's care. Long after oil had completely disappeared from their invoices to him, candles moved in his direction in undiminished volume. Conspicuous as were candles in their trade to New York, to Philadelphia, to the Caribbean, and to certain of the merchants in Newport, it was undoubtedly through Henry Lloyd's commission agency that the Brown family found the most important single outlet for the finished product of their spermaceti works.

The dimensions of the candle trade with Henry Lloyd may be illustrated by examples taken at random. On July 22, 1769 he rendered an account of the sale of 165 boxes of candles, whose net proceeds were £494 lawful money. On August 2 he accounted for the sale of 90 boxes for £251. A month later he forwarded the account of 120 boxes which had netted £344, a total of £1089 lawful money within less than two months. In the year 1766 Lloyd disposed of 475 boxes for £996 lawful money net.[65] From December 16, 1767 to the corresponding date in the following year he sold 685 boxes for £2166 net.[66]

To list the names of those to whom Henry Lloyd sold the candles would be to compile a register of the great merchant families of Boston on the eve of the Revolution. At very frequent intervals throughout the years 1763-1775 Lloyd rendered his accounts, listing not only the proceeds of the sales but also listing the names of those who had purchased the candles. Among those repeatedly appearing were Jonathan and John Amory, William Palfrey, William Vernon, Fortesque Vernon, John Winslow, Jr., Joshua Winslow, Thomas Apthorp, Isaac Codman, Peter Livius, William Vans, Thomas Amory, George Brinley, Robert Auchmuty, Ellis Gray, Thomas Boylston, Richard Lechmere, John Rowe, John Apthorp, John Codman, Patrick Tracy, John Cushing, and William Vassall. On January 1, 1769 twenty-four Boston merchants, including many named above, owed Henry Lloyd £1000:8:9½ lawful money for the account of Nicholas Brown and Company. On October 2, 1770 twenty of the Bostonians owed £519:11:5½ lawful money. These men shipped the candles thus purchased to New York, Philadelphia, and the West Indies, where they were frequently sold in competition with Brown-made candles consigned directly by Nicholas Brown and Company.

Because of this large market, Henry Lloyd's sales of candles almost always exceeded his purchases on the Browns' account. His books usually showed a balance in their favor. On March 1, 1769 the balance amounted to £1042 lawful money.[67] As of August 3 of the same year it was £1420, of which Lloyd was "in cash" for £634:10, leaving £785:10 outstanding.[68] Against these balances Nicholas Brown and Company drew in favor of their creditors, including those at Nantucket. On May 16, 1763 they wrote to Lloyd that Moses Brown had just returned from Nantucket, where he had drawn on Lloyd for £200 lawful money.[69] A month later they requested Lloyd to pay Green and Boylston, of Boston, £133 lawful money on account of Silvanus Hussey of Nantucket.[70] In September they asked him to send "us what money you have in your hands of ours," after reserving £700 for Messrs. Hussey.[71] In August of the following year Henry Lloyd wrote that he would pay Silvanus Hussey, Jr., "what I am in cash for your account."[72] At another time the Browns asked for "1000 dollars for our friends Messrs Hussey immediately."[73] In 1772 Lloyd wrote that their draft for £180 in favor of Samuel Starbuck and Company, at Nantucket, "shall be duly honored."[74] A year later he advised the Providence house that he would "take up Christopher Starbuck and Company's order for £800, which was about the sum he was "in cash" for the Browns' account.[75] In this way Nicholas Brown and Company were enabled to settle, in part, their head matter accounts at Nantucket.

Henry Lloyd, like other correspondents of the Browns, rendered many other kinds of fiscal service. They asked him, as they asked Van Horne, to negotiate Dutch bills of exchange to the best advantage. On one occasion they sent Dutch paper amounting to 2330 Holland guilders.[76] They hoped to net par on them but would take the most Lloyd could get in cash. When they sent him £800 in bills on Philadelphia, they requested him to sell them and remit to "the several persons" at Nantucket.[77] On another occasion Lloyd sent £756 lawful money, £600 of which "I am in cash for your account and £156 I advance for what Mr. Melville still owes."[78] To simplify one of their transactions at New York, Lloyd might send them a draft for £400 New York currency, "amounting to £300 lawful money."[79] Or, to make matters more complicated, he could dispatch four drafts drawn by John Watts and Company, of New York, on "The Right Honorable Thomas Harley & Henry Drummond" for £1100 Sterling, "equal to £1356:13:4 lawful money."[80] To such lengths might they be put to obtain Sterling bills for use in England. In November 1773 Henry Lloyd wrote that, should he meet with any good bills at par, he would purchase them to the amount of £1200 Sterling;[81] and he added that he expected about "£700 Sterling from Quebec which I design for you."[82]

Commissions such as these were an integral part of the correspondent's responsibility. But some of the requests made of Henry Lloyd did not have to do with company finances. They once asked him to supervise the carving of a piece of woodwork; at another time he arranged for the execution of a copper plate for engraving purposes. But one of their most extraordinary requests had to do with the finances of the Colony of Rhode Island. In 1766, the General Assembly of Rhode Island ordered the Treasurer to hire £1000 lawful money, provided it could "be got" by a stipulated date at 6 per cent; for which he was to give "his obligation in behalf of the Colony" payable in one year. "As hard money is very scarce in this Colony," the Browns wrote to Lloyd, "a number of members of the assembly propose writing to their friends in your Province in order to procure the sum." Could the money not be "hired," it was to be "struck off, on which account," they added, "we are more particularly induced to write you on the subject, as we should be very sorry that new emissions should be made at a time when all the rest is just expiring." The Browns believed that "could the present call be supplied we shall hereafter have an established currency."[83] Should Henry Lloyd or any of his friends be able to supply any part of the sum desired it would be very helpful. This letter provides further evidence of the hard money stringency in Rhode Island as compared with neighboring colonies.

In reply to this request Henry Lloyd soon wrote that although he had not had time to "Consult many People" in Boston, he was not without hope of succeeding, having some encouragement from Mr. John Hancock, "whose answer I expect in two or three days." A week later Lloyd informed the Browns that "Mr. Hancock cant yet resolve me whether he can Lend your Colony any money or not but says he will soon determine." Some time later came word from Lloyd that "Mr. Hancock cant yet determine whether the money can be furnished to your Colony or not, but thinks it more likely it will not, than that it will. I have try'd most of the moneyd People in this place, who one and all except Mr. Hancock decline, thinking if there was no Risque the moneyd people of your Government would be glad of the opportunity to do it." Some five weeks after the original request, Henry Lloyd expressed his belief that "you can have no dependence on Mr. Hancock supplying the money for your Government."[84] Hancock, however, seems never to have given a definite reply. This evidently was another of the many situations which he met in an oblique manner!

Although Henry Lloyd was the Browns' only official commission agent in Boston in the decade before the Revolution, he by no means had a monopoly of their trade with the town. Numerous other Boston merchants engaged regularly in the outright purchase and sale of goods with the Providence firm over substantial periods of time.[85] Among these was John Hancock himself. In the late 1760's when Hancock was trying to corner the supply of whale oil in North America, he was glad to obtain that article from every possible source. As Nicholas Brown and Company, of all the manufacturers, received the largest quota of head matter, they naturally had the largest quantities of drained oil to be disposed of. This was Hancock's opportunity. In April 1768 the Browns shipped to him all the oil they then had on hand, amounting to from 40 to 50 tons. They asked in return a bill of exchange on England for £326 Sterling, one for £177 Sterling, and a third for "the remaining amount of the oil."[86]

In March of the following year they delivered to him 69 tons of oil, for which he was to pay £1294 Sterling, plus 40 tons of pig iron which he agreed to ship aboard his vessel to London, Bristol, Liverpool, or Hull at 5 Shillings per ton. Within two weeks they asked him to send them £300 lawful money "by the bearer." On April 25 they advised Hancock that Silvanus Hussey, of Nantucket, wished to borrow £200 lawful money from them "until fall."[87] They requested him to advance the money to Hussey on account of the oil. At the end of May they asked the payment of the balance on the oil which was £476:17 Sterling.[88] Transactions of a similar character continued between the two houses until 1771, when the Browns asked Hancock for the payment of the balance of £130 which he then owed on 40 tons of oil.[89]

Another Bostonian to whom Nicholas Brown and Company sold oil was Joshua Gardner. In the spring of 1768 Gardner purchased 50 tons of oil at £14 Sterling per ton. He paid £350 Sterling in cash, giving his note for the balance.[90] Finding it difficult to pay the note, Gardner authorized Samuel Nightingale, of Providence, who was indebted to him, to make payments on the note. This Nightingale did to the amount of £189:19. The Browns then requested Gardner to give them a draft on Nightingale for the latter's balance. "And the remainder," they added, "we will discount with Messrs C. Hussey & Co. if agreeable to you," a rather good illustration of the complicated business transactions of the time.[91]

The Browns also found Joshua Gardner of service to them in negotiating Dutch bills which came into their hands in consequence of their trade at Surinam. Sending him 7136 guilders, the equivalent of £872 lawful money, they asked him to negotiate them in England through his own correspondent, "as if you sell them they may fall into hands unknown." They requested Gardner to receive the bills on account of Christopher Hussey and Company at Nantucket.[92] From Gardner the Browns bought goods from time to time. In one letter to him they acknowledged the receipt of nails and ink pots. At another time they ordered from him nails, wool cards, cotton cards, raisings, silk, "taffity," together with primers, spelling books, psalters, and "2 doz. Testaments."

Relations with Nantucket, of course, were not confined to the movement of head matter in one direction and of specie and bills of exchange in the other. Concentrating as they did on the whale fishery, the Nantucket men must depend on the "Off-Islanders" for many things, some of which were necessary to the fitting out of the whaling fleets. Originally these articles had come from Boston and Newport merchants. But in the late 1750's the young and enterprising firm of Obadiah Brown and Company began to invade the Nantucket market, not merely to buy head matter but to sell goods. For several years their Sloop *Charming Molly* alternately visited Philadelphia and Nantucket. To the latter she carried assorted cargoes consigned to John or Moses Brown, who served their apprenticeships in business as supercargoes aboard the sloop. On February 23, 1759 the Browns shipped by *Charming Molly,* bound for Nantucket, 41 barrels of brown sugar, 6 barrels of coffee, 2 hogsheads of tobacco, 18 bolts of Russia duck, 4 reams of writing paper, 2 chests of Bohea tea, 25 coils of cordage, 6 coils of spun yarn, 6 bars of German steel, 1 barrel of "Contrays," 21 barrels of molasses, 40 casks of New England rum, 106 barrels of flour, 32 casks of ship bread, 20 firkins of butter, 1095 pounds of hemp, and 1 ton of bar iron.[93] These goods they consigned to John Brown. On April 13 and May 3 of the same year similar cargoes were shipped to the care of Moses Brown.[94] The supercargoes sold these goods principally to the men from whom the Browns obtained their head matter—the Rotch family, Christopher Hussey and Son, Silvanus Hussey and Company, Samuel Starbuck and Company, Christopher Starbuck and Company, and representatives of the Folger, Gardner, and Coffin families. After 1762, when the young supercargoes became members of Nicholas Brown and Company, the goods were shipped directly to these houses. But regardless of the method employed, the merchandise sold seldom equaled in value the head matter purchased. Hence the need for specie or good bills of exchange to cover the balance.

The process is illustrated by three transactions of 1769 with Christopher Starbuck and Company, perhaps the Browns' closest friends on the Island. On June 13 they sent Starbuck 3 barrels of sugar, 1 hogshead of West India rum, 2 hogsheads of molasses, and 4 hogsheads of stone lime. In August they forwarded £400 in cash, two hogsheads of New England rum, 1 barrel of cider, and 4 hogsheads of lime. They advised Starbuck on October 28 that they were shipping 4 hogsheads of molasses, some hollow ware from the Furnace, and £305 lawful money.[95]

The Browns had numerous contacts in Connecticut, but they were chiefly with farmers, village and small-town storekeepers, or ironmasters, such as Dr. Benjamin Gale and Aaron Eliot. Perhaps their most notable experience with the coastal merchants was with Gurdon Saltonstall, of New London. Hearing that Nicholas Brown and Company made candles "of the best quality," Saltonstall arranged for the purchase of a large quantity "to make experiment of in the European market," for which he gave his note.[96] Subsequent relations between the two houses were largely confined to efforts of the Browns to secure payment of the note. To avoid payment Saltonstall resorted to Fabian tactics. He asked what the Browns would allow him for beef and pork toward payment, but without waiting for a reply he announced that he would pay from the proceeds of a cargo of West India goods which he daily expected.[97] But nothing came of this. The Browns then tried to persuade "Connecticut people" to take Saltonstall's note in payment for beef and pork which he would then ship to Providence by way of liquidating his debt.[98] But "Connecticut people" evidently knew Saltonstall too well to be impressed by this proposal. The Browns then suggested that he pay with the 200 barrels of head matter which his whalemen had just brought in. Two months later they acknowledged the receipt of 23 casks of head matter "which have leaked." Once more they asked payment in beef and pork, of which Saltonstall had none. More than four years after the purchase of the candles he was still unable to pay because his whaling voyages had been disappointing.[99] In April 1772 Saltonstall advised Nicholas Brown and Company that, virtually his entire estate having been attached by his other creditors, he had petitioned the General Assembly of Connecticut to appoint commissioners in bankruptcy to take charge of his affairs.[100]

With Charleston, South Carolina and with Virginia the Browns' connections in the pre-Revolutionary period were not particularly important. For a brief season they shipped candles to Nathaniel Russell in Charleston, receiving rice in return. The correspondence did not flourish for the simple reason that Russell was unable to sell the candles. In Virginia they dealt with Colonel Archibald Cary and with Adams and Griffin. But the Virginians tended to fall in debt to the Browns, as to London merchants. In the end the Providence house was forced to commission Thomas C. Williams of Annapolis, Maryland, to collect these debts. Colonel Cary's obligation of £347:17:2 was finally paid early in 1776.[101]

Commercial relations of the Browns with other colonies reveal with great clarity the unity in diversity which characterized their scheme of business. Basically, the Brown family were manufacturers rather than merchants, and their commerce was largely ancillary to their spermaceti plant, and to a less extent to Hope Furnace. In their trade with the Caribbean area they kept constantly in mind the exigency of the candle manufacture. From every voyage they expected good bills of exchange acceptable at Nantucket in payment for head matter. But every voyage also brought back molasses which, with the rum made from it, was sent to other colonies in exchange for flour, forest products, beef, pork, and other articles for a West Indian cargo. More important, however, were the bills of exchange and the specie which came from the neighboring provinces, for the supplying of which the Browns maintained "settled correspondents" in the leading coastal towns. It was the funds thus obtained that enabled them to balance their payments at Nantucket. In this way, too, they obtained cash with which to pay wages at the furnace.

If the major purpose of their commercial activity was to obtain the funds required for their manufactures, the products of the latter in turn served the Browns advantageously in their maritime trade. Candles they sent to Philadelphia, New York, and Boston, as well as to the Caribbean. Pig iron they shipped extensively to New York, receiving flour, bills, and specie in return; and pig iron, together with oil, a by-product of the candle manufacture, furnished them with their two chief forms of remittance to England in payment for manufactured goods. Thus no one of the parallel lines of business activity in which they were engaged was unrelated to any other. Every line was part of a well-integrated pattern; and all lines taken together formed a harmonious whole.

But the story of the Browns' dealings with merchants in other colonies does more than to illuminate the interrelations of their manifold forms of business endeavor. It also brings out in bold relief the economic interdependence of the colonies north of Chesapeake Bay. It shows that they were balancing their economies in terms of each other; that they were interchanging products, utilizing each other's skills and techniques in launching new business ventures, and drawing upon one another in effecting payments. Thus the Browns relied in turn upon Philadelphia, New York, and Boston to obtain the means of meeting their payments at Nantucket. So regular, so vital, and so long sustained were such transactions that they could not fail to bring to businessmen an awareness of interdependence. Such a community of interest in economic affairs was but a preliminary to intercolonial action in the political realm.

Unlike many colonial mercantile firms, the Browns developed their business without making use of family connections or close friends, either in other colonies or in England.[102] The intimate personal relations with men such as Tench Francis and Henry Lloyd came after the business association, not before. With the personal element so largely lacking, their contacts were wholly economic in character; and those contacts continued only so long as they proved mutually advantageous. That the Browns were thus able to exchange products with distant areas over a period of many years bears witness both to their own skill and ingenuity, and to the growth of economic specialization within the colonies.

CHAPTER 8

"Dry Goods from London and Bristol"

IN the early 1730's Captain James Brown was shopkeeper as well as shipowner. Customers at his store could find fish, beef, pork, butter, hoops and staves produced in the colonies; molasses, rum, and salt, the staples of his West India trade; and British goods—cotton, wool, linen, Osnaburgs, silk, grindstones, and a multitude of other items obtained from merchants in Boston and Newport. As Captain Brown's own vessels made no voyages to England, he may not have understood that in a larger sense the real purpose of his own maritime trade with the West Indies was to enable him to pay for the manufactured goods which his customers demanded. He wanted to keep his store well stocked with these English goods. So long as he could secure them from other merchants who did send their vessels to London and Bristol, he was satisfied. The purchase of imported linen at a warehouse in Boston seemed no more significant to him than the purchase of codfish at one of the city's wharves; both helped to increase the profits at his Providence shop.

For many years Obadiah Brown managed his mercantile affairs in the same manner. He procured his manufactured goods from neighboring towns. But later he came to realize, as his older brother had not, the value of direct trade with England. In 1750 he had dispatched the Ship *Smithfield* to London for a cargo of English goods. By 1753 he was in touch with the London merchant, William Stead, from whom he received "an Iron Screw & Brass Box" for the spermaceti works then under construction.[1] By 1756, Obadiah was trading regularly with Stead, sending him "refined spermaceti and whale oil, and receiving from him consignments of British goods."[2] The invoice of merchandise shipped from London on May 10, 1756 amounted to £511:6:10 Sterling.[3] It included, besides the hardware and dry goods usually listed in such documents, the titles of more than two hundred books. These volumes and a smaller number shipped in 1759 appeared on the shelves of the Providence Athenaeum many years later.[4] Obadiah also purchased English wares, mostly hardware from Abraham Hart of London.

Obadiah did not import English goods on a lavish scale. His orders amounted to hundreds rather than thousands of pounds Sterling. One of Abraham Hart's invoices, for instance, amounted to £315 Sterling;[5] and at another time Obadiah owed Hart £508 Sterling.[6] These were modest transactions befitting a small-town merchant just breaking into a new commercial game. Except for the voyage of 1750, he did not use his own ships in the English trade. He freighted the goods aboard vessels owned elsewhere; oddly enough these frequently belonged to men in New York rather than in nearby Newport or Boston. Even so, the payment of the modest sums involved placed a considerable strain upon Obadiah's ingenuity. His shipments of "refined spermaceti" and whale oil were never equal in value to the merchandise received from London. There was always a balance to be settled by bills of exchange which were not always easy to obtain. His correspondence with Stead is largely filled with a discussion of this problem of procuring bills of acceptable quality.

If Obadiah continued to trade with London after 1759, no record of it has been found; and the abrupt termination of all correspondence with London agents in that year probably means that the trade closed at that time. It is apparent that in 1761, the last full year of his life, Obadiah was not regarded by his correspondents in other colonial centers as an importer of English goods. In that year Francis and Relfe, writing from Philadelphia, advised him that they had just received "a complete assortment of dry goods of every kind"; and they were "fully persuaded" that they could give him "perfect satisfaction in what you want in that way, as likewise teas, pepper, china, wine, lemons, etc."[7] Walter and Samuel Franklin, in New York, had learned from Captain Douglas "That you keep a dry goods store and buy considerable quantities at Boston and Philadelphia in order to keep up an assortment." They were prepared to supply Obadiah with "any quantity" on as good terms "as you can have them from either" of those cities. They would sell the goods on "either 6 or 12 months credit."[8] The small lots of merchandise which Obadiah had purchased directly from London were not enough to make him an importer in any real sense of the word. The established firms continued to regard him as a likely purchaser of such wares.

Nicholas Brown and Company did not reopen the London trade until five years after Obadiah's death. During those years they continued to obtain their English goods from importers chiefly in Newport and Boston. In spite of flattering offers from their correspondents in New York and Philadelphia, they did not buy English goods from those sources in large quantities. In 1764 Francis and Relfe of Philadelphia offered "a complete assortment of dry goods just imported which will sell extreme low."[9] Even offers such as this did not succeed in winning much of the business of the Browns away from Newport and Boston. As late as 1766 they were purchasing manufactures from Joshua Gardner, in Boston, to whom they were then selling oil in considerable volume. They complained to him that goods he shipped were "packed up in a very luce extreonary manner, such as Iron and pewter along with cotton velvit, chaffin dishes in a cask with Fiddles." One of the large brass kettles, they said, was "Worn out all around the bottom," while the "fiddles are very much broken to pieces, as is all the toys."[10]

Perhaps it was easier to buy to good advantage in cities so near to each other and to Providence. At any rate, Nicholas Brown and Company showed considerable skill in playing one Newporter against another, and the two of them against a Bostonian. On one occasion after John had gone to Boston to inquire as to the "terms dry goods are sold upon," his brothers wrote to Aaron Lopez of Newport. John, they told him, would not buy goods in Boston unless he could purchase them 30 per cent above the Sterling cost, "expecting we can get them of you at that price, but if he can have them under that price he will probably supply us."[11] John obtained the goods from Boston at 25 per cent above the Sterling cost. This highly satisfactory figure was promptly reported to Lopez, who in turn offered to supply fall goods from Britain at the same price. But the Browns did not immediately place their order with Lopez. They wrote to their lifelong friend at Newport, Benjamin Mason, "give us a line whether you will supply us with such goods as you have & expect this fall at the same rate as we bought them in Boston & now have Mr. A. Lopez's offering them on the same" terms—25 per cent added to the Sterling cost with 9 months' credit. But "this," they continued, "you needn't mention as perhaps Mr. Lopez may think a little hard if we don't give him the preference to you, as he first offered to supply us on those terms." Nevertheless, the Browns thought it their duty, "from the long and good friendship we have had with you . . . to let you know on what terms we are offered to be supplied." Should Mason "incline to supply us on the same terms you may assure yourself that we shall first apply to you for every article we want that we think probable you have."[12] As a result of this chicanery the Browns were assured of dry goods from all three sources on the most favorable terms available to nonimporters.

It was not until 1766 that Nicholas Brown and Company purchased their first shipment of manufactured goods directly from England. Placing an order with Isaac Hazelhurst of Welch, Wilkinson and Startin, of Birmingham, they wrote: "if these goods come to our liking we doubt not but shall import very largely from your house for the future . . . as we are situated in the center of a large and full inhabited country and no goods imported from England to this place." The statement in this letter which implies that no other house in Providence was importing British goods may have been persuasive in arousing the interest of the Birmingham firm but it was not strictly accurate. The Browns must have known that other men in Providence either had already imported goods from England or were preparing to do so. Advertisements of various houses were appearing in the *Providence Gazette and County Journal* for the sale of newly arrived cargoes of English goods.

It would not have been in character for the Browns to have stayed out of this trade too long after other Providence merchants were committed to it. Moreover they were well equipped to make the importation of English goods a successful part of their over-all business plans. Hope Furnace was emerging from the experimental stage. Whale oil had for a long time been acceptable in the English market. They were confident that their pig iron would prove equally tradeworthy. With two products available for remittances, the Browns could import English goods, and at the same time build up valuable outlets for the output of their factories. In the letter to Hazelhurst they stressed this ability to pay for English wares, pointing out that they were "largely concerned in the spermaceti manufactory and have from 100 to 150 tons of strained oil to sell every year, which article always sells for cash or Sterling bills, so that we make no doubt but that we shall make you a satisfactory remittance."[13]

On February 14, 1767, Welch, Wilkinson and Startin shipped the goods which the Browns had ordered through Hazelhurst. It was a large order and seems to indicate that the Browns were entirely confident of their ability to develop the English trade to advantage. Included in the shipment were brass nails, needles, "1 gross best sailors palms," 12 pairs of cooper's compasses, 4 dozen brass dividers, 4 dozen saw sets, 6 dozen brass cocks, 12 dozen dovetail hinges, 24 brass desk sets, 12 dozen steel key rings, steel-plate hand saws, keyhole saws, marking irons, "waiters & trays," 1 dozen mill saws "6 foot)," 12 bundles of spades and shovels, 5 dozen whips, a box of pins, a cask of glue, 6 anvils, 42 casks of nails, and 1 dozen wood saws "4 foot)." Guns and ribbons were to follow. The value of the goods was £826:4:1 Sterling.

Orders to other British firms followed in rapid succession. During 1767-68 the Browns made brief business connections with various houses in London, Liverpool, and Manchester. Most of these relationships were short-lived.

Early in 1767 Hugh Pringle, of Liverpool, shipped the Browns two boxes and one bale of merchandise, amounting to £193:17:1 Sterling.[14]

In September of the same year the Browns made a tentative suggestion to Pringle about handling two of the products from their manufacturing plants in Rhode Island. Speaking of spermaceti candles, they wrote: "If you could procure a price that would net us 1/4 [one shilling, fourpence] Sterling here clear of all charges we could ship you 20 or 30 thousand" pounds yearly. And they added "we are also concerned in a furnace for making pigg iron. Please to give us a price current of that article and what quantity would sell with the charges (if any) attending importation."[15] Nothing seems to have come from these suggestions. There is no indication that trade in candles or pig iron ever developed with Hugh Pringle. When the Brown brothers on May 5, 1768 enclosed a bill of exchange drawn by John Hancock on George Hayley, in London, for £177 Sterling, with the promise that the "balance if any shall be duly paid," their business relations with Pringle came to an end.[16]

At about the same time Nicholas Brown and Company were in touch with a third British firm, that of Robert and Nathan Hyde, of Manchester. From the Hydes they received a consignment of goods filling 36 chests and 1 hair trunk, amounting to £318:17 Sterling.[17] In payment for this shipment they forwarded a bill of exchange for £336 Sterling, drawn by John Hancock on George Hayley.[18] On the same day they sent another of Hancock's bills on Hayley to Welch, Wilkinson and Startin, in Birmingham, in part payment for the goods received from them.[19] By this method, Hancock's bills on his London correspondent, given to the Browns in payment for oil purchased from them, provided the Providence house with a very convenient means of remittance to their English friends.[20]

Through Henry Lloyd, of Boston, the Browns corresponded with Williams and Bellamy, a house specializing in the printing of calicoes bought in large quantities at the "East India sales" in November of each year. Following the receipt of a small shipment in the spring of 1770, Nicholas Brown and Company sent a large order to the London firm in the autumn of that year. Included were calico cloths of a great variety of patterns, together with "18 Doz. Maps of England Handkerchiefs" in red, white, and purple hues.[21] Although Williams and Bellamy supplied the Browns with some goods as late as 1773, no regular correspondence ever developed between the two houses.

While these transactions in various English cities were in process, the Browns were also in contact with Hayley and Hopkins of London. This company had distributed samples of the pig iron from Hope Furnace for trial in English forges. Some reports on these tests were unfavorable, but that of Hayley and Hopkins was distinctly encouraging. They had been successful in selling 14 tons of Hope pigs which the Browns had shipped to them. Hayley and Hopkins had written that "whatever quantity of that article you may at any time send shall be always disposed of at the best market price & believe will not sell better at any port in England than at London."[22]

The apparent eagerness of the London company to handle Hope pig iron, together with their confident prediction of a steady market, must have been gratifying to Nicholas Brown and Company. The Browns counted heavily on pig iron in developing their English trade. None of the other British firms had displayed much interest in handling the product. Moreover, Hayley and Hopkins had justified their enthusiasm by selling the first shipment consigned to them. If they could sell pig iron they could easily sell the other important staple, whale oil. In London, the great entrepôt of European trade, they had an advantage over the merchants in Birmingham or Liverpool. They could buy assorted cargoes of British and continental goods more cheaply than any number of different correspondents in as many different cities in England. Common sense seemed to indicate that the firm of Hayley and Hopkins, of London, was the ideal correspondent for Nicholas Brown and Company, of Providence. The connections in other English cities were not developed to any large extent; and until 1776 Hayley and Hopkins conducted the bulk of the Browns' business in the British metropolis.

When the correspondence between the two houses began, the English firm was very popular in New England. George Hayley, the more active partner, was well known as an alderman of London, a friend of the colonies, and a merchant of distinction. An increasing number of colonial merchants were placing their affairs in his hands. Even John Hancock of Boston had recently deposed a London agent of long standing in Hayley's favor. When the Browns made their initial gesture in the London merchant's direction, they were in fashionable company.

Hayley and Hopkins were, of course, the British analogue of the Browns' correspondents in Philadelphia, New York, and Boston. To them Nicholas Brown and Company shipped regularly consignments of Hope pig iron and oil and, occasionally, potash and candles. In the year 1771 the shipments of oil amounted to £3468:18:3 Sterling.[23] As Hayley and Hopkins explained, the "oil if sold immediately upon arrival cannot be in cash under four months." In the meantime, the Browns were free to draw their bills on Hayley and Hopkins. In June 1769 Hayley wrote "we shall have no objection to paying your draft . . . for £500 as often as you may be circumstanced as you describe, having the most entire dependence upon your punctuality in replacing the money as soon as you conveniently can." The only terms required were the payment of 5 per cent interest for the time "we may continue in advance," plus the usual commission of ½ per cent on paying "your bills on us and the like for negotiating any bills you may remit us."[24]

The analogy between the London and American correspondents appears the more complete when we discover that Nantucket cast its shadow to the British capital as well as to Philadelphia. Bills drawn by Nicholas Brown and Company on Hayley and Hopkins were frequently used to settle head matter accounts at the Island. In 1771 Hayley wrote that "we observe what you say upon the subject of . . . your proposal to draw upon us for £800 if you find it convenient for laying in your stock of head matter." Giving unqualified approval to the proposition, he added that "we have the utmost confidence in your honor and have so fair experience in your punctuality that we should hold ourselves culpable if we did not by any means in our power give you every assistance we are able for the ease and convenience of your business."[25] This bit of correspondence offers convincing evidence of the integrated and balanced nature of the Brown brothers' scheme of business. Spermaceti oil, a by-product of the candle manufacture, was one of their chief forms of remittance to London in payment for British goods. But the oil, along with the pig iron produced in another of their manufacturing plants, did more than pay for European wares; it also gave them credit, which enabled them to draw on their London correspondent in making payment at Nantucket for the raw material which went into the making of candles. Thus every part of the business helped to balance every other part.

Along with the pig iron and the oil, and the potash and the candles which Nicholas Brown and Company remitted to Hayley and Hopkins, there went pieces of paper—Dutch bills of exchange obtained in the course of their trade at Surinam. As negotiation of these through their American correspondents had not always been particularly easy, the Brown brothers were naturally pleased with the willingness of the London house to perform this service for them. Letters from Hayley constantly referred to remittances from Amsterdam for Dutch bills received from the Browns; and the latter firm continued to forward them to London for negotiation even after Hayley's admonition of 1773 that "Dutch bills will be very hazardous and we would advise you if possible not to take any of those. Hardly a bill drawn on Amsterdam now meets acceptance." In April 1774 Hayley acknowledged the receipt of nine "setts" of Dutch bills "which are gone over" to Amsterdam for acceptance. Three months later he wrote that "six setts of Dutch bills are gone over and and you shall be informed of their success."

The types of business transacted between the two houses may be easily illustrated. The account current of December 31, 1770 shows that in the course of the year the Browns had shipped oil, iron, beeswax and Dutch bills to the amount of £2027 Sterling. They had received goods from and drawn bills on Hayley and Hopkins to the value of £3540, leaving a balance of £1513 Sterling due to Hayley and Hopkins. Thereafter the scale of their transactions with Hayley and Hopkins expanded rapidly. Between January 1 and May 14, 1771 they shipped 60 tons of pig iron, a quantity of oil, and 20,000 Holland guilders (equivalent to about £1800 Sterling), a total remittance of £3306:14 Sterling in less than five months. In the same period the Browns had drawn on Hayley and Hopkins to the extent of approximately £2400 Sterling. The calendar year 1771 was notable in that it closed with a balance of £1238 Sterling in favor of the Browns.

The large quantities of goods which Hayley and Hopkins purchased for the Browns were diverse in character. Hayley's letters for the year 1770 give a general idea of the scope of the business. On August 21 he forwarded the invoice of 4 bales and 5 casks of merchandise, with 10 half-barrels of gunpowder, 6 sheets and 65 bars of lead, and 5 tons of hemp shipped aboard the Snow *Tristram* on account and risk of the Brown brothers. The bales contained Osnaburgs and ticklenburgs, Russia duck, and raven's-duck. The contents of the casks included cod lines, twine, wool cards, water glasses, watch mainsprings, silver pendants, "Blue Melting Pots," and a "Watchmakers bright Bench Vice."[26] A month later Hayley advised of goods shipped aboard the Ship *Dione* amounting to £1302:14 Sterling. Remarking upon the care taken in purchasing the goods, Hayley assured the Providence house that "you shall at all times be supplied as well as any house in America."[27] On October 8, Hayley and Hopkins enclosed the invoice of 3 casks, 1 case, 1 bale, 1 chest, and 1 box of merchandise shipped in *Mary* for Rhode Island.[28] This consignment included hardware from Birmingham, such as brass handles, locks, files, and hinges. Also among these articles were 29 dozen escutcheons, and brass knobs by the gross, probably for the doors of the "College Edifice" of Rhode Island College (now Brown University) which was then under construction. Two weeks later came the invoice of 2 boxes, 7 bundles, and 2 casks of merchandise, again largely hardware. Listed were 44 dozen cabinet box locks, 6 six-foot saws, 6 smith's vices, 6 smith's anvils, and 6 dozen brass ink pots, to name only a few of the items.[29] Thus within two months Hayley and Hopkins had shipped four consignments of manufactured goods, amounting to somewhat more than £2000 Sterling.

The invoice of goods shipped by Hayley and Hopkins aboard *Providence* in January 1771 came to £1569:11:2 Sterling.[30] The shipment of July of the same year, representing only part of the order received from the

Browns, amounted to £2465 Sterling.[31] The invoice by *Tristram* in August 1772 was for £1051:8 Sterling; those of *Charlotte* in May 1772 and August 1774 came to £1626 and £2252 Sterling respectively.[32] Consignments in February and August 1773 were for £1778:19 and £2095 Sterling. Two shipments of 1774 amounted to more than £4000 Sterling.

In the 1770's large shipments of oil, iron, and Dutch bills by the Browns were by no means equal to the value of the English goods received from, and the bills drawn upon, Hayley and Hopkins. As a result, the balance ran heavily against Nicholas Brown and Company. On December 31, 1772 it was £6745:4 Sterling; a year later it had increased to £8018:3:10. For a firm which was comparatively new to the London trade these balances were heavy in the extreme. In 1768 John Hancock owed George Hayley only £6700;[33] and his adverse balance of £11,000 in 1774 not only caused Hayley to refuse to honor his bills, but occasioned ugly rumors in regard to his solvency.[34] Yet, so confident were Hayley and Hopkins of the integrity of their Providence friends that they seem to have felt no concern whatever over the magnitude of the sums due them. Never a word of importunity in that regard appeared in their letters. They filled the orders of Nicholas Brown and Company with the utmost care and with every indication of pleasure. "These goods . . . are bought upon the best terms we could possibly procure them and we will venture to assure you that nobody in America can be better supplied than you are," they wrote on one occasion.[35]

As became a faithful correspondent, Hayley and Hopkins did not restrict their services to those arising in the regular course of the trade between the two houses. They responded readily to special requests from Providence. In 1770 they procured for the Brown brothers large quantities of glass, again probably for the "College Edifice." In the same year they arranged for insurance of £2000 Sterling on *Sultan*, which John Brown and two associates were jointly fitting out for a slave voyage.[36] At another time they wrote that "we have endeavored to procure the Theodolite agreeable to your instructions but some difficulties having arisen about the execution of it, we have thought best to defer . . . until we have your further instructions."[37] They assured the Browns that "we shall never think anything troublesome but have great pleasure in the execution of any of your personal commissions as well as those in trade and whenever you have a desire for anything for your own family convenience please freely apply to us."[38] In 1775 they promised that "all possible attention shall be given to the execution of the order for the Bell and clock," no doubt for the First Baptist Meeting House in Providence, then under construction.[39]

Events ultimately were to prove that Hayley and Hopkins' lack of concern over the size of the Browns' balance was more than justified. On March 19, 1776 Nicholas Brown wrote George Hayley that he was determined, "notwithstanding the distressed state of the times" to remit to him as fast as possible "and to be once more clear of debt if in my power." Although expressly contrary to the resolve of the Continental Congress, he was taking the risk of sending Hayley a shipment of oil and candles. He asked the latter to dispose of both the cargo and the schooner, and to place the net proceeds to his credit. Nicholas added that "the populace would certainly destroy her [the Schooner] and me too," should knowledge of the voyage get about; but as she "goes from Nantucket, I hope to escape censure." As no oil had been lately shipped from Providence, "nor no more to go," he hoped for a good price in London. He would not have sent so large a quantity of candles "had not they have lain dead on my hands owing to the stoppage of trade from hence to the West Indies."[40]

From a heavy debtor, which he had been two years before, Nicholas Brown, by this last supreme effort, transformed himself into George Hayley's creditor to the tune of some £400 Sterling. Many colonial merchants at this same time were ignoring their debts in England. They depended upon the probable separation of the colonies from Britain to relieve them of the necessity of paying the debts at all.[41] Nicholas Brown's code of ethics would not permit him to avail himself of this opportunity to side-step an honest obligation. He chose to violate an edict of the Continental Congress and to risk the censure of the populace rather than to default on the payment of his debt. On the other hand, he was equally determined in collecting the balance due him from George Hayley's widow after the war was over.

In the correspondence with Hayley about this final shipment of oil and candles, Nicholas spoke of two vessels; a schooner unnamed and the Brig *Liberty*, both of which Hayley was to sell. This is the only time that vessels owned by the Browns were mentioned in connection with the London trade. The Browns for the most part did not dispatch goods to England in their own ships. With their own craft engaged in the traffic to the Caribbean area, they had been content to freight their goods on board vessels belonging to Newport, Boston, or, sometimes, Nantucket men.

The new rôle of the Brown brothers as importers of English goods was quickly reflected in other aspects of their business. Late in 1767 their friend Christopher Starbuck of Nantucket wrote: "If you have lately imported any dry goods from London & Bristol & could furnish us at any time with some articles which we may want on the same terms as we have from Boston please to let us know & send us a list of some of the articles

& we will write to you for some."[42] He then named Russia duck and raven's-duck, Osnaburgs, twine, shot, "duffils," bar lead, sail needles, palms, blankets, hats, caps, and linen and silk handkerchiefs as some of the articles of which he would have particular need.

At another time, Starbuck, referring to "English goods," said "we may want some early in the spring and will then send." He would mention the Browns' assortment of British manufactured goods to some of "our shop keepers . . . who perhaps, may take some articles of you instead of sending to Boston."[43]

In 1772 Nicholas Brown and Company advised Christopher Starbuck and Company that they had "a very general assortment of dry goods, etc. Shall at all times be obliged for any of your or your friends orders in that way."[44] On the same day they confided to Samuel Starbuck and Company that "we have now by us the best assortment of European goods in the place and expect a fresh supply in the spring with which shall be glad to furnish you or any of your friends."[45]

It may well be that this invasion by the Brown brothers of a market long supplied with English goods by the Bostonians accounts for the improved state of their fiscal position at Nantucket on the eve of Independence. Upon the dissolution of Samuel Starbuck and Company in 1773 the balance in favor of Nicholas Brown and Company was £403 lawful money.[46] In 1774 Christopher Starbuck and Company appealed to the Browns for aid in the fitting out of their whaling fleet. "It is likely," they wrote, "we shall take or want £200 or £300 L. Money more [in supplies] than we may be able to pay you for this fall & if it was agreable & you could help us this way . . . we would pay head matter as usual at the return of our vessels in the spring and we mean also to allow the interest on whatever we may have at cash price longer than the usual credit."[47] This sounds a new note in Nantucket correspondence. The Browns had long been the debtors at the Island, requesting special consideration in the financing of their purchases of head matter. It is possible that the sale of English goods on the Island had finally tipped the scales in their favor.

But the most promising potential market for importations of English goods was that provided by the small-town stores within a forty- or fifty-mile radius of Providence. The Brown brothers were alert to this opportunity. On June 15, 1771 they informed Nathanael Greene at Coventry, Rhode Island, that their fall importation of goods from Britain would give them as complete an assortment "as ever come to New England." Some of the goods, they hoped, would "sute your Customers." They asked Greene's "assistance in noting down every article thats inquired after at your shop," as they were determined "to give timely attention in preparing this summer a compleat invoice to be forwarded in time that they may be bot and put up for next spring importation."[48]

They were especially eager to stock the shelves of stores newly opened. Hearing that Jonathan Wheeler of Grafton, Massachusetts, planned to open a shop, they advised him that they had just received "from London as compleat an assortment of all kinds of goods as any body has," with which they would supply him "on as good terms as they can be got in New England."[49] They would "want in pay for them besides cash," good pork, beef, pot and pearl ash, fats, butter, "cheese & most all other country produce which we will take upon as good terms as they can be sold for in Boston." They wrote in similar vein to John Reid, who was opening a store.[50] As his brother Seth, of Uxbridge, Massachusetts, was one of their regular customers, they asked him to use his influence with John in their behalf.[51]

To Captain John Childs, residence unknown, Nicholas Brown and Company wrote: "As no body in your town keeps a full assortment of goods we had thought of supplying some suitable person with a compleat assortment of English, India & other goods upon the very lowest terms, so that they may afford to retail as cheap as any shop in New England." As they knew of "no more suitable person than you, if you would engage in it we hereby give you the preference to any other person."[52]

Having staked Andrew Waterman and Son, of Smithfield, Rhode Island to English goods to the value of £354 lawful money, Nicholas Brown and Company agreed to accept part payment in staves, boards, hoops, beef, pork, cheese, butter, flaxseed, "or any other they want that the said Watermans have." Whatever money the Watermans received for goods sold was to be paid to the Browns in cash, as was any balance due at the expiration of one year. The avowed purpose of this provision was to prevent the Watermans from using the money "to pay other debts with, or to be laid out at other stores."[53]

When Elihu Williams of Gageborough, Massachusetts desired European goods amounting to one-half the value of his farm, the Browns asked him to have the farm appraised by three "indifferent men." If he would then "make a proper mortgage of the whole" to them, they would gladly supply him with "any sort of goods we have on as good terms as we do our other customers."[54]

On October 27, 1774 Colonel Joab Stafford, of New Providence, Berkshire County, Massachusetts, purchased from Nicholas Brown "a parcel of European goods" and a Negro boy, giving for the latter his note to the amount of £45 lawful money. Nicholas agreed to accept in payment all the pearl ash Stafford could deliver at Providence "before the spring ships sail next year."[55] The value of the pearl ash was to be reckoned at £35 lawful money per ton, "provided no fall of that article that we may hear of at hom in England" should occur in the meantime.

English piece goods the Browns regularly sold to shopkeepers at an advance of 60 per cent from the Sterling cost; stationers' wares, at 66⅔ per cent; and hardware at 73½ per cent. They allowed a credit of four months, after which there was an interest charge of 6 per cent.[56] As it was the pride and boast of the Browns that they supplied British manufactures as cheaply as their Boston competitors, we may assume that these were also the terms offered by the merchants in the metropolis of the Bay Colony. If the Browns were ever disposed to forget the competition of the Bostonians, their customers did not hesitate to remind them of it. Jonathan Hale, of Sutton, Massachusetts, protested the price they had charged him for two bundles of card wire. He had expected the wire at the "Boston price upon my delivering you cards at . . . as low a price as ever any was sold in New England." He hoped they would reduce their wire to "the Boston price or I shall not be able to follow the card making business."[57]

It was important, of course, that the brothers should be able to say "no" to customers who were in arrears for the purchases of goods. They supplied books to Benjamin West, the Providence almanac maker and astronomer, who kept a dry goods store and bookshop. When asked by West to send "another invoice of Books" amounting to some £40, they replied that the importation of "Books in this town in such quantitys" was not justified. As West had paid them nothing from the sale of goods in his first invoice, they advised him to send "for but few if any books this fall."[58]

In the hands of Nicholas Brown and Company the retail trade once centered in Captain James Brown's little shop in Providence was expanded. The original store remained, but others were added in Providence and in Grafton in the Bay Colony. Through their own importation of goods they were able to go into the wholesale field on a wide scale.

Stores the Browns are known to have stocked with English goods were located in Providence, Coventry, Cumberland, and Smithfield in Rhode Island; Uxbridge, Mansfield, Grafton, Sutton, and New Providence in Massachusetts; and Woodstock, Killingly, East Guilford, Willington, and Stonington in Connecticut.

In the score of years preceding Independence, the Browns became one of the outstanding business families in New England. They had welded their manufacturing, maritime, and mercantile affairs into an interlocking business machine. They dispatched their ships to ports where there were prospects for profitable trade. They were active in the Caribbean. They made the most of the poor tobacco of the Narragansett country as the mainstay of their commerce with Surinam. They tried their hand at the slave trade. They fitted out their vessels as privateers. Along with the other merchants of the period they took their chances with the law when they smuggled molasses into the colonies and traded with the enemy in wartime.

But hand in hand with all these maritime ventures went continued effort to build secure foundations at home. They understood that the natural products of Rhode Island were not sufficiently diversified to provide the means of exchange which an expanding business would demand. They turned their bent for manufacture to good account to secure a steady supply of necessary staples for their seaborne trade. They became the leading producers of spermaceti candles in the colonies. At Hope Furnace they turned the inferior iron ore of Rhode Island into a useful and profitable product. In Philadelphia, New York, and Boston, correspondents sold the Browns' manufactures and helped to provide them with the means of meeting their payments at Nantucket.

When the time was ripe, they entered the trade with England. As a result of this they became wholesalers of imported goods while maintaining and expanding their retail business. By the early seventies Nicholas Brown and Company were importing British manufactures to the amount of £5000 Sterling per year.[59] This figure does not include the imports of John Brown who had disassociated himself from the Company in 1771. Since John habitually thought in larger terms than his brothers, there is every reason to believe that his purchases of British goods were even larger. The Browns were late in entering the London trade; but their own manufactures served them in good stead. They could send steady shipments of oil and pig iron in exchange for British goods. On the eve of the Revolution the volume of their importations equaled or surpassed that of many of the great merchants in Boston and Newport who had been in the business for decades.

CHAPTER 9

"Gentlemen of Publick Responsibility"

ALTHOUGH primarily known as a business family, the Browns by no means confined their attention to trade. They found time to maintain an active interest in Rhode Island politics, to hold public office on occasion, to participate in colonial protests against British policies, to have their avocations, and to play an important part in the civic and cultural life of Providence.

Activity of the Browns in the political life of Rhode Island was closely connected with the increasing importance of the town of Providence. Newport, by virtue of its greater commercial maturity, had long exercised a controlling influence in the government of the colony. From 1663 to 1755 all but two of the governors were Newport men; and one of the exceptions was closely identified with the interests of that town. The one Providence man who did occupy the office established his residence in Newport as an acknowledgment of its dominant position within the colony.

The election of Stephen Hopkins, of Providence, to the governorship in 1755 marked the advent of a new era in the politics of Rhode Island. For the first time Providence seriously threatened the hegemony of Newport. But the men of Newport were not to relinquish control without a struggle. They sent forth to the fray young Samuel Ward, son of an earlier governor. For a decade Rhode Island was torn by bitter strife between two rival political factions, one led by Ward, the other by Stephen Hopkins. Rabid partisans "appeared in towns throughout the colony, and families were divided by all the bitterness of party rancor." In these years, it has been said, "Rhode Island politics were little else than an annual propounding and answering of one question: Shall Stephen Hopkins or Samuel Ward be governor of the colony?" Stated in other terms, the question was: Shall Providence or Newport exercise a dominant influence in the affairs of Rhode Island? In the ten annual electoral contests between the two leaders in the years 1758-1767 inclusive, Samuel Ward, in every respect a worthy foe, was victorious only three times, a result which affords a rough measure of Providence's successful challenge to her more populous rival.

In view of the friendly relations and close business associations which the Brown brothers long maintained with Stephen Hopkins and his family, they could not well be neutral in the Ward-Hopkins political feud. And perhaps their zeal for Hopkins was made the more extreme by the fact that their uncle, Elisha Brown, was not only the leader of the Ward faction in Providence, but was twice elected to the Deputy Governorship on the Ward ticket.

The Browns must have found numerous opportunities to render aid to the Hopkins cause. On one occasion they were assured that "it woul[d] be a Grait help to our party" if they should make Levi Potter first mate on board one of their sloops.[1] At another time Nicholas and John issued an "Address" to the "Freemen of the Town of Johnston," a manifesto reminding the voters that their deputies in the Assembly had, "for the Sake of Party," joined "immediately against the Interest of those that chose them for their Representatives."[2] The document enjoined upon the freemen, therefore, the importance of "choosing Deputies who are in Mr. Hopkins's Interest."

However, the outcome of Rhode Island elections in those years depended upon something more substantial than mere rhetoric or exhortation. In an age when British politics were characterized by "bribery elevated into an art," Rhode Island political factions paid British party leaders "the sincere tribute of imitation." Then, as now, parties vied with one another in the collection of campaign chests. But in mid-eighteenth-century Rhode Island the funds thus procured were not employed to finance speaking tours by candidates, to defray the cost of printing and distributing leaflets and broadsides, or yet to purchase full-page advertisements in the newspapers of the day. On the contrary, they were used in a more direct manner to aid doubtful voters in making up their minds.

A campaign document of the Hopkins faction for the year 1765 reads: "We the Subscribers Promise to pay the Sums we have Severaly freely Set to our names in Such articles as may be the most usefull in procuring the free Votes of the poorer Sort of Freemen in this Country . . . and more particularly them Who's Curcumstances does not admit of their Time to ye Injury of their Familys."[3] Twenty-four contributors thus donated £6167 Old Tenor, or 771 dollars, for the benefit of "the poorer Sort of Freemen." Heading the list was Stephen Hopkins himself with £960. The Brown brothers collectively gave £1870.[4]

The itemized account kept by Nicholas and John indicates the articles which were thought to be "most usefull in procuring the free Votes of the poorer Sort of Freemen."[5] To Timothy Willmouth they dispensed one barrel of rum and twenty-two pounds of sugar. A freeman of Cranston received fifteen bushels of corn, while one in Glocester obtained rice and molasses. Loaf sugar, brown sugar, wine, codfish, cheese, lime, and cash went to other voters according to their needs. Daniel Cahoone received £6 Old Tenor for the hire of his horse, used by John Dexter in the town of Cumberland. The latter wrote that he "had only one Day to Ride and That in the Rain, which was very uncomfortable, but do not Repent it, for I am well essured that my So Doing made Twenty more [votes] than if I had Staid at home."[6]

In the campaign of 1765 the efforts of the Brown brothers went unrewarded. They failed to win the "free Votes" of a sufficient number of the freemen. Samuel Ward defeated Stephen Hopkins for the governorship, while Uncle Elisha Brown won the deputy governorship. The following year the brothers were confident that their party would be victorious. To one of their friends they wrote that "Their never was a prospect of Beeting Mr. Ward more than this year & we Doubt not but you'l take the proper Care of Your Town Meeting." They added that "nothing will save Mr. Ward this year Butt a Large Sum of Money which we are advised . . . they cant Git."[7] But, with or without the "Large Sum of Money," Ward and Elisha Brown were again victorious.

The four brothers redoubled their efforts in the campaign of 1767; and they made a play for the "free votes" in the towns of Kent County. To Thomas Aldrich of Greenwich John Brown wrote: "We now send by . . . the Barrer hereof 100 Dollars which with what you and our other Friends in Greenwich or their abouts adds to The Sum will we Hope Give us both Deputys" in the Assembly.[8] John added that "we have Concluded to Send a person from this Town with the money for West Greenwich who will we Expect be with you Sunday Evening and Desire You'l go with him in to the near part of West Greenwich in order to Introduce him to Sum of our Friends." The letter concluded with the cheerful remark that "we are in Gratest Expectation of Giveing our Inemys a Good Drubbing."

In the same campaign the Browns sent to one Beriah Brown, Sheriff of Kings County, at North Kingston, "100 Dollers Cash," with the hope that he "and our other Good Friends" in the town would add "the Same Sum to it" and thus "obtain both Deputys and a Considerable majority . . . in favor of Mr. Hopkins."[9] The brothers would also "take Care that the money to go from here to Covintry is Sent timely."[10] John Brown believed that by the judicious use of the funds thus provided "their may be many persons that is Stranious for Mr. Ward who may be agreed with for a Small Sum to Lay Still."[11] The cash thus dispensed by the Brown brothers may well have induced numerous Ward supporters to "Lay Still"; or, it may have converted them into outright adherents of Stephen Hopkins. In any event, Samuel Ward received the "Good Drubbing" of which John Brown had had the "Gratest Expectation."

In this election Ward and Hopkins were pitted against each other for the last time. For some years the Brown brothers, and the Hopkins faction generally, had been impressed with "the Necessity of putting an End to the party Disputes" in the colony. To their way of thinking, "Mr. Ward and Uncle Brown" had kept the "Government in a Rage for This 7 or 8 years past," although they knew that the "Majority of the Freeholders" were in favor of Stephen Hopkins. Joseph Wanton, leader of the Hopkins party in Newport, and sometime deputy governor, early in 1765 proffered the olive branch to Elisha Brown. Specifically, Wanton offered to "Resine his pretentions to the office" of deputy governor provided Elisha "would agree to Resine his." To this "Uncle Brown made no Answer but avaded it by Introducing other Taulk," which, John Brown believed, was "Suffitient to Shew all men his Determination to keep the Colony in its present Unhappy Scituation."[12]

In 1767 nine Providence friends of Stephen Hopkins, of whom Moses Brown was one, believing the "Spirit of Faction does so prevail in the Colony that there is scarcely the appearance of Government remaining," proposed that the two parties form a coalition with a view to bringing an end to the unhappy state of affairs.[13] To effect such a coalition, they suggested that Hopkins and Ward "resign & give up their pretensions" as candidates for governor. They further proposed that Ward name the governor in 1767, while Hopkins should name the deputy governor. Thereafter the magistrates were to be nominated alternately by Hopkins and Ward. When this compromise arrangement was spurned by the Ward party, Stephen Hopkins wrote that "Unhappy Necessity compels us once more to contend for the government, as all terms of peace have been rejected." Ward's defeat in the election of 1767 seems to have made him more receptive to compromise. The next year he joined with Hopkins in renunciation of all gubernatorial aspirations, thereby making possible a coalition government which put an end to the factional strife which had so long racked the colony.

Support of Stephen Hopkins in his numerous campaigns for the governorship, and of candidates of the Hopkins party for the Assembly, was not the extent of the four brothers' interest in the political scene. At one time or another, all except Nicholas held elective office. Moses was a member of the Rhode Island Assembly in the years 1764 to 1771. Joseph sat in the Assembly during the War for Independence. Although chosen a Rhode Island delegate to the Congress of the Confederation, John seems never to have attended a session of that body. In the years 1799 to 1801, however, he represented Rhode Island in the National House of Representatives.

The Browns were no exception to the rule that sooner or later most men who acquire wealth develop a sense of social responsibility to the community in which they have achieved material success. Although they displayed their civic consciousness in numerous ways, it was perhaps in the realm of education that they made their most notable contribution to the improvement of their home town.

The colony in which they lived had not been outstanding in its devotion to learning even in its elementary forms. As late as 1843 a Providence historian could say with truth that "it is a matter of regret, that education has not always received the same degree of attention in Rhode Island, as in other New England states."[14] He added that the "soil of Rhode Island has never been peculiarly favorable to schools, or institutions of learning." Although Providence had shown more interest in education than the other towns in the state, he could "find little to boast of even in her case."[15]

On December 2, 1767, there was a town meeting in Providence, at which the question of schools received consideration. In his capacity as moderator of the meeting, John Brown presented an address to the freemen of the town.[16] In it he called attention to the "Grait Want of a Publick School House in this Town, That is so publick that Every Inhabitant of S^d Town may have Liberty of Sendg. his Children to it." As a result, many children had "been obloiged to go unlarnt." John was "Sensible that it would be an Easy Matter to Raise Money by subscription from a Very Fue persons to be proprietors to build a School House to their own privit use." But as this would "not be of Servis to Hundreds their is in this Town who is not able to Build a House to School their Children in" John thought it "much Better to Incorage a Town School as that will certainly be the Most Serviceable to the publick." He was sorry to see "so Grand an attempt to Searve the publick opposed by Aney Gentlemen of Learning & much more so from Gentlemen from whoes Stations of Authority the Publick have Reasion to Expect the Graitest Incoragement."

Whether or not as a result of John's exhortation, at a town meeting held a few days later, a committee was appointed "to select locations for the houses, to purchase land and make contract for their erection."[17] Of this committee John Brown was a member. At the same meeting Moses Brown became one of a committee "to prepare an ordinance for the building, supporting and governing the school."[18] On January 1, 1768 the committees submitted reports which were rejected. If we may believe Moses Brown, the plan was defeated, not by "Gentlemen of Learning" or of wealth and influence, but by "the poorer sort of the people."[19] So ended in failure this attempt to establish free public education in the town of Providence.

In the field of higher education the Brown brothers were more successful. In 1762 the Philadelphia Association of Baptists came to the "apprehension that it was practicable and expedient to erect a college in the Colony of Rhode Island, under the chief direction of the Baptists."[20] The considerations which lay back of this "apprehension" were the lack of a "publick School or College" in Rhode Island, the founding of the colony by "persons of the Baptist persuasion," and the control which the members of that sect still exercised over its government.[21]

The following year James Manning, "a young Jersey-man," en route to Nova Scotia, touched at Newport, where he made known the design of the Baptists with respect to the college.[22] There he found a congenial soil for the planting of the idea. Newport was the metropolis of Rhode Island, a busy commercial center, a town of considerable wealth and leisure. It possessed a cosmopolitan population, boasted an excellent library, was frequented by philosophers, artists, and architects, and was the home of numerous patrons of the arts. Among its distinguished citizens was Ezra Stiles, then a scholarly clergyman of the town, but later the distinguished president of Yale College. The wonder was not that such a community should welcome the idea presented by young Manning, "but rather that such a project had not already been realized."

So prompt was the response to Manning's proposals that a charter for the college was drafted and submitted to the General Assembly in August 1763.[23] When action was deferred, another charter was presented at sessions in October 1763 and January 1764. The charter was finally granted in March 1764, and was signed and sealed by the Governor and Secretary on October 24, 1765.[24]

Among those named in the charter as original incorporators of the College of Rhode Island were some of the most distinguished men in the colony: Stephen Hopkins and Samuel Ward, long political rivals, Joseph Wanton and Josias Lyndon, destined to be governors within the next decade, Daniel Jenckes of Providence, and Nicholas Brown.

At a meeting of the corporation held in Newport in September 1765 James Manning, whose visit to Newport had aroused the interest of Rhode Island people in the college, was named President and Professor of Modern Languages.[25] Young Manning had graduated from the College of New Jersey in 1762. The following year he was ordained as a Baptist minister. In 1764 he had located in the town of Warren, Rhode Island. He was pastor of the Baptist Church there and principal of a Latin school.[26] Warren became the first and temporary seat of the college.

At the first commencement in 1769, when a class of seven was graduated, the corporation made an effort to agree upon the permanent location of the college.[27] They first decided in favor of Bristol County, in which Warren is situated. They reconsidered, however, when it was found that the County of Kent, on the west side of the Bay was subscribing funds for the endowment of the college. A special meeting of the corporation called for November 14-16, at Newport, proved to be a lively one.[28] Providence and Newport had now entered the contest. Each of the four contestants presented memorials setting forth its claims to the college. Newporters stressed the town's relatively large population, its reputation for health, ease of communication with other parts of Rhode Island and with the colonies to the West and South, low living costs, and the advantages of the Redwood Library.[29] The memorial from Providence was signed by three men, one of whom was Moses Brown. A preliminary draft of it in the handwriting of Moses referred to the 9000 dollars subscribed by the town, to its central location, transportation facilities, and moderate cost of living.[30] The town had four schoolhouses, a public library, libraries for students of law and medicine, and two printing offices. The memorialists concluded "by observing that it is necessary in the execution of all matters of a public nature, That the undertakers have a zeal for promoting it. This qualification we are conscious we have . . ."

As a result of the pressure from the rival claimants, the corporation rescinded the vote in favor of Bristol County. They agreed that "the College Edifice be at Providence," but the decision was so qualified as not to be binding should "the County of Newport or any other County," subscribe a sum "equal or Superior to any now offered."[31] This in effect reduced the contestants to two—Providence and Newport—and invited them to increase their subscriptions. Describing the rivalry between the two towns, an informed contemporary wrote: "Providence bid high for it which made the County of Newport, which is jealous of Providence on account of trade, assert itself to the utmost."[32]

In the ensuing contest between the two towns, the Brown brothers and Stephen Hopkins led the Providence forces. Appealing to the residents of Scituate and Glocester for funds, they remarked that "building the college here will be the means of bringing great quantities of money into the place, and thereby greatly increasing the markets for all kinds of the Countrys produce, and consequently increasing the value of all estates to which this town is a market."[33] They did not allow their case to rest merely on the narrow ground of self interest. They were sure that locating the college at Providence would "much promote the weight and influence of this northern part of the Colony in the scale of government in all times to come . . ." Newport people were leaving nothing undone

in their efforts "to carry the prize from us . . ." Building materials would
be gladly received in payment of subscriptions to the college.

Meanwhile, Newport was not idle. In mid-January 1770 came the
report that "the County of Newport hath raised a larger Sum than any
that hath yet been offered to the Corporation . . ."[34] A call accordingly
went forth for a meeting of the Corporation at Warren on February 7
to consider action appropriate to the new developments. Partisans of
Providence tried hard to prevent this meeting, contending that the time
for reconsideration of the vote had expired on January 1. When it became
apparent that this effort was in vain, "the Browns and other leaders of the
Providence party" distributed a handbill asking "The Inhabitants of this
Town and County" to meet at the Courthouse "to hear and consider of
some effectual Plan for establishing the College here."[35] This meeting convened on February 5 and was well attended. Stephen Hopkins was in the
chair. A committee, of which Moses Brown was a member, was appointed
to handle subscriptions.

President Manning appears to have thrown his support to the Providence group. In an unsigned, undated letter attributed to him, he indicated to Nicholas Brown the strategy to be followed.[36] Believing that
Newport would almost certainly subscribe the larger sum of money, he
urged the Browns to make the most of certain other advantages which
they enjoyed. "Now," he wrote, "as I think you have the good of the college at heart more than They, it will stand you in hand to demonstrate
this in the clearest light; and this you can do by proffering to build the
college yourselves, without even taking their unconditional subscriptions
in Newport." Continuing, he remarked that "you can here make all the
advantage to your selves from lying handy to materials . . ." The Browns
could "promise just as much more than they can, as the edifice can be
erected cheaper with you than them, . . . as you will prosecute it with
more spirit and do the bargaining and work with less expense." Here
again they would have the advantage over Newport, "as you have made
out bills of everything and bespoke the materials and workmen, and can
push it immediately into execution." He believed they "might reason a
month on these advantages and not make some dull souls see the force of
it, so well as you can demonstrate it in this way in ten minutes."

Thus President Manning expressed his faith in the efficacy of figures,
as opposed to abstract reasoning, in determining the ultimate decision of
the Corporation. That "bills of everything" were available, that complete
data showing the comparative cost of building the college in the two
towns were at hand, was characteristic of the painstaking and methodical
manner in which the Brown brothers informed themselves concerning
business ventures. In their papers has been preserved the document demon-

strating in detail the cost differential between the two rivals.[37] Moses wrote that ". . . reckoning the whole of their sum and the whole of ours they were 158 £ more than we. We presented a calculation in the arguments of the amount of the building if at Newport more than Providence, amounting to £574 L.M. which we insisted should be added to ours which leaves a ballance in our favour of £415."[38]

After they had "maturely considered the several Sums offered, and all the arguments used by all the parties concerned," the Corporation voted not to rescind the earlier vote fixing the location of the college at Providence. Thus that town won the victory, although her rival had actually contributed a larger sum of money. This decision was doubtless the result of several factors. Providence was a more important Baptist stronghold than Newport. "The business energy which was already so conspicuous among her leading men" was unquestionably a significant factor in her favor. And in the display of "business energy" none had been more notable than the Brown brothers, who contributed £760 of the £4175 subscribed by Providence.[39] Indeed, the variety and persistence of their collective efforts may well have been decisive.[40]

The triumph of Providence over a rival possessing "superiority in numbers, library facilities and general culture" was added proof of the readiness of the Brown and Hopkins families to challenge the supremacy of Newport. It was also prophetic of the future when, with the restless energy exemplified by those two families, Providence would emerge as the business and commercial metropolis of Rhode Island. As industrialization proceeded, the college "for liberal Education" helped to prevent Providence from becoming merely one more New England factory town.

Once the Corporation had selected Providence as the permanent seat of the college, it remained for them to decide upon a site for the college edifice. In apparent anticipation of this decision, John and Moses Brown had in the previous month purchased land on the hill at the head of Presbyterian Lane (now College Street), part of which had been included in the original home lot of Chad Browne, their first ancestor in America.[41]

This land they resold to the college for 330 dollars. On March 26, 1770 ". . . the Committee for settling the spot for the College" chose this tract of land on the present College Hill as the site of the college building (now known as University Hall). This was done notwithstanding a memorial, accompanied by a generous subscription, which was presented by residents on the other side of Weybosset Bridge. The memorial strongly urged the advantages of another location which today is in the heart of the Providence business district.[42] The next day digging of the "Cellar" began.

The College Edifice was modeled after Nassau Hall at the College of

New Jersey, whence President Manning had come.[43] In the words of the historian of Brown University, "credit for the rapid yet thorough execution of the work belongs chiefly to the firm of Nicholas Brown and Company, . . . who volunteered to take entire charge of erecting the college building and the president's house."[44] Continuing, he wrote that "their final account, presented to the Corporation in September, 1771, shows their minute care in performing this labor of love, which they pushed forward with characteristic energy and skill." The first "Foundation Stone" was laid by John Brown "in Presence of a Number of Gentlemen, Friends to the Institution."

Closely interwoven with the history of the college thus established is that of the First Baptist Meeting House in Providence. In 1774 a committee, which included Nicholas, Joseph, and John Brown, representing the Baptist Society of the town, informed the General Assembly of the Colony that the Society had "purchased a convenient lot, to build a meeting house upon, for the public worship of Almighty God, and holding the public commencements in." As the acquisition of the lot, together with "the building a proper house for the purposes" would entail a "very great expense," they prayed authorization to conduct a lottery "to raise the sum of £2,000" to enable the "Society to carry their pious designs into execution."[45] The prayer of the petition was granted and Nicholas Brown became one of the directors of the lottery.

Although less conspicuously connected with the building of the Meeting House than with the College Edifice, the Brown brothers followed its progress with a friendly interest. Joseph was a member of a committee "to make a draught of a house 90 by 70 feet together with a tower and steeple and make an invoice of the timber and other material, and ascertain the price of the same."[46] He also went to Boston "to view the different churches and meeting-houses there, and to make a memorandum of their several dimensions and forms of architecture."[47] The final working drawings for the building were adapted by Joseph from plans in James Gibbs's *Book of Architecture*. The steeple was modeled after one of the rejected plans for St. Martin's-in-the-Fields in London.

Nicholas Brown arranged with George Hayley, his London correspondent, for the purchase of some of the materials for the Meeting House, notably the bell and the clock. The completed structure, in which the College Commencement was held for the first time in 1776, still stands as "a noble example of colonial church architecture." With two exceptions, the Meeting House has been the scene of all subsequent commencements of Brown University.

Among the proposed civic improvements advocated for Providence during the dozen years before the Revolution was a market house, the lack of which occasioned much inconvenience to the inhabitants. Provisions often were "almost spoiled by being carried about the streets through wet and heat."[48] In August 1771 the Assembly authorized a lottery for this purpose and appointed Moses Brown one of the directors thereof.[49] The town placed Stephen Hopkins and Joseph Brown in charge of the construction of the building, the latter in his capacity as amateur architect providing the design. Nicholas Brown laid the foundation stone on June 11, 1773.[50] Subsequently enlarged by the addition of a third story and a basement, the building still stands in Market Square.

In 1753 there was organized in Providence a library company which ultimately became the Providence Athenaeum. To this, Obadiah, Nicholas, John, and Moses Brown were original subscribers, while Obadiah procured through his London correspondent the initial collection of books for the infant institution. Nicholas Brown was the first Librarian. The mystery as to how he was able to steal sufficient time from the counting-house for the performance of his new duties is explained by the decree of the board that "'every Saturday, from two to Five of the Clock in the Afternoon, be the Times for opening the Library."

Besides his participation in the architectural planning of the College Edifice, the Meeting House, and the Market House, Joseph Brown in 1774 designed a residence for himself which still stands at 50 South Main Street, Providence, and is now the office building of Brown and Ives. He planned the house which John Brown built at the corner of Power and Benefit Streets (considered at the time to be one of the finest in the country), and which is presently occupied by the Rhode Island Historical Society. Joseph played a prominent part in the observation of the transit of Venus in 1769, for which his expense "was little less than 100 pounds sterling, besides near a month's time of himself and servants in making the necessary previous experiments and preparations." He was interested in pure science, including astronomy, chemistry, and electricity. He became Professor of Experimental Philosophy at the College of Rhode Island. In 1772 he directed the construction of the first fire engine built in Providence. A pump and steam engine (the latter one of the very few made in America to that time) built under his direction will be discussed in another connection.[51]

At the outbreak of the War for Independence the Brown brothers were not only the most important business family in Providence, but they had taken their place in the front rank of those interested in the intellectual and spiritual nourishment of the town in which they lived. Their descendants were to continue and to enlarge upon the work which they had so well begun.

CHAPTER 10

"American Grievances"

ALONG with their participation in the political life of Rhode Island, the Browns maintained a lively interest in the relations of the colony with the British government. As prominent merchants, actively engaged in maritime trade, they could not be indifferent to British commercial policy as it affected the colonies in the years 1763 to 1775.

News of the proposed Sugar Act, reducing the duty on foreign molasses, but providing for the enforcement thereof, arrived in Rhode Island late in September 1763.[1] No doubt Rhode Island merchants generally and the Browns in particular, shared the concern so well expressed by Tench Francis, who wrote from Philadelphia: "What are the people of England now going to do with us? Nothing but Ruine seems to hang over our heads."[2]

After their recovery from the first shock which the news occasioned, merchants addressed their attention to the problem of relief. However much Uncle Elisha and the four brothers might differ on domestic politics, they seem to have been on better terms with regard to British policy. On October 2 Elisha wrote to Nicholas suggesting a meeting of all the merchants of Providence.[3] Although such a foregathering may have occurred, it obviously led to no decision of great moment.

Reaction of the merchants to the Sugar Act was not restricted to any one method of procedure. To many the prospect of continued evasion of the duties was doubtless attractive. Among these were the Brown brothers. After inquiring discreetly of their friends in Newport and Boston as to the attitude of British customs and naval officers, they quietly set about to circumvent the law. Ample illustrations of the devices employed by them to avoid payment of the duty on molasses have been given elsewhere in this volume.[4]

The other procedure open to the merchants was to draft a memorial to the British government setting forth the evil consequences of the Sugar Act and praying that it be not enforced. The idea of colonial protest against the Act seems to have been first suggested in New York. In Massachusetts a committee of merchants prepared a memorial bearing the title "State of the Trade," which they sent in late December 1763 to merchants in other colonies and to colonial agents in Great Britain. A copy of this, with a covering letter, went to two prominent residents of Newport. Merchants of that town then circulated a petition asking Governor Stephen Hopkins to convene the Assembly for the purpose of drafting a memorial to the home government. On January 13, 1764 the Governor signed the warrants calling the legislature into session.

Meanwhile, the merchants of Providence were not idle. It is very probable that signatures of some of them appeared on the Newport petition when it was finally presented to Governor Hopkins. In any event, it is certain that the mercantile element in the town was fully aware of developments and sympathetic to the idea of a remonstrance. A Providence committee drafted a "State of the Trade of this Colony," setting forth the alleged adverse effects of the Sugar Act. This document was carried to Newport, where a committee jointly representing the two towns used it as one of the sources from which they composed the Rhode Island Remonstrance.

Although there is no evidence that the Brown brothers had a hand in the drafting of either the "State of the Trade" or the Remonstrance, it is clear that they were closely in touch with the situation. On January 24, 1764 Nicholas Brown, close friend of Stephen Hopkins and probably a member of his political club, wrote to David Van Horne of New York advising him that the Rhode Island Assembly was convening on that day "in order to give our Agent Instructions to Join with Those of the other Colonys to Lay a State of the Trade of these Northern Colonys before the Parliament and to prevent if Possable the Continuance of the Sugar Act."[5] It was his hope that "Your Government has Joind this so Interesting an Affair."

When the Rhode Island Assembly adopted the Remonstrance on January 27, 1764 it became the first colonial legislature to make an official protest against the Sugar Act, and it was the only one to take action before the new duties went into effect. Within a few months official committees constituted in the various colonies were actively corresponding with one another, thereby providing the groundwork for the later and better-known committees of correspondence. The Rhode Island Assembly appointed such a committee in July 1764, its three members being Stephen Hopkins, Nicholas Brown, and Daniel Jenckes. Soon this committee was in correspondence with similar organizations in Pennsylvania and Boston.[6]

Meanwhile George Grenville had introduced into Parliament a resolution contemplating a stamp tax to be imposed on the colonies. Official word of this intention arrived in Rhode Island in August 1764. In October the Assembly appointed a committee, with Stephen Hopkins at the head of it, to draft an address to the Crown. The next month the committee submitted to the Assembly an address, and a tract written by Stephen Hopkins, bearing the title "The Rights of Colonies Examined." Both documents were sent to England, but the second was to be printed and made available to the colonies generally. As Hopkins' pamphlet was one of the most cogent statements of the rights of the colonies ever penned, it, of course, marked him as the leading opponent of the proposed Stamp Tax in Rhode Island. Once the Stamp Act had passed Parliament in March 1765, Hopkins continued his opposition. He was a conspicuous figure in the Providence town meeting of August 1765 when it adopted resolves against the Stamp Act strikingly similar to those which Patrick Henry had introduced into the Virginia House of Burgesses.[7] No one had a better claim than he to speak for Rhode Island at the Stamp Act Congress which assembled in New York in October 1765.

While their good friend and business associate, Stephen Hopkins, was playing so important a part in the opposition to the Stamp Act, the Brown brothers clearly shared his sentiments with respect to the tax. But they had little opportunity to express their opposition in any dramatic way, as the stamps produced in Providence none of the rioting which occurred in Newport and Boston. As the Browns were not yet regularly engaged in the direct importation of goods from England, they could not express their disapproval of the Stamp Act by countermanding orders previously sent to London. For that reason the only evidence of their reaction to the tax is to be found in their correspondence with their friends. In letters to Tench Francis and John Relfe in Philadelphia and to Henry Lloyd in Boston they frequently revealed their point of view. Writing to Relfe on August 3, 1765, they referred to the forthcoming Stamp Act Congress, in which they hoped Pennsylvania would "hartily joyn."[8] They believed that, should the spirit of Virginia "unanimously prevail," there was a good chance of averting the evil "that almost Accomplish't Ruin of N. America." In a letter to one of their ship captains they described in considerable detail the damage done by the mobs in Newport and Boston. Following their mention of the destruction of Thomas Hutchinson's house in the capital of the Bay Colony, they remarked that "the whole Town of Boston begin to be Terefied as much by them [the mob] as had before bin of the Stamp Act."[9] This latter comment seems to reflect the fear which mob violence of the period increasingly engendered in the breasts of men of property. In short, while the Browns thoroughly disapproved of the Stamp Tax, they preferred that opposition to it should not get out of hand. Both they and their correspondents in the other towns, therefore, breathed a sigh of relief when they heard the news of the repeal.

Nicholas Brown and Company had scarcely established themselves as regular importers of goods from England, when a serious interruption to trade with the mother country began to threaten. In 1767 the British Parliament passed the Townshend Acts which not only tightened the customs service in America but also imposed duties on glass, red and white lead, painters' colors, paper, and tea imported into the colonies. As in 1764, the merchants in the commercial colonies faced trade restrictions which were a serious threat to business profits. In New England "evidences of hard times" quickly became apparent. People began to consider ways to reduce the cost of living. As a means to this end a Boston town meeting on October 28, 1767 adopted a nonconsumption agreement pledging subscribers to purchase colonial manufactures and to boycott a long list of imported articles.[10] The movement thus begun quickly spread within the Bay Colony, where other town meetings took action similar to that in Boston.[11]

At this time Rhode Islanders were also feeling the pinch of hard times, largely because of the declining profits of the traffic in molasses and rum. They, too, desired to reduce the cost of living. The initiative was taken by Providence. On December 2, 1767 a town meeting adopted an agreement more rigorous than that of Boston. Not confined to mere nonconsumption, it pledged subscribers not to import, after January 1, 1768, an imposing list of articles, to eschew the use of teas, chinaware, spices, and costly mourning raiment, and to encourage domestic wool and flax production.[12] Two days later a town meeting in Newport adopted a nonconsumption agreement very much like that of Boston, except that it was to become operative one month later.[13]

Although towns in Connecticut took similar steps, it became apparent early in 1768 that the "sumptuary regulations of the New England towns would fail to secure relief from hard times."[14] There then followed the effort of the Boston merchants to bring about a "non-importation league of the leading ports" within the colonies.[15] When this failed, they resolved to act independently. On August 1, 1768 they agreed to send no further orders for fall goods from England and to import no wares from Britain for one year after January 1, 1769, except for a few articles stipulated in the covenant.[16]

Thus action by the merchants supplanted that by town meeting, and nonimportation succeeded nonconsumption. Within less than a month the merchants of New York emulated the example of Boston. By spring of the next year the mercantile fraternity of Philadelphia had done likewise.[17]

Nonimportation then spread to the planting colonies as well as to other provinces north of Chesapeake Bay. By the autumn of 1769 only Rhode Island and New Hampshire had failed to use nonimportation as a weapon against British trade restrictions.[18] Given the importance of the mercantile interest in Rhode Island, one would suppose that the merchants would have turned readily to commercial retaliation against Britain. "But the temptation in hard times to turn the self-denial of their neighbors to their own immediate advantage proved too great."[19] Reports were rife in Boston and New York papers of "large Importations of British Goods into Rhode Island with Intent to take an Advantage of Sister Colonies." Merchants of Newport and Providence were said to be selling English goods to shopkeepers in western Massachusetts hitherto supplied from Boston.[20]

Stung, perhaps, by such criticism, the people of Providence assembled in town meeting on October 24, 1769, where they pledged themselves not to import or purchase any of the items named in the town agreement of December 2, 1767. Although this covenant had been relatively drastic when originally proclaimed, it was mild when compared with the nonimportation regulations which the other commercial centers had since adopted.[21] As several merchants of the town were expecting "from England in the Snow *Tristram* . . . divers parcels of goods, among which are many of the articles enumerated in the aforementioned agreement not to be imported," they, in the presence of the town meeting, "cheerfully" agreed to deliver up such goods to a committee of three, who were to store them pending the repeal of the Townshend duties.[22]

Merchants of Newport were more indifferent to the criticism of their neighbors. They remained unmoved until advised by the Merchants' Committee of Philadelphia, on October 21, 1769, of a plan to discontinue trade with them unless they united with the other colonies in nonimportation.[23] In the face of similar pressure from Boston and Charleston, the Newporters met on October 30 and promised to import neither British manufactures nor East India goods after January 1, 1770. But the Philadelphians were quick to see the catch in this. As the Newporters had foresworn only English and East India goods, they still could freely import from Britain goods produced in Continental Europe. Furthermore, by deferring the effective date of nonimportation until January, they left themselves at liberty to import vast quantities of goods in the interim. They were informed, therefore, that unless these defects were removed and a "determinate answer" given by December 10, the Philadelphia merchants would boycott them.[24] New York merchants proclaimed an immediate boycott, which they would lift when the Newport merchants complied with conditions not unlike those prescribed by Philadelphia. In the face of these threats, Newport merchants drafted a new agreement, which was satisfactory except for the absence of a provision requiring recent importations to be stored. Philadelphia merchants, with some misgivings, resumed trade with Newport, but only upon the promise of strict compliance in the future.[25] A few weeks later the New Yorkers lifted their boycott against the Rhode Islanders. But merchants who conformed so grudgingly as those of Newport, were likely to seize upon the slightest pretext for the abandonment of the nonimportation.

News of the partial repeal of the Townshend duties arrived in America in May 1770. During the next several months the merchants in most of the commercial centers were undecided as to the proper policy with respect to the importation of English goods. Among the few exceptions were those in Providence and Newport, who promptly made the repeal Act an excuse for a repudiation of their agreements.[26] When New York, Philadelphia, and Boston declared an absolute boycott against Rhode Island merchants, those in Providence quickly resumed nonimportation. Although the Newporters also reënacted their agreement, other provinces questioned their good faith. Soon commercial centers in eight provinces had embargoed the trade of Newport and coastwise vessels from the town were turned back at many ports. Both Newport and Providence were visited by a committee from Boston who induced the merchants to adopt new agreements. Upon recommendation of Boston merchants, other towns resumed trade with Rhode Island.[27]

But the days of nonimportation were now numbered. The very essence of the policy was to be found in the agreements of the three important commercial towns—Boston, New York, and Philadelphia. Should the merchants in any one of them regard partial repeal of the Townshend duties as sufficient reason to lift the boycott of English importations, further self-denial by the others would be pointless. The merchants of New York were the first to weaken; and although their action elicited strong protests from other provinces, everyone realized that this was the beginning of the end. In September 1770 Philadelphia revoked the nonimportation agreement; on October 12 the Merchants' Committee of Boston voted to resume importation of all British goods except tea or other dutiable articles. This action of the commercial centers was quickly emulated by the planting provinces. By the end of the year nonimportation was a thing of the past.[28]

From this brief survey of the policy of nonimportation it is apparent that the conduct of Rhode Island merchants generally was not calculated to fill their descendants with pride. Particularly equivocal had been the course pursued by the mercantile element in Newport, who clearly had sought to profit from the distress and self-sacrifice of their neighbors. The behavior of Providence, while far from exemplary, was less objectionable than that of the Newporters.

In November 1769, David Van Horne, New York correspondent of the Browns, severely criticized their course with respect to nonimportation, and threatened on that account to withhold an advance of £500 which he had promised them.[29] This drew a sharp rejoinder in which the Browns protested that they had "ever been as forward In Acting in opposition to the American Revenue Acts as any upon the Continent."[30] Just prior to the adoption of nonimportation in 1767 they had opened an extensive correspondence with various merchants and manufacturers in England, and had imported some goods, "but Sincerely Disposed" to serve the interests of America at the expense of their own, they had written their friends in England and refused further goods until the affairs between Britain and the colonies "were Settled upon more Equitable Conditions."[31]

The following summer Van Horne again wrote in critical vein.[32] Admitting that the New York Committee of inspection believed the Browns had always been "zealous for the Non-Importation Agreement" and had "more Strictly adhered to it than any one" in Rhode Island, he relayed to them the rumor (current in New York) that Providence was full of English goods. This elicited from the Browns an emphatic denial.[33] There was not "in all this Town an assortment of goods." Proof of this lay in the fact that "Customers to this Town from Connecticut and the Massachusetts as well as within the Colony have Left us and gone to Newport." The Browns knew of "houses that are Raised and Stand uncovered for Want of Nails," so great was the popular repugnance to importation from England.

Although the Snow *Tristram,* Captain Shand, had brought British goods to Rhode Island, the bulk of her cargo had gone to Newport. In Providence only three houses, "out of the number of persons that had before Imported," had received goods by *Tristram.* One of these was Nicholas Brown and Company. But, as the Browns quickly pointed out, their importation had consisted wholly of duck, ticklenburgs, Osnaburgs, cotton and wool cards, and mackerel and cod lines, "all which were allowed."

The Browns felt that Providence had been made to suffer for the sins of Newport. While not desiring to point an accusing finger at the merchants of that town, the principal ones of whom were "as uneasy at the Conduct of Some among them as we or you can be," they were sorry that any among them "Should Take So Much pains as they have done with you and at Phila. to Ubstruct our Intercourse, and have Actually prevailed at Philadelphia to Return one Vessel." They further alleged that by virtue of the action of the Newporters, some of the Southern colonies, where a proper distinction between the conduct of Providence and Newport could not be made, had refused to trade with Providence vessels. On the other hand, at Boston, where the behavior of the two towns was well understood, Providence enjoyed an uninterrupted intercourse "while Newport is Ubstructed."

Nicholas Brown and Company evidently felt keenly the strictures directed at Providence by the other towns when she made the partial repeal of the Townshend duties in the spring of 1770 the occasion for abandoning nonimportation. It is understandable, therefore, that they should react critically when in July of that year the New York merchants led the way to a general repudiation of nonimportation throughout the colonies. Writing to Van Horne in August they chided the New York merchants who "have behaved Scandalously in Braking threw their non Importation agreements," for which the Providence house thought they "ought to be Ridiculed by all the Colonys."[34] They were "men of Grait Vertue . . . to be one Day Resolving in the Strongest terms . . . against this Colony" for breaking "their agreement and Immediately after be Guilty of a worse action if Possable." The Browns charged that the New Yorkers "only waited a Good oppertunity for forwarding their orders for Fall Goods at a Time so late that the other Colonys could not Git knowledge in Season to forward theirs."

It was true that Providence merchants, including the Browns, had forwarded orders for fall goods in June 1770, a month before New York merchants had taken the lead in the wholesale abandonment of nonimportation. But the orders were contingent upon the shipment of similar goods to Philadelphia, New York, or Boston. This meant, of course, that inasmuch as the Yorkers had ordered wares for fall delivery, the orders from Providence could be filled by British houses in conformity with the provisions of the orders. This, the Browns admitted, would "Lay us under Sevear Reflections" in Boston, whose merchants had been less forehanded than those in New York and Providence. But, they regretfully observed, it was too late for Providence merchants to "alter their orders."

After due allowance is made for the understandable desire of the Browns to place their own conduct, and that of their Providence neighbors, in the most favorable light possible, there remains little evidence to support the charge that during nonimportation Providence was full of English goods. There exists in the Brown papers but one invoice of British wares ordered by them prior to the partial repeal of the Townshend duties. It covers the articles brought by Captain Shand in *Tristram,* and it agrees exactly with the Browns' statement to Van Horne of goods imported by them.[35] If Providence importers were supplying goods to shops in western

Massachusetts once stocked from Boston, the Browns were not among them.

The effect on the Browns of nonimportation was undoubtedly less serious than on many colonial merchants, because their business was more diversified. They had but recently established a regular correspondence with Hayley and Hopkins of London when the Townshend duties were imposed Nonimportation of English goods in no way affected their shipments of oil and pig iron to London. And, as they had not been regular importers of European wares, the boycott on imports from England did not interfere directly with an essential trade of theirs, although it must have made it more difficult for them to obtain English goods in other commercial towns. For the Browns, therefore, nonimportation was more in the nature of a postponement of extensive importations rather than an interruption to the accustomed flow of English merchandise.

With the breakdown of the nonimportation movement, the colonies entered upon a three-year period of "material prosperity and political calm."[36] So satisfactory were business conditions that "outside the ports of New York and Philadelphia the tea duty was universally acquiesced in, notwithstanding the widespread resolutions of boycott that had been adopted against customed teas in 1770."[37] Yet, so diligently did the merchants of those two towns apply themselves to the smuggling of tea that in the year 1771 "more than nine-tenths of the tea consumed was illicitly imported."[38] Other articles were also smuggled but "probably in lesser volume than ever before." Revenue from duties on wines and molasses increased steadily in all the colonies. As a result of increased activity of men-of-war along the coast, seizures of merchant craft more than doubled in 1772. And resentment against the vigilance of the customs service issued in the one important untoward incident which broke the "political calm" of the early seventies.

In March 1772 His Majesty's armed schooner *Gaspee*, Lieutenant Dudingston, made her appearance in the waters of Narragansett Bay. The purpose of her visit was "to prevent breaches of the revenue laws, and to stop the illicit trade, so long and so successfully carried on in the colony."[39] Her commander displayed unrestrained zeal in the performance of his duties. Not content with stopping all shipping without showing his authority for such action, he sent the property thus illegally seized to Boston for trial, notwithstanding an act of Parliament requiring all such trials to be held in the colonies where the seizures occurred.[40] Complaints of Providence people regarding his conduct soon became so numerous that the Deputy Governor, a resident of that town, procured from Chief Justice Hopkins an opinion that the Lieutenant had completely transcended his powers.[41] Thereupon the Deputy Governor submitted a report of the situation to Governor Wanton at Newport. Following an inconclusive exchange of letters between the Governor and the Lieutenant, the latter submitted the correspondence to Admiral Montagu, then in command of His Majesty's fleet at Boston.[42] The Admiral then addressed an insolent letter to Governor Wanton who curtly replied that he did not "receive instructions for the administration of my government, from the King's admiral, stationed in America."[43] The Governor laid the Admiral's letter before the General Assembly of Rhode Island at the May session of 1772. That body then adopted a resolution requesting Governor Wanton to transmit to the secretary of state in London copies of his correspondence with the Admiral.[44] Although the Governor promptly complied with this request, the controversy was not destined to be settled in a legal or amicable manner.

At about noon on June 9, 1772 Captain Thomas Lindsey sailed from Newport in his packet for Providence. *Gaspee* followed in close pursuit, continuing the chase to Namquit (now Gaspee) Point, some six miles from Providence, where she was grounded. Captain Lindsey arrived at Providence about sunset, where he immediately informed John Brown of the plight of *Gaspee*.[45] Believing the vessel would remain grounded until after midnight, John resolved upon her destruction as a way of freeing himself and his fellow merchants from the annoyance she had caused. He directed one of his ship captains to procure "eight of the largest long boats in the harbor," to muffle the oars and rowlocks to avoid noise, and to place them in readiness at Fenner's Wharf.

Shortly after sunset a man walked through the street, beating a drum and informing people that *Gaspee* was grounded, and inviting those who desired her destruction to foregather at the tavern of James Sabin in the evening There a considerable crowd assembled, including Captain Abraham Whipple, one of the Browns' shipmasters. About ten o'clock the men embarked in the boats from Fenner's Wharf. When within sixty yards of *Gaspee* they were challenged. According to the recollections of one of the party, recorded 67 years after the event, Captain Abraham Whipple replied in the following manner: "I am the sheriff of the county of Kent, G-d d-n you; so surrender, G-d d-n you." Before Lieutenant Dudingston had an opportunity either to reject or to comply with this demand, he was felled by a shot from one of the boats, which were soon alongside *Gaspee*. The mob boarded the vessel without opposition, removed the crew, and set her on fire. John Brown not only instigated the affair of *Gaspee*, but was also a member of the party which destroyed her.

The King appointed a commission of inquiry to investigate this act of lawlessness and to transport to England for trial those responsible for the burning of *Gaspee*.[46] Although the identity of those involved in the incident was known to more than a thousand persons, no one could be found to testify against them. And Stephen Hopkins, chief justice of Rhode Island and close friend of the Brown family, stood firmly against the removal of anyone to Britain for trial. The royal commission had no alternative, therefore, but to allow the investigation to lapse and to confess their failure to the government in London.

The burning of *Gaspee* contributed substantially to the movement toward colonial union. "The presence of the Commission of Inquiry in Rhode Island was widely pictured as an attack upon liberty in all the colonies, and Americans were told that in this crisis they must unite and stand their ground . . ."[47] The Virginia House of Burgesses took official notice of the Commission and in March 1773 suggested that Committees of Correspondence be appointed in all the colonies for the purpose of resisting British policy.[48] It was in response to this proposal that the Rhode Island Assembly in May of that year appointed a Committee of Correspondence, of which Moses Brown was a member.

Thus at a time when the conservative reaction was in full swing among colonial merchants generally, and when even John Hancock was throwing "his influence and vote in favor of conciliation" with Britain, John Brown had taken the lead in an act of violence against the authority of the home government. It was not likely that he and his brothers would ever find it possible to retreat from this advanced position of opposition to British policy.

Although Providence is not conspicuously associated with the opposition to the Tea Act of 1773, granting a monopoly of tea distribution in America to the East India Company, the town was not indifferent to the course of developments. On January 19, 1774 at a town meeting the people of Providence condemned the Tea Act; branded as an enemy to his country anyone "unloading, receiving, or vending" tea while it remained subject to the payment of a duty; declared their readiness to coöperate with other towns in the colony, and with other colonies, in opposition to all other unconstitutional measures; approved of the actions of their brethren in Boston, Philadelphia, and New York in resisting the introduction of the tea; and appointed a committee to correspond with "the towns in this and the neighboring governments."[49] This committee, of which John Brown was a member, promptly waited upon the various importers in the town and found that but one chest of tea had been ordered for the next spring, and that this had been countermanded before the meeting. And the committee assured the public, "from the best authority," that only nine chests had been imported into the town since the "memorable non-importation agreement."

We may be sure that the Brown brothers followed subsequent developments of that year with a lively interest. Their long-time friend, Stephen Hopkins, was one of the Rhode Island delegates to the First Continental Congress which convened at Philadelphia in September. At a Providence town meeting in December there was appointed a committee of inspection "to see that the association entered into by the general Continental Congrss be strictly adhered to." Joseph Brown was a member of this Committee.[50]

While the Association was still in force, the colonies and the mother country gradually drifted into hostilities which began in April 1775. Within a week after the firing of the first shot John Brown was once again in the limelight.

On April 25, 1775 the General Assembly of Rhode Island created an army of observation of 1500 men. Apprised of this fact by a "Tory informer" in the Assembly, Captain Wallace, then in command of the British patrol at the entrance to Narragansett Bay, decided to interfere with the supply of the army. On April 26th John Brown arrived at Newport with two packets loaded with flour. Some, if not all, of the flour was placed aboard the British men-of-war, while John himself was sent in one of the packets to Admiral Graves at Boston. The seizure of John Brown could have been in revenge for his part in the burning of *Gaspee;* or it could have been the result of Captain Wallace's belief that John, as agent of the colony, had purchased the flour for the benefit of the army of observation. Perhaps both considerations were in the captain's mind. But, whatever the motive may have been, the arrest and spiriting away of so conspicuous a figure as John Brown could not fail to produce a stir among his brothers and other influential persons in the colony. Prompt and numerous, therefore, were the steps taken to obtain his release. Within a week John was released, payment for the flour was ordered, and damages awarded for the detention of the two vessels.[51]

Efforts in John's behalf began with an attempt to intercept the ship carrying John to Boston. Leader of this undertaking, if not its originator, was young Elkanah Watson, a native of Plymouth, Massachusetts, who was to be closely associated with the Browns during the Revolution, and who was destined to make his mark in later life. Elkanah was apprenticed to John Brown in 1773 when a lad of fifteen. Years afterward he wrote that "Mr. Brown had occupied a father's place" to him. He shared with other people in Providence the sense of outrage at the capture of his benefactor. At a hurried consultation it was decided to dispatch a messenger to Plymouth "in order to fit out two armed schooners" to go to the rescue of John Brown. As a native of Plymouth and an apprentice of John Brown,

Elkanah Watson seemed clearly indicated for this mission.[52] With his musket at his back, and mounted on a fleet horse, he arrived in Plymouth at 2 o'clock in the morning. He alarmed the town by the cry of fire, awakened the Committee of Safety, and joined a band of volunteers for the attempted interception. The afternoon of the same day the rescue party embarked in two antiquated fishing schooners, each equipped with two old cannons and "with powder loose in barrels." After a fruitless cruise of ten days they returned to the safety of the harbor at Plymouth.[53]

A more calculated effort to secure John's release was that made by a group of influential Providence men, including Nicholas and Joseph Brown. In a letter of April 27th, addressed to their "Distressed brethren at Newport," they remarked that a communication from Lord Dartmouth suggesting an "Accomodation of the unhappy Difference Subsisting between the Two Countries" had prompted them "to recommend a speedy, but Cool & Dispassionate Meeting of the Town of Newport, to take into Consideration the Contents of the Letter [Dartmouth's], and Mediate Some Pacifick & Consiliating Measures for the Liberation of the Colony's Agent [John Brown] Now on bord the Man of War."[54]

This letter was delivered at Newport by Moses Brown. While there, he probably sought the aid of Governor Wanton, as the latter wrote to General Gage on that same day strongly interceding in behalf of John Brown, whose arrest by Captain Wallace he termed "so extraordinary a Proceeding."[55] Moses then, with brother Joseph, hastened to Boston, where they entreated their friends to use their influence to secure John's freedom.

In the meantime, other persons of influence had not been overlooked. Stephen Hopkins had on April 26th advised the Provincial Congress in Massachusetts of John's arrest.[56] Two days later the Congress directed that certain British officers who were prisoners of war be placed in custody of Hopkins at Providence ". . . to be made such use of as they shall think proper for obtaining the liberty of said Mr Brown."[57] Stephen Hopkins provided Moses and Joseph Brown with a letter of introduction to the Provincial Congress of Massachusetts, bespeaking their assistance to the brothers in securing John's release. His letter rejected the suggestion that British prisoners be used as hostages.[58]

On May 1st General Gage replied to Governor Wanton. Although the vessel bearing John Brown had not yet arrived, the General expected his release, as he saw no reason "for his detention."[59] John finally arrived in Boston on May 2. The following day Moses wrote Nicholas advising him of John's release "after much Intercession of Many & very kind friends and much sollisitation to the General and Admiral . . ."[60]

As a Quaker, Moses was ideally suited to intercede with British authorities in John's behalf. Naturally, and without affectation, he could speak in the spirit of compromise found in Lord Dartmouth's proposal. And, with or without persuasion from Moses, John Brown also assumed an attitude of moderation and restraint. The result was an agreement in writing, signed in the presence of witnesses and "binding both upon the Browns and the British officials." Although no copy of this agreement has been found, its provisions may be inferred from other sources. Ezra Stiles states that John Brown appeared before the General Assembly of Rhode Island on May 7, four days after his liberation. In the words of Stiles, "By Mr Brown, Gen. Gage recommended that Rd. Isld. Assembly shd send Delegates to him to negotiate on the present Crisis. This passed in the Lower House but negatived in the upper—who refused to have any Negotiations with him [Gage] of this Nature . . ."[61]

In his appearance before the Assembly, John reaffirmed "American Grievances" against the mother country. On the subject of taxation he asserted that "the Parliament of England have no more Just right to Tax America than the General Assembly of any One Colony has to Tax another." But, believing that Lord Dartmouth's proposal showed evidence of British inclination toward a compromise, John gave it as his "Opinion, that it is now in the power of this Colony and Continent to make such propositions to his Excellency General Gage, as will effectually put a stop to any Hostilities till the Continental Congress and each Colony can consider of, and Answer the Secretary of States Letter . . ."[62]

More specifically, John suggested that they tell "the General of our Determination of Defence," but that they really wished "there would be no occasion of our Forces going into the Field." He would have the Massachusetts forces, already "Assembled round Boston," return to their homes. All prisoners on both sides should be immediately delivered up and a "free Passage into and out of Boston should be immediately established." There should be no "further Hostilities Committed . . . till answer be received from his Majesty, to what the Colonists may send to him in answer to the Secretaries [Lord Dartmouth's] Letter aforesaid."[63]

It was not illogical that the Browns, a prominent mercantile family, should at that time favor an accommodation of the differences between Britain and the colonies. Their long record of opposition to specific acts of British policy was entirely consonant with a desire to avert a continuation of hostilities which might issue in a separation from the mother country. Even John's part in the burning of *Gaspee* was not inconsistent with a preference for a continued connection with Britain.

Nevertheless, John Brown soon made a move which cast serious doubt upon his good faith in appearing as an advocate of accommodation. This action was in violation of his agreement with British authorities and was likely to cost him the good will of family and friends who had loyally supported him in his time of trouble.

On June 6th he instituted suit against Captain Wallace for £10,000 lawful money damages alleged to have resulted from his seizure and detention. The following day he apprised Moses of the fact, pleading in justification the rather lame excuse that he, and his brothers collectively, were being branded as Tories because he had not brought suit.[64] This prompted a very long letter from Moses adducing many reasons why John should not press legal action.[65] Besides being detrimental to the business interests of John, and of Providence merchants generally, it would place in jeopardy Moses' reputation for "Sincerity & Honnesty," of which that good Quaker gentleman was ever jealous. In his rejoinder, under date of June 21st, John asserted that he was now "so clear in opinion that the Measures now taking to Force America are Rong that it is out of my power to Restrain my Self from wishing Success to the Countery in which I was Born."[66] A rather abrupt change of heart! The more so, since in the interim nothing had happened to justify it.

Another year was to pass before the colonies declared their independence. In those months John became so completely identified with the patriot position that ultimate separation could have occasioned him little, if any, mental anguish. Moses Brown as a Quaker, and a man of moderation, could view the approaching conflict with no satisfaction. Like many others who shared his views, he made the most of a difficult situation. Nicholas contemplated the onset of strife with a feeling of concern. Writing to Henry Lloyd on June 2, 1775, he referred to the "destruction awaiting our kingdom."[67] Several weeks later he remarked that ". . . divine Providence hath Left the Two Countries to be Scurges to Punish Each other for their Sins. May both lay the Cause to heart, be Humble Repent the turn & receive the Divine favour in a happy Tranquility in Peace."[68]

Thus, the Brown family became Conservative Whigs, reconciled to independence, but not committed to the leveling tendencies of the radicals, so evident in the Pennsylvania Constitution of 1776. When, a decade later, this same "leveling spirit" began to run riot in Rhode Island, the Browns opposed it with all the resources at their command.

CHAPTER 11

"Warlike Stores for the Continental Congress"

IN the Revolution, far more than in any war, this country was in urgent need of strategic materials from beyond the seas. The era of a high degree of self-sufficiency was far in the future. Saltpeter, gunpowder, cannon, mortars, cloth, uniforms, blankets, and a host of other items essential to the conduct of the war were not available; nor could they be produced at home in sufficient quantities.

The first and most critical need was for powder. Foreseeing the probable outbreak of hostilities, the British Government in 1774 forbade the export of gunpowder to the colonies. After the fighting began there was a mad rush by both the British and the colonials for control of the magazines within the colonies. From these stores and from the West Indies the colonials gathered a modest supply of powder which was wasted in reckless fashion by the raw recruits before Boston. Shortly after taking command of the Continental army, Washington directed that an inventory be taken of the powder supply. This inventory showed that, aside from what the men then had in their horns, there was a reserve of only nine rounds per man, with none at all available for the artillery. Six months later the situation was no better. On Christmas Day, 1775, Washington wrote that "our want of powder is inconceivable."[1]

Meanwhile the Continental Congress was giving consideration to this "inconceivable" shortage of ammunition. But the members of Congress decided that the manufacture of saltpeter and powder was primarily the prerogative of the colonial governments. They contented themselves with drawing up printed "systems" describing the processes of manufacture.[2]

These they sent to the various colonial governments, requesting prompt attention to the subject. In response to this appeal, several of the colonies, especially Massachusetts and Pennsylvania, attacked the problem with considerable success. Prior to the autumn of 1777, 15,000 pounds of powder were produced from saltpeter extracted locally.[3]

This result may have been gratifying but it was not enough. It was evident that domestic manufacture of saltpeter and powder must be supplemented by very extensive importation from abroad. To this task the Congress, the State authorities, and private individuals gave their earnest attention. Up to the Battle of Saratoga imports of saltpeter amounted to 478,000 pounds, from which 698,000 pounds of powder were manufactured. In addition, 1,454,000 pounds of powder were imported. Thus, directly or indirectly, "well over 90 per cent of all the powder available for carrying on the Revolution during the first two and a half years of the struggle for independence was obtained from outside the country."[4] More than half of the imported powder came into the country through the port of Philadelphia; but every colony, except Georgia, received substantial amounts.

The powder and other "warlike stores" were largely imported from France. From the beginning of the conflict, the Americans realized that their maritime trade was a most valuable asset in purchasing the aid of European powers. And the Bourbon monarchy had the greatest respect for a commerce which had contributed so much to the preëminence of its arch-rival, England. The hope of winning their trade was perhaps the most compelling reason for French assistance to the American rebels. This hope of French officialdom was shared by many merchants of Bordeaux, Le Havre, and Nantes, who had ambitions to supplant the great mercantile houses of London and Bristol in the control of American commerce. Especially alluring to the French merchants was the American tobacco crop, of which approximately 100,000,000 pounds went annually to Britain, where the processing, and the reëxport of vast quantities to continental Europe yielded a handsome profit. Here the Americans had an export potentially capable of balancing the large imports from France which the conduct of the war required.

Aid from France during the Revolution falls into two stages: before and after the signing of the Treaty of Alliance on February 6, 1778.[5] Prior to that date it was unofficial and secret; subsequently it was official and open. In both periods cargoes came from France direct and also by way of the West Indies. In the first year of the war much of the powder, saltpeter, and other military stores came into the country on the private account of colonial merchants. In December 1775 and January 1776, however, the Secret Committee of Congress entered into contracts with merchants authorizing them to import munitions and supplies on the account of Congress. In the spring of 1776 the participation of Congress in the trade became more active and direct, when Arthur Lee and Silas Deane went to France as government purchasing agents. Title to many of the cargoes thus obtained was actually vested in the Congress, as was also true of the goods sent in payment therefor.

After the summer of 1776 the French and Spanish governments were secretly involved in these shipments. Vergennes, the French Minister of Foreign Affairs, advanced a million livres to the Americans for the purchase of munitions, Spain contributed a like sum, and private citizens in the two countries provided additional funds. To conceal the real nature of the transaction, the business was conducted by Caron de Beaumarchais, the French playwright, through the fictitious commercial firm of Rodrique Hortalez & Co. The promoters of the scheme hoped that American goods would be returned in sufficient volume to render the project self-sustaining. By the spring of 1777 no less than nine vessels outfitted by Beaumarchais had arrived at Portsmouth, New Hampshire direct from France. Among them was *Mercury* from Nantes with 1000 barrels of powder, about 12,000 muskets, 11,000 flints, a quantity of shoes, and 46 cases of cloth.[6]

At Nantes the firm of Basmarein & Rambeux, a *bona fide* mercantile house, was also interested in the American trade. The first of its ships to sail carried a cargo which is said to have netted a handsome profit in Boston. In the early stages of the war some eight of every nine cargoes shipped from France direct to American ports arrived safely.[7] But as the British fleet became more vigilant, the proportion of captures increased markedly. Between February 1777 and August 1778, the British captured thirty-eight of sixty-five cargoes dispatched by Basmarein & Rambeux from Nantes.

Although the voyages from France direct to American ports were comparatively successful, the indirect trade by way of the West Indies was far more popular. For every vessel that "went straight overseas" from a French port, "scores sailed to the French, Dutch or Spanish islands" with European goods. "The big vessels, from those nations in Europe that were neutral during the early part of the war, could shuttle back and forth between the home ports and the Caribbean with relative safety. From these islands these European cargoes were carried to the United States in the numerous little vessels which the Americans had long had in the West Indian trade."[8] Cargoes of every description, assembled from various ports of Europe and America, mingled in the "warehouses of Cape Francois, Port au Prince, Martinique, St. Eustatius, Havana and St. Croix."[9] From those ports were transshipped the vast quantities of military stores of European origin and the tobacco, indigo, and naval stores produced in the United States. Most notable of these West Indian entrepôts was the Dutch colony of St. Eustatius. Located in convenient proximity to the insular possessions of several European nations, and readily accessible from the mainland of North America, this little island was ideally situated for this broken voyage trade. Thoroughly aware of this fact, Holland had made it a free port and had thrown it open to the trade of all nations. As a result no less than 3182 vessels cleared from it during a period of thirteen months in the middle period of the war.[10]

The British were exasperated with the aid which the Americans thus received; but they were unable seriously to interfere with it until their declaration of war upon Holland late in 1780. Shortly thereafter Admiral Rodney surprised the busy little port at St. Eustatius and seized a vast booty on shore and in the harbor, including a large convoy just sailing for Holland. By keeping the Dutch flag flying on the captured fleet, he tricked some fifty American ships into the port still supposed to be neutral.[11] During the remainder of the war the Dutch islands were overshadowed by the French, Danish, and Spanish West Indies as centers of this trade. In 1782 Havana attracted much attention, as it was not only a market for flour but a source of much-needed specie as well.[12]

Not all the American trade with Europe, whether direct or by way of the West Indies, was with France. A certain amount of traffic with Spain was carried on through the port of Bilbao. More important was the commerce with Holland. Because of the proximity of Amsterdam to British shores, not much of the Dutch goods went direct to American ports; but the merchants of Holland, of course, enjoyed with those of other countries, the full use of their colony of St. Eustatius. In the later stages of the war American merchants also established commercial contacts with Copenhagen and with Gothenburg in Sweden.

After the Franco-American alliance was formed, the European trade of the Americans enjoyed the benefits of direct loans from the French Government, as well as some assistance from the French fleet. By degrees the traffic became less restricted to military stores and assumed the aspect of a more normal commercial intercourse. More and more the requirements of the military ceased to be the sole governing consideration in the selection of goods to be imported, as the needs and preferences of the consuming public came to dictate the choice of many of the wares shipped from France and the other countries. "Luxury" goods, strangely out of place in a country fighting for its very existence, appeared more frequently on the invoices; and, after the first burst of patriotism had spent itself, American merchants did not blush when indicating their desire for English goods rather than those from the Continent.

Nicholas and John Brown were actively engaged in trade within this wartime framework. After Lexington and Concord they were alert to every opportunity which the situation offered. They combined service in the common cause with advantage to themselves, and on occasion they allowed their own business interests to take precedence over the general welfare of their country. They appear to have been active in the munitions trade almost from the inception of the war. Referring to their efforts to obtain military stores by way of the West Indies, Nicholas remarked late in 1775 that "several Voyages we have as Merchants ben conserned in that way . . . have Intirely failed," although a Brig "of Brother John Browns" had lately brought in from Surinam about 45 hundredweight of powder, "which was all she could get (as the Dutch are bot off)."

Doubtless it was some of this powder lately imported by John which he offered to sell to the Continental Army at Cambridge. On November 27, 1775, Stephen Moylan, Muster-Master General to the Army, wrote to John: "In your letter of the 21st you make an offer of one ton of good pistol powder at six shillings per pound. The General [Washington] will take it, though it is a most exorbitant price. He is willing to encourage the importation of that necessary article."[13] In a postscript Moylan added that "there are two companies ordered from your quarter to this place . . . You will please to send the powder under their guard, in a covered wagon. Should they have set out before this reaches you, you must get a few of the minute or militia men of your Colony to guard it to this place."[14] It seems likely that the "two companies" referred to by Moylan departed before John received the letter, thus requiring the detail of "minute men" to guard the powder. It is probable that one of these was young Elkanah Watson, then apprenticed to John Brown.[15] In his *Memoirs,* Elkanah tells how he took with him "Six or eight recruits" to guard powder which he delivered to General Washington at Cambridge on the account of John Brown. He further tells how the General directed a young officer to super-intend the delivery of the precious freight at the powder house. When Elkanah remarked that he was glad to see so many barrels of powder, the officer replied that the barrels were filled with sand "to deceive the enemy should any spy by chance look in."[16] Obviously the General felt impelled to replace the sand in these barrels with John Brown's powder, even at the "most exorbitant" price of six shillings per pound.

Probably the failure of the West Indian voyages in 1775 helped to turn the Browns' attention to the French trade. Largely under the direction of Nicholas, an experimental voyage was planned to secure a cargo in St. Pierre (the French colony off the Newfoundland coast) or in France, at the discretion of the men in charge of the vessel. The Sloop *Liberty* sailed from Providence for St. Pierre on November 16, 1775.[17] Captain Dou Veille carried with him £657 lawful money in gold and silver, together with a letter of credit for £150 provided by Nicholas. John supplied him with £690. The captain and his factor, Jonathan Clark, were to purchase an assorted cargo. Good merchantable codfish, Nicholas believed, would bring a handsome price in Rhode Island, as would liver oil, coarse linens, checks, and pins. Good "soldier guns," completely fitted with iron or steel ramrods and bayonets, were worth ten dollars apiece in the colonies, with "pistles" and swords in like proportion. But the article "most wanting" was "Canon and Pistle Powder." With an eye to "Future Trade" Dou Veille and Clark were to gather all possible data about prices of New England goods in St. Pierre and in France, and about French merchandise available for the American market. And it was most important that they "find out if there be any probable way of Geting Spermaceti Candles into any port of France by running or Otherways." And to insure a safe return they were to be "sure to get proper papers for Two or more Vessels . . . so Calculated that they may be Briggs or Sloops."

What actually transpired at St. Pierre is unknown, but Dou Veille and Clark continued the voyage to Nantes in France, where they evidently procured French papers which transformed *Liberty* into *Amiable Maria*.[18] On the return voyage, when in sight of the New England shore, they were captured by "a little Cruizer of Four Swivell Guns." Nicholas wrote that Captain Dou Veille was "'Foolishly if not Voluntarily taken'" when "he might have run in with his Vessell and saved his Valuable and Much Wanted Cargo." Nicholas was "much Disstaisfyed with our Captain's Conduct."

In the early stages of the war this idea of protecting his vessels from British men-of-war by the use of false papers of neutral countries seems to have had a strange fascination for Nicholas Brown. Not long after *Liberty* sailed for France, he wrote to one Edmond Jennings in St. Eustatius that he had a plan for "making a very grand voyage from here direct to Amsterdam" with a large quantity of spermaceti candles, tobacco, and oil. Besides the profit to be expected from the sale of this cargo, Nicholas assured Jennings that "many articles from Holland would afford more than 100 per cent profit" in America. For the execution of his plan, he said, "it would be necessary to have a set of Dutch papers for a sloop of about 80 tons or other bigger vessel with a Dutch Captain that could talk English." The captain could bring with him the "proper papers & clearance with blank room to fill up the cargo, etc." in Providence. "But," Nicholas added, "as doubtless you understand the nature of such trade I shant enlarge."[19] Nicholas invited Jennings to take a quarter interest in the proposed voyage. Should he decline to coöperate, however, Nicholas hoped he would "procure me a proper set of papers and a suitable Captain," for which he would satisfy Jennings "at any reasonable rate." And "if a few Dutch seamen could be got 'twould be much best." On his copy of the letter Nicholas recorded his conviction that "this being a confidential affair it ought not to be known whether executed or not." So well did he keep the secret that to this day we know not whether the "affair" was executed. But we do know that the ship captain who carried Nicholas' letter to Jennings brought back a "Sett of Dutch papers for N.B.," for which he paid forty pieces of eight at St. Eustatius.[20]

Nicholas was at this time very much concerned about finding suitable cargoes to send to France. The master of the Sloop *Liberty* had been instructed to bring back information about prices of American merchandise in the French markets. Nicholas had also been hopeful that they would find a way to ship spermaceti candles into France, even if they had to be "run." In a long letter to Stephen Hopkins and Samuel Ward, the Rhode Island delegates to the Continental Congress, he discussed this problem and made some general suggestions about the conduct of the war. He urged the importance of keeping Narragansett Bay open as a channel of communication to the "Grand Continental Army" then engaged in the siege of Boston. Rhode Island "of it self," he wrote, "is Insignificant compared with the whole or some Single Colonys," but its situation with respect to the troops in Cambridge made it imperative that the enemy be prevented from occupying both sides of the Bay.[21]

Nicholas asked whether the Continental Congress, "who sitts at the fountain Head of Welth," was sufficiently vigilant in "sending into all parts of the World" where powder was to be had. "From any knowledge we have," he said, "the Salt Petter Business seems . . . to be a work of Time." Should anything new on the subject "Turn up to the Westward," he hoped it would be published. And he advised his correspondents that the Rhode Island Assembly had appointed a committee, of which his brother Joseph was a member, "to carry on" the manufacture. "Is there any known place in Europe," he asked, "where it may be got with anything we have to purchase it with?"[22]

The supply of money was a subject always dear to the heart of Nicholas. He warned Hopkins and Ward that draining the "Continent of all its Hard Cash" would have a "fatal Tendency to Depreciate all its paper Currency." To this very process Nicholas and John, and their associates in the voyage of *Liberty* to Nantes, had contributed their bit. Of the £4103 lawful money invested in the venture, goods accounted for but a small part. Nicholas himself had sent £657 in gold and silver. But Nicholas knew that this could not continue. He urged upon Hopkins and Ward the importance of exporting goods in lieu of specie as a means of procuring military stores. Then he came to the point. He and his brothers, he wrote, had on hand upwards of eight hundred boxes of spermaceti candles, "all made from last years Stock," which they would be glad to send for arms and powder, "if permitted to send them to the most likely places."[23]

Shortly afterwards Nicholas presented a similar argument in a letter to John Brown, who was visiting in Philadelphia. Referring to spermaceti candles as a "Superfluity" which tended "to Impoverish the Consumer," he asked why they could not be carried to "any part of the English Islands to Raise Money" with which to purchase necessary foreign manufactures, "among others Powder." All this, he said, would "help to save the Hard Money in the Country."[24]

Whether as a result of this letter or not, John used his time at the seat of government to good advantage so far as the disposal of surplus candles was concerned. Both he and Nicholas had large consignments of candles in the hands of Josiah Hewes, their Philadelphia correspondent. Reports from the city indicated "a Miserable Dule market. No demand nor is there Like to be any as None are Exported from here."[25] Nor could they be sold in Philadelphia itself, as there "is not 40 famalies in this City that burn them" in their homes. "Consumption," wrote Hewes, "is but Trifling" now that "no assemblies, Dances or plays" were any longer tolerated by the regime of austerity which patriotism imposed upon the city. He had tried "every means to sell them, but to no purpose." They could not be sold within six months "if our ports are not opened." Hewes had "been with Sum of the Congress but they wont purchase." He wished Nicholas had sent oil in lieu of candles, as its sale was "permitted."

Within one week the gloomy outlook described by Josiah Hewes had completely changed for the better. The government had entered the picture. Hewes reported the sale of 90 boxes of Nicholas' candles, "to be Shipt for the Use & by order of the Congress." For the improved situation, Hewes gave the entire credit to the persuasive powers of John Brown, who "first put them [the Congress] On shipping Candles, Sold his to them, and Recommended them to me for yours." What was more, John had fixed the price of candles at 3/3 per pound, with 2/ for the box. "A Lucky Affair this," was the way Hewes described this latest stroke on John's part.[26] Hewes was evidently unaware of the part that Nicholas had played in suggesting the plan to John or of the influence his letter may well have had upon Ward and Hopkins.

But Nicholas intended to use every available outlet for the disposal of the candles in his warehouses. Notwithstanding the very indifferent results of his West Indian ventures earlier in the year, he decided in December 1775 to have another try at trade in that quarter. The Ship *Unity* was chartered for the voyage.[27] Paul Allen was selected as captain. Whatever Allen's nautical talents may have been, he had the merit of being the son-in-law of Nicholas Cooke, then Governor of Rhode Island. The latter kindly gave Captain Allen a letter of introduction to the Governor of Martinique.[28] Cooke wrote the French official that all hope of an accommodation between Britain and the colonies was at an end, and declared that colonial resistance was "perfectly justified by Charters and by the fundamental Laws and Principles of the British Constitution." The Governor realized that to obtain French aid the colonials would have to offer something more tangible than the abstract justice of their contention. His compatriots, he said, had men, provisions, and "everything necessary to the War excepting Powder and Some Other warlike Stores." Supposing that France should "not interfere in the War," it surely could not be inconsistent with her interests to supply the colonies with arms. He tempted the French official with the lure of the great American trade. Colonial imports from Britain, he said, had amounted to about £3,000,000 Sterling annually, while their exports to the mother country came to a "Still graiter Sum." Like most men of that day, the Governor thought Britain was about to lose forever this great and lucrative prize; like them, too, he looked to France "as the Nation best capable of carrying on this Commerce which will be so beneficial to her as well as the Colonys."

Three hundred boxes of Nicholas' candles went aboard *Unity*.[29] Along with the candles and other goods, Nicholas Brown sent £58 in hard money and a letter of credit addressed to "all Gentlemen Merchants and others of Whatever Nation in any of the foreign Islands in the West Indies." The letter asked them to furnish Captain Allen with "as much Cash, or any Such Goods or Merchandize as he shall Require," for which they were asked to take the captain's bills on Nicholas.[30]

In the office of the Secretary of the Colony of Rhode Island, Nicholas Brown and Captain Paul Allen lodged a bond pledging *Unity* to shun every "port or place in the British West Indies," the danger of the seas and "Seizour by an Enemie Allways excepted."[31] Captain Allen was to lay out the proceeds of his cargo in gunpowder, saltpeter, sulphur, duck, or arms. But in the event of his inability to invest the entire amount in those articles, he was free to "bring back the remainder" in paper, Osnaburgs, ticklenburgs, lead, flints, twine, Jesuits' bark, rhubarb, or in cotton, linen, or woolen cloth. Upon his return to Rhode Island, Captain Allen must lodge with the Secretary a "True Manifest" of his cargo.

Having provided this guarantee that the voyage of *Unity* would neither redound to the advantage of the enemy nor issue in the importation of goods needless to the war effort, Nicholas Brown procured from Governor Cooke a "Certificate of Credit," affirming that Nicholas was a merchant of "principal Note, Reputation and Estate in Providence," and that any bills which Captain Paul Allen might draw on him would meet due honor.[32]

The sailing orders which Captain Allen received from Nicholas Brown authorized him to touch first at St. Eustatius, St. Lucia, Martinique, or

Guadeloupe, although he was at liberty to go to any of the "foreign Islands."[33] Should the letter of credit be acceptable, he might purchase to the amount of £2000 lawful money such articles "as will answer best or sell here for the most profit from the cost in the West Indies." As the *Unity* carried a cargo to the Caribbean valued at approximately £2000, there was the possibility that, should the fates be kind, Captain Allen might bring home military stores to the value of some £4000, a not inconsiderable cargo.

Captain Allen arrived at St. Pierre, Martinique, after a "Tedious Passage of 19 days" in which *Unity* was buffeted about by two or three hard "Gails of Wind." The leaky vessel which made "a Hundred Tons of Water" for every 24 hours taxed to the utmost the energy and vigilance of the six-man crew. Many times the good captain despaired of making port, but "Going from the Pump to the Helm . . . and incouraging" his men, he managed to "Keep their Spirits up" until they reached the "Desired Heaven."[34]

Had they arrived at a good market they could quickly have "forgot their late troubles," and he added, with the pessimism so characteristic of sea captains, that markets were never worse than at St. Pierre. Nevertheless, Captain Allen sold there all of his tobacco and flour, 200 boxes of spermaceti candles, and substantial portions of the other articles in his cargo. Although the items he wished to purchase were "very dear & scarce," he laid out "about 1000 Dollars" in twine, rhubarb, nutmeg, cinnamon, Jesuits' bark, handkerchiefs, etc. Reports of a bad market at St. Lucia deterred him from going there, as Nicholas Brown had suggested; while "8 ships of War" cruising between Granada and St. Eustatius persuaded him to avoid the latter.[35] Instead, he decided to try his fortunes at Curaçao. Details of what took place at that Dutch port are very meager, but Captain Allen presumably obtained better terms there than at St. Pierre. The sale of the remainder of his cargo brought the total proceeds to 6716 pieces of eight. And there he purchased the bulk of his return cargo, which, exclusive of arms and military stores, absorbed almost exactly the sum realized from his sales. It seems evident, therefore, that he made use of his letter of credit to pay for the munitions he brought back to Providence. These consisted of 117 casks of powder, the net weight of which was 3080 pounds, 129 small arms, 60 pistols, 11,000 flints, 48 cutlasses, 4 swivel guns, and 1900 pounds of lead in "Shot & Bullets."[36] In the invoice these were valued at £1468 lawful money.[37] Captain Allen also procured at Curaçao 68 bolts of Osnaburgs, 102 blankets, considerable amounts of "checks, stripes and Hollands," nails, pins, cocoa, coffee, and pepper, and a quantity of "Course Baging Cloth fit for knap sacks."

This voyage of *Unity,* made in a little more than two months, was a substantial contribution to the war effort. Nicholas had shipped candles to a "likely place" and had received in exchange munitions and other much needed goods. As the account of the sales of the return cargo has not been preserved, it is impossible to determine with any degree of accuracy the success of the voyage as a business venture on the part of Nicholas Brown. But since *Unity* brought goods urgently needed by a people preparing for war, her cargo could hardly fail to command a satisfactory price at Providence.

These voyages to the West Indies and to Nantes had been undertaken by Nicholas and John Brown on their own accounts. Later, they sent out vessels on the account and risk of the Continental Congress. In 1775 that body appointed a Committee of Secrecy, whose membership at different times included Benjamin Franklin, Robert Morris, Samuel Ward, John Langdon, and other well-known figures of the day. One of the functions of the Committee was to procure arms and munitions from every possible source. Accordingly, the Committee entered into contracts with merchants in the various coastal towns authorizing the importation of military stores on a commission basis. The firm of Willing and Morris of Philadelphia, Silas Deane of Connecticut, and John Alsop, Philip Livingston and Francis Lewis of New York were among those receiving such contracts. Before many months had passed the Congress was "disturbed by rumors that the house of Willing and Morris stood to make £12,000 on powder deliveries."[38] Forty-four other American merchants residing in the more important commercial centers obtained commission contracts from the Committee. The conspicuous absence of Boston and Newport names from the list was, of course, the result of British occupation of those towns during the early stages of the war.

During his visit to Philadelphia in December 1775, John not only persuaded the Committee to purchase the candles which he and Nicholas then had in that city, but also negotiated a commission agreement authorizing him to import military stores on the account of the Committee.[39] In consideration of 20,000 dollars in Continental currency which the Committee advanced to him, John agreed to undertake a voyage or voyages for "the Speedy procuring" of thirty-six tons of good gunpowder. Should the powder not be available, he was to purchase "as much Salt Petre" as would be sufficient to make that quantity of gunpowder. He was also to obtain one thousand stand of good arms, one thousand double bridled gun locks, twenty tons of lead, and one thousand bolts of Russia duck. If the arms were not to be had he might lay out their value in gunpowder or salt peter and sulphur. If neither of these could be procured, ticklenburgs,

Osnaburgs, or "vitreys" would be acceptable. Failing to obtain these, John was to return the net proceeds of his outbound cargo in gold or silver.

The vessel or vessels were to be chartered for the use of the United Colonies, the freight to be paid on their return. Except for the "risque of the sea," the United Colonies assumed the "whole risque of the . . . adventure," including insurance against British capture. John's commission was to be 5 per cent on the cargo purchased for export, 2½ per cent on its sale in Europe or the West Indies, and a similar amount for the purchase of the return cargo. He promised to put the powder or other supplies on shore in "some safe and convenient place" to the eastward of Chesapeake Bay.

From John's point of view this appeared to be a pretty safe proposition. He received from the Committee the funds with which to purchase a cargo for export and was to be paid a commission on every transaction involved in the venture. He was to collect the freight on the cargoes. Except for the hazards of the seas, he assumed no risk whatsoever. In January 1776 Nicholas became "one third Consern'd" in this contract.

On February 6, 1776 John and Nicholas jointly signed a second contract with the Committee of Secrecy.[40] By it the Committee advanced to them the sum of 24,000 dollars. On their part the brothers agreed to undertake voyages to "Some proper port or ports" in Europe "for the speedy procuring" of ten thousand good striped blankets "for soldiers" at "four Shillings and Six pence or five Shillings" Sterling per blanket. They further undertook to purchase 9200 yards of broadcloth, "the Collours to be Brown and Blue for Officers and Soldiers Uniforms," and 800 yards of broadcloth of "Different Colours Suteable to face them." For the "Cloths" for enlisted men, constituting the "graitest part" of the total, John and Nicholas were to pay about four shillings Sterling per yard; for cloth for officers' uniforms they might pay as much as six shillings per yard. The contract also authorized the importation of ten tons of lead, 250 stands of good arms "such as are used by the infantry of France," and 50 barrels of good gunpowder (each of 100 pounds). Should any of the articles enumerated be unavailable, "then a graiter proportion of such as are at market" was to be procured. "In default of any of these," the brothers were to purchase Russia duck, raven's-duck, ticklenburgs, Osnaburgs, or "vitrys or other Course Linnens or course Woolens fit for Soldiers or Sailers use." Other provisions of the contract were almost identical with those of the one previously signed, except that Governor Cooke of Rhode Island was to "value" the vessels and to estimate their monthly hire, "or the freight to be given on the Goods exported and imported."

Fortified with two contracts with the Secret Committee, Nicholas and John lost no time in arranging for the fulfillment of their obligations. A few days before the signing of the second contract, they leased from Benjamin and Joseph Comstock of Providence, for the "Use of the United Colonies, Seven Eighth Parts" of the Sloop *Polly,* which they planned to send on a voyage to the West Indies.[41] They were to pay the owners at the rate of one dollar a ton per month for the "Whole Vessel." In the event of the loss of the Sloop "by any Means whatsoever saving the Danger of the Sea," they were to reimburse the Comstocks at the rate of 800 dollars for the "Whole Vessel," but in such case they were to pay no "Hire or Freight Money." By a significant provision of the agreement, the owners assumed all risk against the "Dangers of the Sea." As the contracts which Nicholas and John had signed with Congress protected them against all other risks, this clause actually assured them of complete immunity from loss on the forthcoming voyage of *Polly.*

Command of the Sloop was vested in Captain Benjamin Comstock. Her cargo comprised 100 boxes of spermaceti candles, 60 barrels and 45 half barrels of pork, 8 barrels of beef, 53 barrels of flour, 30 barrels of oil, and 350 bunches of onions.[42] The candles were charged in the invoice at 2/6 per pound, Rhode Island currency, which was only a trifle less than the 3/3, Pennsylvania currency, at which John Brown had recently sold them to the Congress in Philadelphia. The charge for the entire cargo was £932 lawful money.

Captain Comstock's sailing orders directed him to go to sea "Secunnit way" and to proceed with all possible dispatch to St. Eustatius, where he was to dispose of his cargo, provided he could procure powder and other munitions.[43] Should none of these articles be obtainable there to the amount of his cargo, he was at liberty to visit "any other of the French or Neutral Islands." If he could not procure the powder or arms at any of these ports he was to purchase any of the other items mentioned in the contracts with the Committee of Secrecy. His instructions called for the use of circumspection on the approach to home waters. He might stop at "Stoningtown" in Connecticut or at any harbor on "The Eastern Shore from Secunnit to bedford." But should he deem it wise he might run "Directly to this town by Coming in by Night Secunnit way as the wind may permit."

Polly's voyage to St. Eustatius and back was made in surprisingly good time. Leaving Providence on January 3, 1776, she had returned before the 20th of March. Captain Comstock disposed of his cargo at St. Eustatius for 3764 Spanish pieces of eight. Powder and arms were in extremely short supply, although a large quantity was "Soone Expected there." The captain therefore invested the bulk of his funds in 193 bolts of Russia duck and 43 pieces of Russia sheeting.[44] After her departure from St. Eustatius *Polly* was chased "very clost" for some ten hours by a small armed cutter, but "being well Fitted with Lite Sails & a prime sailor escaped being tacon." She evidently approached Narragansett Bay "Secunnit way," as on March 20th John Brown wrote the Committee of Secrecy that she was then at Howland's Ferry on the east side of Rhode Island. Captain Wallace's fleet, stationed between Bristol and Prudence Island, prevented her from continuing to Providence. John Brown assured the Committee that "we shall take care to watch the motions of the enemy, so as to secure the Duck, etc. till we have your orders what to do with them." John expected early instructions from the Committee with respect to the disposition of the goods *Polly* had brought. He assumed that the duck and sheeting would be wanted immediately for the ships then building in New England on the account of the Congress. In this expectation of prompt action John showed his lack of experience with governmental red tape; for, of course, the Committee of Secrecy itself could not make disposition of the goods. Robert Morris, Chairman of the Committee, wrote to John that he would advise the Marine Committee of the arrival of the duck; that body, in turn, would ultimately instruct the Browns as to the disposal of it. Meanwhile, John and Nicholas were to keep it safely in their possession.[45]

The voyage of *Polly* affords striking evidence that wartime trade did not always return a large profit. Her cargo to the Caribbean cost £932 lawful money of Rhode Island. It sold for 3764 pieces of eight, or approximately £1129, Rhode Island currency. There remained, therefore, the sum of £197 to pay for all the expenses of the outbound voyage. Assuming that *Polly* was of 60 tons burden, the lease of her amounted to £36. This left a balance of £161 with which to meet the food and wage bills of the captain and crew, and to defray port charges at St. Eustatius. The profit must have been modest in the extreme.

But the goods brought back by *Polly* were only a beginning. To fulfill the government contracts, the Browns had to arrange for additional voyages. Conditions at the moment made it imprudent to attempt to secure the rest of the "war-like stores" from the West Indies. Captain Comstock's report of the capture of many vessels, including several from Rhode Island, trading with the neutral Islands in the Caribbean had temporarily dampened their ardor for this uncertain traffic. And *Polly*'s own narrow escape from the armed cutter could hardly rekindle their enthusiasm. Added to this was the fact that spermaceti candles would not "fetch near the first cost at St. Estacie or Martinica & the Other Neutral Foreign Islands." Other sources of supply must be found if the Browns were to satisfy the commitments they had made in the interest of "the Publick Good & a Small Commission."

Just a few weeks before *Polly* sailed for the West Indies, the Browns had a unique opportunity to explore the advantages which French ports had to offer. In December 1775, without any advance notice or fanfare, "Two French Gentlemen" arrived in Providence.[46] They disembarked from a vessel which had returned from a voyage to the West Indies on behalf of the colony of Rhode Island. The good supply of powder aboard the sloop was very welcome; but for the moment everyone from Governor Nicholas Cooke down to the humblest citizen forgot about the vital cargo and concentrated their attention on the travelers. Frenchmen were a rare sight in Colonial Providence, and these two were an unusually imposing pair. On the first evening after their arrival they were taken to meet President James Manning of the College of Rhode Island and David Howell, a tutor in the same institution. President Manning reported that both the visitors were "Gentlemen and Schollars."

Fortified with this information, Nicholas Brown called upon M. Penet and M. de Pliarne the following evening. Howell went with him, obviously as an interpreter, because the strangers could "talk no Inglish but French & Lattin." Nicholas learned that one of the men was from "Parris" and the other the "Kings Armerer of the Cape" François in Hispaniola. Except for these rather nebulous identifications, the past of both men seemed shrouded in mystery. Nicholas may have been persistent in trying to learn more, but he had to be content with this meager information. He did discover, however, that they had come to the Colonies on a definite mission which called for an immediate conference with no less a person than the Commander-in-Chief of the Continental Army. They were much "Inclining to Secrecy till they can see the Genl."

Nicholas and other dignitaries of Providence were much impressed. In very short order, arrangement had been made for their two mysterious guests to see General Washington who was then engaged in the siege of Boston. Governor Cooke provided them with a letter to the General. "M. Penet," wrote the Governor, "comes extremely well recommended to our committee for providing powder from a merchant of character at the Cape." The other gentleman, too, was a "person of some consequence."

Pliarne and Penet waited upon Washington at his headquarters in Cambridge. They presented him with an elaborate plan for supplying the United Colonies with powder and arms. These stores were available in France, they argued, and no one was better equipped than they to get muskets and rounds of ammunition into the hands of the American soldier. Washington was interested. He thought the plan as outlined was a "very Eligible" one. But he declined to negotiate because he was not "acquainted with the extent of schemes already formed by Congress for the attainment of the necessary articles." In addition, he believed that he did not have the authority to enter into contracts for such material. But Washington did the next best thing, or from the standpoint of Pliarne and Penet, the all-important thing. He gave them a letter of introduction to the President of the Congress. And so that they might lay their plans before that body without delay, he arranged for them to travel from Cambridge to Philadelphia at public expense.

En route to Philadelphia to complete their mission, the two Frenchmen paused long enough in Providence to secure a letter from Nicholas Brown to Stephen Hopkins and Samuel Ward.[47] They left Providence apparently convinced that the advance reports which they had heard about the business reputation of the Browns were true. While they were in Philadelphia busy with their congressional interviews, they kept in close touch with Nicholas; and they expressed deep disappointment that John, who had been in Philadelphia, had departed the day before their arrival in that city.[48]

Members of Congress were easily persuaded of the soundness of the proposition made by the two self-appointed envoys from France. The Committee of Secrecy affixed the necessary signatures to a contract with them for the supplying of arms and powder to the Continental cause. Negotiations completed, M. Penet embarked for France early in February 1776. Later Silas Deane wrote that Penet "returned to France (copy of the contract excepted) almost as empty handed as he had come to Philadelphia."[49] Nevertheless, within a very short time after his return he "had found the means to collect a very considerable quantity of stores," part of which he actually shipped to America. Deane said Penet had been indefatigable in the business. His heart seemed to be entirely in it and Deane thought him honest. Although "his connections, either commercial or political" were not equal to such an undertaking, "the cause he was imployed in had in a great measure . . . supplied the deficiency."

Deane's reference to Penet's lack of business connections suggests that the two Frenchmen had undertaken their American project too casually. Deane may not have been the most creditable witness, but there is other evidence to suggest that in this case his judgment was substantially correct. If, however, Penet and his companion had begun their negotiations with nothing save their own wit, charm, and enthusiasm, they later were at pains to regularize their activities. As early as February 8, 1776 Pliarne writing from Philadelphia to Nicholas Brown mentioned two addresses for the firm of "Pliarne, Penet & Compagnie," one at Nantes, and the other at Le Havre. He also spoke of the company's connections in the West Indies, especially at St. Eustatius and at Martinique;[50] and he established their relationship with Jacques Gruel "upon the Isle of Feydeon," to whom he referred as "one of the richest and first houses for business in Nantes."[51]

Regardless of the circumstances under which Pliarne and Penet entered into business, their choice of Nantes was fortunate. At that port, they were in a favorable position to carry out their agreements with the Americans. Merchants in Nantes, among them J. Gruel, had formed some commercial connections with the American colonies before the outbreak of the War for Independence, with the result that the port was already favorably known to a number of colonial business firms. For purposes of trade with the colonies in wartime, Nantes enjoyed an advantageous situation. Unlike Le Havre, it was not openly exposed to the vigilant scrutiny of the British fleet in the English Channel. Its location on the estuary of the Loire, which extends into the very heart of France for a distance of 150 leagues, made the markets of the entire kingdom accessible to a degree which Bordeaux could not equal. Moreover, Nantes had long been a slave port; and slave ships required arms and powder.[52] Supplies of these articles, therefore, were customarily on hand; and additional supplies of guns and powder could be concentrated at Nantes without unduly exciting the suspicions of the British. Thus, in this port which was rapidly becoming the center of the munitions trade in France, Pliane, Penet & Compagnie were ideally situated to carry out their plans for arming the United Colonies.

But propitious as the location of the two French gentlemen seemed to be, John and Nicholas Brown were not convinced that all of their vessels should be sent to Nantes. The Sloop *Liberty* which they had dispatched on their own account had been lost with all her cargo on her return voyage from that French city. Perhaps the total failure of that experiment made them a little wary of counting too heavily on any one port of supply. At any rate, as late as March 22, Nicholas in a letter to Thomas Boylston in Boston wrote that they were looking for "the proper markets in Europe for procuring all the articles wanted as also of the best Place for the sale of the Goods for Export & the most safest places to go on account of our most Unnatural Enemies who we are assured will take us wherever they find us."[53] The Dutch ports did not appear practical, Nicholas went on to say, because the "Influence of the [British] Ministry have stoped" the export of powder and arms therefrom. There was some suggestion of shipping to Hamburg. But they had "pretty much Determined" to send one vessel to Bilbao in Spain. They believed that oil and candles could be shipped from that port, while the articles wanted for the Committee could be procured at the Spanish and French ports in the Bay of Biscay.

The Browns persisted in this plan. The first of three vessels sent to Europe to secure materials under government contract was dispatched to Bilbao in Spain, although she eventually discharged her cargo at Bordeaux. The other two went directly to Nantes, to the care of "Pliarne, Penet &

Compagnie." The Schooner *William* was chartered for the first voyage, with Captain Joshua Bunker in command.

Captain Bunker's sailing orders which bore the date of April 12, 1776 directed him to chart his course to Bilbao with his cargo of oil, sperma-ceti candles, codfish, and staves.[54] Should he meet with "obstruction" there, he was to call at any other port in Spain or France which seemed to answer. After disposing of his cargo for the most it would "fetch," he was to lay out the proceeds in powder, sulphur, saltpeter, arms, gun locks, Russia duck, various kinds of cloth or blankets in that order.[55] To avoid the enemy on his return he was to "Indever to Fall in on the back of Nantucket or the Vineyard to know the safest place to proceede too with the Schooner." If at Nantucket, he was to call on Christopher Starbuck; if at Martha's Vineyard, on John Pease, with both of whom the Browns would lodge instructions for his "Further Government." Evidently Captain Bunker encountered some sort of "obstruction" at Bilbao, which forced him, in accordance with his instructions, to seek another Spanish port or a French port. In the end he put in at Bordeaux, in France, where Nicholas and John Brown had no business connections of any kind.

On April 24, the Browns dispatched a second vessel, the Brigantine *Happy Return,* in pursuance of their contract with the "Honorable Continental Congress." *Happy Return*'s master was Captain Gideon Crawford. Her cargo consisted largely of oil and spermaceti. Captain Crawford's orders directed him to proceed to Nantes, "taking care to avoid the enemy as much as you can."[56] There he was to commit himself to the mercy of Pliarne, Penet & Compagnie who, "being well Recommended to us," would undoubtedly transact his business well. As, according to the latest accounts, spermaceti oil was worth £48 Sterling in London, Nicholas and John hoped the captain would obtain as much at Nantes. Should the oil and spermaceti promise to command a better price if held for some time, he must persuade Pliarne, Penet & Compagnie to advance the expected proceeds of the cargo and dispatch the vessel on her way. In exchange for his cargo Captain Crawford was to make a special effort to obtain blankets and broadcloth; but, of course, any of the many articles authorized by the Committee of Secrecy would be very acceptable. On his return, Captain Crawford must "get in the First safe Harbor you can aney Ware in the United Colonys," and send an express by land advising what he had on board.

Captain Crawford carried with him to Nantes a significant letter from Nicholas Brown to Pliarne, Penet & Compagnie.[57] It contained the announcement that the Congress "have resolved to open a free trade with all the World except Great Britain and her dependencies." Nicholas expressed the hope that the voyage of *Happy Return* "will be but a Specimen for our Future & lasting Commerce if it can be carried on to our Mutual Advantage."

Close in the wake of *Happy Return,* Nicholas and John dispatched a third vessel to Europe. The Schooner *Sally,* of 112 tons, was the property of Aaron Lopez, the once-great Newport merchant, now forced by the British to take refuge in Portsmouth, Rhode Island, and Francis Rotch, of Bedford (now New Bedford), scion of the prominent Nantucket family of that name.[58] With Captain Samuel Avery in command, *Sally* sailed on May 23, carrying a large quantity of oil and spermaceti.[59] It was the hope of the Browns that at Nantes the oil could be exchanged for about 6000 blankets and some 6000 yards of broadcloth.[60]

Like Captain Crawford of *Happy Return,* Captain Avery carried a letter from Nicholas Brown to Pliarne, Penet & Compagnie.[61] In it Nicholas explained the reasons for dispatching two cargoes of oil and spermaceti to Nantes within a single month. He realized that the market there might be surfeited with these products, and that the supply of blankets and cloth on hand might prove insufficient for the two vessels. But, he added, "Your House at the Havre being so Dangerous to be Come at on account of the Crewsers in the English Channel, we thot it not prudent to Address them there." Nicholas asked Pliarne, Penet & Compagnie to advise Captain Avery as to the state of the markets. Should those at Nantes not answer they were to direct him to "Rochell or Other Where in the Bay of Biskey," as they might think best.

Thus, between April 13 and May 23, 1776, Nicholas and John Brown had dispatched three vessels to France in pursuance of their contracts with the Committee of Secrecy. Of these, one had deposited her cargo at Bordeaux; the other two, at Nantes. Numerous questions concerning these voyages suggest themselves. Did the outbound cargoes answer in the French markets? Did the French merchants transact the business efficiently and with dispatch? What "warlike stores" were the Browns able to procure? To what extent did these three voyages, combined with that of *Polly* to St. Eustatius, provide the quantity of goods which their contracts with the Committee of Secrecy authorized Nicholas and John to import?

At Bordeaux, Captain Bunker of the Schooner *William* fell into the hands of one J. Lafitte, who "accepted with pleasure" the captain's suggestion that he transact the business of *William.* M. Lafitte was confident that he would have no difficulty in handling the cargo as he had previously disposed of consignments from some merchants in New York. But, to his surprise, he found that the importation of the candles and whale oil was prohibited, while the articles desired by Captain Bunker could not be legally exported from France to any foreign port. However, M. Lafitte found a way of circumventing the impediments of the law. It was his good fortune to have a brother with very good connections at the Court of France. The brother appealed to these friends for permission to sell Captain Bunker's cargo and to ship the goods he desired in return. "After a long and tedious piece of work," M. Lafitte received the necessary authorization, so that he flattered himself "to be the Protector" of the American trade "to this part of the kingdom." In the future any goods which Nicholas and John Brown might think proper to send him would be admitted, subject only to the payment of a duty. In return, he would be able to supply them with anything they might desire.[62]

If M. Lafitte required time to win over French officialdom, he needed it no less to effect a sale of the cargo brought by *William*. After the lapse of several months he had sold only 34 of the 300 boxes of candles. For these he had received 55 sous per pound, instead of the 3 livres he had expected, and he saw no prospect of further sales at that figure. Two and a half months later he had sold an additional 24 boxes at 50 sous. But he could not hope to maintain even this low price, as the people gave preference to wax candles which sold at the same figure and "wear ⅓ Better." His friends in Holland and Spain gave him no encouragement to send them there, where the "Rich folks" preferred the wax candles. He then sent small parcels to Versailles, Paris, Rouen, Toulouse, Marseilles, and all the larger "places in the Kingdom," but to no avail. Everywhere there was a prejudice against spermaceti candles. In the end, M. Lafitte was forced to reduce the price as low as 20 sous per pound.[63] He sold the oil more quickly, but only by allowing the white spermaceti variety to go at the same price as the right whale oil. In France, no distinction was made between the two. Furthermore, the tare on the casks was 20 per cent, and the casks were not the right size. M. Lafitte advised Nicholas to send only ordinary whale oil in future, and he indicated that French customs officials frowned upon the casks of the dimensions preferred in England.[64]

The French customs service proved to be exasperating in its procrastination. Nicholas and John undoubtedly expected to pay duties on the cargo of *William;* but they were not prepared for the endless delay in the computation of these duties. This apparently was entirely beyond the province of the local officials in Bordeaux, as M. Lafitte repeatedly mentioned the lack of word from Paris on the subject. On one occasion he had written the "Court" to ask for an abatement; on another, he had appealed to the "King's Council" concerning the duty on candles. In the end the duties were very heavy.

As M. Lafitte found it necessary to send Captain Bunker on his way long before he had sold *William*'s cargo, he advanced the funds for the purchase of the bulk of the goods she had carried from Bordeaux. This not only compelled Nicholas and John to pay interest on the "advance," but it also kept them in ignorance of pertinent facts without which it was difficult to plan further voyages. *William* sailed from Bordeaux on September 4, 1776, after long delay; it was not until September 4th of the following year that M. Lafitte was able to forward his account of the sales of the cargo she brought to France. Although such a leisurely course of trade could not be fatal to Nicholas and John so long as they were protected by congressional guarantee, it might well be ruinous to commercial intercourse of purely private character.[65]

The cargoes of *Happy Return* and *Sally*, both committed to the care Pliarne, Penet & Compagnie at Nantes, proved slightly more acceptable than that of *William*, principally because they included no candles. But, for a variety of reasons, oil at Nantes was low in price. The *pêche de Baleine* had been unusually successful in France and Holland that year, thus depreciating the price of whale products. Furthermore, the uses of sperm oil were very limited in France. Woolen manufacturers were unwilling to use it in scrubbing their wool, as did the manufacturers in England. For that purpose the French made extensive use of olive oil, while in Languedoc, Provence, and Flanders oil of *Rabette* was much approved for that purpose. Nor was whale oil used for burning, for which the French relied on olive, walnut, and linseed oils, as well as oil of *Rabette*. In France, whale oil was used only in the dressing of skins. But even for that purpose the oil brought by *Happy Return* was not well suited, as there was a "Grose matter" or sediment in every cask. To the British this was no drawback, but to the French tanners and curriers it was so obnoxious that they commonly "exacted a deduction either in Measure or in price" on all such oil.[66]

In lieu of candles, *Happy Return* and *Sally* had carried white spermaceti, from which candles could be made, and which could also be used for medicinal purposes. But since the French were prejudiced against spermaceti candles, the Browns' correspondent wrote dolefully that "let me look which way I will I cannot but see with sorrow that the sale of that cargo will differ much from your expectations." He also reported that the spermaceti brought by the two vessels was greatly inferior in quality to that used by the apothecaries in France. The purchaser of a parcel of it had submitted samples to "a Public inspector" in Paris, who announced that it was "unctious and loaded with oily particles" which rendered it unfit for the apothecaries.[67]

A further hindrance to the trade was the high duty on oil and spermaceti at Nantes. The oil on board *Happy Return* sold at Nantes for 39,911 livres, out of which a duty of 7674 livres was paid. Although Pliarne, Penet & Compagnie held out some hope that the duty might be circumvented by importing whale oil under another name, a privilege which would be restricted to their own clientele, this was merely another example of the unwarranted optimism in which Pliarne, Penet & Compagnie, as well as M. Lafitte, indulged themselves at intervals. Seeing that the combination of low price and high duties on oil made it not worth shipping, Nicholas Brown in turn indulged himself in a bit of fantasy. To Pliarne, Penet & Compagnie he suggested that perhaps they could avoid the duty by entering it at Nantes for exportation, and reshipping it for the London market on the account and risk of Nicholas and John Brown, the net proceeds to be negotiated by bills of exchange. "Whither Pollicy of London would admit oil from a foreign market," Nicholas did not know; but if so, and Pliarne Penet & Compagnie would advance the value of the oil until remittance came from London, he thought it would be a fine idea.[68]

Enough has been said to indicate that the efforts of M. Lafitte and of Pliarne, Penet & Compagnie to sell the products of the whale fishery had not been attended with the happiest results. As a consequence, the subsequent letters of the two houses to Nicholas and John Brown were largely filled with suggestions regarding articles the latter should ship in lieu of whale products. M. Lafitte wrote that rice was "the best thing" they could send to Bordeaux; but any quantity of wheat "you could send me . . . will be sold immediately." He reported a great demand for superfine flour. "Barril Beef" of "Large oxen" would command a handsome price, as would indigo, various kinds of skins, "Specially the Beaver," undressed deer skins, fox skins, and "all kinds of Furrs." Other letters from the two firms stressed beeswax, hemp, staves and heading for sugar hogsheads, and, especially, tobacco. Both houses dangled before the eyes of the Browns the alluring prospect of a special dispensation by which they would be allowed to import tobacco duty free. Indeed, Pliarne, Penet & Compagnie wrote flatly that "we have agreed or Contracted with the fermiers general of France for Twenty Thousand Tons Tobacco. Consequently have power to Enter it Freely in our port of Nantes." Then followed the fantastic suggestion that if Nicholas and John could "furnish us the whole quantity, it is the Best Cargo You Can Send us."[69] Of course no American merchant was in a position to supply them with forty million pounds of tobacco, least of all one in New England, laboring under the impediments of war and of distance from the Chesapeake. Nicholas and John could have been pardoned had they interpreted this and other proposals of the two houses as calculated to impress them with the Frenchmen's facilities for obtaining preferential treatment from the French Court.

If the cargoes which the brothers Brown sent to France proved disappointing, that was less true of those which they received in return. *William* brought from Bordeaux 30,000 pounds of lead, 110 pieces of

Russia duck, about 5500 ells of "Bretaigne" cloth, 500 bayonets, a large quantity of nails, and 18,000 pounds of powder.[70] From Nantes *Happy Return* carried 1820 yards of brown cloth, 1810 yards of blue cloth, together with smaller amounts of yellow, green, red, white, gray, and dove cloth for facing the uniforms of brown and blue. She also brought 96 pigs of lead, 12 boxes of sulphur, a small quantity of lead "bullets," 1500 gun flints, 40 dozen blankets, and some salt.[71] The cargo of *Sally* consisted chiefly of brown and blue cloth, with small amounts of yellow, green, and white facing. The total was about 2400 ells.[72] She also carried a quantity of salt. The Browns found little if any fault with the goods. Indeed Nicholas was of the opinion that the cargo of *Happy Return* from Nantes was "well bought and as good as from England."[73] But he might have viewed French wares with a more critical eye had he imported them on his own account rather than that of the Committee of Secrecy.

These three cargoes, together with that of *Polly* from the Caribbean, were imported in pursuance of the two contracts which Nicholas and John had signed with the Committee of Secrecy. A comparison of the cargoes with the terms of the contracts shows that the four voyages yielded but nine of the thirty-six tons of gunpowder authorized by the Committee. The vessels brought approximately one-half of the 30 tons of lead, 40 dozen of the 10,000 "good striped blankets," and about 300 of the 1000 bolts of Russia duck which the contracts called for. Of the 1000 stand "of good arms" and the 1000 double bridled gun locks none was forthcoming, although 500 bayonets appeared. Of the sulphur and saltpeter to be imported in default of gunpowder, only a small amount of the former was shipped. On the other hand, the ships brought somewhat more than the 10,000 yards of cloth mentioned in the covenants. The scarcity of military stores at St. Eustatius undoubtedly accounts for the slender cargo of *Polly*. The low price of candles and oil, high duties on these articles, heavy interest charges, and other costs so reduced the net proceeds of the three cargoes sent to France that the volume of goods purchased therewith fell short of the amount stipulated in the contracts.

To the Committee of Secrecy, the four voyages must have been somewhat of a disappointment, the more so by virtue of British seizure of *William* while homeward bound. To Nicholas and John, who had undertaken them merely for "the publick Good" and a small commission, they could not have been of vital concern. The commission largely vanished in the face of the necessity of sharing it with the ship captains who transacted the business for them. Although the Committee of Secrecy ultimately allowed an "advance" of 25 per cent on the proceeds of the outbound cargoes, this almost certainly does not represent profit to the Browns.[74] This advance was made necessary by the disparity between the net returns on the goods exported and the cost of the cargoes bought for importation. Although the candles and oil from *William* sold at Bordeaux for 63,903 livres, the duties and charges reduced this sum to 45,786 livres. The return cargo cost 65,149 livres, leaving a balance of more than 19,000 livres due M. Lafitte.[75] The goods carried to Nantes by *Happy Return* sold for 46,294 livres, of which 24,119 livres remained after all charges were paid. The cost of the cargo brought home was 36,154 livres, leaving an adverse balance of 12,000 livres.[76]

The balance due M. Lafitte had a somewhat unpleasant sequel. As their contracts with the Committee of Secrecy gave Nicholas and John no authority to import more than they exported, they were naturally displeased with this balance. But their displeasure was the greater because of the capture of *William*. Making no effort to conceal their disapproval of his handling of the business, they reminded Lafitte that they had undertaken the voyage solely on the account of the Committee, that the payment of the balance must come from Congress, and that "sum time" doubtless would elapse before the matter could be settled.[77]

It is possible that M. Lafitte never received this letter, as he appears to have persisted in the belief that the Browns had fitted out *William* on their own account.[78] During the next four years he wrote them "plus de cent lettres," partly to ask payment of the balance, partly to proffer his services to them. To these the Browns made no reply. Tiring eventually of this one-way correspondence, Lafitte drew a bill of exchange on Nicholas and John in June 1781. This they protested, solemnly swearing before a notary that the voyage of *William* had been made at the risk of the Committee of Secrecy. Advising M. Lafitte that he must look to Congress for payment, they thought it was not to his interest to seek a settlement while hard money was in hiding. For this reason they had not applied for the balance which the Congress owed them. In 1782 Robert Morris proffered payment to Lafitte in a bill on France, which the latter refused. Thereupon Nicholas and John seem to have dismissed the matter from their minds, but not so M. Lafitte. In 1788 he was in this country threatening them, in his ever-gracious manner, with the attachment of their property in the "Dominions of France and Spain." In April of that year Nicholas and John drafted a letter to the Treasury Board of the United States, giving a detailed history of the long overdue balance. This letter they read to M. Lafitte who "would take nothing short of pay." The Browns decided not to send the letter, the draft of which they filed with the notation in Nicholas Brown's hand that the payment of M. Lafitte "being a matter for Congress to settle is yet to be Done."[79] So far as the Browns were concerned, this seems to have terminated the affair of J. Lafitte.

The importation of cloth by Nicholas and John Brown, under their contracts with the Committee of Secrecy, for a short time involved them in their first and only experience with the putting-out system. In October 1776, the Committee instructed them to deliver all the cloth on hand or expected from France, to Thomas Mifflin, Quarter Master General of the army.[80] A few days later, a letter from Mifflin requested them to "employ as many Taylors as you judge necessary in making up the coarse Cloth." The cloth was to be tailored into double breasted waistcoats or "Jackets" (with "long plaited Skirts, Sleeves with small Cuffs, and a small Cape of the same Colour with the Jacket") and into "Breeches," with an equal number of each.[81] As soon as 100 suits had been made, they were to be forwarded to Thaddeus Burr at Fairfield, Connecticut. In accordance with these instructions, the Brown brothers distributed cloth and buttons to some 32 different persons, male and female, residing in Providence, North Providence, Glocester, Pawtucket, Cranston, and Pawtuxet in Rhode Island, and Rehoboth and Attleboro in Massachusetts, each one receiving from 20 to 65 yards.[82]

Nicholas and John Brown must have viewed with mixed emotions the results of the voyages made under contract with the Committtee of Secrecy. They could take a pardonable pride in their support of the Continental cause. But as businessmen they could hardly continue in a trade which, while it guaranteed them against loss, offered so little prospect of profit. They were doubtless relieved therefore when more effective ways of procuring munitions from France rendered further contracts between Congress and American merchants unnecessary. The Brown brothers were thus free to participate on their own account and risk in any trade which promised to yield a profit. And to them, as to Americans generally in the Revolutionary era, France appeared to be the obvious commercial substitute for Britain.

CHAPTER 12

"Bills on France"

COMMERCIAL opportunities of American merchants during the war were not confined to the importation of military stores, whether on their own accounts or under commission contracts with the Committee of Secrecy. In April 1776 the Continental Congress issued a "commercial declaration of independence" from England and opened American commerce to the world. Most colonial import duties were soon repealed. Colonial customhouse monopolies previously enjoyed by Annapolis in Maryland and Newport in Rhode Island were abolished, much to the satisfaction of Baltimore and Providence.

Merchants in this country were not slow to take advantage of this new dispensation in trade; nor were mercantile interests in the countries of continental Europe any less alert. Just as Americans looked to France as the chief source of military supplies, so they regarded that country as the place to procure the great variety of consumer goods needed by the civilian population—goods which hitherto had come chiefly from England. Between January 1777 and March 1778 ninety-five vessels cleared from Bordeaux for the American states. The Franco-American Treaty of 1778 quickened the tempo of commercial relations between the two countries. Numerous Americans now settled in France with a view to promotion of trade with the states. At Nantes, men who had come from Boston, Philadelphia, and Providence were soon to be found in business. At L'Orient were merchants from Boston, Philadelphia, Newburyport, Hartford, and Albany. Merchants from New York and Newport were not represented, doubtless because of the British occupation of the two ports.

Business firms in Holland also eagerly sought commercial connections with American merchants. The Crommelins of Amsterdam engaged in trade with "patriotic merchants, and doubtless with their loyalist relatives in New York." John de Neufville and Son of Amsterdam sent sixteen ships to the States in 1780 and 1781. In May 1783 there were twenty-one

Dutch ships in the harbor at Philadelphia. On the other hand, ships owned by American merchants were frequent visitors at Dutch ports.

Although American commercial connections with Spain were important during the war, especially those with Gardoqui and Sons at Bilbao, this trade was not new; merchants in the English colonies had long engaged in this traffic. However, the opening of Spanish colonial ports in the Caribbean to American ships in 1780 marked a new departure; and there lumber and provisions from the States found a profitable market.

Nicholas and John Brown had sent their first voyages to France to secure war materials under government contract. But they were well aware of the importance of consumer goods to the beleaguered Americans, and they could not afford to abandon that phase of their business. At the time of the arrival of *Happy Return* and *Sally* from Nantes, late in 1776, Nicholas and John were already preparing to dispatch vessels to France on their own account; and because of the British occupation of the Island of Rhode Island they fitted them out at Nantucket. One of these was the Brig *Chester,* which carried a cargo of whale oil and whale fins to the care of Pliarne, Penet & Compagnie at Nantes.[1] Whether they shipped those particular articles in spite of, or in the absence of, contrary advice from their French correspondents is not clear. By March 1777, *Chester* was back in Nantucket with a cargo comprising salt, large quantities of builders' supplies, brandy, nails, painters' colors, tea, hemp, twine, cod-hooks and cod lines, spices, and the inevitable supply of cloth for ladies' dresses.[2] The invoice of these goods came to 42,000 livres, a cargo of greater value than that of *Happy Return*. To the Browns, whose Nantucket friend, Christopher Starbuck, had given her "over for lost or taken" because she was six weeks overdue, the safe arrival of *Chester* must have been particularly welcome.

About the time of the departure of *Chester* for Nantes, Nicholas and John dispatched Captain Andrew Brock from Nantucket in the Sloop *Ushant.* By design or by chance, Captain Brock ultimately found himself in Bordeaux. There he committed his cargo to the care of S. & J. H. Delop, rather than to J. Lafitte. His spermaceti oil sold at a loss, but whalebone commanded such a satisfactory price as to prompt the Delops to encourage further shipments of it.[3] Sailing from Bordeaux on January 27, 1777, *Ushant* arrived at Nantucket on March 5, "a very extraordinary good passage for winter," wrote Christopher Starbuck. She was "running many times 10 & 11 knots which is great Sailing for a Single deck Sloop."[4] *Ushant* carried 23 tons of dry goods on freight for Stephen Higginson, of Salem, thereby earning £69 Sterling, which, in the words of Starbuck, was "like so much clear gain."[5] Captain Brock also brought the glad tidings that Nicholas' bill of exchange on London for £100 Sterling had been accepted and paid at Bordeaux, although many bills, including some drawn by Willing & Morris, of Philadelphia, had been returned under protest.[6] The cargo of *Ushant* included paper, lead, German steel, 8 tons of Holland yarn, and many yards of cloth, some of it for the carriage trade; broadcloth, taffeta, dimity, and silk were listed in large quantities in the invoice.[7]

It was the good fortune of Nicholas and John that Christopher Starbuck was on hand to take charge of the goods brought by *Chester* and *Ushant,* and to offer advice which was the product of his wisdom and long business experience. When the news of the arrival of the two vessels was noised about "Merchants from all Quarters," starved for European goods, quickly gathered at Nantucket in the hope of satisfying their wants.[8] Although the Browns had probably expected to run the cargoes to the mainland as opportunity offered, they could not well ignore the opinion of Starbuck that the goods would sell as well at Nantucket as elsewhere, thereby obviating any further charge or risk of transportation. Accordingly, they decided to dispose of the bulk of the articles on the Island, reserving for subsequent shipment to Providence some "particular" items requested by Nicholas.

By April 14, 1777 Christopher Starbuck had sold all the tea, paper, linen handkerchiefs, dressmaking supplies, cod lines, and some of the lead.[9] Still on hand, aside from the articles set apart for Nicholas, were the brandy, glass, salt, building materials, much of the lead, duck, and yarn. Thus dry goods seem to have been in great demand, doubtless to restock shelves largely depleted of British wares. The nails had not sold because "the smiths" made them more cheaply. As for the Holland yarn, Starbuck had expressed a desire to "work it up" in his ropewalk. The slow sale of the salt may have been the result of the prejudice against French salt and a popular predilection for the coarse West Indian variety.[10] By October 15, 1777 the duck and cordage were gone, but the nails and steel were still on hand. The salt was not finally disposed of until December 31, 1777. Starbuck sold the brandy slowly, not because of lack of demand, but in compliance with instructions from Nicholas Brown. During the first few weeks he had sold about 600 gallons at 15 shillings, when Nicholas requested him to hold the remaining 800 gallons for a higher price. The last of it was sold in December 1778.[11]

From reports submitted by Christopher Starbuck from time to time we have partial information regarding the proceeds of the sale of Nicholas' one-half interest in *Ushant* and his one-quarter "concern" in *Chester.* Exclusive of the goods Nicholas reserved for himself, the returns were

£6673 lawful money.[12] Whether John was the sole owner of the remainder of the two cargoes it is impossible to say. In the absence of complete data as to the cost and sales of the cargoes shipped to France, there is no way of determining the profits of the ventures accurately. In April 1777, before receipt of the account of *Chester's* sales at Nantes, Christopher Starbuck estimated Nicholas' profits at £3000 lawful money.[13] Subsequently, he tempered his optimism to the point where he merely hoped that the "Voyages will yield a Satisfactory & handsome Profit."[14] He then added that "had the oil only neated first cost in France there would have been twice as much Returns." Piecing together the various comments, however, it seems likely that two vessels actually returned a substantial profit.

If the voyages of *Chester* and *Ushant* provided Nicholas and John with fresh and convincing evidence that consignments of whale products would not answer in the markets of France, the prompt sale of their return cargoes of tea and dry goods at Nantucket demonstrated conclusively that the war had destroyed neither the demand nor the ability to pay for European goods. The problem of the Brown brothers, therefore, was to find exports with which to pay for the European wares the people of New England so much desired. The solution to the problem had been suggested by their correspondents in France. M. Lafitte had written the year before that rice was "the best thing" to send to Bordeaux; and indigo stood high on the list of recommended articles.

Early in 1777 John and Nicholas purchased the Brigantine *Live Oak*, recently brought into Nantucket as a prize.[17] A few weeks later they were planning to send her to Charleston, South Carolina, where, before the Revolution, they had done business with Nathaniel Russell, a native New Englander who had established a mercantile firm in the southern metropolis. They now took steps to renew their contacts with Russell. With the aid of Christopher Starbuck, they fitted out *Live Oak*, named Captain Andrew Worth to her command, loaded her with loaf sugar, and started her on her way to Charleston.

Captain Worth sailed in *Live Oak* about June 10, 1777.[16] He carried a letter from Nicholas and John to Nathaniel Russell, requesting the latter to load the vessel with about 1000 casks of rice and four to five thousand pounds of indigo.[17] Russell might draw bills of exchange on the Brown brothers to cover the difference between the proceeds of the loaf sugar and the cost of the rice and indigo. His bills would meet payment with the utmost punctuality, but, should he think there was the "Least kind of Risque" involved, he was to insure the vessel and cargo for the amount of the bills drawn. Nicholas and John flattered themselves, however, that Russell was so well acquainted with them that he would not be "Fearful of the Bills meeting due Honour." No other person had authorization to draw on them, although they had "Contenentell" securities sufficient to discharge several such drafts.[18]

Live Oak arrived at Charleston on July 8th. Almost immediately Nathaniel Russell wrote that he would be able to sell bills "on any of the Northern States" only at a ruinous discount.[19] Loan office notes would not "pass" because "no such office" had as yet been established in South Carolina. Russell therefore urged the Browns to send "Continental Money" by land.[20] Writing again on July 26th he said *Live Oak* had about 750 barrels of rice and somewhat more than 5000 pounds of indigo on board. He was also shipping about 20,000 staves. The cargo would cost about £30,000 as indigo was then very dear. Russell had sold the loaf sugar at vendue, although it was "more like powder" than otherwise. Because three men-of-war had appeared in sight of the town daily for fifteen days, he could not insure the Brigantine and her cargo for less than 40 per cent. Although she would be ready to sail by the first of August, he would advise Captain Worth "not to go unless the coast is clear."[21] Russell reiterated that "no paper Currency that you can send will answer but Continental Dollars," and he begged his correspondents to lose no time in sending them. He had given his note for the indigo, payable in two months, while for the rice he was obliged to pay cash. If the money were not forwarded soon it would be a "great hurt" to him.

Captain Worth's orders directed him to proceed from Charleston to Nantes, to present himself to Pliarne, Penet & Compagnie, and to receive their instructions as to the loading of the vessel. The only article he was specifically requested to bring from France was salt, of which he was to procure some 4000 bushels. On his return from Europe (should he be so fortunate), he was to put in at the "First Safe port you can come at Within the United States, but we Reither Recommend Portsmouth or Newbury Port."

The master of *Live Oak* also carried with him a letter to Pliarne, Penet & Compagnie.[22] It asked them to send the unsold spermaceti they had on hand to Amsterdam, where the Browns were sure it would command a good price. The brothers expressed their hope for a remission of the heavy duties charged on their previous cargoes of whale products, "or the Voyages will Turn out very unprofitable." They rejected an astounding suggestion, evidently made by Pliarne, Penet & Compagnie, that they send materials and workmen to France to "set up the Spermaceti candle Manufactory," for the making of candles which were not in demand in that country. Nicholas and John complained of the "very grait Expense Arising in Our Trade to France on Account of the Grait Delay in Dispatching Vessels which make the Voyage much longer than they used to be with the Same Cargo out & Home from London." As they desired the prompt loading of *Live Oak,* they were confining their orders to a few articles which they hoped Pliarne, Penet & Compagnie could procure without delay. They even suggested that their correspondent obtain the tea from the "Indemen" at L'Orient while the Brigantine was loading with the other articles at Nantes. Aside from tea and salt, the only article mentioned for the return cargo was "woolens" of various sorts. If it could be done for 20 per cent, Pliarne, Penet & Compagnie were to insure the goods for 150,000 livres, which seems to indicate high hopes for a successful voyage.

Presumably, Nathaniel Russell sent *Live Oak* on her way from Charleston to Nantes. But thereafter she disappeared from the records of Nicholas and John Brown. As Pliarne, Penet & Compagnie were equally silent upon the subject, it is doubtful that Captain Worth ever delivered at Nantes the letter which he carried from the owners of his vessel. It seems not unlikely that *Live Oak* was the Brigantine belonging to John Brown which is said to have burned "in sight of the town" of Charleston.[23]

Although *Live Oak* was almost certainly lost, she had left her legacy to Nicholas and John Bown—a heavy debt to Nathaniel Russell for the rice and indigo shipped aboard her. Upon word of Russell's inability to draw bills on them in Charleston, they sought unsuccessfully to purchase bills on that city as a means of paying for *Live Oak*'s cargo. They were compelled, therefore, to comply with Russell's request that they send the money overland, and without delay.

For this mission the Browns selected young Elkanah Watson. Since his efforts in behalf of John Brown in the first year of the war, Watson's life had been dull in the extreme. Although he was eager to take part in the campaign of 1777, his "father interdicted the measure" and his "indentures" to John held him "enchained." He was "languishing . . . without employment for . . . hands, or occupation to . . . mind" when the appeal from Nicholas and John aroused him from his lethargy.[24] They entrusted him with "Twenty Six Thousand Six Hundred Continental Dollars in Cash," together with a letter to Nathaniel Russell.[25] With a view of "Convenient Carage" they were at particular pains to "Exchange the Money all in 20 and 30 Dollar Bills." Of this sum, Watson was to deliver 20,000 dollars to Russell, to be applied toward payment for the rice and indigo purchased for *Live Oak*'s cargo. Believing that numerous articles, such as tea, indigo, shirtings, linens, silk thread, and broadcloth might be procured more cheaply at Charleston than in New England, they authorized Watson and Russell to consult with regard to a speculation in those items.[26] For the guidance of their two agents in such a venture, they listed prices current at Providence showing "good Green Tea" at £4 to £4:10

per pound, with other things in proportion. Should prices in Charleston be such as to allow a 25 per cent profit at Providence, Russell and Watson were to invest 6000 dollars in the articles named. And should the chances for a profit appear exceptionally bright, Russell might draw bills of exchange on the Browns to the amount of 6000 to 8000 dollars, provided he could do so at a small discount. The brothers thus contemplated a possible speculation to the extent of 12,000 to 14,000 dollars. That they could calmly consider transporting goods overland to Providence at a "half Dollar" per pound indicates the extent to which inflation had developed as early as the autumn of 1777.

Watson, his money "securely quilted in the lining" of his coat, a good horse under him, a hanger at his side, and a pair of pistols in his holster, "crossed the great bridge at Providence" on September 4, 1777, and set out on a journey entailing a heavy responsibility for a youth of nineteen.[27] He arrived at Charleston on November 18, after a lapse of seventy-five days. There he delivered the letter and funds to Nathaniel Russell. Following extensive travels in South Carolina and Georgia, he returned overland to Providence, where he arrived on April 29, 1778, after an absence of almost eight months.

From all available evidence it appears that Watson's journey served no immediate or tangible purpose other than the reimbursement of Nathaniel Russell for his outlays on account of Live Oak's cargo. The proposed speculation in goods at Charleston seems to have come to naught. Perhaps the entire 26,000 dollars which he carried was needed to square accounts with Russell. But whatever the facts may be, the young agent had so conducted himself as to retain the complete confidence of John and Nicholas Brown, who were soon to offer him an opportunity to resume his travels.

Shortly after Watson's twenty-first birthday in January 1779, "Mr. Brown and others" proposed that he visit France as their agent.[28] "Mr. Brown," of course, meant John Brown; while Nicholas was definitely one of the "others." Watson embarked from Boston on August 4, 1779, in the Packet Mercury, built in his native Plymouth and partly manned "by unfortunate schoolmates and companions" of his youth.[29] He carried a letter of introduction to Benjamin Franklin, written by the good Doctor's sister, Jane Mecom, at the request of Silas Casey of Warwick, Rhode Island, together with official dispatches to the philosopher-diplomat. With him there also went 1518 dollars in twenty-five bills of exchange placed in his hands by Nicholas Brown, as well as funds of undetermined amount entrusted to him by John.[30]

Upon his arrival in France he hastened to Paris where he delivered his letter of introduction and dispatches to Franklin. Watson remained the guest of the American agent for fourteen days while awaiting dispatches to be delivered at Nantes for carriage to America by *Mercury*. During this interval he attended the wedding of Franklin's grandnephew, Jonathan Williams, thereby making a contact which was to be valuable to him later. He arrived at Nantes on September 28th, where he delivered the "dispatches on board" *Mercury*.[31]

Writers have assumed that Watson originally intended to return to America on *Mercury;* and that his decision to settle himself in the mercantile business in Nantes was the result of a sudden inspiration.[32] This conclusion seems questionable, however, in the light of a letter which he wrote to Nicholas Brown after he had been domiciled in Nantes for some time. In this letter he expressed the hope that "the tour I made in America under your patronage will be attended now with the most agreeable consequences."[33] On that tour he had made it his "object (having an idea at that time of coming into Europe) to contract acquaintances with the most principal merchants in the several ports to all which I have tendered my services." In other words, the idea of this business career in France came to him while on his journey to Charleston in 1777.

Nor do Nicholas' instructions regarding the bills of exchange bear out the view that Watson's visit was a flying one, designed merely to convey dispatches to and from France. He authorized Watson to lay out funds "in France, Spain or Holland."[34] In return he wished good Bohea tea, "course and middling fine Linnen," calicoes, Barcelona handkerchiefs, "or sum other Handkerchiefs," fashionable silks for bonnets, German steel, and so forth.[35] He hoped to receive the goods "airly in the fall," which would enable him to purchase "a Handsome Sum in bills."[36] Thus the tenor of his words is that Watson was expected to remain abroad for some time, even though no precise location was designated.

The directions which Nicholas gave to Watson also contained a suggestion which may have been instrumental in determining the place at which the latter was to establish himself. Nicholas believed that the execution of Watson's business commission would be facilitated by the endorsement of the bills of exchange to some well-known mercantile house in France, and he mentioned in this connection Franklin's kinsman, Jonathan Williams, whose wedding Watson later attended.[37] Jonathan Williams, a native of Boston, had gone to London in 1770 to complete "his training and make contacts" under his great-uncle's tutelage. There his devotion to duty earned for him the respect of the Doctor as well as success in business. When in 1776 Franklin went to France as a Commissioner of the Continental Congress, Williams abandoned his London career and followed him to Paris. The American Commissioners immediately employed him as their agent at Nantes to inspect the arms and munitions being shipped to America from that port. In this capacity he became an innocent victim of the celebrated controversy between Arthur Lee and Silas Deane; and as a result of Lee's "unjustified denunciations" of him he lost his position in the public service, although he was later "several times employed to purchase supplies."[38]

At the time of Watson's arrival in France, Williams had been located at Nantes for about three years. In February 1780 he sent a circular letter to American merchants, including the Brown brothers, announcing that he had decided "to remain & settle" there for the purpose of transacting American business which he earnestly solicited.[39] His choice of Nantes was the result of several considerations: its safety, as compared with channel ports; its water communication with the interior of France; its importance as a "Resort for the Dutch and other Northern nations," whose ships were always there to purchase the tobacco, rice, and indigo imported from America. But residence in Nantes was not Williams' only asset. He had "the honour of being well known to Doctor Franklin, and in consequence of his Recommendations" had made "many good & extensive Connections" in France. This circumstance "added to a sufficient Knowledge of the Language" encouraged him to believe he could give satisfaction to all who might honor him "with their Commands."

Meanwhile, in December 1779 Elkanah Watson dispatched a circular letter to American merchants advising them that he had united with Jonathan Williams "under the firm of Williams & Watson, to transact American business."[40] He chose Williams because of his knowledge of the French language and "very extensive correspondence with the most principal Manufactures" in the kingdom. The precise nature of this business association is difficult to describe. Williams subsequently denied that he and Watson were partners; yet he signed numerous business letters jointly with Watson, while he subscribed others as "Jonathan Williams, for self & Elk. Watson." But regardless of the nature of the relationship, the two men jointly transacted business for the Brown brothers over a period of two years.

Williams and Watson thus supplanted the earlier correspondents of Nicholas and John at Nantes. M. de Pliarne's death in 1778 dissolved the firm of Pliarne, Penet & Compagnie. Shortly thereafter M. Penet discontinued the informal association which his company had maintained with Jacques Gruel at Nantes. The announced reason for this was the "Slow and Careless Manner he Conducted the Business from North America," a judgment quite out of accord with the high praise which Penet had once bestowed upon Gruel. M. Penet then formed the new firm of Penet, d'Acosta & Compagnie, and solicited the continued patronage of Nicholas and John.[41] To this invitation there was no response, as *Live Oak* seems to have been the last ship which the Brown brothers ordered to M. Penet's care.

With Williams and Watson as their new correspondents at Nantes, Nicholas and John entered upon the last phase of their wartime trade with France. They undoubtedly expected much from this new connection. The fact that both members of the firm were American born, that Watson had American contacts, and that Williams was thoroughly conversant with the language, customs, merchants, and manufacturers of France all seemed to make them a redoubtable combination entirely capable of transacting business to the satisfaction of the most discriminating American taste.

In certain respects their traffic with Williams and Watson differed from the commerce which Nicholas and John had previously carried on with France. To their new agents they seldom shipped goods in payment for French wares. Whale products having long since been discredited in the French markets, they sent no oil, fins, or bone, and only twelve boxes of spermaceti candles. The loss of *Live Oak* with its costly cargo of rice and indigo evidently so dampened their enthusiasm for the products of the Palmetto State that they made no further effort to ship those articles. Nor did they attempt to send Virginia or Maryland tobacco to Williams and Watson. Instead, they tried a consignment of Rhode Island tobacco which in prewar days they had largely sold in Surinam. Reports that no Virginia tobacco had been lately shipped to Nantes tempted them to make the experiment. In advising Williams and Watson of the shipment, Nicholas wrote that "altho it looks Black and Seems moist its from the Nature of it & at Present is Sound & Good."[42] Williams first tried to sell the Rhode Island weed to French merchants, who declined it at any price. Next he offered it to the Farmers General, who were no more interested. He then offered it at "publick Sale," but the bids were so low he was ashamed to sell it. After holding it for almost a year he finally sold it for a mere pittance.[43] Williams wrote that unless "the Tobacco of your State is differently prepared for our markett, it must inevitably Sink into Such disrepute as will greatly obstruct the future sales of it."[44] He assumed, perhaps incorrectly, that the fault lay with the methods of curing and packing rather than in the quality of the tobacco. True, the European taste was not educated to the packing of the product "moist" in molasses hogsheads, as was done for the Surinam market, but it is doubtful that the Rhode Island tobacco, cured and packed the Virginia way, could have commanded the price of that grown in the Old Dominion. In any event, the Browns shipped no more tobacco of any sort to Nantes.

Nicholas was concerned in only one other shipment of goods to Williams and Watson. He and others had dispatched the Schooner *Betsey* to

Cap François in Hispaniola with a cargo which sold for 14,505 livres.[45] There, however, *Betsey* was condemned "as not fit to proceed home." Nicholas then entered into an agreement with the owners of the Brig *Dolphin,* by which Captain Earl of that vessel carried to Cap François a bill of exchange for 1800 livres belonging to Nicholas. This, together with the proceeds of *Betsey*'s cargo, was to be laid out there in sugar and coffee for shipment on board *Dolphin* to Williams and Watson at Nantes. The latter were to "pay or credit Captain Earl with forty per cent for the freight" of the goods. The funds remaining from the sale of the coffee and sugar the captain was to invest in Bohea tea or other articles of no greater average "bulk and weight." The freight charge on the return cargo was to be 10 per cent. Under otherwise ideal conditions, the exorbitant freight charge on the sugar and coffee could hardly have allowed Nicholas more than a modest profit from this venture. But the subsequent silence of Nicholas and of Williams and Watson with respect to *Dolphin* creates a doubt that she ever arrived at Nantes.

Since Nicholas seldom shipped American produce to Williams and Watson, there was little if any occasion for him to dispatch to them ships owned or chartered by himself. Unless assured of a full freight on the outward voyage, it would have been economically unsound to employ his own vessels in this trade. Thus the meager flow of goods to Nantes and the more substantial volume therefrom moved as freight in bottoms owned by other men. In the years 1780-1782 Nicholas preferred to employ his own ships in other trades.

But how were the European goods imported through Williams and Watson paid for if not by the export of American produce? There obviously were but two possible ways—in specie or in bills of exchange; and of these, the latter was the only practicable means. As we have seen, Elkanah Watson carried with him to France in 1779 bills of exchange entrusted to him by Nicholas and John Brown. Many of these were drawn by Direk ten Brock of New York in favor of various members of the de Peyster, von Schaick, Beekman, and other families in the Empire State. Two of them were drawn in favor of Nicholas Brown himself.[46] The vast majority of the bills which Nicholas subsequently sent to Watson, however, were the so-called "bills on France," which were quite plentiful in this country after the signing of the Franco-American Treaty of Alliance in 1778. Nicholas found little difficulty in obtaining them in the course of his various business ventures. According to the final accounting between the two men in 1786 Nicholas had remitted the following sums:[47]

	Bills		Livres
1779	25		8,370
1780	30		22,890
1781	16		23,437
	1		1,500
1782	12		30,700
	9		14,300
Remittance			11,528

Total   112,725

During the same period Watson had shipped various consignments of goods to Nicholas:[48]

			Livres
1779	By the Packet *Mercury*	Invoice	3,481
1780	" " Brig *Katy*	"	720
1781	" " Ship *Mars*	"	2,766
	" " " *Sally*	"	723
	" " " *Sally*	"	9,172
	" " " *Aurora*	"	4,726
1782	" " " *Sally*	"	30,982
	" " " *Polly*	"	23,782
	" " " *Hope*	"	14,007
	Tea from Gothenburg		2,319
1781	Remittance to George Hayley in London		9,558

102,236

The type of goods in demand in New England during the later years of the war is well illustrated by a memorandum which Nicholas forwarded to Watson in June 1781. This document is worthy of consideration in some detail. Among the items mentioned were broadcloth, cloth for "cotes," 6 beaver "cotings," 4 bear skins, baize, shalloons, durants, "mareens," ratteens, German serges, camblets, cambletines, "fallons," flannels, silk twist, buttons, cotton velvet, callemanco, black "sowing" silk, crepes, ribbon, "taffety," checks, pelong satin, Bengal's muscrade, worsted gloves, thread gauze, morocco pocket books, feathers or "plooms," grey sable tippits, "paste pins for ladies hair," "cambrick," "shoo" buckles, knee buckles, shoes, shoe patterns for silk shoes, "a riding hat like the one Watson found for JB's daughter," fashionable hats, lutestrings, pins ("English if to be had"), needles, black laces, tapes, handkerchiefs, knives, forks, screws ("English if possible"), brass inkpots, "dandriff combs," crooked combs for ladies hair, whips, gloves, and Bohea tea.[49]

Of the economic situation in New England as the end of the war approached, this memorandum says much and says it eloquently. The goods mentioned therein are not those required by a beleaguered people desperately striving to avert defeat. They are rather the wares desired by a community in the midst of a period of business expansion and speculation, of optimism and rising prices, a community caught in the boom which usually accompanies the closing months of a victorious war. This is an order for goods to satisfy the wants of a people on a spending spree for which they were to pay dearly when the bubble of postwar prosperity collapsed. Doubtless, too, this order reflects the increased confidence born of the merchants' knowledge that the depreciated Continental currency had been abandoned in favor of a safer circulating medium.

Although Nicholas continued to trade with Watson to the end of the war, he was not always pleased with the service he received. Having previously suffered heavy loss through lack of insurance, as in the case of *Live Oak*, Nicholas was emphatic in his orders that all goods shipped to him must be insured. But, as insurance on goods from France to New England then averaged from 45 to 55 per cent, Watson sometimes chose to obey his own sense of thrift rather than the commands of Nicholas. When he considered the rates too high, he delayed shipment, hoping for a decline in the premium rate. Greatly annoyed by this procedure, Nicholas wrote on the back of one of Watson's letters: "he ought to have shipped my Effects by this Oppy. for when he did ship he had no further orders." After holding another consignment in expectation of lower rates, Watson was forced to send the goods without any insurance whatsoever. To Watson's explanation of this delay Nicholas appended the notation: "he owns he had 2 opportunities before & had my Express orders to Insure why did he not." Yet Nicholas seems to have been more annoyed by the belated arrival of his goods than by the lack of insurance. He was especially irritated when he found himself unable to purchase "bills on France" (then circulating freely in this country) because his funds were tied up in the European goods which Watson had not shipped from Nantes. He reminded his correspondent that this delay had worked to their mutual disadvantage.[50]

The other bone of contention between the two men was the rate of commission charged by Williams and Watson. Nicholas had been fortunate enough to find a correspondent in Gothenburg who negotiated bills of exchange gratis and charged but 5 per cent on goods purchased for export. Brother John had discovered a Swedish merchant who exacted only 2½ per cent for transacting all business.[51] Compared with this, Watson's 10 per cent commission (five for bills and five for goods purchased) seemed unreasonably high to Nicholas. Watson replied that the standard commission on bills in France was 5 per cent, although he did not doubt that it would be reduced upon the return of peace. He believed the higher commission in France was justified because that country, unlike England, had no single entrepôt of trade such as London, where an assorted cargo of goods for the American market could be procured. In France, invoices had to be filled from as many different places as there were varieties of goods.[52]

For a time, however, Watson weakened in the face of the repeated complaints by Nicholas. If the latter would consign the bills to him alone, he would negotiate them for 3 per cent. But Watson's conversion was not to last. Within four months he was again demanding 5 per cent, since the filling of Nicholas' orders involved so much effort. Nicholas then wrote that he hoped "each of your *separate private* Business will not Ingrose all your Personal Attention from my order as by an Means to injuor my best Interest." He had received an offer "to have any bills negotiated & Goods shipped by as good a House as any in France" for a commission of $2\frac{1}{2}$ per cent "on the goods shipped only." He added, however, that for the present he chose "to continue with my old Friends."[53] But, "as a professed Friend," he felt obliged to warn them that their rate of commission would drive business away from French ports.[54]

After maintaining a benevolent neutrality during two years of controversy, Jonathan Williams finally entered the fray. With respect to French houses who solicited Nicholas' business at a lesser commission, Williams wrote: "I would my Self be contented to have no more on the Same kind of Business; but if you will make a trial by sending an assorted American order to a French House I shall probably be applied to translate it, choose the goods, and direct the mode of packing, Shipping and making out the Invoice."[55] He meant this as no reflection upon French houses, which in general were very respectable, especially those in Nantes. They could ship supplies to their own colonies

perhaps better than I can, but as to the American Trade, they are not only ignorant of the Taste in patterns, and the quality of the Goods that suits our Countrymen, but all the Dictionaries in the world could not translate the names of the goods ordered. Order a French Merchant to ship a piece of Book Muslin and he would endeavor to find a piece of Mouseline de Livre, but no Manufacturer in Europe would be able to furnish him, and he would write in answer that it was not be found unless some American were to tell him that a piece of Goods called ourgandi answers to Book Muslin, except in the folding it.

Williams added that it had cost him five years of experience and close attention "to acquire this kind of commercial translation." Although he was the first American to settle in Europe after the outbreak of war, he found something new every day. In short, Williams denied that profits varied directly with the amount of the commission; a higher rate of commission was the merchant's reward for more skilled and competent service.

In January 1782, Elkanah Watson wrote that so far as the "long contested point of commission" was concerned, he was sure his 5 per cent was just and reasonable. However, "if finally you should determine to thro' your business into this new channel, rather than allow what *Justice* & *Reason* must dictate, I will receive your particular bills in preference to losing your correspondence & do your business at 5% as usual upon the Invoice & credit you in Acct. as profit and loss half this amt."[56] Elkanah added that this was a delicate point because he was determined not to make the concession general. Therefore, if Nicholas chose to accept it, he must let "the matter rest a secret in your own breast."

This gesture of coöperation on Watson's part came rather late. The next month he and Jonathan Williams severed their relationship. Watson then entered into partnership with one M. Cassoul, whose knowledge of French commerce, together with Watson's extensive American connections, seemed to augur well for their success in the American trade. Within a few months the new firm had forgotten Watson's special dispensation in favor of Nicholas Brown. In a letter accompanying an invoice of goods shipped to him they remarked that "we Know you are too liberal in yr. Sentiments to wish any Body to do yr. business . . . Short of what it is worth, and what Reason & custom will both justify."[57] This called forth from Nicholas the comment that "they flatter abot. the comissn. & goods coming cheeper etc.," whereupon he proceeded to deduct 2½ per cent from the commission.[58]

By January 1783, Watson and Cassoul were beginning to read the signs of the time. With peace in sight, they decided to open a house in London and also to reduce their rate of commission. But this eleventh-hour repentance came too late to retain the patronage of Nicholas Brown. He would gladly place his orders in London, but not with Watson and Cassoul. This coolness developed into a bitter controversy when Watson returned to this country still owing Nicholas a balance of some £110. When Nicholas demanded payment Watson reminded him of his earlier offer of a farm in liquidation of the debt; and he added that he had "nothing else to offer . . . except you wish to vendue my cloaths, or take off my skin . . . Is it possible after all you have said about benevolence, humanity etc. . . . you can find it in your heart to hold an unfortunate Son of . . . fate in fetters and misery?"[59] So ended the trade of Nicholas Brown with France.

Important as traffic with that country was to him in the war years, his European contacts were not entirely confined to the Bourbon Monarchy.

As early as 1773 Nicholas Brown and Company had transacted business with John Turner and Son at Amsterdam.[60] It was in February 1776 that Nicholas had entertained the idea of a "very grand voyage" from Providence direct to that city.[61] Although there is no evidence of such a voyage by one of his ships at that time, Nicholas did dispatch *Polly* to Surinam in May 1776 with a consignment of refined white spermaceti suitable either for candles or for medicinal purposes, spermaceti candles, and Dutch bills of exchange to the amount of 1200 Holland guilders. From Surinam the goods were to be shipped, presumably in a Dutch vessel, to Turner and Son in Amsterdam. In return, Nicholas requested Turner to ship to Surinam, to his account, 4 tons of Russian steel, 1 ton of cardwire, 50 pieces of Russia drab, 150 pieces of Russia duck, 40 pieces of ticklenburg, 20 pieces of Osnaburg, 100 pounds of nutmegs, 150 pieces of linen, 100 pieces of silk, and 100 dozen handkerchiefs.[62] Some of these articles were doubtless for military use, but others were obviously consumer goods.

Although Turner and Son received the goods consigned to them, they delayed the shipment of the return cargo for reasons which are not quite clear. After the lapse of two years Nicholas disgustedly transferred his business affiliation in Amsterdam to John de Neufville and Son. After assigning to them the funds and the order in the hands of Turner and Son, he and John ordered the Sloop *Diamond* to Amsterdam with a quantity of indigo and somewhat more than 12,000 dollars in Loan Office certificates.[63] They directed de Neufville and Son to invest one-third of the total funds in good Bohea tea and added to the previous order china, black "taffity," calicoes, scarlet broadcloth, cambrick, lawn, "plooms," feathers, "shew" bindings, and fine Irish linen. In compliance with these directions, de Neufville and Son sent two shipments of merchandise to the Browns in the summer of 1779. The first was freighted to Boston aboard the Sloop *Independence*, and consisted of a large quantity of china and three chests of tea.[64] Of the 2098 guilders at which the goods were charged in the invoice, tea represented 681 guilders, or just about one-third of the total. Much of the larger consignment, including 50 chests of Bohea tea, went on board the Browns' own Sloop *Diamond;* also included were such items as German steel, "Sweeds edge" and flat iron. The tea accounted for more than 14,000 guilders out of a total of 20,808.[65] Thus "warlike stores" were relatively much less conspicuous in the shipments of 1779 than in the original order of 1776. Between these dates the Browns' trade with Holland showed the same increase in demand for consumer goods that characterized their commerce with France.

As the indigo shipped on board *Diamond* met with a poor sale in Amsterdam, Nicholas and John squared accounts with de Neufville and Son by means of the loan certificates. But they were still without a satisfactory product for remittance to continental countries. Unsuccessful in their rice and indigo ventures, they next made a trial of Virginia tobacco. In March 1780 they arranged for Captain John Updike to take the Sloop *Crawford* on a voyage to the Old Dominion. The vessel's rather novel cargo of cannon cast at Hope Furnace consisted of 14 six-pounders, 12 four-pounders, and 4 three-pounders.[66] John Brown believed the cannon would more than suffice to pay all of Captain Updike's expenses and load the sloop with tobacco, "as six pounders was Five Thousand pounds per pair when Tobacco was one Dollar per lb. and Four pounders in proportion." The captain was to lay out the overplus in snake root, beeswax, or bills of exchange, and proceed to Amsterdam, where the house of De la Lande and Fynje bore an excellent reputation. Besides the European goods to be brought back on the Brown brothers' own account, Captain Updike was to procure "as much valuable Frate home" as he could. His owners recommended, however, that he take no freight "of Less Value than Tea according to the Bulk."[67]

In Virginia Captain Updike purchased 95 hogsheads of tobacco, the net weight of which in Amsterdam was about 87,000 pounds, which sold for 38,339 guilders clear of all charges. The return cargo of *Crawford* may well have been the largest and most costly imported by the Browns in the course of the war.[68] As in the invoices from France in the later years of the war, consumer goods predominated; and the amount and variety of the wares indicate a state of comparative well-being within the trade territory of the Browns.

In 1780 the brothers also ordered the Brigantine *Betsey,* Captain Joseph Cooke, to Virginia and thence to Amsterdam. The contents of the cargo she carried to the Old Dominion are not known; nor the means by which the master purchased the 105,000 pounds of tobacco with which he embarked from the James River for Amsterdam. He, too, entrusted his goods to De la Lande and Fynje, who procured for him a return cargo which met with approval in Providence, except that the "small chests of tea were exceeding poor." As the tobacco by *Betsey* shrank some 30 per cent in weight, its proceeds failed to balance the homeward cargo by about 9000 guilders. This deficit Nicholas promptly made up by forwarding bills on France to the amount of 21,635 livres.[69]

While *Crawford* and *Betsey* were absent on their successful voyages to Holland, Nicholas, John, and Joseph Brown, together with Nicholas Power, made large additional purchases of James River tobacco with a view to sending the two vessels on similar voyages in the year 1781.[70] *Crawford* actually proceeded to Virginia, but the captain discovered that the presence of British forces in that State made it very difficult, if not impossible, to ship the tobacco. There is no evidence that either of the vessels made a voyage to Amsterdam in that year, nor is it clear as to the disposition which the brothers made of the large stocks of tobacco owned by them in Virginia.

In the course of the war, Nicholas Brown engaged in trade with at least one other country in Continental Europe. Believing that tea and cordage were more expensive in France than in the Scandinavian countries, he asked Williams and Watson to invest £300 Sterling for him in either Denmark or Sweden.[71] He requested that the cordage range from the smallest size to five-inch rope. In compliance with his request, his correspondents in Nantes obtained the desired articles from Dickson and Company in Gothenburg, Sweden.[72] In June 1780 Nicholas sent to Henry Grieg, also at Gothenburg, an order for tea, dry goods, German steel, cardwire, Russia duck, and hemp.[73]

No discussion of the Brown brothers' relations with Europe during the Revolution would be complete without some attention to their attitude toward British goods. In the early stages of the conflict the assumption was that, of course, no one would think of importing English wares. When he forwarded his order to John Turner and Son at Amsterdam in May 1776 Nicholas was obviously very much aware of his correspondent's English name and nationality. He expressed the belief that, whatever Turner's sentiments were in regard to the "Present Troubles" between England and America, they should not prevent the "Utmost Dispatch" in a purely mercantile transaction.[74] But he quickly added that "You must Observe not to send any Goods by any means of the English Manufactory." For the moment patriotism would not admit of the purchase of enemy products.

As time passed and the stock of English goods on merchants' shelves became increasingly depleted, this attitude changed. Writing to de Neufville and Son at Amsterdam in 1779 Nicholas directed that "all the Articles to be purchased . . . is to be English Manufactory or such as resembles it as near as Possible & to purchase such articles only of the above as is nearly the same in appearance & quallety to English."[75] He requested De la Lande and Fynje to procure glass and nails from Bristol on the cheapest terms possible, and to purchase other articles from London or Ireland and "have them ready in your store for Capt. Cooke."[76] The same change of attitude is evident in the trade with France. In correspondence with Pliarne, Penet & Compagnie at Nantes there was never any suggestion with respect to British goods, although Nicholas did mention the possibility of reshipping to England the whale oil that sold so poorly in France. His orders to Williams and Watson, however, abound in reference to English products. In January 1781 he urged them to obtain the best possible terms on the articles purchased because English goods, which were much more salable, were being offered on the market in New England.[77] His orders were dotted with notations such as "1 dozen of silk womens shoes if these fashion is like the English"; or he might stipulate that the cutlery be of English manufacture. The greater ease with which English goods could be obtained from Holland and Sweden doubtless explains in part the increased trade with those countries in the later stages of the war.

In August 1781 Nicholas received a letter from George Benson of Boston, later his partner in the firm of Brown and Benson.[78] Benson had lately interviewed the captain of a Boston ship bound to North Faro, "Composed of a number of Small Islands situated between Iceland & the Orkneys." The captain had visited North Faro the previous year and had bought tea there more cheaply than in Amsterdam. There was "an easy & Constant Communication from those Islands not only to all Parts of Denmark but to many Ports of England in the Clandestine Way." So tempting did Nicholas find this opportunity to obtain English goods that on August 18, 1781, a little more than two months before Yorktown, he drafted an order to an unnamed person at North Faro, which he sent to George Benson for transmittal to the Boston ship captain. He enclosed 7024 livres in bills on France, to be invested in good Bohea tea, cutlery, English knives, wire for knitting needles, 6 boxes of English tin, 20 pieces of black calminico, 50 to 100 dozen Scotch Bibles, ravens duck, ticklenburgs, cordage, etc.[79] Because of an alteration in the ship's voyage this order never passed beyond the hands of George Benson.[80] That fact, however, in no way detracts from the significance of the incident as an indication of the desire of American merchants to procure English goods, even if they had to be obtained in "the clandestine way." Small wonder that they were so eager to reëstablish commercial ties with Britain as the war drew to a close!

Before the war the Browns had sold much of their English goods to the little shops dotting the countryside in their territory. They had been at considerable pains to build up this wholesale trade. But during the war the merchandise imported from Continental Europe sold itself for the most part. In the seller's market which the war created it was unnecessary to solicit the business of the small-town merchants. With the return of peace, the Browns realized that continued success in the importing business would require them again to develop markets for the goods they imported. They had largely lost contact with the shopkeepers of prewar days. But they succeeded in establishing relations with a new group of customers in the village and crossroads stores of Rhode Island and nearby areas.

Trade of the Browns with France began in 1776. It continued throughout the War. The Browns also traded with other countries in continental Europe but this traffic was less constant and less significant. On both sides of the Atlantic this new commerce was inaugurated with high hopes. To the French this was an opportunity to capture permanently the rich American trade. To the Americans the time had come when they could break the bonds which had so largely confined their commerce within the limits of the British Empire, and thereby reap a greater harvest. On both sides of the Atlantic these high hopes were destined to disappointment. To the Browns trade with France was disillusioning. The French market for New England products was not a good one. French goods received in return were less prized than English wares. French procrastination, French ways of transacting business, and French disinclination to grant credit proved annoying. Confronted with this situation, the preference of the Browns for English manufactures asserted itself long before the end of the War. With the end of hostilities, they, and other American merchants, hastened to beat a path back to London.

CHAPTER 13

"Grait Zeal and Indefatigable Industory"

JUST as the war shifted the Browns' trans-Atlantic commerce from London to Nantes, so it brought profound dislocations in their enterprises on this side of the water. Their Caribbean trade had to be adjusted to new problems in securing outgoing cargoes and new hazards in the shipping lanes. The whale fishery was crippled and with it the candle manufacture. But there were compensations. If war cut off the supply of spermaceti for making candles, it left intact the local deposits of bog iron. Hope Furnace came into its own as a source of weapons for the soldiers in the grim struggle for the "Grait Cause" and for the privateers in the business of preying upon the enemy's commerce.

It was the good fortune of the Browns and other Providence merchants that they lived in a town not occupied by British forces in the course of hostilities, a distinction which Providence shared with Baltimore. But if they thus escaped the direct ravages of war, their relations with other coastal towns were seriously disrupted. British possession of Boston during the first year of the war completely severed the Browns' business connections with that town; and with the departure of the King's troops went their Loyalist friend, Henry Lloyd, long their most important correspondent there. During the remainder of the war, contacts of the Browns with Boston were occasional rather than constant. With the candle manufacture in a state of collapse, they needed no one to take the place of Henry Lloyd, who had not only supplied them with specie and good bills for use at Nantucket, but had also sold their candles on commission.

During the first two years of the war Philadelphia was important to the Browns as a source of supply for flour, which they imported in large quantities. British occupation, of course, abruptly terminated these relations, which were not renewed after the evacuation of the town by the enemy. With the spermaceti plant in disuse in wartime, the Browns required no "settled correspondent" at Philadelphia to supply them with funds for the purchase of head matter.

The prolonged presence of British forces at New York completely destroyed the contacts of the Browns with David Van Horne and Peter Curtenius. Enemy occupation of Newport for a period of almost three years broke the ties of the Browns with the great merchants there, and, probably more important, prevented access to the sea from Providence. When Newport was finally evacuated by the British, the town was too demoralized to be of immediate significance in a business way.

In prewar days no spot on the earth's surface had been more important to the Browns than Nantucket; and with no other place had their business connections been so numerous. The war completely destroyed their accustomed commercial relations with the Island, and left Christopher Starbuck as their only correspondent there. During the period of British control of Narragansett Bay, however, Nantucket served as a fitting out point for numerous Brown voyages, in some of which Starbuck was directly concerned in a small way.

As it was largely through their intercolonial trade in prewar times that the Browns had procured the assortment of goods suited to a West Indian cargo, shrinkage of their trade with the coastal towns during the war years could not fail to affect both the character and the extent of their commercial relations with the Caribbean area. In the early stages of the war, however, the flour which they were then importing in large quantities from Philadelphia was used effectively in their trade to the Islands. In exchange for the flour they procured not merely the molasses, rum, sugar, coffee, and salt of the West Indies, but also supplies of European goods which were usually available there. Ships in which the Browns were concerned made numerous voyages to Surinam, St. Croix, and St. Eustatius. Later in the war Nicholas tried his fortunes in the French colonies of Martinique and Hispaniola, and at the Spanish port of Havana. With Newport in the hands of the British, Providence was for all practical purposes a land-locked city. Cargoes often were carted overland to Bedford (now New Bedford) and then shipped to Nantucket. This added to the cost of the voyages. But when the vessels returned safely, laden with such supplies as molasses, coffee, or English dry goods for which the local demand was great, the profits were gratifying. On the other hand, the loss on a vessel which did not return was proportionately high.

But trade with the Caribbean, like all business of the period, was carried on within a framework of price controls and embargoes. Every war brings with it shortages of certain commodities with resulting appreciation in prices. In the War for Independence this normal tendency of prices to increase was greatly accentuated by rapid depreciation of the currency. As a result, there soon developed a widespread demand by the humbler folk for price regulation, as a means of protecting the poor from the "oppression of Rich merchants." When the prestige of the Continental Congress was thrown in support of this demand, State legislatures felt impelled to act. In 1776 Connecticut enacted laws establishing ceiling prices on the necessities of life, justifying the action on the ground that the sharp advance in the price of such articles was chiefly caused by monopolizers.[1] Similar acts were passed in Massachusetts, where price increases were attributed to machinations of the merchants.[2]

Meanwhile, the general movement for price control was spreading. In December 1776 a Convention of delegates from all the New England States assembled in Providence to launch a concerted attack upon rising prices.[3] This Convention recommended that the various states establish "stated" prices for wheat, rye, Indian corn, wool, pork, swine, beef, hides, salt, rum, sugar, molasses, cheese, oats, flax, coffee, and other commodities.[4] On December 31, 1776 the General Assembly of Rhode Island enacted the recommendations into law.[5] New Hampshire, New York, Pennsylvania, and New Jersey all took similar action.

By 1777 the demand for price controls seems to have weakened temporarily. In accordance with the recommendation of a Convention at Springfield in the summer of that year, all the New England States temporarily abandoned price-fixing, Rhode Island taking action in August to repeal the law of the previous December.[6] The respite, however, was of brief duration. In January 1778 an interstate Convention at New Haven recommended price ceilings allowing a 75 per cent advance on the prices of 1774. In October of the next year a Convention at Hartford was attended by delegates from the New England States and New York. This in turn was followed by the proposal of a nation-wide Convention to meet in Philadelphia in January 1780.[7] The complete failure of this Convention brought to an end the citizens' pressure for price control.

Except sporadically, the effort to maintain price ceilings was a failure. Although enraged housewives of Beverly, Massachusetts might raid merchants' warehouses and compel a temporary observance of "stated" prices; and although many persons were accused of forestalling and monopolizing, there is little evidence that prices were effectively held in check.[8] On the lists of the accused the great merchants were usually conspicuous by their absence. As early as June 1778 the Congress began to waver on price controls, the result of their realization of "a change of circumstances in the commerce of these states." A congressional committee, of which Robert Morris was the chairman, dissented from the recommendations of the New Haven Convention of 1778, although Congress as a whole was evasive.[9] A year later the members were more favorable to price controls, but it was then too late. The public had lost interest.

Hand in hand with interstate attempts to maintain direct price controls went efforts by individual states to avert the shortages which induced higher prices. If the necessities of life sold at prohibitive figures in one of the sovereign states, there was nothing to prevent that state from placing an embargo upon the shipment of such commodities beyond its borders. In this manner the scarcities which sent prices soaring could be avoided.

In spite of congressional recommendations to the contrary, such embargoes by the states were common. In May 1777 the Rhode Island Assembly forbade the shipment from the state of rum, sugar, molasses, cotton-wool, coffee, tanned leather, sheep's wool, and sheep.[10] In August of the same year the Assembly lifted the embargo. In a state so void of flour and meat products as was Rhode Island, embargoes by neighboring states upon these articles proved serious in the extreme. During the winter of 1778-79, the food situation in Rhode Island became desperate. Hundreds of people in Providence had neither bread nor the means of procuring it. A thousand refugees from Newport were almost completely destitute. Corn sold at eight dollars per bushel. Confronted with this situation, the Governor appealed frantically to Connecticut to permit the shipment of foodstuffs into Rhode Island.[11] His appeal was not in vain. The Assembly of the Nutmeg State provided relief in abundance.

Conditions such as these afforded plenty of opportunities for engrossing and speculation, opportunities which businessmen often turned to good advantage. Apparently the "limited" prices caused the Browns little inconvenience in conducting their affairs. State embargoes were more troublesome. It was the embargo which Connecticut had laid upon the export of West Indian goods that brought the Browns into one of their first encounters with the law.

In 1776-77 Nicholas Brown and Christopher Starbuck of Nantucket joined forces in several voyages to the West Indies. Starbuck was of great service to the Browns in connection with their wartime trade to France. The Browns were in a position to be very helpful to him in securing supplies from the Caribbean area.

Few places were harder hit by the war than Nantucket. With the destruction of the whale fishery, economic paralysis settled upon the Island. There is perhaps no better picture of this collapse than that which Starbuck painted in a letter to Nicholas Brown in 1777.[12]

Many of our people [he said] have Continued to get small sail Boats . . . by Rhode island in the Night to Connecticut & bring cheese & provisions here which they exchange for Salt . . . Mostly. Query whether thou Wd permit me to take a few Bushels of thy Salt Just to get a few Necessarys of life for my own familys use. I dont mean many bushels but any qt. from 10 or 12 to 20 Bushels allowing what price thou please or might get for the Remainder.

To such a plight had the fortunes of war reduced this once prominent Quaker merchant of Nantucket! Starbuck added that he had purchased a part interest in one of the small boats "with a good Smart Young man on purpose," believing it to be the most satisfactory trade "in the small way" in which he could engage. If Nicholas had "amind to own one-half such a small sail Boat" with him, Starbuck could build or buy another and "employ her . . . to good Advantage." It was even possible that Nicholas might "make as much of thy salt or some of it this way as any."

In the pre-refrigeration era, the lack of salt might mean near starvation for New Englanders during several months of the year. Starbuck's anxiety about his own isolated island was well justified. He was eager to secure every possible aid from Nicholas in an effort to improve the situation and to capitalize upon it. Late in 1776 the two men chartered or purchased the Schooner *William* (not to be confused with the vessel of the same name which Nicholas and John Brown sent to Bordeaux earlier in the year, and which was captured on her return voyage), Nicholas holding a three-quarter interest in her. After loading her with provisions probably brought to Nantucket from Connecticut through the traffic "by Rhodeisland in the Night," Starbuck ordered her to the Bahamas where she was to procure a cargo of salt.[13]

But this voyage did little to relieve the salt shortage at Nantucket. On the return voyage Captain Coffin brought *William* into Stonington, Connecticut. Whether this was by design or because of stress of the weather it is impossible to say. The fact that Nicholas had ordered other vessels to put in at "Stoning Town" or elsewhere, while determining whether the Rhode Island coast was clear, makes it not improbable that he and Starbuck had given such directions to Captain Coffin. But, when he met the forces of the law at Stonington, the Captain protested that "a very hard wind & a Terible bad Sea . . . that Loged our vessell filled our Cabbin & Sterage full & . . . obliged [us] to cut our Jib & fore Stasail away for preservation of vessell & Lives," had forced him to seek shelter in the harbor.[14]

Whatever the truth of Captain Coffin's allegation, the city fathers of Stonington were unimpressed. When he refused to retail the salt to the people at the price of ten shillings per bushel, "agreeable to the Law of the State of Connecticut," recourse was had to a Justice of the Peace.[15] The latter advised the captain "that there is an Embargo laid, that West India goods shall not be Exported out of this State," and he enclosed "the Act relative to the price of Salt." He recommended that Captain Coffin "emediately proceed to unlay your Hatches & retail Out the Salt at the Price affixed by Law." Refusal to comply with this request would entail a warrant taking the salt into the hands of the "Civil Authority & Selectmen," who would sell it at ten shillings per bushel and "account with you for the avails," which the Justice thought, after deducting charges, would not "neet you more than 9/ per Bushel." The answer, "Emediately requested," of Captain Coffin was, of course, a complete capitulation to the "Civil Authority."

However disagreeable the enforced sale of the salt may have been to the captain and his owners, the voyage of *William* was not an unprofitable one. A cargo costing £272 lawful money at Nantucket had purchased in the Bahamas goods which sold in Stonington for £875 lawful money.[16] These included 1454 bushels of salt, a barrel of limes and a quantity of Osnaburgs, duck, checks, stripes, drab and cotton cloth. The profits were sufficient to encourage Nicholas to plan other West India voyages.

In June 1777 Starbuck, acting merely as Nicholas' agent, fitted the Sloop *Bonetta* at Nantucket, loaded her with boards and staves, and sent her on her way to the Bahamas, with Captain Macy in command.[17] The Sloop's long outward passage of 46 days proved a blessing in disguise, as she thereby escaped probable capture by a man-of-war which had been cruising off the Bahamas until about ten days prior to her arrival.[18] Partly because of the poor sale of his boards, and partly because he was obliged to advance some 50 pieces of eight to repair his leaky vessel, Captain Macy was unable to return to Nantucket "full loaded." But this was also good fortune, as Christopher Starbuck believed *Bonetta* escaped capture "by reason of not being deep laden." She was "Chased by a Frigate most all one day." Her would-be captor was within three or four miles of her in the morning but "before Night" was "most out of Sight." Starbuck found it easy to be philosophical about the short cargo, "as we pretty much expected" Captain Macy to be taken. "I believe," he wrote, "no body here wd have Insured at 75 per cent Yesterday."[19] And he could also be pleased that much of the short cargo was salt.

Nicholas Brown had every reason to share his friend's satisfaction with the outcome of *Bonetta*'s voyage. The cargo for which they had paid about £300 lawful money in June 1777 bought, in the Bahamas, 1080 bushels of salt which in December sold at Nantucket for £2519 lawful money.[20] Some of it "fetched" as much as 84 shillings per bushel, an advance of 73 shillings over the price at which *William*'s salt had been sold at Stonington, only a few months before. To determine the actual profit of the voyage, however, allowance must be made for the depreciation of the currency between the two dates. By December it would have required £775 to purchase the cargo which cost only £300 in June. Even so, however, the voyage of *Bonetta* returned a good profit.

"There is nothing at present," wrote Christopher Starbuck, "seems more valuable than Salt & Molasses." He added that he supposed "the greatest proffit by it is Sending of it from here to Connecticut in small Vessels & Boats, where it is said 1 Bushel Salt Buys 1 barrel flour."[21] The "limited price" on salt in Connecticut, combined with the embargo upon its export from that state, discouraged its legal importation. The result was a bootleg traffic in salt from Nantucket by means of the small craft which Starbuck said passed by "Rhodeisland in the Night." One of these boats, the Sloop *Bounty,* carried 190 bushels of Nicholas' salt from Nantucket to Connecticut.[22] Starbuck remarked that if she "should get back safe will by being exchanged for Flour & Corn yield a good Profit." He understood that Connecticut people were offering 200 pounds of flour or 12 bushels of corn for one bushel of salt. The anticipation of the high purchasing power of salt smuggled into Connecticut was justified. *Bounty* returned with 80 barrels of flour, 3763 pounds of pork, 830 pounds of beef, 19 bushels of wheat, 110 pounds of cheese, 104 pounds of lard, 82 pounds of flax, 23 pounds of tallow, and 25 bushels of oats.

Confident that Nicholas could find no better employment for *Bonetta,* Christopher Starbuck fitted her for another voyage to the Bahamas in quest of salt. Under command of Captain Barnabas Starbuck, she sailed from Nantucket on December 10, 1777, carrying boards, onions, beef, and pork brought from Connecticut in exchange for salt.[23] *Bonetta* arrived in the Bahamas;[24] but when she had not returned by late February 1778, Starbuck expressed the fear that she had been captured.[25] His fear was the stronger because seven other vessels which had sailed from Nantucket for the Bahamas at about the time of *Bonetta's* departure were known to have been taken. Although she failed to return to Nantucket, her cargo was not a total loss. In September 1778 Starbuck advised Nicholas that her captain had stored about 240 bushels of salt from her in the Bahamas, which might suggest that shipwreck rather than capture was *Bonetta's* fate.[26]

Undoubtedly the ventures of Nicholas Brown in salt were among the most profitable undertaken by him during the war. True the loss of *Bonetta* was a heavy blow; but certainly not one which the illegal salt traffic with Connecticut could not soften.

Another commodity in short supply in New England during the first years of the Revolution was flour. Early in the war Nicholas and John began to build up their supply. In December 1775 Josiah Hewes of Philadelphia shipped 300 barrels of this commodity to Nicholas.[27] In January 1776 Nicholas, together with Clark and Nightingale and Brown and

Power, chartered the Schooner *Two Brothers,* belonging to Phineas and Joseph Potter, and sent her to Philadelphia. She returned with a large quantity of flour, cocoa, pepper, butter, and bottled porter. The flour was deposited in Joseph Brown's store.[28] By March 9, 1776 Josiah Hewes had shipped an additional 455 barrels of flour to Nicholas and John jointly, and 265 barrels to John's individual account. Thus within a period of three months Hewes had forwarded well over 1000 barrels to Nicholas and John, not to mention the shipment by *Two Brothers,* in which others were also concerned. On April 8, 1776 the Sloop *America* brought another 341 barrels of flour and varying quantities of ship bread, crackers, hams, and pork.[29] Until the British occupation of New York Nicholas and John also eagerly purchased commodities, especially flour, through Peter T. Curtenius in New York. The importations of flour continued through the year 1776. When British control of Newport prevented further shipments to Providence, the consignments were directed to Bedford and Nantucket. On April 8, 1777 Captain John Waterman, writing to Nicholas from Nantucket, enclosed the invoice of 345 barrels of flour which he had brought on Nicholas' account from the Delaware country in the Schooner *Bonaventura.* Waterman had reshipped 235 barrels to Leonard Jarvis at Bedford, who was to store it for Nicholas.[30]

Although much of this flour went into cargoes for West India voyages, Nicholas had considerable quantities still on hand when in May 1777 the selectmen of Nantucket appealed to him to sell some of his stock for the relief of the poor and hungry people on the Island.[31] Nicholas replied that he was "truly sorry" for the plight of the people, and he expressed the belief that the scarcity was equally acute in Providence, "as there is not a barrel as I know except what I have at Bedford." He attributed the shortage to "the limiting of the price" in both Massachusetts and Rhode Island, since flour could not be imported at the stipulated price. With reference to the flour he had stored at Bedford, Nicholas observed that it would "fetch" 50 shillings per hundredweight in Providence. The lowest price, therefore, at which he could sell it was 38 shillings, clear of all charge "since the delivery of it by Captain Waterman from the vessel which brought it."[32] These terms, he thought should prove to the satisfaction of "all thinking men capable of considering both sides." He authorized Captain Waterman to sell the flour to the Islanders on these terms. Subsequently the captain wrote Nicholas that he was "exceeding glad you consented to sell the flour. It gave great satisfaction to the people in general especially the poor who mostly wanted bread."[33]

But negotiations in regard to flour were not so amicable in another community in Massachusetts. In that same summer of 1777 the town Committee of Safety of Attleboro invoked the resolve of the General Court forbidding the export of commodities from the Commonwealth to justify the seizure of twenty barrels of Nicholas' flour while being carted from Bedford to Providence.[34] Appealing to the Committee for a second time in a vain effort to secure the release of the flour, Nicholas asked how "any set of men [could] stand forth without blushing after so manifestly showing the design of wickedly taking and holding other mens property." And he remarked that "this is so far from the true spirit of the laws that all honest men will reproach it."[35] This incident, combined with a similar experience in Rehoboth, Massachusetts, indicates a strong popular antipathy to those believed to be holding essential commodities in anticipation of higher prices.

Nicholas and his brother Moses on another occasion came into conflict with the Connecticut embargo upon the export of flour. In April 1780 they accepted the bond of Elijah Hollister and Roger Bull of Wethersfield for approximately nineteen tons of flour, payable in four equal installments. Later in that year they appealed in vain to the Governor and Council of the State for permission to remove the flour to Providence. In July 1781 they renewed the request, explaining that the flour was due them in satisfaction of a debt incurred by the Connecticut men through the purchase of "land and mills" near Glastonbury.[36]

When in 1777 the capture of Providence by the British seemed probable, the Browns considered it the part of wisdom to move stores of oil and sugar to neighboring towns for safekeeping. In April they carted some 10,000 gallons of oil, chiefly to Attleboro, although they stored some of it at Mansfield and Rehoboth in Massachusetts and at Smithfield in Rhode Island.[37] Sugar which they had bought to stock a sugar house erected by them "at great expense," they moved to nearby Rehoboth. As the oil was not edible, the civil authorities in the towns where it was stored made no demands upon the owners with respect to it. But as sugar was much wanted, a delegation of the selectmen of Rehoboth appeared in Providence in June 1777, giving notice that they "had determined upon a distribution" of some of the sugar. Outraged by this bit of impudence, Nicholas wrote John (who was then in Boston) asking him to apply to the General Court for "a stop" to the proceedings. "Otherwise," he said, "you must get a permit to bring it back into our state again," a rather remote possibility in view of his own experience with the flour at Attleboro and Rehoboth.[38]

Nicholas was not to escape the displeasure of consumers in his own state. An unnamed person, with whom he had deposited a quantity of sugar, was told it would be seized as soon as the Rhode Island limited act went into effect.[39] To forestall such action Nicholas promptly offered it for sale to his friend William Foster of Boston. This, he said, would serve to disappoint those who were disposed "wrongfully to obtain property to my injury under the color of the law."

Whether the sugar house to which Nicholas referred was built merely to justify the large accumulation of sugar, or whether it was part of a plan to increase the profits, already large because of the wartime demand, is not clear. Details of the project are lacking. One incident, however, seems to indicate that the Browns did have plans to monopolize the making of loaf sugar in their own community.

With a view to the operation of the sugar house which the Browns alleged they had erected at "great expense," they engaged one Jonathan Pike to "cut & fetch" one hundred cords of pine wood to be delivered at the sugar house "formerly the Baptist Meeting house near the Mill Bridge in Providence."[40] The following day John Mumford, "Sugar Baker," agreed to serve as master workman in the manufacture of loaf sugar in the sugar house.[41] For his services in this capacity Mumford was to receive a salary of 444 "Continental" dollars per month. He also leased a quarter interest in the business, for which he was to pay the Brown brothers 600 dollars per year. Mumford pledged himself "not by any means to let out or Carry on the Business of Sugar Baking in his Sugar House on the Point" without the consent of the Browns. Thus Nicholas and John acquired the services of an experienced sugar baker who, by a self-denying contract, removed himself and his own sugar house from competition with them.

Commerce with Europe and trade to the Caribbean, with the interstate exchange of the staples involved, kept the Browns busy with one hand; with the other, they developed their manufacturing facilities to meet the demands and opportunities of war. The conflict was not many months old when the question of converting Hope Furnace to military purposes arose. As early as November 1775 the Rhode Island Assembly appointed a committee to consider the matter of cannon "to be made here or got else where." This prompted Nicholas Brown to write to Stephen Hopkins and Samuel Ward, Rhode Island delegates to the Continental Congress at Philadelphia, asking the price at which cannon could be made in the "Western Colonys" of New Jersey, Pennsylvania, and Maryland.[42] Besides ascertaining the cost, Hopkins made inquiry concerning workmen who understood the art of casting cannon. He had heard of only one man in the entire Province of Pennsylvania who could qualify—an "Old Country-man" whom he was unable to persuade to go to New England on any terms whatever. As Hopkins had learned of "but one other man in America who understands Foundery of that kind"—a man living "somewhere in Maryland"—he advised Nicholas not to depend on "any workmen from this way."[43]

By January 1776 "the necessary additional works" were under construction at the furnace to equip it for making cannon. The Browns, as principal owners, informed the Committee of the Assembly that they were prepared to cast cannon for the Colony at the rate of £35 lawful money per ton, as compared with £40 Pennsylvania currency asked by the furnaces in that Province.[44] Although the price quoted was equivalent to £43-15 in Pennsylvania currency, the higher figure for Rhode Island may well have been justified by one or more of the factors determining the cost of production. The Browns, however, would expect the Committee to take the number of guns agreed upon, even though the war might terminate before they were needed. The Government was to be "at the expense of proving them," except where the guns burst in the process.

After the Assembly had contracted for 60 twelve- and eighteen-pounders, on these terms, the search for experienced workmen began in earnest. Nicholas wrote to his old friend, Peter T. Curtenius in New York, asking him to send two men whom he would employ on terms which Curtenius might name.[45] Locally, men of somewhat lesser skills accepted employment at the furnace. One agreed to serve as overseer of the ore beds in Cranston.[46] Joseph Brown engaged five other men to serve in various capacities; and he also employed young Elkanah Watson to go to Newport to purchase three tons of "Good English Hay . . . to be used in the business of making the Cannon . . ."[47]

Within a short time, the Marine Committee of Congress placed an order for the casting of 60 twelve-pound cannon with which to arm the two Continental frigates which were building in Providence. Before many months had passed the Browns received an inquiry from John Langdon of New Hampshire regarding guns for the Continental vessel under construction at Portsmouth. In reply they drew up a proposed agreement for the sale to Langdon of 26 twelve-pounders and six-pounders at £100 lawful money per ton.[48]

After refusing to sign this covenant because of the price quoted, Langdon promptly wrote an account of the incident to Josiah Bartlett, one of the New Hampshire delegates in Congress. This letter Bartlett in turn submitted to the Marine Committee of the Congress, of which Robert Morris was a member. On October 9, 1776 this Committee addressed a letter to Stephen Hopkins, previously one of its members, informing him of John Langdon's "extraordinary account" of the conduct of the furnace owners during his negotiations with them.[49] The Committee fully concurred in Langdon's opinion that the price demanded for the cannon was exorbitant and "extravagant." And they added that "no consideration shall induce us to submit to such extortion as was attempted with Mr. Langdon." Should the owners of Hope Furnace persist in their demands, the Marine Committee would have the guns for the New Hampshire frigate cast at the "Hughes works" in Maryland or at one of the Pennsylvania furnaces.

The Browns soon took cognizance of the "many accusations . . . alledged against" them. In a letter (drafted but not sent) to Robert Morris, dealing primarily with blankets and other supplies imported by the Brown brothers on the account of Congress, John Brown was moved to attempt a refutation of the charges made by the Marine Committee. He asserted that guns at Providence had recently sold at double the price demanded of Langdon; and that the owners could sell all their cannon at 25 to 50 per cent in excess of the figure quoted to him. The proprietors felt that to be branded as "Extortioners," notwithstanding their desire "of supplying the Continental Ships So much to the prejudice of their own Interest" was "Indecent as well as uncharitable." They knew themselves, he stoutly asserted, "to be as Deeply Ingauged in the Cause of the United States as any other men on the Continent." John reminded Robert Morris that the "Gentlemen of the Mareen Committee are but men tho they are of that August body the Congress." [50]

Somehow, this statement of protest would seem more convincing if it had actually been sent to Morris. The blast at the Marine Committee might then have appeared as an expression of righteous indignation at an unwarranted insult to the integrity of the Providence cannon-makers. But the deletion of this portion of the letter before it was posted seems to indicate that upon reflection their confidence in the rightness of their position weakened. By their silence they seem to have given consent to the charge of an attempt to exact an exorbitant charge for the cannon.

Besides unpleasant incidents of this sort, the Browns faced other problems in connection with the furnace during the year of Independence. Although the evidence is fragmentary, it appears that the original furnace, even with "the necessary additional works" provided earlier in the year, was not ideally suited to the casting of cannon. Further adjustments were therefore required. In October 1776 a boatload of "Good Merchantable Bricks" was purchased with which to construct an air furnace. [51] Preoccupation with the new construction undoubtedly accounts for the lack of any reference to the making of cannon during the next year. But in June 1777 the work had progressed to the point where the workmen were ready for hearth and lining stones for the project. At the end of the year Solomon Perkins and Daniel Keith were employed to "Mould Cannon Or any other Castings at the Air Furnace now building here." The two men engaged to find "a sufficiency of hands" to carry on "all parts of the Mouldings" in order to "take off all the Iron into Guns" at rates stipulated in the agreement. The owners of the furnace in turn promised to find the necessary patterns and all the materials for carrying on the business, to find board and lodging for all the workmen, and at the completion of the work to pay cash for the workers' services.[52] Actual operation of the new air furnace, however, appears not to have begun until the summer of 1778. In June of that year Thomas Pratt agreed to work "at cutting off the Heads of Guns."[53] At that time the Browns and the lesser proprietors agreed among themselves that no one would draw any pig iron from the common stock "without the consent of the majority part of the owners."[54]

One of the first orders for cannon from the air furnace came from the Navy Board of Congress, and controversy soon developed with respect to these guns. When the captain of the Frigate *Alliance* visited the furnace to witness the proving of the cannon, he and Rufus Hopkins, the furnace manager, disagreed sharply regarding the method of proving. According to Hopkins, the accepted procedure was to place the guns upon two blocks; but the captain insisted that the "Britch shall Lay upon the Ground with a Block under the Forepart." Furthermore, the captain believed that should the cannon "Bust with the Second or Third Charge" they were at the owners' risk, which Rufus "never Before understood to be the Intentions of the Contractors."[55] Stephen Hopkins, on behalf of the company, thereupon wrote to the Navy Board, expressing his associates' surprise at the captain's conduct in this affair.[56] En route from the furnace, Hopkins said, the captain had passed through Providence without speaking to any of them about the incident, and without leaving with them a letter which Rufus Hopkins had entrusted to him. The Board was asked to send the captain again "or some other Person to see the Cannon proved as soon as possible."

This was merely one of several bones of contention with the Navy Board. Nicholas Brown complained that the rapid depreciation of the currency made adherence to their contracts a hardship; that before the cannon could be completed the purchasing power of the sum named in the covenant, in terms of labor and materials, had declined by 50 per cent.[57] In December 1779 the owners grudgingly agreed to complete for the Board 24 twelve-pounders at £2600 each. "The terms," they wrote, "are not so good for us as we sell to private persons." They had recently sold 16 six-pounders and 16 fours at a higher price "though the purchasers find all the powder to prove them at their own expense."[58]

The effects of currency depreciation upon the proprietors were the more onerous when the Navy Board was dilatory in making payment. When one Captain John Deshon, on behalf of the Navy Board, contracted for cannon for the Ship *Trimble* the agreement stipulated that full payment must be made when the guns were ready for delivery. The money was not forthcoming at the appointed time; but in order to "forward and Promote the Publick Servis as far as they Can Consistent with the Security of their Interest," permission was given for the cannon to be carted to Providence, placed on "Sum Convenient Wharfe," and guarded at the expense of the Navy Board until full payment was made.[59]

The most prolonged of the various disagreements began with the allegation by the Providence men that the Board had changed the patterns after signing a contract for cannon. Close on the heels of the delay and expense thus occasioned came General Sullivan's campaign in Rhode Island, in the course of which he commandeered the furnace for a time.[60] When the proprietors regained control of their property, wages and materials had advanced so sharply that they requested an allowance of £60 per ton to cover the increased cost of making the guns.[61] Refusal of the Board to comply promptly with this request caused Joseph Brown to refer to the suffering which the "Shameful neglect of the Navy Board" had caused to the owners. But the latter persevered in their demands. In March 1782 Jabez Bowen was in Boston pressing the owners' claim upon the Board. Writing to Nicholas Brown, he remarked that should the Board "Make an award Tho it should not be to our minds we must be quiet."[62]

In their controversy with the Navy Board the proprietors of the furnace had a good case. In view of the persistent advance in the price level consequent to currency depreciation, they had the same strong claim to a review of their agreements as did various state works which obtained substantial revisions in contracts for the delivery of firearms. Their experience with the Board, however, was not without its benefits. It taught them to be wary. To avert the evil effects of future currency depreciation, they "Determined to fix no price to . . . Cannon, only when payment is made at the Time of Contract or at the Delivery, as the Purchaser may Choose."[63] By keeping their prices flexible they would compel the procrastinator to pay the penalty for his delay.

In spite of a substantial amount of work done on government account, by far the greater number of cannon cast at the furnace were for men fitting out privateers in the port towns from Portsmouth, New Hampshire, to Suffolk, Virginia. Typical of the inquiries and orders for cannon were those of William Creed of Salem. Enclosing a memorandum from a fellow townsman calling for 14 four-pounders or 16 three-pounders, he requested complete information as to price, time of delivery, and so forth. He remarked that there were several privateers on the stocks at Salem, most of which were to carry four-pounders. Later in the same year he asked for

8 pairs of six-pounders and 8 pairs of four-pounders. He added that "Salem and Beverley will take all the guns you can spare." After the lapse of a few months he ordered an additional 4 pairs of six-pounders.[64]

Captain Isaac Freeborn and Colonel John Cooke ordered 24 four-pound cannon, to be in readiness "in five weeks from date."[65] Captain Samuel Newhall, of Newburyport, contracted for 10 four-pounders and 10 six-pounders, at £1050 and £1500 respectively.[66] Because of currency depreciation the prices advanced to £1400 and £2000 respectively within six weeks.[67]

An agreement was made with John Murray and Captain Francis Fearis, of Philadelphia, for the delivery of 32 six-pound cannon on the wharf in Providence, "where the Ship *True Blue* may be."[68] Gabriel Holman, of Salem, agent for the owners of the Ship *Pulaski*, desired 18 six-pounders.[69] Captain Lamb ordered a "suite of nine pounders" for a vessel he was building at Norwich, Connecticut. Howland and Coit, of New London, purchased 14 guns to be paid for in good West India Rum.[70]

As Providence was an important center of privateering during the war, its sons were not absent from the list of those purchasing cannon. Nicholas and John Brown frequently bought guns from Hope Furnace of which they were principal owners. On April 6, 1780 Rufus Hopkins wrote that he had "proved fourteen 6 pounders yesterday afternoon for N. & J. Brown," that he intended to prove the same number "this day," and that he expected to have the "Remainder of the 4 pounders and nine or ten threes bored out by Saturday."[71] The firm of Clark and Nightingale also made several purchases. Rufus Hopkins reported that their six-pounders were ready, and that he understood they desired an additional 4 pairs of four-pounders.[72] By an agreement of April 8, 1780 Clark and Nightingale and John Brown jointly contracted for 17 nine-pounders, for which they promised to pay in good bills of exchange at thirty days' sight drawn by the American commissioners in France.[73]

In the later stages of the war the proprietors of the furnace seem to have taken an added precaution against loss through currency depreciation. This took the form of a clause in their contracts fixing the price in "hard money," "lawful silver money," bills of exchange on Europe, or in Continental currency at the current rate of exchange. Thus, in June 1780 they agreed to supply William Cowper and Company, of Suffolk, Virginia, with four- and six-pound cannon, to be paid for in hard money, bills of exchange, or "the exchange in Continental money which at this time is 60 for one hear."[74] Two months later they contracted to provide the owners of the ship *Le Marquis de la Fiette*, who resided in Norwich, Connecticut, with 6 pairs of six-pounders delivered at the furnace at £76-6-8 lawful silver money per pair, "to be paid for in such price goods as the owners of the Furnace may choose." Or, they would allow three months' credit "to have the cash paid at the end of that time." The purchasers were to find the powder for proving the guns, while the furnace proprietors would procure teams to transport the guns to Providence at the shipowners' expense.[75]

An agreement was made with Captain Ichabod Nichols, of Portsmouth, New Hampshire, under date of January 5, 1781 to cast 14 six-pound cannon at £66-13-4 hard money per pair, "to be paid at Providence as soon as it can conveniently be got from Salem." Nichols was to bear the cost of proving the guns and carting them to Boston. This sale resulted in disagreement and controversy because of the discovery of an error in computing the cost. Captain Nichols' disappointment at having to pay an added £7 per pair was not diminished by the thought that he had let go an opportunity to buy guns at £74 hard money, the guns to be delivered to him at Portsmouth.[76]

In the same month Joshua Ward, of Salem, wrote that the "bearer," Captain Rolland wanted 14 four-pounders, if he could have them at "what your price was last week," an interesting commentary on the relation between currency depreciation and prices.[77] In September 1781, when the Continental currency had ceased to circulate, Nicholas Brown offered to supply William Cowper and Company, of Suffolk, Virginia, with 8 pairs of six-pound cannon at £73 lawful silver money per pair on three months' credit.[78]

Money due in payment for cannon delivered was sometimes collected only after long negotiations. Among the many purchasers of cannon cast at Furnace Hope were John and Andrew Cabot, of Beverly, Massachusetts, older brothers of George Cabot, later a prominent Federalist political leader in the Bay State. The Furnace Company held their note for £990, dated January 20, 1780, which may have been on account of cannon purchased. On February 15, 1781 the Cabots purchased 10 pairs of six-pounders. The charge for casting and proving the guns, and for carting them to Boston, was not paid at the date of delivery. A year passed and the debt was still unpaid. In March 1782 Jabez Bowen, while in Boston on business for the furnace, paid a visit to Beverly in an effort to collect. He returned to Boston with the report that he "had no success in applying to Mr. Gabbet."[79] The Cabots expected the money from Philadelphia within three weeks, when they would liquidate the debt. When another year passed without payment, Nicholas Brown reminded them of the many letters written and personal applications made by the furnace proprietors in a fruitless effort to collect the debt, notwithstanding the fact that "very grait sums" had passed through the hands of Mr. Prince, the Cabots' agent in Boston.[80] A reply from Boston pointed out that although the Cabots had "Considerable Property arrived from Europe . . . the Difficulty of raising the Money and the Multiplicity of the Clamorous Demands upon their House" proved an "Insuperable impediment to the payment of the debt."[81] Thanks to a complicated arrangement negotiated by Nicholas Brown's friend, George Benson, of the Boston firm of Eaton & Benson, the debt was finally adjusted after the lapse of more than three years.[82]

Besides the custom casting of cannon, the furnace made guns which were sent to Eaton & Benson in Boston for sale on a commission basis. Among the purchasers of these guns were Joseph Head, Joshua Ward, Thomas Russell, Elisha Sigourney, Farris & Russell, William Gray, Daniel Sargent, John Jenckes, "Monsieur D'Luce," and John Callahan, all of the Boston area.[83]

Unfortunately, it is impossible to determine from the records of the furnace the precise number of cannon cast there during the course of the war. Many years later, John Brown wrote that the furnace produced "about 3000 . . . of the best Cannon ever made in the Nation."[84] Assuming that this statement reflects something of John's tendency to think and speak in superlatives, it would still seem to indicate that the number of guns supplied by the furnace was very large. If there is uncertainty as to the number of cannon made at the furnace, that is no less true in regard to the profits of the business. In view of the fluctuating and inflated state of the currency it is difficult to estimate even the gross revenue of the furnace for the war years. On April 13, 1780 there was an accounting among the several owners for cannon cast in the weeks immediately preceding. It shows that they had sold 78 guns of various sizes for £78,687, and partial payment of 47 others brought the total to £97,793. Assuming the rate of exchange to be 60 to 1, this represents about £1630 in hard money.[85] There was another accounting on March 22, 1781, probably covering a longer period. For this the gross returns reach the fantastic figure of £351,879, which, at the rate of exchange then prevailing, amounts to £5000 in hard money.[86]

It can hardly be doubted, however, that operation of the furnace in war time was a profitable undertaking. The action of the proprietors in advancing the price of cannon from £35 to £100 in the course of a few months in 1776 reflects their resolve to charge what the traffic would bear. An analysis of their contracts and their correspondence shows that they continued this policy throughout the war years. Joseph Brown remarked that "Upon the whole Cannon is an article we can make as cheepe as aney body & it is my opinion to gitt as good a price for them as we can."[87] By frequent upward revision of prices and by restrictive clauses in contracts, the Browns and their partners not only took full advantage of the extraordinary demand but also largely safeguarded themselves against the evil effects of inflation. That they made a good thing out of the furnace is indicated by another observation made by Joseph to Nicholas:

You know it is only when there is a dull sail for an article that the low price it can be made for is computed but when it comes in grate demand then is the Manufacturers or Vendor's Time & he always gitts as much as he can in order to make him some sattisfaction for his past labour when he rubed hard to hold his own etc. And what disintrusted Person if he knew every circumstance attending the building stocking & carriaing on the Furnace the Vast deal of Business Labour trouble & time about it and the small profits on the whole which we have made by it . . . Would think we have ever bin paid what so much exertion & Trouble in any Business deserves . . .[88]

By making the most of the seller's market for cannon, Joseph would compensate for the more modest profits of the earlier years of the furnace.

The operations of the furnace during the war years threw into relief the personality of Joseph Brown. Although he had managed the spermaceti works before the Revolution, he had remained a nebulous figure who seldom committed himself in writing with respect to any of the manifold business enterprises of the family. In the midst of the war, however, he wrote a series of letters to Nicholas, some from his retreat at Grafton, Massachusetts, some from Newport where he sat as a member of the Assembly, in which he expressed himself with great clarity and vigor on matters of furnace policy generally.[89] But, given his mechanical bent, his talents were most conspicuously displayed in connection with the technical aspects of the enterprise.

Joseph played a leading role in the original conversion of the furnace to the uses of war, as well as in the construction of the air furnace in 1776-77. In February 1780 plans were made to rebuild the air furnace "adjoining the Moulding House of the Blast Furnace," and to construct pumps with which to raise water from the pits at the ore beds in Cranston. It was in pursuance of these plans that Joseph made the most notable mechanical contributions of his career. Writing to Nicholas he said: "You ask me whether the pumps I talked of should not be a makeing it is my opinion they should accordingly I now send the dimentions of the Loggs to make them of And if you and the othir owners are willing they should be got you will ingage the pum[p] makers to gitt the Loggs as soone as they can by which time I will send the directions for makeing the pump."[90] The plan for building the pumps at the Furnace led to a discussion among the managers and workmen alike as to the relative merits of pine and oak pumps. A prevailing opinion that pine was the more durable was effectively disposed of by Joseph with the assertion that it would not last "half as long for our use."[91]

The pumps thus designed by Joseph Brown were driven by a steam engine which he also built. The only description of the engine and pumps is that by the Reverend Doctor Manasseh Cutler, who paid a visit to the furnace in June 1787 while en route to New York, where he was to lobby so effectively before Congress for the sale of land to the Ohio Company and for the enactment of the famous Ordinance of 1787. Because of its uniqueness, Dr. Cutler's account merits a full statement. He wrote:

I arrived at the ore-beds at 12 o'clock. The engine was at work, raising water from a well 80 feet deep. The iron flue is 2½ feet wide and six feet long, with a square hearth at the mouth, secured from fire by large thick, iron plates. On the back part of the flue is a winding funnel, which passes into a chimney on the back part of the building. A wooden boiler of 6 feet diameter is placed above the flue, which is constantly kept full of water when the engine is in motion. The boiler rises above the first story of the building, much in the form of the large cisterns in distilleries, where it receives at the top the condensing cylinder, 2½ feet in diameter, and made of plated iron. From this cylinder a large worm passes with many windings down the boiler. The valve that passes into this cylinder is more than 2 feet in diameter, and rises and descends by means of an iron rod made fast to one end of the large beam. Around the top of the boiler are numerous leaden pipes, some connected with the condenser and some not, furnished with stop-cocks for admitting and excluding air or water, as necessary in working the machine, but they are too numerous and complicated to admit of any description from a mere view of the machine. A large reservoir of water is placed in the third loft of the house, constantly affording water to the works below, and as constantly supplied (with a pump for the purpose), by the working of the machine. The large beam is a massive piece of timber, near 4 feet in diameter and 20 feet long, being two very large oak timbers nicely forged together. It moves on a large bolt in the center, like the beam of scales, and has two arching timbers at each end forming the segments of a circle, along which two chains of a prodigious size play as the beam moves. One of these chains leads to the piston or valve of the condenser, and the other, at the opposite end, to the pumps in the well. There are four cold water pipes, one feeding pipe and one venting pipe. By the same motion of the beam which raises water out of the well, all these pipes open or close, by the means of stop-cocks and valves, as the design of them requires. There are two large pumps in the well, which is 80 feet deep and 23 feet wide. The sides of wells are supported by large timbers, laid horizontal, so as to make the form of the wells quintangular, and the ends of the timbers let into one another. The engine raises 7 hogsheads of water in a minute, and the flue consumes 2 cords of wood in twenty-four hours. The immense weight of the beam, the cast-iron wheels, large chains, and other weighty parts of the works, occasion a most tremendous noise and trembling of the large building in which it is erected, when the machine is in motion. By the sides of the wells from which the water is drawn are two other wells of the same form 70 feet deep. These are sunk in the bed of ore; and in these are the workmen, about ten or twelve in number, digging ore. The ore is raised in large buckets, which hold about one ton weight, let down and drawn up by large chains, carried from the well to a large capstan, which is constantly turned by an ox. As one bucket rises another goes down. These wells are kept dry by the water continually drawing off into the well where the pumps are fixed, and the pumps keep the water below the height where the men work. This curious machine was made under the direction of Mr. Joseph Brown, of Providence, and is a standing proof of the abilities of that able philosopher. The invention was not new but he has made many valuable improvements, in simplifying and making the working of it more convenient, above what has yet been done in Europe. It cost upward of one thousand pounds sterling.[92]

As Dr. Cutler stated, Joseph Brown's steam engine at the furnace was not an original invention; it was rather an improvement upon the Newcomen engine, built in England about 1712, for the purpose of pumping water from mines. It probably was one of the first two successful Newcomen engines built in this country.[93] Unfortunately, it is impossible to date it precisely; but as Joseph built it to operate the pumps which he made in 1780, it must have been contemporaneous with them.

But while Joseph was deep in the financial and mechanical aspects of the furnace, Nicholas and John were engaged in another enterprise which put some of the cannon produced there to a practical use. It was not in the nature of things that they would be satisfied merely to equip the ships of their friends and neighbors for the exciting business of privateering. They were very vigorously engaged in those adventures themselves. After the decision of the Congress early in 1776 to authorize the issuance of letters of marque and reprisal, a wave of privateering quickly swept over the eastern states, engaging the attention of the mercantile classes frequently to the detriment of other interests of a private or public nature. In no state was this more true than in Rhode Island. Robert Morris, who later was influential in stopping so much of the corruption and extravagance of the Revolutionary period, took Rhode Island merchants to task late in 1776. Writing to the American commissioners in France, he referred to the Frigate *Raleigh,* built at Portsmouth, New Hampshire, for the Continent, as "a very fine ship, completed in every particular, except the want of cannon." These, he added, were "to have been cast in Rhode Island, but the spirit of privateering has prevailed so eminently there, that they have sacrificed every other pursuit to it, both public and private, as I am informed." As a result, the Marine Committee of Congress had ordered the guns cast in Connecticut.[94] As two of the principal owners of Furnace Hope (where the guns were originally to have been cast), Nicholas and John clearly were objects of Morris' criticism.

Nor was this the only instance in which the Brown brothers were alleged to have permitted privateering to take precedence over the public interest. On December 13, 1775 the Congress authorized the building of thirteen men-of-war. It was decided to construct two of the ships in Rhode Island, and a local committee of Providence men was appointed to be responsible for them. As early as January 1776 this committee, of which Nicholas, Joseph, and John Brown were members, decided upon the dimensions of the vessels which they named *Warren* and *Providence*.[95] Although the frigates were launched in May, they were not ready for the sea until October 1776, at which time the local building committee received a severely critical letter from the Marine Committee of Congress. As a result of this letter, and of reports which bore "hard on the character of the committee, as merchants and as gentlemen," the local group divested themselves of all authority over the vessels and delivered them to Stephen Hopkins, recently one of the Rhode Island delegates to the Congress.[96]

One of the "reports" which the local committee regarded as derogatory to their characters was that of Esek Hopkins, one-time ship captain for the Browns, but then Commander-in-Chief of the Continental Navy. He charged the members of the local committee, especially John Brown, with the diversion of labor from the frigates to the construction of their own privateers.[97] This circumstance may well have been responsible for the slowness with which the building of the two vessels proceeded. Perhaps the Marine Committee of Congress could have forgiven the delay had the ships embodied the finest in materials and craftsmanship. On this point the best witness again is Robert Morris. In his letter to the American commissioners in France, mentioned above, he not only commends the quality of the ship built at Portsmouth, but he refers to the "two fine frigates" constructed in Boston, the "fine ship" from Connecticut, "two very fine frigates" blocked up by the British in New York, and a "very fine frigate" at Baltimore "now only waiting for an anchor and men." Referring to the Providence vessels, he wrote that "in Rhode Island were built the two worst frigates, as I have been informed by those that have seen the whole."[98] Thus the Providence frigates suffered from something more than the delay resulting from the diversion of labor to other projects. It seems quite logical to assume that the skills and materials which should have gone into them were also diverted to privateers.

Once the vessels were ready for the sea, there remained the problem of manning them, and here again privateering allegedly interfered. Sailors on Continental ships received a wage of eight dollars per month, and shared one-third of all prizes, except armed vessels, of which they received one-half. But so great were the profits, real or fancied, that sailors on privateers readily secured a wage of twelve to sixteen dollars, with a share of one-half of all prizes taken. Competition between Continental ships and privateers for seamen led to unpleasant incidents and to controversy "about men claimed, on either side, as deserters." Doubtless it was from such a situation that came some of the reports which bore "so hard" upon the "characters" of the local committee members.

Although the Brown brothers and their fellow committeemen must accept the blame for the tardy and shoddy construction of the two vessels, they hardly deserve unqualified censure for the delay in manning them. Rhode Island was not unique in its shortage of sailors for the Continental fleet, nor did the lack stem wholly from the competition of privateers. As early as December 9, 1775, three months before the Congress authorized privateering, the need for seamen was acute in other localities. Writing at that time on behalf of Congress, Stephen Hopkins appealed to Nicholas and John Brown to use their "utmost influence for the procuring of . . . seamen, it being slowly that we raise" them in Philadelphia.[99] He added that "as this is an essential service to your country, we have no doubt of your engaging zealously in it." Specifically, he asked them to send the sailors to Philadelphia aboard the Sloop *Fly,* belonging to Clark and Nightingale of Providence. Should they recruit more than *Fly* could carry, they might charter another vessel which would be allowed to return to Providence with a load of flour.

Stephen Hopkins' appeal to the patriotic and profit motives of the Browns did not go unanswered. Rhode Island did not let Philadelphia down. Having other irons in the fire, Nicholas and John enlisted the aid of Captain Nicholas Power, brother-in-law of Joseph Brown. On January 2, 1776 Nicholas Brown was able to inform Stephen Hopkins that Captain Power's "Grait Zeal and Indefatigable Industory" had sufficed to recruit 64 seamen who would sail immediately for Philadelphia.[100] Captain Power "out of choice" had "advanced the whole money out of his own Pocket, Supposing it may be less Trouble to settle the affair." Nicholas Brown looked upon this as "a piece of singular Servis to the Grand cause," and he had no doubt that the "Honorable Congress will readily reimburse Capt. Power with some future Notice of him."

If the lure of privateers was not solely responsible for the paucity of seamen for Continental vessels, it certainly intensified the shortage everywhere. So great was the pull of Rhode Island's sixty-five privateers upon seamen, actual or potential, that in December 1776 the Assembly deemed it necessary to place an embargo upon the further enlistment of sailors upon such vessels.

Among the privateers which Nicholas and John sent to sea in that year were *Yankee Ranger, Diamond,* and *Sally.* In September it was reported that the first of these, together with *Montgomery,* had taken three large brigs bound from the West Indies to England with rum, sugar, coffee, cotton, and oil, and that all the prizes had arrived in a safe port.[101] The Sloop *Diamond* embarked upon her first cruise in July. To whet the appetites of Captain William Chace and his crew, John Brown reported to them the news of "Three Grand Prizes brot in to the Eastward one a Three Decker which with one other Ship is supposed to be worth £30,000 Sterling."[102] These had been captured by a privateer of "Little or no more Strength" than Captain Chace's sloop. John added that "no Time ought to be Lost before you Git on the Ground for prizes." He hoped in a few weeks to have the satisfaction of going on board a prize ship from Captain Chace, and if it should be agreeable to the officers and men to appoint him as their agent, he would do his utmost to see that "the prize shall net as Large a Sum of money as possible to Every one Concerned." Captain Chace's orders directed him to "Crews off Bermudose, the Bay of Mantancis, Cape St. Anthonys or Crooked Island Passage"; to send all his prizes home under "Good Commanders"; and to order the prize masters to come in between Nantucket and the Vineyard, "as being much the Safest from the Enemy"; then to Buzzards Bay, by way of "Woods Hoole," and finally to Bedford or to Providence if they should have "Good Intelligence of our Coast being clear."[103] Because of the "Grait Expense as well as Trouble in Giting away" on a privateering cruise, the Browns recommended that the captain remain out with the "Sloop as Long as you possibly can."

Within a week *Diamond* had captured the Ship *Friendship*. Little is known about this prize except that the master whom Captain Chace placed on board had to be removed because of disobedience and the "Scirilous language" he employed.[104] On her second voyage in 1776 Captain Stacy commanded *Diamond*.[105] He was directed to cruise "on the Bermudos Stations" until he had reason to believe all the West India vessels "air Gone by"; then he was to proceed to Newfoundland "after Fishing Vessels," not returning home until he had disposed of all the men he could spare "on Board of prizes." Should he not finish his "Crews sooner," he was at liberty to go to "Cannedy River about the Strats of Billile or of hallefax." What success *Diamond* achieved on her West India cruise we do not know; but she later shifted her operations to the northward where she captured a vessel bound from Quebec to England with "coal, copper kettles, etc.," which seems to have been a case of "carrying coals to Newcastle."[106] *Diamond* made a third cruise in 1777, but of its results nothing is known.[107]

The Sloop *Sally* was at sea in the years 1776-1778. Her record is fragmentary but she captured one prize, and probably two.[108] One of these was a "wine ship." Being desirous of having his part of the prize cargo stored in some "safe and cheap" place, Nicholas asked his friend Bossenger Foster, of Boston, to hire for him a store which would meet those require-ments.[109]

In 1776 it may have appeared to the residents of Nantucket that Nicholas Brown's privateers were more interested in plundering the property of loyal Americans than in waging war upon the enemy. In the summer, *Ranger*, in which Nicholas was concerned, seized *Somerset*, at Nantucket, as British property. In reality the vessel was owned by the Coffins of Nantucket, and the oil which she had on board was the property of William Hussey, also of the Island. In a hearing at Providence on August 2, 1776 no evidence was forthcoming to show that *Somerset* was guilty of a breach of the resolves of the Continental Congress or of the laws of Rhode Island.[110]

Another incident at Nantucket in the same year involved an un-named privateer in which Nicholas was also interested. The complainant in this case was none other than William Rotch. Prefacing his letter of pro-test with an appeal to Nicholas to "exert every faculty that may conduce to the extirpation of such atrocious Villany," he explained that the harbor at Nantucket had been frequently infested by a "small Sloop, her name I know not, but she is known here by the Name of the *Willful Murther,* an appellation not very unbecoming the carrecteristic of her Crew."[111] One of the victims of *Willful Murther* was the Schooner *Nightingale*, entirely owned by Nantucket people, and chartered for a voyage to the West Indies by Rotch and Captain Timothy Folger. According to Rotch, she arrived at Mole St. Nicholas, on Hispaniola, much in need of new sails which were not to be had at that port. In the guise of a whaling vessel and with nothing but oil on board she was proceeding in the direction of Jamaica when she was captured and condemned by the British, causing a loss of 3000 dollars to her owners. Captain Folger bought *Nightingale* back at a high price, sailed her to the Mole again, loaded her and returned to Nantucket. As she was discharging her cargo at her home port the commander of *Willful Murther,* with his company, boarded her in a "Ruffion like manner," took possession of her, and held her and the cargo, notwithstanding the fact that her cargo had been purchased at a neutral port and belonged entirely to people at Nantucket.[112]

Rotch could not believe that Nicholas would acquiesce in

such conduct nor be partaker of the Spoils of such wicked plunderers. [Con-tinuing, he wrote that] if thou art concerned in the Privateering business, I beg thee to consider the consequences of it & how often honest Men are de-prived of their Rights; it is not sufficient in my opinion to say that the inno-cent must suffer with the guilty . . . I entreat thee & that from pure good will to let the consideration of those things pass over thy mind & endeavor to bring to thy View the cries of innocent parents & of their tender Off-spring, perhaps for the want of bread . . . I really believe I have seen thee seeking better things & wish still to see thee pursuing such.[113]

From Nicholas this brought a letter expressing his unqualified disapproval of the action of the commander of *Willful Murther*.[114] In a somewhat lame apology for his involvement in the privateering game he said that injury to neighbors or friends had ever been contrary to his inclinations. But after Rotch's protest *Willful Murther* did no more marauding.

On October 22, 1776 it was reported that thirty-two prizes had been brought into Providence since the authorization of privateers in March of that year.[115] Of these, the Browns had their fair share. This "pretty good beginning" was about to bear bigger and better fruit. Two twenty-gun ships were then fitting out in the town; and two new brigs, each mounting 18 six-pounders were soon to be built especially for the privateering business. According to the Reverend Ezra Stiles, privateering and related activities were believed to have brought into Providence in the year 1776 spoils of war to the amount of £300,000 Sterling. That year probably saw the heyday of privateering for the Rhode Islanders, as the occupation of Newport by the British placed the commerce of the state under a substantial handicap for the next two years. Nevertheless, just as Nicholas and John were able to continue in other branches of their trade through the assistance of their friends at Boston, Bedford, and Nantucket, so were they able to fit out privateers.

John was interested and successful in privateering voyages almost to the end of the war. On November 27, 1779 he advertised with pride in the *Providence Gazette* "The new ship *General Washington,* built on purpose for a fast sailing privateer to mount 20 six-pounders, commanded by Captain James Munro. Will sail on a four months' cruize from Boston by the 15th of December next. All persons inclining to enter for said cruize are desired to apply to said Commander or to Mr. John Brown, both at Providence." In the same paper on July 29, 1780 three prize vessels and their cargoes are listed for sale at John Brown's Wharf: the Brig *Barrington* (formerly called *Monmouth*), the Schooner *Spitfire,* and the Sloop *Surprise.*

So diverting and apparently so profitable did John find the privateering game that even the new ship *General Washington* with her 20 six-pounders did not seem large enough to satisfy his ambitions. In September 1779 he was giving serious consideration to the construction of a ship of one thousand tons, which with sails, rigging, provisions, guns, powder, and all other stores would cost a million dollars.[116] Such a vessel would carry 28 or 18 eighteen-pound cannon on each deck and 8 or 10 nine-pounders on the quarter-deck and forecastle. This grandiose scheme was entirely in harmony with John's tendency to think in superlatives. The only fly in the ointment was his attempt to make the building of the ship contingent upon participation of the other furnace owners in the venture, and upon a bargain price for cannon. This latter proposal elicited from Joseph some rather caustic comments reflecting the suspicion with which the brothers so frequently viewed John's propensity for driving a hard bargain. There is no evidence that this ambitious plan was ever carried out.

It is apparent that the Brown brothers neglected few of the business opportunities offered by wartime conditions. The story of their numerous and varied activities is pretty much the business history of the Revolutionary Era in microcosm. That often the history reveals more of self-interest and less of concern about the outcome of the war, there can be little doubt. Once during the war when John Brown wrote to General Greene complaining bitterly of the conduct of the campaign on the Island of Rhode Island, the General replied: "I cannot help feeling mortified that those that have been at home making their fortune, and living in the lap of luxury, and enjoying all the pleasures of domestic life, should be the first to sport with the feelings of officers who have stood as a barrier between them and ruin."[117] Such an exchange as this between business men at home and soldiers in the field has a familiar ring. The conflict of interests between the two appeared in the days of the musket loaded with "pistle powder" as it does in the days of jet planes and atom bombs.

But in contrast to Nicholas and John, and their absorption in the business side of the war, Moses was engrossed in a significant humanitarian undertaking. He was a leader in New England of the organization which the Quakers set up for the relief of suffering among the civilian population during the war.[118] He and his Committee were responsible for collecting and administering the funds which took care of almost seven thousand distressed people in various communities. His activities made a vital contribution to the beginning of the work which the Quakers have expanded so successfully so "that our religious Testimony against wars may be preserved pure."

To many merchants of the day, the War for Independence was an event of decisive importance. It encompassed the financial ruin of many proud mercantile families of the late colonial period. It elevated to a position of economic importance many persons hitherto comparatively unknown. In the annals of the Brown family it had no such epoch-making significance. It did not greatly change their position in the scale of business prominence. At its beginning they belonged to the somewhat select group of long-established, successful businessmen. At its end they were still in that category. In the interval, they neither suffered catastrophic reverses nor achieved astonishing successes. But they easily held their own, and they emerged from the war with prestige undiminished and with resources unimpaired. Nicholas, John, and Moses were all to play new and important rôles in the business life of New England in the decades to come.

CHAPTER 14

Back to London

THE Revolution, by severing the ties which had bound the colonies to England, wrought a complete transformation in the political fortunes of the American people. In the economic sphere, however, the change was less abrupt and less complete. Trade with Continental European countries during the war had not been entirely satisfactory to American merchants. When, therefore, British mercantile firms at the close of hostilities solicited their business, Americans were not reluctant to accept the opportunity thus offered. Convincing evidence of their prompt return to the older channels of trade is found in the fact that their importations of British goods in 1784 were roughly equal in value to those of prewar years.

As they reaffirmed economic allegiance to Great Britain, merchants in the northern states assumed that independence involved no fundamental change in the economic *status quo ante bellum*. Before 1776 they had found the means of paying for English manufactures; with the return of peace they expected to employ the same methods of making remittance. Little did they realize that the accustomed ways and conditions of commerce might, for a time at least, be so dislocated as to complicate the problem of paying for imports from Britain. Before they discovered their mistake their country had slipped into the great depression of the 1780's, and they were themselves overwhelmed by their debts to English exporters.

A variety of circumstances combined to bring on the depression. The withdrawal of British and French forces from American soil stopped the flow of foreign specie into the pockets of American merchants and farmers; and the large importations from Britain in 1784 drained from the country most of the gold and silver that remained. Exclusion of American ships from the British West Indies temporarily dealt a blow to northern merchants; while restrictions by France upon trade to her Islands in the Caribbean were a further complicating factor.

With prewar channels of commerce partially closed to them, American merchants began the search for new types of trade. In 1784 they sent their first ship to China. Soon they were trading with India and the East Indies. Their ships visited the Baltic countries with increasing frequency. In France they found a market for tobacco and other products. The threat of starvation on West Indian sugar plantations forced the French government to relax its regulations with respect to trade with that area. Trade with Holland assumed a new importance. Even the ban on American ships in the British West Indies was at least partially nullified by an indirect and illicit trade to those Islands.

As a result of these new trades, complete prosperity had virtually returned to the young nation by 1790; and Americans once more had the means with which to purchase manufactured goods abroad. But while they welcomed the opportunity to profit from trade with other countries, they still preferred to spend their money for British wares. In 1790 they imported and paid for British goods approximately equal in value to those brought into the country on credit in 1784.

Of the immediate postwar behavior of many merchants, Nicholas Brown offers an excellent illustration; and surely none has left a more complete record of his trials and tribulations during those fateful years which have come to be known as the "Critical Period." To Nicholas, trade with the Continent during the war had never been satisfactory. Whenever possible in the later stages of the conflict he had sought to obtain English wares through European countries. As early as January 1781 he was anticipating a return to the London trade. In November 1782 he forwarded bills of exchange to Watson and Cassoul at Nantes, with the request that they hold them pending further instructions from him. He might lay the bills out in France or Holland, or he might employ them "Sum where else," by which he obviously meant England.[1] Early in 1783 Watson and Cassoul expressed to him their apprehension lest England should command the bulk of the American trade after the war. In anticipation of this, they were establishing a London branch of their house, and Elkanah Watson was surveying the British market to determine the American products most in demand.[2]

In his choice of a London correspondent Nicholas found it unnecessary to limit himself to Watson and Cassoul. In spite of large sums owed them by American debtors, and notwithstanding Lord Sheffield's warning against too great generosity to Americans seeking to evade payment of their debts, London merchants eagerly solicited business connections with American firms. In the spring of 1783 Nicholas Brown was visited by representatives of no less than six English houses.[3] Among them was one William Burgess, agent for Champion and Dickason, who were reported to be creditors of Boston merchants to the amount of more than £150,000 Sterling.[4] Although other houses offered terms in some respects more liberal, such was the reputation of Champion and Dickason that Burgess secured for them the business not only of Nicholas, but also of other prominent Providence men, including John Brown, Welcome Arnold, Clark and Nightingale, Joseph and William Russell, and Thomas Lloyd Halsey.[5]

Nicholas formally inaugurated his trade with Champion and Dickason in that same spring of 1783, when he shipped two large consignments of whale oil to them.[6] This article having provided him with one of his chief means of remittance to London before the war, it was natural that he should seek to make it a staple item in his business with his new correspondent in London. On May 1, 1783 Nicholas forwarded to Champion and Dickason a memorandum of English goods to be shipped to him for the fall and winter trade.[7] Explaining the magnitude of this order, which included everything from playing cards to Bibles, he wrote:

Altho it's now Impossible to know what Goods may be vended in the course of the next fall & Winter I concluded it better to have sum left of the first importation than for want of a sufficient assortment for the retailers to go to N. York & form Connections there and Elsewhere. [He added that the] present Importation will doubtless be much larger than is Common to be expected hereafter as many Shop keepers will be supplyd anew that after will only want to be Sorted.[8]

Meanwhile, Nicholas was conducting a search for a partner. While he regarded the formation of a copartnership as a way of divesting himself of certain of the personal cares and responsibilities of business, he doubtless considered it more important as a means of establishing a mercantile house of some permanence. Such a house would then serve as a training school in business for his young sons, Nicholas Jr. and Moses, should the "Almighty" see fit to remove him from "This Transitory Life" before the boys attained to man's estate.[9]

His choice fell upon George Benson, one-time clerk in the firm of Nicholas Brown and Company in the days before the Revolution. The copartnership of Brown and Benson was to endure for a term of seven years. For the "Use Improvement and advantage" of the Company, Nicholas agreed to deliver into the hands of Benson "the full and Compleat Sum of Ten Thousand Spanish Silver Milled Dollars in solid coin," to be held in the company's stock "free from any charge of Interest."[10] Nicholas also "put into the stock" of Brown and Benson his interest in Hope Furnace, the spermaceti manufactory, and the sugar refinery.[11] He further promised to furnish from time to time all funds "necessary & requisite, from his own private Stock or Capital, so far as may be Convenient and Possible," for which he was to receive 6 per cent interest. Finally, he covenanted to

"Use Imploy and fully Pledge all his Credit, Estate or Property for the Use Benefit & advantage" of Brown and Benson.

George Benson was to invest in the partnership "whatever Stock he can spare & thinks fit and Proper," Nicholas adding "Double that amount," over and above the 10,000 dollars and "other Stock . . . already herein Specified."[12] Nicholas was to bear the entire cost of the employment of his sons as apprentices in the firm. Young Nicholas, upon the attainment of his majority, might be admitted into a "New Continuance of Partnership."

Of the "Advantage and Gains" of the business, Nicholas was to receive two-thirds, Benson one-third. The agreement required Benson to take upon himself all the "Care & attention of Conducting the whole of the Business," while Nicholas need assume no greater part than was agreeable to him."[13] Thus Nicholas contributed the bulk of the capital to the venture, while Benson gave the time and energy which management entailed. Nicholas' hard sense and wealth of experience were at the command of the partnership at all times.

Benson became a partner in the new firm after a somewhat checkered career. After leaving the service of Nicholas Brown and Company, he had engaged in business in Newport. There he was alleged to have conducted an illicit trade with the enemy during the later stages of the War for Independence.[14] According to Benson, this charge resulted from the fact that he had sold on commission goods which he had not known to be of English origin. Later, he was accused of publishing an advertisement calculated to reflect upon the dignity and honor of a Rhode Island court.[15] As a result of this, the Rhode Island Assembly in 1781 ordered his prosecution, should he return to the State following a sojourn in Boston.

Although the details are somewhat hazy, the entire incident seems to have been in the nature of a tempest in a teapot. It probably ill-behooved Benson's traducers to charge him with trade with the enemy simply because he had, wittingly or unwittingly, sold on commission goods of British production. Few were the people who, in the later years of the war, scrupled at the enemy origin of the goods they so much desired. As for the other charge, Benson's return to Rhode Island in 1783 indicates that it was not pressed.

Certain influential persons had never wavered in their faith in Benson. Among them was the elder Jonathan Williams, whose son played such a prominent part in mercantile affairs in France during the American Revolution. One of the leading merchants of Boston, the senior Williams, in complete disregard of the accusations against Benson, had made possible by his moral and financial support the formation of the partnership of Eaton and Benson in 1781.[16] Joshua Eaton, the senior partner, was the son-in-law of Williams.[17] For the next two years this new Boston firm had freely received the commission business of several Providence houses, including the various owners of Hope Furnace. Nicholas Brown showed his confidence in Benson not merely by entering into partnership with him, but even more by his remark that "from my many years experience of his integrity, I choose him from all the young men of my acquaintance."[18]

The articles of copartnership provided for the assumption by the new firm of responsibility for the generous supply of goods which Nicholas had ordered from Champion and Dickason in the spring of 1783. One of the first moves of the partners was to enter into an agreement with the other leading mercantile houses of Providence with respect to the importation and sale of European goods.[19] By this covenant, signed in October 1783, the ten subscribers agreed upon their "Honors with each other to sell no European Goods on a longer Credit than Four months without Interest being allowed after that time at the rate of six per cent." More important, the document stipulated the price at which they would sell various kinds of wares. Piece goods were to sell at 60 per cent above the Sterling cost. On nails, pewter dishes, plates and basins, brass kettles, steel pins, writing paper, ink cake and powder, sealing wax, wafers, quills, account books, Bibles, and "all other books" the advance was to be $66\frac{2}{3}$ per cent. The agreement called for an increase of $73\frac{1}{3}$ per cent on hardware "in General," sewing twine, cotton and wool cards, women's chip hats, playing cards, slates and pencils, cod and mackerel lines, blankets, white flannel, baizes, looking glasses "by the case," and a variety of other items. The subscribers promised to sell crates, hogsheads, and cases of crockery and glassware, boxes of pipes, corks, time glasses, "looking glasses opened or loose" bellows, "allum," copper, brimstone, and iron staves and spades at 100 per cent above Sterling cost. On bar lead, shot, gunpowder, and certain other articles the prices were to be "mutually agreed on hereafter." On May 14, 1784 representatives of fifteen Providence mercantile concerns subscribed to a renewal of this agreement, with the proviso that it was not to be binding unless signed by all the importers in Providence.[20] Among the new signers were Welcome Arnold, Holroyd and Tillinghast, and Power and Tillinghast, all of whom were to be prominent in the business affairs of the community for many years to come.

By this early example of a markup agreement did the mercantile elite of Providence seek to make the most of the anticipated demand for English goods. Could they have foreseen the dull times which lay just ahead, perhaps they would have felt even more strongly the need for some form of insurance against the evils of price cutting.

Within a month after the signing of the original agreement, Brown and Benson transmitted to London another order for a very large assortment of goods to be delivered the following spring. Included was an item of 150 dozen silk handkerchiefs, an interesting commentary upon the nature of the expected demand for British wares. Of these, 10 dozen were to be "half brown and without fringe or border, suitable for Quakers."[21] With this order they enclosed a sharp complaint regarding the manner in which Champion and Dickason had shipped their order of the previous spring. They had forwarded the goods in installments over a period of months rather than in one large consignment. As a result Brown and Benson had been compelled to disappoint many of their customers who had promised to take all their supplies from them; and they had sold their goods on credit because the retailers with cash had had recourse to importers having no connection with Champion and Dickason.[22] In short, whoever received the first importation enjoyed every advantage, in that he attracted all the shopkeepers and secured all the money. Brown and Benson, and the other Providence merchants who were suffering from the partial shipments from London, lost the business of shopkeepers who were forced to go to Boston and New York for their European goods.

Brown and Benson decided that the best insurance against the belated arrival of shipments from England was to carry them in their own vessel. They accordingly began construction of the Ship *Hope*, designed especially for the London trade; and they eventually persuaded Champion and Dickason to take a three-eighths interest in her.[23] But as the completion of *Hope* would require several months they felt it necessary to take some immediate step to prevent a recurrence of their recent unsatisfactory experience. On November 13, 1783 they joined with four other mercantile houses of Providence in a letter urging upon Champion and Dickason "the absolute necessity of having each of our invoices of goods come in one bottom as early in the spring [of 1784] as may be."[24] This brought a response under date of March 10, 1784 in which Champion and Dickason said they had taken up a vessel especially for the shipment of the goods.[25] But they added that the orders had come too late by many weeks; that they should have been in London at the time they were dispatched from Providence; and that there must be delay in filling them. The reasons assigned for the delay present an excellent picture of the American trade with Britain during the first full year of peace between the two countries:

The severe winter and such a demand as this country never before experienced for its manufactures of any description have rendered goods both scarce and dear. This delay is absolutely unavoidable on our part and will be greatly experienced, and the orders are of such magnitude and consist of such a multiplicity of articles that they call for much time at any season, but more particularly the present when the tradesmen and manufacturers are so glutted

with orders that they must at this pressing moment be courted instead of commanded to obtain anything out of their hands.[26]

The letter concluded with the gentle note of warning: "We wish our
friends may not feel the bad effects of too great importations."

Champion and Dickason pursued the same theme in a letter written
two weeks later.[27] Calicoes and India goods generally were very scarce
and dear in England, and the same was true of many other items. They
added " 'tis pity our friends should import them from hence while they
go so much cheaper from France and Holland," an interesting revelation
of the American preference for British goods and, even more, for British
credit. The invoice of this latest shipment to Brown and Benson amounted
to almost £10,000 Sterling. Speaking of this, together with the sum owed
for the shipment of the previous year, Champion and Dickason remarked:
"We will not disguise that it exceeds our wishes . . . We must entreat and
rely on your strenuous endeavors that our advances do not extend far beyond the limited time of our credit. It does not at this time appear clear
to us how America can supply remittances to discharge the astonishing
export, particularly the Northern States."[28]

This discouraging word from London was but a foretaste of the disappointment which Brown and Benson were to experience in that same
year. In the middle of May they were complaining that they had received
not a line with respect to their orders for spring goods. Timely arrivals
at Boston were replenishing many shops which they should have supplied.[29] In June they observed that the "winter is past and the rain is over
and gone . . . but no amount of our summer goods."[30] Again their customers were turning to Boston and New York where they were leaving
the sums of money which should have been expended in Providence.

Eventually their goods did arrive, but so late that they had lost all the
shopkeepers with ready cash. They suffered also from the Connecticut
impost on goods imported from other states, which cost them the patronage
of shopkeepers in Pomfret, Woodstock, and other towns in the Nutmeg
State.[31] Confronted with this discouraging prospect, they decided to cur-
tail greatly their importations for the following year, confining them to
the supplementary articles necessary to provide a general assortment of
wares.[32] This decision to retrench was well-advised, as on December 31,
1784 Champion and Dickason forwarded their account current, showing
a balance due them from Brown and Benson of £26,144 Sterling.[33] In
their covering letter Champion and Dickason strongly urged their debtors
to exert themselves to place remittance in their hands.[34]

At first glance, this large sum, owed by just one of numerous mercantile houses in a small New England commercial town, would seem to indicate that the irresponsibility and improvidence of Brown and Benson had been exceeded only by the gullibility of their correspondent in London. Actually, however, the debt was not the result of negligence by either party; it had grown out of a combination of circumstances which neither had foreseen.

Brown and Benson had not incurred this obligation blindly or without definite plans for its liquidation. Like other American merchants at the close of the war, Brown and Benson expected to pay for imports from England in much the same fashion as before the war. Before the Revolution the Browns had paid for English manufactures partly by the export of pig iron from Hope Furnace, partly by shipments of whale oil to London, and partly by bills of exchange. They obtained Dutch bills through their trade with Surinam and bills on London through their commercial relations with Boston, New York, and Philadelphia. They had shipped candles to Henry Lloyd in Boston. He had sold the candles on commission to the Boston merchant aristocracy, who in turn had shipped them in large quantities to the British Islands in the Caribbean. In this manner bills on London had found their way to the Providence house with considerable regularity. Although the Browns must have realized that Britain would not remit the duty on pig iron from the independent United States, as she had on colonial iron, they little suspected that there would be other British policies which would affect adversely their ability to pay for English goods.

No commercial measure of Britain aroused greater protest by the Americans in the 1780's that the British Order in Council of July 2, 1783 closing British West Indian ports to American ships. It permitted the shipment of a long list of American products to the Islands, but only in British bottoms. Prominent, however, among items excluded from the Islands was salt fish, which was a serious blow to Boston merchants. Goods of West Indian production could be imported into the United States only in His Majesty's ships. Although American merchants soon discovered ways of circumventing the Order in Council, there is little doubt that for a time it occasioned serious dislocations in trade to the British Islands.

Assuming that Nicholas and his new partner were planning to establish their trade in the channels frequented by the Browns in prewar days, they were probably less directly affected by this British decree than many other American merchants, since the Brown brothers had sent their ships more largely to Surinam and the French Islands than to British West Indian ports. But indirectly Brown and Benson stood to lose heavily. In proportion as their correspondents, actual or potential, in Boston, New York, and Philadelphia felt the adverse effects of the exclusion of their ships from the Island ports, so did they themselves suffer loss. It became increasingly difficult for Brown and Benson to procure in those cities either the specie or the bills of exchange which had been so important to them before the war. Twice within a single month they wrote plaintively to Champion and Dickason about the scarcity and high price of bills on Europe. "Can you," they asked, "help us to any bills or point out any mode of speedy remittance?"[35]

Just as they were beginning to feel the effect of the Order in Council, Brown and Benson discovered another regulation affecting them more obviously and directly. We have seen that prior to his first order for goods from Champion and Dickason in 1783, Nicholas Brown had shipped them two large consignments of whale oil. Although the London house experienced some difficulty in the sale of this oil, their reports seemed to indicate nothing more serious than the slack demand for oil in the summer months, combined with some deterioration in its quality as a result of age. Not one word from Champion and Dickason in that first year of peace could be construed as an effort to discourage further oil shipments. This fact is made the more significant by the promptness with which they threw cold water on the Providence firm's plan for a tobacco speculation as a means of providing remittance.[36]

Thus Brown and Benson went confidently forward with their plans for the shipment of whale oil to London. On January 20, 1784 they wrote that they were contracting "for several vessels proper for the whale fishery from which we principally expect to furnish our remittances."[37] As the acquisition of a whaling fleet would require some considerable time, they purchased whale oil for shipment to Champion and Dickason. For 100 tons bought at Nantucket they paid £40 Sterling per ton. They procured another 60 tons at Boston at an equally high price. Although they made these purchases with the knowledge that in December 1783 the British Government had imposed a duty of £18-3 per ton on whale oil, they did so only because of assurance from Champion and Dickason that the so-called alien duty would be either greatly abated or wholly abolished.[38]

The first portent of evil came in a letter from London bearing date of July 30, 1784, saying that "the heavy duty on oil continues and is likely to remain, so that we wish to recommend your declining speculations in that article."[39] Exactly one month later Brown and Benson's worst fears received confirmation when Champion and Dickason wrote that "after our sanguine expectations that the oil duty would be relaxed, we find ourselves severely mortified that it is enforced. We have in vain labored to persuade the government to lessen it and are now under the disagreeable necessity of paying down £18.3.0 per ton for three or four cargoes."[40] But this intelligence came too late to forestall the shipment of the two large purchases of oil which Brown and Benson had made. On one of these they incurred a loss of approximately £2000 Sterling.[41] Champion and Dickason appear to have entertained the hope that the duty on whale oil would at least have the merit of increasing the price of the article in England. But in this belief they were also mistaken, and they finally admitted reluctantly that the duty diminished the price by encouraging large numbers of adventurers from various British ports to fit out for the whale fishery.[42]

Deeply in debt to Champion and Dickason, thwarted in their efforts to remit in kind, unable to procure bills on London in the ordinary course of trade, and discouraged from purchasing them because of their scarcity and prohibitive price, Brown and Benson appeared helpless in the extreme. To add to their woes, Champion and Dickason refused to honor their order for spring goods in 1785, even though they had confined the invoice to such articles as would, with the stock on hand, give them a general assortment capable of attracting shopkeepers fortunate enough still to have some cash on hand.[43] Referring to Champion and Dickason's refusal to ship the goods, they wrote: "Our sales are in consequence very small this spring, our customers having repaired to those who could supply them. The general prejudice in favor of fresh importations is such that the arrival of a very small quantity of goods each season will promote the sale of many articles which are otherwise neglected as old goods."[44] This letter, which began an unpleasant exchange which continued between the two houses for several years, drew from Champion and Dickason the rejoinder that

it gave us infinite concern to decline the shipping of your order last spring, but surely you will allow it was high time to put a stop to the increasing magnitude of an account already swelled to the enormous sum of £26,000 ... The length of credit you and other houses in your State have and are taking is absolutely impossible to be borne. On reciprocal terms we have no objection to the continuance of trade with you, but we are constrained to observe that you seem to expect every advantage it is capable of.[45]

They then pictured the excessive exports to America, lack of pay for which had led to the distress and ruin of many respectable families in Britain. This letter, of course, was merely an invitation to Brown and Benson to observe that much of their difficulty was the result of the faulty advice which Champion and Dickason had given them regarding the purchase and shipment of whale oil.

Among the charges and countercharges which passed between the two firms, none was more unfair and none more resented than Champion and

Dickason's statement that "in every commission engagement made by us on your side we never built on the circumstance that the sale of the goods shipped [by us] should produce the means of remittance, but that the means existed prior to the shipment, having declined all connections where it was supposed the property shipped was to produce the remittance."[46] This implication that Brown and Benson were attempting to conduct their business on a shoestring brought this rebuke from them: "The most ample means and resources cannot be at all times applied to advantage and a debtor possessed of ten times the amount he owes may be so situated that an emergency would oblige him to sacrifice his all in paying his debt. But this we are persuaded your House can neither wish nor expect from any of your friends."[47] It may have been true, as Champion and Dickason asserted, that no other American house was so heavily indebted to them, and none had received such great attention from them as Brown and Benson. But it surely was not true that the latter had possessed insufficient means, misrepresented their resources, or been callous and indifferent about their debt. They had merely sought to avert an unnecessary sacrifice of their capital fund.

The refusal of Champion and Dickason to ship their goods in 1785 was a bitter pill to Brown and Benson; but they soon were able to solace themselves with the thought that their situation was no worse than that of other importers in Rhode Island. In 1786 the importation of British merchandise into the State virtually came to a standstill. Shopkeepers with cash on hand had resort to Boston and New York to replenish their stocks. This generally adverse situation within the State was made worse by the paper money evil. Referring to the emissions of paper, Brown and Benson wrote to Champion and Dickason in July 1786:[48]

This iniquitous procedure has absorbed all our attention and must apologize for our apparent remissness in addressing you. Our situation at present is extremely disagreeable. Having a very large amount in debts due to us for the discharge of which 'tis in vain to apply while the Tender Law or even paper money exists. Hence we are obliged to adopt the most gentle and persuasive measures with our debtors in order to divert them from availing themselves of the advantage which the law courts to them embrace. A paper emission even suppose it to obtain a currency in this State must be very detrimental to the merchant, as nature has denied us those valuable exports with which the Southern States abound, and of course no money can be of use to us but what will circulate in those quarters to which we are obliged to have recourse for the objects of our remittance. It is painful to us to reflect on the magnitude of our debt and on the variety of impediments which crowd to obstruct our most vigorous exertions to abate the sum. The alien duty on oil, the impossibility of securing hard money, the great scarcity and advanced rate of bills, the exorbitant price of Southern production, and superadded to all, the present deranged and unhappy state of political affairs in this government all conspire to defeat our best exertions.

That Brown and Benson were exaggerating neither the size of the large sums due them nor the difficulty of collecting from their debtors is abundantly clear. Under date of March 15, 1786 they compiled a list of persons and firms whose promissory notes they then held.[49] There was due on the 117 notes a balance, exclusive of interest, of £16,177 lawful money, the equivalent of nearly half the amount which they owed Champion and Dickason.[50] This imposing list of debtors also bears out the contention of Brown and Benson that the loss of cash customers, resulting from the belated arrival of their goods in 1782 and 1784, had forced them to sell on credit to shopkeepers who lacked cash. When the increasing severity of the depression interfered with the payment for these wares, Brown and Benson had accepted the notes as evidence of the debts.

The catalogue of debtors has yet another significance. It is proof of the vigor with which Brown and Benson had lately pushed the sale of British goods into areas previously closed to Providence firms. Among the makers of the notes were some of the most prominent men in the State. Some were shopkeepers in Newport which had not been frequented by Providence importers in pre-Revolutionary days. Merchants of neighboring towns in Massachusetts and Connecticut were liberally represented. Prominent on the list were Ward and Sanderson of Petersham, in the Bay State, a town normally in the trade territory of Boston.[51]

Brown and Benson reached the bottom of the pit of economic adversity in 1786; and their situation showed only the slightest improvement in the following year. They were still handicapped by the continued refusal of Champion and Dickason to send them fresh supplies of British goods. In May 1787 they wrote: "We have a considerable quantity of goods on hand but for want of a few articles to complete an assortment we cannot sell them and shop keepers in town and country are repairing with all the money they receive to New York and Boston, where they purchase goods of British agents as low or lower than what the same articles are charged in your invoices."[52] As letters in similar vein arrived from other Providence merchants, Champion and Dickason finally became aware that the economic situation in Rhode Island was even more adverse than elsewhere. Accordingly, they granted preferential interest, commission and insurance rates to Brown and Benson, John Brown, Clark and Nightingale, Joseph and William Russell, and Welcome Arnold on all goods purchased prior to October 29, 1787.[53]

Meanwhile, the building of the Ship *Hope* had not improved the relations between the two houses. The vessel, built to carry English goods im-

ported by Brown and Benson, was scarcely off the stocks when Champion
and Dickason rendered her temporarily useless by refusing further shipments of goods. Brown and Benson asserted that "no better ship was
ever built in New England, if not in all the country," but Champion
and Dickason thought her "the dearest we ever heard of."[54] After much
bickering, the latter finally sold their interest in the vessel for £1000
Sterling. In other times and circumstances the building of *Hope* might
have been a master stroke. But, as Brown and Benson regretfully wrote, it
was "unfortunate considering the new system or rather no system of commerce between this and your country." With obvious reference to the
alien duty on oil and the exclusion of American ships from the West
Indian ports, they added that this had "deranged all our plans and had the
difficulties been foreseen we imagine the trade of importation from Great
Britain would not have existed or at least in a very small degree."[55]

Instead of using *Hope* to freight new cargoes of British goods to Providence, Brown and Benson employed her in various ways in a rather for-
lorn effort to pay for the wares already received from London. In November 1785 they advised Champion and Dickason that they were sending the
vessel to Charleston for a load of rice, which they planned to consign to
their care.[56] Upon the receipt of this intelligence, the London house expressed their regret; they were sure the "speculation must be attended with
loss."[57] When *Hope* arrived in London with the rice, Champion and
Dickason sent her to Amsterdam, where much of the rice proved badly
damaged, or even rotten. Nevertheless, sale of the cargo at public auction
netted almost £1700 Sterling for remittance to Champion and Dickason
on the account of Brown and Benson.[58]

Late in 1786 *Hope* was dispatched to the French West Indies with
a cargo of hoops, beef, and codfish. After obtaining a quantity of
rum and sugar, she proceeded to Charleston, where she loaded with
tobacco which she carried to L'Orient in France.[59] From there, Lanchon
Frères, to whom the cargo was consigned, remitted at various times a total
of about £2500 to Champion and Dickason.[60] In 1787 Brown and Benson
assembled a quantity of New England goods which they shipped to Virginia aboard the Brig *Rising Sun*. With the proceeds of these wares, they
purchased tobacco for consignment to a mercantile firm at Bordeaux. Sale
of this cargo not only provided funds for a return cargo of brandy, claret,
dry goods, and cordage, but also a substantial balance for remittance
to Champion and Dickason.[61] With the knowledge that John Brown
had lost £2000 Sterling on a single consignment of tobacco at London,
Brown and Benson disregarded Champion and Dickason's suggestion that
they ship the tobacco to them. Nor did they accept their correspondents'
advice that they ship flaxseed to Ireland. They sent some potash to Cham-

pion and Dickason who urged them to augment their shipments of that product. This they declined to do because of the very limited supply in Rhode Island, where its production, along with that of other commodities, was largely neglected, as the people had found the Tender Law an easier and less painful means of paying their debts.[62]

In 1789 Brown and Benson returned to the whale fishery and resumed the purchase of whale oil on a limited scale, but not with a view to shipment to England. In that year the French government revoked the edict prohibiting the importation of oil in American bottoms.[63] Shipments of oil and whalebone to Bordeaux and L'Orient soon provided Brown and Benson with another means of making modest but frequent remittance to Champion and Dickason.

Thus in the year the new Federal Constitution went into effect, conditions were looking up somewhat for Brown and Benson, even though their State had not ratified the document. The wheels of business had slowly begun to turn for them once more. They had made considerable recovery from the almost total stagnation of 1786. New avenues of trade were gradually opening to them. Yet, despite all the activity described above, the liquidation of their debt to Champion and Dickason was proving a painfully slow process. On December 31, 1789 they still owed £23,706 Sterling, a net reduction of but £2438 from the figure of five years before.[64]

In 1790 Thomas Dickason and Company (successors of Champion and Dickason as of December 31, 1789) decided that the improved state of economic affairs in this country, together with the even more promising outlook for the future, made the time opportune for them to employ more rigorous measures to collect from their American debtors. In May of that year they remarked that "the happy turn of public affairs on your side and the rise of State securities we hope will enable you shortly to do something handsome for us, and we have the pleasure of hearing that you are considerable holders of that paper."[65] In the same month Thomas Dickason, Jr. arrived in this country as the representative of Thomas Dickason and Company. His mission was that of facilitating the collection of the debts owed by the many American merchants to his principals in London. He established his headquarters in Boston and for the next four years he roamed north to Portsmouth, New Hampshire, and south to Philadelphia. The length of his sojourn and the geographical range of his travels attest to the magnitude and difficulty of his task, as well as to the wide distribution of those indebted to his house.

He soon paid a visit to Providence, where he outlined to Brown and Benson his plan for the payment of their debt to his firm, "whose sufferings," he said, "from the detention of their property has been greater than it might be prudent to relate."[66] His specific demands were that Brown and Benson sell at once sufficient public securities to yield a payment of ten thousand dollars and that the balance due from them be reduced to ten thousand pounds in the course of a year by stated payments according to their convenience.[67] "But," he added, "I expect that you lodge such securities [with Dickason and Company] as to insure payment at the time agreed upon, and from this I will not depart . . . I do not hesitate to say that I know, gentlemen, you have such funds as will enable you to do this with ease to yourselves."[68]

The first reaction of Brown and Benson to young Dickason's proposition was noncommittal. While acknowledging the magnitude of their debt, they refused to pledge any particular time of payment. But they gave assurance "that we are fully determined to diminish the sum by all means in our power."[69] Their means, however, were strictly limited by the impossibility of recovering money for debts owed them, as well as by the many legal impediments and prohibitions to remittance, all so entirely unanticipated by either party when the business connection between the two houses was established years before.[70] A large proportion of the goods imported in 1784 was still unsold, and a far greater amount unpaid for by their customers. They added that "it is still hard to collect debts in Rhode Island," even though the State had now ratified the Constitution. Not only were "the most gentle and conciliatory measures necessary to collect," but a "debt must be a considerable one to avail ourselves of a federal court."[71]

The question of public securities introduced by young Dickason became an added source of unpleasantness between the two houses, largely because of his allegation that Brown and Benson had purchased the depreciated paper with funds which they should have applied to the payment of their debt. On September 17, 1790, however, the Providence firm advised Dickason and Company in London that they had paid Thomas Dickason Jr. in Boston £2250 Sterling.[72] "This money," they wrote, "was the produce of some public securities sold by our Mr. N. B. at less than the current price so desirous are we to evince the sincerity of our wishes to reduce our debt."

Concurrently, Brown and Benson were able to announce that, as a result of the success of their whaling vessel, they were shipping 90 tons of oil and 6000 weight of bone to Fenwick and Mason in Bordeaux.[73] In consequence, they immediately drew upon the latter house in favor of Dickason and Company to the amount of £1200 Sterling; and they instructed Fenwick and Mason to make further remittance to London as the sale of the cargo proceeded. On October 31, 1790 their debt to Dickason and Company was approximately £19,000 Sterling, a net reduction of almost £5000 in the course of the year.[74]

Although this fell far short of young Dickason's original demand,

Brown and Benson's evidence of good faith caused him to adopt a more indulgent attitude toward them. During the next year he took no steps to enforce his demand for the deposit of securities as a guarantee of payment. In April 1791 Brown and Benson sold 30,000 dollars of Continental securities, netting £5400 Sterling, which they promptly placed to the credit of Dickason and Company.[75] "Nothing," they wrote, "but a wish to pay would induce us to part with that species of property, which promises an increasing value from the resources of the country and the disposition of the government to support the public credit." In the same month they made a payment of 3000 dollars to Thomas Dickason, Jr.[76] Writing of this to the house they said:

> He assured us he was in pressing want of the money and we hired that sum at a peculiar inconvenience, so difficult is it to obtain money. But the desire with which we are impressed to reduce our debt, combined with the pleasure we enjoy in complying with his wishes, induced us to submit to a sacrifice rather than disappoint him. We feel that he presses extremely hard for payment, but we conceive it a duty at the same time to acknowledge that he conducts with all that delicate propriety that marks the character of a gentleman.[77]

In the spring of 1791, Brown and Benson shipped to Fenwick and Mason at Bordeaux 200 hogsheads of good tobacco, 40 casks of oil, and 17,000 weight of whalebone.[78] They directed that the proceeds of this cargo should be remitted to Dickason and Company. At the same time they were expecting their whalemen from the coast of Brazil, from which they planned to ship to Bordeaux at least 100 tons of oil and a quantity of bone. Dickason and Company were also to receive the returns from this shipment.[79] Somewhat encouraged by their prospects, they wrote to London that

> we have not yet recovered from the embarrassed & detrimental state into which the Paper Money system plunged us. We have large sums due to us & a large amount of our old importations on hand but we hope that we are gradually Emerging from the various and multiplied Difficulties which Continually baffled our wishes & endeavors to reduce our Debt.[80]

The various payments and remittances made in the course of the year reduced the debt by £8000 leaving a balance of £10,912 due to Dickason and Company on December 31, 1791.[81] Although this represented substantial progress in debt reduction, it failed to satisfy Thomas Dickason, Jr., who recurred to his earlier plan of a deposit of public securities as a pledge of payment. On May 12, 1792 he entered into an agreement with Brown and Benson by which they transferred to Dickason and Company 48,000 dollars in deferred stock issued in pursuance of Hamilton's funding plan, together with 30,000 dollars in 3 and 6 per cent stock of the United States.[82]

The agreement stipulated that Dickason and Company were not to sell the stock in less than one year from the date of its receipt in London, unless it would command an average price of 75 per cent of its nominal value. After that date, however, the London Company was free to sell it at the current market price, should the debt still be unpaid.[83]

On the face of it this agreement seemed to provide adequate protection to Thomas Dickason and Company, as well as reasonable assurance against the sale of Brown and Benson's stock at a sacrifice. It was the latter's belief that the threat of war in Europe would cause the price of the stock to rise above the limits set by them. But in this expectation they were disappointed. The ominous situation in Europe had precisely the opposite effect. Prices soon declined so sharply as to make it certain that a forced sale would result in a heavy loss. This seemed to render prompt payment of the balance imperative.

To all outward appearance the year 1792 was prosperous and successful for Brown and Benson. Their business was expanding in all directions. They were building new ships for the China, the East India, and the Baltic trades. But the ever-widening scope of the activities called for the reinvestment of the greater portion of their profits in the business. As a result, on December 31, 1792 their debt was £9000 Sterling, a reduction of only about £2000 for the year; and the date for final payment was but five months away, unless they were willing to sacrifice the stock.[84]

On April 16, 1793 Thomas Dickason, Jr. advised Brown and Benson: "It is with much concern I inform you that American stocks are likely to be much below your last limits and most earnestly request that you would adopt some plan of redeeming those in Champion and Dickason's hands . . . to prevent sacrifice that will be distressing to them and injurious to you."[85] As the time was getting late, Brown and Benson now urged Thomas Dickason, Jr. to intercede with the London office to prevent the sale of the stock on June 1st, pending the submission of another plan for the payment of the debt.[86] On June 20, 1793 they offered to pay an additional 6 per cent interest and a 3 per cent commission on their balance from July 1st of that year on condition that Dickason and Company would hold the stock until January 1, 1794.[87] The London firm accepted this proposal with the remark that "we should receive no pleasure in selling your property at so great a loss."[88]

Once more Brown and Benson submitted a detailed plan according to which expected remittances from various of their correspondents in this country and continental Europe would extinguish the debt by the latest dead line. To make payment doubly certain they purchased, at a very high premium, bills of exchange on the Sierra Leone Company.[89] But again their expectations were not realized because of the failure of Bordeaux

and Amsterdam correspondents to remit in time.[90] It was necessary, therefore, to prepare still another plan of payment and to ask of Dickason and
Company another extension of time.[91] To this request the latter readily
acceded, once again refraining from selling the stock. This was the last
postponement. Within a few months remittances from the continent had
finally extinguished the debt. On November 14, 1794 Thomas Dickason
and Company wrote that they had closed the account.[92]

The debt of £26,144 Sterling, as of December 31, 1784, had required
almost exactly ten years for its liquidation. Nicholas Brown, Sr., founder
of the partnership of Brown and Benson, was now dead, and the partnership had become Brown, Benson and Ives. Throughout the long years of
the unpaid balance, Champion and Dickason and, later, Thomas Dickason
and Company had been patient in the extreme. During the black depression of the 1780's they had merely entreated their debtors to do their
utmost. Only when better times set in at the close of the decade did they
adopt a sterner attitude. Even then, however, they had shown no disposition to take advantage of their position as creditors. They had confined
their demands to assurance of reasonably prompt payment through the
posting of 78,000 dollars in government stock.

Once the stock was in their hands, they had been as considerate of it
as if it had been their own; and through repeated deferment of the ultimate date of payment they had enabled Brown and Benson to salvage their
property. The liquidation of the debt, however, had not been without its
cost to Nicholas Brown, Sr., who had been forced to sell in this country
public securities sufficient to yield somewhat more than 40,000 dollars. As
the correspondence between the two houses fails to indicate either the
total nominal value of the paper thus sold or the price at which it was
sold, it is impossible to say precisely what loss he suffered through his inability to hold the securities until the date of their maturity. There is,
however, some fragmentary evidence on this point. One block of stock
with a nominal value of 30,000 dollars yielded £5400 Sterling, which represents a relatively slight loss. On the other hand, there appears to have been
a loss of 10,000 dollars on another sale of stock; and this conclusion is
supported by a subsequent statement by Nicholas Brown, Jr., that at one
time his father had saved the partnership by the sacrifice of 10,000 dollars
in public securities.[93]

The decade required for the payment of the debt was one of great
significance in the annals of Brown and Benson. At its beginning they
were conspicuous importers of English goods. By the end of the decade
they were no longer concerned in such trade. Their experience as importers in the postwar period was unhappy in the extreme. After falling deeply
into debt in the London trade they found it extremely difficult to liquidate

their obligations. It does not follow, however, that it was merely their debt which caused them to forswear the importing business. Although most American merchants contracted heavy debts in England during the critical period, not all of them discontinued the importation of goods from that country. Before Brown and Benson had paid their debt they were launched on other kinds of trade which largely engrossed their energies. Perhaps these left them neither time nor inclination to deal in British wares.

While engaged in the painful process of extinguishing their debt to Dickason and Company, Brown and Benson's relations with that firm were undergoing a transformation. The London house had in the beginning sold American products and purchased English goods on commission for their Providence correspondents. But as the latter entered new channels of commerce, involving new and widely scattered connections on three continents, Dickason became the clearing house for all the widespread maritime ventures of Brown and Benson. This new relationship between the two firms was to continue for another generation.

CHAPTER 15

The End of an Era

IF the decade following the peace of 1783 marked a transformation in the relations of Brown and Benson with England, it was no less a period of transition with respect to other features of their business. Pre-Revolutionary forms of activity were slowly retreating in the face of new types of trade, new business institutions, and new kinds of manufacture. At the end of the decade some of the older forms had entirely disappeared, some were on the verge of oblivion, while still others lingered on for a time in a state of diminishing significance.

Trade to the Caribbean area never regained its prewar importance to the Browns. Although they resumed traffic with Surinam, it lacked both the volume and the regularity of an earlier day. They sent vessels to St. Croix and St. Eustatius, and sometimes to the French Islands, but such voyages no longer played the vital rôle of their West Indian ventures of colonial times.[1] Their commerce with the Islands became increasingly an adjunct to trade with Virginia and the Carolinas, where they obtained the tobacco, rice, and indigo which they needed in their new and growing peacetime traffic with continental Europe.

The years of the Critical Period were also a time of transition in the coastwise trade of the Browns. Both the identity and the function of their correspondents in the seaport towns changed. Gone were Van Horne and Curtenius in New York, Henry Lloyd in Boston, Tench Francis in Philadelphia, Lopez and Mason in Newport, and the Starbucks, Husseys, Macys, Folgers, and Rotches in Nantucket. Death had doubtless claimed some of them, while the hazards of war account for the absence of others. Their disappearence tends to support Richard Hildreth's assertion that "one large portion of the wealthy men of colonial times had been expatriated and another had been impoverished by the Revolution."

The change in function of the correspondents was only less marked than that in personnel. The gold, silver, and good bills of exchange which these men had provided in colonial days had partly compensated for the deficiency of hard money in Rhode Island, and supplied the Browns with the means of making payments at Nantucket and London. For a decade after the war this function ceased and the correspondents were more important chiefly as a means of enabling Brown and Benson to procure better rounded cargoes for the Caribbean and continental European markets.

Brown and Benson's correspondent in Philadelphia in the Critical Period was the firm of Hewes and Anthony. Josiah Hewes, the senior member, had begun to transact business for Nicholas and John Brown in the Quaker City in 1775. Despite interruptions, he continued to serve their interests there throughout the war. With the return of peace, he was joined by Captain Joseph Anthony, originally a resident of Newport. To them, Brown and Benson shipped the molasses and rum whose sale at Philadelphia purchased the flour so essential for cargoes to Surinam. So enthusiastic were Hewes and Anthony about the potentialities of the Philadelphia-Providence traffic that they suggested the joint ownership and operation by the two firms of a "coaster" to ply regularly between the two ports.[2] They had a small sloop which they were prepared to share for purposes of this trade. But, under the spell of the buoyant optimism which characterized American merchants generally in 1784, Brown and Benson countered with an offer to build a new vessel, of which they would own one-half, while the Providence house of Holroyd and Tillinghast would share the other half equally with Hewes and Anthony.[3] Accepting this proposal, the last-named firm remarked that since "the Newport Packet does very handsome . . . certainly as much may be done at Providence. We have from long experience found that for people in extensive trade one coaster answers many good purposes, as it helps their other branches of business."[4]

In January 1785 Brown and Benson wrote that the "Sloop we intend for the Packet is now building of very good timber and plank."[5] They were convinced they were getting her at a bargain price in view of the sharp advance in the cost of shipbuilding at Providence, occasioned by the decision of John Brown and others to build immediately a "large number of vessels for the cod fishery," a new branch of business for a member of the Brown family, but one which Brown and Benson believed would "conduce much to the interest of this town."

Under more favorable conditions a "coaster" or packet service between Providence and Philadelphia, with calls at intermediate points, might have done well. But it was the misfortune of *Delaware,* as the new Sloop was named, to begin her career in 1785 when the country was rapidly slipping into the abyss of depression. With business all but stagnant for the next several years, she was foredoomed to failure. Unable to find profitable employment for the vessel, her owners soon quarreled among themselves over the disposition to be made of her. In the end, Hewes and Anthony became her sole owners.

One service rendered by Hewes and Anthony was of a novel character. Brown and Benson believed that real estate mortgages which they held were particularly vulnerable to the provisions of the Rhode Island Tender Law, according to which a debtor could discharge his debt by the proffer of paper money to his creditor. To protect themselves, they proposed to transfer this species of property to persons in other states. They accordingly suggested a fictitious sale to Hewes and Anthony of a mortgage of "upwards of £300 lawful money" which they held on a certain property in Providence, and of one "on the estate of Metcalf Bowler, Esq. . . . for about £600 lawful money."[6] After outlining the plan, they added that "if you approve of the proceeding we think it may afford us a plausible security to give us an opportunity to transfer the mortgage from you to others as the emergency of future occasions may require." Deciding that they could "approve the proceeding," Hewes and Anthony negotiated the "purchase" of the lesser of the two mortgages, "the . . . estate that was mortgaged" by Metcalf Bowler having been so "adjusted" that Brown and Benson believed no difficulty was "to be apprehended from that quarter." That this device served the purpose desired is indicated by a subsequent letter by Brown and Benson to their Philadelphia friends: "As our Assembly have at length suspended the tender law and which we suppose will expire we now enclose a conveyance of the estate back to us which we conveyed to you to prevent a tender in paper money." They requested that "where it now appears as your property you will please sign it before witnesses & return it to us under cover by some safe hand"; and they were "gratefully obliged" to Hewes and Anthony for their "friendly services in this instance," which they believed "was the principal means of averting the tender."[7]

Apart from Hewes and Anthony, the most important of Brown and Benson's correspondents in the decade after Yorktown was the firm of Thayer and Bartlett in Charleston, South Carolina. Although the Browns had occasionally dealt with the southern metropolis both before and during the Revolution, it acquired a new significance for them in the Critical Period. As it became evident that whale oil could not serve as a remittance to London, they were compelled to ship Southern produce to continental Europe, whence remittance was made to London. Beginning in 1785 Thayer and Bartlett sold New England and West Indian goods in Charleston on account of Brown and Benson, and purchased for them rice, tobacco, and indigo for the continental European markets.[8]

Brown and Benson's relations with New York were of minor importance compared with their connections at Manhattan before Independence.

Their only regular contact was with Murray, Mumford and Bowen, whose services were undoubtedly a convenience but hardly a necessity to the Providence house.[9] The latter derived from this correspondence neither goods in large volume nor bills of exchange for use elsewhere. It was only in the next decade that New York again began to play a significant part in the affairs of Brown and Benson.

In colonial times the Browns had traded with the Old Dominion frequently, but not with great regularity. They had great difficulty in collecting the bills owed them as a result of this traffic. It may have been for this reason that Nicholas and his new partner sought other correspondents in Virginia after the war. Of these the most important were Jenckes, Winsor and Company at Alexandria, and Campbell and Wheeler at Petersburg.[10] For a time Brown and Benson also maintained Joseph Butler, a native Rhode Islander, as their factor in Virginia, where he sought to dispose of indents in payment for tobacco.[11]

It was in relations with Boston, Newport, and Nantucket that the war brought the most profound change. When Henry Lloyd became a Loyalist and expatriated himself, no one at Boston took his place in the service of the Browns, although during the war Nicholas and John kept in touch with several merchants there, including Bossenger Foster. After the return of peace, Brown and Benson had no established correspondent in that city, nor did they transact business of importance with any Boston house. For the time being, Boston virtually vanished from the business world of the Providence firm. Only after 1790 do we find Brown and Benson again in close and regular touch with Boston houses.

At Newport the change was no less marked. For a decade no one replaced Aaron Lopez, Benjamin Mason, and the numerous other merchants with whom the Browns had exchanged goods and services in colonial times. Not until 1792 did Brown and Benson establish a regular correspondence with a Newport house—the new firm of Gibbs and Channing.[12]

The most complete break of all came at Nantucket. There the contacts of the Browns had been varied, constant, and close, a fact well attested by the multitude of Nantucket letters preserved in their papers. Probably no colonial economic interest suffered more in the war than the whale fishery of the Island. Prompt reëstablishment of it at the end of the war was made impossible by the prohibitive duty on whale oil imposed by England, the chief market for the product in prewar days. William Rotch, perhaps the greatest of the Nantucket whaling merchants, thereupon sought to establish the industry in Britain. To the end he had interviews with the younger Pitt and with Lord Hawkesbury, both of whom refused to make concessions to him. He then established the business at Dunkirk, in

France, where he was able to avoid the French prohibition upon the importation of whale oil in foreign bottoms.[13]

After the war the relations of Brown and Benson with Nantucket were only intermittent. They occasionally dealt with Christopher Starbuck, now an impoverished figure. The name Rotch disappeared from the records of the Browns in 1781, to reappear ten years later in the person of William Rotch, Jr., who had long since abandoned Nantucket in favor of New Bedford, destined to be the new seat of the whale fishery.[14] The other names so familiar in Nantucket's palmier days fail to make any appearance at all.

Demoralization of the whale fishery, of course, diminished the flow of head matter into the candle manufacture. This largely explains the restricted scale of operation of the Browns' spermaceti candle works in the decade following the war, just as it accounts for the declining importance of candles in the cargoes which they sent to the Caribbean region.

In pre-Revolutionary times the scarcity and high price of head matter had prompted the candle manufacturers to combine for the purpose of fixing its price. But after the war the demoralization of the business was such that the short supply of head matter seems to have provided little incentive to combination. We have found but one reference to the subject of a union of the candle makers in the postwar years. Replying to a letter from Nathaniel Appleton, of Boston, Brown and Benson wrote on May 24, 1784 that

as the Sperm Works in this Town are not yet repair'd & but few Vessels out a Whaling its thought there will be but little Sperm bot [bought] in this Season Amongst us, so that a Meeting Will be Unnecessary as Its Supposed the price you propose will be as Much as Can well be afforded. We think it best by all means to keep the Price within bounds, and if it be thot necessary to have A meeting we will give you timely advise.[15]

This faint suggestion of an informal understanding in regard to the price of head matter is but a pale imitation of the articles of union which were an annual affair before 1775. When this letter was written Americans still hoped either for the total repeal or a drastic abatement of the British duty on whale oil. When the disappointment of this hope doomed the Nantucket whale fishery, there was no longer any need for price-fixing by the manufacturers.

It is disappointing that the demise of the candle manufacture is not better documented. Yet the very brevity of the record is evidence of the industry's moribund state during and after the war. The manufacture of spermaceti candles belonged to the past. In their efforts to keep it alive the Browns were endeavoring to reconstruct an era that was already at an end. They would never again find fame or fortune in the spermaceti works—a fact that they were slow to accept.

A return to the distilling of rum represented another effort of Brown and Benson to revive prewar days; and this attempt is the more remarkable in that it came after a twenty-five-year interval. The four brothers had foresworn the rum distillery after Obadiah's death in 1762. Although John in the postwar era built a gin distillery, Nicholas and his new partner did not return to the distilling of rum until 1788. In that year they signed articles of agreement with Welcome Arnold, of Providence, providing for the construction and equal ownership of a distillery. Erected at a cost of approximately 25,000 dollars, its owners alleged that it was the finest establishment of its kind in the country. The reasons which impelled Brown and Benson to take this step were stated in a letter to Hewes and Anthony. They "were induced to be concerned in a distillery because we are often obliged to receive our debts in molasses and have great occasion for rum in the course of our business; and are also obliged to receive country produce for debts which we ship to the West Indies and cannot find sale for all the molasses & the demand for rum is almost constant."[16]

Hewes and Anthony were unable to "conceive what can be your inducement to build a distillery." In Philadelphia it was a branch of business "much on the decline" and one of the last things they would "meddle with." And they wrote that "in the States East of you we find they are at a loss what to do with their rum."[17] This must have been rather discouraging news to Brown and Benson, who hoped to ship much of the rum to Hewes and Anthony. The returns from the rum they would invest in Philadelphia flour which, when shipped to Surinam, would purchase further quantities of molasses to feed the distillery.

Notwithstanding their doubts as to the wisdom of the distilling venture, Hewes and Anthony soon had an opportunity to sell some of the rum in the Philadelphia market. Explaining the ease with which they disposed of a consignment of 62 hogsheads, they wrote that

we must do the manufacturers [Brown and Benson] the justice to own that the rapid sale was in some measure owing to the extreme neatness and good order of the casks and the superior good quality of the liquor which on all accounts is presumed equal to any ever brought from any of the New England states. When rum is at a low price, such as this would often times command a penny per gallon more than the common kind. We sincerely wish you every success in the business and advise your keeping up its reputation.[18]

This flattering report with regard to the product of the distillery was doubtless very pleasing to Brown and Benson. It should have encouraged them to concentrate upon the maintenance of a reputation for quality. But that was not to be. For reasons which are not apparent, but of which the example and advice of John Brown may have been one, they soon enlarged the distillery with a view to the production of gin.[19] But, for reasons which again are not clear, the enlarged capacity was not utilized for that purpose.

Disagreement among the partners played a part in the ultimate abandonment of the distillery. Relations of Brown and Benson with Welcome Arnold seem never to have been especially harmonious. The former contended that, since the charges for "labor and wood," as well as the interest "on a very Costly Estate" were constant, considerations of economy required the operation of the distillery at capacity.[20] They adduced data to show that between November 30, 1789 and April 25, 1794 the distillery produced 517,655 gallons of rum. Of this amount, 284,610 gallons were distilled from molasses supplied by Brown and Benson, leaving 233,045 gallons as Welcome Arnold's share. Thus Brown and Benson had received 51,565 gallons more than Arnold. The latter took the view that since this excess had been produced in a plant in which he had a half interest and bore one-half the charges, he should be compensated by Brown and Benson. Brown and Benson argued, in turn, that they had suffered financial loss because of Arnold's refusal to supply stock necessary for capacity operation of the distillery. Had it been kept going at full blast, they said, the total output of rum would have been increased by 186,121 gallons. Of this, their half would have been 93,060 gallons. By this reasoning, Brown and Benson argued that they were entitled to compensation for this loss.

Because of this dispute, the partners ceased to operate the distillery after April 1794. But it was not until approximately one year later that they agreed to submit the controversy to the judgment of three impartial arbiters who unanimously decided that Brown and Benson "for their having Distilled a larger Quantity of Rum Than the Said Welcome" should pay him the sum of £88:10.[21] Within a few months Brown and Benson disposed of their half interest to Cyprian Sterry for 11,250 dollars.[22] With this sale they divested themselves of one more form of pre-Revolutionary business activity.

Another inheritance of the Brown family from colonial days was Hope Furnace. When it was reconverted to the uses of peace at the close of the war, Nicholas, Joseph, and John each had an interest in it. In 1787 the owners were Jabez Bowen, Brown and Benson, Rufus Hopkins, Nicholas Power, Brown and Francis (the firm name of John Brown and his son-in-law, John Francis), and Brown, Rogers and Brown (the partnership formed a few years earlier by Joseph Brown and his son Obadiah).[23] In the decade following the war the operations of the furnace seem to have been on a somewhat restricted scale. No longer was pig iron an article of remittance to London. Nor was there anyone in New York to take the place of Peter T. Curtenius as a purchaser of Hope pigs. Gone also was Aaron Lopez of Newport, once a regular buyer of pig iron. The market for the furnace product appears to have been purely local.

Only two brief periods of revival served to relieve the monotony of gradual decay in the postwar era. In the summer of 1794 the owners signed a contract with the Government for the casting of 128 cannon.[24] When it was charged that some of the guns made in pursuance of this agreement were defective, the proprietors expressed their regret that they had ever entered into the covenant. But they added that their "Principal Workmen" had been instructed in the art by a French officer in the late war; and they assured the Secretary of War that the guns remaining to be delivered were "the best cannon ever cast in America."

The other period of notable activity came at the time of the undeclared naval war with France in 1798. In April of that year, Brown and Ives, writing to their Boston correspondent, Head and Amory, enclosed a number of handbills advertising cannon for sale, which they asked the Boston house to "put up in the most conspicuous places."[25] Evidently these handbills, or other media of information, did their work well. Replying to advice from Head and Amory that they had received an application for eight pairs of four-pounders, Brown and Ives said that "the metal of which the guns are made in Scituate is of a superior quality. Several setts of them have been sent to Boston and the public ships fitted in New England have all been furnished from that Foundry."[26] A few days later they again sent to Head and Amory "some advertisements respecting the Cannon Foundry in Scituate in which we are concerned," and they requested that the advertisement be inserted in the *Centinel* and one other paper."[27] Head and Amory soon wrote that they could sell five pairs of four- or six-pounders, but they "must be cast in the mould of those which your furnace cast for the *Pickering* and *Herald*." The furnace owners could supply the number of guns requested "but not of the pattern by which the *Pickering* & *Herald* guns were made."

Meanwhile, Head and Amory had received application from the "agents who superintend the building of the Frigate" in Boston for an estimate of the cost of 26 twelve-pounders for the main battery of the ship. Brown and Ives, in behalf of the owners of Furnace Hope, indicated their readiness to deliver this number of guns at 500 dollars per pair, to be of the same pattern as the cannon they were casting for the ship under construction at Warren, Rhode Island.[28] They were also making the guns for the frigates being built at Newburyport, Massachusetts, and Portsmouth, New Hampshire, as well as for the "U. S. Ship of War" building in Connecticut.[29] "All the public ships fitted in New England," they said, "have been supplyed from this Foundry except the *Washington*," only part of whose guns had been cast at the Hope.

But the market for cannon was not restricted to New England. The owners made at least one shipment of 12 six-pounders to Baltimore, and another of 16 six-pounders to Philadelphia.[30] In 1799 the War Department forwarded signed contracts for the purchase of cannon to be cast at the furnace, which seems to indicate that the reputation of Hope Foundry guns was not confined to the builders of ships, whether public or private.[31]

This was the last brief season of glory that Hope Furnace was to know. At a meeting of the Company on March 18, 1803 the owners voted to sell a "sufficiency of the Lands belonging to the Company" to pay the outstanding debts.[32] Three years later it was decreed that all the lands belonging to the Company should be sold at public auction.[33] On July 12, 1806 Silvanus Hopkins and his "Associates" undertook to purchase "the Furnace Hope Estate with the Mill Privilges" at 7000 dollars and the "Potter Farm so called" at 2000 dollars.[34] So ended the Browns' connection with an enterprise whose post-Revolutionary history, like that of the spermaceti works and the distillery, was anticlimactic.

PUBLIC SECURITIES*

The decade following the close of the War of Independence was the era of conservative "counterrevolution" carried through by a "consolidated group whose interests knew no state boundaries and were truly national in scope."[35] On the political side the great achievement of this conservative group was the framing and adoption of the Constitution. In the economic sphere they sought bank charters in the various states, explored new routes of commerce, and endeavored to foster the commercial interests by "shifting the burden of taxation upon the land-owner."[36] But the greatest economic triumph of the Counterrevolutionists lay in the funding and assumption plans of Alexander Hamilton; for these were the policies which transformed the doubtful state and federal securities of the time into fluid capital, with its wonderfully stimulating effects upon the entire economic organism.

Before the close of the war these securities, once so widely held, gradually became concentrated in fewer hands. Hard times in the middle 1780's accelerated the trend. "A race of stockjobbers and speculators" appeared, as soldiers and other small holders found themselves obliged to part with their paper at a mere fraction of its face value.[37]

---

*Although the dollar symbol is technically incorrect when used in connection with events prior to 1784, it is employed in this section in order to avoid the frequent repetition of the word "dollars."

The depreciated securities first began to pass into the possession of shop-keepers and merchants, doubtless in partial payment of debts.[38] But un-disguised speculation soon made its appearance. Availing themselves of the opportunity offered by the Pennsylvania funding law of 1785, "inter-state combinations were organized to buy up her securities at debased prices." William Bingham of Philadelphia remarked that the profit to be derived from the ultimate redemption of the depreciated paper was "like holding a lucky number in a lottery." Robert Morris, financier of the Revolution, was reputed to have bought the depressed obligations freely from their distressed owners. In January 1785 it was reported that brokers quoted the price of Pennsylvania securities as freely as those of commodi-ties. Newspapers carried advertisements of speculators who bought and sold both state and Continental paper.

Securities were extremely depressed in 1786, and the buying of them continued unabated. The next year, probably because of hope engendered by the Federal Convention, the price of the paper increased, as did specu-lation in it. The price of loan office certificates advanced 25 per cent, and a wave of buying followed the adjournment of the Convention.

By 1790, when the funding process began, Northern merchants, finan-ciers, and speculators had thus acquired a large portion of the Continental debt originally held by others, as well as securities of States other than those in which they resided. Notably marked had been the purchase by men in the North of the debt of Southern States. South Carolina securi-ties were especially attractive to speculators; those of Virginia only some-what less popular. "Southern State Securities" are said to have yielded to the Barrells of Boston a very handsome profit in the years between 1790 and 1795.

Unfortunately, there is no complete study showing the degree of con-centration in the ownership of State and Continental securities; probably no such study can ever be made, because of the loss or destruction of neces-sary records. Conclusions of a tentative nature may be drawn, however, on the basis of such documentary evidence as has survived.

Of 160 holders of Continental securities in Massachusetts, 37 were "yeomen," 29 were referred to as "esquire" or "gentlemen," 21 were "mer-chants," while brokers, widows, physicians, clerks, druggists, brickmakers, and cordwainers each enjoyed a lesser representation. On their face, these figures do not indicate an undue concentration of paper in the hands of capitalists. But if the average holding per person in each of the various categories be taken as the criterion, the concentration is very apparent. The average yeoman held paper to the value of only $752, compared with average holdings of $5851 for the esquires, $5712 for the merchants, and $4408 for the brokers.[39]

A more pertinent consideration is the extent to which the holdings of these individuals represented loans to the government in wartime. Or, stated in different terms, were those persons primarily original investors in Continental securities, or were they speculative holders of the paper? Yeomen were the original holders of 37 per cent of their funded paper. The corresponding figure for the esquires is 31 per cent; for the merchants, 24 per cent. The brokers had originally held none of the securities funded by them. Thus, of the paper held by the 160 persons in 1790, only about one-quarter represented original investment by them.

One of the important holders of securities in Massachusetts was Harvard College, whose $102,923 of funded paper had once belonged to more than 80 different persons. One Boston merchant turned in certificates which had originally been issued to 47 persons; another funded securities obtained from 95 individual holders.[40]

If the situation prevailing in Massachusetts may be regarded as fairly typical of the States north of Chesapeake Bay, it is apparent that the benefits of Hamilton's funding and assumption plans were very unevenly distributed through the country. The result was a concentration of much of the "pure" capital in the hands of a comparatively few persons. In the possession of these people, the new paper served to provide the capital for banks, insurance and turnpike companies, manufacturing enterprises, investment in wild lands, and other promotional ventures of the day.

High on the list of holders of public paper within the young nation were Nicholas and John Brown. Joseph and Moses held relatively small amounts. Few, if any, persons have left such a complete record of their dealings in securities as Nicholas. Less is known in detail, unfortunately, of John's activities in this respect.

Nicholas began his investment in securities early in the war. Between March 26 and June 7, 1777, 85 certificates with a total specie value of $29,600 were issued to him by the Continental Loan Office in Rhode Island.[41] On June 25, 1777 he received from the Continental Loan Office in Massachusetts 31 Loan Certificates, each with a specie value of $400, or a total of $12,400.[42] Within a period of three months, therefore, he had staked more than $40,000 on the future of the young nation.

But while he was thus extending financial assistance to his country and state, Nicholas was alert to the opportunities for traffic in securities originally owned by others. In 1778-79 Bossenger Foster of Boston sold merchandise for Nicholas, some of which came from a prize captured by a privateer in which the latter was interested.[43] Foster's remittances were partly in Continental Loan Certificates and partly in Massachusetts State notes. On September 25, 1778, Nicholas acknowledged receipt of $4800 in Continental Certificates from Foster.[44] He added that "you will be improving every opportunity of turning the balance [which Foster owed him] into continental certificates with as much interest on them . . . as you can get . . . Perhaps some after receiving the first years interest . . . may incline to sell them." A month later he wrote Foster that he "should be glad to have the account of . . . all my goods sold and the balance invested in continental certificates dated before the first of March last . . . if any will sell after they have received the first years interest . . . purchase them."[45] Nicholas suggested that Foster ask "Mr. Appleton," Loan Commissioner for Massachusetts, with whom he had "some small acquaintance," to "make some enquiry of the possessors of the certificates as they call for . . . the interest." Such "enquiry" would reveal the identity of those who were inclined to sell their certificates before depreciation could take further toll.

These and other letters which passed between Nicholas and his Boston correspondent indicate his eagerness to acquire depreciated loan certificates from owners already in distress or desirous of averting further loss through depreciation. In this way he came into possession of at least a portion of the large amount of Massachusetts Loan Office certificates and state notes of the Bay State which he held at the time of his death.

By 1782 Nicholas was beginning to take depreciated paper in part payment of debts. In April of that year William Newman of Boston, whose note of hand for an undisclosed sum was held by Nicholas, wrote that he had some consolidated notes amounting to about £60 which he had "bought at 2/5^{ths}."[46] He added that if it were agreeable to Nicholas "to take them at that I will send them by the first opportunity and shall be glad to know if I can procure a larger sum upon them terms if you will take them as it may be of mutual advantage."

In January 1783 Ephraim Willard, of Fairfield, Connecticut, "paid" Nicholas in Pennsylvania notes to the amount of £319-10-5 in the currency of that State.[47] In November of the same year Brown and Benson accepted Continental Certificates from Gideon Sisson to the nominal value of $60,200 in payment for European goods amounting to £246 lawful money of Rhode Island.[48] Sisson reserved the right to redeem all or part of the certificates within four months. At another time Nicholas wrote that there were some debts due to him which he "could get paid in final settlement notes."[49]

Several years later Brown and Benson held £1363 in Rhode Island State notes, valued at the time of assumption at over $6000. As they were the original holders of virtually none of this, it is probable that the securities were received in payments of debts owed to them. In 1786 they owned final settlement notes with a specie value of $17,981.65. As these notes had originally been issued to other persons, they, too, must have been acquired by Brown and Benson largely in satisfaction of debts.

Not until 1784 did Nicholas begin to deal systematically in depreciated paper. By that time the adverse economic conditions of the postwar period had debased the price of securities to the point where speculators began to buy them in quantity. Among these enterprising men was one Jonathan Wheeler of Grafton, Massachusetts. Wheeler evidently dealt in all sorts of public paper, but he appears to have been particularly zealous in the pursuit of final settlement notes.

On May 8, 1784 Nicholas bought from Wheeler twelve of these notes with an aggregate specie value of $1901.[50] The following year he made six different purchases from Wheeler, ranging from $1718 to $8593, with a total value of $24,832.[51] During the same period he bought final settlement notes to the value of $5591 from Edmund Fowler and Samuel Myrick, while on August 30, 1785 he acquired $3505 in final settlements from ·Abijah Holbrook.[52] In 1786 he made two additional purchases of those notes, the combined value amounting to about $1400.[53] From these three sources within a period of less than three years he procured final settlement notes with an aggregate specie value of somewhat more than $35,000.

The transactions described above account for little more than half the final settlement notes which Nicholas Brown possessed late in 1786. He then held well over 600 of these certificates originally issued to almost as many different persons and having a specie value of $61,790. In that year he received from William Ellery, Continental Loan Officer in Rhode Island, indents to the nominal value of $6702, covering interest on these notes to December 31, 1784.

Unfortunately, the documents relating to his purchases of final settlement notes fail to indicate the price he paid for them. It is possible, however, to draw some reasonable inferences. As he acquired most of them in 1785, he probably paid less than three shillings on the pound, as the average price of securities in that year was below that figure. For those bought in 1786 he undoubtedly paid even less, as the price of the paper then reached rock bottom.

Nicholas did not long retain possession of his large assortment of final settlement notes. In June 1787 he delivered $5353 of them to Joseph Bennett, who was to buy lands in New York State with them.[54] The following year Nicholas loaned $30,000 in securities to William Constable and Richard Platt of New York City, two of the most conspicuous speculators and financial operators of the day.[55] In return Constable and Platt deposited in the hands of John Mumford of New York "Three Thousand Dollars in Specie," together with a bond for $30,000 as surety for the return of the securities.[56] The securities were still in the hands of the New Yorkers in April 1791 when Thomas Dickason and Company of London were pressing Brown and Benson hard for payment of the large sum which they still owed the London house. Accordingly Nicholas sold Constable and Platt's bond to Dickason and Company for £7200 lawful money, or £5400 Sterling, this being the amount of the bond less the $3000 in specie deposited at the time the securities were loaned.[57] As these securities were final settlement notes, this transaction, combined with that with Joseph Bennett, reduced by more than $35,000 the amount of that species of paper held by Nicholas.[58]

Soon after the new constitution went into effect, Nicholas found other ways to dispose of final settlement notes—ways which he evidently felt were of advantage to him. One way was by exchange of these notes for South Carolina State securities, which were so popular with Northern speculators at that time. In May 1790 he turned over to Jonathan Wheeler (from whom he had purchased so much of this type of paper) approximately $2000 in final settlements in return for South Carolina certificates, the rate of exchange being £100 of the former for £135 of the latter.[59] By another transaction with Wheeler in the same month he traded £2872 lawful money in final settlements for South Carolina paper at the same rate of exchange.[60] A month later he transferred to Wheeler $9574 in final settlement notes for the same purpose.[61]

While thus making use of his final settlement notes to acquire South Carolina securities, Nicholas did not neglect paper issued by states nearer home. In that same spring of 1790 he parted with $4371 in final settlements in exchange for Massachusetts State notes at the rate of £100 for £125.[62]

This trading of Continental for State paper, which was doubtless encouraged by the favorable rate of exchange, did not take place without the knowledge that Hamilton's plan for Federal Assumption of State debts would materially enhance the value of securities issued by the states. Nicholas had thus diversified his holdings of public paper by handing over some $25,000 in final settlements in return for obligations of two of the states. This, combined with his earlier transactions with Bennett and with Constable and Platt, reduced his holdings of that species of notes by about $60,000, approximately the amount of final settlements which he owned in 1786. He, therefore, could have had very little of this particular paper on hand when the funding operation began.

When we turn to other kinds of securities held by Nicholas we find that there, too, he had acquired large amounts originally issued to others. Toward the close of the Confederation period he compiled a list of certificates in his possession emanating from the Continental Loan Office in

Rhode Island. Of the 279 certificates, with a specie value of $69,315, he was the original recipient of 98 with a specie value of $35,152, issued chiefly in 1777 before depreciation had begun.[63] He turned in to the Loan Office 153 of the depreciated certificates with a specie value of $27,068. Of these he had been the original holder of only eight certificates valued at $2387.[64] In return for the 153 certificates he received six new ones bearing his own name. From this it is clear that the names appearing on loan certificates at the time of the funding of the debt were frequently those of speculative purchasers. Nicholas was thus the original holder of only about one-half of the amount which he funded in certificates issued by the Continental Loan Office in Rhode Island.

Of certificates issued by the Continental Loan Office in Massachusetts, Nicholas' holdings at the time of his death amounted to $26,089 specie value, represented by 74 certificates.[65] Of these, 21 for $400 each were issued to him on June 25, 1777, before the onset of depreciation. The bulk of the certificates, however, were depreciated and were obviously the sort of securities which Nicholas urged his Boston friend, Bossenger Foster, to buy for him. A good deal less than half of his "Massachusetts Continental certificates," therefore, represented his own original investment.

Nicholas was the first owner of a large part of the Rhode Island State debt which he held. Of the 53 notes with a combined value of £6569 in his possession, he was the original recipient of 10, representing £4840.[66] The remaining 43 notes had been the property of 37 different persons. At the time of Assumption of State debts, Nicholas' Rhode Island State notes were valued at $29,411, of which $17,085 were assumable.

On one list of his holdings of Massachusetts State notes there are 86 certificates for £7818 Massachusetts Currency, of which six, with a value of approximately £3100, had been issued to him.[67] Subsequently he made further acquisitions of this paper, in part by the exchange of final settlement notes. Ultimately he owned Massachusetts State notes to the amount of £17,460 Massachusetts Currency, less than one-fifth of which had been issued to him.

From this discussion it is apparent that Nicholas Brown was interested in several different kinds of public securities—final settlement notes, Rhode Island Continental Loan certificates, Massachusetts Continental Loan certificates, and the State notes of Rhode Island, Massachusetts, and South Carolina. He was the original owner of none of his final settlement notes. These he had used in various ways to purchase lands, to exchange for State securities, and, indirectly, through the Constable and Platt bond, to make payment on his debt to Dickason and Company. Of his Rhode Island Continental Loan certificates, he was the first owner of about one-half. Of his Continental Certificates issued by the Massachusetts Office, he was the original holder of a good deal less than one-half. About 73 per cent of his Rhode Island State notes were issued to him, but he was the first recipient of less than one-fifth of his Massachusetts State notes. None of his South Carolina securities were issued to him. He had therefore owned originally less than one-half of these various forms of paper.

Very shortly after Nicholas' death in 1791 an "Account of Public Securities of different Descriptions" belonging to his estate was prepared.[68] This shows that he owned no less than 23 "different" kinds of public paper in various amounts. Included were New York State notes, Pennsylvania depreciation notes, impost orders, teaming certificates, Connecticut State notes, "40 for one Money," and Rhode Island "funded money." But six categories—Rhode Island State notes, Massachusetts Loan Office certificates, Massachusetts State notes, Pennsylvania Loan Office certificates, South Carolina State notes, and United States stock issued to him under the funding plan—account for 95 per cent of the total value. It will be observed that he then held no Rhode Island Continental Loan Office certificates. It was largely in exchange for these that he had received the 6 per cent, 3 per cent, and deferred stock of the United States in the sum of $88,463.

This "Account" or inventory lists the nominal amount of each of the 23 different "Descriptions" of securities in lawful money. Their combined nominal value was £68,318-19-8. They were estimated to be worth "on an Average" thirteen shillings and fourpence on the pound, which was equivalent to £45,545-19-9 lawful money. As the pound in lawful money was worth $3.33⅓, the estimated value of Nicholas Brown's securities was slightly in excess of $150,000. In short, the securities were appraised at two-thirds of their face value, which seems to have been sufficiently conservative. In the case of the Rhode Island State notes this figure proved to be far too low.

The inventory, however, does not reveal the full extent of the securities which Nicholas owned a short time before death. It leaves out of account $20,000 worth of paper which he sold at ten shillings on the pound to relieve the financial distress of the partnership of Brown and Benson.[69] Nor does it include the $30,000 in securities loaned to Constable and Platt, and for which he received the latter's bond, the bond which he later sold to Dickason and Company. From these securities he realized the approximate face value.[70] It appears, therefore, that a year before his death Nicholas held public securities worth close to $200,000.

During the years when Brown and Benson were so heavily indebted to Dickason and Company, the latter indirectly charged that Nicholas and his partner were investing in public securities money which they should apply toward the liquidation of their debt. The partners indignantly denied the allegation, and asserted that they, as a partnership, held only a small amount of securities and that these had been acquired in payment of debts owed to them. The records confirm this statement. The firm of Brown and Benson owned comparatively little of the paper. Dickason and Company obviously confused the personal holdings of Nicholas with those of the partners. In the end, of course, Nicholas drew on his own holdings in order to relieve the pressure on the partnership.

Unfortunately, John Brown's dealings in public securities are less well documented than those of Nicholas. It is apparent, however, that he was a large-scale operator in State and Continental paper. John would have been acting out of character had he bought securities on a modest scale. Writing in 1785, Nicholas referred to "Brother Jno. B. who is here the largest in Trade & has the most Securities."[71] This seems to indicate that John was then preëminent among security holders of Rhode Island. But whether he kept pace with Nicholas in the enlargement of his holdings during the next six years, it is impossible to say.

For reasons not easy to explain, John's name does not appear among the Rhode Island subscribers to the Continental domestic loan of 1790-91, toward which he could have applied any Continental Loan Office certificates issued by the Rhode Island Office. Yet, a few years before he had held 320 such certificates with a specie value of $68,232.[72] John then held more of these certificates than did Nicholas—more in fact, than any other person in Rhode Island.

John at one time held large amounts of other securities. In 1786 he had $58,260 in final settlement notes, an amount somewhat less than that held by Nicholas.[73] He was, of course, the original owner of none of this paper. On June 23, 1777, before the beginning of depreciation, the Continental Loan Office in Massachusetts issued to him 31 certificates for $400 each, a total of $12,400.[74]

To the assumed debt of Connecticut John subscribed $10,931 in notes obtained from one Joshua Lathrop.[75] Of the 89 Rhode Island State notes amounting to £5,935, which he owned, he was the original holder of eight with a value of £3661.[76] At assumption these notes were valued at $26,943, of which $15,652 was assumable.

Joseph and Moses Brown were very modest owners of public securities. Joseph held five certificates issued by the Continental Loan Office in Rhode Island, their total specie value being $1500.[77] Moses had four of the same variety, with a combined value of $553.[78] Their respective holdings of the assumed debt of Massachusetts were £1,218 and £1,734, most of it originally issued to them.[79] Of Rhode Island State notes they held £1875 and £182 respectively.[80] Joseph was the original owner of all his notes, while most of those belonging to Moses had been issued to other persons.

There is evidence that the Browns followed closely the course of events in Congress which affected them as security holders. Nicholas and John were conspicuous in a movement to assemble the Providence owners of public paper "at Mr. Aldrich's Tavern" on the afternoon of December 7, 1790, "to Consult and Determine on the Propriety of Forming a Memorial to Congress on the Subject of a punctual Complyence of the payment of both Principle & Interest of the Public Securitys according to the Originell Contract between the Public & Individuels."[81] The notice promised that the Memorial of a Committee of the "Public Creditters" of Pennsylvania would be at the meeting for a general perusal. Forty-four men were invited to the meeting, of whom seventeen actually appeared. Among them were Nicholas and John Brown, Obadiah Brown (son of Moses), and John Francis, son-in-law and partner of John Brown.

This record of the dealings of the Brown brothers in public securities provides further evidence of the fact that as businessmen they came through the war, and the "Critical Period" which followed, in handsome fashion. In no sense the product of the wartime boom and inflation, the business of the Browns emerged from the years of conflict in a fundamentally strong position. The adverse conditions of the postwar years were perplexing but not seriously menacing to their situation. At the very moment that Nicholas and John were so heavily indebted to their London creditor, they were, by judicious acquisition of public securities, building a financial backlog which was to stand their successors in good stead.

Nicholas was not one of the more glamorous and spectacular figures of the Revolutionary era. But, in his quiet, cautious manner, he had missed few business opportunities that came his way; and, when some of those who had enjoyed the limelight lingered in debtors' prisons, he was able to hand on to his son and son-in-law an established business, buttressed by a large fund of the "pure" capital provided by the funding and assumption plans.

THE NEW CONSTITUTION

From the foregoing discussion it is apparent that the Browns were substantial beneficiaries of the conservative counterrevolution which swept away the Articles of Confederation and established the Constitution. The essence of the new document was its provision for a stronger frame of government. One might suppose, therefore, that the Brown family had always believed that the general government should be endowed with powers adequate to its needs. Yet, in the early eighties they opposed the grant of the taxing power to the Congress of the Confederation.

Early in 1781 the Congress asked that the states authorize it to impose a 5 per cent duty on all imports coming into the United States. As this was in the nature of an amendment to the Articles of Confederation, it required unanimous consent of the states. Rhode Island was one of two which refused to approve this change. Thereupon the Congress submitted to the states a modified version of the Impost, designed to meet the objections of Rhode Island. But the Rhode Island General Assembly found this Impost Act of 1783 quite as unacceptable as its predecessor. Not until 1786 was the Legislature willing to approve the Impost, and then only on condition that interstate trade be entirely free of state duties. As the Congress of the Confederation had authority neither to regulate trade among the states nor to prohibit the enactment of impost laws by the states, it could not accept the Rhode Island stipulation. Only through a new Federal Constitution could Rhode Island obtain the interstate free trade which its commercial interests required.

Rhode Island opposition to the Continental Impost, 1781-1786, was dictated by the mercantile element, to which the Browns belonged.[82] Opposition to the new Constitution, 1788-1790, came from the country party, the merchants being heartily in favor of the new frame of government. Why, then, had the group who were to support the new charter of government, with its more sweeping delegation of powers to the general government, opposed a limited grant of the taxing power to the Confederation Congress?

The most recent student of this problem has found the answer in the "peculiar nature of Rhode Island commerce."[83] Before the Revolution, merchants of the colony had complained of the dearth of products for export. In a sense they were forced to import in order to export. The bulk of the articles imported into Rhode Island were reëxported either abroad or to other colonies. The postwar years brought no immediate change in this "peculiar" situation. Merchants feared, therefore, that the Continental Impost would be detrimental to their reëxport trade. As it allowed no drawback on goods reëxported, Rhode Island exporters, in order to compete with merchants abroad, would be compelled to absorb the 5 per cent tax instead of adding it to the cost of the articles reëxported. Thus merchants had selfish reasons for preferring a state impost system to the one proposed by Congress; and the suggestion that Rhode Island should tax the people of other states by a duty on imports was not lacking in popular appeal.

That the mercantile fraternity at the time of the Impost were aware of the "peculiar" character of Rhode Island's commerce is evident in the correspondence of Nicholas Brown. Writing to David Howell, one of the Rhode Island delegates in Congress, he remarked that "Our State do the most in Coasting according to the Bigness of any State in the Union, indeed our Navigation for foreign ports far exceeds any State in proportion."[84] Confessing his dislike of the Impost, he added that "I look upon myself as one Amongst us who has done about as much Mischief as most amongst us if the Opposit'n Can be so Called."

In their campaign against the Impost the merchants were careful to emphasize the political rather than the economic ills it would inflict upon Rhode Island. "The major premise of the opposition to the Impost was the very popular idea that all political power must be jealously guarded and cautiously distributed."[85] History showed that in periods of crisis "people are often led to give up powers which, once surrendered, could not be regained." Such might be the case with the Impost. The other argument was that the Impost would render Congress independent of the people—a somewhat specious view to be expounded in a state where the delegates to Congress were elected annually by direct popular vote. Nevertheless, the majority of the voters became "convinced that the adoption of the Continental Impost would destroy democracy and individual liberty."[86]

Within a few years Rhode Island merchants had occasion to regret their part in the defeat of the Continental Impost. Even from the point of view of their own selfish interests they had been short-sighted in the extreme. In the postwar years, the states, in an effort to obtain funds with which to pay the interest on their revolutionary debts, resorted to state tariffs. As these laws generally exempted from duty articles of American growth or manufacture, they did not directly affect the farmer.[87] But they imposed a heavy burden on the merchant who must pay not only the Rhode Island impost on goods imported but also a similar duty on wares he reëxported to neighboring states. The tariff duties imposed by Connecticut and Massachusetts were especially burdensome to the trade of Rhode Island.

Defeat of the Continental Impost proved a boomerang to Rhode Island merchants in another sense. Denied the necessary funds, Congress was able to pay only a fraction of the interest on the Continental debt, a circumstance which greatly depressed the price of securities. As the paper was largely in the hands of merchants, notably Nicholas and John Brown, ʹhey came to see that an adequate revenue for the general government was a first requisite for any rise in the value of securities. The result was Rhode Island acceptance of the Continental Impost of 1786, on condition that interstate trade should not be impeded by state tariffs.

This changed attitude of the merchants with respect to the powers of the general government was much accentuated by the triumph of the paper money party in Rhode Island in the spring of 1786. The Assembly then issued £100,000 in bills of credit.[88] Although the paper was declared legal tender in payment of all past or future debts on a parity with specie, and nonacceptance entailed heavy penalty, it almost immediately began to depreciate.

Holding notes of hand of many persons in Rhode Island, Nicholas Brown and his partner, George Benson, were greatly concerned over a measure which seemingly offered debtors a glorious opportunity to liquidate their indebtedness at a mere fraction of its face value. Their papers not only abound in denunciations of the Tender Law but also in evidence of their efforts to circumvent it. When a Newport debtor threatened to discharge his debt by resort to the Tender Act, George Benson, "reasoned, persuaded, persisted & prevailed" upon him instead to convey to them title to a tract of land.[89] They treated their debtors with forbearance in order to avoid a tender of paper.[90] On occasion they might sell a debt to a person in another state, so strong was their resolve not to be paid in paper.[91] They vigorously refuted false reports circulated in Newport that John Brown was freely accepting the paper and then using it to pay the workmen engaged in the building of his mansion on the hill in Providence.[92] And there is evidence that they and other merchants sought, by means of a concerted refusal to give currency to the paper, to hasten its depreciation with a view to defeating the entire plan of the paper money crowd.[93]

"Deeply affected with the evils of the . . . unhappy times," the merchants and tradesmen of Providence looked hopefully to the Convention which was to assemble at Philadelphia in May 1787 for the purpose of amending the Articles of Confederation. Great was their disappointment, therefore, when the Upper House of the Assembly refused to concur in a vote of the Lower for naming delegates to the Convention. Nevertheless, merchants of Providence, speaking through a Committee of thirteen, including Nicholas and John Brown, resolved to make their views known to the Convention, even though their state was unrepresented therein. Accordingly, on May 11, 1787 the Committee penned a letter to that Assembly for the avowed purpose of preventing "any impressions unfavorable to the Commercial Interest of this State from taking place in our Sister States" as a result of "our being Unrepresented" in the Convention.[94] They believed the deliberations of the delegates at Philadelphia would have a tendency "to strengthen the Union, promote the Commerce, increase the power & Establish the Credit of the United States." Specifically, they believed that full power to regulate the commerce of the United States, "both Foreign & Domestick," should be vested in the "National Council." They were further of the opinion that "effectual arrangements should . . . be made for giving operation to the present power of Congress in their Requisitions upon the States for National purposes." In short, they believed Congress should have effective power for raising a revenue.

This communication was to be handed to the Convention by General

James M. Varnum, prominent Rhode Island political leader, who was then in Philadelphia, and to whom the merchants wrote under date of May 14th.[95] Varnum was to deliver the letter to the Convention "in such way as you may think best." Should the Delegates be "so condescending" as to permit him to take a seat with them "when the Commercial Affairs of the Nation" were discussed, the Browns and their fellow merchants would think themselves "highly favored" to have him there to speak for them.

To Varnum the Providence group expressed themselves as in favor of interstate trade "free of any Duty or Excise." All goods imported from "any Foreign Nation" paying the "National Impost" at the first port of entry might then be "Transported to any of the United States free of any further Duty or Impost." The carrying trade should be "insured" to vessels belonging to "subjects" of the United States. It was their hope, too, that "Consideration of a General Currency throughout the United States" would not be forgotten by the Convention, as it was "so nearly Connected with Trade & Commerce."

Should Varnum find that he could render service to the merchants of Rhode Island by "tarrying" in Philadelphia after the completion of his other business, they would gladly reimburse him for any extra expense. On the chance that Varnum should leave the Quaker City before the arrival of the letters, they sent Tench Francis a duplicate of the communication to the Convention "to be by him delivered."

On May 28th the letter addressed to the Convention was read before that body; and it was accompanied by one from Varnum, strongly supporting the views set forth by the Providence merchants.[96] The General informed the delegates that "the majority of the administration [in Rhode Island] is composed of a licentious number of men, destitute of education and many of them void of principle." Their views were "equally reprobated and abhorred by gentlemen of the learned professions, by the whole mercantile body, and by most of the respectable farmers and mechanics." With this information in hand, it was unlikely that "any impressions unfavorable to the Commercial Interest" of Rhode Island would take form in the minds of delegates from "Sister States."

In September the completed Constitution was submitted to the states for ratification. If the Providence merchants hoped for prompt action by Rhode Island, they were doomed to disappointment. Rather than call a Convention, the Assembly referred the document to the towns, where it was rejected by a heavy majority. Repeatedly the legislators refused to summon a Convention. In the summer of 1788 New Hampshire became the ninth state to ratify, and the Constitution became effective. Virginia and New York soon followed. When in November 1789 North Carolina ratified, the isolation of Rhode Island was complete.

Meanwhile, in July the lower house of the new Congress of the United States passed a tariff providing no exemption for Rhode Island. Fearing the commercial consequences of this action, the town of Providence presented petitions to Congress praying that the maritime interests in the state be not punished for the sins of other groups. James Manning, President of the College of Rhode Island and one of a committee selected to wait upon the Congress, kept his friend Nicholas Brown carefully informed of the efforts to persuade that body to exempt the coastal towns of Rhode Island from the provisions of the tariff. On September 12, 1789, he wrote that "The 15th of January was the utmost limit we could prevail on Congress to extend this indulgence to. After that, if still out of the Union, both Towns & Country will to all intents and purposes be considered & treated as foreigners."[97]

On January 17, 1790 the Rhode Island Assembly finally voted to call a convention. This assemblage met on March 1, discussed at length, and adjourned to May 24. Meanwhile the pressure for ratification increased. The Federal Senate adopted a resolution calling for a severance of relations between the United States and Rhode Island. Providence threatened secession from the rural areas of the state. Alarmed by the prospect of complete commercial isolation, the reassembled Convention ratified the Constitution on May 29.

Rhode Island thus gave belated recognition to the fact that an older political and constitutional regime within the nation had come to an end. In the economic sphere there was no break of comparable significance, although the new political order was to provide marked stimulus to economic change and development. The Confederation period just closed had been a time of commercial readjustment made necessary by dislocations of the war and postwar years. In the process some long-familiar forms of business activity disappeared, to be replaced by those more suited to the conditions of the new day. The Brown family well illustrates this transition which occurred in the ten years following the close of the War for Independence. Their fortunes had been bound up with the West India trade, the traffic in molasses and rum, the manufacture of spermaceti candles, the production of pig iron, and the importation of English goods. By 1790, when Rhode Island joined the Union, these forms of business were in process of liquidation. Already the family had turned to the China, the East India, and the Baltic trades. They were at that moment introducing cotton manufacture into the United States. Soon they would give their attention to banking, to insurance, to canals, to turnpikes, to investment in wild lands on many different frontiers, and to manufacture on a more elaborate scale. The story of these activities will provide the subject matter of a later volume.

CONCLUSION

The Browns went into business in 1723 as merchants engaged in the maritime trade. Before the Revolution, they had become well-established manufacturers with subsidiary commercial and mercantile interests. The decisions which led to this shift in emphasis seem to have followed each other in logical sequence. That this is evident in retrospect is not to suggest that the development came about through some uncanny ability of the Browns to project their plans far into the future. But motivated by the desire to build a business which could be passed on to future generations of the family, they were bound whenever possible to take the long view. They sought stability rather than short-term profits, and their day-to-day plans were geared to this general objective.

A fortuitous circumstance gave the Browns their first opportunity to experiment with manufacture. It was only by accident that the spermaceti candle industry in America had its beginnings in Rhode Island. There was apparently no more substantial basis for it than the chance acquisition of the knowledge of the process. But within a few years after Obadiah Brown built his first spermaceti plant, the making and marketing of candles was exercising a controlling influence over every facet of the family's business. The development of Hope Furnace provided additional evidence of a primary concern with manufacture.

The Browns made constructive use of the occasional kindness of fate. But the secret of their long-sustained success lay primarily in the personal qualities and business methods of the family. The continuity of the Browns in business throughout the eighteenth century was the result of careful planning from one generation to the next. A younger brother, a son, or a nephew well trained by his elders was always ready to assume the responsibilities of leadership at the proper time. But the rules of succession were not rigid and inflexible. Members of the family were not forced to undertake jobs for which they were not suited. Particular responsibilities were assumed as a result of individual preferences and skills and were not superimposed by arbitrary rule. When differences of opinion arose, they were settled amicably. Moreover the Browns did not attempt to extend the family control by placing relatives in important auxiliary positions. No member of the family was ever sent to take over a permanent assignment outside of Rhode Island. The correspondents in the other colonies and in Europe were chosen for their ability and general usefulness to the business and not because of family connection. Through this policy of moderation, the Browns were able to derive maximum benefit from family control, and to avoid some of the pitfalls which this type of management often entails.

The same moderation characterized their over-all business planning. The Browns as a business family rarely thought in superlatives. John was, of course, the exception, but his success in some of his more ambitious undertakings probably came in part as a result of the experience and resources he had acquired in coöperation with his more conservative brothers. Compared with that of many of their contemporaries, the Browns' West Indian trade was of medium proportions. Although they were the most important of the candle manufacturers, this part of the business was not allowed to develop out of proportion to the other branches. This same sense of balance appears in the handling of the extensive intercolonial trade which they developed largely as a result of the candle business. Hope Furnace was by no means the largest furnace within the colonies. The Browns did not become large-scale importers of English goods until long after their fellow merchants were well established in a lively trade in goods brought in from London and Bristol. They waited until they were certain that the general state of their business justified this phase of expansion.

Another important factor in the success of the Browns was the element of rationality. The fact that their business papers have survived in such large measure is probably an indication of this very quality. They saved their records for a purpose: to use them in making their plans for future undertakings.

Their papers afford many illustrations of the care with which they gathered all possible information before embarking upon a new venture. Their attempts to monopolize the tobacco market in Surinam were made only after they had been at pains to inform themselves regarding crop conditions in Rhode Island and Connecticut, together with probable shipments from the two colonies. Similarly, before embarking upon trade with Continental Europe during the War for Independence, they asked Nicholas Boylston, of Boston, the merchant reputed to be the best informed on the subject, for the necessary data upon the trade.

The classic example, of course, of their careful planning is Hope Furnace. From their friend, John Relfe, of Philadelphia, they procured detailed information with respect to Pennsylvania iron furnaces; and from the iron manufacturers in Connecticut and Massachusetts they borrowed freely both the personnel and the techniques needed in establishing the furnace. When difficulties arose as production proceeded, they sought out every possible source of help in solving their problems. It was only after careful study and consideration of the best advice available, that new plans were formulated or old procedures abandoned.

If the family achieved strength through moderation and caution, they also built securely through diversification. The Browns were unwilling to place all their chances of success in a single enterprise. They were very skillful, however, in organizing the various branches of their business into a well-knit entity. Risks were so well distributed that they were not likely to suffer catastrophic losses in the ordinary course of events. Losses in one line of business could readily be absorbed by another.

Through a rare stroke of good fortune, the Browns were able to continue in business during the Revolution with their resources unimpaired. But this situation of itself is not the whole explanation for their continued success after the war. Colonial forms of manufacture were almost outmoded by the time peace was restored. In the era of transition which followed, the Browns' varied business experience stood them in good stead. They were able to develop the necessary techniques to build another integrated system of business adapted to the conditions of the new day.

The conduct of the Browns as a business family must be judged by the standards of the times in which they lived. Students of history have frequently commented upon the prominence of Rhode Islanders in some of the less ethical forms of eighteenth-century commercial activity. Although no colony had a monopoly of smuggling, men of Rhode Island seem to have enjoyed a special form of notoriety in that regard. Participation of northern colonial merchants in the African slave trade was widespread, but by common consent Rhode Islanders appear to have attained a greater eminence in the traffic than did their contemporaries in other colonies. Colonial trade with the enemy was a commonplace in the Anglo-French wars of the eighteenth century, but, in proportion to their numbers, Rhode Island merchants were more strongly attracted to it than those in neighboring governments. So conspicuous were the sons of Rhode Island in these activities that, in the eyes of British officials in America, the very name of the colony was but a byword for lawlessness.

The prominence of Rhode Islanders in illicit trades has often been attributed to the particular form of government which prevailed in the Colony. It is true that under its charter the Colony enjoyed comparative freedom from British control. Yet the citizens of Connecticut, whose charter was equally liberal, were obviously less conspicuous in the forbidden trades than were the Rhode Islanders. Nor can the Rhode Island charter explain the Colony's addiction to the African slave trade, as that traffic was in no way contrary to British laws or regulations.

There may be another explanation for the fondness of Rhode Island merchants for these various types of trade. It may be found in the lack of a hinterland, in the scarcity of "natural produce," and in the chronic lack of hard money within the Colony. Rhode Island merchants were convinced, rightly or wrongly, that these deficiencies were much more acute in Rhode Island than in the neighboring colonies. Under these circumstances, they may have been willing to go to greater lengths and to more serious hazards to maintain themselves in business. They may have believed that the illicit trades and the slave trade would in some measure offset the disadvantages inherent in the Rhode Island economic situation.

The Browns had a modest share in all these illegal activities. But alongside this participation in lawless procedures must be set their long record of meticulous honesty and fair dealing in their other business transactions. Their reputation for honesty is well attested by the liberal terms of credit which they received in London, both before and after the War for Independence. Unlike many of his contemporaries, Nicholas Brown was at pains to liquidate his debt in London at the outbreak of the war. And if his postwar debt was paid slowly and painfully, that fact in no way detracted from his reputation as a man of honesty and integrity. The other members of the family appear to have shared the reputation of Nicholas in this respect. Although John's propensity for recklessness in a business way sometimes involved serious financial losses, his credit was never seriously impaired. A record such as this can hold its own with that of the best of businessmen of the period.

Notes

NOTES

CHAPTER 1. THE BROWNS OF PROVIDENCE PLANTATIONS

1. Abby Isabel Bulkley, *The Chad Browne Memorial. Consisting of Genealogical Memoirs of a Portion of the Descendants of Chad and Elizabeth Browne—1638-1888* (Brooklyn, 1888), pp. 7-8. This volume provides the fullest statement of the beginnings of the family in this country. The final "e" has long since been dropped by most of the descendants of Chad and Elizabeth Browne.

2. Ibid., p. 10.

3. Ibid., pp. 11-12.

4. Ibid., p. 16.

5. This book is in the Library of the Rhode Island Historical Society, hereafter referred to as RIHS. Except where otherwise indicated the manuscript materials referred to in this volume are to be found in the Brown Papers in the John Carter Brown Library.

6. Gertrude S. Kimball, *Providence in Colonial Times* (Boston, 1912), p. 233.

7. The last ten pages of James Brown's book of geometrical and nautical problems contain the log of *Truth and Delight.*

8. This ledger is in RIHS.

9. This ledger is in RIHS.

10. The Manuscript Letter Book is in RIHS. It has been published as *The Letter Book of James Brown of Providence Merchant, 1735-38* (with an introduction by George Philip Knapp and a biographical sketch by John Carter Brown Woods). (Providence, 1929.)

11. All the letters from which the foregoing passages are quoted are to be found in *The Letter Book* in RIHS.

12. The letter bears the date of May 18, 1736. See *Letter Book.*

13. The letter is dated March 6, 1735/6. See *Letter Book.*

14. This volume is in RIHS.

15. For this letter see Moses Brown Papers, I, 4, RIHS.

16. Moses Brown Papers, I, 5, RIHS.

17. This letter is in a bundle of uncalendared Brown Papers which recently were deposited in the John Carter Brown Library.

18. This letter is also in the bundle mentioned above.

19. These ledgers are in RIHS.

20. Kimball, *Providence in Colonial Times,* p. 255. The invoice is in the unbound Moses Brown papers in RIHS.

21. See Obadiah Brown's *Manuscript Letter Book, 1751-1752,* RIHS.

22. These letters were dated May 4, May 4, and May 27, 1752, respectively, in *Letter Book.*

23. The letter was dated March 13, 1752, in *Letter Book.*

24. The Day Book is in RIHS.

25. In unbound papers of Moses Brown in RIHS there is "Benjamin Crabb's scheme for a contract with Obadiah Brown," with figures as to cost of a ton of oil, cost of separating head matter. Crabb was to have ⅛ part of candles for finding and supporting all utensils in the manufactory. This document is undated but is found with an invoice of a shipment of 8 boxes of candles by Benjamin Crabb, dated August 21, 1751, which suggests that it may be contemporaneous with the invoice.

26. The Day Book is in RIHS.

27. In unbound Moses Brown Papers in RIHS.

28. See Obadiah Brown's Manuscript *Receipt Book, 1750-1760* in RIHS.

29. U-SA- Spermaceti Accounts—undated to 1761, Invoice of February 25, 1754.

30. See Obadiah Brown's Ledger, in RIHS.

31. Obadiah Brown's *Insurance Book #1, 1753,* in RIHS.

32. This is in RIHS.

33. In the John Carter Brown Library.

34. In his book of *Geometrical Problems* he kept a journal of various voyages.

35. Moses Brown Papers, I, 7, in RIHS.

36. See the journal he kept in his book of *Geometrical Problems.*

37. Joseph Brown to Nicholas, May 24, 1774, Miscellaneous Letters, 1774.

38. This is in RIHS.

39. See sketch of him by Lawrence C. Wroth in *Dictionary of American Biography,* (20 vols., New York, 1928-1936) III, 129.

40. This letter is undated but very probably was written in 1770, Miscellaneous Letters, 1770, vol. I.

41. For the agreement see Miscellaneous Letters, 1771.

42. For this agreement see Miscellaneous Letters, 1771.

43. Moses Brown Papers, II, 18, RIHS.

44. Moses to his brothers, September 15, 1773, *Moses Brown Papers,* II, 18, RIHS.

45. Nicholas Brown to Hayley & Hopkins, May 24, 1774, P-H2.

46. Ibid.

CHAPTER 2. "MOLASSES AN ENGINE IN THE HANDS OF THE MERCHANT"

1. For the West Indian trade of the Continental colonies of England see Herbert C. Bell, "The West India Trade before the American Revolution," *American Historical Review,* XXII, 272-287 (January 1917); Frank Wesley Pitman, *The Development of the British West Indies, 1700-1763* (New Haven, 1917); and Worthington C. Ford (ed.), *The Commerce of Rhode Island,* Massachusetts Historical Society *Collections,* 7th series, vols. IX and X (1914-15).

2. For the text of the "Remonstrance of the colony of Rhode Island to the Lords Commissioners of Trade and Plantations," see *Records of the Colony of Rhode Island and Providence Plantations in New England* (7 vols., Providence, 1856-1862), VI, 378-383. (Hereafter referred to as *Rhode Island Colonial Records.*)

3. See the Invoice, dated July 16, 1768, in V 68-69 BG.

4. See copy of the Agreement, Miscellaneous Letters to 1761.

5. Miscellaneous Letters, 1764.

6. For the papers of this voyage, see V 64 SN.

7. See V 64 BG.

8. Nicholas Brown & Co. to Capt. Christopher Sheldon, July 16, 1768, V 68-69 BG.

9. Ibid.

10. Nicholas Brown & Co. to Capt. Abraham Whipple, September 16, 1764, V 64 BG.

11. Ibid.

12. Ibid.

13. Capt. George Hopkins to Nicholas Brown & Co., March 10, 1764, V 64 SN.

14. Capt. Christopher Sheldon to Nicholas Brown & Co., November 20, 1768, V 68-69 BG.

15. Capt James Burrough to Nicholas Brown & Co., October 2, 1766: "The craft that bring the molasses are all engaged so that the last comers are obliged to wait till others are served." On November 2, 1766 he wrote: "It requires the patience of Job to wait the return of the crafts that fetch our molasses." Both letters are in V F6.

16. The Agreements with Isaac Tripp are dated March 11, June 10, and October 2, 1765, Miscellaneous Letters, 1765.

17. Miscellaneous Letters, 1765 and 1766.

18. Miscellaneous Letters, 1764.

19. Orders and instructions of Nicholas Brown & Co. to Capt. Abraham Whipple, September 16, 1764, V 64 BG.

20. Nicholas Brown & Co. to Capt. Abraham Whipple, October 9, 1764, V 64 BG.

21. Ibid.

22. Ibid.

23. The letter is to be found in V Misc.

24. This clearly indicates that the competitive selling of the tobacco by the various ship captains at Surinam had depressed the price.

25. Letter to Esek Hopkins, September 5, 1766, V Misc.

26. For the agreement, dated October 19, 1766, see V Misc.

27. Ibid.

28. Joseph & William Wanton to Nicholas Brown & Co., December 7, 1766, in L 58-69 J & WW.

29. The letter is to be found in V Misc.

30. Ibid.

31. Ibid.

32. Ibid.

33. Ibid.

34. See Invoice of sundry merchandise shipped by Nicholas Brown & Co. on board the Sloop *Mary Ann,* October 29, 1766, V 66 SMA.

35. This letter is dated October 29, 1766, in V 66 SMA.

36. Ibid.

37. Ibid.

38. Capt. Esek Hopkins to Nicholas Brown & Co., March 22, 1767, V 66 SMA.

39. See Nicholas Brown & Co. to Capt. Christopher Sheldon, October 17, 1767, in V G4, vol. I, Brig *George* to Surinam, 1767-68. Nicholas Brown & Co.'s instructions to Capt. Christopher Sheldon directed him "to consult and advise with Capt. Crawford about Disposing of the Tobacco as you are to average with him for the whole you both have on board in proportion to ye quantity and price, Each owner Risking their own Tobacco. In your selling it you'l consider it Distinct from Aney other article so that the price may not be Inlarged nor Lessend their by, which you'l observe more fully by our agreement with Messrs Jenckes, a copy of which is delivered you."

40. See Capt. Christopher Sheldon to Nicholas Brown & Co., December 13, 1767, in V G4, vol. I.

41. *Ibid.*

42. Capt. Christopher Sheldon to Nicholas Brown & Co., September 16, 1768, V 68-69 BG.

43. A copy of the agreement is to be found in OL 59-72 M.

44. *Ibid.*

45. *Ibid.*

46. *Ibid.*

47. Capt. Simon Smith to Nicholas Brown & Co., November 10, 1770, V 70-71 BS.

48. Nicholas Brown & Co. to Capt. Christopher Sheldon, November 15, 1770, V G4, vol. II.

49. Capt. Christopher Sheldon to Nicholas Brown & Co., March 22, 1771, *ibid.*

50. Capt. Simon Smith to Nicholas Brown & Co., December 2, 1771, V 70-71 BS.

51. Vessels usually brought home from 20,000 to 25,000 gallons of molasses.

52. For the papers of this voyage see V 68-69 BS.

53. Account current of Nicholas Brown & Co. with Capt. Christopher Sheldon, Brig *George,* January 14, 1769, V 68-69 BG. The balance remitted in bills of exchange does not represent the profit of the voyage, since it does not take into account either the cost of the voyage or the proceeds of the sale of the return cargo.

54. Nicholas Brown & Co. to Capt. Nicholas Power, April 30, 1767, V 66 SMA.

55. Esek Hopkins to Nicholas Brown & Co., March 22, 1767, V 66 SMA.

56. Capt. John Burrough to Nicholas Brown & Co., August 27, 1768, V 68 SMA.

57. Capt. Simon Smith to Nicholas Brown & Co., November 10, 1771, V 70-71 BS. Capt. Nicholas Power wrote: "We are all under contract to fall molasses to 6st. Two days ago it was offered for 7. Though the contract has been standing but a week I am in hopes we shall be able to get it for 6st in 8 or 10 days." Captain Power to Nicholas Brown & Co., December 13, 1767, V F6, vol. II.

58. Capt. Christopher Sheldon to Nicholas Brown & Co., January 15, 1768, V G4, vol. I.

59. Capt. Abraham Whipple to Nicholas Brown & Co., January 4, 1766, V F6, vol. II.

60. Capt. Nicholas Power to Nicholas Brown & Co., November 17, 1767, V F6, vol. II.

61. *Ibid.*

62. Capt. Nicholas Power to Nicholas Brown & Co., December 13, 1767, V F6, vol. II.

63. Capt. Simon Smith wrote to Nicholas Brown & Co. on November 10, 1770: "I expect some of the bills I carried from here last voyage will be protested as there is no less than eight million gilders in bills that has been & will be protested, chiefly drawn by the principal men here, so that at present there is hardly telling who is good among them." V 70-71 BS.

64. See U—C 1775-1785 for lists of these.

65. See letters of Capt. John Peck, January 25, 1771 and Capt. Joseph Tillinghast, January 22, 1772, both from St. Eustatius. L 53-74 M.

66. Nicholas Brown & Co. to Capt. Peter Ritto and Stephen Gregory, July 4, 1772, V G4, vol. II.

67. The bill of sale is in V G4, vol. II.

68. Nicholas Brown & Co. to Stephen Gregory, July 7, 1772, V G4, vol. II.

69. The "Writing of Defeasance" is in V G4, vol. II.

70. Stephen Gregory to Nicholas Brown & Co., August 28, 1772, V G4, vol. II.

71. See the bill of lading in V G4, vol. II. On another occasion when the Brig was bound for Hispaniola, the owners wrote the Captain as follows: "If you are obliged to Imploy a French man settle his commission before hand on as good terms as you can." They also instructed him on his arrival "in the Bite" on Hispaniola "to use your utmost indeavors to get a permit from the General of the Island to trade to any part of it." Nicholas Brown & Co. to Capt. Christopher Whipple, January 2, 1772, V G4, vol. II. These instructions indicate the employment of various means to overcome the obstinacy of local French officials on the Island.

72. Gertrude S. Kimball, *Providence in Colonial Times,* pp. 276-277.

73. See "Agreement of Partition among the children and widow of James Brown, March 15, 1760," P B7.

74. John Brown to Nicholas Brown, October 20, 1770, Miscellaneous Letters, 1770.

75. Nicholas Brown & Co. to Shaw & Long (New York), October 13, 1773, Miscellaneous Letters, 1773.

76. Nicholas Brown & Co. to Capt. George Hopkins, January 21, 1764, V 64 SN.

77. *Ibid.*

78. William Barnet (Boston) to Nicholas Brown & Co., September 11, 1764, Miscellaneous Letters, 1762-1764.

79. Nicholas Brown & Co. to Capt. Abraham Whipple, October 9, 1764, V 64 BG.

80. *Ibid.*

81. *Ibid.*

82. Nicholas Brown & Co. to Capt. Abraham Whipple, January 13, 1765, V 64 SF.

83. *Ibid.*

84. Nicholas Brown & Co. to Capt. Peter Ritto, December 23, 1772, V G4, vol. II.

85. *Ibid.*

86. Nicholas Brown & Co. to Mr. Fales, April 17, 1773, V G4, vol. II.

CHAPTER 3. "PROHIBITED TRADE WITH THE VASSALLS OF THE FRENCH KING"

1. George Louis Beer, *British Colonial Policy, 1764-1765* (New York, 1907), p. 73. This volume contains the most satisfactory general account of colonial trade with the enemy in the Seven Years' War.

2. *Ibid.,* p. 81.

3. *Ibid.,* pp. 82-83. "Rhode Island especially paid no respect to the orders from England."

4. *Ibid.,* p. 88.

5. *Ibid.,* p. 90.

6. *Ibid.,* p. 94.

7. *Ibid.*

8. *Ibid.,* pp. 96-99.

9. *Ibid.,* p. 99.

10. *Ibid.*

11. *Ibid.,* p. 103.

12. *Ibid.,* pp. 90-91.

13. See Obadiah Brown's Ledger in RIHS. The entry is under date of January 14, 1747/8.

14. Beer, *op cit.,* p. 92.

15. *Ibid.*

16. *Ibid.,* p. 93, note.

17. The Insurance Book is in RIHS.

18. The papers of *Prudent Hannah* have not been preserved. This account of her capture and condemnation is based chiefly on the long letter which Capt. Paul Tew wrote to Obadiah Brown & Co. from Williamsburg, Virginia, August 26, 1758, in L 58-84 Priv.

19. Obadiah Brown & Co. to Capt. Paul Tew, September 16, 1758. The Company wrote two letters to him on this day. Both are to be found in V Misc.

20. *Ibid.*

21. *Ibid.* The letter of credit is also dated September 16, 1758. A copy of it is in V Misc.

22. See letters of Tench Francis to Obadiah Brown & Co., October 29, 1758 and January 10, 1759. Both are in L 58-87 TF.

23. For the surviving papers of this voyage see V 58 BB.

24. This certificate is in V 58 BB.

25. This receipt is also in V 58 BB.

26. See copy of the orders to Captain Rhodes, dated July 4, 1758, V 58 BB.

27. The orders to Captain Bardin bear the same date.

28. Tench Francis to Obadiah Brown & Co., October 27, 1758, L 58-87 TF.

29. Tench Francis to Obadiah Brown & Co., November 27, 1758, L 58-87 TF.

30. Tench Francis to Obadiah Brown & Co., July 9, 1759, L 58-87 TF.

31. The Charter Party bears the date of November 10, 1758. For a copy of it see V 58 SS.

32. See sworn statement of Daniel Jenckes and Elisha Brown, November 11, 1758, V 58 SS.

33. *Ibid.*

34. See Memorandum of the cargo, V 58 SS. There is nothing in the papers of *Speedwell* to indicate that she carried any prisoners; but in the Brown Papers there is a document signed by Kerlérec, the governor of Louisiana, authorizing Captain Updike to take two English prisoners in exchange for two Frenchmen. As this document is dated at New Orleans, March 1, 1759, it obviously refers to this particular voyage of *Speedwell.*

35. *Ibid.*

36. See orders and instructions from Obadiah Brown & Co. to Capt. John Updike, November 14, 1758, V 58 SS.

37. *Ibid.*

38. The account current is in V 58 SS.

39. See the account current.

40. Francis & Relfe to Obadiah Brown & Co., September 20, 1759, L 58-87 TF.

41. The Charter Party is dated June 8, 1759, V 59 SS.

42. See Invoice of goods shipped on the Sloop *Speedwell,* May 16, 1759, V 59 SS.

43. These are dated May 16, 1759, V 59 SS.

44. These are dated May 24, 1759, V 59 SS.

45. Capt. John Updike (at Monte Cristi) to Obadiah Brown & Co., March 23, 1760, L 60 M, in which he refers to this incident of the preceding year.

46. Ibid.

47. Ibid.

48. Ibid.

49. Capt. John Updike (at Cap François) to Obadiah Brown & Co., May 18, 1760, L 60 M.

50. For the record of these later voyages of *Speedwell,* see V 61 SS.

51. For the first voyage of this *Speedwell,* see V 59-C SS.

52. The entire history of this unhappy voyage is related in "Condemnation Proceedings, Court of Vice Admiralty, at New Providence," Bahama Islands. This is an imposing document with many exhibits. The document is mistakenly filed with the papers of the other Sloop *Speedwell,* which made the three voyages to the Mississippi, V 58 SS.

53. See the Condemnation Proceedings, V 58 SS.

54. Capt. Silas Cook (at St. Mark) to Capt. John Randall, March 22, 1760, V 59 BP.

55. Condemnation Proceedings, V 58 SS.

56. Ibid.

57. For the Agreement, see V 59 BP.

58. Ibid.

59. Obadiah Brown & Co. to Francis & Relfe, January 26, 1760, V 59 BP.

60. Orders and instructions of owners to Capt. John Randall, January 4, 1760, V 59 BP.

61. Ibid.

62. V 58 BP.

63. Capt. John Burgess to Capt. John Randall, February 14, 1760, V 59 BP.

64. Capt. John Burgess to Capt. John Randall, February 28, 1760, V 59 BP.

65. Ibid.

66. Capt. John Randall to Obadiah Brown & Co., March 5, 1760, V 59 BP.

67. For the letter see V 59 BP.

68. Capt. John Randall to Obadiah Brown & Co., April 25, 1760, V 59 BP.

69. Bill of Lading for 15 hogsheads and 12 barrels of molasses shipped by Capt. John Randall on the Snow *Winsor* from Port-au-Prince, April 25, 1760, V 59 BP.

70. Bill of Lading of the Brigantine *Providence* from Port-au-Prince, May 9, 1760, V 59 BP.

71. Capt. John Randall to Obadiah Brown & Co., June 2, 1769, V 59 BP.

72. Ibid.

73. Capt. John Randall to Obadiah Brown & Co., July 22, 1769, V 59 BP.

74. See the Condemnation Proceedings in the Vice Admiralty Court at New Providence, June 3, 1760, V 59 BP.

75. Ibid.

76. Sworn statement by Nicholas and John Brown before Daniel Jenckes, November 25, 1766, vouching for accuracy of copy of the invoice of the Brigantine *Providence,* V 59 BP.

77. A copy of this decision is in V 59 BP.

78. A copy of the decision of the Privy Council is also in V 59 BP.

79. See copy of sworn statement, May 19, 1767, in V 59 BP.

80. See copy of sworn statement, June 1, 1767, in V 59 BP. It was signed by Daniel Jenckes, John Cole, Nathan Angell, Thomas Greene, Jabez Bowen, Daniel Tillinghast, Nathaniel Greene, and Nicholas Cooke.

81. Statement by Will Shaeffer, Collector of Customs at Boston, June 1, 1767, V 59 BP.

82. Copy of decision of Supreme Court of Pennsylvania, in case of John Brown & Samuel Purviance, April 11, 1767, V 59 BP.

83. Tench Francis to Nicholas Brown & Co., May 5, 1767, V 59 BP.

84. Obadiah Brown & Co. to William Earle, February 16, 1760, V G45, vol. I.

85. Capt. Abraham Whipple to Obadiah Brown & Co., November 20, 1762; also Captain Whipple's protest before Notary at St. Pierre on November 20, 1762, both in V G45, vol. III.

86. Obadiah Brown & Co. to Detruce & Lecount, October 14, 1761, V 61 SS.

87. By an agreement dated February 18, 1754, Samuel Lee of Swansea, Massachusetts, sold *Speedwell,* then on the stocks, to Obadiah Brown, Esek Hopkins, John Hawkins, and Ephraim Bowen. Obadiah had first employed her in the whale fishery. See the

Agreement of Sale in unbound Moses Brown Papers in RIHS.

88. The papers of these five voyages are to be found in the unbound Moses Brown Papers in RIHS. For Captain Wheaton's rôle as factor at Monte Cristi see his letters to Obadiah and Nicholas Brown, dated July 24, August 5 and 20, and September 24, 1758.

89. For this voyage see letter of Obadiah Brown & Co. to Capt. William Earle, May 22, 1761. Also Capt. William Earle to Obadiah Brown & Co., June 29, August 1, and September 13, 1761, V G45, vol. II. Captain Earle's letters were written from Monte Cristi.

90. The record of *Providence* is found in V 57 BP.

91. For the invoice see V 57 BP.

92. Silas Cook to Nicholas and John Brown, January 11, 1757, V 57 BP.

93. Ibid.

94. For the text of the agreement see V 57 BP.

95. This phase of *Desire's* history is related in two letters by Tench Francis & Son to Obadiah Brown & Co., May 4 and 18, 1758, L 58-87 TF.

96. Ibid.

97. For the invoice see V 57 BP.

98. For the computation of the value see V 57 BP.

99. Kimball, *Providence in Colonial Times,* pp. 268-270.

CHAPTER 4. "THAT UNRIGHTEOUS TRAFFIC"

1. Rhode Island Colonial Records, IV, 54-55. Governor Samuel Cranston to the Board of Trade.

2. Ibid.

3. For the text of the Remonstrance see *Rhode Island Colonial Records,* VI, 378-383.

4. This letter is found in the Letter Book of James Brown in RIHS.

5. James Brown to Obadiah Brown, March 10, 1737, in Letter Book of James Brown in *Rhode Island Manuscripts,* VIII in RIHS. This is not the same Letter Book as the one referred to in the previous note.

6. James Brown to "Mr. Marcey," May 26, 1737. *Ibid.*

7. Obadiah Brown's Insurance Book contains a reference to the "Sloop *Cumberbus* from ye coast of Africa to Jamaica" in 1753. This could have been a slave trader in which Obadiah was concerned. One cannot be certain of this, however, as numerous vessels referred to in the Insurance Book were craft on which he had written the insurance.

8. For the letter see L 57-87 TF.

9. Ibid.

10. Obadiah Brown & Co. to Tench Francis & Son, June 27, 1759, P F7.

11. That John Brown drew his brothers into the trade appears evident from a letter written on January 30, 1800 by Moses Brown to Dwight Foster, *Moses Brown Papers,* X, 1, in RIHS. There is a typed copy of this letter in the John Carter Brown Library.

12. Carter Braxton to Nicholas Brown & Co., February 1, 1763, Miscellaneous Letters, 1762-1764.

13. Nicholas Brown & Co. to Carter Braxton, September 5, 1763, Miscellaneous Letters, 1762-1764.

14. For the letter, see Miscellaneous Letters, 1762-1764.

15. For the papers of this voyage, see V F6, vol. I.

16. For this letter, see *Moses Brown Papers,* I, 60, in RIHS.

17. For the invoice, see V S2.

18. For the list of stores, see V S2.

19. For Captain Hopkins' orders, see V S2.

20. This letter is in V S2.

21. The Trade Book is found with the other papers of this voyage of *Sally* in V S2. This account of Captain Hopkins' trading on the African coast and of his loss of slaves on the Middle Passage is based on the entries in the Trade Book.

22. This letter is in V S2.

23. Letter of Moses Brown to Capt. Esek Hopkins, July 17, 1765, V S2. In this letter Moses refers to the report that Hopkins had "Lost all Your Hands in the River Basa."

24. Ibid. In which Moses refers to the letter from Hopkins.

25. Ibid.

26. The details of the passage are recorded in Esek Hopkins' Trade Book.

27. Letter of Nicholas Brown & Co. to Capt. Abraham Whipple, Capt. George Hopkins, and Capt. Nicholas Power. These men, all masters of the Company's ships, were then in the West Indies. The letter related to them the details contained in Esek Hopkins' letter.

28. The letter is found in V S2.

29. Nicholas Brown & Co. to Capt. Esek Hopkins, November 16, 1765, V S2.

30. Ibid.

31. Joseph Wanton to John Brown, June 20, 1766, P W2.

32. Nicholas Brown to Joseph and William Wanton, June 28, 1766, OL 57-73 M.

33. This conclusion seems warranted by the letter which Moses Brown wrote to Dwight Foster, member of the lower House of Congress from Massachusetts on January 30, 1800, *loc. cit.* In it Moses, referring to John Brown, says: "He . . . has often appeared in Support of a Trade which his Love of Money and Anxiety to acquire it Long Since Drew his Brothers with him into a Voyage in that Unrighteous Traffic, but hapily they and I may say we Lived to Regret it, and to Labour to have it Relinquished in this State; but my Brother John, the only one Living, has most Unhapily as I think both for himself and others Continued Obstinately bent to Encourage the Trade. . ." The slave voyage into which John's "Love of Money . . . Drew his Brothers" was undoubtedly that of *Sally* in 1764-65.

34. John Brown to Benjamin Mason, December 12, 1769, P M2, vol. III.

35. Ibid.

36. The Reverend Samuel Hopkins wrote of Moses Brown: "Moses Brown is a man of a respectable character, as an honest, sensible man. He is a man of interest. He was not educated a Quaker, but joined that sect some years ago. He is a brother to the famous John Brown, the rich merchant in Providence. This Moses was once concerned in the slave trade; but for many years has been convinced of the iniquity of it, and his sin in practicing it has lain heavy on his conscience. He thinks it his duty to do all in his power to put a stop to this traffic, and an end to the slavery of Africans, and to assist them to obtain their freedom in all the ways he can. And he is active and unwearied in his endeavors to promote these ends. And I must say, that he and a number of his brethren, who join him in this matter, have acted a judicious, faithful and honorable part. We have no men of any denomination in these states, who appear so conscientious, discerning, faithful, and zealous in this matter, as these Quakers do." This statement is found in a letter of Hopkins to Levi Hart, November 27, 1787. Quoted in Elizabeth Donnan, *Documents Illustrative of the History of the Slave Trade to America* (4 vols.; Washington, 1930-1935), III, 335, note.

37. Rhode Island Colonial Records, VII, 251-253.

38. Records of the State of Rhode Island and Providence Plantations (3 vols.; Providence, 1863-1865), III, 7-8, hereafter referred to as *Rhode Island State Records.*

39. Moses Brown to Samuel Hopkins, March 3, 1784, *Moses Brown Papers,* IV, 314, in RIHS.

40. Ibid.

41. Irving B. Richman, *Rhode Island: A Study in Separatism* (Boston and New York, 1905), p. 268.

42. John Brown to Moses Brown, August 18, 1787, *Moses Brown Papers,* VI, 11.

43. Ibid.

44. Rhode Island State Records, III, 262.

45. Ibid. Moses Brown Papers, XI, 43, 45, 49.

46. For the act of incorporation, see *Rhode Island State Records,* III, 383-385.

47. Letter of Moses Brown to Dwight Foster, January 30, 1800, *loc. cit.*

48. John Brown to Moses Brown, July 31, 1797, *Moses Brown Papers,* IX, 711. Also John Brown to Moses Brown, July 28, 1797, *Moses Brown Papers,* IX, 710.

49. John Brown to Moses Brown, July 31, 1797, *loc. cit.*

50. At the bottom of John's letter of July 31, 1797 Moses penned a notation that he had answered to this effect.

51. Ibid.

52. John Brown to Moses Brown, August 28, 1798, *Moses Brown Papers,* IX, 729.

53. Letter of Moses Brown to Dwight Foster, January 30, 1800, *loc. cit.*

54. Statutes at Large, II, 70-72.

55. For the purport of the speech, see *Annals of Congress,* X, 686-687.

CHAPTER 5. "SPERMACETI CANDLES WARRANTED PURE"

1. Works of Edmund Burke (Boston, 1839), II, 30.

2. See Agreement between Samuel Lee of Swansea, Massachusetts, on the one hand, and Obadiah Brown, Job Hawkins, and Ephraim Bowen, on the other, February 18, 1754, by which Lee sold the Sloop *Speedwell* to them. This document is in the unbound Moses Brown Papers in RIHS.

3. John Brown to Joseph Nichols, December 24, 1764, P N2, vol. I.

4. Nicholas Brown & Co. to Capt. Abner Coffin, December 7, 1769, P C55.

5. Gauge of the oil and head matter brought by Captain Coffin in Sloop *A,* September 20, 1770, L & A 63-75 Sp. C.

6. Instructions of Nicholas Brown & Co. to Capt. Abisha Luce, November 13, 1773, V 65-74 SA.

7. For the various voyages of Sloop *A,* see V 65-74 SA.

8. For the figures, see L & A 63-75 Sp. C.

9. Nicholas Brown & Co. to Capt. Christopher Folger, November 12, 1772, V 65-74 SA.

10. Nicholas Brown & Co. to Isaac Knight, October 21, 1773, Miscellaneous Letters, 1773, vol. II.

11. For the various versions, see I. B. Richman, *Rhode Island: A Study in Separatism* (Boston and New York, 1905), p. 127; Obed Macy, *The History of Nantucket* (Mansfield, Mass., 1885), p. 78; George F. Dow, *Whale Ships and Whaling* (Salem, 1925), pp. 35-37; and *The Chad Browne Memorial* (Brooklyn, 1888), p. 16.

12. See "Account of head matter received by Nicholas Brown & Co. for the year 1769." The document is dated February 20, 1770. It is in L & A 63-75 Sp. C.

13. Henry Lloyd to Nicholas Brown & Co., April 9, 1764, L 62-64 HL.

14. Nicholas Brown & Co. to Henry Lloyd, May 11, 1764, P L5. One of the labels is preserved in the Brown Papers.

15. Gurdon Saltonstall to Nicholas Brown & Co., July 2, 1770, L 51-72 M.

16. John Relfe to Nicholas Brown & Co., February 20, 1765, L 58-67

17. Henry Lloyd to Nicholas Brown & Co., March 22, 1774, L 71-75 HL.

18. Henry Lloyd to Nicholas Brown & Co., April 26, 1774, L 71-75 HL.

19. Ibid.

20. For this memorandum, see P U5.

21. Nicholas Brown & Co. to Tench Francis, March 11, 1765, P F7.

22. Tench Francis & Son to Obadiah Brown & Co., September 6, 1759, L 58-87 TF.

23. Tench Francis to Obadiah Brown & Co., May 18, 1758, L 58-87 TF. Also Tench Francis to Nicholas Brown & Co., November 11 and December 24, 1764, L 63-65 FR.

24. For the letter, see L 60 M.

25. Obadiah Brown & Co. to John Brown, October 8, 1761, P U5.

26. There is no copy of this agreement in the Brown Papers. It is printed in Worthington C. Ford (ed.), *The Commerce of Rhode Island*, Massachusetts Historical Society *Collections*, IX, 88-92.

27. Copy of letter of Collins & Rivera, Naphtali Hart & Co., and Aaron Lopez to Richard Cranch & Co., July 29, 1762, L & A 59-92 Sp. C.

28. Richard Cranch & Co. to Nicholas Brown & Co., August 16 and 23, 1762, L & A 59-92 Sp. C.

29. Nicholas Brown & Co. to Joseph Palmer & Co., February 21, 1763, P U5.

30. Joseph Palmer & Co. to Nicholas Brown & Co., March 7, 1763, P U5.

31. For the text of the agreement, see L & A 59-92 Sp. C.

32. Joseph Palmer & Co. to Nicholas Brown & Co., May 16, 1763, L & A 59-92 Sp. C.

33. For the agreement, see L & A 59-92 Sp. C.

34. Joseph Palmer & Co. to Nicholas Brown & Co., July 12, 1763, P U5.

35. Nicholas Brown & Co. to Joseph Palmer & Co., July 24, 1763, P U5.

36. Thomas Robinson & Co. to Nicholas Brown & Co., October 11, 1763, P U5.

37. Copy of letter of Mr. Stocker (Philadelphia) to J. R. Rivera, October 20, 1763, L & A, 59-92 Sp. C.; also copy of letter of Stocker to Rivera, December 25, 1763, P R5.

38. Tench Francis to Nicholas Brown & Co., November 15, 1763, L 63-65 FR.

39. J. R. Rivera to Nicholas Brown & Co., December 8, 1763, P R5.

40. Tench Francis to Nicholas Brown & Co., February 22, 1764, L 57-67 FR.

41. Moses Brown to Obadiah Brown & Co., February 24, 1761, V Misc.

42. For a copy of the Mifflins' letter to Wilkinson, see P U5.

43. Nicholas Brown & Co. to J. R. Rivera & Co., October 8, 1763, OL 52-31 M.

44. Ibid.

45. Jacob R. Rivera (Newport) to Nicholas Brown & Co., October 17, 1763, L 58-70 M.

46. Ibid.

47. Ibid.

48. Nicholas Brown & Co. to Joseph Palmer & Co., October 10, 1763, P U5.

49. Copy, letter of Israel Wilkinson to Benjamin and John Mifflin, October 18, 1763, P U5.

50. Ibid.

51. Ibid.

52. Ibid.

53. Thomas Robinson (Newport) to Nicholas Brown & Co., October 17, 1763, quoting Thomas Richardson's words, P U5.

54. Ibid.

55. Ibid.

56. Thomas Robinson to Nicholas Brown & Co., December 3 and 9, 1763, P U5.

57. Nicholas Brown & Co. to J. R. Rivera, January 29, 1767, P R5.

58. Ibid.

59. John Brown to "Messrs. Jenckes," June 24, 1772, P U5.

60. Ibid.

61. Ibid.

62. Edmund Quincy to Nicholas Brown & Co., September 3, 1762, L & A 59-92 Sp. C.

63. For the inventory, see L & A 59-92 Sp. C. under date of September 3, 1762. A copy of the inventory of the buildings of the Quincys' works, as well as of the utensils is found with the letter of Joseph Palmer & Co. to Nicholas Brown & Co., August 26, 1763, P U5.

64. Joseph Palmer & Co. to Nicholas Brown & Co., August 26, 1763, P U5.

65. Ibid.

66. Ibid.

67. Nicholas Brown & Co. to Joseph Palmer & Co., September 2, 1763, P U5.

68. William Rotch to the "Manufacturers of Head Matter at Newport and Providence," January 24, 1774, P U5, vol. II. Rotch demanded this larger proportion only in principle, as he admitted that such a division would bring him a "much larger quantity than I want."

69. See the Articles of Agreement for the various years in L & A 59-92 Sp. C.

70. See "Account of Head Matter Received by Nicholas Brown & Co. in the year 1769," bearing date of February 20, 1770, L & A 59-92 Sp. C.

71. See "Account of Head Matter Purchased by Nicholas Brown & Co. and obtained in their own vessels, 1774," L & A 59-92 Sp. C.

72. Henry Lloyd to Nicholas Brown & Co., March 19, 1772, L 71-75 HL.

73. Henry Lloyd to Nicholas Brown & Co., June 30, 1773, L 71-75 HL.

74. Henry Lloyd to Nicholas Brown & Co., February 6, 1774, L 71-75 HL.

75. Copy of letter of Joseph Rotch to Rivera & Co., Napthtali & Isaac Hart, Thomas Robinson & Co., and Aaron Lopez, July 3, 1764, P U5. Rotch later specifically accused Robert Jenkins of Newport of informing on him. See copy of letter of Joseph Rotch to Robert Jenkins, August 16, 1764, P R6.

76. See letter of Hayley & Hopkins (London) to Nicholas Brown, February 20, 1775, in which they say that "these inspectors (who are Custom House officers) have never seen a single cask of head matter from its first importation here till this winter," L 1770-75 HH.

77. Copy of letter of P. Dumersque (Boston) to Jacob Polock, October 2, 1769, L & A 63-75 Sp. C.

78. Copy of Circular of Rhode Island manufacturers to Joseph Rotch & Son, October 12, 1769, P U5, vol. II.

79. See copy of the letter, P U5, vol. II.

80. See copy of it under date of October 25, 1771, P U5, vol. II.

81. See copy of the letter, dated October 25, 1771, P U5, vol. II.

82. See copy of the letter in P U5, vol. II.

83. For the letter, see L 71-75 HL.

84. This is made evident in the letters of Henry Lloyd to Nicholas Brown & Co., April 29 and May 13, 1772, L 71-75 HL.

85. Hayley & Hopkins (London) to Nicholas Brown, February 20, 1775, L 1770-75 HH.

86. Louis M. Hacker, *The Triumph of American Capitalism* (New York, 1940), pp. 136-140.

CHAPTER 6. "A FURNACE FOR MAKING PIGG IRON"

1. Quoted in J. L. Bishop, *A History of American Manufactures from 1608 to 1860* (2 vols.; Philadelphia, 1864), I, 476. Also Arthur C. Bining, *British Regulation of the Colonial Iron Industry* (Philadelphia, 1933), pp. 9-10.

2. Bishop, *op. cit.,* I, 502.

3. Bishop, *op. cit.,* I, 503.

4. See *Dictionary of American Biography,* XX, 227-228 for sketch of Jeremiah Wilkinson.

5. Bishop, *op. cit.,* I, 502.

6. Edward Field, *State of Rhode Island and Providence Plantations at the End of the Century: A History* (3 vols.; Boston, 1902), III, 331. Also Bishop, *op. cit.,* p. 502. Bishop gives Waldo's name as "Samuel."

7. Both Field and Bishop evidently assume that there was a direct and unbroken connection between Waldo's establishment and the later Hope Furnace. There is nothing in the Brown papers to indicate that there had been a furnace on the Pawtuxet prior to 1765.

8. There is an excellent survey of the Colonial iron industry in Bining, *British Regulation of the Colonial Iron Industry,* pp. 5-31.

9. For an exhaustive study of this, see Arthur C. Bining, *Pennsylvania Iron Manufacture in the Eighteenth Century* (Harrisburg, 1938).

10. Bining, *British Regulation of the Colonial Iron Industry,* p. 19.

11. Bining, *Pennsylvania Iron Manufacture,* pp. 33, 79-80.

12. Ibid., pp. 33-34.

13. The points discussed above are set forth in the "Articles of Co-partnership," signed by Stephen Hopkins, Israel Wilkinson, Nicholas, Joseph, John, and Moses Brown, Job Hawkins, and Caleb Arnold, July 9, 1765, P H6, vol. I.

14. Ibid.

15. Nicholas Brown & Co. to John Relfe, May 21, 1765. PH6, vol. I.

16. See "Estemate on Pennsylvania Furnaces" (undated), P H6, vol. I.

17. Stephen Hopkins to Nicholas Brown & Co., July 28, 1765, P H6, vol. I.

18. Nicholas Brown & Co. to John Relfe, August 3, 1765, P H6, vol. I.

19. Joseph Remington's Promise of a Deed for the Furnace Land, August 9, 1765, PH6, vol. I.

20. See the Document bearing date of August 10, 1765, P H6, vol. I.

21. For this see P H6, vol. I.

22. Ibid.

23. Ibid.

24. See the Agreement between the owners of Hope Furnace and Mathew and Job Manchester, September 3, 1765, P H6, vol. I.

25. See Minutes of Meeting of Furnace Owners, October 1, 1765, P H6, vol. I.

26. See Memorandum of Agreement, November 9, 1765, P H6, vol. I.

27. Agreement between Owners of Hope Furnace and Francis Brayton, January 18, 1766, P H6, vol. I.

28. Nicholas Brown & Co. to Jeremiah Lippitt, January 4, 1766, P H6, vol. I.

29. Elisha Painter's Agreement to make bellows for Hope Furnace, September 23, 1765, P H6, vol. I.

30. James Sturdefant's Agreement with the Owners of Hope Furnace, P H6, vol. I.

31. Nicholas Brown & Co. to Martin Gay, January 6, 1766, P H6, vol. I.

32. Minutes of Meeting of Furnace Owners, December 23, 1765, P H6, vol. I.

33. Resolves of the Furnace Company, January 5, 1766, P H6, vol. I.

34. See Letter of Joseph Washburn, Jr., to Nicholas Brown and Co., August 16, 1766, P H6, vol. I. For the data from Abner Lapham of Cumberland, see the notations on the letter from Washburn.

35. Nicholas Brown & Co. to Paris Simmons, June 20, 1766, P H6, vol. I.

36. Ibid.

37. Nicholas Brown to Nicholas Brown & Co., October 2, 1766, P H6, vol. I.

38. Stephen Hopkins to Nicholas Brown & Co., October 7, 1766, P H6, vol. I.

39. Nicholas Brown to Nicholas Brown & Co., October 14, 1766, P H6, vol. I.

40. Nicholas Brown to Nicholas Brown & Co., November 6, 1766, P H6, vol. I.

41. See the Report of the Meeting of the Owners of Furnace Hope, September 22, 1766, P H6, vol. I.

42. See Agreement between Owners of Hope Furnace and Rufus Hopkins, November 7, 1766, P H6, vol. I.

43. Nicholas Brown & Co. to Rufus Hopkins, August 3, 1767, P H6, vol. II.

44. Resolves of Furnace Hope Owners, May 30, 1767, P H6, vol. II.

45. John Brown (at Lime, Connecticut) to Nicholas Brown & Co., June 1767, P H6, vol. II.

46. Copy, John Brown (at Philadelphia), to Mr. "Hick," June 11, 1767, P H6, vol. II.

47. John Brown (at Philadelphia) to Nicholas Brown & Co., June 12, 1767, P H6, vol. II.

48. John Brown (at Philadelphia) to Nicholas Brown & Co., June 20, 1767, P H6, vol. II.

49. See Dictionary of American Biography, XVIII, 16-17.

50. See the Agreement, June 28, 1767, P H6, vol. II.

51. Rufus Hopkins to the Owners of Furnace Hope, August 20, 1767, P H6, vol. II.

52. Rufus Hopkins to the Owners, August 24, 1767, P H6, vol. II.

53. Furnace Owners to Rufus Hopkins, October 12, 1767, P H6, vol. II.

54. Rufus Hopkins to Owners, November 17, 1767, P H6, vol. II.

55. Rufus Hopkins to Owners, November 26, 1767, P H6, vol. II.

56. Rufus Hopkins to Owners, December 5, 1767, P H6, vol. II.

57. Rufus Hopkins to Owners, December 13, 1767, P H6, vol. II.

58. Rufus Hopkins to Owners, December 20, 1767, P H6, vol. II.

59. William Burton (Cranston) to Nicholas Brown & Co., November 20, 1767, P H6, vol. II.

60. Rufus Hopkins to Owners, January 5, 1768, P H6, vol. II.

61. Nicholas Brown & Co. to Welch, Wilkinson & Startin (Birmingham, England), May 13, 1767. Miscellaneous Letters, 1767.

62. Nicholas Brown & Co. to William Russell, May 23, 1767. Miscellaneous Letters, 1767.

63. Nicholas Brown & Co. to Capt. John Burrough, August 10, 1766, V F6, vol. II.

64. Henry Lloyd (Boston) to Nicholas Brown & Co., September 25 and October 18, 1766, L 64-67 HL.

65. Christopher Hussey & Co. to Nicholas Brown & Co., August 25, 1766, P H8.

66. Peter T. Curtenius (New York) to Nicholas Brown & Co., October 29, 1766, P C8.

67. Nicholas Brown & Co. to William Russell, May 23, 1767. In the letter the Browns wrote: "And as we apprehend our Iron (being very fine and strong) will be suitable for making the best of steel, we desire you to enquire after a person acquainted in that business and if you can procure a workman brot over we will assure him employ but as we are unacquainted with that Branch can't advise what terms to engage," Miscellaneous Letters, 1767.

68. Copy of letter of Benjamin Parker (in England) to Vardon T. Franklin, August 29, 1767, P H6, vol. II.

69. Henry Cruger (Bristol, England) to Nicholas Brown & Co., November 5, 1768, P H6, vol. II.

70. See copies of Letters of these "Manufacturers" to Henry Cruger re Hope Pig Iron, from February 3, 1769 to February 17, 1770, P H6, vol. III.

71. Nicholas Brown & Co. to Henry Cruger (Bristol, England), June 9, 1770, P H6, vol. III.

72. Hayley & Hopkins (London) to Nicholas Brown & Co., September 22, 1770, L 68-72 HH.

73. Andrew Oliver's letters to English authorities were among those obtained by Benjamin Franklin and returned to Massachusetts Bay where they created such a sensation.

74. Nicholas Brown & Co. to Peter Oliver, August 17, 1768, P H6, vol. II.

75. Nicholas Brown & Co. to Peter Oliver, October 18, 1768, P H6, vol. II.

76. Peter Oliver to Nicholas Brown & Co., January 1769, P H6, vol. III.

77. Nicholas Brown & Co. to Peter Oliver & Son, January 25, 1769, P H6, vol. III.

78. Peter Oliver, Senior & Junior, to Nicholas Brown & Co., February 9, 1769, L 68-69 M.

79. Nicholas Brown & Co. to Peter Oliver, January 27, 1770, P H6, vol. III.

80. Ibid.

81. Henry Lloyd to Nicholas Brown & Co., August 10, 1779, L 67-72 HL[2].

82. Nicholas Brown & Co. to Griffin Greene, December 8, 1769 and March 4, 1771, P H6, vol. III.

83. Silas Wood to Moses Brown, March 13, 1770, P H6, vol. III.

84. Nicholas Brown & Co. to Peter Oliver, April 25, 1769, P H6, vol. III, in which they report this judgment of various forgemen.

85. For the Memo of the Agreement, dated October 25, 1771, see P H6, vol. III.

86. Nicholas Brown & Co. to James Obiel

(New York), July, 1771, P H6, vol. III. This may well be a misspelling of "Abeel," as a family of that name was then in the iron business in New York. See Virginia D. Harrington, *The New York Merchant on the Eve of the Revolution* (New York, 1935), p. 151.

87. See Memo of Agreement, October 20, 1772, P H6, vol. III.

88. Nicholas Brown & Co. to Archibald Cary, May 23, 1770, Miscellaneous Letters, 1770.

89. Nicholas Brown & Co. to Archibald Cary, April 17 and June 25, 1771. Miscellaneous Letters, 1771.

90. Nicholas Brown & Co. to Dr. Benjamin Gale, December 12, 1768, P H6, vol. II.

91. Dr. Benjamin Gale to Nicholas Brown & Co., January 23, 1769, L 67-69 M. The sketch of Dr. Gale in the *Dictionary of American Biography,* VII, 97-98, makes no mention of his experiments in the manufacture of steel.

92. See Memorandum of Agreement, October 27, 1774, P H6, vol. III.

93. It should be noted that Henry Lloyd in Boston handled Hope pigs on commission; he did not purchase the iron from the Browns.

94. Aaron Lopez to Nicholas Brown & Co., May 16, 1769 and Nicholas Brown & Co. to Aaron Lopez, May 20 and 22, 1769, P L6.

95. Aaron Lopez to Nicholas Brown & Co., October 18 and 27 and November 8, 1769, P L6.

96. Nicholas Brown & Co. to Aaron Lopez, July 10 and August 5, 1770; Aaron Lopez to Nicholas Brown & Co., August 30, 1770, P L6.

97. Aaron Lopez to Nicholas Brown & Co., March 22, 1770 and January 11, 1770, P L6.

98. Aaron Lopez to Nicholas Brown & Co., October 5 and 9, 1774, L 74 M.

99. Peter T. Curtenius to Nicholas Brown & Co., September 24, 1766, P C8.

100. See the Agreement, P C8.

101. Peter T. Curtenius to Nicholas Brown & Co., May 9, 1771, P C8.

102. Peter T. Curtenius to Nicholas Brown & Co., May 29 and July 23, 1771, P C8.

103. Peter T. Curtenius to Nicholas Brown & Co., July 23, 1771, P C8.

104. Nicholas Brown & Co. to Peter T. Curtenius, March 13 and 30, June 19 and July 20, 1772, P C8.

105. Peter T. Curtenius to Nicholas Brown & Co., November 5, 1774, P C8.

106. Nicholas Brown & Co. to Peter T. Curtenius, March 15, 1773 and December 9, 1771, P C8.

107. Peter T. Curtenius to Nicholas Brown & Co., March 24, 1774, L 74 M. On another occasion Curtenius forwarded a bill of lading for "Specie amounting to £145-8 Currency." See Peter T. Curtenius to Nicholas Brown & Co., July 9, 1768, L 63-74 M.

108. Peter T. Curtenius to Nicholas Brown & Co., March 21 and May 20, 1774, L 74 M.

109. Peter T. Curtenius to Nicholas Brown & Co., August 3, 1774, L 74 M.

110. Peter T. Curtenius to Nicholas Brown & Co., August 28, 1774, L 74 M.

111. See P H6 Uncal., vol. III, for "Account Hibernia pig—Who Sold to & Who Delivered," for 1774-75. This lists the names of some 88 individuals and firms to whom 52 tons of Hibernia pigs had been delivered. Presumably these purchasers were forgemen. Included in the list was Aaron Eliot of Killingworth, Connecticut. In Harrington, *op. cit.,* p. 151, there is the conjecture that "Mount Hope" pig iron, advertised in New York in 1774, was the product of "a mine" in the Province of New York. This writer suggests that they may have been Hope pigs which the Browns were then shipping to New York in large quantities.

112. Peter T. Curtenius to Nicholas Brown & Co., October 24, 1774, L 74 M.

113. It is significant that the success was achieved in spite of the depression prevailing in the Colonial iron industry during 1768 and the years which followed. The depression resulted from the too rapid expansion of the business. See Arthur C. Bining, *British Regulation of the Colonial Iron Industry,* p. 77, note.

CHAPTER 7. "SETTLED CORRESPONDENTS IN THE
NEIGHBORING GOVERNMENTS"

1. See C. M. Andrews, *The Colonial Period of American History* (New Haven, 1938), IV, 413; Virginia Harrington, *The New York Merchant on the Eve of the Revolution,* p. 206.

2. W. T. Baxter, *The House of Hancock: Business in Boston, 1724-1775* (Cambridge, 1945), p. 189.

3. Nicholas Brown & Co. to David Van Horne, May 24, 1763, P-V2.

4. Obadiah Brown & Co. to Tench Francis, May 25, 1761, P-F7.

5. Aaron Lopez to Nicholas Brown & Co., May 16 and November 8, 1769, P-L6.

6. Nicholas Brown & Co. to Aaron Lopez, July 3, 1773, P-L6.

7. Nicholas Brown & Co. to Aaron Lopez, July 7, 1766, P-L6.

8. Nicholas Brown & Co. to Aaron Lopez, September 27, 1767, P-L6.

9. Joseph and William Wanton to Obadiah Brown & Co., August 3, 1758, L58-69 J & WW.

10. Joseph and William Wanton to Nicholas Brown & Co., June 20, 1766, L58-69 J & WW.

11. See the Agreement, dated September 15, 1769, L59-72M.

12. Joseph and William Wanton to Nicholas Brown & Co., February 4, 1766, L58-69 J & WW.

13. Nicholas Brown & Co. to Benjamin Mason, October 31, 1763, P-M2.

14. Benjamin Mason to Obadiah Brown & Co., June 4 and 11, 1759, P-M2.

15. Nicholas Brown & Co. to Benjamin Mason, December 10, 1763, P-M2.

16. During the period 1756-1765 Tench Francis was alone in the business part of the time; for a period he and his son were partners in the firm of Tench Francis & Son; and for a season he was a partner of John Relfe in the firm of Francis & Relfe. By 1766 he had retired from the business and John Relfe was the Philadelphia correspondent of the Browns. In the text Tench Francis is commonly referred to, regardless of the official name of the firm at any give time.

17. See Francis & Relfe's account of sales, August 18, 1759, L58-67FR.

18. Francis & Relfe to Obadiah Brown & Co., October 12, 1759, L57-67FR.

19. Compiled from Francis & Relfe's accounts of sale for the year.

20. See Francis & Relfe's accounts of sales dated July 31 and December 14, 1764, L58-67FR.

21. Obadiah Brown & Co. to Francis & Relfe, September 23, 1759, P-F7.

22. Francis & Relfe to Obadiah Brown & Co., October 12, 1759, P-F7.

23. Nicholas Brown & Co. to Tench Francis, September 14, 1762, P-F7.

24. Nicholas Brown & Co. to Tench Francis, October 28, 1762, P-F7.

25. Nicholas Brown & Co. to John Relfe, September 24, 1765, P-F7.

26. Francis & Relfe to Obadiah Brown & Co., March 28, 1761, L57-67FR.

27. Francis & Relfe to Obadiah Brown & Co., April 9, 1761, L57-67FR.

28. Francis & Relfe to Obadiah Brown & Co., July 9, 1761, L57-67FR.

29. Francis & Relfe to Obadiah Brown & Co., October 28, 1761, L57-67FR.

30. Nicholas Brown & Co. to Francis & Relfe, September 14, 1762, P-F7.

31. In 1763 there was discussion between the two houses with respect to the shipment of oil to London, but little seems to have come of it. See Nicholas Brown & Co. to Francis & Relfe, February 28, 1763 and Francis & Relfe to Nicholas Brown & Co., February 11, 1763. P-F7 and L57-67FR. Francis & Relfe wrote that they wanted spermaceti oil to load to vessels for London.

32. Clement Biddle & Co. to Nicholas Brown & Co., June 23, 1768, L68-72CB&Co.

33. Walter and Samuel Franklin to Obadiah Brown & Co., February 16, 1760, acknowledging receipt of the goods, P-F75.

34. Walter and Samuel Franklin to Obadiah Brown & Co., March 10, 1760, L60-67W&SF.

35. Nicholas Brown & Co. to David Van Horne, May 24, 1763, P-V2.

36. David Van Horne to Nicholas Brown & Co., June 7, 1763, P-V2.

37. It would be pleasant to believe that Van Horne's suggestion had prompted the manufacturers to fix a minimum price for candles. However, the price in New England had been fixed in 1761, while the fixing of the price in New York and Philadelphia had been discussed prior to the receipt of Van Horne's letter of June 21, 1763.

38. Nicholas Brown & Co. to David Van Horne, September 24, 1763, P-V2.

39. Nicholas Brown & Co. to David Van Horne, October 18, 1763, P-V2.

40. David Van Horne to Nicholas Brown & Co., October 24, 1763, P-V2.

41. Nicholas Brown & Co. to David Van Horne, November 1, 1763, P-V2.

42. Nicholas Brown & Co. to Henry Lloyd, December 16, 1763, P-L5.

43. Nicholas Brown & Co. to David Van Horne, May 14, 1764 and Van Horne to Nicholas Brown & Co., August 4, 1764, P-V2.

44. Nicholas Brown & Co. to David Van Horne, July 21, 1764 and Van Horne to Nicholas Brown & Co., August 4, 1764, P-V2.

45. Nicholas Brown & Co. to David Van Horne, October 1 and 30, 1764, P-V2.

46. Nicholas Brown & Co. to David Van Horne, October 30, 1764, P-V2.

47. Nicholas Brown & Co. to David Van Horne, December 14, 1764, P-V2.

48. Nicholas Brown & Co. to David Van Horne, February 20, 1768, OL 68 DVH.

49. Nicholas Brown & Co. to David Van Horne, February 20, 1768, OL 68 DVH.

50. David Van Horne to Nicholas Brown & Co., February 28, 1768 · and Nicholas Brown & Co. to Van Horne, March 15, 1768, P-V2 and OL 68 DVH.

51. David Van Horne to Nicholas Brown & Co., October 24 and 25, 1768, P-V2.

52. Nicholas Brown & Co. to David Van Horne, November 28 and 30, 1768, OL 68 DVH.

53. Nicholas Brown & Co. to David Van Horne, March 15, 1773, P-V2.

54. Nicholas Brown & Co. to David Van Horne, November 6 and December 10, 1771, P-V2.

55. Nicholas Brown & Co. to David Van Horne, March 5, 1765, P V2.

56. Nicholas Brown & Co. to David Van Horne, March 27, 1769, OL 59-03 M.

57. It is dated January 21, 1763, L 59-66 WH.

58. Henry Lloyd to Nicholas Brown & Co., November 9, 1764, L 62-64 HL.

59. Henry Lloyd to Nicholas Brown & Co., November 14, 1764, L 62-64 HL.

60. Henry Lloyd to Nicholas Brown & Co., November 26, 1764, L 62-64 HL.

61. Henry Lloyd to Nicholas Brown & Co., December 11, 1764, L 62-64 HL.

62. Henry Lloyd to Nicholas Brown & Co., December 17, 1764, L 62-64 HL.

63. Henry Lloyd to Nicholas Brown & Co., April 4, 1765, L 63-66 HL.

64. Henry Lloyd to Nicholas Brown, June 13, 1763 L 62-64 HL.

65. See accounts of sales rendered by Lloyd on January 21, May 29, November 18, 19, 20, and 25, and December 22, 1766, L 63-66 HL and L 64-67 HL.

66. See accounts of sales rendered by Lloyd on December 16 and 31, 1767, and January 27, February 13, March 10 and 16, June 11, September 13, November 18, December 7 and 16, 1768, L 67-72 HL and L 67-69 HL.

67. See the account of Nicholas Brown & Co. with Henry Lloyd, March 1, 1769, L 67-69 HL.

68. Henry Lloyd to Nicholas Brown & Co., August 3, 1769, L 67-72 HL².

69. Nicholas Brown & Co. to Henry Lloyd, May 16, 1763, P-L5.

70. Nicholas Brown & Co. to Henry Lloyd, June 17, 1763, P-L5.

71. Nicholas Brown & Co. to Henry Lloyd, September 22, 1763, P-L5.

72. Henry Lloyd to Nicholas Brown & Co., August 25, 1764, L 62-64 HL.

73. Nicholas Brown & Co. to Henry Lloyd, November 22, 1765, P-L5.

74. Henry Lloyd to Nicholas Brown & Co., November 30, 1772, L 71-75 HL.

75. Henry Lloyd to Nicholas Brown & Co., November 4, 1773, L 71-75 HL.

76. Nicholas Brown & Co. to Henry Lloyd, September 13, 1763, P-L5.

77. Henry Lloyd to Nicholas Brown & Co., October 18, 1763, acknowledging the receipt of their instructions regarding the bills, L 62-64 HL.

78. Henry Lloyd to Nicholas Brown & Co., September 27, 1763, L 62-64 HL.

79. Henry Lloyd to Nicholas Brown & Co., October 10, 1763, L 62-64 HL.

80. Henry Lloyd to Nicholas Brown & Co., February 7, 1775, L 71-75 HL.

81. Henry Lloyd to Nicholas Brown & Co., February 10, 1775, acknowledging receipt of the specie, L 71-75 HL.

82. Henry Lloyd to Nicholas Brown & Co., November 18, 1773, L 71-75 HL.

83. Nicholas Brown & Co. to Henry Lloyd, March 4, 1766, P L5.

84. Henry Lloyd to Nicholas Brown &

Co., March 10, 17, and 26, and April 7, 1766, L 64-67 HL.

85. At Philadelphia and New York the Browns dealt only occasionally with merchants other than their "established correspondents," although, first and last, they traded with a substantial number of houses in the two cities.

86. Nicholas Brown & Co. to John Hancock, April 25, 1768, P-H15.

87. Nicholas Brown & Co. to John Hancock, March 27 and 28, and April 13 and 25, 1769, P-H15.

88. Nicholas Brown & Co. to John Hancock, May 22, 1769, P-H15.

89. Nicholas Brown & Co. to John Hancock, June 12, 1771, P-H15.

90. Joshua Gardner to Nicholas Brown & Co., April 16, 1768, P-G25.

91. Nicholas Brown & Co. to Joshua Gardner, October 3, 1769, P-G25.

92. Nicholas Brown & Co. to Joshua Gardner, August 23, 1766, P-G25.

93. For the invoice of this cargo see I 57-62 M.

94. This invoice is also in I 57-62 M.

95. For these various transactions see Nicholas Brown & Co. to Christopher Starbuck & Co., June 13, August 29, and October 28, 1769, P-S7.

96. Gurdon Saltonstall to "Elisha Browne," June 25, 1767, P-S2. Saltonstall's letter was turned over to Nicholas Brown & Co. by their relative, Elisha Brown. Nicholas Brown & Co. to Gurdon Saltonstall, July 7 and 24, 1767, P-S2.

97. Gurdon Saltonstall to Nicholas Brown & Co., January 3, 1770, P-S2.

98. Nicholas Brown & Co. to Gurdon Saltonstall, January 5, 1770, P-S2.

99. Nicholas Brown & Co. to Gurdon Saltonstall, October 8 and December 18, 1770, and February 21, 1771. Gurdon Saltonstall to Nicholas Brown & Co., July 11, 1771, P-S2.

100. Gurdon Saltonstall to Nicholas Brown & Co., April 22, 1772, L 72-73 M.

101. Nicholas Brown to Thomas C. Williams, January 27, February 16, April 16, and May 21, 1773, June 24, 1774, August 19 and December 16, 1775, and Thomas C. Williams to Nicholas Brown, February 9, 1776, Miscellaneous Letters, 1773-1776.

102. Members of the Lloyd, Wendell, and Apthorp families, to mention only a few, were to be found in business in several different colonial seaport towns. See Virginia Harrington, *The New York Merchant on the Eve of the Revolution,* pp. 218-220.

CHAPTER 8. "DRY GOODS FROM LONDON AND BRISTOL"

1. William Stead (London) to Obadiah Brown, April 16, 1756, in unbound Moses Brown Papers in RIHS. Stead says that "about three years since I sent an Iron Screw & Brass Box to your Parts for Spermaceti Works, which cost about £80."

2. Invoice of Sundry Merchandise shipped by Obadiah Brown on board the Ship *Noble Galley,* consigned to William Stead, September 23, 1756. In unbound Moses Brown Papers, RIHS.

3. In unbound Moses Brown Papers, RIHS.

4. See the invoice dated August 10, 1759, in unbound Moses Brown Papers, RIHS.

5. Invoice of goods shipped by Abraham Hart, August 25, 1758, in unbound Moses Brown Papers, RIHS.

6. Account current of Obadiah, Nicholas, and John Brown with Abraham Hart, September 25, 1758, in unbound Moses Brown Papers, RIHS.

7. Francis & Relfe to Obadiah Brown & Co. March 4, 1761, L 57-67 FR.

8. Walter & Samuel Franklin (New York) to Obadiah Brown & Co., February 25, 1760, P-F75.

9. Francis & Relfe to Obadiah Brown & Co., February 22, 1764, L 57-67 FR.

10. Nicholas Brown & Co. to Joshua Gardner, August 15, 1766, P-G25.

11. Nicholas Brown & Co. to Aaron Lopez, July 18 and 29, 1766, OL 66-75 AL. The figure of 25 to 30 per cent above the Sterling cost evidently was a special one granted to the Browns, as importers habitually sold European goods to small retail shops at a much greater advance above the Sterling cost.

12. Nicholas Brown & Co. to Benjamin Mason, August 19, 1766, P-M2.

13. Nicholas Brown & Co. to Isaac Hazlehurst, July 15, 1766, Miscellaneous Letters, 1766.

14. Hugh Pringle to Nicholas Brown & Co., February 4, 1767, L 67 M.

15. Nicholas Brown & Co. to Hugh Pringle, September 15, 1767, L 67 M.

16. Nicholas Brown & Co. to Hugh Pringle, May 6, 1768, L 68-69 M.

17. Nathan Hyde to Nicholas Brown & Co., 1768, L 68-69 M. See also account current of Nicholas Brown & Co. with Robert and Nathan Hyde, July 24, 1768, L 68-69 M.

18. Nicholas Brown & Co. to Robert and Nathan Hyde, May 6, 1768, L 68-69 M.

19. Nicholas Brown & Co. to Welch, Wilkinson & Startin, May 6, 1768, L 68-69 M.

20. In spite of the brevity of their direct business relations with the Hydes of Manchester and with Welch, Wilkinson & Startin at Birmingham, the Browns evidently held the two houses in high esteem. In 1770 they asked Hayley & Hopkins to purchase goods from these two houses on their account, a request which met with ready compliance. See Hayley & Hopkins to Nicholas Brown & Co., January 10, 1771, L 70-75 HH.

21. Williams & Bellamy to Nicholas Brown & Co., February 1 and September 24, 1770, L 70 M; Nicholas Brown & Co. to Williams & Bellamy, November 24, 1770, L 70 M.

22. George Hayley to Nicholas Brown & Co., July 23, 1768, L 68-69 M. See also account of the sales, June 30, 1768, L 68-72 HH.

23. See Account Current of the two houses, December 31, 1771, L 70-75 HH.

24. Hayley & Hopkins to Nicholas Brown & Co., May 13 and June 24, 1769, L 68-72 HH.

25. Hayley & Hopkins to Nicholas Brown & Co., July 30, 1771, L 70-75 HH.

26. Hayley & Hopkins to Nicholas Brown & Co., August 21, 1770, L 68-72 HH.

27. Hayley & Hopkins to Nicholas Brown & Co., September 22, 1770, L 68-72 HH.

28. Hayley & Hopkins to Nicholas Brown & Co., October 8, 1770, L 68-72 HH.

29. Hayley & Hopkins to Nicholas Brown & Co., October 20, 1770, L 68-72 HH.

30. Hayley & Hopkins to Nicholas Brown & Co., January 24, 1771, L 70-75 HH.

31. Hayley & Hopkins to Nicholas Brown & Co., July 30, 1771, L 70-75 HH.

32. Hayley & Hopkins to Nicholas Brown & Co., May 16 and August 26, 1772, L 70-75 HH; and August 11, 1774, L 70-75 HH.

33. Baxter, *The House of Hancock,* p. 252.

34. Ibid., p. 285.

35. Hayley & Hopkins to Nicholas Brown & Co., August 29, 1771, L 70-75 HH.

36. Hayley & Hopkins to Nicholas Brown & Co., February 22, 1770, L 68-72 HH.

37. Hayley & Hopkins to Nicholas Brown & Co., August 21, 1770, L 68-72 HH.

38. Hayley & Hopkins to Nicholas Brown & Co., August 29, 1771, L 70-75 HH.

39. Hayley & Hopkins to Nicholas Brown & Co., May 10, 1775, L 70-75 HH.

40. Nicholas Brown to George Hayley, March 19, 1776, P H2.

41. Baxter, *op. cit.,* p. 285.

42. Christopher Starbuck & Co. to Nicholas Brown & Co., November 13, 1767, P-S7.

43. Christopher Starbuck & Co. to Nicholas Brown & Co., November 20, 1771, P-S7.

44. Nicholas Brown & Co. to Christopher Starbuck & Co., April 6, 1772, P-S7.

45. Nicholas Brown & Co. to Samuel Starbuck & Co., April 6, 1772, P S7.

46. Joseph Nichols (for Samuel Starbuck & Co.) to Nicholas Brown & Co., April 26, 1773, L 72-73 Nantucket.

47. Christopher Starbuck & Co. to Nicholas Brown & Co., August 25, 1774, P-S7.

48. Nicholas Brown & Co. to Nathanael Greene, June 15, 1771, Miscellaneous Letters, 1771.

49. Nicholas Brown & Co. to Jonathan Wheeler, November 9, 1771, Miscellaneous Letters, 1771.

50. Nicholas Brown & Co. to John Read, November 5, 1771, Miscellaneous Letters, 1771.

51. Nicholas Brown & Co. to Seth Read, November 5, 1771, Miscellaneous Letters, 1771.

52. Nicholas Brown & Co. to Capt. John Childs, November 16, 1771, Miscellaneous Letters, 1771.

53. Agreement between Nicholas Brown & Co. and John Waterman, January 21, 1772, Miscellaneous Letters, 1772.

54. Nicholas Brown & Co. to Elihu Williams, April 28, 1773, Miscellaneous Letters, 1773.

55. Agreement between Nicholas Brown and Col. Joab Stafford, October 27, 1774, Miscellaneous Letters, 1774.

56. Nicholas Brown & Co. to Solomon Owens, November 9, 1771, Miscellaneous Letters, 1771.

57. Jonathan Hale to Nicholas Brown &

Co., July 3, 1771, Miscellaneous Letters, 1771.

58. Nicholas Brown & Co. to Benjamin West, December 9, 1771, Miscellaneous Letters, 1771.

59. John Hancock and "his satellites" received goods from England in 1767-68 to the value of £8250 Sterling. Baxter, *op. cit.*, pp. 251-252.

CHAPTER 9. "GENTLEMEN OF PUBLICK RESPONSIBILITY"

1. William Warner (Johnston, R. I.) to Nicholas Brown, February 23, 1767, P P6.

2. For a copy of the "Address," which is undated, see P P6.

3. "List of subscriptions to the political campaign in Rhode Island," L & P 58-70 RIP.

4. *Ibid.*

5. Nicholas and John Brown's bill for campaign of 1765, L & P 58-70 RIP.

6. John Dexter (Cumberland) to Stephen Hopkins, April 17, 1766, L & P 58-70 RIP.

7. Nicholas Brown and Company to Joseph Holway, April 15, 1766, P P6.

8. Nicholas Brown & Co. to Thomas Aldrich, April 10, 1767, L & P 58-70 RIP.

9. Nicholas Brown & Co. to Beriah Brown, April 10, 1767, P P6.

10. Nicholas Brown & Co. to Richard Greene, April 10, 1767, P P6.

11. Nicholas Brown & Co. to Gideon Tripp, April 9, 1767, P P6.

12. John Brown to Joseph Winsor, April 8, 1765, L & P 58-70, RIP.

13. See copy of their plan, bearing date of March 12, 1767, in P P6.

14. William R. Staples, *Annals of the Town of Providence* (Providence, 1843), p. 492.

15. *Ibid.*

16. "Copy of John Brown's address to the freemen of Providence," December 2, 1767, P P6.

17. Staples, *op. cit.*, p. 496.

18. *Ibid.*

19. *Ibid.*, p. 500, quoting Moses Brown.

20. Walter C. Bronson, *The History of Brown University* (Providence, 1914), p. 8.

21. *Ibid.*, p. 9.

22. *Ibid.*

23. *Ibid.*, p. 14.

24. *Ibid.*

25. *Ibid.*, pp. 35-36.

26. *Ibid.*, p. 36.

27. *Ibid.*, pp. 43-44.

28. *Ibid.*, p. 44.

29. *Ibid.*, p. 45.

30. The part played by the Brown family in bringing the college to Providence is discussed in an article by William Greene Roelker, "The Browns and Brown University," *Brown Alumni Monthly*, vol. XLIX, No. 4 (December 1948), pp. 3-7. Bronson, *op. cit.*, p. 45. The draft of the Memorial is in Moses Brown Papers, Box 2, Brown University Papers, RIHS.

31. Bronson, *op. cit.*, pp. 45-46.

32. The Reverend Mr. Morgan Edwards, quoted in Roelker, "The Browns and Brown University," *loc. cit.*, p. 5.

33. Committee for erecting the College Edifice to residents of Glocester and Scituate, December 8, 1769, in John Carter Brown Library, Loose Papers. Also quoted in Roelker, "The Browns and Brown University," *loc. cit.*, pp. 5-6.

34. Bronson, *op. cit.*, p. 46.

35. *Ibid.*

36. Quoted in Roelker, "The Browns and Brown University," *loc. cit.*, p. 6. This letter is in Moses Brown Papers, Box 2, Brown University Papers, RIHS.

37. These calculations in John Brown's handwriting are in Moses Brown Papers, Box 2, Brown University Papers, RIHS. Also see Roelker, "The Browns and Brown University," *loc. cit.*, p. 6.

38. This document is dated Warren, February 7, 1770, Moses Brown Papers, Box 2, Brown University Papers, RIHS. Also see Bronson, *op. cit.*, p. 48. Roelker, "The Browns and Brown University," *loc. cit.* p. 6.

39. Nicholas, Joseph, and John each subscribed £200. Moses gave £160. See "Subscriptions for the College to be Built in the Town of Providence," Brown University Manuscripts, John Carter Brown Library.

40. William G. Roelker, in "The Browns and Brown University," *loc. cit.*, p. 6, after a careful examination of the evidence, says "it was the force and strategy of the Brown family, led by brother Moses" which brought the college to Providence.

41. Bronson, *op. cit.*, p. 55.

42. This memorial is in Brown University Manuscripts, in the John Carter Brown Li-

brary. It is printed in *Brown Alumni Monthly*, vol. XLIX, No. 4 (December 1948), p. 8.

43. Joseph Brown, an amateur architect, was a member of the committee "to draught instructions and prepare a model of the house." He was also one of three men whose "passage" to Cambridge the college paid for in order that they might "view the colleges" there. See J. Walter Wilson, "Joseph Brown, Scientist and Architect," *Rhode Island History*, IV, 67-79, and 121-128.

44. Bronson, *op. cit.*, p. 56.

45. *Rhode Island Colonial Records*, VII, 248-249.

46. J. Walter Wilson, "Joseph Brown, Scientist and Architect," *loc. cit.*, p. 71.

47. *Ibid.*

48. *Rhode Island Colonial Records*, VII, 36.

49. *Ibid.*

50. William R. Staples, *Annals of the Town of Providence* (1843), p. 202.

51. For a good account of these interests and activities of Joseph Brown, see J. Walter Wilson, "Joseph Brown, Scientist and Architect," *loc. cit.*

CHAPTER 10. "AMERICAN GRIEVANCES"

1. This discussion of the Sugar Act is based largely upon the excellent article by Frederick B. Wiener, "The Rhode Island Merchants and the Sugar Act," *New England Quarterly*, III, 464-500.

2. Tench Francis to Nicholas Brown & Co., September 16, 1763, L 63-64 FR.

3. Elisha Brown to Nicholas Brown & Co., October 28, 1763, L 55-76 M¹.

4. See Chapter 2, *supra*.

5. Nicholas Brown & Co. to David Van Horne, January 24, 1764, OL 63-74.

6. Tench Francis to Nicholas Brown & Co., October 25, 1764, L 57-67 FR. He wrote, "I gave the Resolve you sent me to one of our Committee, who has promised to let me have a Copy of what they have been doing, which I will transmit to you." Tench Francis to Nicholas Brown & Co., November 11, 1764, L 63-65 FR. "Our Committee have sent yours an Acct of their Proceedings." Also Nicholas Brown to Joseph, John, and Moses Brown, September 12, 1764, *Moses Brown Papers*, I, 60, in Rhode Island Historical Society. In this letter Nicholas refers to correspondence with a committee in Boston.

7. William R. Staples, *Annals of the Town of Providence*, pp. 210-214.

8. Nicholas Brown & Co. to John Relfe, August 3, 1765, P F7, vol. 2.

9. Nicholas Brown & Co. to Capt. George Hopkins (at Surinam), September 8, 1765, L 61-64 M. The boycott of British goods at the time of the Stamp Act brought no such decline in imports into New England as in New York, Pennsylvania, and the tobacco colonies. In 1764 imports into New England from England amounted to £451,299

Sterling; for 1765 the figure was £409,642 Sterling. See David Macpherson, *Annals of Commerce* (London, 1805), III, 410 and 435.

10. Arthur M. Schlesinger, *The Colonial Merchants and the American Revolution, 1763-1776* (New York, 1918), p. 107.

11. *Ibid.*, p. 110.

12. The report of the Committee which drafted the agreement was in the handwriting of Moses Brown. William R. Staples, *Annals of the Town of Providence*, p. 217. Also Schlesinger, *op. cit.*, p. 111.

13. Schlesinger, *op. cit.*, p. 112.

14. *Ibid.*, p. 113.

15. *Ibid.*, p. 114.

16. *Ibid.*

17. *Ibid.*, p. 131.

18. *Ibid.*, p. 149.

19. *Ibid.*, p. 152.

20. *Ibid.*, p. 152, note.

21. William R. Staples, *Annals of the Town of Providence*, pp. 223-224. Schlesinger, *op. cit.*, p. 153.

22. See the resolve in Staples, *op. cit.*, p. 224.

23. Schlesinger, *op. cit.*, p. 154.

24. *Ibid.* A copy of the letter from the Philadelphia Merchants' Committee under date of November 17, 1769 is in the Brown Papers, P P6.

25. Schlesinger, *op. cit.*, pp. 154-155.

26. *Ibid.*, pp. 214-215.

27. *Ibid.*, pp. 215-216.

28. For the ultimate breakdown of non-importation see Schlesinger, *op. cit.*, pp. 217-236.

29. Van Horne's letter has not been found but its purport may be inferred from the reply to it. See Nicholas Brown & Co. to David Van Horne, November 29, 1769, OL 59-03 M.

30. Ibid.

31. Ibid.

32. David Von Horne to Nicholas Brown & Co., June 18, 1770, L 57-74 M, vol. II.

33. Nicholas Brown & Co. to David Van Horne, July 3, 1770, OL 59-03 M.

34. Nicholas Brown & Co. to David Van Horne, August 8, 1770, OL 59-03 M.

35. See Hayley & Hopkins to Nicholas Brown & Co., March 8, 1770, enclosing the invoice.

36. Schlesinger, *op. cit.,* p. 240.

37. Ibid., p. 244.

38. Ibid., p. 249.

39. Rhode Island Colonial Records, VII, 59-60.

40. Ibid., p. 60.

41. Ibid.

42. Ibid., pp. 61-62.

43. Ibid., pp. 62-63.

44. Ibid., p. 64.

45. For two accounts of the burning of *Gaspee* by men who participated in the affair, *ibid.,* pp. 68-76.

46. Extract of a Letter from Lord Dartmouth to the Governor of Rhode Island, September 4, 1772, *ibid.,* pp. 103-104. For documents pertaining to the investigation by the Commission, *ibid.,* pp. 107-189.

47. John C. Miller, *Origins of the American Revolution* (Boston, 1943), p. 329.

48. Ibid. Also *Rhode Island Colonial Records,* VII, 189-190, for the request to the Rhode Island Assembly.

49. Ibid., pp. 272-274.

50. William R. Staples, *Annals of the Town of Providence,* p. 242.

51. The only careful and connected account of the seizure of John Brown and the circumstances attending his release is William Greene Roelker, "The Patrol of Narragansett Bay (1774-76)," *Rhode Island History,* VIII, 45-63. The discussion here given is based chiefly on Mr. Roelker's article.

52. For Elkanah Watson's account of this attempt to rescue John Brown, see Winslow C. Watson (ed.), *Men and Times of the Revolution; or Memoirs of Elkanah Watson* (New York, 1856), pp. 21-23.

53. Joseph Brown (at Dedham, Massachusetts), to Nicholas Brown, May 1, 1775. Uncalendared Brown Papers in the John Carter Brown Library.

54. The letter is in *Moses Brown Papers,* Miscellaneous, I, 26 in RIHS. It was signed by Nicholas and Joseph Brown, William Smith, Job Smith, Elisha Brown, Ephraim Bowen, and Daniel Tillinghast.

55. The letter is quoted in Roelker, "The Patrol of Narrangansett Bay," *loc. cit.,* p. 48. The original is in the Gage Papers in the Clements Library.

56. Ibid., p. 50.

57. Ibid.

58. Ibid. Roelker quotes the letter in part.

59. Ibid. Roelker quotes the letter.

60. Moses Brown to Nicholas Brown, May 3, 1775, P B7. Also quoted by Roelker.

61. Quoted in Roelker, "The Patrol of Narragansett Bay," *loc. cit.,* p. 52.

62. Ibid. Roelker quotes from an abstract of John Brown's address to the Assembly which exists in transcripts of the British Admiralty records in the Library of Congress. A copy of the address has recently been discovered in the State Archives of Rhode Island.

63. Ibid.

64. John Brown to Moses Brown, June 7, 1775, *Moses Brown Papers,* II, 34, RIHS. Quoted in Roelker, note, p. 61.

65. Moses Brown to John Brown, June 16, 1775, *Moses Brown Papers,* II, 35, RIHS. Quoted in full in Roelker, pp. 54-56.

66. John Brown to Moses Brown, June 21, 1775, *Moses Brown Papers,* II, 36, quoted in Roelker, note, pp. 61-63.

67. Nicholas Brown to Henry Lloyd, June 2, 1775, OL 71-75 HL.

68. Nicholas Brown to Sharp, Curtenius & Co., July 10, 1775, OL 75-76 M.

CHAPTER 11. "WARLIKE STORES FOR THE CONTINENTAL CONGRESS"

1. O. W. Stephenson, "The Supply of Gunpowder in 1776," *American Historical Review,* XXX, 272-274.

2. Ibid., p. 275.

3. Ibid., p. 276.

4. Ibid., p. 277.

5. For French aid before the Alliance, see C. H. Van Tyne, "French Aid before the Alliance of 1778," *American Historical Review,* XXXI, 20-40. Also E. S. Kite,

Beaumarchais and the War of American Independence (2 vols., Boston, 1918); R. G. Albion, *Sea Lanes in War Time* (New York, 1942), chap. ii; and Robert A. East, *Business Enterprise in the American Revolutionary Era* (New York, 1938).

6. Albion, *op. cit.*, p. 46.

7. *Ibid.*

8. *Ibid.*, p. 51.

9. *Ibid.*, p. 52.

10. *Ibid.*, p. 54. On the trade of St. Eustatius generally during the war, see J. F. Jameson, "St. Eustatius in the American Revolution," *American Historical Review*, XIII, 683-708.

11. Albion, *op. cit.*, p. 57.

12. *Ibid.*

13. Peter Force, *American Archives* (in six series, III, Washington, 1837-1853), Fourth Series, 1688.

14. *Ibid.*

15. Elkanah Watson, *Men and Times of the Revolution; or, Memoirs of Elkanah Watson*, p. 20.

16. *Ibid.*

17. For details of this voyage, see Nicholas Brown to Charles Jouett, November 15, 1775; also undated, unaddressed letter, but evidently written by Nicholas to Jouett at about the time of the one mentioned above. Both are in L 75-77 C & F. Also "Memorandum of all the persons in the Douville & Clark voyage to France, May, 1776," in L 70-82 C & Rev. Also "List of money sent by Nicholas Brown in the concern for a powder voyage, Nov. 14, 1775" and "Letter of Credit of N. B. to Dou Veille and Clark, Nov. 15, 1775," both in L 75-77 C & F.

18. See "Memorandum of all persons concerned in Dueval Voyage to France taken coming Home May 1776" in L 70-82 C & Rev. See also Nicholas Brown to Plombard et Legris & Co, June 6, 1776 and Nicholas Brown to Tardieu & Bennet, June 6, 1776, both in L 75-77 C & F, in which he describes the capture of *Amiable Maria*. The conclusion that the Sloop *Liberty* became the Sloop *Amiable Maria* rests upon the following considerations: (a) Dou Veille and Clark were instructed to obtain "proper papers" for two or more vessels, which undoubtedly meant French papers; (b) Nothing more is heard of *Liberty;* (c) Although Dou Veille and Clark could conceivably have sold her and purchased *Amiable Maria* in France, this is improbable since they had no such

instructions; (d) Since only about six months elapsed between the sailing of *Liberty* on November 16, 1775 and the capture of *Amiable Maria* in May 1776, Dou Veille and Clark are not likely to have made a complete voyage in *Liberty* plus another voyage in *Amiable Maria* from Providence to Nantes and return. Furthermore, there is no evidence that *Amiable Maria* ever sailed from Providence.

19. Nicholas Brown to Edmond Jennings, February 2, 1776, V 75-76 S U.

20. Capt. Benjamin Comstock's account current for the Sloop *Polly* to St. Eustatius, 1776, V 76 S P. Captain Comstock carried Nicholas Brown's letter to Jennings.

21. Nicholas Brown to Stephen Hopkins and Samuel Ward (at Philadelphia), November 21 and December 18, 1775, L 75-77 C & F.

22. *Ibid.*

23. *Ibid.*

24. Nicholas Brown to John Brown (at Philadelphia), December 11, 1775, L 75-77 C & F.

25. Josiah Hewes (Philadelphia) to Nicholas Brown, December 23, 1775; also Joseph Anthony (Philadelphia) to Nicholas Brown, December 15, 1775, in L 75-77 C & F. Also Josiah Hewes to Nicholas Brown, December 9, 11, 16, and 27, 1775, L 75-87 J H. Undoubtedly the bulk of the candles which the Browns shipped to Philadelphia in prewar days were reëxported, largely to the West Indies.

26. Josiah Hewes to Nicholas Brown, December 23, 1775, L 75-77 C & F.

27. V 75-76 S U.

28. Governor Nicholas Cooke to Governor of Martinique, December 20, 1775, L 70-82 C & Rev.

29. Bill of Lading, December 30, 1775, V 75-76 S U.

30. Copy of Letter of Credit given Capt. Paul Allen, December 30, 1775, V 75-76 S U.

31. Copy of the Conditions of the Bond given in the Secretary's Office, December 29, 1775 by Nicholas Brown and Paul Allen, V 75-76 S U.

32. Certificate of Credit from Governor Cooke, December 31, 1775, V 75-76 S U.

33. Orders and instructions of Nicholas Brown to Capt. Paul Allen, December 31, 1775, V 75-76 S U. Also Nicholas Brown to Capt. Paul Allen, January 12, 1776, V 75-76 S U.

34. Capt. Paul Allen to Nicholas Brown, January 26, 1776, V 75-76 S U.

35. Capt. Paul Allen to Nicholas Brown, January 26, 1776, V 75-76 S U.

36. "Manifest of the War ammunition, arms, duck, etc. imported in the Sloop *Unity,* March 1776." Also invoice of sundry merchandise imported in the Sloop *Unity,* both in V 75-76 S U.

37. Memorandum of the value of the powder and arms imported in the Sloop *Unity,* April 1776, V 75-76 S U.

38. Robert A. East, *Business Enterprise in the American Revolutionary Era,* pp. 130-131.

39. Copy of John Brown's Contract with the Secret Committee of Congress, January 1776, L 70-82 C & Rev.

40. Contract of Nicholas and John Brown with the Secret Committee of Congress, February 6, 1776, L 70-82 C & Rev.

41. "Agreement between Benjamin and Joseph Comstock on the one hand and Nicholas and John Brown on the other hand, who in this matter act for the Continental Congress in pursuance of contract entered into with the Secret Committee of Congress," February 1, 1776, V 76 S P.

42. Invoice of cargo of the Sloop *Polly,* February 2, 1776, V 76 SP.

43. Orders of Nicholas and John Brown to Capt. Benjamin Comstock, January 31, 1776, V 76 SP.

44. Copy of letter of John Brown to the Committee of Secrecy, March 20, 1776, L 70-82 C & Rev. Also Account Current of Captain Comstock, V 76 SP. *Polly* also brought 1 pair of swivel guns, 12 small arms, 12 barrels of powder, and 30 barrels of cannon balls.

45. Robert Morris to Nicholas and John Brown, April 3, 1776, L 70-82 C & Rev.

46. For the visit of the two French gentlemen see Nicholas Brown to John Brown (at Philadelphia), December 11, 1775, L 75-77 C & F. Also Governor Nicholas Cooke of Rhode Island to General Washington, December 14, 1775; Governor Cooke to the President of the Congress, December 18, 1775, all in Peter Force, Fourth Series, IV, 235, 261, 264, and 310.

47. Nicholas Brown to Stephen Hopkins and Samuel Ward, December 18, 1775, L 75-77 C & F.

48. Pliarne and Penet (at Philadelphia) to Nicholas Brown, December 31, 1775, L 75-77 C & F.

49. See the long letter by Silas Deane (Paris) to the Committee of Secret Correspondence, August 18, 1776 in Peter Force, *op. cit.,* Fifth Series, I, 1011.

50. Pliarne, Penet & Co. (Philadelphia) to Nicholas Brown, February 8, 1776, L 70-82 C & Rev.

51. See letter of Pliarne, Penet & Co. to the New York Convention, October 21, 1776, in Peter Force, *op. cit.,* Fifth Series, II, 1146-1147. This arrangement explains the presence in the Brown papers of letters from J. Gruel to Nicholas and John Brown, along with those from Pliarne, Penet & Co.

52. Martin Gaston, "Commercial Relations between Nantes and the American Colonies during the War of Independence," *Journal of Economic and Business History,* IV, 812-829.

53. Nicholas Brown to Thomas Boylston, March 22, 1776, L 70-82 C & Rev.

54. For the orders see V W55.

55. "Extract from the Books of the late Secret Committee lodged in U. S. Treasury Office," February 10, 1787, in L & P 76-89 Cadet. This lists the cargoes of all vessels sent out by Nicholas and John Brown under their contracts with the Secret Committee.

56. Bill of Lading of the Brigantine *Happy Return,* April 24, 1776, V 76 BHR. See also orders to Capt. Gideon Crawford, the Brigantine *Happy Return,* April 24, 1776, V 76 BHR.

57. See copy of letter of Nicholas Brown to Pliarne, Penet & Co. (Nantes), May 23, 1776, covering copy of letter by Nicholas to the same house, April 23, 1776, V 76 S. It was the letter of April 23, 1776 that Captain Crawford carried.

58. "Charter Party for hire of the Schooner *Sally,* signed by Aaron Lopez and Francis Rotch (owners) and by Nicholas and John Brown, in pursuance of contract with Committee of Secrecy," May 6, 1776, V 76 S.

59. Invoice of Sundry Merchandise shipped by Nicholas and John Brown on board the Schooner *Sally,* on the account and risk of the Continental Congress, May 23, 1776, V 76 S.

60. Instructions of Nicholas and John Brown to Captain Samuel Avery, Schooner *Sally,* May 23, 1776, V 76 S.

61. Nicholas Brown to Pliarne, Penet & Co., May 23, 1776, V 76 S.

62. J. Lafitte (Bordeaux) to Nicholas

and John Brown, September 4 and October 30, 1776 and January 13, 1777, L & P 76-89 Cadet.

63. J. Lafitte to Nicholas and John Brown, February 15, May 2, and September 4, 1777, L & P 76-89 Cadet.

64. Ibid.

65. J. Lafitte to Nicholas and John Brown, September 4, 1777, L & P 76-89 Cadet.

66. On the subject of the sale of the two cargoes sent to Nantes, see Pliarne, Penet & Co. to Nicholas and John Brown, August 3, 1776, V 76 BHR; Pliarne, Penet & Co. to Nicholas and John Brown, August 19 and September 28, 1776, V 76 S; J. Gruel to Nicholas and John Brown, August 3 and 22, and September 28, 1776, V 76 S. Also Pliarne, Penet & Co. to Nicholas and John Brown, September 20, November 9 and 30, December 3 and 7, 1776, and February 1, 1777, in L 76-77 PP & Co. Also J. Gruel to Nicholas and John Brown, January 25, 1777, L 76-77 PP & Co.

67. On this subject see Pliarne, Penet & Co. to Nicholas and John Brown, September 28, 1776, V 76 S and J. Gruel to Nicholas and John Brown, September 28, 1776, in V 76 S. Also Nicholas and John Brown's account Current with J. Gruel & Co., September 1778, L & A '78 PD & Co.

68. Nicholas Brown to Pliarne, Penet & Co., November 5, 1776, L 76-77 C & F.

69. Pliarne, Penet & Co. to Nicholas and John Brown, August 3, 1776, V 76 BHR.

70. Account of sales of the cargo of the Schooner *William* and invoice of goods shipped to Nicholas and John Brown by J. Lafitte, September 1776, L & P 76-89 Cadet.

71. Invoice of merchandise brought from Nantes in the Brigantine *Happy Return,* 1776, V 76 BHR.

72. Invoice of return cargo of *Sally,* September 1776, V 76 S.

73. Nicholas Brown to Robert Morris, October 13, 1776, L 70-82 C & Rev.

74. "Extract from the Books of the late

Secret Committee lodged in the U. S. Treasury Office," February 10, 1787, L & P 76-89 Cadet.

75. Account of sales of cargo of the Schooner *William,* and invoice of goods shipped to the Browns by John Lafitte, September 1776, L & P 76-89 Cadet.

76. Account of sales and net proceeds of sundry merchandise received by the Brigantine *Happy Return,* Capt. Gideon Crawford, 1776 V 76 BHR.

77. Nicholas and John Brown to J. Lafitte, June 10, 1777, V 77 B L O.

78. For this whole affair see J. Lafitte to Nicholas and John Brown, June 22, 1781, February 28, May 25, and September 4, 1782. Nicholas and John Brown to J. Lafitte, April 8, and November 20, 1782. Copy of Bill of Exchange drawn by Lafitte on Nicholas and John Brown, June 22, 1781. Copy of statement by Nicholas and John Brown before a Notary in regard to bill drawn by Lafitte on them, March 1, 1782. Also "Extract from the books of the late Secret Committee lodged in the U. S. Treasury Office," February 10, 1787. "Copy of a certificate given under an extract from a letter from Robert Morris concerning Captain Bunker (Schooner *William*), made out and given to J. Lafitte *Cadet,*" March 7, 1788. All of the above documents are in L & P 76-89 Cadet.

79. "Rough Draft of a letter designed to be sent to the Treasury Board of the United States," April 13, 1788, L & P 76-89 Cadet.

80. Secret Committee of Congress to Nicholas and John Brown, October 13, 1776, L 70-82 C & Rev.

81. Thomas Mifflin to Nicholas and John Brown, October 18, 1776, L 70-82 C & Rev.

82. Account of cloth and buttons delivered to the various persons to be made up for the Continent, December 2, 1776, L 70-82 C & Rev.

CHAPTER 12. "BILLS ON FRANCE"

1. Account of sales of 486 casks of sperm and whale oil sold at Nantes, April 2, 1777, V 76-77 M.

2. Invoice of sundries from Nantes for the account of Nicholas and John Brown, 1777; and Invoice of sundries in *Chester* for

account of Nicholas and John Brown, April 26, 1777. Both in V 76-77 M.

3. S. & J. Delop to Christopher Starbuck, January 23, 1777, L 75-77 C & F.

4. Christopher Starbuck to Nicholas Brown, March 5 and 6, 1777, L 75-79 CS.

5. Christopher Starbuck to Nicholas Brown, March 6, 1777, L 75-79 CS.

6. Christopher Starbuck to Nicholas Brown, March 5, 1777, L 75-79 CS.

7. Christopher Starbuck to Nicholas Brown, March 6, 1777, L 75-79 CS.

8. Christopher Starbuck to Nicholas Brown, April 8, 1777, L 75-79 CS.

9. Christopher Starbuck to Nicholas Brown, April 14, 1777, L 75-79 CS.

10. Christopher Starbuck to Nicholas Brown, April 22 and 28, 1777, L 75-79 CS.

11. See various letters by Christopher Starbuck to Nicholas Brown, April to December 1777, L 75-79 CS.

12. Christopher Starbuck in account with Nicholas Brown, July 27, 1777, L 75-79 CS.

13. Christopher Starbuck to Nicholas Brown, April 22, 1777, L 75-79 CS.

14. Christopher Starbuck to Nicholas Brown, May 19, 1777, L 75-79 CS.

15. Nicholas and John Brown to Capt. Abraham Pease, February 28, 1777, V Misc., vol. IV.

16. Instructions of Nicholas and John Brown to Capt. Andrew Worth, June 10, 1777, V 77 BLO.

17. Nicholas and John Brown to Nathaniel Russell (Charleston, S. C.), June 9, 1777, V 77 BLO.

18. Ibid.

19. Nathaniel Russell to Nicholas and John Brown, July 10, 1777, L 76-77 Cong. & France.

20. Nathaniel Russell to Nicholas and John Brown, July 11, 1777, L 76-77 Cong. & France.

21. Nathaniel Russell to Nicholas and John Brown, July 26, 1777, V Misc., vol. IV. Because of the prohibitive premium, *Live Oak* was not insured.

22. Nicholas and John Brown to Pliarne, Penet & Co., June 10, 1777, V 77 BLO.

23. Elkanah Watson, *Men and Times of the Revolution; or Memoirs of Elkanah Watson,* p. 44.

24. Ibid., p. 25.

25. Nicholas and John Brown to Elkanah Watson, August 31, 1777. Watson's receipt for the money is at the bottom of the sheet, P-W25. See also Nicholas and John Brown to Nathaniel Russell, August 31, 1777, V 77 BLO. In his *Men and Times of the Revolution* Watson says the total amount of money was "about $50,000," which seems to be an excessive figure. According to an entry in Nicholas' "Pocket Memorandum Book," un-

der date of September 3, 1779, he entrusted Watson with two continental notes for 500 dollars each, to be delivered to Pliarne & Compagnie at Alexandria, Virginia (a branch of Pliarne, Penet & Compagnie in Nantes); an order on Josiah Hewes of Philadelphia for 1100 dollars and an order on Wiley & Seixas for "my money in their hands." Unless the latter held some 21,000 dollars belonging to Nicholas (which seems unlikely) the amount named by Watson is inaccurate.

26. Nicholas and John Brown to Elkanah Watson, August 31, 1777, P W25. Also Nicholas and John Brown to Nathaniel Russell, August 31, 1777, V 77 BLO.

27. Elkanah Watson, *op. cit.,* pp. 27 and 44.

28. Ibid., p. 75.

29. Ibid.

30. See *The Letters of Benjamin Franklin and Jane Mecom,* Edited with an Introduction by Carl Van Doren (Princeton, 1950), pp. 192 and 198, for Jane Mecom's letter to Franklin and for his reply. Also Nicholas Brown to Elkanah Watson, June 23, 1779, OL 79-86 EW. "Your commission is to be the same as you have for doing Brother John's Business."

31. Elkanah Watson, *op. cit.,* pp. 86, 88, 92.

32. Dictionary of American Biography, XIX, 541.

33. Elkanah Watson (Nantes) to Nicholas Brown, May 2, 1780, L 79-86 EW.

34. Nicholas Brown to Elkanah Watson, June 23, 1779, OL 79-86 EW.

35. Ibid.

36. Nicholas Brown to Elkanah Watson, June 25, 1779, OL 79-86 EW.

37. Ibid.

38. For a sketch of Jonathan Williams' life see *Dictionary of American Biography,* XX, 280-282.

39. Jonathan Williams (Nantes) to Nicholas Brown, February 21, 1780, L 79-86 EW.

40. See the letter, L 79-86 EW.

41. Penet, d'Acosta & Co. to Nicholas Brown, September 1778, L & A 78 PD & Co.

42. Nicholas Brown to Williams & Watson, June 27, 1781, OL 79-86 EW.

43. Jonathan Williams to Nicholas Brown, October 20, 1781, L 79-86 EW.

44. Ibid.

45. Agreement between Captain John Earl and owners of the Brig *Dolphin* on the one hand and Nicholas Brown for himself and the owners of the Schooner *Betsey* on the

other, whereby Captain Earl is to take on
board at Cap François sugar and coffee for
Nantes, June 5, 1781, L 79-86 EW. Also
Nicholas Brown to Mr. Brasher, June 5,
1781, and Nicholas Brown to Williams &
Watson, June 5 and 27, 1781, all in OL 79-
86 EW.

46. Elkanah Watson to Nicholas Brown,
June 23, 1779, L 79-86 EW. He lists the
bills in his receipt for them.

47. Account current of Nicholas Brown
with Elkanah Watson, March 11, 1786, OL
79-86 EW.

48. Ibid.

49. Memorandum of an order sent to
Williams & Watson, June 27, 1781, OL 79-
86 EW.

50. On the insurance controversy see
Nicholas Brown to Elkanah Watson, June
25, 1779 and Nicholas Brown to Williams
& Watson, January 4, 1781, both in OL 79-
86 EW. Also Elkanah Watson to Nicholas
Brown, October 1779 and November 20,
December 12, 14, and 20, 1780, all in L
79-86 EW.

51. Nicholas Brown to Elkanah Watson,
January 4, 1781, OL 79-86 EW.

52. Elkanah Watson to Nicholas Brown,
February 10, 1781, L 79-86 EW.

53. Nicholas Brown to Williams & Watson, October 9, 1781, OL 79-86 EW.

54. Ibid.

55. Jonathan Williams to Nicholas Brown,
January 6, 1782, L 79-86 EW.

56. Elkanah Watson to Nicholas Brown,
January 13, 1782, L 79-86 EW.

57. Watson & Cassoul to Nicholas Brown,
July 10, 1782, L 79-86 EW.

58. Ibid. Nicholas penned this notation
on the back of the letter from Watson &
Cassoul.

59. Elkanah Watson to Nicholas Brown,
March 1, 1786, L 79-86 EW.

60. John Turner & Son to Nicholas Brown
& Co., September 28, 1773, L 73-81 J & N.

61. See p. 220, *supra.*

62. Nicholas Brown to John Turner &
Son, May 11, 1776, OL 76-79 M.

63. Nicholas Brown to John Turner &
Son, June 13, October 21, and December 25,
1778; and Nicholas Brown to Captain Hatha-
way, December 19, 1778, all in OL 76-79 M.
Also Nicholas Brown to John de Neufville

& Son, December 25, 1778 and April 20,
1779; and Nicholas Brown to Capt. Joseph
Cook, April 20, 1779, all in OL 76-79 M.

64. Invoice of sundry goods shipped on
board the Sloop *Independence* by John de
Neufville & Son on account of Nicholas
Brown, June 30, 1779, L 73-81 J & N.

65. Invoice of sundries shipped on board
the Sloop *Diamond* from Amsterdam, July
16, 1779, L 73-81 J & N.

66. "Account of Cannon sold from Furnace Hope since the last Division among the
Owners," April 13, 1780, V C7.

67. Orders to Capt. John Updike, Master
of the Sloop *Crawford,* for a voyage to
Virginia and Amsterdam, April 18, 1780,
V C7.

68. Invoice of goods purchased by De la
Lande & Fynje and shipped on board the
Sloop *Crawford,* for the "account & risque"
of Nicholas Brown, September 28, 1780,
V C7.

69. Nicholas Brown to De la Lande &
Fynje, December 30, 1780, Miscellaneous
Letters, 1777-1780.

70. See papers of *Crawford,* V C7. Also
John Brown to Nicholas and Joseph Brown,
November 15, 1781, L 73-81 J & N.

71. Nicholas Brown to Williams & Watson, June 20, 1781, OL 79-86 EW.

72. David Dickson & Co. (Gothenburg)
to Nicholas Brown, October 12, 1781. This
letter is found with the Watson correspondence, L 79-86 EW.

73. Nicholas Brown to Henry Grieg, June
8, 1780, Miscellaneous Letters, 1777-1780.

74. Nicholas Brown to John Turner &
Son, May 11, 1776, OL 76-79 M.

75. Nicholas Brown to John de Neufville
& Son, April 20, 1779, OL 76-79 M.

76. See the letter, December 30, 1780,
Miscellaneous Letters, 1777-1780.

77. Nicholas Brown to Williams & Watson, January 4, 1781, OL 79-86 EW.

78. George Benson (Boston) to Nicholas
Brown, August 8, 1781, L 80-83 GB.

79. Nicholas Brown to ———, North
Faro, August 18, 1781, Miscellaneous Letters,
1781-82.

80. See notation in Nicholas Brown's
handwriting on the back of his copy of the
letter, Miscellaneous Letters, 1781-82.

CHAPTER 13. "GRAIT ZEAL AND INDEFATIGABLE INDUSTORY"

1. Robert A. East, *Business Enterprise in the American Revolutionary Era,* p. 203.

2. Ibid.

3. Rhode Island State Records, I, 85.

4. Ibid., pp. 86-87.

5. Ibid., p. 88.

6. Ibid., p. 289.

7. Ibid., p. 634.

8. East, *op. cit.,* p. 204.

9. Ibid., pp. 205-206.

10. Rhode Island State Records, I, 242 and 284.

11. Irving B. Richman, *Rhode Island: A Study in Separatism,* p. 236.

12. Christopher Starbuck to Nicholas Brown, June 27, 1777, L 75-79 CS.

13. Invoice of sundries shipped by Christopher Starbuck on board the Schooner *William,* George Coffin, Master, for the Bahamas, October 3, 1776, V 76-77 SW.

14. Capt. George Coffin's protest at Stonington, Connecticut, December 13, 1776, V 76-77 SW.

15. Order of Justice of the Peace, Stonington, Connecticut, directing Capt. George Coffin to sell at ten shillings per bushel or deliver it up to the Civil Authority for sale, December 20, 1776, V 76-77 SW.

16. Nicholas Brown, Jonathan Burnell, and Christopher Starbuck, owners of the Schooner *William,* Nantucket to the Bahamas, and thence to Stonington, Connecticut, in account with Capt. George Coffin, January 3, 1777, V 76-77 SW.

17. The Sloop *Bonetta*'s account with Christopher Starbuck, June 1777, V 76-77 M.

18. Christopher Starbuck to Nicholas Brown, September 17, 1777, L 75-79 CS.

19. Ibid.

20. Account of the sale of the Sloop *Bonetta*'s cargo of salt, December 31, 1777, L 75-79 CS.

21. Christopher Starbuck to Nicholas Brown, September 17, 1777, L 75-79 CS.

22. Christopher Starbuck to Nicholas Brown, February 23, 1778; sales of 190 bushels of salt by Prince Gardner in Connecticut on account of Nicholas Brown, March 15, 1778; account of sale of sundries received from Connecticut by *Bounty* on account of Nicholas Brown, September 15, 1778, all in L 75-79 CS.

23. Invoice of sundries shipped by Christopher Starbuck on the Sloop *Bonetta* for the Bahamas on account of Nicholas Brown, December 10, 1777, L 75-79 CS.

24. Account of sales of the Sloop *Bonetta*'s cargo in the Bahamas, 1778, L 75-79 CS.

25. Christopher Starbuck to Nicholas Brown, February 23, 1778, L 75-79 CS.

26. Christopher Starbuck to Nicholas Brown, September 14, 1778, L 75-79 CS.

27. Josiah Hewes to Nicholas Brown, December 23, 1775, L 75-87 JH.

28. See Charter Party for the Schooner *Two Brothers,* January 16, 1776, and invoice of sundry goods shipped by Josiah Hewes on board the Schooner *Two Brothers,* February 23, 1776, V 76-77 STB.

29. Invoice of sundries shipped by Josiah Hewes on board the Sloop *America,* April 8, 1776, V 76-77 SA.

30. John Waterman (Nantucket) to Nicholas Brown, April 8, 1777, P N2.

31. Nicholas Brown to Selectmen of Nantucket, May 20, 1777, in which he acknowledges receipt of their letter of May 10, 1777, Miscellaneous Letters, 1777-1780.

32. Ibid.

33. John Waterman to Nicholas Brown, July 5, 1777, Miscellaneous Letters, 1777-1780.

34. Copy of the Oath taken by Nicholas Brown about the flour stopped at Attleboro, August 1777, L 77-88 Cong.

35. Nicholas Brown to the Committee of Correspondence at Attleboro, Massachusetts, August 20, 1777, Miscellaneous Letters, 1777-1780.

36. Nicholas and Moses Brown to the Governor and Council of the State of Connecticut, July 5, 1781, Miscellaneous Letters, 1781-82.

37. "Account of oil and the places where it is in the country belonging to Nicholas and John Brown," April 6, 1777, L & A 59-92 Sp. C.

38. Nicholas Brown to John Brown, June 25, 1777, Miscellaneous Letters, 1777-1780.

39. Nicholas Brown to William Foster, June 5, 1777, Miscellaneous Letters, 1777-1780.

40. See Memorandum of Agreement, September 20, 1779, Miscellaneous Letters, 1777-1780.

41. Contract between Nicholas and John Brown on the one part and John Mumford, September 21, 1779, Miscellaneous Letters, 1777-1780.

42. Nicholas Brown to Stephen Hopkins and Samuel Ward, November 21, 1775, L 75-77 C & F.

43. Stephen Hopkins (at Philadelphia) to Nicholas Brown, December 9, 1775, L 75-77 C & F.

44. For the letter to the Assembly Committee, January 12, 1776, see L & A 73-88 HF.

45. Nicholas Brown to Peter T. Curtenius, January 20, 1776, OL 74-77 M.

46. Benjamin Handy's agreement to be the overseer of the ore bed in Cranston for the owners of Hope Furnace, March 13, 1776, P-H6, vol. IV.

47. Joseph Brown to George Irish (Newport), May 18, 1776, introducing Elkanah Watson, L & A 73-88 HF.

48. For a copy of the proposed agreement, see L & A 73-88 HF.

49. Marine Committee to Stephen Hopkins, October 9, 1776, in Peter Force, *American Archives,* Fifth Series, II, 954.

50. See copy of the letter in John Brown's handwriting, November 17, 1776, L 70-82 C & Rev.

51. Nicholas Power to Joseph Brown, October 29, 1776, P-H6, vol. IV. Power says he and Jabez Bowen agreed "vorbelly" with Peares Hall for the bricks.

52. Agreement between Solomon Perkins and Daniel Keith on the one hand and the owners of the furnace on the other, in regard to molding cannon, December 6, 1777, L & P 69-84 Fur.

53. Memorandum of agreement made between Jabez Bowen, in behalf of the owners of the Air Furnace, and Thomas Pratt, June 12, 1778, P H6, vol. IV.

54. Agreement of Furnace Owners, June 13, 1778, P H6, vol. IV.

55. Rufus Hopkins to Furnace Owners, October 27, 1778, P-H6, vol. IV.

56. Stephen Hopkins to Navy Board, October 29, 1778, P-H6, vol. IV.

57. Nicholas Brown to Navy Board, January 23, 1779, P-H6, vol. IV.

58. Nicholas Brown to John Manley, December 8, 1779, P-H6, vol. IV.

59. See the agreement bearing date of March 30, 1780, P-H6, vol. IV.

60. Furnace Owners to "Naval Board"

about an "allowance on the Guns," 1779, P-H6, vol. IV.

61. *Ibid.*

62. Jabez Bowen (at Boston) to Nicholas Brown, March 25, 1782, A 80-84 HF.

63. Nicholas Brown to William Creed, November 15, 1779, P-H6, vol. IV.

64. William Creed to Nicholas Brown, February 25, April 11, and October 13, 1779; and March 22, 1780, all in P-H6, vol. IV.

65. See the Agreement, September 18, 1779, P-H6, vol. IV.

66. See Memorandum of Agreement, October 26, 1779, P-H6, vol. IV.

67. Memorandum of Agreement with William Creed, December 4, 1779, P-H6, vol. IV.

68. See the Agreement, February 22, 1780, P-H6, vol. IV.

69. Gabriel Holman (Salem) to Nicholas Brown, March 7, 1780, P-H6, vol. IV.

70. Rufus Hopkins to Nicholas Brown, May 25, 1780, L & P 69-84 Fur; and account of guns sold to Howland and Coit, July 1781, A 80-84 HF.

71. Rufus Hopkins to Nicholas Brown, April 6, 1780, L & P 69-84 Fur.

72. Rufus Hopkins to Nicholas Brown, April 17, 1780, L & P 69-84 Fur.

73. See the agreement, P-H6, vol. IV.

74. Nicholas Brown to William Cowper & Co. (Suffolk, Virginia), June 12, 1780, P-H6, vol. IV.

75. See the Agreement, August 11, 1780, P-H6, vol. IV.

76. Agreement between owners of Furnace Hope and Capt. Ichabod Nichols, January 5, 1781; Nicholas Brown to Ichabod Nichols, January 9, 1781 and Ichabod Nichols to Nicholas Brown, January 22, 1781, all in P-H6, vol. IV.

77. Joshua Ward to Nicholas Brown, January 22, 1781 and Nicholas Brown to Joshua Ward, January 25, 1781, P-H6, vol. IV.

78. Offer by the Owners of Hope Furnace to supply Cooper & Co. with cannon, September 14, 1781, P-H6, vol. IV. Although the name is spelled "Cooper" it is almost certainly Cowper & Co. of Suffolk, Virginia.

79. Jabez Bowen (at Boston) to Furnace Owners, March 25, 1782, A 80-84 HF.

80. Nicholas Brown to John and Andrew Cabot, January 29, 1783, A 80-84 HF.

81. Eaton and Benson (Boston) to Furnace Owners, May 28, 1783, A 80-84 HF, in which they explain the Cabots' difficulties.

82. Eaton and Benson in account with Hope Furnace Company relative to the payment of John and Andrew Cabot's debt, May 29, 1783, A 80-84 HF.

83. Eaton and Benson to Nicholas Brown, August 19, 1782; and account of Sales of Cannon by Eaton and Benson, January 16, 1783, A 80-84 HF.

84. Brown and Francis to Benjamin Bourne, January 1, 1796, in the Peck Papers, Box X, no. 27, in Rhode Island Historical Society.

85. "Account of cannon sold from Furnace Hope since the Last Devition of money among the owners," April 13, 1780, A 80-84 Fur.

86. Owners of Furnace Hope in account current settled March 22, 1781, A 80-84 Fur. The rate of exchange was then somewhat in excess of 70 to 1.

87. Joseph Brown to Nicholas Brown, September 13, 1780, L & P 69-84 Fur.

88. Joseph Brown to Nicholas Brown, October 8, 1779, L & A 73-88 HF.

89. Joseph Brown to Nicholas Brown, February 20 and 28, 1780, and September 13, 1780, all in L & P 69-84 Fur. Also Joseph Brown to Nicholas Brown, September 30 and October 8, 1779, L & A 73-88 HF. The figure of one million dollars is in terms of depreciated currency, of course.

90. Joseph Brown to Nicholas Brown, February 20, 1780, L & P 69-84 Fur.

91. Joseph Brown to Nicholas Brown, February 28, 1780, L & P 69-84 Fur.

92. Life, Journals and Correspondence of Rev. Manasseh Cutler, LLD. (2 vols.; Cincinnati, 1888), I, 205-207. J. Walter Wilson, "Joseph Brown, Scientist and Architect," *Rhode Island History,* IV, 76-79 (July 1945).

93. Arthur C. Bining, *Pennsylvania Iron Manufacture in the Eighteeth Century,* pp. 99-100. Bining does not refer to Joseph Brown's engine, but he discusses the one built by Sharp & Curtenius in New York in 1775. He mentions no other engine which antedated that built by Joseph Brown.

94. Peter Force, *American Archives,* Fifth Series, III, 1335.

95. The other members of the Committee were Nicholas Cooke, Joseph Russell, William Russell, John Smith, Daniel Tillinghast, John Innes Clark, Joseph Nightingale, Jabez Bowen, and Rufus Hopkins, all of Providence.

96. William R. Staples, *Annals of the Town of Providence,* pp. 267-269.

97. Ibid. Also Irving B. Richman, *Rhode Island: A Study in Separatism,* p. 220.

98. Peter Force, *American Archives,* Fifth Series, III, 1335-1336.

99. Stephen Hopkins (at Philadelphia) to Nicholas and John Brown, December 9, 1775, L 75-77 C & F.

100. Nicholas Brown to Stephen Hopkins, January 2, 1776, L 75-77 C & F.

101. Peter Force, *American Archives,* Fifth Series, III, 338. For scattered papers of *Yankee Ranger,* see V R2. She was also referred to as *Ranger.*

102. John Brown to Capt. William Chace, July 1776, V D5.

103. Orders to Capt. William Chace, July 7, 1776, V D5.

104. Memorandum of Captain Freeborn's disgrace, July 13, 1776, V D5.

105. Orders to Captain Stacy, August 21, 1776, V D5.

106. Peter Force, *American Archives,* Fifth Series, II, 1260.

107. For papers of the third voyage, see V D5.

108. See Memorandum of stores taken out of the Ship *Louisa,* 1778; and Memorandum of sundries delivered Captain Bishop for use of the Sloop *Sally* out of stores belonging to the Sloop *Retaliation,* 1778, both in V 76-78 SS.

109. Nicholas Brown to Bossenger Foster, June 14, 1776, P-F6. In this letter Nicholas does not mention *Sally* by name, but refers to the "privateer Capt. Bishop that took the wine ship." Captain Lemuel Bishop was the master of *Sally.*

110. See the opinion in L 58-84 Priv. This vessel was commanded by Captain Warren and is not to be confused with *Yankee Ranger,* commanded by Capt. William Wall.

111. William Rotch to Nicholas Brown, November 26, 1776 and Timothy Folger to Nicholas Brown, November 29, 1776, L 58-84 Priv.

112. Rotch to Nicholas Brown, November 26, 1776, L 58-84 Priv.

113. Ibid.

114. Nicholas Brown to William Rotch, December 3, 1776, OL 74-77 M.

115. Peter Force, *American Archives,* Fifth Series, II, 1194.

116. John Brown to Furnace Owners, September 11, 1779, L & P 69-84 Fur., and Joseph Brown to Nicholas Brown, October 8, 1779, L & A 73-88 HF. This estimate was made, of course, in terms of depreciated Continental dollars.

117. Quoted in I. B. Richman, *Rhode Island: A Study in Separatism,* p. 233.

118. For the wartime activities of Moses Brown, see Rhode Island Historical Society Manuscripts, XII, 110; and *Moses Brown Papers,* II, 47 and 48. Also Augustine Jones, *Moses Brown: His Life and Services* (Providence, 1892), p. 34.

CHAPTER 14. BACK TO LONDON

1. Nicholas Brown to Elkanah Watson, November 28, 1782, L 79-86 EW.

2. Watson & Cassoul to Nicholas Brown, March 1, 1783, L 79-86 EW.

3. Nicholas Brown to Champion & Dickason, May 17, 1783, P C5, vol. I.

4. George Benson (at Boston) to Nicholas Brown, March 15, 1782, L 80-83 GB.

5. Nicholas Brown to Champion & Dickason, May 17, 1783, P C5, vol. I. Also Letter of Brown & Benson, Joseph & William Russell, Clark & Nightingale, John Brown, and Thomas L. Halsey to Champion & Dickason, November 13, 1783, P C5, vol. I.

6. See invoices dated Spring, 1783 and May 16, 1783, OL 83 C&D.

7. For Memorandum, see OL 83 C & D. The goods ordered included lawns, cambrics, calicoes, gauzes, Irish linens, sheeting, linen, apron and shirting checks, pelongs, velvets, corduroys, ribbed velvets, crepes and poplins, Spittlefield silk handkerchiefs, "bandano" and "Rametts" handkerchiefs, black cravats, ferretings, mitts and gloves, knee straps, cambletts, baizes and shaggs, serge, denim and everlastings, ribbons, hose, children's red morocco shoes, flannels, blankets, Persians, "tafities," breeches, "canvis" for samplers, muffs and tippits, aprons, "shallons," topes, tablecloths, Bibles and Testaments, sealing wax, playing cards, shoe and knee buckles, cupboard and chest locks, tin tea pots, tin spoons, ink powder, dishes, fiddle strings, spurs, iron candlesticks with "brass nubs," thumb latches, pocket looking glasses, double wormed gimlets, warming pans, brass kettles, screws, hunting knives, cups, saucers, and many other articles.

8. Nicholas Brown to Champion & Dickason, May 20, 1783, OL 83 C & D.

9. Nicholas Brown to Champion & Dickason, November 6, 1783, P C5, vol. I. Also Articles of Agreement for copartnership between Nicholas Brown and George Benson, 1783, L 81-04 M. Also Minutes of agreement of copartnership for establishing a commercial house between Nicholas Brown and George Benson, with Benson's comments on the minutes, Miscellaneous Letters, 1783.

10. Articles of Agreement for copartnership, L 81-04 M.

11. Ibid.

12. Ibid.

13. Ibid.

14. For detailed, but by no mean clear, accounts of his difficulties see his letters to Nicholas Brown, June 5, 7, 11, 12, and 18; July 3, 5, 6, 11, and 12; and August 8 and 25, 1781, all in L 80-83 GB.

15. Ibid.

16. See especially Benson to Nicholas Brown, July 3, 4, and 6, 1781, L 80-83 GB.

17. See various letters of Eaton & Benson to Nicholas Brown, August 8, 1781 to December 12, 1782, L 81-82 E & B. These deal principally with the services of Eaton & Benson as commission agents of Nicholas Brown and the other owners of Hope Furnace. Many of them relate to the sale of cannon on commission by Eaton & Benson.

18. Nicholas Brown to Champion & Dickason, November 6, 1783, P C5, vol. I.

19. See "Original Agreement respecting Terms of selling Goods," October 1783, Miscellaneous Letters, 1783. The signers of this agreement were Brown & Benson, Joseph & William Russell, Clark & Nightingale, Thomas Jenkins, Joseph Brown, John Rogers, Ebenezer Thompson, John Brown, John Jenckes, and Thomas Lloyd Halsey.

20. See the agreement, Miscellaneous Letters, 1784, vol. I.

21. Brown & Benson to Champion & Dickason, December 13, 1783, P C5, vol. I.

22. For examples of this disappointment of customers see letter of Nicholas Brown to William Morris, Woodstock, Connecticut, October 31, 1783, in which he informs Morris that he will be unable to supply him and his partners with goods "this fall . . . as Capt. Coffin . . . did not bring near all the Goods we Expected." See also letter of Croode & Tisdale, Warren, R. I., to Brown & Benson, November 25, 1783, asking when their goods from London will be for sale. Both of these letters are in Miscellaneous Letters, 1783.

23. Champion & Dickason to Brown & Benson, December 9, 1784, P C5, vol. I.

24. See the letter in P C5, vol. I.

25. The letter is in P C5, vol. I.

26. Champion & Dickason to Brown & Benson, March 10, 1784, P C5, vol. I.

27. Champion & Dickason to Brown & Benson, March 24, 1784, P C5, vol. I.

28. Ibid.

29. Brown & Benson to Champion & Dickason, May 12, 1784, P C5, vol. I.

30. Brown & Benson to Champion & Dickason, June 7, 1784, P C5, vol. I.

31. Brown & Benson to Champion & Dickason, November 9, 1784, P C5, vol. I.

32. Brown & Benson to Champion & Dickason, November 1, 1784, P C5, vol. I.

33. Champion & Dickason to Brown & Benson, December 31, 1784, P C5, vol. I.

34. Ibid. John Brown also fell heavily in debt to Champion and Dickason. As late as 1789 this debt had not been paid. See Champion & Dickason to Moses Brown, April 16, 1789, in *Moses Brown Papers,* vol. VI, in which they refer to John's debt to them.

35. Brown & Benson to Champion & Dickason, December 30, 1783 and January 20, 1784, P C5, vol. I.

36. Champion & Dickason to Brown & Benson, July 9, 1783, P C5, vol. I.

37. For the letter see P C5, vol. I.

38. Champion & Dickason to Brown & Benson, March 24 and May 28, 1784, P C5, vol. I, in which they express their hope for an amelioration of the duty. See Brown & Benson to Champion & Dickason, September 29, October 25, and November 9, 1784, P C5, vol. I, for their accounts of the purchase of the whale oil.

39. For the letter, see P C5, vol. I.

40. Champion & Dickason to Brown & Benson, August 30, 1784, P C5, vol. I.

41. Brown & Benson to Champion & Diekason, December 10, 1785, P C5, vol. I.

42. Champion & Dickason to Brown & Benson, January 31, 1785, P C5, vol. I.

43. Brown & Benson to Champion & Dickason, June 1, 1785, P C5, vol. I, in which they lament the failure of the London firm to ship their goods.

44. Ibid.

45. Champion & Dickason to Brown & Benson, August 10, 1785, P C5, vol. I.

46. Champion & Dickason to Brown & Benson, January 31, 1785, P C5, vol. I.

47. Brown & Benson to Champion & Dickason, June 1, 1785, P C5, vol. I.

48. Brown & Benson to Champion & Dickason, July 12, 1786, P C5, vol. II.

49. For the list, see U-C 1786-1792.

50. Ibid.

51. For the correspondence of Brown & Benson with Ward & Sanderson, see P W24.

52. Brown & Benson to Champion & Dickason, May 17, 1787, P C5, vol. II.

53. See agreement of William Burgess (for Champion & Dickason) with Providence importers, October 29, 1787, and agreement between Brown & Benson and Brown & Francis, on the one hand, and William Burgess (for Champion & Dickason) on the other, October 30, 1787, both in P C5, vol. II.

54. Brown & Benson to Champion & Dickason, November 9, 1784 and Champion & Dickason to Brown & Benson, January 31, 1785, both in P C5, vol. I.

55. Brown & Benson to Champion & Dickason, December 29, 1786, P C5, vol. II.

56. Brown & Benson to Champion & Dickason, November 23, 1785, P C5, vol. I.

57. Champion & Dickason to Brown & Benson, January 4, 1786, P C5, vol. II.

58. Champion & Dickason to Brown & Benson, May 27 and June 7, 1786, P C5, vol. II.

59. Brown & Benson to Champion & Dickason, December 29, 1786 and June 13, 1787, P C5, vol. II.

60. Champion & Dickason to Brown & Benson, October 8, 12, and 25, 1787 and January 2, May 22, and October 7, 1788, P C5, vol. II.

61. Brown & Benson to Champion & Dickason, August 27, 1787, P C5, vol. II, also V R5, vol. II.

62. Brown & Benson to Champion & Dickason, May 7, 1789, P C5, vol. II.

63. Ibid.

64. Champion & Dickason to Brown & Benson, January 26, 1790, P C5, vol. III.

65. Champion & Dickason to Brown & Benson, May 31, 1790, P C5, vol. III.

66. Thomas Dickason, Jr. (at Boston) to Brown & Benson, August 7, 1790, P C5, vol. III.

67. Ibid.

68. Ibid.

69. Brown & Benson to Thomas Dickason, Jr. (at Boston), August 9, 1790, P C5, vol. III.

70. *Ibid.*

71. *Ibid.*

72. Brown & Benson to Thomas Dickason & Co., September 17, 1790, P C5, vol. III.

73. *Ibid.*

74. Thomas Dickason & Co. to Brown & Benson, January 4, 1791, P C5, vol. III.

75. Brown & Benson to Thomas Dickason & Co., May 28, 1791, P C5, vol. III.

76. *Ibid.*

77. *Ibid.*

78. *Ibid.*

79. *Ibid.*

80. *Ibid.*

81. Thomas Dickason & Co. to Brown & Benson, January 4, 1792, P C5, vol. III.

82. Agreement between Thomas Dickason, Jr. and Brown, Benson & Ives, Providence, May 12, 1792, P C5, vol. III.

83. *Ibid.*

84. Thomas Dickason & Co. to Brown & Benson, January 12, 1793, P C5, vol. IV.

85. For the letter, see P C5, vol. IV.

86. Brown, Benson & Ives to Thomas Dickason & Co., April 19, 1793, P C5, vol. IV.

87. "Proposal of Thomas Dickason, Jr. for the liquidation of Brown & Benson's debt by January 1, 1794," dated Providence, June 20, 1793, P C5, vol. IV.

88. Thomas Dickason, Jr. to Brown, Benson & Ives, July 13, 1793, P C5, vol. IV.

89. Brown, Benson & Ives to Thomas Dickason, Jr., September 11, 1793 and Brown, Benson & Ives to Thomas Dickason & Co., November 29, 1793, both in P C5, vol. IV.

90. Brown, Benson & Ives to Thomas Dickason & Co., January 3 and 24, 1794, P C5, vol. IV.

91. Brown, Benson & Ives to Thomas Dickason & Co., June 27, 1794, P C5, vol. IV.

92. For the letter, see P C5, vol. IV.

93. He wrote that his father "sold twenty thousand dollars of stocks at ten shillings on the pound at a period a little before his decease, whereby his heirs immediately sustained the loss of ten thousand dollars and that solely for the good of the Company," Nicholas Brown, Jr. to George Benson, September 22, 1796, Miscellaneous Letters, 1796, vol. II.

CHAPTER 15. THE END OF AN ERA

1. They employed the Brigantines *Commerce, Harmony,* and *Rising Sun* with more or less regularity in the trade to the Caribbean region. On occasion they dispatched the Sloops *Polly, Sukey, Delaware,* and *Betsey,* the Brig *Mary,* the Brigantine *Betsey,* and the Schooner *James* to ports in that area. In addition they used the Ship *Hope* in the European trade in such a fashion as to make her an auxiliary to their traffic with the West Indies. For the various voyages of these vessels, see V C6, V H2, V R5, V P65, V S9, V D45, V B4, V M2, V B35, V J2, and V H6.

2. Hewes & Anthony to Brown & Benson, August 26, 1784, P H4, vol. I.

3. Brown & Benson to Hewes & Anthony, September 24, 1784, P H4, vol. I.

4. Hewes & Anthony to Brown & Benson, October 11, 1784, P H4, vol. I.

5. Brown & Benson to Hewes & Anthony, January 24, 1785, P H4, vol. I.

6. Brown & Benson to Hewes & Anthony, October 23, 1786, P H4, vol. II.

7. Brown & Benson to Hewes & Anthony, October 2, 1789, P H4, vol. III.

8. For the relations of Brown & Benson with Thayer & Bartlett, see P T45.

9. For the correspondence with Murray, Mumford & Bowen, see P M8.

10. See P J4 and P C2. Jenckes and Winsor were Rhode Islanders.

11. See U PS, vol. II.

12. For the correspondence with Gibbs & Channing, see P G52.

13. *Dictionary of American Biography,* XVI, 186.

14. See P R6.

15. For this letter, see Miscellaneous Letters, 1784, vol. I.

16. Brown & Benson to Hewes & Anthony, March 9, 1789, P H4, vol. III.

17. Hewes & Anthony to Brown & Benson, February 14, 1789, P H4, vol. III.

18. Hewes & Anthony to Brown & Benson, June 26, 1790, P H4, vol. III.

19. See "estimate of rum distilled in one year in the distillery, and remarks thereon

for the consideration of Messrs. Mason, Sterry and Bowen," March 13, 1795, P P5, vol. II.

20. For this dispute see George Benson to John Mason, Ephraim Bowen, Jr., and Cyprian Sterry, March 13, 1795; Nicholas Brown, Jr. to the same men, March 13, 1795; four papers bearing the date of March 1795, regarding various aspects of the dispute; and "Statement of the rum that could have been made in the distillery and the rum each owner has drawn out," March 1795—all in P D5, vol. II.

21. See the decision of the arbiters under date of April 22, 1795, P D5, vol. II.

22. Brown, Benson & Ives to Cyprian Sterry, August 3 and 11, 1795, and Sterry to Brown, Benson & Ives, August 12, 1795, all in Miscellaneous Letters, vol. II, 1795.

23. Agreement by the owners of Hope Furnace on the price of pig iron, February 3, 1787, P H6, vol. V.

24. Hope Furnace owners to Tench Coxe, August 20, 1794, and Hope Furnace owners to Timothy Pickering, November 23, 1795, both in P H6, vol. V. Tench Coxe was then Commissioner of Revenue. Timothy Pickering was Secretary of War.

25. Brown & Ives to Head & Amory, April 19, 1798, P H35, vol. VI.

26. Brown & Ives to Head & Amory, November 12, 1798, PH35, vol. VI.

27. Brown & Ives to Head & Amory, November 15, 1798, P H35, vol. VI.

28. Brown & Ives to Head & Amory, November 30, 1798, P H35, vol. VI.

29. *Ibid.* Also Brown & Ives to Head & Amory, November 15, 1798, P H35, vol. VI.

30. Peter Blight (Philadelphia) to Rufus and Silvanus Hopkins, May 17, 1798, and Rufus and Silvanus Hopkins to Peter Blight, May 26, 1798, both in P H6, vol. V.

31. James McHenry to Jabez Bowen, July 30, 1799, P H6, vol. V.

32. Minutes of Meeting of the Furnace Company, March 18, 1803, P H6, vol. V.

33. Minutes of meeting of Furnace Company, July 7, 1806, P H6, vol. V.

34. Silvanus Hopkins and Jabez Bowen's Agreement *in re* sale of Furnace Hope Estate with mill privileges, July 12, 1806, P H6, vol. V. This sale did not include the "oarbed Estate" in Cranston.

35. Charles Beard, An *Economic Interpretation of the Constitution of the United States* (New York, 1935), p. 325.

36. Robert A. East, *Business Enterprise in*

the *American Revolutionary Era* (1938), p. 265.

37. *Ibid.*, p. 269, quoting Pelatiah Webster.

38. The next two or three pages of the text are based upon East, *op. cit.*, pp. 263-284.

39. These calculations are found in East, *op. cit.*, p. 279.

40. East, *op. cit.*, p. 280.

41. See list of certificates in U PS, vol. I.

42. *Register of Loan Office Certificates Issued at the United States Loan Office in the State of Massachusetts from 1st of July to 1st of September 1777 previous to Commencement of Depreciation*, National Archives. The writer is indebted to Professor Hillman M. Bishop of the College of the City of New York, who kindly allowed him to make use of material on Brown family security holdings found in the National Archives.

43. Nicholas Brown to Bossenger Foster, June 14, 1778, P F6.

44. Nicholas Brown to Bossenger Foster, September 25, 1778, P F6.

45. Nicholas Brown to Bossenger Foster, October 26, 1778, P F6.

46. William Newman to Nicholas Brown, April 17, 1782, L 81-83 M.

47. Account of Pennsylvania State notes received from Ephraim Willard, January 23, 1783, L & P 83-88 Cont. Sec.

48. See the agreement, dated November 5, 1783 in Miscellaneous Letters, 1783.

49. Nicholas Brown to David Howell, March 26, 1785, RIHS Manuscripts, XIV, 53.

50. List of final settlement notes bought by Nicholas Brown from Jonathan Wheeler, May 8, 1784, U PS, vol. I.

51. For the various lists, under date of May 4, May 19, June 7, August 30, September 26, October 6, and November 12, 1785, see U PS, vol. I.

52. For these transactions, see U PS, vol. I.

53. See L & A 84-91 M, under date of February 27, 1786 and November 1786.

54. See L & A 84-91 M for the list of notes.

55. See U C 1786-92, under date of October 10, 1788. For an account of the activities of Constable and Platt, see Robert A. East, *op. cit., passim.*

56. U C 1786-92 under dates of October 10, 1788 and January 14, 1791.

57. U C 1786-92 under date of April 20, 1791 for the agreement.

58. For evidence that the securities in question were final settlement notes see letters of Murray, Mumford & Bowen (New York) to Brown & Benson, August 13 and 28, and September 14, 1790, P M8, vol. II.

59. See the agreement under date of May 26, 1790, U PS, vol. II.

60. See the agreement in U PS, vol. II.

61. The agreement is in U PS, vol. II.

62. See U PS, vol. II.

63. For this list, see U PS, vol. I.

64. For this list, see U PS, vol. II.

65. See list of "Massachusetts Continental Certificates" in U PS, vol. II.

66. "List of State notes issued from the State of Rhode Island, belonging to Nicholas Brown," U PS, vol. I.

67. See "A list of Massachusetts State Notes," U PS, vol. I.

68. For this document, see U PS, vol. II.

69. See Chapter 14, note 93.

70. At the time Nicholas Brown had loaned the securities, Constable & Platt posted $3000 in specie along with their bond for $30,000 as surety for their return. Nicholas later sold the bond to Thomas Dickason & Co. for £5,400 Sterling. This sum, together with the $3000 in specie, is approximately the equivalent of the $30,000 in securities.

71. Nicholas Brown to David Howell, March 26, 1785, RIHS Manuscripts, XIV, 53.

72. Consolidated Value of Loan Office Certificates belonging to the following persons in this State per Order of the Honble Assembly at May Session, Rhode Island State Archives (FC4).

73. Register of the Certificates of the oaths and affirmations administered to persons who have applied for the liquidation of interest at the Loan Office in the State of Rhode Island, Newport Historical Society (#85).

74. Register of Loan Office Certificates Issued at the United States Loan Office in the State of Massachusetts from the 1st of Feby to 1st September 1777 previous to Commencement of Depreciation, National Archives.

75. No. 495 Connecticut Ledger "A" 6 per cent, National Archives.

76. Subscribers to Loans, Loan Office, RI 1791—Loan Book State Debt. National Archives.

77. Consolidated Value of Loan Office Certificates belonging to the following persons in this State, etc., Rhode Island State Archives (FC4).

78. Ibid.

79. Massachusetts Assumed Debt, vol. II (#280 Massachusetts), National Archives.

80. Subscribers to Loans, Loan Office—RI 1791—Loan Book State Debt., National Archives.

81. For a statement of the purpose of the meeting, together with a list of those invited and of those who attended, see U PS, vol. II.

82. Hillman M. Bishop has made a fresh study of Rhode Island's opposition to both the Continental Impost and the Constitution in "Why Rhode Island Opposed the Constitution," Rhode Island History, VIII (January 1949), 1-10; (April 1949), 33-44; (July 1949), 85-95; and (October, 1949), 115-126.

83. Hillman M. Bishop, "Why Rhode Island Opposed the Constitution," loc. cit., pp. 4-6.

84. Nicholas Brown to David Howell, March 26, 1785, RIHS Manuscripts, XIV, 53.

85. Hillman M. Bishop, "Why Rhode Island Opposed the Constitution," loc. cit., p. 7.

86. Ibid., p. 9.

87. Ibid.

88. Ibid., p. 40.

89. George Benson (at Newport) to Nicholas Brown, June 22, 1786, P B45.

90. See p. 297, supra.

91. See p. 308, supra.

92. George Benson to Nicholas Brown, June 22, 1786, P B45.

93. George Benson to Nicholas Brown, June 19, 1786, P B45.

94. For a copy of this letter, see P P6. Besides Nicholas and John Brown, the signers of the letter were Jabez Bowen, Welcome Arnold, John Jenckes, John Barton, Joseph Nightingale, William Barton, Thomas L. Halsey, Philip Allen, Levi Hall, Paul Allen, William Russell, and Jeremiah Olney. The letter is printed in Publications of the Rhode Island Historical Society, II, 169, and in Irving B. Richman, Rhode Island: A Study in Separatism, pp. 250-251. See also Frank G. Bates, Rhode Island and the Formation of the Union (New York, 1898), p. 157 for quotations from the letter.

95. For a copy of this letter, see P P6.

96. Bates, op. cit., p. 158.

97. For this and his letter of September 16, 1789, see Miscellaneous Letters, 1789.

Index

INDEX